1992

Early Antiquity

Early Antiquity

I. M. Diakonoff
Volume Editor

Philip L. Kohl
Project Editor

Translated by Alexander Kirjanov

The University of Chicago Press
Chicago and London

I. M. Diakonoff is a senior research scholar of ancient history at the Institute of Oriental Studies, Leningrad Academy of Sciences.

Philip L. Kohl is professor of anthropology at Wellesley College.

The University of Chicago Press, Chicago 60637
The University of Chicago Press, Ltd., London
© 1991 by The University of Chicago
All rights reserved. Published 1991
Printed in the United States of America

00 99 98 97 96 95 94 93 92 91   5 4 3 2 1

Originally published as *Istoriya Drevnego Mira*, volume 1: *Rannyaya Drevnost'*, revised edition. © 1982, 1989 Chief Division of Eastern Literature, Nauka Press.

Library of Congress Cataloging in Publication Data

Istoriĩa drevnego mira. 1, Ranniaĩa drevnost'. English
    Early antiquity / I. M. Diakonoff, volume editor ; Philip L. Kohl, project editor.
        p.   cm.
    Translation of: Istoriĩa drevnego mira. 1. Ranniaĩa drevnost'.
    Includes index.
    ISBN 0-226-14465-8
    1. History, Ancient. I. D'iakonov, Igor' Mikhaĭlovich.
    II. Title.
    D57.I88   1991
    930—dc20   90-24148
                                                            CIP

⊚ The paper used in this publication meets the minimum requirements of the American National Standard for Information Sciences—Permanence of Paper for Printed Library Materials, ANSI Z39.48-1984.

Contents

Foreword *by Philip L. Kohl*   vii

Introduction *by the Editorial Board*   1

1   General Outline of the First Period of the History of the Ancient World and the Problem of the Ways of Development

     I. M. DIAKONOFF   27

2   The City-States of Sumer

     I. M. DIAKONOFF   67

3   Early Despotisms in Mesopotamia

     I. M. DIAKONOFF   84

4   The Old Babylonian Period of Mesopotamian History

     N. V. KOZYREVA   98

5   Sumerian Culture

     V. K. AFANASIEVA   124

6   The Predynastic Period and the Early and the Old Kingdoms in Egypt

     I. V. VINOGRADOV   137

7   The Middle Kingdom of Egypt and the Hyksos Invasion

     I. V. VINOGRADOV   158

8   The New Kingdom of Egypt

     I. V. VINOGRADOV   172

9   The Culture of Ancient Egypt

     I. A. LAPIS   193

10   The First States in India and the Pre-Urban Cultures of Central Asia and Iran

     G. F. IL'YIN and I. M. DIAKONOFF   214

11   Asshur, Mitanni, and Arrapkhe

     N. B. JANKOWSKA   228

12   Mesopotamia in the Sixteenth to Eleventh Centuries B.C.

     V. A. JAKOBSON   261

13   The Hittite Kingdom

     G. G. GIORGADZE   266

14/, 8 23

14 Syria, Phoenicia, and Palestine in the Third and
    Second Millennia B.C.
    I. M. DIAKONOFF   286

15 The World of Crete and Mycenae
    YU. V. ANDREYEV   309

16 Greece of the Eleventh to Ninth Centuries B.C. in the
    Homeric Epics
    YU. V. ANDREYEV   328

17 Phoenician and Greek Colonization
    YU. B. TSIRKIN   347

18 India, Central Asia, and Iran in the First Half of the
    First Millennium B.C.
    G. F. IL'YIN AND I. M. DIAKONOFF   366

19 The First States in China
    T. V. STEPUGINA   387

20 China in the First Half of the First Millennium B.C.
    T. V. STEPUGINA   420

    Maps   433

    Index   441

Foreword

On the English translation

The organization and nature of this book, *Early Antiquity*, and its conceptual relation to the two remaining volumes in the three-volume Soviet study on *The History of the Ancient World* are discussed in the Introduction. This Foreword explains some difficulties associated with the English translation of this work and tries to familiarize its English-reading audience with certain characteristics of Soviet Marxist historiography on antiquity. First, a brief description of the history of the translation is required.

I first learned of the three-volume study *The History of the Ancient World* while visiting Leningrad in fall 1983 as a member of an American delegation of archaeologists to the Soviet Union. Dr. I. M. Diakonoff of the Leningrad Branch of the Oriental Institute of the USSR, Accademy of Sciences, provided the delegation with a single copy of the first edition of the work and suggested that it would be worthwhile to translate this recent synthesis of his and, primarily, fellow Leningrad colleagues' historical studies of the ancient world. This single copy of the limited first edition ended up gathering dust in my library in Wellesley, dutifully having been set aside in my "To Do" file on collaborative research with Soviet scholars. It might have remained there had I not had the opportunity the following year to travel to Leningrad to participate in the *Rencontre Assyriologique Internationale,* where I again met with Dr. Diakonoff and discussed with him at length his desire to have a major work of his translated into English. Several possibilities presented themselves, including the recently published work primarily written by him: *Istoriya drevnego Vostoka: Zarozhdenie drevneishikh klassovykh obshchestv i pervye ochagi rabovladel'cheskoi tsivilizatsii* [The history of the ancient East: The birth of the most ancient class societies and the first centers of slave-owning civilization] (Moscow, 1983), but he reaffirmed his desire to have the multi-authored three-volume *The History of the Ancient World* translated, since it was in his opinion more up-to-date, better represented his current understanding of developments in ancient Mesopotamia, and offered the inestimable advantage of providing a synthetic overview to antiquity as a whole. Its introductory chapters (see the Introduction and Lecture 1, this volume) attempt to structure and interpret the discussed historical materials according to an explicit, consistent, and expanded historical framework as evolved by Soviet scholars in the general Marxist tradition, which, Dr. Diakonoff believed, would be of considerable interest to Western readers.

In fall 1984 the University of Chicago Press contacted me about the possibility of translating this work, which had by then appeared in its second revised edition in the Soviet Union, and details, as acknowledged below, concerning the translation and editing of the final text eventually were hammered out among the interested parties in Chicago, Leningrad, and Wellesley. Some of these details, as well as specific problems related to the translation of a general popular work of this kind, should be explicated further. All of volume 1, *Early Antiquity*, initially was translated by Mr. Alexander Kirjanov and then entered by Ms. Daria Kirjanov, his daughter, into my file on the Wellesley College mainframe computer. These rough translations were then sent lecture by lecture to Dr. Diakonoff in Leningrad for corrections and revisions, a process complicated not only by long-distance mail service but also by the fact that a substantially revised third edition, upon which this English translation is ultimately based, appeared in the Soviet Union during the course of this editing. I then incorporated the revised and edited text on my word processor and mailed the corrected copy once more to Dr. Diakonoff for his final approval.

Though necessary, such a laborious procedure is, to say the least, time-consuming and helps explain why so few outstanding works of Soviet historical scholarship are translated. Some particular difficulties beset the translation of the *The History of the Ancient World* because it is intended for a general educated lay audience. First and fundamentally, the reading publics of different countries differ, and this fact is particularly striking when contrasting the potential "market," if you will, for this book in the Soviet Union to that in the United States. A cursory comparison of the reading materials available for purchase in a subway stall or street corner kiosk in any major Soviet city with those on sale at equivalent locations in American cities would quickly convince anyone of this difference. The interested Soviet reader does not expect a novel approach to the data or the advancement of a new all-encompassing theory to provide the latest perspective on ancient history; a product is not expected to be sold, but current knowledge is to be presented in a straightforward, accessible form within an understood and generally unquestioned theoretical framework. It is for such an audience that *The History of the Ancient World* was originally written. The English-reading audience is likely to be considerably diverse, consisting of specialists from a range of disciplines—anthropology, history, Assyriology, classical studies, etc., interested in a theoretically distinctive materialist interpretation of the past—as well as university students interested in a general overview to antiquity.

The expectations of such potential readers necessarily will differ. As explained in the Introduction, this book was not primarily written for specialists; it is not annotated or extensively footnoted and, not infrequently, controversial theories and interpretations are presented as unproblematic, as givens. Let me just mention two examples in which theories of American scholars are cited favorably in this fashion; D. Schmandt-Besserat's theory (itself originally based on an idea of P. Amiet) on the use and significance of "tokens" for understanding the beginnings of writing (see Lecture 2); and D. McAlpin's thesis that ancient Elamite and the Dravidian language family are cognate (Lecture 10). Scholars familiar with the literature will immediately realize that such interpretations are either sharply contested or inconclusively demonstrated.[1] Such controversy also occasionally concerns fundamental questions of interpretation and classification, such as the scale and nature of the private/communal sector in ancient Mesopotamia. Debates on some of these issues also rage within the Soviet specialist literature (see below).

A related difficulty is due to the lack of access to or familiarity with the latest results of Western research on particular problems. Thus, for example, H. Weiss's fundamental work on the beginnings of urbanism in northern Mesopotamia and his writings on the productivity/unit area of the dominantly rainfall-based agriculture in northern Mesopotamia compared with the exclusively irrigation-based agriculture in the south are not presented here.[2] There is an inevitable lag time in the diffusion of knowledge across the still-significant political frontier that separates Soviet from Western scholarship, though fair recognition of this fact admits that this temporal gap works in the opposite direction as well; indeed, we tend to be far more ignorant of recent Soviet scholarship on antiquity than they are of our work. In any event, one of the primary purposes of this volume is to facilitate the transmission of knowledge across this unfortunate boundary.

The editor of the English edition, thus, is presented with a problem. Should one flag such debatable theories by reference to the rele-

1. For serious criticisms of the former theory, see M. J. Shendge, "The Use of Seals and the Invention of Writing," *Journal of the Economic and Social History of the Orient* 26, part 2 (1983); for reservations concerning McAlpin's thesis, see the thoughtful (and largely sympathetic) review of McAlpin's *Proto-Elamo-Dravidian: The Evidence and Its Implications* by the Dravidian scholar K. V. Zvelebil in the *Journal of the American Oriental Society* 105, no. 2 (1985).

2. See, e.g., *The Origins of Cities in Dry-Farming Syria and Mesopotamia in the Third Millennium B.C.*, ed. by H. Weiss (Guilford, Conn.: Four Quarters Publishing Co., 1986).

vant opposed literature? Should one note recent research that supports or contradicts an interpretation made in one of the "lectures"? In my opinion, two arguments militated against such interference. First, given the considerable time and geographic areas covered in this collectively written study of antiquity—literally stretching in time from Neolithic origins to the fall of Rome and in space from the western Mediterranean to East Asia—no single editor could possibly note all controversial areas of interpretation. Collective editorship was not feasible. Second and more important, the documentation required to address this problem would change the character of the work. The introductory chapters of each volume and all the lectures are clearly synthetic interpretations of a vast corpus of data. Final truths never should be expected in history, and intelligent readers will immediately recognize that their approximation will be rougher and less precise in a generalizing work of this kind. In a very few cases I took the liberty of noting some relevant research. These always occur in the footnotes and are marked "Editor's note (PLK)"; the other, more numerous instances designated "Editor's note (IMD)" refer to additions made by the principal Soviet editor, I. M. Diakonoff.

One must not exaggerate the problem; nearly all of what is presented is consensually accepted by all historians. For the remainder, it should suffice simply to let the reader beware of these difficulties at the outset and seek on his or her own alternative perspectives on particular topics of interest.

Early Antiquity, volume 1 of *The History of the Ancient World*, is a work written by a group of historians and linguists largely working at the Oriental Institute in Leningrad. Difficulties associated with collective authorship are discussed in the Introduction, but it is important to emphasize here that substantial differences of interpretation exist even within this closely collaborating circle of scholars. Some lectures devote more, some less, space to straightforward political history or cultural description. Others focus more intensely on socioeconomic reconstruction. Such diversity in perspective and presentation, of course, may constitute more a strength than a liability, and the reader should evaluate each lecture on its own.

The historical/linguistic perspectives of the authors also should be noted; we are told that the study of languages provides the key for penetrating the mental processes or spiritual world of antiquity, whereas archaeological data, the material culture record, often are implicitly or even explicitly regarded as of relatively limited value for reconstructing the socioeconomic structure of ancient societies. Such a perspective, of course, has merit and may indeed be more right than wrong, but again *caveat lector*.

Finally, the overall organization of the work, the sequence of lectures, should be mentioned: materials are presented roughly in chronological order, though each individual lecture treats separately a specific area of early civilization. Thus, fourth through early second millennia B.C. developments in Egypt are presented after a comparable review of the early history of Mesopotamia but before treatments of the beginnings of civilization in South Asia, Central Asia, and, finally, East Asia. Such a framework is logical and, given the collective authorship, constitutes perhaps the only feasible structure. However, by its very nature this structure tends to minimize historical interconnections among separate areas; it threatens to obscure the single "world historical" process of development in which all the societies were involved. Thus, paradoxically, this comprehensive history of antiquity can be read from a perspective that stresses the internal evolution of separate societies, each of which finally reaches the same typological stage of development (see below).

Despite this inherent, if not inevitable, limitation, the work fulfills its main purpose. The format of the lectures, the periodization and typology elucidated in the introductory lectures, and the guiding hand of Dr. Diakonoff and the editorial board are all responsible for the creation of a unified work; the fundamental goal of presenting the histories of separate early civilizations as part of an integral or universal historical process *(vsemirnaya istoriya)* is achieved, despite the problems associated with collective authorship and organizational framework. Certain questions, however, inevitably emerge and must be addressed. How are separate early states with their incipient class structures temporally, typologically, and historically related to one another? How satisfactory or complete is this canvas that purports to sketch in broad strokes the main features of the ancient world? What is the vision of the past, the view of history, that permeates this study and how does it conform to or distinguish itself from an orthodox stage theory of development? And, finally, how does this macrohistorical collective Soviet overview compare with the overviews of Western macrohistorians—be they explicitly Marxist-inspired or not?

Soviet Historiography on Antiquity: Common Problems, Particular Solutions

An outside observer attempting to describe any complex "school" or relatively unified corpus of scholarship always confronts the double-edged difficulty of disentangling common features, more or less universally shared by adherents of the school, from those characteristics and concerns specific to individual scholars. This difficulty is particularly pronounced when generalizations are made concerning Soviet scholarship, for the Western observer must be aware of and somehow consciously correct for stereotypic prejudices that permeate Western understanding of all things Soviet. One such grossly inaccurate, albeit all-pervasive, image is that of a monolithic, dogmatic, highly entrenched orthodoxy to which everyone submits either through brainwashing or coercion. Whether applied to society at large or to a branch of scholarship, such as ancient history, this image distorts reality, actually shedding more light on Western prejudice than Soviet practice. Yet, it is also legitimate to describe national traditions of research in the historical sciences, and Soviet scholars themselves consciously refer to "the Soviet school of economic historians of the ancient Orient"[3]—a phrase that explicitly acknowledges the existence of such a school and, correspondingly, some commonality of interest or approach that defines it.

Before attempting to list some of the features characteristic of Soviet writings on antiquity, one first must demolish the abovementioned caricature. Soviet historical and social science writings abound in polemic, sharply contested points of view, the articulation of which often shocks uninitiated Western readers. As illustration of this penchant for polemic within Soviet historiography on antiquity, one can cite two recent debates that were featured in major Soviet journals. *Vestnik drevnei istorii* [The journal of ancient history] devoted several issues[4] to the presentation and criticism of a new, detailed linguistic theory purporting to reconstruct Proto-Indo-European language and culture. Disagreements ran deep and were baldly expressed. Similarly, two recent issues of *Narody Azii i Afriki* [Peoples of Asia and Africa] (1984, nos. 2–3) presented a roundtable discussion *(kruglyi stol)* on "the state and law in the ancient East" led by V. A. Jakobson, one of the contributors to *Early Antiquity.*[5] Many fascinating issues were raised in this discussion, some of which are also discussed in *The History of the Ancient World:* including the origins of law; the re-

3. See I. M. Diakonoff's prefatory remarks to his edited volume in English *Ancient Mesopotamia* (Moscow: Nauka, 1969).

4. *Vestnik drevnei istorii,* 1980, no. 3; 1981, no. 2; 1982, nos. 3–4; and 1984, no. 2. Fortunately, these and related articles have been translated into English, initially published in *Soviet Studies in History* 22, nos. 1–2 (1983), and in *Soviet Anthropology and Archeology* 23, no. 2 (1984), and subsequently reprinted with the response of T. V. Gamkrelidze and V. V. Ivanov to I. M. Diakonoff's criticisms in *Journal of Indo-European Studies* 13, nos. 1–2 (1985). An English translation of the definitive statement of Gamkrelidze and Ivanov's thesis, *Indoevropeiskii yazyk i indoevropeitsi: Rekonstruktsiya i istorikotipologicheskii analiz prayazyka i protokul'tury* [Indo-European and the Indo-Europeans: A reconstruction and a historical-typological analysis of a proto-language and a protoculture] (2 vols., Tbilisi, 1984), is currently being prepared.

5. Fortunately, this was also translated and appeared in *Soviet Anthropology and Archeology* 24, no. 4 (1986); and 25, no. 4 (1987).

lationship or relative dependence/independence between religion
and ethical and moral norms, on the one hand, and law or legal justice, on the other; culturally based differences in the expression of
law, which is defined in classic Marxist terms as written codes that express and sanction the interests of the ruling class. During this discussion, specialists, utilizing different source materials, differed sharply
in their views on fundamental questions of interpretation; similarly
structured presentations with rebuttals in Western jounals may wan in
comparison to the tone and tenor of this debate.

One of the major points of contention in this roundtable discussion
on ancient law also forms the major theoretical question addressed in
the Introduction to *Early Antiquity:* namely, the distinctiveness of historical development in the East relative to the West (i.e., for antiquity—classical Greece and Rome). There is no reason to recapitulate
the history of scholarly writings on this seemingly timeless, peren-
nially recurring question; the summary in the Introduction sketches
its main contours quite adequately, though it also may partially mis-
lead the unfamiliar reader. The Introduction discusses the debate
over the distinctiveness of the East, the phenomenon of Oriental despotism, the validity of the Marxist concept of an Asiatic mode of production, and so on, as a problem intially formulated and today still
raging primarily within Western scholarship.[6] In its review of Soviet
writings on the subject, the Introduction is uncharacteristically mild,
intentionally conciliatory, as it glosses over very real and profound
differences among Soviet scholars that appear regularly—indeed,
with increasing frequency—in their literature.[7] *The History of the Ancient World* aims at presenting developments in antiquity as part of
a single, unified process—the universal history of humanity; its intent
is to emphasize the common, shared features at the expense of the
particular and, in so doing, lump together disparate civilizations into
similar typological categories. From this perspective, classical Greece
and Rome theoretically *must* resemble ancient Near Eastern civilizations.

The disagreements within Soviet historiography on such funda-

6. One might add that today this debate in the West experiences perhaps its clearest
manifestation in the battle raging over the question of Western scholarship on the East,
the phenomenon of Orientalism or disciplines that took shape under, and presumably
were permanently affected by their association with, Western colonial rule, the resul-
tant image being that of a distinctive, unchanging, and monolithic Orient. See E. W.
Said, *Orientalism* (New York: Random House, 1978).

7. For a thorough review of the earlier Soviet debate on the Asiatic mode of produc-
tion from its appearance in the thirties through the sixties and early seventies, see S. P.
Dunn, *The Fall and Rise of the Asiatic Mode of Production* (Boston: Routledge and Kegan
Paul, 1982).

mental issues of interpretation, however, are real; and it is healthy
that they are debated openly in their literature. Those who have followed English translations of several of Diakonoff's major theoretical
studies on the private/communal sector in ancient Mesopotamia, the
nature of the dependent labor force, and the phenomenon of "helots"
in early antiquity, for example, will also realize that his interpretations
have been critcized (almost predictably) by Soviet theorists and historians, particularly by the Georgian scholar G. A. Melikishvili, whose
criticisms are mentioned only in passing in the Introduction.[8] The dis-
agreement between these two scholars continues, as reflected in
Melikishvili's recent summary article "Ob osnovnykh etapakh razvi-
tiya drevnego blizhnevostochnogo obshchestva" [On the basic stages
of the development of ancient Near Eastern societies],[9] which, among
other points, attacks the periodization of antiquity presented in *The
History of the Ancient World*. Other issues of contention include the scale
and significance of the so-called private/communal sector in third millennium B.C. Mesopotamia and the related problem of the relative
size and dominance of the temple/state sector in early Near Eastern
irrigation civilizations; the character of the later military states of the
second millennium B.C. (or Diakonoff's "third way of development,"
see Lecture 1); the nature of the classical Greek *polis* compared with
contemporary and later Near Eastern cities; and property relations in
classical Greece and Rome and how they should be distinguished
from those present in Near Eastern societies. The interested reader
should consult Melikishvili's cited works and contrast his interpretations with the overview presented in *The History of the Ancient World*.
Here, one should only be aware that the debate on fundamental questions of interpretation both outside and within the Soviet Union continues and that *The History of the Ancient World* provides only *a
particular perspective* on a vast corpus of data, *a particular reading* set
forth in a logically consistent, economical, and readable form.

    If answers to fundamental questions differ, what then unites Soviet
historical writings on antiquity? Can one legitimately refer to a Soviet
school of economic historians of the ancient world? It is insufficient

8. Contrast, e.g., I. M. Diakonoff's "The Commune in the Ancient East as Treated in
the Works of Soviet Researchers," *Soviet Anthropology and Archeology* 2, no. 2 (1963), and
"Slaves, Helots, and Serfs in Early Antiquity," *Soviet Anthropology and Archeology* 15, nos.
2–3 (1976), with G. A. Melikishvili's studies: "On the Character of the Most Ancient
Class Societies," in *Introduction to Soviet Ethnography*, ed. by S. P. Dunn and E. Dunn,
vol. 2, pp. 549–73 (Berkeley: Highgate Road Social Science Research Station, 1974);
"The Character of the Socio-economic Structure in the Ancient East," *Soviet Anthropology and Archeology* 15, nos. 2–3 (1976); and "Some Aspects of the Question of the Socioeconomic Structure of Ancient Near Eastern Societies," *Soviet Anthropology and
Archeology* 17, no. 1 (1978).

    9. *Vestnik drevnei istorii*, 1985, no. 4.

simply to label Soviet scholarship on the ancient world as Marxist or to find a common denominator in historical materialism as an answer to these questions for, at least, two reasons. First, not all Soviet historians are Marxists, though it probably would be fair to say that those who are not Marxists, have pursued their historical researches without challenging Marx's or Lenin's writings, indeed often without referring to this paradigm and its classic literature at all. That is, the debates— occasionally vitriolic—that have occurred and continue to rage in the Soviet literature have taken place within recognized limits; whether or not Soviet historical writings will be as self-circumscribed in the future is unclear, though it, at least, is questionable whether this silence or default by omission will continue as Soviet society evolves and accepts and openly debates more of its own internal contradictions.

Second, as any observer of Western Marxism immediately recognizes, not all Marxists, including Soviet historians, interpret Marx and his successors in the same fashion. In the West, tremendous, at times irreconcilable, differences exist among scholars professing to write within the Marxist tradition;[10] in the Soviet Union, this tendency may be muted, but it is still possible to detect differences, and one may find relatively more deterministic or vulgar materialistic interpretations alongside others emphasizing the more voluntaristic, class struggle side of Marxism.

The Introduction to *Early Antiquity* stresses the shared interests and common perspectives of the numerous contributors to *The History of the Ancient World,* asserting that it was the conscious decision of the editorial board to select scholars sharing a particular approach or orientation to historical data. This claim too should be tempered somewhat, at least insofar as it is fair to judge the orientation of specific contributors in terms of their other published works.

For example, the views of M. A. Dandamaev, a contributor to volume 2 of *The History of the Ancient World, The Florescence of Ancient Societies,* on the slave-owning character of Neo-Babylonian and Achaemenian societies differ markedly from the long-accepted, more orthodox position of Diakonoff that more or less slavelike dependents were the major exploited labor force throughout all periods of antiquity. The contrast is explicitly drawn by Dandamaev in his recently translated *Slavery in Babylonia: From Nabopolassar to Alexander the Great (626–331 B.C.):*

> Slavery never reached in Babylonia such a degree of development that one can speak of slave labor as having the leading

10. For divisions within Western Marxism, see P. Anderson's fine studies: *Considerations of Western Marxism* (London: NLB, 1976), *Arguments within English Marxism* (London: NLB, 1980), and *In the Tracks of Historical Materialism* (London: NLB, 1983).

role in the economy. Slave labor was only one of several types of forced labor and not always the most significant. . . . That there was no predominance of slave labor in any branch of the Babylonian economy is not the main point; more important is that labor in agriculture was furnished primarily by free farmers and tenants and that free labor also dominated in craft industries.[11]

Certainly, not all the contributors consider themselves representatives of a particular "school," though, as noted, it is not without interest for both theoretical and obviously practical reasons that nearly all the contributors work in Leningrad. Dr. Diakonoff and his editorial board have chosen scholars whom they personally have known and collaborated with for years. Given this context, it would be surprising if one could not detect certain common themes and frameworks for understanding the past that characterize the works of this Leningrad circle of historians of the ancient world.

Even outside this circle, within Soviet historiography as a whole, one can detect a common sense of problem, a common arena of debate that unites scholars as sharply opposed as Diakonoff and Melikishvili. Here, reference to a particular reading of Marx is appropriate. Melikishvili writes that

in order to arrive at a characterization of the socioeconomic system of any society, it is quite important to identify its class structure, particularly the status of the direct producers. However, one must not forget that the class structure of society is itself derivative and depends on the division of labor operative in that society—the economic base, the fundamental expression of which is property relationships. . . . since it is the economic base—the totality of the relationships of production—that defines a system (society), it will be understood that one system may be distinguished from another above all in terms of that base, of the relationships of production, which, in the words of Marx, are expressed in property relations. Proceeding from this assumption, researchers are en-

11. Trans. by V. A. Powell, ed. by M. Powell (co-editor D. B. Weisberger), (DeKalb: Northern Illinois University Press, 1984), p. 660. Also, see his review of the slave-owning debate in Soviet Orientalist literature through 1977, "Problemy istorii drevnevostochnykh obshchestv v trudakh sovetskikh vostokovedov (1967–1977 gg.)" [Problems of the history of ancient Eastern societies in the works of Soviet Orientalists (1967–1977)], *Vestnik drevnei istorii*, 1977, no. 4. For a recent defense of the slave-owning concept by another contributor to *The History of the Ancient World*, see G. F. Il'yin, "Drevnevostochnoe obshchestvo i problemy ego sotsial'no-ekonomicheskoi struktury" [Ancient Eastern society and the problem of its socioeconomic structure], *Vestnik drevnei istorii*, 1983, no. 3.

tirely justified in recognizing property relationships as the system-forming element of a given society.[12]

This is developed from a straightforward, unambiguous interpretation of Marx's famous "Introduction" to *A Contribution to the Critique of Political Economy* and summarizes the orthodox, or classic, Marxism espoused by most Soviet Marxist historians of antiquity. Certain emphases, however, are apparent. The primary task of the historian is to *characterize* the socioeconomic system of a society. Thus, there is a concern for definition, a need to construct a typology that reduces the bewildering kaleidoscopic array of historical data into a manageable, understandable whole. Primary effort is expended on defining stages of development and describing their characteristics; less energy is devoted to explaining processes of change or how societies evolve from one developmental stage to another. The Marxism shared by many Soviet historians of antiquity is certainly not vulgarly materialist in the sense of reducing social complexity to features of the environment or of explaining institutions in terms of the functions they perform to solve problems ultimately posed by nature. Nor is theirs a Marxism emphasizing changes in the forces of production. The general disparagement of archaeological data already has been noted;[13] while mentioned, technological developments are not emphasized relative to the reconstruction of social groups in terms of their access to means of production. The concern, quite properly, is with the reconstruction of direct primary production, which for antiquity always meant agricultural production—thus, the emphasis on the critical variables of landownership and land use.

As the reader soon will discover, *The History of the Ancient World* is not a speculative account but a rich summary based on the distillation of primary source materials. Most contributors are internationally known specialists in their fields, and their lectures here detail current historical knowledge. As emphasized in the Introduction, however, source materials for antiquity often are so incomplete that they cannot serve as the sole basis for reconstruction, and consequently, the theoretical perspectives of the authors help them fill in the lacunae and guide them consciously or not in fleshing out their portraits of past societies and epochs. One aid frequently employed in this task is the use of an evolutionary theory that finds its Marxist origins in F.

12. G. A. Melikishvili, "Some Aspects of the Questions of the Socioeconomic Structure of Ancient Near Eastern Societies," p. 26.

13. It is instructive, for example, to contrast the once-popular summary of ancient history to the fall of Rome *What Happened in History*, written by the Marxist archaeologist V. Gordon Childe (rev. ed. [London: Penquin Books, 1954), with that presented here by Soviet Marxist linguists/historians.

Engels, *Origin of the Family, Private Property, and the State*. For the Western reader, the terminology associated with this particular evolutionary perspective may have a slight anachronistic ring. For example, in the second section of Lecture 1, we read that "accelerating progress distinguishes the early class society from barbarism, the level that even the most developed primitive society cannot exceed." Societies are ranked on an ascending *scala societatis*, and it may not always be clear how they can mutate or so transform themselves in order to be classified at a new evolutionary level.

Evolutionary theory also sometimes serves as the basis for reconstruction when the texts are silent. For his controversial interpretation of a large and important private/communal economic sector in third millennium B.C. Mesopotamia, Diakonoff utilizes a variety of arguments, one of which is based principally on his understanding of the final stage of advanced patriarchal barbarism:

> In the same way as the medieval society inherited certain features of the ancient society structure, the ancient society did also inherit certain still more ancient structures from the society which preceded it. Arising from the primitive pre-urban, pre-class society, the ancient society could not have been divided solely into slave-owners and slaves; the numerically predominant part of the population could not fail to consist of what had been inherited from the mass of the population of the pre-class society. . . . it certainly was a mass of personally free persons, at least in so far as the family heads were concerned.[14]

Although the texts themselves do not inform us that this was the case, such a mass of free citizens theoretically *must* have continued to exist during the time when the state and temple sectors first slowly developed; later it was the impoverished members of this citizenry who hired themselves out as laborers for the large centralized economies. The point is not to question this reconstruction, which may seem logical and convincing, but to emphasize its epistemological basis: a vision of preclass society that is derived ultimately from Engels's *Origin*, though bolstered, of course, with later historical and ethnographic evidence.

Evolutionary teminology permeates the created ordering of antiquity. We are presented with different "ways of development" along which preclass societies evolved into stratified states. Mesopotamia and Egypt are thus distinguished and both are separated from the military states (Hittite, Mitannian, etc.) that arose later outside the ir-

14. I. M. Diakonoff, "The Rural Community in the Ancient Near East," *Journal of the Economic and Social History of the Orient* 28, part 2 (1985): 122.

rigated heartlands of the Nile and Euphrates valleys. On the one
hand, these types are abstracted from history, transcending strict
chronological limits:

> . . . societies belonging typologically to early antiquity do
> not necessarily arise only in the chronological framework of
> the classical ancient Orient: in certain places the same ty-
> pology can also be traced in the first millennium B.C. and—
> albeit for a short time—in the first millennium A.D., as, for
> instance, in northern and eastern Europe. In the tropics, in
> mountainous zones, and in piedmont regions, the same ty-
> pology may linger and even reemerge as late as the second
> half of the second millennium A.D.[15]

On the other hand, specific discussions always emphasize and make
clear that the factor of time—the period when early states emerge—is
crucial. In reference to the later second millennium military states (or
his third way of development), Diakonoff writes that

> the fact that these societies took longer to attain the level of a
> class society and of civilization gave Egypt and Lower Meso-
> potamia the time to exert a powerful cultural influence on
> these areas—an influence aimed precisely at strengthening
> the authority of temples and of the royal power.[16]

These "types," thus, are related to one another historically (i.e., they
mutually influence one another), as, undoubtedly, also would be true
for areas for which we cannot adequately reconstruct their early ways
of development from the available historical evidence (e.g., India and
China).

The question arises as to whether or not an unnecessary tension has
been fostered between the historical account and the abstracted
evolutionary types. Are the latter really necessary for writing a universal history? The purpose they serve must be the simplification and
ordering of data, but their use exacts the price (reinforced by the organizational framework of the work) of minimizing the historical relationships and interconnections among the separate societies that
transformed themselves into states during the course of the same
"world-historical" time.

Marxism and Beyond: The Missing Dialogue

The History of the Ancient World does not concern itself solely with the
reconstruction of socioeconomic systems. Its Marxism is not the crude

15. Lecture 1, p. 46.
16. Lecture 1, p. 45.

variety that cleanly separates phenomena of the base from those of the superstructure. Some of the most fascinating sections attempt to reconstruct ancient thought: mythologies, worldviews, early systems of "proto-ethics," and later philosophies. In these sections, ancient ideology is not simply reduced to "false consciousness," though ancient thought is viewed as related to and ultimately derivative of social reality; that is, social experience determines consciousness, more than the reverse. The discussions of how reality colors consciousness and, in turn, is changed by it under the relatively low level of development of productive forces in antiquity are insightful and stimulating.

In Lecture 1 Dr. Diakonoff adumbrates an agenda for a future generation of historians. As the mature reflections of a great scholar, his suggestions deserve careful attention; as recommendations for a more complete accounting of the past by a leading Soviet Marxist historian, whose writings over a long and distinguished career have substantially refined and sustained their still-dominant stage theory of successive socioeconomic formations, they are of great intellectual interest. The attempt is to provide a more comprehensive understanding of the past than that obtained from an exclusive focus on the interplay between changes in the forces and changes in the relations of production.

Maintaining his materialism by citing the well-known dictum that an idea becomes a material force once it is seized by mass consciousness, Diakonoff argues for a history of emotions that utilizes and extends analytical techniques developed by social psychologists. Major historical events of universal historical significance, such as the initial spread of Islam or the French Revolution, cannot be adequately explained by nor deduced from a consideration solely of developments in the forces and relations of production. Why some movements have succeeded and others failed and why they occurred precisely when they did cannot be explained simply by consideration of economic phenomena. His is a call for a historical social psychology, a new, much more comprehensive history of culture that considers everything "that . . . has an impact upon society and that induces men and women to socially valid actions."[17]

These thoughtful, provocative suggestions are offered to future historians of antiquity, but they are of interest to other specialists concerned either empirically or theoretically with macrohistorical developments: anthropologists, archaeologists, historical sociologists, economic historians and historically minded economists, social psychologists, and, of course, medieval and modern historians. It is impossible to read this section without reflecting upon the unfortunate

17. Lecture 1, p. 63.

absence of reference to trends in contemporary Western historiography and to Western macrohistorical studies and critiques and defenses of historical materialism.

One would like to know, for example, how Diakonoff would evaluate the macrohistorical works of certain French *Annales* historians in terms of his called-for historical social psychology. Would Braudel's use of a plurality of times from the *longue durée* to the event be considered a useful or a confused and obfuscatory analytical technique for ordering history on a macroscale? Superficially, at least, the well-known attempts to write histories of the *mentalités* of given periods (e.g., the studies of G. Duby, J. LeGoff, P. Aries) seem to have already set in practice Diakonoff's recommendations for a more complete understanding of the past. Or do they? Would Diakonoff criticize them on fairly obvious materialist grounds? Diakonoff undoubtedly would insist that whether one writes an *histoire des mentalités* or a historical social psychology of the sort he envisages, the critical task is to relate the collective representations or psychology of a society at a particular point in time to its social structure, internal contradictions, and class antagonisms. He would correctly assert that if these connections are not made, the result may be a kind of muddled, imprecise history of ideas in which the *mentalités* are viewed either as inexplicably resisting change or teleologically exhibiting a gradual "drift towards enlightenment."[18]

In certain respects, Diakonoff's discussion of the limitations of previous socioeconomic historical research and suggestions for a history of emotions and a broadened history of culture seem to anticipate or independently voice many of the objections articulated by M. Sahlins in his not-insensitive and—to a Marxist purist—disturbing critique of "practical reason."[19] Conceptual differences, of course, are manifest. Sahlins emphasizes the symbolic ordering of Western (or, here, industrial) society and its nonreflective, culturally conditioned belief in "ob-

18. The phrase is M. Gismondi's. See his penetrating analysis of the *histoire des mentalités*, or what he sarcastically refers to as this "new approach to illuminating the role of the common people in history." See his "'The Gift of Theory': A Critique of the *Histoire des Mentalités*," *Social History* 10, no. 2 (1985). For an extended discussion of the early development of the *histoire des mentalités* in the *Annales* and the divergent emphases given it by L. Febvre and M. Bloch, see A. Burguiere, "The Fate of the History of Mentalities in the *Annales*," *Comparative Studies in Society and History* 24, no. 3 (1982). In a personal communication, Dr. Diakonoff has informed me that he evaluates the contribution of Braudel and the *annalistes* in a generally positive light.

19. See M. Sahlins, *Culture and Practical Reason* (Chicago: University of Chicago Press, 1976), as well as his later historical essays on Polynesia: *Historical Metaphors and Mythical Realities: Structure in the Early History of the Sandwich Islands Kingdom* (Ann Arbor: University of Michigan, 1981), and *Islands of History* (Chicago: University of Chicago Press, 1985).

jective" reality and the dominance of pragmatic activities and seeks a historical synthesis of conventionally posed alternatives, such as structure and history, materialism and idealism, or infrastructure and superstructure. Diakonoff appeares unaware or, at least, unconcerned with the problem of subjectivity and never abandons an essentially historical materialist position, though attempting to extend the traditional reading of Marx among Soviet historians. Nevertheless, certain points of similarity remain. It can be argued that with some modification, Diakonoff's recommendations might be rephrased to incorporate the anthropological concept of culture initially developed by F. Boas, a change that for Sahlins would represent the initial, minimally necessary emendation to Marx. If this were attempted, one could, perhaps, more clearly detect and understand the differences that separate a more sophisticated historical materialism from the symbolic anthropological or "culturological" approach of Sahlins.

Unfortunately, this exercise is unlikely ever to be undertaken, for these possible protagonists carry on totally different scholarly discourses. Here, one can only note and regret the lack of common conceptual ground, the absence of a shared vocabulary and literature among scholars concerned with essentially similar theoretical problems on either side of the East-West political divide. The absence of dialogue is as apparent as it is unnecessary. Western readers of *The History of the Ancient World* will appreciate the quality of historical research on antiquity conducted by Soviet specialists, a fact long recognized by ancient Near Eastern scholars. However, when one turns to broader theoretical concerns, an unfortunate vacuum exists in which Soviet and Western scholars seem to be either unaware of or out-of-date with each other's works. There are for example, more recent Western overviews and macrohistorical theories than those advanced by Spengler and Toynbee (as intimated in the Introduction). In reality, though, the problem is more serious on the Western side, where the tendency is to dismiss out of ignorance (including the inability to read Russian) Soviet writings as dogmatic and uninteresting. The condemnation is not only uninformed but paradoxical: how can such benighted theory produce such quality scholarship? One is reminded of the equally illogical political view that fears a Soviet Union bent on world domination while at the same time predicts the imminent collapse of its economy—a thought that inexorably leads one to the gloomy, if realistic, expectation that communication among scholars, as well as politicians, is likely to improve substantially only when the objective conditions for its persistence themselves change; that is, when both sides move beyond the cold war realities of the last forty years and define a new relationship. Translation of *Early Antiquity*, obviously represents no such breakthrough, but it does provide us with a unified current overview of antiquity and constitutes a small step toward maintaining and extending a sadly underdeveloped dialogue among interested, open-minded scholars and laypersons on the nature of long-term historical developments. For the moment, all we should do is simply sit back and enjoy this integrated vision of ancient history presented to us by a group of Soviet specialists.

Many people worked on the English translation of *Early Antiquity*. A. Kirjanov provided a rough translation of the entire volume and completed his task in the time promised. My duties as project director and final editor were immensely simplified by the fact that Mr. Kirjanov's translations were entered into the Wellesley computer by Ms. Daria Kirjanov, a former student at the College. Initially, I must confess to being somewhat intimidated by the rigorous standards of editing insisted upon by Dr. Diakonoff; his command of English and impeccable sense of grammar, no doubt, increased my consternation. Obviously, he is primarily responsible for the standards of consistency and editorial uniformity present in the work. Wellesley College must be acknowledged for the support it provided, especially for covering the expenses of mailing rough and edited drafts to Leningrad; the help of the Department of Anthropology's secretary at Wellesley, Ms. Edna Gillis, in the final preparation of Lectures 11 and 19 also must be mentioned. Publication would have been impossible without the assistance, indeed encouragement, of the University of Chicago Press, particularly of its most able and understanding editor Ms. Karen Wilson. I would also like to thank Dr. Norman Yoffee at the University of Arizona for his support and for originally suggesting to people at the University of Chicago Press that I actively participate in this project and Dr. C. C. Lamberg-Karlovsky of Harvard University for critiquing the initial draft of this Foreword. My wife, Barbara Gard, son, Owen, and daughter, Mira (who was born during the long gestation of this work), must be praised for their tolerance of my sequestering myself for inexplicably interminable hours in our "computer room." Without their unreasonable patience and encouragement this work would not have appeared.

And, finally, I wish to acknowledge that it has been a privilege to have worked with Dr. I. M. Diakonoff on this project. The breadth of his erudition and stature as a scholar require no more comment. Once we had agreed upon a system of editing and regularly corresponded, all work proceeded smoothly. I like to believe this was accomplished not only because we shared the same professional goal of producing a scrupulously accurate and readable translation but also because we grew to appreciate each other as colleagues and friends. I am most grateful to have had this opportunity.

Introduction

THE EDITORIAL BOARD

General Remarks

The occasion to write this book arose out of work conducted over many years by a large group of collaborators at the Oriental Institute of the USSR Academy of Sciences and other scholarly institutions during the preparation of the extensively documented, multivolume *Istoriya drevnego Vostoka* [History of the ancient orient]. As the latter publication is oriented toward specialists, our editorial board and group of authors decided to write the present work in the interest of reaching a broader public. Directed at a wider audience, this work examines the history of ancient class societies and states that once existed in Asia, Europe, and North Africa as part of the process of the historical development of humanity. Scholars of numerous scientific and educational institutions from all parts of the Soviet Union participated in this effort.

Thus, our publication, which will consist of three volumes (*Early Antiquity*, *The Florescence of Ancient Societies*, and *The Decline of Ancient Societies*), is an attempt to create a historical account involving the entire ancient world. It is based on contemporary knowledge and a clearer understanding not only of the individual features of specific societies but also of the general features characteristic of ancient class societies as a whole. We hope that it also will contribute to the solution of ongoing theoretical controversies on this subject. The authors believe that the idea that specific ancient societies exhibit an absolute dissimilarity among themselves has arisen through examining them according to unsuitable reference scales that are either too restricted spatially or too narrow temporally. The authors contend that a comprehensive view of all ancient societies, seen in relation to each other, will reveal general outlines of a regularity in the historical development of humanity. The readers will judge whether or not we were right.

Today's universities offer separate courses on the specific histories of Greece, Rome, and the ancient Orient. In the case of the Orient, the courses end abruptly at arbitrary periods in the development of the various Asian or African societies, and their histories are not presented as integral parts of a universal historical process. *Vsemirnaya istoria* [Universal history] (vols. 1–2, Moscow, 1955–56) does permit a comparison between the more significant societies in the context of universal historical development; however, it is too voluminous and, therefore, does not offer a general perspective. Moreover, new data have made this work, to a considerable degree, obsolete.

Other than *Vsemirnaya istoria,* no general, comprehensive survey of the history of the ancient world has appeared in the Soviet Union. This lack is due to the difficulty of treating material covering so many societies and periods (a fact that sometimes leads to general textbooks being written by authors insufficiently versed in the historiography of some of the societies treated). It was therefore decided to assign the writing of each section of the book to specialists in particular fields. Keeping in mind the experience gained in the publication of *Vsemirnaya istoria,* we tried to avoid excessive unification of the authors' texts. Thus, the present publication is actually a collection of lectures in book form, read by different experts, each in his or her own way, but presented so as to create a general overview. Without supplying exhaustive data (because the contents of each lecture were determined by the specific interests, abilities, and resources of the individual lecturer), such a series should ideally offer a general notion of the subject matter with which it deals. The contents of the book, however, are ultimately determined by the staff of "lecturers" available. Our book, thus, suffers from inevitable gaps, and there are some differences in the views adopted by the various writers on specific questions, as well as some dissimilarities, for example, in treating cultural questions concerning different societies. Each lecturer presents his or her own point of view; and depending on an author's individual interests and preferences, the character of the presentation, as well as the relative emphasis on the different materials presented (e.g., the amount of information on political, ethnic, or cultural history relative to socioeconomic information), changes from lecture to lecture. The editorial board assumes responsibility for the overall scientific and methodological quality of this book without necessarily agreeing with the individual authors or particular questions.

On theoretical issues, there is no unanimity among Soviet historians (the problem is discussed in more detail below). This lack of agreement naturally is reflected in our text. The editorial board did not consider it possible to impose its own viewpoint, though a general editorial statement appears in the introductory chapter to each volume. In order to ensure a certain degree of structural integrity for the book, however, the editorial board preferred to invite scholars to contribute who share most of their theoretical positions and who work within the mainstream tradition of Soviet scholarship. Such authors would, we believed, reflect more or less faithfully the views of the majority of Soviet scholars. However, other opinions on a number of important theoretical questions do exist among scholars, as we will attempt to show below.

Notwithstanding the closeness of their theoretical viewpoints, it is quite understandable that there are disagreements among our authors, as an attentive reader will easily discover. Yet, it is important to emphasize that despite disagreements on minor points, the authors based themselves on similar theoretical premises and had a similar understanding of their task, so that these lectures by no means constitute a shapeless collection. Rather, it represents a well-defined entity whose parts, ultimately, are closely knit together.

During the editing process, the editors made various suggestions and asked the authors for certain modifications of their texts. The final decision, nevertheless, lay with the author. In the interest of unity, the editorial board also took the liberty of expressing its own opinion about the material presented by the individual authors— namely, in the general theoretical sections preceding each of the three volumes of the work. The editors actually intervened only where the designed length of the book or other technical considerations warranted such action. The suggestions and factual corrections of numerous scholars who read the manuscripts were taken into careful consideration.

Given the character of this publication as lectures in book form, the sections are called "lectures" rather than "chapters." There are four reasons justifying such a designation: the independence of the sections; the fact that some of them are actually based on lectures delivered at universities or other institutions; the fact that the amount of material, in most cases, fits into the time span normally allotted to a lecture; and, finally, the fact that such a format may be helpful in using this book as a reference manual. It is necessary to emphasize that this book does not pretend to replace existing textbooks, particularly university texts on Greece and Rome, which develop the material in more detail but fail to show the position of the societies treated within the overall human historical process. As we have already stressed, this book does not claim to be an exhaustive treatment of all regions and problems of the ancient world. At the same time, the lectures, written independently by different authors, partially overlap. We hope, nevertheless, that this book conveys an integral and more or less internally consistent view of the ancient world.

Convinced of the unity of the historical process, the authors considered it possible to adopt a single periodization system for the history of ancient class societies and divided the materials into three stages, constituting three separate volumes. The first stage (the formation of class society and the state and the early forms of this society) encompasses a long time span, stretching from the end of the fourth to the end of the second millennium B.C. The second stage (the florescence of ancient societies and the highest development of the "slave" economy) begins with the introduction of iron at the end of the second and beginning of the first millennium B.C. and lasts throughout the entire first millennium B.C. The third stage (the decline of ancient societies and the appearance of features indicating the transition to feudalism) occupies approximately five centuries of the first millennium A.D.

The detailed characterization of each stage, of its economic, political, and cultural features, is given in the introductory lectures preceding each of the three volumes. Within each volume we tried to examine the individual countries chronologically. Each volume is subject to a typological principle of periodization. As far as possible, we characterized the various countries according to their respective stage of historical development. Expecting a wide readership (i.e., students, teachers, and anyone interested in ancient history), the staff of writers aimed for simplicity, clarity, and an accessible presentation (based on scientific data available in the early 1980s).

Discussion of Theoretical Problems in Contemporary Ancient Historiography

Any textbook on history in our country is usually preceded by an introductory section defining the subject under consideration and stating the fundamentals of the Marxist approach to history. The present work is not a textbook; it is intended for readers with a sufficiently high educational background who are sufficiently versed in the fundamentals of historical materialism. Today, the Marxist method maintains a dominant place among Soviet historians and occupies an important position all over the world. As admitted by many Western scholars, there does not exist in the West any complete and consistent theory of history regarded as a single process, a theory comprehensive enough to match that of historical materialism. We will assume that the latter is known to the readers and will attempt to acquaint them with those theoretical problems that today remain unresolved.

The central questions of the discussion, which some years ago concerned Soviet historians, can be formulated in philosophical terms as follows: What is the correlation between the general and the particular in the development of the different societies and civilizations during the precapitalist period? The question can be rephrased in terms of historical science as follows: Is there a single, common path of development for all precapitalist societies (unavoidably with local variants), or are there several? Of course, all Marxist historians adhere to the concept that, in the final analysis, the relations of production are determined by the level of development of the means of production. Yet, in theory, it is quite possible to accept that specific local features of the means of production (e.g., those depending on geographical factors) can lead, under certain specific conditions, to peculiar trends in production relations, thus producing typologically different societies. In its most general form, this question asks whether the "West" (i.e., Europe) and the "East" (i.e., virtually the rest of the world) have been developing in more or less the same way, or whether the course of development each has followed is radically different.

The idea of a radical difference between the East and the West arose in European scholarship long ago. European philosophers, historians, and writers of belles-lettres became interested in the East as early as the seventeenth century. They built their theories on the Bible, on the sparse and not always reliable information of Graeco-Roman writers, and later on information acquired from European ambassadors at the courts of Oriental rulers, from travelers, missionaries, and, since the middle of the eighteenth century, from colonial functionaries. These theories were used by ideologues of the growing bourgeoisie for their political aims. The attitude toward the political order of the East swung from idealization, which presented the social and state order of Oriental societies (especially of China) as models to be emulated (L. Levalier, Voltaire, F. Quesnay), to sharp condemnations of and warnings against any attempts to follow these examples (F. Bernier, Ch. Montesquieu, and J. J. Rousseau in France and D. Defoe in England). On the whole, however, the dominant viewpoint was that the fundamental difference between the East and the West consisted in the absence of private property in the Orient. It was assumed that all the land in that part of the world belonged to the monarchs as their property, and that this supreme proprietorship was the foundation of "Oriental despotism" and of "general slavery."

The same point of view, with sundry variations, predominated in the beginning of the nineteenth century. Representatives of pre-Marxian political economy (Adam Smith, J. Stuart Mill, et al.) and philosophy (G. F. W. Hegel) subscribed to this idea, despite information available at that time about the existence in many nations of community relationships, private property, and so on.

In studying the problems of capitalist society, Marx and Engels inevitably became interested in societies that had not yet reached the level of capitalist development—hence, their interest in the Orient. However, they began studying the Orient only in 1853, with most of their efforts concentrated between 1857 and 1859. Their opinions stemming from these studies were outlined in a draft of a manuscript by Marx, *Precapitalist Economic Formations* (not published during Marx's lifetime). The Preface to *The Critique of Political Economy* offers a more succinct review of this subject. In his analysis, Marx formulates the regular succession of modes of production: "In broad outlines Asiatic, ancient, feudal, and modern bourgeois modes of production can be designated as progressive epochs in the economic formation of society."[1] This is the first expression of a dialectical materialist view of history as a single developmental process. This conclusion, of course, was drawn from the scientific data accumulated up to that time. Let us point out, however, that Marx's formula assumes that an "Asiatic" mode of production precedes the ancient—that is, the slave-owning mode of production. Also his formula lacks another natural human developmental stage: the primitive mode of production. The later works of Marx and Engels developed the fundamental principles of historical materialism in more detail, and as new data became available, these principles evolved further, and particular features of historical processes were better understood.

Information about the work of historians during the period in question (i.e., about writings that were used by Marxist theoreticians), can be found in special publications dedicated to historiography. Here we will only mention the work by L. H. Morgan: *Ancient Society; or, Researches in the Line of Human Progress from Savagery through Barbarism to Civilization* (1877). In his *Origin of the Family, Private Property, and the State*, Engels notes that Morgan's book has "the same significance for the history of primitive society as Darwin's theory of evolution has for biology."[2] Morgan's book was written from an independently derived materialist position and contained considerable data about preclass social structure as well as about approaches to the emergence of class society; that is, about data illustrating the fundamental positions of historical materialism, which could and did lead to further and deeper studies.

We must point out that after the appearance of the first volume of *Capital*, the term "Asiatic mode of production" disappears from the writings of Marx and Engels. It is also absent from Lenin's works (except, of course, in references to the earlier publications of Marx and Engels). On the whole, the development of historical materialism led to the conclusion that society passed through three consecutive developmental stages or formations in the precapitalist period: primitive order, slave-owning order, and feudalism.

The end of the nineteenth century and the first decades of the twentieth century saw a rapid development of Oriental studies and an accumulation of enormous amounts of new information, which was not easy to sort out. Among the professional historians of that time, there was no unified conception of history, except for the hypothesis of cyclical development, a theory that was rapidly losing its support-

---

1. K. Marx and F. Engels, *Selected Works* (Moscow: Progress Publishers, 1973), 1:504.

2. Ibid., 3:201.

ers. According to this hypothesis, development occurred from primitive feudalism to Graeco-Roman capitalism, from capitalism back to feudalism, from there to a new capitalism, and so on. This hypothesis was most vividly presented by Eduard Meyer in the several volumes of his *History of Antiquity* (published between 1884 and 1902; numerous reeditions appeared until the middle of the twentieth century). A somewhat similar cyclical theory was suggested by Oswald Spengler (*The Decline of the West*, 2 vols., 1918–23). Based on his theory, Spengler thought it possible to present "the spiritual form, duration, rhythm, meaning, and product of the still unaccomplished stages of our Western history." However, Spengler's predictions did not come true. In the West the views of the philosophers W. Dilthey, B. Croce, and R. Collingwood became most important. They thought that history could be understood only insofar as it is made comprehensible by professional historians working on specific problems; nothing more can reasonably be expected. Most historians limited themselves to the accumulation of new data.

That the cyclical theory of history is unsatisfactory for explaining the latest events of world history soon became evident. It followed from this that its explanation of any stage of history could be questioned. This lack of satisfaction contributed to a great degree to the rise among Russian historians of an interest in the Marxist theory of the historical process, which had already had its adherents in Russian academic circles as early as the 1890s to 1910s (e.g., N. I. Sieber and A. I. Tyumenev). This interest continued to grow in the 1920s and 1930s, when historians began to seek, along with the rest of the intelligentsia, their niche in the emerging Soviet society.

A general interpretation of newly acquired data from the perspective of the fundamentals of historical materialism was urgently required. After long discussions in which different solutions were suggested within the framework of Marxist theory, a general interpretation was proposed in 1933 by V. V. Struve (originally, a student of E. Meyer) in his address "Problem of the Origin, Development, and Decline of Slave-Owning Society in the Ancient Orient" and in his article "Plebeians and Helots." Struve's outstanding erudition (he used Egyptian, Mesopotamian, and classical sources) allowed him to support the conclusion that ancient Oriental society, despite all its specific features, belonged to the slave-owning type. This theory was not immediately accepted. One of Struve's most active opponents, A. I. Tyumenev, learned Sumerian in order to verify this conclusion. For fifteen years he investigated Sumerian administrative and economic documents; his findings, however, can be regarded as not fundamentally disagreeing with those of Struve.

From then on, especially during the postwar period, the concept of the slave-owning character of ancient Oriental society was dominant among Soviet historians.[3] This viewpoint affirms the unity of the universal historical process, leaving no ground for the "Europe-centered" and "Orient-centered" concepts of universal history. Almost all the authors of our book have worked in the tradition established by Struve and Tyumenev.

In the West during this period and slightly later, Arnold Toynbee's theory of universal history was most popular. He presented it in the ten volumes of his *A Study of History* (1934–57). According to Toynbee, "civilizations"—twenty-one in number—successfully emerged and grew in response to certain sociocultural "challenges," under the leadership of creative minorities. Civilizations declined when the leaders failed to act according to the demands of the historical situation. Actually, Toynbee's theory is simply an elaborate rationalization of the popular notion that history is a multicolored kaleidoscope of irregular events. Despite a number of useful ideas and acute observations, Toynbee's theory, on the whole, has made little impact on the discipline of history.[4] Lately, however, the necessity of regarding the historical process as a series of identical stages in all parts of the world has also been recognized in the West; human history is now currently subdivided into pre-urban, urban, and industrial societies.

The postwar period saw an even more active development in Oriental and African studies. Recently collected data naturally required new theoretical generalizations, since the new facts did not always fit the old historical schemes. When such a situation arises in science, two solutions are possible; either the old theories must be adjusted or modified, or if this is not feasible, new theories must be substituted. (The latter solution may also consist of a return to older, formerly rejected theories that now appear more consistent with the new evidence.) Many Marxist historians considered, and still consider, that new facts do not require revision of existing theories, particularly of the theory of ancient society as slave-owning. More accurate definitions are all that is required. This group of historians accepts the existence of multiple development variants in ancient society similar to

3. The most complete defense of this perspective on ancient history can be found in G. F. Il'yin, "Rabstvo i drevnii Vostok" [Slavery and the ancient Orient], *Narody Azii i Afriki*, 1973, no. 4.

4. Perhaps, one also should mention the theory of hydraulic (irrigation-based) Oriental civilizations that was popular in the West about the same time. According to this theory, the complete monopoly of state economies, supposedly typical of the Orient, was a form of state socialism. Regardless of the obvious political bias of this theory, we may state that it was largely mistaken, since most of the ancient Oriental societies were not based on irrigation, and their state economies usually coexisted with the private/communal economic sector. Today, this theory essentially has been abandoned.

those, for example, that characterized nineteenth–twentieth century capitalism (except that during antiquity the differences between the variants were more pronounced). They do not regard the variants as different socioeconomic formations characterized by different modes of production but merely view them as variants of one and the same ancient mode of production. Hence, they adhere to the position that emphasizes the "unity of human historical development." Most of the authors of this book belong to this group.

On the other hand, many scholars considered and still consider that a radical revision of views about ancient Oriental societies is necessary in order to overcome the danger of overschematization and dogmatism. Several works criticizing the slave-owning view of ancient Oriental societies have been published. In addition, the concept of an Asiatic mode of production, which was based on an early work of Marx and which was popular in the 1920s, has again become a subject of discussion.

The first works supporting this latter concept appeared in print at the end of the 1940s, but debate started in our country only after the 1964 publication of the French Marxist theoretical journal *Pensée*, which contained several articles on the Asiatic mode of production. J. Chesnaux, for example, wrote that the Asiatic mode of production "is characterized by a conjunction of the productive activity of village communities with the economic intervention of the state authorities, the state simultaneously both exploiting and ruling these communities." In brief, he defined this mode of production as "despotic-cum-village community." According to Chesnaux, the fundamental difference between the Asiatic despotic state and other precapitalist states consists in the fact that the former "is itself the organizer of production." The main contradiction of such a society is not between classes but between the state and the communities.[5] Subsequently, Chesnaux revised his views.

In 1965, the Soviet journal *Narody Azii i Afriki* published the theses of two French Marxist scholars, the Africanist J. Suret-Canal and the theoretician M. Godelier, as well as Struve's responding thesis. This publication actually triggered new discussions among scholars in our country. The controversy developed in two directions. The first was a more profound study of the classic Marxist-Leninist writings in order to demonstrate that Marx, Engels, and Lenin actually adhered consistently to the "Asiatic mode of production" concept. These attempts, however, must be regarded as failures, since in their later writings, as

5. According to Marxist philosophy, any process is moved by some main inner contradiction. For example, capitalist development is moved by the contradiction between the capitalist and the working class.

already mentioned, Marx and Engels never again referred to this concept. Moreover, the fundamental Marxist work on the subject belongs
among these later writings, namely, *The Origin of the Family, Private
Property, and the State,* which was written by Engels on the basis of
Marx's own notes.

The other side of the controversy was supported by a number of
authors who criticized the slave-owning concept of ancient Oriental
society, proposing their own models and using supporting data from
their particular areas of expertise without always paying attention to
materials from other regions. Unfortunately, many of these authors'
publications were based on secondary and even tertiary sources.

We cannot enumerate all the participants in this debate or all their
arguments. We shall only mention the most typical and important ones.

First of all, we must note that the concept of an Asiatic mode of production implies that a special structure (or "formation") existed parallel to the slave-owning structure (formation). This particular developmental path was determined by special geographical conditions,
particularly by the need for artificial irrigation. It generated the centralized power of a despotic ruler and was also the cause of the long-
term preservation of the primitive community, which was subject to
exploitation. Although private property did not appear in such societies, it is assumed that the existence of the Asiatic mode of production is "everlasting" (apparently since the disintegration of the
primitive community order?). E. S. Varga supported this view,[6] and
Struve admitted the validity of the above-mentioned theses (with certain caveats), though as applied only to the early period of antiquity.

More complex structures were also proposed. L. S. Vasil'ev and
I. A. Stuchevskii proposed their own concept of a "secondary" formation; that is, a formation positioned between the primitive order and
capitalism.[7] According to these authors, a society emerging from the
primitive order can proceed along one of three, almost equally possible, paths: slave ownership, feudalism, or the Asiatic order (the last
combining features of the first two). The actual path is not determined by the developmental level of the forces of production (it is
about equal in all cases.) but by the type of community, which, in turn,
is determined mainly by environmental conditions.[8]

6. *Ocherki po problemam politekonomii kapitalisma* [Essays on the politicoeconomic problems of capitalism] (Moscow: Nauka, 1964).
7. "Tri modeli vozniknoveniya dokapitalisticheskikh obshchestv" [Three models for
the origin of precapitalist societies], *Voprosy istorii,* 1966, no. 6.
8. In his recent work *Istoriya drevnego Vostoka* [History of the ancient Orient],
vols. 1–2 (Moscow: Nauka, 1985), L. S. Vasil'ev bases his arguments, on the one hand,
on Hegel and early Marxian work and, on the other, on social anthropology and con-
tends that all class societies are stagnant except those based on private property in the
means of production, as, for example, ancient Greece. Not distinguishing between sov-

A similar perspective is advanced in a number of writings by the prominent Soviet historian and philologist, G. A. Melikishvili.[9] In Melikishvili's opinion, the most common manifestation of precapitalist class society is feudalism. The slave-owning order appears only in exceptional cases (Phoenicia, Greece, Rome), culminating in a return to the main road; that is, to feudalism. During the early developmental stages of a class society, the Asiatic mode of production can also come into existence. This mode of production is defined by Melikishvili as a "protofeudal" complex of exploitation methods.[10]

Although Melikishvili's view differs from the one adopted in this book, it is nevertheless close to it in many respects. We actually agree with him on the existence of various types of development within the framework of ancient society. However, we try to stress common features, defining the different types of ancient societies as ways of development of one and the same ancient mode of production. Melikishvili puts more emphasis on the distinguishing characteristics, which he considers different production structures. Yet Melikishvili emphasizes, to a greater extent than we do, the similarity between the mode of production of antiquity and that of the Middle Ages. To us the difference in this case is more substantial. (At the same time, doubtless no one could dispute the fact that ancient society differs less from medieval society than both differ from capitalism; capitalism, in other words, is separated from feudalism by a sharper break.)

The picture of world history drawn by another Soviet historian and philosopher, V. P. Ilyushechkin, seems to us oversimplified.[11] He studies the forms of exploitation attested in antiquity and in the Middle Ages and concludes that the number of possible methods of exploita-

ereignty and property, Vasil'ev asserts that only state property existed in all other ancient and medieval societies.

9. "K voprosu o kharaktere drevneishikh klassovykh obshchestv" [On the problem of the nature of the most ancient class societies], *Voprosy istorii*, 1966, no. 11; "Kharakter sotsial'no-ekonomicheskogo stroya na drevnem Vostoke (Opyt stadial'no-tipologicheskoi klassifikatsii klassovykh obshchestv)" [The nature of the socioeconomic formation in the ancient Orient (An attempt at a typological-stage classification of class societies)], *Narody Azii i Afriki*, 1972, no. 4; "Nekotorye aspekty voprosa o sotsial'no-ekonomicheskom stroye drevnikh blizhnevostochnykh obshchestv" [Some aspects of the problem of the socio-economic formation in ancient Near Eastern societies], *Vestnik drevnei istorii*, 1975, no. 2; and others.

10. It should be noted that G. G. Giorgadze, one of the authors of this book and Melikishvili's pupil, adheres to the theory that the different types of ancient societies cannot simply be reduced to varieties of the same slave-owning mode of production.

11. See his *Sistema vne-ekonomicheskogo prinuzhdeniya i problema vtoroi osnovnoi stadii obshchestvennoi evolyutsii* [The system of extraeconomic coercion and the problem of the second major stage of social evolution] (Moscow: Nauka 1970); *Sistemy i struktury doburzhuaznoy chastnosobstvennicheskoy ekspluatatsii* [Systems and structures of precapitalist exploitation by private proprietors] (Moscow: Nauka 1980).

tion was limited and the application of one or another depended on differences in specific historical conditions. From this, Ilyushechkin deduces that all precapitalist societies constitute a single "precapitalist formation," or "the second stage of social evolution."[12] At the same time, however, the author virtually ignores the forms of property in the means of production—especially land (real) property. But only the combination of the form of property in the means of production with the form of exploitation determines the dominant mode of production and its place in the historical process. Moreover, the author fails to consider the development of ideas, which depends on the processual development of socioeconomic history. It is well known that an idea becomes a material force as soon as it possesses the consciousness of the masses; but the ideational structure typical of antiquity is quite dissimilar from that of the Middle Ages, which also means that the incentives for mass behavior were different.

Finally, we also mention that new formations have been postulated (though without sufficiently convincing argumentation) during the course of this discussion (e.g., by Yu. I. Semenov).

Participants in this debate variously interpret the character, role, and significance of the factors that are fundamental to the theory of historical materialism. Such factors include property in the means of production (especially land); the character of exploitation: economic (via the market, where the labor force becomes a commodity) and noneconomic (by compulsion); and the correlation of these two factors (i.e., forms of property and exploitation): whether the persons exploited are deprived of property in the means of production or not. In our view, property as a relationship of classes must not be confused with simple physical possession, especially in the case when the possessor cannot legally dispose of the object in his own interest and at will.[13] Our position is that the character of a society is determined by the mode of production, which is realized in the developmental level of the means of production and is achieved and reflected (on the social level) in the character of property. This relation determines both the character of the exploitation and the class structure of the society. We believe our position to be in agreement with the tenets of historical materialism and that opposing theories have not offered clear answers to the problem of the correlation of these decisive factors in ancient societies.

12. Ilyushechkin's precapitalist formation or second stage of social evolution corresponds to the preindustrial or urban society.

13. That is, property can be defined as an object that an owner can use, possess, and dispose of in his own interest and at his own will, and can exclude any nonproprietor from using, possessing, or disposing of.

We will not offer further detailed presentation of the views and arguments produced by opponents of the slave-owning formation in the ancient Orient but will limit ourselves to outlining the fundamental directions taken by the discussion. Those desiring to familiarize themselves with its course are referred to V. N. Nikiforov's book *Vostok i vsemirnaya istoriya* [The East and world history] (Moscow, 1975). This work contains a thorough and, on the whole, well-argued analysis of all the viewpoints expressed in the discussion, as well as a comprehensive bibliography. In recent years, this debate has subsided. Its main utility lay in the fact that many of the participants (as well as historians who did not take a direct part in the discussion) subjected the arguments used to support their proposed historical constructions to a new thorough analysis, redefining their concepts where necessary. However, obviously, not all the questions of the history of the ancient world have been resolved. Uncertainty and incompleteness in our views are due mainly to the unequal quality and quantity of information regarding different periods and countries, as well as to an uneven elaboration of some trends of the historical process.

The greatest wealth of documented data about the entire period of antiquity, from the beginning of class civilizations to the start of the medieval era, comes from the Near East. We would like to point out that the taxonomic rank of early antiquity and late antiquity remains uncertain. Were there four taxonomically equivalent stages of one precapitalist society (early antiquity, late antiquity, early Middle Ages, late Middle Ages) or were there two consequent formations—an ancient and a medieval one, each of them subdivided into an early and a late stage (as has been assumed in this book)? Or is one dealing with three consequent precapitalist formations: early antiquity, late antiquity, and the Middle Ages? Here we arrive at an important theoretical difficulty, which is due to a certain vagueness in our constructions. We still actually do not know the mechanisms by which a society passes from one form to another, nor can we even establish whether the change in each case is from "formation" to "formation" or whether it is less important.

Naturally, because of the vast amount of historical information that students of the ancient Near East have amassed, many authors of our book have used Near Eastern data as a kind of standard. But, in the future, when our knowledge of the ancient societies in India, China, Central Asia, Iran, Egypt, and other African countries attains the same scientific level as our present knowledge of the Near East, Greece, and Rome, we hope that historical science will advance without the need for extrapolations from data acquired in one region to other regions.

The Problem of Sources for Ancient History

Sources of information on the history of the ancient world are manifold. In a number of cases, more information is available from certain early periods than from epochs much closer to our own time. These sources, however abundant, are incomplete, a fact that presents serious difficulties for the objective study of ancient history.

The history of ancient Mesopotamia, from the beginning of the third millennium B.C. to the beginnings of the Christian era (first century B.C. to first century A.D.), is reconstructed from original contemporary texts, written on clay tablets and other objects made of clay, stone, and metal. The script is called cuneiform, and the writing system is a complex, "word-syllabic" one. The quantity of cuneiform texts is enormous—hundreds of thousands, their number increasing every year as a result of new archaeological excavations. Yet it would be wrong to think that these discoveries give a completely satisfactory view of ancient Mesopotamian society, of its life and historic events. Royal inscriptions praise the gods and the king and inform us of the temples he built (and, less frequently, other structures). The inscriptions of Hittite and Assyrian kings relate only their military triumphs; their accounts are very much biased. (Defeats are, of course, ignored.) Texts recording laws are incomplete in terms of the social relations regulated by them and, as often as not, are poorly preserved; moreover, such texts have not been recovered for all historical periods and all countries. Religious-literary texts are mostly preserved only in fragments. They are difficult to date and usually illustrate only the official ideology. It is rarely possible to extract from them any information about the real life and views of the population. Administrative-economic texts, which represent the vast majority of the available cuneiform material, originate from state economies or the economies of government employees, merchants, and others. Again, the result is a one-sided view of society. It is not surprising that historians believed for a long time that only state or temple economies existed in Mesopotamia during the third millennium B.C. Texts recording private legal contracts appear on those relatively rare occasions when the social relations were in the process of change and when verbal contracts based on customary law were inadequate for a number of reasons. The periods that are illustrated by numerous written documents alternate with centuries from which not a single written document has reached us. The Hittite civilization, which existed in Asia Minor during the second millennium B.C. and also used the cuneiform script, left us only one royal archive, containing accounts of royal victories, treaties between states, legislative texts, instructions to employees, and innumerable magic rituals—but not a single document dealing with the private lives of men and women. From the second half of the first millennium B.C., when such new writing materials as parchment, pottery sherds (ostraca), and papyrus came into use in the Near East, practically no documents have reached us; parchment and papyrus disintegrate rapidly, and inscriptions in ink or sherds rub off or fade with the passage of time.

Let us now turn to the archaeological remains from the ancient Near East. Until recently, extensive excavations were conducted only on temples and palaces. Before the beginning of the twentieth century the unearthed sites of ancient towns were razed in search of tablets and statues and other "art" objects. Later excavations in Mesopotamia and other parts of the Near East were conducted by architects. Consequently, the cities began emerging with more clarity (although residential houses still attracted only minimal attention), but the circumstances surrounding such finds as domestic utensils and even tablets remained mostly unrecorded. For a long time, the excavations of towns and cities did not proceed stratum by stratum to lay bare the remains of the different periods. Even today, many pottery fragments, bones of domestic animals, and other artifacts are sometimes discarded—materials that could provide clues to aspects of the daily life and the diet of the inhabitants. Yet, even when the excavations are conducted in the best possible way, archaeology without the support of written records cannot provide a complete picture of the social structure or the spiritual culture of a past society. While archaeologists were gaining on-the-job training in the mastery of the complex digging techniques necessary to furnish proper material for historians, they often managed to destroy many interesting sites. As a rule, early archaeologists dug the best preserved ancient sites, and after having destroyed them, they left less significant sites to the next generation of scientists, whose methods were more sophisticated.

The history of Egypt has its own sources. The vast majority of written material is represented by prayers and invocations recorded on the walls of tombs and on funeral stelae (at times with much embellished, though standardized, biographies of the deceased). In relatively rare cases, inscriptions dedicated to the exploits of pharaohs were engraved on temple walls. More important even than the inscriptions are the wall paintings and reliefs illustrating the religious ideas of ancient Egyptians, who imagined the afterlife to be a copy of their earthly existence. In these pictures, we find numerous scenes of everyday life, although it is difficult to use them to re-create the social aspects of this life. The texts written on the well-known Egyptian papyri stem from relatively later times (second millennium and especially first millennium B.C. through the first millennium A.D.). A few ostraca containing economic and legal information have survived.

The first code of law was found recently but has not yet been fully published.

It was mainly religious, literary, and, occasionally, scientific subjects that were recorded on papyri, although documents originating from state administrative institutions have also come down to us. (Most of them are from the end of the second through the first millennium B.C., as well as from the Hellenistic and Roman periods.) A relatively small number (except for later periods) of legal contracts also exist. Keeping in mind that scholars understand Egyptian texts with less accuracy than they do the Babylonian texts, one may say that reconstruction of socioeconomic life in ancient Egypt is a very difficult matter, and much remains unclear. Art experts, as well as comparatively narrowly oriented philologists, have more success in their efforts than economic historians.

The smaller the number of documentary sources, the more difficult it is to reconstruct the history of a society. Documentary sources have two invaluable advantages. First, they are, as a rule, contemporary with the events they relate and, thus, provide more objective accounts of what really occurred. Second, given that the number of texts is sufficiently large and that we can ascertain that the large or small number of a certain type of document reaching us is not the result of the fortuitous conditions under which these documents were found, we can draw conclusions as to whether a particular social phenomenon was common or unusual during the period in question.

With regard to the so-called narrative sources (both purely literary works and works by ancient historians), it is important to realize that they do not inform us of actual facts but, rather, only of what the authors, or the group to which they belonged, thought about the subject. Though such information is certainly useful to the historian, we can rarely check the correctness of the data transmitted by a narrative source. Details describing sundry events and quotations of pronouncements made by historical figures are, in particular, nearly always fictitious.

The history of Palestine is known almost exclusively through narrative sources, although recently discovered archaeological data can, to some extent, be used in checking their validity. The narratives have been preserved in the Bible—the holy scriptures of the Jewish and Christian religions. The Bible is not a book but an entire library containing a number of writings dating from the twelfth to the second centuries B.C. (Old Testament) and from the first to the second centuries A.D. (New Testament). The Bible includes mythological and legendary accounts relating to the creation of the world and to the life of the peoples in and around Palestine (mainly Jews). It also includes criminal, civil, and ritual legislation; prosaic historical accounts (these can be verified to a substantial degree by comparing them with archaeological data, as well as with Assyrian, Babylonian, and Egyptian royal inscriptions and, occasionally, even with documents); religious and secular poetry; fragments of epic poems; religious and secular didactics; rhythmical religious (prophetic) sermons—actually often speeches on political events of the day (these can also be substantiated by historical information from other Near Eastern countries); fictional stories; and more. Clearly, this diverse material is of quite unequal historical value, but with the aid of historical criticism, biblical texts provide a great deal of reliable information. Unfortunately, the almost complete lack of documental sources severely limits the investigation of ancient Palestine, despite the fact that the number of documents has, in the past few years, increased, especially with the sensational discovery of the Dead Sea scrolls, dating from around the second century B.C. to the second century A.D.

The historiography of India presents a very difficult problem. Despite the flourishing of numerous sciences in ancient India—philosophy, mathematics, astronomy, grammar, and others—the science of history did not come into being. The ancient religious hymns, the *Veda*, ritual-legislative collections, epics, and philosophical and other treatises that have reached us can be dated only with the greatest difficulty. Although there are some royal inscriptions carved in stone (dating from a time not earlier than the third century B.C.), in most cases, they are not very informative. Documental sources are completely lacking. In the past half-century, Indian archaeology has made great progress. One of its major successes was the discovery of the ancient, previously unknown Indus civilization, which existed during the third and second millenia B.C. Unfortunately, its written texts consist only of very brief inscriptions on seals and other such items; they are insufficient to decipher the script. The structure of the grammar can be ascertained, but we are unable to read the words.

The ancient history of China is based almost exclusively on narrative sources. In contrast to India, historical literature flourished in China. Nevertheless, it only covered the period starting with the second half of the first millennium B.C., although historians of that time had access to more ancient records, which have not reached us. Inscriptions from earlier periods are preserved on bronze vessels of various kinds; divinatory texts, dating from the second millennium B.C., are also inscribed on sheep shoulder blades, turtle shells, etc. We also have ancient hymns and legends, but they have reached us in versions written down much later than the original compositions. There are numerous philosophical, scientific, economic, and military treatises, but until lately, there were scarcely any documentary sources available. Despite the fact that important discoveries have already been made, the archaeology of China is still in its initial phase. The most sensational discovery was that of the tomb of the first Chinese emperor, Ch'in Shih Huang-ti, which remained hidden throughout antiquity. It was surrounded by an entire army of realistically and brightly colored terra-cotta warriors of the imperial guard with all the details of their arms, clothing, and horses' accoutrements. Less sensational finds also promise a considerable increase in our knowledge about ancient China. Much has also been accomplished in the historical criticism of the written sources.

Until recently, the most ancient period of Greek history could be studied only from nontextual archaeological objects; just a few decades ago, the mysterious Mycenaean word-syllabic writing of the second half of the second millennium B.C. was deciphered. But the texts appeared to be accounts of the palace household, and for a number of reasons, scholars believe that the Greeks of that time did not record anything else. In addition to archaeological materials, the next period is illuminated by epics, which were composed during the eighth to seventh centuries B.C. and are attributed to Homer: *The Iliad* and *The Odyssey*. These poems pose a most complex problem in historical criticism: how to separate the poet's imagination from historical reality.

Almost no original documents written on perishable materials and contemporary with the events described have reached us from Greece and Rome. However, two fortunate circumstances neutralize this drawback. First, the Greeks (and later the Romans) produced a very rich and most diverse narrative literature, including some remarkable works of history that will be frequently quoted in our book. Thucydides (ca. 460–396 B.C.) can rightly be regarded as the founder of scientific historical criticism. Unfortunately, all these writings have reached us only in the form of medieval copies or on papyri, mostly from Egypt, of the first centuries A.D. They have required a huge amount of critical work. Second, in Greece and later in countries influenced by Greek culture (essentially the entire Near and Middle East and the Roman Empire), it was customary to record on stone all sorts of private and social events. Among these inscriptions we can find a detailed account of the reign of Augustus written by the Roman emperor himself, as well as a few heartfelt words in memory of a slave's concubine; or an enormous customs tariff on international trade, as well as the record of a private sacrifice to a deity. In some cases private deeds were also reproduced on stone. A large number of documentary materials from the times of Graeco-Macedonian and Roman rule have reached us on papyri from Egypt. Numerous legislative records and legal commentaries (mainly Roman) have also been preserved (again as medieval copies).

Today's scholars of Greek and Roman history and of culturally and politically related countries (including the ancient Black Sea littoral) have a great advantage over those researching the Oriental countries, because the sources for Greek and Roman history began to be studied about four hundred years earlier. The result is a truly enormous accumulation of scholarly work and historical criticism. However, new discoveries and interpretations of old materials continue to appear every year.

Graeco-Roman archaeology has achieved brilliant results. Everyone is familiar with the excavations of Pompeii—the city that perished under hot ash during a volcanic eruption in the first century of the Christian era. It was preserved almost intact, including inscriptions (graffiti) on the walls of the houses. Other discoveries are equally fascinating and successfully complement the abundant written sources. Modern science has developed underwater archaeology, making possible the discovery of the remains of sunken cities, as well as virtually intact ships that went down with all their freight two thousand years ago.

In the last few years, the field of comparative historical linguistics has advanced considerably. We may reasonably hope that this source will enable us to make at least a partial reconstruction not only of the material (archaeological) culture of humanity far beyond the range of written history but also of its mentality, its ideology and cultural values, and certain social features. The migration routes of the speakers of the most ancient languages are still hard to reconstruct. However, it seems that a collaboration of linguists with archaeologists, physical anthropologists (who, using the latest discoveries in genetics, have made spectacular progress), palaeobotanists, palaeozoologists, historians of the climate, and others will enable us to create a base for the science of *ethnogenesis* (the study of the origins of nations). Let us note that finding the origin of a nation implies the discovery of its *three distinct roots:* the history of its physical anthropological characteristics; the history of its language; and the history of its culture. We very rarely have information about all three.

This brief survey cannot, of course, replace a comprehensive summing up of research based on ancient sources. But it may provide at least an approximate idea about the character of the sources that served as a basis for the lectures in our book, about the degree to which the reported facts can be regarded as reliable, and about the obstacles confronted by scholars in their historical research.

In addition to the difficulties in studying these sources, we must mention the philological difficulties. Historians investigating the ancient world cannot afford to work with materials prepared for them

by philologists or archaeologists. It is crucial that the historians themselves read in the original, sort out, and interpret the necessary passages of ancient texts. They must also learn to interpret the results of
archaeological excavations.

The ancient historical sources are recorded in many, often complex
writing systems designed for dozens of languages, some of which are
not yet well understood. Some writing systems have not been fully deciphered, so that their interpretation is controversial. The languages
themselves were always changing and are still changing, so that fifth
century B.C. Latin differed considerably from the Latin of the first
century B.C. to the first century A.D., and the latter was notably distinct
from medieval Latin, which, in turn, was different from Renaissance
Latin. Akkadian, which existed for two and a half millennia, and Chinese, which existed for three and a half millennia, were, of course,
subject to still more drastic change.

To end with the problem of sources, it is worthwhile to dwell upon
the following question: Is it not a fact that the sources reach us accidentally, so that we may miss the more important ones? To this
legitimate question there is no unequivocal answer. Some countries
and some epochs are, one can assume, elucidated satisfactorily. Thus,
we know more about Rome under Emperor Augustus than about
seventeenth-century Russia. Our knowledge about, say, the time of
Nebuchadnezzar II or about the Old Babylonian Period is considerable but fragmentary. We know by name hundreds and thousands of
persons and the life histories of a few. Of other epochs we know, alas,
next to nothing, and considerable errors in reconstruction are possible and even probable. However, we can be sure that human society
lives and develops in accordance with certain uniform socioeconomic
and sociopsychological laws. Therefore, with great caution, we may
sometimes allow ourselves to extrapolate from the known without too
great a possibility of falling into error. In any event, there is no science that does not have its share of unknown or erroneously interpreted facts. Science is a *way* to truth, a gradual approach to it;
complete, absolute truth is unattainable.

History first emerged in antiquity as a genre of narrative art, and
it still retains some features of its literary origin. There is nothing
wrong in this, so long as it allows the historian to present a living picture of the past not only to the reader's intellect but also to the reader's
imagination. However, a subjective-emotional approach to the facts of
history can do incalculable harm to science and to society. One must
deduce from the fact what really happened, not what the historian
thinks ought to have happened. The scientist's task is the objective
cognition of facts; emotions induced by facts are antithetical to science.

Thus, the readers of our book must clearly understand that it does not contain absolute and final truths but, rather, just what can be said about the different subjects involved on the basis of present-day knowledge. Development of the historical sciences does not stop; our ideas about the past are changing and will continue to do so. Maybe it is the gradual revealing of truth that makes history so fascinating.

Problems of Ancient Chronology

Anyone approaching the study of ancient history will probably ask, How does one fix the time at which a particular event in ancient history took place? How reliable are the assigned dates? In the specialist literature, one actually finds numerous disagreements as to the dates of individual events and entire ancient epochs, not to mention the approximate nature of the datings. The difficulties in establishing the chronology of ancient history are due to the absence of adequate systems of year reckoning in most ancient lands, as well as to the character and condition of many sources, which are not always dated and which frequently cannot be dated even by circumstantial evidence (such as references to events for which the dates are known from other sources or spelling and writing peculiarities).

Such is the case especially with the dating of the most ancient periods of oriental societies. The establishment of the chronology in ancient oriental history is complicated by the fact that there was no single reference point from which to count the years. Each country had its own, very imperfect way of determining elapsed time.

Thus, in the Mesopotamian states it was customary, at one time, to designate a year according to some important event that took place during that year. Lists of such year designations (date formulae) were kept. Sources mention such dates as, for example, the year when a certain building was erected, the year of a war against a certain tribe, and so forth. In other cases, the years were counted according to the duration of the reign of each king. In Assyria, the count was kept by the annual tenures of certain functionaries—the so-called *limmu*. Scholars also refer to these Assyrian functionaries by the Greek word *eponym*. In order to correlate events that occurred at different times, it was necessary to compile lists of all the dating formulae (names of years) or lists of eponyms, or enumerations of kings with the lengths of their reigns. Such lists could be interrupted by wars or enemy conquests of the capital city, and they could contain both accidental and intentional errors: approximation of numbers and exclusion of some names, as well as of entire dynasties that, for political reasons, were not considered desirable to mention.

Such records can be correlated with our own chronological system only when they can be related at some point (better yet, at several) to firmly dated astronomical events, the dates of such events depending entirely on the laws of celestial mechanics. The most reliable reference points are solar eclipses. That is why all historical events that took place in the Near East starting from 1073 B.C. are usually dated with an average error no larger than one to two years. Less reliable are references to other astronomical time measurements, such as those based on the quite imperfect ancient observations of the planet Venus. This particular reference is used to date events in the history of Babylonia from the twenty-fourth to the sixteenth centuries B.C. After a series of corrections that resulted in lowering the proposed dates, we are left with a probable error of sixty-four years, forward or backward, for the end of the period in question, and up to one hundred years for its beginning. Historians have agreed to assign a conventional date, 1792–1750 B.C., to the reign of King Hammurapi of Babylon, from which the dates of other events, preceding or following, are calculated based on their distance in time from Hammurapi's rule. This dating system is called the middle chronology.

When a certain local chronology has a point of astronomical reference, it may also help to establish absolute dates for the ancient chronological systems of other countries. This determination depends on finding synchronisms between them; that is, historically verified indications that two specific public figures, one from each country, were contemporaneous or indications of battles, wars, and agreements between the two countries. A chronological system based only on synchronisms with another system (as are the chronological systems of ancient Asia Minor, Palestine, and other areas) is less accurate than a system directly tied to the astronomical time scale.

An additional difficulty in establishing an exact chronology for the ancient New East is that the year used in that region was mostly not solar (approximately 365 days) but lunar-solar, consisting of 12 months, with successive months alternating between 29 and 30 days, amounting to a total of 354 days in a year. The deviation from the natural calendar was compensated for by intercalating leap months, first irregularly and then, since the sixth century B.C., according to a rigorously applied system.

Today, our chronology is strictly correlated with astronomical time. Small errors caused by the somewhat imprecise coincidence between the civil and the astronomical year are corrected by adding one day during leap years.

In Egypt, time was counted by the length of reign of each pharaoh, and the count was renewed with each new ruler. A list of pharaohs indicating the duration of their reigns has not reached us in its complete form; it also contains gaps owing to scribal errors. Moreover, there was another shortcoming in this list that led to unjustified chronological extensions: reigns of pharaohs who ruled simultaneously (coregents, as well as contemporaneous kings, each governing part of the country during periods of political division) are presented as sequential. (The same happens sometimes in the king lists of Mesopotamia.) As a result, the estimate of dates during the third millennium B.C. oscillates within a 300-year range. It is only at the beginning of the second millennium B.C. that the estimates improve to the range of one or two decades. The dating becomes reliable from the middle of the first millennium B.C. on.

The situation with the dating of ancient Indian history is very poor. The reason is the nature of the preserved sources. Not a single example of historical work in the proper sense—be it chronicle, historical account, or treatise—is available from this region. Nor have any royal archives or any other official written documents yet been discovered. Virtually the only dated sources available for ancient India are inscriptions on stone and metal. But even these are few and stem from a relatively late time, beginning with the third century B.C. Let us remember that the oldest dated written sources of Egyptian and Mesopotamian history (although these dates are only approximate) are from the third millennium B.C.

In contrast to Indian sources, those of China contain numerous dates. This is because China, like Greece and Rome, is one of the few ancient countries where historical works were written. Ancient China has left us chronicles, dynastic histories, and valuable generalizing historical books. In his voluminous work *Shih Chi* [Historical notes], Ssu-ma Ch'ien (145–87 B.C.), the prominent historian of ancient China, paid great attention to chronology. This work, which encompasses the time from the mythological creation of the world to the end of the second century B.C., gives a chronological outline of ancient Chinese history. However, the basis for the system of dating that Ssu-ma Ch'ien and other Chinese authors use is often unclear. Therefore, their dates are not always quite reliable.

The situation with the chronology of Greek and Roman history is quite satisfactory because of the great number of historical works that have reached us and that contain sufficiently reliable datings. These works were based on several different chronological systems. Thus, a system of dating after yearly tenures of certain high state functionaries (the system also known from Assyria) was used in Athens, where years were counted by archon eponyms. In Rome the year count was based on the yearly terms of consuls. Partial records of archons and consuls inscribed on stone have been preserved. Furthermore, there was a pan-Greek year count based on the Olympiads—festivals that bound together the union of Hellenic communities. The Olympiads took place regularly every four years. The first Olympiad occurred, according to Greek legend, in 776 B.C.[14]

Later, the Romans established their year count from the legendary date of the foundation of Rome. The Roman historian Marcus Terentius Varro (first century B.C.) dated the foundation of Rome to the third year of the sixth Olympiad; that is, to 754–753 B.C. Attempting to determine the date of the foundation of Rome, Varro utilized synchronisms between the year count based on the office terms of consuls with the Greek count based on the Olympiads.

Claudius Ptolemaeus, the great Greek mathematician and astronomer of the second century A.D., connected the Greek chronology with the Babylonian, which, as mentioned above, has an exact astronomical point of reference. Moreover, the Graeco-Roman chronology has a number of other independent astronomical points of reference. Ptolemaeus's "Canon" includes references to several astronomically identifiable solar eclipses.

Beginning with the sixth to fifth centuries B.C., a new independent historical and chronological source appears, namely, coins. Numismatics is a field of scholarship devoted to the study of coins from the point of view of their metallic content, weight, area of diffusion, the declared and the actual face value, inscriptions (called legends), and the character of depicted objects and persons, including portraits of the heads of state who issued the coin. During archaeological excavations, coins are often found that have inscriptions of kings known from narrative sources (and sometimes unknown), and in a number of cases the portrait on the coin can be identified with already known sculptural portraits. Such coins constitute a link between archaeological data and the data of the inscriptions and narrative sources. Besides, numismatics supply diverse historico-economic, politico-geographic, and other data to the historian. This is especially important for periods on which other sources cast little light.

In the sixth century A.D., the Italian monk Dionysius Exiguus proposed a new chronological system based on the birth of Jesus Christ. For his point of orientation he used the date for the foundation of Rome. Dionysius proposed December 25 of the 753d year after Rome's foundation as the date of Jesus' birth. Accordingly, the foundation of Rome began to be dated in the year 753 before the birth of

14. It should be mentioned that the legendary character of the first Olympiad does not in any way invalidate the correctness of the Olympiad-based chronology. It is important that the initial point from which the years are counted be defined at some definite astronomical point. There is no need for such a reference point to correlate with any real historical event. The date of any event calculated from an astronomical reference point can easily be recalculated into our chronological system.

Christ. Now it is agreed that Dionysius made an error and that, in reality, Jesus must have been born a few years earlier, perhaps in the fourth or even fifth year before our era.

The new year count "from the birth of Christ"—A(nno). D-(omini).—did not take root immediately. During the entire Middle Ages it coexisted with the biblical tradition of counting years "from the creation of the world" adopted earlier in Christian nations.[15] Gradually, the calculation in years from the birth of Christ or, more correctly, from the beginning of our era was accepted in many countries, including Russia. A significant portion of the world's population uses this system, which is also universally accepted in history. Other chronological systems also exist, but there is no need to discuss them here.

In recent times, historians have relied on an archaeological method to establish absolute dates with the aid of radioactive carbon dating. Carbon dating is based on measuring the concentration of radioactive carbon in excavated artifacts. For instance, a felled tree ceases to take up the radioactive 14 isotope of carbon, and thus, the time when the tree was cut can be determined according to our present chronological scale. Unfortunately, radioactive carbon dating is imprecise, leading to unavoidable errors, which sometimes amount to tens and even hundreds of years and which preclude its application to cases that require more accurate dating.[16] At the present time, a potentially important absolute dating method called thermoluminescence is being developed for ceramics, as well as other physical methods such as archaeomagnetism.

For the time being, however, all dates for ancient Near Eastern history earlier than the second millennium B.C. and for Europe and China earlier than the middle of the first millennium B.C. remain uncertain; they only provide relative orientation. The situation is even worse for India, where even the dates in the first millennium B.C. are frequently approximate and inaccurate, because they are primarily based on objects imported from other countries with a better established chronology or on late king lists of doubtful accuracy or on establishing that certain literary works influenced certain others, rather than the reverse. Generally speaking, the farther away a territory is from ancient Mesopotamia, the less accurate is its chronology and the more recent its reliable datings.

15. During the Middle Ages, the mythological date of the creation of the world based on the biblical legends was calculated in various ways. The Greek Orthodox church adopted the year 5508 B.C., and the Anglican, the year 4004 B.C.

16. Most of the radiocarbon dates relevant to the history of the ancient world need to be recalibrated by adding a certain correction factor based upon dendrochronologically determined dates. The radiocarbon dates for ancient history are too young due to past variations in the production of radioactive carbon in the earth's atmosphere.

1441 833

1

General Outline of the First Period of the History of the Ancient World and the Problem of the Ways of Development

I. M. DIAKONOFF

Preconditions for the Formation of the First Class Society

The genus *Homo* separated out of the rest of the animal kingdom roughly two million years ago. Our species, *Homo sapiens sapiens,* has existed at least since the end of the Middle Palaeolithic, some forty thousand years. From his ancestors, who belonged to more ancient human species, *Homo sapiens sapiens* inherited the ability to produce simple tools for labor. But for thirty thousand years of history, humans, with the aid of the tools they made, still derived benefits solely from nature, just like their ancestors; for thirty thousand years, they did not sow or reap. Their means of sustenance were gathering wild plants, hunting, and fishing, all of which are activities that are certainly work. In order to exist, however, it was not sufficient for them to merely produce the necessary work tools: they had to be reproduced. But they could not reproduce the products they had extracted from nature. For this reason, the life of human groups (communities usually based on kinship) depended largely on environmental conditions, such as climate, on the abundance or scarcity of game, and on pure luck. Successes alternated with periods of hunger; mortality was very high, especially for children and the elderly. The surface of the enormous planet was inhabited by very few people, and if their number increased at all, it did so very slowly; indeed, sometimes it may have even decreased.

This situation changed about ten to twelve thousand years ago, when in certain ecologically favored regions, some human communities learned to plant grain, ensuring their year-round food requirements, and to raise sheep, goats, and cattle, allowing for regular consumption of meat, as well as for provision of milk and cheese (curds). The domestic animals also provided leather, which was superior to that from hunted animals, and supplied wool, which people learned to spin and weave. Soon after, humans were able to abandon

cave dwellings, twig and mud huts, or dugouts and to live in permanent houses made of clay or clay-coated rocks and, later, of adobe
bricks. Community life became safer: the mortality rate decreased
somewhat. Population growth, though never exceeding about 0.01
percent, became noticeable from generation to generation, and the
first farmers and livestock herders began to expand gradually over
the earth's surface.

The first humans to achieve these successes inhabited the North
Temperate Zone of the Eastern Hemisphere. This was the epoch
when the great Ice Age was not yet over in northern Europe and Asia,
but to the south of the glacial zone the cold dry climate of the
Pleistocene had passed. A significant portion of the Eurasian land-
mass was covered by pine forests, separated from the glacial zone by a
zone of tundra. The peninsulas of Italy, Greece, Asia Minor, and most
of China were all covered with deciduous forests. The expanse of
North Africa, Arabia, and other Near Eastern regions as far as northern China (covered today by dry steppes or scorched deserts) was
mostly mixed forest and steppe. Farther to the south, in Africa, southern India, southern China, and Indochina, lush tropical forests were
growing.

The partly wooded steppe regions were the most favorable areas
for human life, but not everywhere even in this zone were the conditions sufficiently conducive for a transition to agriculture and livestock
raising. A region was suitable when it offered wild grains appropriate
for consumption and later for artificial sowing (as documented by
N. I. Vavilov in 1926), as well as wild animals that could be domesticated. The first grains harvested in their wild state (aided by wooden
or bone sickles with embedded flint blades) and later cultivated were
barley and einkorn and emmer wheat. Wild stands of barley and these
early wheats grew in the uplands of Asia Minor, Palestine, Iran, and
southern Turkmenia, as well as in northern Africa. Other cereals were
domesticated later. Though it is difficult to determine where this phenomenon occurred for the first time, it is certain that cereals were
already being sown between the tenth and eighth millenia B.C. in Palestine, in Asia Minor, and on the western slopes of the Iranian uplands.
In Egypt, along the Danube River, in the Balkans, and in southern
Turkmenia, grains were being sown no later than the seventh to sixth
millennia B.C. At about the same time, these regions saw the domestication of goats and sheep. (Late Palaeolithic hunters had tamed dogs
much earlier.) Cattle and, sporadically, pigs were domesticated later.
The standard of living improved even more during the eighth to sixth
millenia B.C. when people learned to make polished stone tools, woven
baskets, woven fabrics, and fired pottery, which permitted better food
preparation and storage.

With the disappearance of the northern glaciers, the climate in the temperate zone of the Northern Hemisphere gradually became drier. Foothill agriculture depended less and less on natural rain irrigation and more on damned brooks channeled to the fields. For a long time, the population of the northern and southern forest zones was still very scanty and was not able to adopt the achievements of the inhabitants of the forest-steppe and the steppe-uplands; with the tools then available, it was still impossible to clear forests for tilling the land.

Archaeologists attribute significant technological progress to three important periods: to the final stage of the Old Stone Age—the Upper Palaeolithic—when *Homo sapiens sapiens* began to prevail; to the Mesolithic Age, which in the temperate zone coincides with the development of agriculture and animal husbandry; and to the Neolithic Age, which saw the development of polished stone implements and the invention of weaving and pottery. But even the most advanced Neolithic communities of northern Africa, the Near East, and the Middle East were unable to reach the level of production necessary for the creation of a civilization. The goal of their agricultural production and animal husbandry was, as before, solely to ensure the survival of the community and its members. Reserves were accumulated only for extreme emergencies, such as unexpected natural disasters. Working the soil with hoes made of stone or horn was very arduous, even in the softest of soils, and provided very meager, although reliable, nutrition. Domesticated goats and sheep still supplied only small quantities of wool and milk. Dairy products and milk had to be consumed quickly, because long-term storage methods were unknown. It was only in Asia Minor, Syria, and Palestine that during the eighth to sixth millennia B.C., there arose wealthy villages with considerable populations and sometimes even surrounded by walls (which means that there was something to protect!). These, however, were exceptions, and the oldest of these cultures—Jericho in Palestine and Çatal-Hüyük in Asia Minor—did not develop into civilizations.

With the growth of agricultural populations in the foothills, some people had to migrate deeper and deeper into the steppes. As these clan or tribal groups migrated away from regions with more or less efficient pluvial or brook irrigation, animal husbandry became a more important factor in their economy, while the cultivation of barley and emmer wheat became economically less reliable and less important. However, since humans had not yet domesticated the horse or the camel, the shepherds were not able to manage the long seasonal migrations necessary for the restoration of the grassland used to graze sheep and cattle; that is, they were not nomads. And since they could not move too far away from water sources, they did not entirely abandon agriculture. When it became impossible to feed the animals as a result of the sheep and goats completely overgrazing the meager southern grasslands or after a catastrophic drought, the shepherds migrated to other places. Thus, during the eighth to the sixth millennia B.C., tribes speaking Afrasian (Afro-Asiatic, Semito-Hamitic) dialects (who, in the opinion of A. Yu. Militarev and V. A. Shnirelman, were the descendants of the Mesolithic population of the Near East) expanded over northern Africa and over the steppe regions of Western Asia (Arabia, Syria, and Upper Mesopotamia, where tribes of the Semitic language family of the Afrasian languge phylum had remained or had immigrated). Beginning with the fifth to third millennia B.C. (i.e., at the beginning of the age of metal), related groups speaking Indo-European languages migrated in different directions from their homeland. Their homeland was previously thought to be between the Elbe and the Vistula (eastern Germany and Poland), but more likely, one should locate it in more southerly areas nearer the Black Sea; for example, in the Danube Valley, the Balkans, or on the Eurasian steppes.[1] By the second millennium B.C., these tribes had passed their languages to the local populations affected by their movements, and these then have passed them on again, over a vast area stretching from the Atlantic to the Indian Ocean.

Minor migrations contributing to the vast spread of language families were, of course, by no means fortuitous. They were mainly connected with secular fluctuations of the climate. Thus, the sixth and the late third to the second millennia B.C. were periods of drought that may have stimulated tribal migrations in search of better living conditions. Drought may have caused the decline of the Early Neolithic agricultural villages in Asia Minor and the rise of animal husbandry and agriculture in the still-forested Balkans or the Danube Valley. But in the fifth and fourth millennia B.C. the climatic conditions were more favorable; the mortality rate in the agricultural pastoral tribes decreased somewhat, and a relative population surplus was created. The population gradually spread in different directions within the general climatic zone favorable to the type of economy of such tribes.

It must be understood that the earth at that time was very thinly populated and that as shown by the data of historical linguistics, the migration of peoples did not result so much in the total destruction or

1. Recently a hypothesis has been proposed, according to which the original home of the Indo-European languages is to be sought in Asia Minor and eastern Anatolia. This hypothesis, which has failed to convince most linguists, cannot be brought into harmony with archaeological data either. More likely, the distant forebears not only of the speakers of Proto-Indo-European but also of some other languages (e.g., South Caucasian) may have inhabited these territories in the eighth to sixth millennia B.C. and later, in connection with the beginning of an arid epoch about 5000 B.C., migrated to Europe and the Caucasus.

displacement of native tribes as in the assimilation of the new arrivals
with the natives, so that the wave of a further migration could differ
ethnically, though not linguistically, from the original one. People
who in the sixth and fifth millennia B.C. brought Afrasian languages
deep into Africa and those who in the second to first millennia B.C.
brought Indo-European languages to the shores of the Bay of Bengal
(present-day Bangladesh) were not at all similar in their culture and
physical features to those who started the first wave of migration of
tribes engaged in agriculture and animal husbandry.

Although these relatively mobile pastoral tribes, who also always
practiced some form of subsidiary agriculture, were not true nomads,
one is justified in stating that the people permanently settled on fertile, irrigated land were a population group opposed to shepherds,
cattle raisers, and semiagricultural transhumants; this separation or
opposition represents the first great division of labor. Exchange was
already established at this early age between the groups engaged in
agriculture and those engaged in animal husbandry. Moreover, there
was need for such an exchange even earlier, because even during the
late Old Stone Age, no group of people was able to provide itself with
all the necessities without exchange. Materials for exchange included
relatively scarce stones suitable for making implements (flint and obsidian). Later, the newly discovered metals—gold, copper, and silver—
began to be exchanged for various handiwork products, such as
textiles. These exchanges involved several intermediaries and covered great distances.

We can trace several ways of the development of stratified (class) societies; each way depended on a specific combination of two economic
sectors, and their ratio, in turn, probably depended on specific ecological conditions.

Societies in Early Antiquity: The First Way of Development

During the resettling of communities from the original agricultural
centers (in the foothill regions of the Near and Middle East), other
events took place imperceptibly. It is possible that they had an even
greater significance for human history.

Between the sixth and third millennia B.C., agriculturalists settled
the valleys of three great rivers in Africa and Asia: the Nile, the Lower
Euphrates, and the Indus.[2] While part of the population belonging to
agricultural communities in the foothills either was displaced or voluntarily migrated further into the steppes, a few were forced to re-

2. They also settled the valleys of the Karun and Kerkheh rivers, located to the east
of present-day Iraq.

treat toward the plains of Lower Mesopotamia. There they found extremely unfavorable conditions owing to the periodic flooding of the land by three rivers—the Euphrates, the Tigris, and the Karun. All three flow through a desert area or through very hot and dry steppes where grain cannot be grown without artificial irrigation. Yet, all three rivers had yearly periods of flood, inundating vast areas for long periods of time and converting them into swamps. Thus, the fields were either flooded at the wrong time (during the spring harvest) or were parched by the sun once the floodwaters receded, making agriculture much less successful here than in the foothills, and food supplies much less secure. The Lower Euphrates Valley lacked building timber (only giant reeds were available) and stone suitable for manufacturing tools. Since there were also no metals, the inhabitants of this valley had to depend on implements made of reeds and clay or had to obtain stone by bartering with neighboring groups. Meanwhile, their neighbors had long since mastered copper smelting. The inhabitants of the Lower Euphrates also, of course, knew copper as an exotic material, but it was much more difficult for them, compared with other groups situated closer to the source areas, to obtain it through exchange. Many dozens of generations passed before the inhabitants of the great river valleys of Mesopotamia managed to take practical advantage of the floods for agricultural purposes. This then became the first victory of humans over the natural elements.

Control over the water supply was accomplished in various ways. In the Nile Valley of Egypt, the river begins to flood in June and remains at a high level until October. People learned to divide the fields with earthen dikes. After the trapped Nile floodwaters deposited their fertile silt, the water was released, leaving the trapped silt with enough moisture to serve as an excellent fertilizer not only for germination but also for the entire growing period of the grain. In Sumer (i.e., the Lower Euphrates Valley) the river overflowed its banks in the spring, but at rather irregular times. Its water was diverted to special reservoirs, and from there it was supplied to the fields several times during the growing season. Special methods of taming rivers were also employed on the Kerkheh, Karun, and Indus rivers (the last of which was brought under control only in the middle of the third millennium B.C.).

It must not be assumed that irrigation and land reclamation systems were being created for the entire lengths of the rivers; only local systems, such as were within the capabilities of a community or an association of a few communities, were developed. But this alone was an enormous accomplishment, which the inhabitants owed to persistence and cooperation. We do not know how this work was actually organized, because writing did not yet exist, and thus, no records have reached us. However, it has been noticed that in those areas where the creation of a productive agriculture required the cooperation of numerous communities at the earliest stages of civilization, the power and wealth of temples and cultic chiefs were much more conspicuous than in regions where agriculture was based on rain or stream irrigation, neither of which required large-scale work projects. It has, therefore, been postulated that the land improvement and irrigation tasks must have been placed under the management of the priests. This is reasonable, since the task of the priests was to ensure the general well-being of the community by way of cultic activities and propitiation of deities. Considering the *Weltanschauung* or *Weltgefühl* at the level of human development in those times, cultic actions were no less important and effective than technical ones, and it was only natural to put the most respected and wisest persons in charge of organizing both the cultic activities and the technical enterprises. The priest-chief, precursor of kings, is represented on some of the most ancient reliefs of Egypt and Sumer performing an agricultural ceremony, and this is significant.

Mastering fluvial irrigation at that level of development of the forces of production (the Chalcolithic Age) was possible only where the soil was sufficiently soft, the riverbanks not too steep and rocky, and the river flow not too swift. This meant that many rivers, including the Tigris, Araxes, Kura, Syr Darya, and Amu Darya rivers, were not suitable for the creation of irrigation-based societies, not even where they flowed through subtropical desert, desert-steppe, steppe, and forest-steppe country. People began to make use of their waters only during much later periods.

But where organized fluvial irrigation was feasible and where the soil was composed of fertile silt deposits, harvests began to increase rapidly. The growth of labor productivity also contributed to more abundant harvests. In addition to tilling with hoes, plowing was practiced (with donkeys or with oxen). There was an overall improvement in soil-working techniques, and these techniques have remained almost unchanged through millennia. In Egypt and Sumer by the end of the fourth millennium B.C., harvest yields had increased tenfold to twentyfold. This meant that each person began to produce significantly more than needed for personal sustenance. The increased harvests were also especially conducive to the development of livestock raising. And a well-developed livestock economy contributed to an even higher standard of living. The community was then able to feed not only the laborers but also those incapable of production, such as children and the elderly, and to create a reliable food reserve, as well as to free some of the able-bodied from agricultural work. This labor reserve fostered the rapid growth of specialized crafts: pottery, textiles and basketry, shipbuilding, stonecutting, copper working, and so forth. The mastering of copper was of the utmost importance. Copper was first used as just another variety of stone, but eventually, it was forged and, finally, cast. Numerous implements and weapons that could not be made of stone, wood, or bone began to be manufactured from copper. Moreover, such objects could be remelted when broken and the raw metal used for new implements. The separation of the crafts from agriculture marked the second great division of labor.

The increased surplus of agricultural and livestock-raising products freed some of the community members from having to perform productive labor. Who were these people who could be so liberated and maintained at the expense of other people's labor? The formation of a ruling class was certainly a complex and nonlinear process. Already in primitive society, the structure of human groups was not homogeneous. The primitive community could be divided into different age-groups and male, female, and cultic associations. Military leaders could keep their own personal armed followers, recruited from among the community members. Sometimes the lives of prisoners taken in skirmishes with neighbors were spared, and they were adopted into the households, acquiring the status of community members. In other cases, they became slaves. However, no antagonistic socioeconomic classes existed during the Chalcolithic Age. (By *classes* we mean here historically developed groups of people with different tasks in the production process and distinguished by their different relationships to property in the means of production and by their opposing social interests.)

A household commune was headed by a patriarch and included his sons and grandsons and their wives and children.[3] While the patriarch was alive, all the commune members and dependent persons were subject to his total, practically unlimited authority. In the event that the household commune did not subdivide following his death, it could gradually grow into an entire clan, including the spouses of the male members. (Marriages within this kinship group were mostly banned to avoid internal strife. As a rule, therefore, the wives belonged to other lineage groups.) In primitive society, a clan was usually part of a tribe—a larger association of people supposed to be related in the maternal or paternal line. But under the conditions of an agricultural society and with the increasing role of exchange between communities, it became more difficult to maintain close organizational and economic unity of very large groups only on the basis of kinship. Thus, tribal ties began to loosen and relations based on resi-

3. Communes organized along matrilineal lines are not attested in the Near East.

dence or ties formed simply on the basis of being neighbors became dominant. Neighbors could be related through kinship or not be related at all. At the time when the first class society was born, the role of the tribal union passed to the territorial community (village or city), which was a group of neighboring household communes that had the land and water more or less at their common disposal. The territorial community decided its affairs in a general assembly of warriors. Such large assemblies could not possibly go into all the details of administration, so important affairs had to be entrusted to a council of elders—the most experienced representatives of the individual household communes, which, in principle, were considered to be equals (although clans could be distinguished as elder and younger). In most cases, the assemblies simply approved the decisions made by the council. The assembly or, more often, the council also chose one or two leaders of the community whose responsibility it was to serve as military commander and community representative before the unknown forces of the world that were personified as gods. Such a system of public administration is often called a military democracy.

Naturally, the amount of the first surpluses could not suffice for everyone. At the same time, not all the people of the territorial community had the same opportunities to ensure their livelihood at the expense of others. The persons in the most favorable situation were, on the one hand, the military chief and his entourage and, on the other, the high priest. (It is assumed that in the lands with fluvial irrigation, the latter was also the manager of irrigation activities.) Not uncommonly, one leader could be both the military chief and the high priest. The members of the council of elders also ranked higher than the rest of the community members, and even different household communes could have unequal authority and power.

The formation of a class society is governed by strictly logical laws. In order to maintain the highest growth of the means of production and cultural and ideological progress, a society requires people freed from productive labor. This certainly does not mean that a society consciously releases the best organizers, the most profound thinkers, and the most outstanding artists from production work. It is not those who are best capable of utilizing the surplus of produce in the most rational way who acquire it. It is, rather, those who are in a position to do so: individuals who possess resources of sheer physical strength or who have the daring or the armed or the ideological power; it is they who also appropriate the organizational power. Most of these individuals exploit the labor of others without thereby benefiting society as a whole. A certain percentage, however, are people who are really able to promote the technical and cultural progress of a society.

It is precisely this accelerating progress that allows us to call the very first class society a *civilization* (from the Latin: *cives*, "citizen"; *civitas*, "community of citizens," "city"). Acclerating progress distinguishes the early class society from barbarism, the level that even the most developed primitive society cannot exceed.

When the society began to produce a surplus, its quantity, of course, was insufficient to raise the standard of living for the entire society. Only a certain fraction of society benefited, which means that economic and social inequality inevitably arose. Moreover, at the level of productivity characteristic of that period, no progress at all was possible without such inequality and without the potential for growth of the production forces, which were inherent in the exploitation of the labor of one group for the benefit of another. It is evident that no one would willingly agree to surrender his portion of the society's product to someone else. A coercive mechanism was therefore necessary to force the exploited class, as well as the entire society, to submit to the socioeconomic order. Such a mechanism was found in the state, which developed simultaneously with the class society. Special administrative personnel; territorial, instead of clan or tribal, subdivision of the administered region; special armed forces separate both from the people at large and from their own popular armed militia; and taxes collected from the inhabitants for the maintenance of the state machinery and the armed forces—these are the features characteristic of a state. The taxes could have different forms, occasionally quite different from those of today.

In Sumer during the third millennium B.C. (we have less information about the other riverine civilizations), the top echelon of society was sustained not so much by requisitioning produce (although there were some requisitions) as by giving large tracts of communal land to the temples and to the most important functionaries (and it must be remembered that the irrigated land belonging to the community was limited). A very large number of people worked this appropriated land, and it is they who constituted the majority of the emerging exploited class. Temples had special significance for the community. For one thing, the produce of the temple economy was originally the community emergency fund. Furthermore, the sacrificial offerings performed in the temple gave the participating population virtually its only opportunity to consume meat. At the same time, the extensive area of temple land made possible the application of advanced agricultural techniques, such as plowing. It was here that the bulk of the surplus was produced. For the majority of the free inhabitants (i.e., those not in the developing state bureaucracy, to which we must add

---

4. We must assume that the temple economies were originally established to serve the gods rather than the priests. In general, the concept of priesthood, at least in Meso-

the nascent priesthood),[4] the segregation of a substantial portion of the most fertile community land for the benefit of this elite was actually a form of taxation. Other forms of taxation were levies for irrigation and construction work, as well as for military service.

It is important to note that during the later stages of the primitive order, whereas tribes could form unions of tribes and confederations, the first states always originated within a small area, within the confines of a single territorial community or, more frequently, within a few closely knit communities. The security of such a state depended on the existence of natural boundaries—mountains surrounding a valley, a sea surrounding an island or a peninsula, or a desert encircling a region irrigated by a master canal. We will call such a clearly distinct region in which an early form of state emerges a nome. The center of a nome was usually a temple of the dominant local deity. Located around this central temple were the homes of the administrative functionaries, warehouses for food and other supplies, armories, and so on. Also, the most important craft workshops were concentrated here. All this was eventually enclosed within a security wall and constituted a city, the center of a small primary state. The form of government in these city-states was usually, though not always, monarchic, although bodies of communal self-government (council of elders, assembly of warriors) were also usually retained.

Since the formation of cities roughly coincides with the appearance of the earliest class society and state, Western scholars frequently term the transition between the primitive community order and the class order the urban revolution. This term is convenient but not unreservedly acceptable, because it focuses on the development of centers of trade and industry and does not take into account the main feature distinguishing the final stage of the primitive society (barbarism) from civilization: the stratification of the society into antagonistic classes. It is precisely this feature that provides the key for our understanding of the course of the subsequent history of ancient society.

The first societal class differentiation is attested in Egypt and Sumer. In both of these countries, the process had certain peculiarities decisive for the future history of each civilization and for their specific ways of development within the framework of the same type of society (conventionally called the slave-owning mode of production). The first way of development of the various types attested in ancient slave-owning societies has been studied satisfactorily in its early stages mostly for Sumer. We have already seen that economically Sumerian

---

potamia, belongs to a much later time; the ancients did not at first distinguish priestly activities or the ceremonial and magical services to the gods from other state and social services.

society was divided into two sectors. One included the great economies of the temples and the top functionaries of the emerging state.
During the first centuries of written history, these economic entities
gradually released themselves from the jurisdiction of the bodies of
the community's self-government. The second sector comprised lands
settled by free inhabitants who participated in the self-government
of the community. The supreme proprietor of the lands of the second sector was the territorial community, but the lands were held by
extended-family households; that is, communes headed by their patriarchs. In the third or fourth generations, such household communes usually divided, though the separated households still regarded
themselves as kin; they had a shared cult of ancestors, and the custom
of mutual aid between them continued.

Later, the economies of the first sector became state property, while
the economies of the second sector remained under the supreme proprietorship of the territorial community and in the possession of the
family heads. In practical terms, the possessions of the latter differed
from full property solely in that only as members of the territorial
(i.e., rural and urban) community could they use and dispose of the
land at will.

The community members themselves—that is, the free members
of the second-sector economies (communal-cum-private)—worked
on the land aided only by their families. Nevertheless, inequalities in
wealth did exist, both within the confines of individual extended-
family communes and especially between different kin-related communes. These inequalities depended on the social status of the heads
of the nuclear and extended families (some of the community members could be priests, elders, etc.); on accidental fortune or misfortune; and on the ability of the individual members to manage their
movable property, because such items, as opposed to house, field, or
date plantation, were considered the personal property of each family
member. By utilizing the custom of mutual aid or by lending some of
their products to less successful community members, the more fortunate families could also profit from the labor of others. Also, slaves
were sometimes owned, but more on this below.

People who were settled on land owned by the state sector held the
land as conditional possessions; it was allotted for their sustenance or
in payment for services or work performed for the temple, the chief,
or other functionary. Such land was granted on an individual basis to
a nuclear, rather than to an extended, family unit. In other words,
sons and grandsons performed their duties individually and were
awarded land separately from their fathers and grandfathers. From
each of them, the land could be taken away or replaced with other

land at the discretion of the administration. Many workers in the state sector did not receive any land at all, just a ration.

Even among state dependents, however, there existed well-to-do persons, according to the standards of that time, who profited from the labor of others and who could own slaves of both sexes. These were state functionaries, the elite military commanders, and specialized craftsmen. By acquiring land and by receiving comparatively generous rations, they actually obtained a portion in the agricultural produce of the temple or of the state economy. Occasionally, they rose quite high on the service ladder; these were the people who supplied the personnel for the administrative machinery. Even when they did not possess any state land or have any landed property of their own, some of them actually managed the state sector economy. On the other hand, state dependents also included slaves, especially female slaves, who could be bought and sold.

Thus, the society that emerged in the third millennium B.C. in the Lower Euphrates Valley was divided into several social estates. The upper estate comprised the members of the communities who participated in the communal ownership of property in land, who had the right to take part in communal self-government, and who, initially, also had the right to elect the chief. A lower estate included temple or state economy personnel who owned no land outright but either possessed land only in return for their services or possessed no land and were allocated rations. In addition, there were slaves, who were outside the social estates and, in principle, could be treated as cattle. Actually the slaves also constituted an estate—one deprived of rights.

This division of society was quite evident and fully acknowledged by the ancients themselves. But there was another, more profound socioeconomic division in society. The society was divided into social classes occupying different positions within the production process and differing in their relationship to the property in the means of production and to exploitation. This division did not coincide with the estates.

The upper class consisted of people who did not engage in productive work and who exploited the labor of others. In our country this class is usually labeled slave owners, although they exploited others besides slaves, in the strict sense of the term. The members of this class owned property in the means of production (if they were members of a community) or they owned property in return for their services. Actually, they managed the economy of the state sector in the interest of the ruling class as a whole.

The middle class comprised agriculturalists and craftspeople who engaged in productive labor but, as a rule, did not exploit the labor of others or, at most, used them only as auxiliary labor. To this class may be assigned, first of all, the less well-to-do landowning community members, although it could also include the conditional landowners (i.e., state sector personnel). But these latter were, in most cases, subject to exploitation, and for this reason, it is sometimes very difficult to draw the line between the middle and lower classes in the state sector.

The lower class was made up of slavelike dependents who owned no property within the economy and who were also subject to extraeconomic exploitation. Extraeconomic exploitation is exploitation by direct physical or ideological coercion. Economic exploitation, on the other hand, occurs when workers within a certain historically conditioned socioeconomic structure cannot sustain themselves except by entering into a contractual agreement with a proprietor of the means of production to sell their labor power. In antiquity, economic exploitation was the exception, not the rule.

Slaves also formed part of the exploited class. Not only did they lack property in the means of production, but they themselves were their exploiter's property, being, as it were, live tools. Since slaves could be most completely exploited, a slave labor force was, in principle, the most desirable for the owners. However, because this labor force had to be constantly supervised and the agricultural implements of that epoch were quite primitive, the productivity of slave labor did not differ substantially from the productivity of a free agriculturalist. A slave, however, was not supposed to have a family, unlike those members of the exploited class who were not slaves and who had to feed their families on their rations or from the crops on their land allotment. It was convenient for the owner not to have to supply his slaves with food for their families. A slave could be given less food than other dependent workers and the worst clothes (or none at all) and could be forced to work more each day. This was such a profitable arrangement for the slave owners that, circumstances permitting, they tried to convert other exploited persons into actual slaves. This is why such an economy may be called a slave-owning one and why the slavelike dependent workers are frequently designated as a slave class in the broad sense of the term.

This scenario of "classic" slave exploitation usually could not be realized in early antiquity for a number of reasons. For example, it was not possible to convert individuals who were members of a community into real slaves, because of their kinship relations and religious ties to other community members, who would come to their aid. During the third millennium, community members of the Lower Euphrates Valley managed periodically to free their members who had been enslaved for debt or for other reasons.

A foreigner could be enslaved only if taken prisoner in battle. However, it was costly to force a male prisoner to work for his enslaver if the latter did not create for him more or less reasonable living conditions. In the fourth to third millennia, a warrior had no defensive arms except for a copper helmet and, on occasion, a very rudimentary shield made of leather or reeds. His offensive weapons consisted of a dagger, a small copper axe hafted to a wooden handle, or a copper-headed spear. If each captured warrior was given a copper pick, spade, or hoe, the soldiers serving as guards would be at a disadvantage—unless each prisoner was guarded by two or three soldiers. Therefore, many captured warriors were killed on the spot. Alternatively, captured warriors could be made dependent workers on state lands and given a ration or a land allotment and allowed to have their own shelters and families. This relatively lenient treatment was intended to maintain order and ensure their subordination.

The private economies of community members could not afford to grant their captive slaves separate households, nor was the community in a position to keep them working the fields under guard. Consequently, under such conditions, only patriarchal slavery could exist. This meant that from the arrived troop of prisoners, a number of girls would be taken into individual homes (where the slave owners would father their children). Boys were also taken, provided that they were at an age when they could accustom themselves to their new home and feel part of the household.[5] Slaves of both sexes were mainly assigned heavy productive labor in the house (making pottery, tending the cattle, spinning and weaving, cooking, and milling grain between two stones, which was an especially heavy task). In the fields, the boy slaves and women slaves were given auxiliary work along with family members, such as driving oxen, weeding, harvesting, and tying sheaves of grain; they were not entrusted with plowing and sowing. The slaves' labor around the house was extremely productive, not only because they were under the constant supervision of their owners but also because they participated in one common production process with the masters. No less important was often the actual kinship of many slaves with their owners, as well as the insignificant difference between the living conditions of the master and the slave. The nourishment of the masters was equally meager and their clothing extremely unpretentious. The same conditions also prevailed for the individuals who received land allotments in the state sector.

5. In any event, there were often more male than female slaves in a private household. But the number of both was small, and probably most households had no slaves at all.

Although small households did not require many dependent workers, the situation in the state sector was different. On temple lands, for example, many workers were required, yet it was impossible to keep large numbers of slaves working the fields, because there were not enough overseers to guard them. Here there were no free agriculturalists who would undertake plowing and sowing. For these reasons, only women were kept as slaves on temple lands, and male prisoners, both adults and boys, worked with the nonslave personnel of the large economies. This labor force consisted of the younger brothers from impoverished households and of refugees seeking the protection of the temple or a neighboring chief when, for instance, their home town had been destroyed by war or when their land had suffered from a catastrophic drought or a flood. Nor can we exclude the possibility that a community, while allocating part of its land to the temple or the chief, would, at the same time, commit a number of its members to working for the economies in question.

Even though workers in the state sector received only a land allotment or a ration, they were not actually enslaved, despite being exploited by extraeconomic compulsion and deprived of property in the means of production. These workers were not necessarily recruited from captives and prisoners-of-war but, perhaps more frequently, may have come from the local population. They were allowed personal movable property, often their own house, and sometimes even sheep and cattle. All of this, however, they enjoyed not as property, but as conditional possessions. (We might use the Roman term *peculium*.)

Because these workers were bound to the estate that employed them (they were not allowed to leave it), they have frequently been classified as serfs. But since they had no part in the property in the means of production, they differed from medieval dependent agriculturalists in that they were, in fact, subject to slave-type exploitation. To avoid confusion, let us from now on use the Greek term for state slavelike dependents who were settled on land and who maintained the members of the ruling class with their labor but who still had their own households: helots. Within state property, the helots are the equivalent of private patriarchal slaves.[6]

6. Note a phenomenon that has been underestimated by scholars. From a very early period, probably not later than the second millennium B.C., a considerable number of eunuchs were employed in the temple and state economies, especially as functionaries and temple singers (these probably were always eunuchs in Mesopotamia) but also as manual workers. Probably it seemed natural to castrate "bipeds" for security's sake, just as one castrated calves at least as early as the sixth millennium B.C. This phenomenon was obvious in the nineteenth century A.D. to the first students of Mesopotamian culture. Thus, for example, Layard, a British consul in the Turkish Empire, had himself met many eunuchs and had no difficulty in identifying them in depictions of numerous

Relying on the personnel of the powerful state economies, the rulers of individual nomes, or city-states, could create large troops of warriors, who were not dependent on the council, the popular assembly, or other community self-governing institutions. This enabled these rulers, supported by a bureaucracy composed of their personal followers, to rise above the individual nomes and establish a despotic royal power—a power not limited by any other legal bodies. Becoming independent of the nomes, a king could gradually consolidate his power over the entire irrigational network of Lower Mesopotamia, the country between the Tigris and Euphrates rivers. The emergence of this power made a single unified royal and slave-owning economy within the state sector possible. Yet, in this "slave-owning" society, private economies continued to survive in the community sector.

Further along in the course of history, it became clear that maintaining the state through an economy of its own, with large numbers of slavelike, exploited laborers (helots), was not profitable; too many nonproductive expenses connected with supervision and management were required. The state began to shift to a system of direct taxation of the entire population and collection of tribute. The distinction between the state and the private/communal sector remained, although the same type of private slave-owning economies now existed on both the state and the community lands. The difference was in the character of property and possession: the possession of state land did not imply property rights to it.

In the field of exchange, the main role in early antiquity was played by international trade. Intermediaries were often necessary, especially when great distances were involved. This trade was conducted at their own risk either by state agents or by professional household communes whose members were not in the state service. Both, however, were closely linked to the state, but the state had under its control not so much the international activities of the traders as revenues from them. The produce was redistributed in the cities and towns, where the industrial and exchange activities of the society were concentrated, where the state administration was located, and where most of the nonlaboring population had their homes. Inside the city community, in-kind exchange was practiced on a small scale (often based on nonequivalent mutual aid relations), along with centralized state distribution.

Such was the first way of development of the most ancient class so-

---

beardless men with fat under their chins on Assyrian reliefs. However, modern Assyriologists identify them, both on reliefs and in texts, and sometimes against common sense, as "young men." In the ancient languages a eunuch was supposed to be identified by a polite term, such as "following (his master) at his foot" or "being before (the king)."

ciety. It was characterized by the coexistence of two economic sectors: state and private/communal, the former being dominant. This way of development was typical of the Lower Euphrates Valley and the valleys of the Karun and Kerkheh rivers (ancient Elam).

The Second Way of Development in Early Antiquity

Another variant of early society to be considered is that which developed in the Nile Valley in Egypt. Unfortunately, early Egyptian economic and legal documents are extremely scarce, and much of the information is not clear to us.

Sumer is traversed by separate branches of the Euphrates, making it possible to construct individual master canals, around which formed many small nomes that endured for long periods; unified kingdoms were short-lived. On the other hand, Upper Egypt stretched like a narrow ribbon along a single main stream of water—the Nile. Only in Lower Egypt does the Nile fan out into many branches of the Delta. Since the Upper Egyptian nomes constituted a chain of bordering territories, squeezed between the Nile and the rocky precipices of the desert edge, it was obviously not possible to form multilateral political alliances by taking advantage of struggles and competition between neighbors. Elsewhere it was such competition that actually ensured sufficient independence for self-governing nomes.

In Egypt, clashes between the nomes invariably led to a unification "along the chain" under the power of the strongest nome or else to the complete annihilation of a quarrelsome neighbor. Consequently, autocratic kings appeared in Upper Egypt already during the earliest epoch. They acquired despotic power over the individual nomes and later over the entire country, eventually conquering Lower Egypt as well. In early Egypt a state sector (temple and royal and, possibly, also "houses" of nobles) must have originally coexisted with a private/communal sector, but the latter, apparently, was gradually swallowed up, without leaving any trace, by the state. In any case, Egyptologists cannot ascertain the existence of communities of free citizens, fully invested with rights and administratively independent from state economies, on the basis of any clear evidence available from the year 2000 B.C. on. This does not preclude the possibility that separate self-sufficient households could have arisen within the state itself.

All this, however, does not constitute an essential difference between the societies of Egypt and Lower Mesopotamia. Here, as there, direct management by the royal power of huge slave-owning economies became, in the end, unprofitable, with the difference that in Egypt the private slave-owning economies developed on what legally were state lands. These private economies had their labor force (helots) allotted to them by the state, and in addition, they may have owned slaves. Each of these laborers, who were state dependents (or what we have termed helots), were assigned a specific task, such as tiller of the soil, craftsman, or the like, to be fulfilled for the economic entity to which they had been allotted. Any production over and above the assigned task could be kept for their own benefit and disposed of at their own discretion. However, such products should not be regarded as property but, rather, as conditional possession (*peculium*). As we already know, patriarchal dependents, even including classical slaves, could also dispose of their *peculium*. Classical slaves, however, were even allowed to amass savings for the purpose of redeeming themselves from their master, a right that the ancient Oriental helots lacked.

Other Ways of Development in the Societies of Early Antiquity

In countries that lacked the high crop capacity of the fertile silt of the great river valleys, the same laws that governed the first way of development in river irrigation societies also applied. But in order to achieve a sufficiently high technological level for generating agricultural surplus, a significantly longer time period was required in these less fertile regions. In addition to mastering the techniques of grain cultivation, such factors as livestock raising, viticulture, olive growing, gardening, and the extraction of metals usually were equally important, helping the local society, through the process of exchange, to partake of the surplus product from the leading agricultural areas. Furthermore, in these regions there was no need to create and maintain vast, labor-intensive irrigation and land improvement systems, a condition that resulted in temples and priest-chiefs playing a much diminished role. The private/communal sector sometimes gained prominence over the state sector. However, the fact that these societies took longer to attain the level of a class society and of civilization gave Egypt and Lower Mesopotamia the time to exert a powerful cultural influence on these areas—an influence aimed precisely at strengthening the authority of temples and of the royal power. Thus, the most ancient societies belonging to this third evolutionary course exhibit a diversity of relationships between the state sector and the private/communal sector but tend to monarchical forms of polity.

In some countries and periods the one economic sector was stronger and, in some, the other.[7] Moreover, since there were no vast or nu-

7. Note that the existence of territorial communities (rural and later also urban) and the existence within these of extended-family communes resulted from the level of development of production in antiquity and was not connected specifically with the necessities of a "hydraulic" society. Usually the private/communal sector is weaker when the state economies flourish, as happens in the riverine irrigation societies. It is stronger in

merous irrigation systems, which would have been profitable to unify, these regions did not generate monolithic and despotic kingdoms like the kingdom on the Nile or the less stable kingdoms of Mesopotamia. The local empires (the Achaean, the Hittite, the Mitannian, the Middle Assyrian, and the Egyptian empire in Syria during the New Kingdom) were more like military alliances in which weaker nomes were obliged to pay tribute and provide military support to a stronger state. In the third and especially in the second millennium B.C., all the societies of Asia Minor and the Near East (with the exception of Lower Mesopotamia and the Kerkheh and Karun plain), as well as the societies around the Aegean Sea in the eastern Mediterranean, belonged to the third way of development of early ancient class societies. It appears that in the first millennium B.C., certain societies in the uplands of the Near East and Asia Minor, in Greece, and probably in Italy (Etruria?) still belonged to this type of society.

From the point of view of universal history, the epoch when the social conditions typical of early antiquity existed are mainly the third and second millennia B.C. We know too little about the societies of India and China during that period to describe confidently their socioeconomic development. Therefore, at the present level of knowledge, we may regard early antiquity as a period when the first, the second, and the third ways of development predominated.

But societies belonging typologically to early antiquity do not necessarily arise only in the chronological framework of the classical ancient Orient: in certain places the same typology can also be traced in the first millennium B.C. and—albeit for a short time—in the first millennium A.D., as, for instance, in northern and eastern Europe. In the tropics, in mountainous zones, and in piedmont regions, the same typology may linger and even reemerge as late as the second half of the second millennium A.D.

The Further Development of the Class Societies
Established in Early Antiquity

The typology of societies of late antiquity differs strongly from that of early antiquity. In many respects, the later period presents more variation of forms than the earlier, and not all of the emerging variations are easily explained by ecological conditions. It seems that there were at least four ways of development. In the field of production, typical of late antiquity is the use of iron and primitive steel, which resulted,

---

the countries of the third way of development, especially in the mountainous regions of the periphery. Often it was the mountain people who controlled the passes over which the population of the lowlands traded and which the latter needed for military purposes.

among other things, in the exploitation of new natural regions for civilization. At the same time, in agricultural technology there is little appreciable development, as compared with development of industries, especially the production of arms and military equipment.

The first way of development in late antiquity, which is the most thoroughly studied, is the Mediterranean one. It emerged from the third way of early antiquity under certain specific conditions and was characterized by the virtually complete abolishment of the state sector during the stormy epoch of ethnic migrations and the fall of the kingdoms that belonged typologically to early antiquity. The *polis* organization now emerged. These were city-state communities, which, for all practical purposes, lacked a state economic sector; state power was conferred on a vestigial monarchical or purely republican administration. The *poleis* grew and flourished on the basis of market-oriented agricultural and industrial production in the private sector. Such production became possible because of the intensification of international trade, which had now become easier and more accessible to the private enterprise of the citizens of the *poleis*. A balance between the communal (that which belonged to the *polis*) and the private (that which pertained to the individual) arose. This contributed to the development of rationality in the mental life and to the emergence of individuality in art, literature, and philosophy; at the same time, the traditional community cults were preserved. For the first time in history there was a notion of the freedom of the individual. The majority of the citizens consisted of the same nonexploited working population of the primitive epoch, but the more well-to-do citizens of the *polis* exploited slave labor not only in its patriarchal form but also in its classical one; namely, as chattel slavery.

After a comparatively short period, a crisis of the *polis* arose that could only be resolved by incorporating all *poleis* into an empire; here the citizens could continue to enjoy their rights and privileges, but at the same time, they could also reap the advantages of belonging to an empire. The most important advantage was that the empires united, under one political authority, both regions of agricultural production (which were also the market for industrial production) and regions of industrial and livestock production. Moreover, in unifying these different economic areas, these later empires did not upset trade routes, as was the case in early antiquity, but actually secured the routes between different regions. The later empires were also able to defend the cities. The zenith of this development was reached in the Roman Empire, which was a very specific formation since it had no state sector. (The emperors' estates were their private property.)

The transition to a new medieval society in which formerly free artisans and agriculturalists constituted the exploited class (first along with the slaves and later in place of them) occurred within the Roman Empire and along its frontiers. Some members of the ancient exploiter class, reappearing now as the protofeudal class of landed magnates, became vested with state power.

The second way of development is represented by the Near Eastern empires, from the Assyrian and Neo-Babylonian through the Hellenistic. As a result of attempts to unify the regions of agriculture with those of livestock and industrial production, and also of certain strong internal processes, conquests were made on a grand scale, and interregional empires were created. All conquered land became state land, providing the base for the state sector of the economy; here the "king's men" and other groups of the helot type were exploited. However, inside the empires there also existed self-governing temple cities and territories, and, later, Hellenistic *poleis* that superficially reproduced the structure of the Greek *poleis*. Personally free citizens, both slave owners and non–slave owners, existed within such structures; slave labor was on a métayage or quitrent basis. At the end of this way of development, as well as of the others, magnate landownership emerged, and state power passed to the magnates; the self-government of the cities was abolished, and the market-oriented economies were destroyed (mainly because of the autarchic character of the magnates' economies).

A third way seems to have developed in India; here the opposition between the king's men and the citizens was not as important as the rigid opposition of social estates, which evolved into the caste system.

Finally, the fourth way is that of the Far East, where the formal social opposition is between literates (functionaries) and illiterates (nonfunctionaries); however, the actual class structure, on the whole, is the same as attested elsewhere. Here also the class of magnates with political power evolves at the end of antiquity.

The attention of the reader should also be directed to the following. The history of *class societies* from the fourth millennium B.C. to the first millennium A.D. is not the same as the history of the world for the same period of time; the ancient class societies always existed within a world that was also populated by primitive societies at various levels of development from simple Neolithic tribes to relatively sophisticated ones with complicated social structures. Moreover, the ancient class societies could not have existed without a preclass periphery where they could exploit seemingly inexhaustible resources of raw materials and, over time, inexhaustible supplies of labor. The presence of the periphery also always implied the threat of invasions and the disruption of cultural and historical traditions. The periphery, paradoxically, also was regarded as a world of primitive "freedom" or "innocence," and it influenced the ideational and emotional life of the class societies.

The first period of early antiquity (Lectures 2–7) is the history of small foci of civilization in a vast world of primitive "barbarism"; continuous areas of civilization only emerge in the second period of early antiquity (Lectures 8–20): the Mediterranean, the Near East, India, and China. But they still continue to be surrounded by the primitive periphery. Even when the zone of class-based civilization occupies an unbroken territory, it remains encircled by this periphery.

Thus, the universal history of humanity, from the fourth millennium B.C. to the first millennium A.D., ought not to be simply a history of civilizations but a history of civilizations encircled by the primitive world. The authors of this work did not feel themselves equal to a task of this kind, nor did they even set for themselves this goal. The reader, nevertheless, must always remember the other, less developed world, which always surrounded the states we are describing.

The Perception of the World at the Passing from Primitive to Ancient Society

It is difficult to comprehend the events of the ancient epoch without attempting to understand, at least approximately, how the ancients thought and felt. What did they think about the world and about themselves?

Unfortunately, it is very difficult to penetrate the spiritual world of ancient times—in fact, almost impossible. The unearthed temples are mute, the images uncertain; only very slowly, in small bits, do we become acquainted with the relics of ancient literature. And, even if ancient art and literature were completely understood, do they really reflect all the thoughts and feelings of the people of those bygone times? After all, artistic accomplishments are just mementos, accidental relics preserved for us by chance of all that the artists of that epoch had created. There are, of course, also oral myths, fairy tales, songs, proverbs, and aphorisms that are rooted in the thought of the ancient world. Yet changes and additions made during the course of time may well distort them before they reach the present. Present-day narrators of folktales whom social anthropologists have studied cannot themselves know what the ancients originally meant by their stories. The hypotheses scholars have formulated on these subjects are usually rejected by those who still keep the old myths alive, such as the tribal peoples of Africa, Australia, and Polynesia.

Perhaps, however, there does exist one objective means that can assist us in penetrating the mental processes of people who lived in primitive times and in early antiquity; namely, the study of languages. Language expresses categories of the mental process: by investigating the structures of the most archaic languages, the modes used to express how humans related to the world and its phenomena, it is possible to recover some of the mental processes of that time.

Based on a comparative study of the most ancient strata of the languages that have reached us and on the structures of the most ancient myths, the following hypothesis about the mentality and worldview of primitive people seems to be the most plausible.

The great difficulty for primitive humans was to comprehend and express abstract concepts. Since no judgment is possible without making certain generalizations, one had to generalize without stating abstract concepts. For this, one had to create associations based on images perceived by the senses (e.g., comparisons). For example, in order to express the idea that the sky is a dome or roof supported by four points on the horizon and, at the same time, something that gives birth to the sun every day and to the stars and moon at night, as well as the place where the sun travels from one end to the other, one could illustrate the concept of "sky" as a cow standing on its four legs, a woman giving birth to the sun, and a river along which the sun travels. This quite adequately illustrated the idea that had to be expressed without anyone being disturbed by the question of how the sky could be a cow, a woman, and a river all at the same time. Everyone clearly understood that this was merely an interpretation and that, in reality, the sky was not a cow, a woman, or a river. But because abstract concepts had not yet developed, such ideas as "comparison," "metaphor," "interpretation," and all that is necessary to express that the sky is actually not any of these objects did not exist. The process of comparing, interpreting, and naming an object or a phenomenon was perceived in material terms. For example, a name was perceived as a material part of the named object. Therefore, we should not be surprised that even without identifying the sky with a real cow or a real woman, the ancient people could still offer sacrifices to the sky personified as a divine cow or a goddess.

Any natural and purposeful phenomena that concerned people (or phenomena imagined to have a purpose) and any phenomena without a known purpose but with a definite cause were mentally and emotionally perceived as caused by an intelligent will. This was the result of the fact that people could, in practical life, observe a relationship between cause and effect essentially only within the context of their own activities, understanding a cause as a willful action. For this reason, some intelligent being was imagined to be behind every phenomenon that took place in the world, and for humanity's benefit, this being had to be propitiated. Such a being, or deity, was not thought of as spiritual (because an immaterial spirit is also an abstraction and could not be verbally expressed or imagined for lack of the means to do so) but as material. It could differ from humanity in its power, in its maliciousness—in anything but its spirituality.

Neither was a deity distinct from humanity in terms of immortality, because people had no means to imagine or describe verbally nonexistence and, hence, could not conceive of being dead as being nonexistent. A deceased person was someone who had passed from life here to another life somewhere else, just as a newborn was transferred from a life in some other place to life here. Another transition from one form of existence to another was the passage from childhood: boys to warriors and girls to marriageable maidens. Such a transition was often celebrated by an initiation ritual, or a consecration, which included testing a young man's or woman's fortitude in confronting fear or experiencing physical pain. (Circumcision of the foreskin and infliction of wounds or burns were typical.) Initiation could also include passing on to the new generation the experience of their forebears, which consisted not only of various practical skills and labor techniques but also of myths. The latter created a sensorial and figurative comprehension of the causes of phenomena and their relationships.

A myth cannot be interpreted out of the context of a ritual. Primitive people interpreted their actions in the same way they did natural phenomena—in a sensorial and associative manner rather than in an abstract and logical one. Practical activities (technical work methods, for example) were, of course, also interpreted associatively but, nevertheless, were understood quite correctly, because such actions are in an obvious way directly affected by human will. Ritualistic actions were conditioned by assumed causes governing universal phenomena, which were conditioned by the will of deities. As we have already seen, deities and their actions were re-created in myths by generating associations. These associations lacked rigorous logic; they were sensorial and emotional. Therefore, it is not surprising that the way to influence the causes (the divine causes!) of phenomena also had to be associative and emotional, not logical. For example, if a name is a material part of a deity, then would whoever uttered this name not also possess this deity to some degree? Would not the act of coition with a woman incarnating (as an "actress") the goddess promote the fertility of the goddess herself and, in turn, the fertility of the land of which she was not only in charge but which she, herself, was? The ritual appeared to be even more effective because the concept of abstract, physical time was nonexistent for primitive humans. Today, of course, we know that physical time unwinds uniformly, always moving in the same direction. Yet, we do not perceive time with our senses; we perceive only the events that fill it, or those we expect to fill it. If many events are taking place or are expected, it seems to us that a long time has passed.

If nothing happens, time seems to have passed quickly. Primitive people experienced time in the same way; that is, in terms that allowed them to relate it to events in their own lives.[8] It was still more difficult to define a point in time not connected with one's own life or even with the lives of remembered ancestors. And mythological events such as, let us say, a goddess giving birth to the sun or a goddess giving birth to cereals are not connected to any point in time, because the sun rises every morning and the grain comes up every year. Thus, a ritual performed today can certainly be thought of as influencing mythological events that took place at any other time and can affect their regular repetition.

We cannot call this mythological attitude a philosophy, nor do we know whether to call it a religion. Nevertheless, it does contain a certain proto-ethic; from the plot of a myth, we can see what is viewed as good or bad. This proto-ethic, however, has a somewhat automatic character, because it is not a logical system. In essence, it shows that what is useful to one's own community, comrades-in-arms, and children is good; since all people beyond the border of the community are enemies, it is certainly good to outwit or kill them. And whatever is bad is usually under a magic spell or taboo; if you do what is prohibited, you will die, not necessarily for fear of being killed but for fear of the taboo itself. Here, ethics are inseparable from primitive magic. Thus, shedding blood (except in the case of war) defiles a person because of blood's magical properties, regardless of whether murder is good or bad. To have eaten a prohibited food, participated in a prohibited ceremony, cohabited with a woman of a prohibited kinship degree, or pronounced a god's dread name in vain may turn out to be a much graver sin than the sin of murder itself, which could, in any event, be redeemed by a ransom or a purifying ritual.

Such was the burdensome load of emotional and ideological heritage that humanity carried over the threshold of civilization. If we add the additional weight of the insecurity of crops, defenselessness against disease and natural disasters, wretched dwellings, clothing, and tools, and lack of any knowledge about hygiene, it becomes clear how difficult life was in that world. We must not assume that some lone genius would have been able to teach the people the falsehood of this or that view and win followers. At a time when development, compared with what we are accustomed to, was extremely slow and gradual, only the collective experience of the ancestors carried any weight. And just that experience was embodied in myths and rituals.

8. We must remember also that at that time there was no fixed point from which to count years, nor was there any definite subdivision of the day. The day was simply divided into morning, noon, and evening, and the night into several "watches" or vigils, depending on the custom of the garrison.

The success of an individual who did not adhere to the ancestral teachings would appear fortuitous or controlled by some sort of unaccounted-for, perhaps ill-boding, magic.

We should not, however, belittle the ancients and their myths. Today, life is also filled with many tenaciously held delusions and prejudices that have no logical basis whatsoever, as in attitudes toward alien nations or beliefs in ominous signs, etc. These, too, qualify as true myths. They do not develop logically but, rather, are based on emotional associations; many erroneous scientific hypotheses are also scarcely more than myths. And despite being limited by mythological reasoning, primitive people's abilities—when the collective experience was sufficient—to make reasonable decisions, to associate ideas correctly, to find the real causes of phenomena, and to verify conclusions were adequate for their needs.

In examining the outlines of the early period of ancient history, we have focused on the particular features of ancient mentality; without understanding these features, we would have difficulty explaining why religion, the temple, rituals, and the priesthood played such an enormous role during the early period of human development. Why was it that the priesthood received the lion's share of the first production surpluses? Of course, the explanation of eighteenth-century rationalists was naive, as was that of many twentieth-century antireligious thinkers, who saw the reason, primarily, in the priests' conscious deception of the public. There is no doubt that the priests never neglected their own interests and, not uncommonly, even placed them above those of others. But let us bear in mind that everyone, without any exception, was a believer. So, of course, were the priests. The particularly important social role played from the very beginning of civilization by the professional performers of religious rituals can be explained by the fact that the entire population regarded the rituals themselves as the supreme means of ensuring the welfare of the entire community. Initially, the wealth of the temples was the insurance fund of the entire community. For millennia, the majority of the farming population ate meat only during sacrifices to the gods.

Let us also remember the creation of the "slave-owning" mode of production was, in those times, a progressive phenomenon that contributed to the highest possible development of productive forces, increasing the standard of living for as large a number of people as was then possible. In the meantime, primitive society was fading into the background, despite its predominantly egalitarian character. (It was mostly a hungry egalitarianism.) But it was for the return of this primitive past that the oppressed people of antiquity longed.

For the mass of the people, myths and rituals were vital. The collective experience of the ancestors, expressed in these myths and rituals, still determined, to a large degree, the interpretation of the world and the social psychology of humans. Such an attitude toward the phenomenal world had an authoritarian character independent of the political order of each individual society. This was because this attitude was based on the absolute authority of "those who ought to know," of those who were regarded as inheriting the power and the wisdom of the ancestors. It was only during a later period in antiquity—in Greece and in some of the advanced societies of the East— that authoritarian thought began to lose its sway over people: no longer would one accept everything on trust and mere faith; each proposition had to be proved. But even when, after 2,500 years, a scientific outlook and philosophy began to emerge alongside the religious worldview, the new philosophy remained alien to most of the population; it was the ideology of the upper class.

However, it was only then that a nonmetaphoric cognition of the world emerged clearly enough as a separate field of creative activity and when it first was divided into science—cognition of the world's phenomena as such—and into art—cognition of our attitudes toward the world.

The Common and the Particular in the Historical Process of Antiquity: History of Ideas and History of Emotions

The last fifty years' experience in the study of the ancient world has shown that by studying the socioeconomic history of antiquity with the help of the methods we have at our disposal, we have apparently been able to find certain very general common laws typical of the whole millennial epoch in question. We have examined them in the second through fourth sections of the present lecture. Meanwhile, discussions about the "formation" to which ancient societies belonged have become more and more concerned with the problem of definitions. We already know in general outline what the ancient societies were like, although details still must be elucidated; the rest is a question of definition and classification.

We know that the ancient epoch was subdivided into, at least, two consecutive periods: early and late antiquity. Both periods are differentiated from the primitive epoch by the fact that two antagonistic classes formed and continued to exist: one of them having property in the means of production or, at least, the possibility to dispose of this property; the other being exploited by the first and being devoid of property in the means of production. Some of the people belonging to the latter class may themselves have been the property of the ruling class or of the state; others could have had certain means of production in their possession but not property.

In the field of production, a division of labor between agriculture (including irrigation agriculture) and industry (including highly specialized crafts and mining, which used mostly bronze tools, although wooden and stone implements had not totally disappeared) was typical for early antiquity. Agriculture and industry are also counterposed to livestock raising, which is not fully divorced from subsidiary agriculture.

The association of people into communities similar to those of the primitive epoch was also characteristic, although such communities came into existence and were maintained by conditions specific to ancient society itself. These were the helplessness of the individual in the production process against natural and social forces and the necessity for close cooperation and reciprocal aid. The emergence of the state economies, typical of early antiquity, was also conditioned by the necessity of cooperation, which was required not only by free people, but also by the dependent and exploited people.

In the field of production relationships, this epoch was also characterized by the preservation, from the times of primitive society, of a considerable stratum of working men who did not exploit the labor of others but who themselves, likewise, were not exploited (if one discounts their utilization for socially necessary work; i.e., that which was necessary for defense and magic [cultic] activities). Here, as the reader may note, we have passed into the field of ideology or, to be more precise, of social psychology. The fact is that magical aid to fertility and social welfare was not perceived by ancient people as belonging to the field of ideas. On the contrary, magic activity was perceived as part of the process of production itself and, of course, was not regarded as some sort of burden imposed by a class enemy. Granted this fact, it follows logically that in order to discover how ancient society actually functioned, it is necessary to enlist the services of social psychology; and this is something ancient historians have not attempted, never knew how to do, and even were not aware that it ought to be done.

Ideology in early antiquity is determined by traditional features of community religions. These are mainly inherited from primitive society and do not so much consecrate the existing social structure (which requires no such justification) as the political and, even, the dynastic structure. The religion of early antiquity is predominantly of a magicoritualistic type with very little ethicophilosophical contribution: each incognizable natural phenomenon, the mechanism or functioning of which is obscure, is *eo ipso* regarded as possibly having an unpredictable ability to influence people; and the more the phenomenon is of everyday occurrence and nearer to one self, the stronger is its supposed active influence. The one factor in the world's structure that is the most important for society is the maintenance of fertility for agricultural production (hence, in Mesopotamia, the sacred marriage rite; in Egypt the renascence of plants in the cult Osiris—rites promoting the activity of the sun, the Nile, etc.). Caring for the dead to keep them satisfied can also be an important factor in maintaining the world's structure. Such care aims to prevent the unfavorable and to promote the favorable influence of the dead over the society of the living.

All this is comparatively clear, but the ideological situation becomes less amenable to explanation as we move from early to late antiquity.

We understand clearly enough the socioeconomic structure of late ancient society, its division into classes. We can also note considerable changes in the ideological field: the emergence of rational forms of scientific thought and philosophy; a flourishing of the exact sciences; and, at the same time, a remodeling of the religious systems in the direction of introducing elements of ethics and developing the motif of the necessity of human salvation, in both the moral and the physical sense.

However, although we seem to understand the static structure of ancient society satisfactorily enough, both in the field of production and in that of ideology, and, lately, we have begun to understand the mechanism of the structures of production, we are still far from understanding the causes inducing human masses to actions. Such actions are those that bring about major shifts in history: changes and developments that operate in all areas of human life. That which is common to the ancient world as a whole is, in many respects, clear, but the causes of the differences are often not apparent. However, such differences—among various periods and regions—are often crucial.

In contrast to other scientists, the modern historian does not aim at the prediction of future phenomena. Because we deal with events that have already happened, we utilize the materialist theory only as a means to *explain* the causes of the social changes and other major events of the past both on the scale of millennial epochs and great continents and on the scale of comparatively small segments of space and time. Nevertheless, a sort of prediction is still sometimes possible: now and again, based upon some known facts, we can extrapolate back to some fact yet unconfirmed, which later can be corroborated when new historical sources are discovered or when sources already known are studied from a novel viewpoint. Such moments in the lives of historians provide a check of the correctness of their concepts and induce them to continue their labors.

We have always proceeded and are still proceeding first from the universal concept that any material process is governed by certain developmental laws and that fact must also be true of the historical process (always taking into account, of course, various fluctuations, some of which are important). And, second, we proceed from the concept of a dialectic connection between productive forces and the relationships in production: the productive forces tend to develop to a limit; and when this limit has been reached, it is sharply overcome by creating new relationships in production, including the formation of new social classes and the destruction and disappearance of the old ones.

Studying the process of history, the generation of historians born in the 1900s to 1920s made certain typical, systematic errors. Thus, for instance, despite many warnings by the greatest thinkers that development does not occur linearly but according to much more dynamic laws, we yielded in the past to the positivist illusion that progress is a constant movement (admittedly, not uniform, but by fits and starts) toward perfection of the society; actually, the development is not from bad to better, but only from less complex to more complex. This greater complexity, of course, may manifest itself in a new "unheard of simplicity," in the words of the poet Pasternak. Moreover, each natural process (which means a process induced by inherent contradictions) is an immanent process, and it cannot be related to ethical categories, as, for instance, the assertion that each new formation of a mode of production means more good to more people.

Thus, contrary to facts in evidence, but in accordance with a simplified concept of progress, we again and again stated in lectures and textbooks that the European Middle Ages did not simply represent a change and a complication of the social mechanism but that it constituted direct progress in the sense of an improvement in the living conditions and morals of a greater percentage of people inside the *socium*.[9]

The same mistake was made for ancient society: the progress from primitive to slave-owning society did not, of course, consist in the betterment of living conditions for the majority, but rather only for the minority. Nor was there improvement in the mechanisms conducive to the further immanent development of productive forces. Moreover, we forgot to keep in mind that progress in the positivist sense would contradict natural laws; namely, the second law of thermodynamics. Obviously, any progressing development presupposes losses, to which we did not give the attention they deserve.

It is evident that the process of socioeconomic development is not fully uniform, and within it we can trace certain specific ways of development. In antiquity, these, to a very considerable degree, were deter-

9. Any sufficiently closed social group—a family, a clan, a professional group, a class, the entire society inside a certain state, etc.—is called a *socium*.

mined by ecological conditions. However, the diversity of the historical process is not limited to these ways of development. This diversity should not, on the other hand, be regarded as absolute, and history should not be regarded (as is often the case in the West) as the inexplicable, irregular, and erratic kaleidoscopic vibration of phenomena. Behind the peculiarities, the common features can always be traced; namely, the dialectics of productive forces and relationships in production. These common features determine the *general* flow of the historical process.

However, we would not have fulfilled our duty as historians if we did not also take into account *peculiarities* in the development of particular societies. It is our obvious duty to be able to explain and—in the future—to predict them. Meanwhile, there are a number of phenomena very essential to the understanding of history that we still do not know how to explain. The more complicated the society, the more such phenomena exist.

For instance, we may notice that events that we usually associate with the passage from one socioeconomic formation to another not uncommonly occur either after or far before the full development of the critical situation in the relation between productive forces and relationships in production. Thus, in English history, the critical situation developed in the industrial revolution of the late eighteenth and early nineteenth centuries. However, on the one hand, the bourgeois revolution, which took a religious form, occurred in England more than a century earlier, and, on the other, the capitalist class gained power (in quite practical forms) as late as the middle of the nineteenth century.

Similar examples could easily be cited from ancient history. It is not easy to determine where the border between early and late antiquity lies, and it is perhaps still more difficult to discover where antiquity ends and the Middle Ages begin. It is even more difficult to synchronize the critical phenomena in the socioeconomic sphere with those in the sphere of ideas and emotions. For instance, we have not satisfactorily explained such phenomena as the unexpected leap in the development of Greek culture in the eighth to fifth centuries B.C.; the failure of some religious movements, such as the religious reforms of Akhenaton in the New Kingdom of Egypt; and the success of other movements that have substantially changed not only the appearance of some particular societies but even the motion of the historical process itself (e.g., the conquest of the Near East, North Africa, and Central Asia by Islam in the early Middle Ages; the importance of Buddhism for the early Indian Empire and of Zoroastrianism for the early Iranian Empire, an importance that had disappeared by the end of the ancient or the beginning of the medieval epoch; or the correlation between the emergence of feudal socioeconomic conditions in the late Roman Empire and the rise of Christianity). Late antiquity is particularly replete with examples of this sort that the historian must confront and attempt to understand.

As the societies of late antiquity developed, the traditional ideologies everywhere proved to be no longer adequate for fulfilling the needs of the more complicated *socia*. These inherited traditional ideologies proved to be insufficient even for supplying the self-governing cities with an ideological base for their special position within the empire. Unavoidably, they were transformed. Also outside the cities, an ideological crisis was felt everywhere, and everywhere there arose new ethicodogmatic doctrines. At first, they did not repudiate the earlier religious traditions but were superimposed on them. Sometimes these doctrines did not even acquire a religious form. But with time they not only developed into dogmatic religions but also began to fix in writing a canon obligatory for all believers (thus, Zoroastrianism, Jainism, Buddhism, the different and constantly renewing forms of Brahmanism-Hinduism, Confucianism, Taoism, Manichaeism, and the doctrines growing out of Judaism—Christianity and, later, Islam, etc.).

The historian finds it more and more difficult to deduce the *changes* in social structure and the *differences* among societies directly and immediately from changes in the forces of production and, hence, from changes in relationships in production. Differences not infrequently appear among societies that are characterized by an approximately similar level of production (or at a similar typological stage of development) or, in other words, among societies where one would expect to, but does not, find roughly similar developments with respect to their ideology.

It is evident that between a critical situation in the process of the development of the productive forces and their result in the form of changes in social structure there has to occur a crisis in social psychology, in the mass psychological motivation of actions. What had once been impossible must now have become both possible and desirable, and what had been possible must now be condemned by the society. It is only then that social masses are brought into action, and society itself is changed.

An idea becomes a material force as soon as it takes possession of mass consciousness. However, there is never a vacuum in mass consciousness; and typically, this consciousness, filled with traditional concepts, does not induce the masses to actions directed toward social change. If the masses are to act in the direction of a change in the conditions of their existence, it is necessary that the dominant psychological tendency of *preservation* should be changed by a psychological tendency toward *development*. Also, the very strong human tendency of *imitation* ("I do as everyone else does") must be overcome, and a new suggested model of behavior should be accepted by the human mass for imitation.

The science of psychology has shown that the need to imitate becomes absolutely dominant mainly in two cases. First, imitation is part of the process of education (or the process of mastering social skills and habits) and occurs in the form of direct imitation of adult actions or in the form of children's play involving, especially, the emotional and even artistic spheres. Second, imitation will occur in a critical situation to which the individual cannot confer meaning by responding independently ("If you do not know what to do, do as everyone else does"). However, the need to imitate is not present only in these two cases; rather, it is always present, sometimes to a high degree. This need actually remains in the background no matter what motivates people to act. (However, it is important to distinguish the situations when this background is, as it were, jammed or negated by less constant but more demanding needs.)

The considerable strength of the need to imitate has been shown in the well-known experiment with the lozenge and the triangle. In the experiment, forty-one people (forty of whom know the secret, one of whom does not) are shown diverse geometrical figures on a display board. Each time, everybody must quickly name the figure. All are unanimous until the experimenter shows a rhombus, and the warned people cry, "Triangle." Only the test subject says, "Lozenge." The experiment continues, and after a time, a lozenge again appears on the board, and again everyone who has been informed cries, "Triangle!" Eventually the sole dissenter, who asserted that he had seen a lozenge, gives up. Of dozens tested, only very few continue to maintain that the figure is a lozenge (if the experiment goes on long enough). Thus, for the majority the need for imitation is stronger than the need for cognition of new objects. This is only natural, because the one who conducts the experiment (in the described case) or the propagandist (as in actual history) does not appeal to reason, which does not enter into play at all, but to the emotions. This is why new ideas created in the rational sphere have such difficulty in gaining recognition—as long as they remain purely rational. If traditional ideas continue to dominate the emotions, owing to some objective historical conditions, a new ideology will not be accepted, even if it is adequate and appropriate to changed conditions in the productive forces. If it succeeds, it is because the new ideology has transformed itself or evolved from a system primarily of conscious reasoning to one of emotional *agitation*. This is why Robespierre was a follower of Rousseau, not of Voltaire;

all the skeptical encyclopaedists appealed to reason, whereas Rousseau appealed to emotion.

But what is true of Robespierre is many times truer of those who
motivated and activated the *socia* of primitive and ancient societies.
The traditional ideologies of early antiquity were mythologies, so here
the historian has to deal with the so-called mythological mentality.

The twentieth century has witnessed a great and manifold interest
in myths and mythological ways of thought, but historians, accustomed as they are to documented facts, find it difficult to agree with
most of what has been said and written on this topic. L. Lévy-Bruhl
treated primitive mentality as prelogical, as opposed to modern logical mentality; but he was unable to explain why primitive people with
their prelogical mentality could achieve sensible results in their activities. S. Freud attempted to construct a system of emotional psychology, also social psychology, but his system was not based on the
physiology of the brain and contained much that was subjective and
one-sided. Instead of this, C. G. Jung was a proponent of a mystical
system that included collective psychological archetypes, the mechanism of which (i.e., how it functioned) cannot, apparently, be specified
in strictly logical terms. C. Lévi-Strauss attempted to lay bare the general laws of the structure of the mind, and his binary oppositions seem
to actually have a physical basis. However, Lévi-Strauss and, especially, his epigones operate with "concepts" supposedly existing in the
mythological mentality, such as the concept of "above and below" or
of "the universal vertical." In this, they resort to terms of rational
logic, which was certainly alien to primitive humanity. Where there is
a concept, there inevitably must exist a word expressing the concept.
However, Lévi-Strauss's concepts cannot be expressed in terms of any
language of early antiquity, which is sufficient proof that the ancients
actually did not have such concepts (if we understand them as logical
categories). At the level of mythological mentality, generalizations are
made not by evolving abstract notions and corresponding terms but
through tropes, mainly image-inducing metonymies. Such a generalization is always emotional; that is, it induces to action certain brain
structures, but *not* those that govern verbal formulations. Therefore,
such generalizations, seen from the logical point of view, are extremely vague. When speaking of primitive people and the people of
early antiquity, we should not make statements in terms of concepts
but in terms of metonymic chains and bundles of images.

Until early antiquity, human mentality could not operate with formulated logical concepts: they cannot be found in the texts, and they
did not exist in the languages. But even when they had been developed, Aristotle and the other great thinkers of antiquity labored only
for a minority, and it was not their ideas that were to move the souls of

the masses. In the last century, scientists and scholars of many nations have written on the history of ideas, but if we want to understand the mechanisms of history, we need a history of emotions.

In order for a new idea to gain acceptance in society, the one who promotes it must resort to propaganda. This term was first introduced by the Roman Catholic church during the Counter-Reformation. (In 1622 Pope Gregory XV established the Roman Congregation of the Propaganda of the Faith.) But we shall now use this term in a broad sense to mean the spreading of controversial ideas. Obviously, when no one disagrees, there is place for ritual but not for propaganda. (Such was the case of the traditional mentality in the primitive epoch and in early antiquity.) Propaganda presupposes a _struggle_—either against tradition or against another propaganda. Already in ancient times, propaganda was not necessarily religious: one could generate propaganda about royalty, a dynasty, or an empire. But whether or not the propaganda was successful (in the historical situations of antiquity) depended on the extent to which it penetrated and affected the sphere of social emotions.

The fact that propaganda acts mainly in the sphere of emotions can be seen from the simple fact that the trump card of any propaganda is justice and fairness. One of the most important statements of an ancient Oriental king when propagandizing in favor of his royalty was the claim that he advocated fairness and justice, _kittum u mīšarum_. Of course, in different historical epochs, there were different notions of what was just and fair: thus, what was meant by justice and fairness in ancient Mesopotamia was a moratorium on incurred debts, the safety of family landholdings, and so on. In any event, agitation for justice—in this and all similar cases—involved an impact upon the emotional sphere; modern psychophysiologists know that a need for justice is inherent in the physiology of human emotions.

It would be possible to cite many more examples showing how social psychology may aid the historian who tries to explain certain situations of social history; for example, why the pupils of Socrates and Jesus were mostly unmarried men. But such examples would occupy too much space; this book is not a special monograph, and here we aim only at pointing out some possible new directions of historical research.

To sum up, a modern historian of antiquity is confronted with the problem of social psychology. It follows from the above that to explain social events and social changes in antiquity, one must not limit oneself to studies in the history of material culture and the history of social structures and machinery, but one should also apply historical social psychology.

Of course, this has been obvious for a long time. However, here we encounter a serious difficulty: up to the present, social psychology has been an experimental science, so that its methods were inapplicable to history.

It seems to us that a possible way to surmount this difficulty lies in an orientation toward such features of psychology—and, first of all, such emotional needs—that are unavoidably present in humanity as a species: those that are always present to a greater or lesser degree, in one form or another, independent of the current social environment. It is, of course, precisely the social environment that determines the concrete form of these psychological features. In studying ideology, one should be required to separate the psychologically universal (whether hyptertrophied or depressed) from the distinctive: those determined by social factors limited in space or in time or by ecological factors, and so on. Thus, for example, it probably will be particularly important to sort out the local and temporally limited factors relevant for the study of the ancient Egyptian religion; here one should establish what is not universal for humanity, and, not restricting oneself just to stating what is distinctive, one should attempt to explain it by the presence or absence of certain impacts (I. P. Pavlov would have said "irritants").

In general, we shall have to treat the factors of ideology and culture not in themselves but by taking account of what psychological needs— emotional, above all—were satisfied by these factors or, contrariwise, suppressed by them. Especially, the impact of propaganda will have to be studied not in itself, but as a response to the input of traditional mentality, and as something inimical to it. We shall have to note the historical moment when the struggle between propaganda and tradition ceases and is replaced by the struggle of more or less particular or private interests. Moreover, in studying propaganda we must, without fail, keep in mind the feedback between the propaganda and the propagandists themselves. Because they typically are the most staunch believers of their own propaganda, they are able to influence and carry away the emotions of the *socium*. Here another very strong sociopsychological factor is involved; viz., the need to be led (and also loved and esteemed), which is stronger and more common than the need to be a leader.

At present, the history of culture is a collection of information on science, literature, art, and, sometimes, religion and, very seldom, everyday life. Actually "culture" is all that, being created by society, has an impact upon society and that induces men and women to socially valid actions. It seems to us that the history of culture should be a history of factors influencing social psychology. In order to accomplish this, we shall have to regard psychology not as a whole but take into account the *different* psychological (even psychophysiological) mechanisms that are subject to *different* impacts. Some attention should be devoted to biological needs, such as the need for satisfying one's hunger and the need for reproduction. More attention should be given to social needs, such as the need to occupy an important place in the *socium;* the need to evade the frustration induced by an impact from the *socium* that is perceived to be unjust; the need to be led, protected, and secure; and only then, finally, the need to lead. An important need is that of cognition of the environment, including new objects, both of the surrounding phenomenal world (which develops into science) and of the world of one's emotional perceptions of the natural and social environment (which develops into art). The dual character of the object of cognition is reflected in the duality of cognition itself: scientific cognition strives to attain and define absolute truth, which is a movement leading to infinity; whereas emotional cognition is subject to "Sherrington's funnel": the stream of emotional stimuli is vastly greater than the ability of efferent nervous tracks to react to each single stimulus. Hence, comprehension of truth in art is manifested only in images intended to induce the pertinent but undefined associations.

The fact that we will have to be oriented not to psychology as a whole (as the mentality of an individual is a whole) but to *specific* needs and to characteristic *groups of responses* seems important to us. Otherwise one might think that, being oriented to what is characteristic of humans as a species, we would receive only uniform, socially non-differentiated answers, insofar as *Homo sapiens sapiens* as a species itself is uniform. This assumption obviously would be incorrect. Just as the individual finds thousands of different responses to the impact of the environment, so also does the *socium*. Inside the *socium* a psychologist will be able to show statistically the needs that are more developed under what conditions and those that are variable and depend upon the character of the environment—the social environment in our case. The study of the influencing factors of culture and of ideology will, correspondingly, allow us to predict which centers in the brain will be subject to the greatest impact. By the character of an impact on an individual, we will be able to assess the probability of his response (if his typological psychophysiological characteristics are known). Thus, confronting the response of the *socium* known from history with the influencing factors that are also known from history, we will be able to assess the statistically probable mechanism of the motivation for social behavior.

Our suggestions, formulated in this way, bear an external similarity with the definitions of early behaviorism. Thus, J. Watson stated "that the goal of psychological study is the ascertaining of such data and laws that, given the stimulus, psychology can predict what the re-

sponse will be; or, on the other hand, given the response, it can spec-
ify the nature of the effective stimulus" (italicized in original).[10]

This position of the behaviorists has been justly criticized. It has
been observed that the behaviorists simply do not take into account all
the intermediary factors, as, for example, all the extremely complicated functions of the different mechanisms of the brain that do not
allow for a simple stimulus-response correlation. However, complex
problems of psychophysiology lie outside the realm of the humanities.
We shall have to take at face value the data (including statistical data)
that the science of psychology, especially experimental social psychology, furnishes us. From these data we must draw sufficiently differentiated information on the reciprocal influence of different psychological needs; for example, information on the relative ability,
under given conditions, of certain needs to stimulate or to suppress
other needs. But the social stimuli and the social responses doubtless
lie within the sphere of competence of the historian of society and
culture.

If we were to regard from this point of view the different ideological and religious movements of antiquity (and since religion is always
emotional, it is always universally ascendant), we would probably be
able to solve a number of problems. For instance, why is it that some
doctrines have greatly influenced the historical development of a society, whereas others have quickly dwindled to nonexistence? We shall
try to adduce a single example—a very crude one, perhaps—that may
illustrate the general direction of our thought. Why did pure monotheism take such a long time to spread, and why did it, in its mass variant, mostly appear as a quasi monotheism? Even medieval Christianity
can actually be regarded as monotheistic only with great reservations.
Why was Akhenaton's monotheism (or quasi monotheism) doomed to
quick extinction, whereas the quasi monotheism of Zoroaster or of
Paul received widespread and long-lived support? To answer that the
society under Akhenaton was not yet mature enough for monotheism
is not to answer at all. What are the criteria of maturity for monotheism? Akhenaton's doctrine was not viable because it did not evoke
positive emotions in anyone.

At present, we already have some knowledge about the emotional
side of human cerebral activity. Apart from addressing sociopsychological problems, one can, in principle, address problems of how a
certain social personality emerges; how certain correlations arise, say,
between the need of cognition and the need to return to a stable place

10. J. B. Watson, *Psychology from the Standpoint of a Behaviorist*, 1st ed. (New York: Lip-
pincott, 1919), p. 10.

in the *socium;* the need of preserving skills and habits and the need of acquiring new skills; the need of self-preservation and the need of aggression. If at some time in the future we are able to assess correctly the formative sociopsychological situation, we shall, ideally, be able to explain why *this* epoch and *this* nation needed the domination of a Chinghiz Khan, another of a prophet Muhammad, while still another of an Ivan the Terrible, an Akhenaton, or a Hammurapi.

Meanwhile, we ought to reorient our research in the history of culture (without detriment to socioeconomic research) toward the understanding of the sociopsychological causes and sociopsychological effects of different cultural phenomena—above all, the emotional effects. Furthermore, there should be research on the relations between tradition and various types of propaganda. Finally we should attempt to understand clearly the connection between cultural phenomena and their substratum of social relations in production. This is a *moving* substratum that is always receiving a certain interpretation and remodeling in people's minds. In other words, we ought to understand better the connection of culture with the dialectics of the productive forces and social relationships in production.

All this is a program for the future. In this book we attempt only to put together what has already been done; in this last section we have just outlined a plan of further work for the next generation of historians.

2

The City-States of Sumer

I. M. DIAKONOFF

The Development of Organized Irrigation
in the Lower Euphrates Valley

The Introduction to this volume described the emergence of the earliest class societies and the particular ways in which they developed in the Lower Euphrates Valley and in the Nile Valley; that is, in ancient Sumer and in ancient Egypt. Now, let us analyze more closely the Lower Euphrates Valley (Lower Mesopotamia) in early antiquity.[1]

We already know that this country is separated from the rest of the Near East by barely passable deserts and that it was already inhabited during the sixth millennium B.C. During the sixth to fourth millennia B.C. the tribes lived here in extreme poverty. Barley, which was sown on the narrow strip of land between the marshes and the burned-out desert and irrigated by irregularly occurring floods of varying intensity, yielded small and fluctuating harvests. Harvests were greater on lands irrigated by channels dug from the Diyala River, a minor tributary of the Tigris. It was only toward the middle of the fourth millennium B.C. that individual community groups managed to create drainage-irrigation systems in the Euphrates basin.

The Lower Euphrates basin is a wide, flat plain, bordered to the east by the Tigris, beyond which stretch the spurs of the Iranian mountains, and to the west by the steep edge of the Syro-Arabian semidesert. Lacking suitable irrigation and land improvement, this plain was a desert in some places and in others was covered by bogs and shallow lakes bordered by thickets of giant reeds swarming with noxious insects. Today, the desert portion is crossed by earthen banks of former canals. When a canal is operating, date palms grow along the banks. Here and there, the flat land is dotted by mounds of clay (*tells*) and by cinder mounds (*ishans*). These are ruins of cities; actually, they are the remains of hundreds of adobe houses and temple towers, reed huts and mud walls—structures that succeeded one another at the same site. In earliest antiquity, however, there were no

---

1. The ancient Greeks used the term *Mesopotamia* to designate the land between the Tigris and the Euphrates rivers. Today, the territory of historic Mesopotamia is part of Turkey, Syria, and Iraq. Lower Mesopotamia is the southern part of present-day Iraq.

mounds or banks. The swampy lagoons covered more surface than they do now, stretching across what is now southern Iraq; it was only in the extreme south that low, uninhabited islands broke up the vast lagoons. Gradually, the silt from the Euphrates, the Tigris, and the northeast–southwest flowing Elamite rivers[2] formed an alluvial barrier, which extended the territory of the plain by some 120 kilometers (almost 75 miles) to the south. Where, at one time, shallow coastal bays communicated directly with the Persian Gulf, the Shatt-al-Arab River now flows. The Shatt-al-Arab was formed by the confluence of the Tigris and Euphrates, both of which once had their own mouths and lagoons.

The Euphrates divided into several branches within Lower Mesopotamia. The most important one in the third millennium b.c. was Iturungal, from which the canal I-Nina-Gena extended to a lagoon in the southeast. The Tigris flowed further east; its shores were bare except where it received the Diyala tributary. In the fourth millennium several smaller canals stemmed from each of the main branches of the Euphrates. With the aid of a system of dams and reservoirs, it was possible to accumulate sufficient water to irrigate the fields throughout the entire growing season. This increased the harvest yields and made it possible to accumulate a surplus. It was a development that led to the second great division of labor; that is, to the segregation of specialized trades. It eventually allowed class stratification: a slave-owning class formed that could exploit slavelike dependents (patriarchal slaves and helots).

It should be mentioned that the extremely strenuous labor of building, cleaning, and maintaining the canals—or of any other earth-moving construction work—was generally not performed by slaves but, rather, by community members serving their conscription duty.[3] Every free adult spent an average of one or two months doing this type of work. This arrangement existed throughout the entire history of ancient Mesopotamia.

The free community members also performed the main agricultural work—plowing and sowing. Those individuals who were invested with authority and performed functions that were considered socially important were the only ones who did not personally participate in these duties and did not work the soil.

Extensive archaeological surveys of the most ancient traces of settlements in Lower Mesopotamia show that the accomplishment of local

2. Like the Tigris and the Euphrates, the Elamite rivers discharged into the Persian Gulf, though perpendicular to the other two.

3. Such work was necessary for the people's very existence. Conscription duty was a form of taxation, much like military duty or the regulation of resources for the maintenance of defense; however, not every tax is exploitative.

land improvement and irrigation systems was attended by an influx of inhabitants from scattered tiny villages, probably made up of extended-family groups, into the regional, or nome, centers, where the principal temples and their rich granaries and workshops were situated. The temple functioned as the collection center for the emergency funds of the nome. From these centers trading agents—*tamkars*—traveled to distant lands to exchange the grain and textiles of Lower Mesopotamia for the lumber, metals, and slaves of other regions. In the beginning of the second quarter of the third millennium, the densely populated perimeters of the main temples were encircled by city walls. Somewhat earlier, around 3000–2900, the temple economies became so large and complex that it was necessary to keep accounts of their activities. In the face of this necessity, writing was born.

Invention of Writing: the Protoliterate Period

At a very early period in history, people felt the need to pass on information not only orally, from one person to another, but also across time and space. For this, they used special reminding (mnemonic) signs that symbolized or depicted the objects of significance or signs that called forth corresponding associations. We know a considerable amount about such signs used by tribes of the nineteenth and twentieth centuries A.D. under primitive conditions, but unfortunately, until recently we knew nothing of those used by ancient Neolithic peoples. Some years ago, the American scholar Denise Schmandt-Besserat discovered that the Neolithic population of the Near East used for communication not only objects that primarily had another purpose[4] (and possibly drawings in paint or soot, which have long since disappeared) but also three-dimensional representations of objects, which have sometimes been found enclosed in special clay containers. The shapes of these clay three-dimensional mnemonic signs used for communicating information is very similar to some of the first Mesopotamian pictorial signs that already constitute a closed system (i.e., a script).

By the end of the fourth and beginning of the third millennium, information was passed on through drawings. They were made on soft clay tablets with the corner of the edge of a reed stick's cutoff stump. Each drawn sign represented either the depicted object itself or concepts associated with the object. For example, a drawing of the sky made with a hatched, arched line meant "night," as well as "black," "dark," "darkness," "ill," and so on. Similarly, the sign of a

---

4. For example, a bunch of arrows might signify a declaration of war. Of course, we are unable to identify objects so used by preliterate peoples.

foot signified such verbs as "to go," "walk," "stand," and "bring." The grammatical forms of words were not expressed; it was not really necessary, since the earliest documents recorded only numbers and the signs of the objects. It was more difficult to express the names of the individuals receiving or delivering the objects. Initially, it was sufficient to identify them simply by their trade: a furnace signified a coppersmith; a mountain (which was the symbol for a foreign land) indicated a slave; a terrace(?) (perhaps a kind of rostrum) meant a chief priest; and so on. Very soon, however, rebuses came into use: if *na* meant "stone" or "weight," then the sign denoting a weight and placed next to that of a foot suggested the word *gena*, "walking"; and the sign for "heap," *ba*, placed next to the same sign suggested the word *guba*, "standing." At times, the rebus method was used to write entire words when their meaning was difficult to represent pictorially. Thus, *gi*, "return, turn in," was represented by the sign for "reed," *gi*. The earliest pictorial mnemonic signs are attested from about 3000 B.C., but it took at least 600 years for this purely mnemonic or suggestive system of sign making to develop into an orderly system that could convey spoken information over space and time. This process was completed around 2400 B.C.

By this time, the signs had developed into combinations of short, straight lines, because it was not possible to draw curved lines on clay with the necessary speed and without causing accidental ridges and other marks. This form of writing made it difficult to recognize the original drawings. Each short, straight line in this system resembles a wedge because of the angle at which the corner of the rectangular stick was pressed into the malleable clay. Hence, the term *cuneiform* (wedge-shaped) script. Each cuneiform sign could stand for several semantically related words and, for this reason, could also have several phonetic (rebus) values. (The signs are commonly referred to as syllabic. Strictly speaking, this is not correct; the phonetic value may also correspond to half a syllable. For example, the syllable *bab* can be written with two "syllabic" signs: *ba-ab*. The value is the same as for the sign *bab*, the difference being in the convenience of memorizing and saving space, not in the reading.) Certain signs could be used as "determinatives"; that is, signs that were not pronounced but that indicated the conceptual category to which the neighboring word belonged (such as wooden or metallic objects, fish, birds, or occupations). Determinative signs helped the reader to select the correct meaning from among several possible options.

Despite the communicative imprecision of the written language during this period of Lower Mesopotamian history, it is now possible to read at least some of the very ancient administrative documents.

The information from these documents and investigations of the drawings used for writing, in conjunction with archaeological data, allow us to partially re-create the ancient social history of this country, even though many events that occurred during this long period of history remain unknown.

Questions inevitably arise. What people created the first civilization in Lower Mesopotamia? What language did they speak? Linguistic studies of later cuneiform inscriptions (from about 2500 B.C.) and proper names mentioned in the inscriptions (from about 2700 B.C.) show that Lower Mesopotamia was then inhabited by people who spoke two completely different languages: Sumerian and Eastern Semitic. The Sumerian language, with its idiosyncratic grammar, is not known to be related to any language that survives today. However, the Eastern Semitic language, which was later called Akkadian or Babylonian-Assyrian, belongs to the Semitic family of the Afrasian linguistic phylum. The following present-day languages belong to the same family: several languages spoken in Ethiopia; Arabic; the language of the Mediterranean island of Malta; Hebrew; and the Neo-Aramaic dialects, spoken by a small group of people who call themselves Assyrians and who are dispersed throughout many countries, including the USSR. The Akkadian, or Babylonian-Assyrian, language died out before our era, as did a number of other Semitic languages. The ancient Egyptian language also belongs to the Afrasian phylum, which includes a number of languages spoken today in northern Africa, Tanzania, Nigeria, and in countries all the way to the Atlantic coast.

There is reason to believe that in the fourth millennium B.C. and, perhaps, even later, there were still people in the Tigris and Euphrates valleys who spoke languages that became extinct in early Antiquity. It is possible that the speakers of one of these languages were the first to have created systematic irrigation works in the Diyala Valley, and they may have taken part also in the development of the lands in Lower Mesopotamia. Although in the latter region the main role was probably played by Sumerians, Eastern Semitic–speaking peoples also participated, particularly on the northern borders of Lower Mesopotamia. The earliest Mesopotamian texts (ca. 2900–2500 B.C.) were written, without doubt, exclusively in Sumerian; the character of the rebus-like use of signs proves this. It is obvious that if the word "reed" coincides with the word "return"—*gi*—then we must be dealing with a language that had just such a phonetic coincidence: Sumerian. This does not mean that at that time and even earlier, Eastern Semites and, perhaps, people who spoke another language, now unknown, did not inhabit Lower Mesopotamia together with the Sumerians or before them.

We have no indications, archaeological or linguistic, to prove that the Eastern Semites were nomads and that they could not jointly participate with the Sumerians in the great task of developing the Euphrates region. Nor do we have reason to believe that Eastern Semites invaded Mesopotamia around 2750 B.C., as many scholars once supposed. On the contrary, linguistic data show that already during the Neolithic, the Eastern Semites must have settled between the Euphrates and the Tigris. Apparently, however, the inhabitants of the southern part of Lower Mesopotamia spoke primarily Sumerian until at least 2350 B.C., whereas the Eastern Semitic language was spoken side by side with Sumerian in the central and northern parts of Lower Mesopotamia and was predominant in Upper Mesopotamia. Judging from the available information, there was no ethnic enmity between the people who spoke these completely different languages. Evidently, people of that time did not think in broad categories of linguistic and ethnic groups; they both made friends and made war only at the level of the smaller units—the tribes, nomes, and territorial communities. At the same time, there could have been a sense of identity on a broader level. For example, all the inhabitants of Lower Mesopotamia, regardless of which language they spoke, called themselves "black-headed people" (*sang-ngiga* in Sumerian and *tsalmat-qaqqadi* in Akkadian).

Since the historic events of such remote times are unknown to us, historians use archaeological periods to classify the earliest ancient history of Lower Mesopotamia. They distinguish a Protoliterate Period (2900–2750 B.C., with two subperiods) from an Early Dynastic Period (2750–2310 B.C., with three subperiods).[5] We have three archives from the Protoliterate Period, not counting occasional isolated documents. Two of the archives, one of which is somewhat older than the other, were found in the city of Uruk (present-day Warka) in southern Lower Mesopotamia, and one is from the archaeological site of Jemdet-Nasr in the north. (The ancient name of the city is not known.) The latter archive is contemporaneous with the second, more recent Uruk archive. Two Soviet scholars, A. I. Tyumenev and A. A. Vaiman, attempted a study into the social order of the Protoliterate Period. Whereas Tyumenev's research was based exclusively on the interpretation of the pictographs themselves, Vaiman's was based on the actual readings of some of the documents.

Note that the system of writing during the Protoliterate Period, despite its unwieldiness, was identical in both the southern and the northern parts of Lower Mesopotamia. This suggests that it origi-

---

5. According to the latest findings, these dates should perhaps be corrected to somewhat earlier ones.

nated in a single center that must have enjoyed considerable authority, since the invention was adopted by different nomes regardless
of the fact that no economic or political unity existed among them and
that their main canals were separated from each other by zones of
desert. This center was, apparently, the city of Nippur, situated between the southern and northern parts of the Lower Euphrates Valley. Here the temple of the god Enlil was situated. Enlil was worshiped
by all "black-headed people," although each nome also had its own
mythology and pantheon (system of deities). At some period during
the pre-urban epoch, Nippur was probably the ritual center of a Sumerian tribal union. Although Nippur was never a political center,
it remained an important cultural center for a long time.

Some of the documents of the Protoliterate Period come from the
economic administrative archive of the Eanna temple, which was dedicated to the goddess Inanna and around which the city of Uruk was
consolidated. The rest of the documents come from an analogous
temple archive found at Jemdet-Nasr. The documents show that the
temple's household was composed of numerous specialized craftsmen
and quite a few captured slaves of both sexes. The male slaves probably were absorbed into the general mass of the temple's dependents.
In any case, such was certainly the case two centuries later. It also appears that the community allotted large parcels of land to its principal
functionaries, such as the soothsayer-priest, the chief judge, the senior priestess, and the chief of the trade agents. But the lion's share
was given to the priest holding the title *en*.

An *en* was the supreme priest in those communities that worshiped
a goddess as their supreme deity. He represented the community to
the outside world and presided over the community council. He also
partook in the "sacred marriage" rite with the chief goddess. (In
Uruk, it was Inanna.) This was a ceremony that evidently was considered necessary in order to ensure the general well-being and fertility
of the land of Uruk. In communities where the supreme deity was
male, there was a priestess, also called *en* (sometimes she was known
by other titles), who also participated in the sacred marriage rite with
the chief local deity. The land assigned to the *en* (called *ashag-en* or
nig-en) gradually became temple land. Its crop became the community's emergency reserve stock and was also used for exchange with
other communities and countries, for sacrifices to the gods, and for
the rations of the temple personnel—its craftsmen, tillers of the soil,
fishermen, and others (sometimes rations were given to personnel in
addition to land). The priests usually also had personal land allotments within the community. It is still not quite clear who worked the
nig-en land during the Protoliterate Period, though we know that it
was later cultivated by different kinds of helots. This appears from

the data of an archive from Uruk's neighboring city, archaic Ur, as well as from certain other archives; they all belong to the next, or Early Dynastic, period.

The Early Dynastic Period

The establishment of an Early Dynastic Period as distinct from the Protoliterate is based on various archaeological reasons that would be difficult to discuss here; but the Early Dynastic Period also stands out quite clearly from a purely historical point of view.

In the third millennium B.C., the Sumerians composed a sort of primitive account of history: the "King List." It recorded all the kings, who supposedly ruled in a consecutive order, succeeding one another in the various cities of Mesopotamia from the beginning of time. The kings ruling one after another in the same city were conventionally regarded as one "dynasty." Actually, mythological as well as historical characters were included in this list, and the dynasties of the individual cities often ruled contemporaneously rather than sequentially. Moreover, most of the enumerated rulers were not kings: some bore the title *en*-priest; some were "Big Men" (Sumerian *lu-gal, lugal*)—that is, chiefs who were military commanders; and some were *ensí*, which possibly meant "priest-founder (of buildings?)." The ruler's adopting one or the other title depended on circumstances and on the local traditions of the city. The number of years assigned in the list to the duration of the individual reigns is rarely reliable; in most cases, it resulted from later arbitrary manipulations of the figures. The King List is essentially based on a count of generations according to two major lines, originally independent lists; one is connected with the cities of Uruk and Ur in southern Lower Mesopotamia, and the other with the city of Kish in the north.[6] If we entirely disregard the imaginary dynasties that, according to the King List, ruled "before the Flood," then the beginning of the First Dynasty of Kish (the first "after the Flood") will approximately coincide with the beginning of the Early Dynastic Period; according to the archaeological periodization, this part of the Early Dynastic Period is referred to as "ED I." This is the time of the previously mentioned archaic archive from Ur, Uruk's neighboring city.

En-Menbaragesi, the penultimate ruler of the First Dynasty of Kish, is the first Sumerian statesman not only included in the King List but also known from his own inscriptions; so there are no doubts about

6. Only in the latter part of the Uruk-Ur list are the durations of reigns based on lists of "date formulae" (lists of designations of years according to events occurring in them). Such assessments of the duration of reigns may be regarded as more or less reliable.

his historical authenticity. He waged war against Sumer's neighboring cities in Elam, in the valley of the Karun and Kerkheh rivers, where the historical development was similar to that of Sumer. Thus, there should not be too much doubt also about the authenticity of Aka, the son of Menbaragesi, also mentioned in the King List. The only other mention of him is in an epic that has reached us in a copy written down about a thousand years later. According to this epic, Aka tried to place Uruk in the south under the control of his native Kish, and the council of Uruk's elders was about to accept it until the popular assembly of the city proclaimed the chief priest (*en*), Gilgamesh, as their chief military leader (*lugal*) and decided to resist Aka. Aka besieged Uruk but did not succeed, and consequently, it was Kish that had to submit to Uruk under the leadership of Gilgamesh. According to the King List, Gilgamesh belonged to the First Dynasty of Uruk.

Eventually, Gilgamesh became the hero of many Sumerian epic songs and, later, of the great epic poem written in the Akkadian language (Eastern Semitic). These literary compositions will be discussed in the lectures dealing with the Sumerian and Babylonian culture. Let us just mention here that the identification of an epic hero with a historic person is a very common feature of ancient literature. However, the myths that were used for the plots in the songs about Gilgamesh are much older than that historical figure. Gilgamesh himself seems to have been a remarkable enough personality to remain in the memories of much later generations. (Soon after his death, he was deified, and his name was known in the Near East even as late as the eleventh century A.D.). The epics glorify his major accomplishments: the building of Uruk's city wall and an expedition to the mountains[7] to obtain cedar. (It is not known whether such an expedition actually took place.)

Gilgamesh begins the second stage of the Early Dynastic Period (ED II). Our knowledge of the socioeconomic conditions of that time stems from yet another archive, which was discovered in the ancient town of Shuruppak. It contains economic and legal documents, as well as educational texts of the twenty-sixth century B.C.[8] One part of this archive belongs to the temple economy, while other documents come from individual houses.

We have learned from these documents that the territorial community (nome) of Shuruppak was part of a military union of communities headed by Uruk. Apparently, the direct descendants of Gilgamesh (the First Dynasty of Uruk) ruled at the time. Some of Uruk's warriors

7. The later version of the epic, in Akkadian, speaks of the Lebanon, but originally some less distant mountains to the east probably were meant.

8. Such texts, as well as the earliest copies of literary compositions so far discovered, were found at another site dating from that time, present-day Abu-Salabikh.

were stationed in the different cities of the union, but the *lugals* of
Uruk did not, in general, interfere in the local community's affairs. At
this time the temple economy was already separate from the territorial community and from the economies of the extended-family communes established on its land. Nevertheless, the connection between
the temple and the community remained conspicuous. When necessary, the territorial community loaned draft animals to the temple
economies (donkeys were most often used for this purpose) and, possibly, even donated the labor of its members; in turn, the temple supplied food for the traditional feast that took place during the general
assembly of the community. The ruler of the Shuruppak nome was an
ensí, a quite unimportant figure. He received a relatively small allotment; it seems that the council of elders and some of the priests were
more important than he was. The years were not counted by the
reigning years of the *ensí* but by the annual periods during which
some sort of duty, apparently ritual, was performed alternately by the
representatives of the different temples and by those of the various
minor territorial communities making up the Shuruppak nome.

Craftsmen, cowherds, shepherds, and agriculturalists of the most
diverse social categories worked in the temple economy. It seems that
they usually received rations for their labor, although some of them
may have obtained service-conditioned land allotments (not as property, of course). They were all deprived of property in the means
of production and were extraeconomically exploited. Some of them
were fugitives from other communities; some were descendants of
prisoners-of-war; but many of the workers were probably local people.
Female workers were automatically labeled slaves.

Outside the temple, the extended-family households sometimes
sold their land. The patriarch of the extended-family commune received the payment for this land; if he happened to be dead, payment
went to the "brothers"—that is, the descendants in the next generation. Other adult community members received gifts or symbolic
treats for agreeing to the transaction. The payment for the land (in
kind or in copper) was extremely low, and it is entirely possible that
after a certain time, the "purchaser" actually had to return the parcel
of land to the household commune of the original owners.[9]

Toward the middle of the third millennium B.C., in addition to the
military and cultic leaders (*lugal*, *en*, and *ensí*) who were under the political control of the councils of elders, a new figure emerged: the

9. Another explanation is that the sales were conditioned by a catastrophically poor
crop; a "sale" would then be regarded as an input in the reciprocal aid fund, and either
the property could be retrieved later or some other services could be requested from
the "purchaser" at a later date. However, the hypothesis as stated in the text tallies with
later Mesopotamian customs.

hegemonic *lugal*. This *lugal* relied on the support of his personal followers and his own military troop, whom he could keep without the
council's approval or consent. With the help of this military detachment, he was able to conquer other nomes and place himself above
the individual nome councils, which continued to act only on the
nome level. In the northern part of the country, the hegemonic *lugal*
usually adopted the title of "*lugal* of Kish" (this was a play on words,
meaning also "*lugal* of the multitudes"),[10] and in the southern part,
the title of "*lugal* of the Country." To earn the latter title, it was necessary to be recognized in the temple of the city of Nippur.

In order for the *lugals* to be independent of the nome bodies
of self-government, they needed independent resources—primarily
land, which they could allot to their followers without bothering about
their daily sustenance. Allowing his followers to sustain themselves
was much more convenient for the *lugal*, because he did not need to
provide them with grain and other rations. Since the temples actually
had both the resources and the land, the *lugals* tried to gain control of
the temples, either by marrying the chief priestess or by forcing the
council to elect them as both military leader and chief priest; it would
then be possible to entrust the administration of the temple to men
personally dependent on the *lugal* instead of to the community elders.

The wealthiest *lugals* were those of the First Dynasty of Ur, which
replaced the First Dynasty of nearby Uruk: these were Mesanepada
and his successors. (The last *lugals* of the First Dynasty of Ur moved
from Ur back to Uruk and founded the Second Dynasty of Uruk.)
Their wealth was based not only on the seizure of temple land (we can
assume this from an indirect reference)[11] but also on trade.

During the excavations at Ur, archaeologists discovered an as-
tonishing burial. A sloping passage led to a subterranean chamber.
There were carts with harnessed oxen in the passage. The entrance
was guarded by warriors in helmets, holding spears; both the oxen
and the warriors had been killed during the preparations for burial.
The funeral chamber itself was a rather large dug-out space; dozens
of women were seated along its walls. (Actually they had *originally*
been seated; archaeologists found the skeletons lying on the floor.)
Some held musical instruments. Their hair had once been gathered in
the back and fastened above their foreheads by silver bands. One of
the women apparently died before she had time to don her silver

10. This title is frequently translated as "King of the Universe." This translation,
however, is probably incorrect.

11. Thus, Mesanepada assumed the title "husband of the (heavenly?) harlot," meaning either "the heavenly harlot, goddess Inanna of Uruk" or "the harlot-priestess of
goddess Inanna." In either case, it means that he claimed authority over Inanna's
temple.

band, and it rested in the folds of her dress; the metal was imprinted with the remains of a valuable fabric.

In a corner of a neighboring funeral chamber there was a small vaulted cell made of bricks with a sort of bed inside. This was clearly no common Sumerian burial; on the bed, the skeleton of a woman lay supine. The woman was dressed in a mantle of blue beads of imported lapis lazuli; she wore rich bead necklaces of carnelian and gold, large golden earrings, and a peculiar headdress made of golden flowers. Judging from the inscription on her seal, her name was Puabi.[12] Also found were a number of gold and silver objects that had belonged to Puabi, including two harps of exquisite workmanship with images (on the one, of a bull; on the other, of a cow) sculpted in gold and lapis lazuli on the resonance box. Archaeologists found some similar burials nearby, although they were not as completely intact. The remains of the central figure were not preserved in any of them.

Puabi's burial stimulated debates among scholars that continue to this day; in its lavishness it is unlike any other of that epoch, including a shaft burial, also uncovered in Ur, of a king whose remains were found wearing a golden helmet in the form of a female coiffure with a rolled-up braid of exceptionally fine craftsmanship. None of the sacrificial victims of Puabi's funeral showed any traces of violence; they were probably put to sleep by poison. It is quite probable that they submitted voluntarily to their fate in order to continue their customary service to their mistress in the other world. In any case, the warriors in Puabi's guard and her maids of honor in their rich attire most likely were not simply slaves. Because of the vegetation symbols on Puabi's headdress, because she lay on what can be described as a bridal bed, and because her golden harps were decorated with representations of a wild, bearded bull, the personification of Ur's tutelary god, Nanna, the god of the Moon, and of a wild cow, personifying Nanna's spouse, the goddess Ningal, some scholars believe that Puabi was not just the wife of a *lugal* of Uruk but that she may have been an *en*-priestess who had participated in the sacred marriage rite with the Moon god.[13]

Whatever the case may be, Puabi's burial and other similar examples from the First Dynasty of Ur (about the twenty-fifth century B.C.) testify to the exceptional wealth of the ruling elite of the Ur king-

12. The reading of the name, as is frequently the case with early Mesopotamian inscriptions, is not certain. It has also been read as "Shub-ad"; this is the form used in most popular and even in some specialized works, but it is almost certainly wrong.

13. Such burials were, however, not part of an annual rite; the funeral gifts were too expensive, even for a royal spouse.

dom, which apparently headed the southern union of Lower Mesopotamian Sumerian nomes. There is no doubt about the source of this wealth: the gold and the carnelian beads came from India, and the lapis lazuli, although from the mines of Badakhshan in northern Afghanistan, probably also reached Ur from India via the sea. It is to be noted that the burials of the *lugals* of Kish were much less lavish: Ur was the seaport for trade with India. The high-prowed Sumerian ships, built of long giant reed beams tied together and coated with natural bitumen, with sails made of reed mats and attached to thick reed masts, sailed along the shores of the Persian Gulf to the island of Dilmun (present-day Bahrain) and then to the Indian Ocean, possibly even reaching the ports of Melakha—a country of the ancient Indus civilization, not far from the mouth of the Indus River.[14]

The First Dynasty of Ur begins the last stage of the Early Dynastic Period (ED III). In addition to the city of Ur, there existed other independent nome communities in Lower Mesopotamia, some of which were headed by *lugals* who, like the *lugals* in Ur, strove for hegemony. The communities constantly clashed with each other; this condition of unremitting warfare was characteristic of the period. They fought for the fertile strips of land, for canals, and for accumulated riches. Among the rival states claiming hegemony, the most important was the nome of Kish in the northern part of Lower Mesopotamia and the nome of Lagash in the south. Lagash was situated on a branch of the Euphrates, the I-Nina-Gena, that reached the Tigris lagoon. Girsu (or, actually, Ngirsu) was the capital city of Lagash.

We have many more documents and inscriptions from Lagash than from any other Lower Mesopotamian nome of that time. Most important is the economic archive of the temple dedicated to the goddess Baba (or Bau). This archive indicates that the land was divided into three categories: (1) The actual temple land, the *nig-en*, which was worked by the temple's dependent laborers. In part, its income went to the maintenance of the economy's personnel. But the greater part of the income went into the sacrificial, reserve, and exchange funds. (2) Land allotted in parcels to some of the temple personnel: to minor administrators, craftsmen, and men responsible for the agricultural work. This group also supplied the soldiers for the temple's military detachment. Frequently, such an allotment was given to an entire group of workers who were considered "men" of their chief. Legally, the allotments did not constitute the property of the holders; they were just a form of personnel maintenance. If, for some reason, it

14. In the specialized literature, it is also called Meluhha. Both readings are acceptable.

suited the administration, the allotment could be withdrawn, or not be awarded in the first place, and the man given a ration instead.[15] The female workers who were employed in spinning, weaving, tending cattle, and so on received rations only, as did their non-adult children and all male unskilled laborers. Men and women of this group could be purchased, and for all practical purposes, they shared the status of slaves, although the children of the female slaves could be eventually transferred to another category of workers. (3) Land apparently rented out by the temple to anyone who wanted and was able to work it, on relatively favorable conditions. The holder's main obligation was to cede a portion of the crop to the temple.

As before, there still existed lands outside the temple that belonged to extended-family households. It does not seem probable that they employed slave labor as a rule.

The higher functionaries of the nome, including the chief priest and the ruler himself, received very substantial allotments for their service. They had their own "men" working for them, who carried the same status as those working the temple land. It is not entirely clear whether the lands allotted to these important persons were part of the state fund or whether they were given to these functionaries as property. Actually, this may not have been clear even to the people of Lagash themselves. The fact is that property, as opposed to mere possession, is characterized by the right of the proprietor to dispose of it at his own discretion, as, for example, by selling it, by bestowing it as a gift, or by leaving it as an inheritance. But the idea of the complete alienation of land contradicted the deep-rooted principles that the Mesopotamians had inherited from primitive times. Moreover, the rich and the noble actually had no need to alienate land. It was the poor of the community who sometimes were forced by circumstance to relinquish their land in order to pay off debts, but such deals may not have been considered fully irreversible. There were also occasional instances when a ruler would force someone to give up his land to him. But the property relationships of Lower Mesopotamia in the third millennium were apparently not yet clearly geared to the needs of class society. However, it is important to realize that the society was already stratified into a wealthy class that had the opportunity to exploit the labor of others, a class that was not yet exploited and did not exploit other people's labor, and a class of people who were dispossessed of means of production and who were subject to extra-economic exploitation. This last class included patriarchal slaves and helots, workers who were bound to the large economies.

15. Actually, the holders of allotments also received rations—not monthly but once in a season.

It is true that this information almost exclusively comes from Lagash (twenty-fifth to twenty-fourth centuries B.C.), but there is some evidence that an analogous situation prevailed in all the other Lower Mesopotamian nomes, regardless of whether their inhabitants spoke Sumerian or Eastern Semitic. However, in many ways, the Lagash nome was in a unique position. For example, Lagash was second in wealth only to Ur-Uruk. The Lagash port of Guaba competed with Ur in overseas trade with neighboring Elam and with India. The trade agents (*tamkars*) were part of the temple economies' personnel, although they also accepted private orders for the purchase of overseas products, including slaves.

The rulers of Lagash, like their counterparts in the other nomes, dreamed of achieving hegemony in Lower Mesopotamia, but access to the center of the land was blocked by the neighboring city of Umma, which was located near the point where the I-Nina-Gena separated from the Iturungal. For many generations Lagash was engaged in a bloody feud with Umma over the fertile region at the border between the two cities. The rulers of Lagash held the title of *ensí* and were granted the title of *lugal* (by the council or the popular assembly?) only temporarily, apparently in conjunction with the transfer of special powers, such as for the duration of a military expedition or when carrying out some especially important measures.

The army of a Sumerian nome ruler at that time consisted of relatively small detachments of heavily armed warriors. The soldiers were protected by cone-shaped copper helmets and by heavy felt cloaks with large copper plates, or by enormous copper-covered shields; they fought in close order, the long spears of the rear rows protruding between the protective shields of the first row like bristles. There were also primitive chariots on solid wheels with quivers containing missile darts or javelins attached to their fronts. The chariots were pulled by onagers (large semiwild donkeys).[16]

The losses suffered in the confrontations between such detachments were relatively small; the dead were only counted in dozens. The warriors of these detachments were allotted parcels on temple land or on the land of the ruler, if they were directly committed to him. A *lugal* could also raise a popular militia from among the temple's dependents, as well as from the free community members. These militiamen formed a light infantry armed with short spears.

Soon after 2400 B.C., the ruler of Lagash, Eanatum, was temporarily elected *lugal;* he led the heavily armed detachments and the militia

16. The horse was known but, most likely, had not yet been domesticated in Mesopotamia. Earlier evidence for the utilization of the horse has been found in archaeological sites in Turkey, Transcaucasia, and, particularly, the Ukraine. Editor's note (PLK).

against Umma, inflicting enormous casualties (at least, by the standards of that time) on the enemy. Although in his native Lagash Eanatum had to be content with the title of *ensí*, he eventually acquired the title of *lugal* of Kish after successes in his wars against Ur and Kish, as well as against other nomes. His successors, however, were unable to maintain hegemony over these nomes.

After some time, the rule of Lagash passed to Enentarzi, the son of the chief priest of the local god, Ningirsu. After his father, Enentarzi also became chief priest of Ningirsu. When he became the *ensí* of Lagash, he merged the state lands with the lands of Ningirsu's temple and of the temples belonging to the goddess Baba (Ningirsu's wife) and their children. In this way, more than half of all the land in Lagash came into the possession of the ruler and his family. Many priests were removed, and the administration of the temple lands passed into the hands of the dependents of the ruler. The ruler's people began exacting various levies from the lower priests and men in the temple service. We must assume that the situation of the community members also deteriorated. There are documents showing that impoverished parents had to sell their children, which gives us some vague information about the indebtedness of the community members. The causes of this impoverishment are not known exactly; increased taxation owing to the growth of government personnel combined with unequal distribution of land and of other resources caused by social and economic stratification may have played a part. In such circumstances it was necessary to get means on credit in order to obtain grain for sowing and tools. But the amount of metals in circulation (silver and copper) was extremely small.

All this caused discontent among different groups of the population of Lagash. Lugalanda, Enentarzi's successor, was overthrown, although it is possible he continued living in Lagash as a private citizen. Uruinimgina (ca. 2318–2310 B.C.)[17] was elected in his place, probably by the popular assembly, and during the second year of his rule, was conferred the authority of *lugal*. As *lugal*, Uruinimgina carried out an important reform that was recorded and described in inscriptions made on his orders. Apparently, he was not the first to accomplish such reforms in Sumer; we know that they had been, perhaps periodically, enacted in the past, though we do not have such detailed evidence of these previous measures as we have from Uruinimgina's inscriptions. Nominally, this reform put an end to the ruling family's ownership of the lands of Ningirsu, Baba, and the other gods and goddesses; it abolished requisitions that contradicted the prevailing customs; it stopped some arbitrary actions of the ruler's men; it im-

17. Earlier, his name was incorrectly read "Urukagina."

proved the conditions of the junior priesthood and of the more well-to-do temple dependents; it eliminated debt contracts; etc. However, despite the revolutionary appearance of the reforms, the situation changed very little. The removal of the temple economies from the ruler's possession was purely nominal—indeed, the entire administration installed by the former ruler remained in place. Whatever were the causes for the impoverishment and indebtedness of community members, they were not eliminated. Meanwhile, Uruinimgina got himself involved in a war against neighboring Umma. This war had disastrous consequences for Lagash.

At that time, Umma was ruled by Lugalzagesi, who had inherited from the First Dynasty of Ur (Second Dynasty of Uruk) the power over all of southern Lower Mesopotamia, except for Lagash. His war against Uruinimgina lasted several years and ended with the conquest of a good half of Uruinimgina's territory and the decline of the remainder of his state. Having defeated Lagash in 2312 B.C.,[18] Lugalzagesi then defeated Kish and succeeded in obtaining free passage for his traders through the territories of the northern rulers. These traders already enjoyed access to India via the Persian Gulf, and now they could travel to the north, toward the Mediterranean Sea, to Syria and Asia Minor, from whence they brought valuable lumber, copper, and silver. But soon Lugalzagesi himself suffered a crushing defeat. This defeat is the subject of Lecture 3.

18. All dates cited in this lecture may be affected by an error of about one hundred years in either direction; but any two dates, in relation to each other, do not diverge by more than one generation. For example, the date of the beginning of the Protoliterate Period (2900 B.C. in this lecture) can oscillate between 3000 and 2800, and the date of the beginning of Eanatum's rule (2400 B.C. in this lecture), from 2500 to 2300. But the time from the start of Eanatum's rule to the end of Uruinimgina's rule (ninety years, or three generations, according to the chronological calculation used in this lecture) cannot be less than two or more than four generations in duration.

3

Early Despotisms in Mesopotamia

I. M. Diakonoff

The Kingdom of the Sargonids

After having subjugated almost the entire southern part of Lower Mesopotamia (Sumer), Lugalzagesi did not attempt to consolidate it into a unified state; having his social base in the elite of the temples and communities of the Sumerian nomes, he limited himself to appropriating the local priestly or princely titles conferred by the nome elders. Lugalzagesi did nothing to bring the struggle against his opponents to a permanent end. Although he defeated Kish, he did not destroy the Kish *lugals*, and having defeated Lagash, he was not able to remove Uruinimgina from power. During Lugalzagesi's rule, Sumer resembled the military confederations of nomes in the times of Gilgamesh and Aka.

Eventually, Lugalzagesi had to confront a new, formidable, and unexpected adversary: Sargon the Ancient. (This is the conventional name that historians give Lugalzagesi's foe.) Sargon descended from the people who inhabited the northern part of Lower Mesopotamia and who spoke the Eastern Semitic language. In this language he called himself *Sharrum-ken*, which means "the king is the true one." Historians assume that this was not his original name and that he appropriated it only after he declared himself king.

Legends of much later times describe Sargon the Ancient as a man of very humble origin, and there is no reason to doubt the credibility of this tradition. It was said that he was a gardener, the adopted son of a waterbearer, and that he became a cupbearer of the *lugal* of Kish. When Lugalzagesi defeated this nome, Sargon carved out of it his own kingdom.

Sargon did not tie his fortunes to age-old community or nome traditions. In his own right, he elevated a small obscure town called Akkade. (This town was probably located somewhere on the irrigated lands that once belonged to Kish.) When Sargon's dynasty fell, the city of Akkade was completely destroyed, leaving no trace. Archaeologists have not yet found the site of its ruins.[1] In its own time, however, this

1. The city of Akkade is mentioned in post-Akkadian texts, so apparently some remnant of it survived. Editor's note (PLK).

city played an important role; and after Sargon the Ancient (ca. 2316–2261 B.C.), the entire northern part of Lower Mesopotamia (between the Tigris and Euphrates and including the lower part of the Diyala Valley) began to be called Akkad. For the next two thousand years the Eastern Semitic language was known as Akkadian.

The fact that Sargon had no roots in the traditional nomes and did not depend on the nobility allowed him to draw his support from the common people, forming a militia that might have been more or less voluntary. Sargon and his successors changed the traditional battle tactics by replacing the small, heavily armed detachments, which fought in closed ranks, with large masses of lightly armed, mobile warriors, who either fought in chain formations or dispersed. Traditionally, the *lugals* did not use bows and arrows in combat, since Sumer lacked the flexible and resilient varieties of wood that were suitable for bows. But Sargon and the Sargonids attached great importance to archers. They had the advantage of being able to shower with a cloud of arrows the clumsy detachments of warriors bearing heavy shields and spears, thus breaking up their ranks and evading hand-to-hand combat by remaining at a considerable distance. It is entirely possible that Sargon had access to yew tree (or hazel tree) groves in the foothills of Iran and Asia Minor or that a composite bow, glued together from horn, wood, and sinews, had already been invented at that time. A good bow is a powerful weapon that can hit a target at 200 yards and even farther; at close range an arrow can pierce a heavy board. Five to six shots can be released in one minute, and a single quiver can store thirty to fifty arrows.

In Lagash, the events that led to the coup of Uruinimgina attest to the accumulation of many grievances against the prevailing order. Sargon could encounter support everywhere. The poorest community members may have been interested in curbing the inordinate growth of the nome aristocracy's power; service in Sargon's army offered them hope for social and material betterment. In the past the means for such personal advancement had been inaccessible to these people. But even within the temple and the state economies, the personnel were stratified to such a degree that it was always easy to find here people who were willing to help destroy the nome order. It was actually from such people that Sargon himself had originated. The unification of the country into one state could appear to be beneficial for the development of productive forces. It could stop the endless, bloody squabbles over canals and the interruptions of irrigation networks. It would also mean more efficient trade.

Apparently, Sargon started by expanding his authority over Upper Mesopotamia, possibly reaching all the way to the Mediterranean. He then offered Lugalzagesi a family alliance. When Lugalzagesi refused,

Sargon resorted to military action and quickly defeated his adversary. Lugalzagesi was captured and triumphantly paraded in copper shackles through the "Gates of Enlil" in Nippur; he was probably executed soon after. Over a short period of time, Sargon conquered all the most important cities of Lower Mesopotamia, including Lagash, which was now taken in its entirety. Having reached the Mediterranean, Sargon's soldiers next washed their weapons in the Persian Gulf. Later, his troops carried on other campaigns into Asia Minor (the "Silver Mountains") and Elam.

The nomes under Sargon retained their own internal structure, but the individual *ensís* now became officials responsible to the king. They took over the management of the temple economies, which were also subjected to the king. Sargon and his successors kept at their court the representatives of the remaining aristocratic nome family lineages, especially the ruling ones; their status was part dignitary, part hostage. Having his own personal standing army (according to tradition, the soldiers were settled around the city of Akkade) and the support of a countrywide militia, Sargon had no need for detachments of soldiers who were allotted land by the temple economies; being useless now, they were disbanded. The Sargonids generally preferred to maintain their workers with rations and to decrease the number of allotments awarded to the state economy personnel. The result was a higher rate of exploitation.

Sargon's introduction of uniform measuring units for area, weight, and so on throughout the country and his maintenance of overland and sea trade routes were also important. During his rule, ships from Melakha (in India) are said to have navigated up the river, bringing exotic goods, such as elephants and monkeys, to the quay of Akkade. This trade, however, did not flourish for long.

Sargon made much of his reverence to the gods, especially to the patron deity of Akkade, Aba (or Amba), and to Nippur's Enlil, and gave rich gifts to the temples in order to sway the priesthood to his side. He had his daughter consecrated as *en*-priestess (*entu* in Akkadian) of the Moon god Nanna of Ur. From that time on, it became traditional for the eldest daughter of the king to become *entu* of Nanna. But despite Sargon's patronage, the relationship between the priesthood and the kings, especially under Sargon's successors, remained cool. The Sargonids broke with the Early Dynastic traditions in all respects—in the use of titles, in their customs, and in artistic tastes. In art, the superhuman, impersonal image of a god or a priest was replaced by images exhibiting a powerful individuality. These images were actually Sargon himself and his closest associates who had achieved power on their own merits. Heroic epic images began to dominate the oral literature. However, very few individuals managed to rise from the lower ranks to positions of power, and those who did seem mainly to have succeeded only in the beginning of Sargon's rule. Eventually, there arose a new aristocracy of royal servants, and its ranks were restricted. Although the soldiers of Sargon's army are said in the legend to have assembled at meetings, the popular assemblies and councils of elders no longer had any significance, being always no more than nome bodies. The king now exercised a despotic power over the entire state; that is, his power did not derive from any outside authority, whether it be a council or a popular assembly. Nor was there any auxiliary authority parallel to the king's and legally checking his power. Thus, the popular masses, who had supported Sargon, gained little from his victory and eventually lost considerably, because a despotic and bureaucratic form of government became firmly established in Mesopotamia and lasted for millennia.

The people sensed and understood their situation very quickly. According to a late legend, some city elders organized uprisings even during Sargon's time. Once, in his old age, Sargon is said to have been forced to flee and hide in a ditch; nevertheless, he was eventually able to subdue the insurgents. But Sargon's sons, Rimush and Manishtushu, who ruled in succession after their father, confronted a unanimous and stubborn resistance throughout all of Lower Mesopotamia. The city *ensís* and noblemen rose in revolt, and they were supported by a multitude of people from all social ranks. In the process of subduing the rebellion, Rimush slaughtered the entire populations of some of his country's cities and executed countless thousands of prisoners.

Let us note that in this case, as in the Early Dynastic Period, there was no ethnic enmity. The Akkade dynasty is frequently called Semitic, as opposed to earlier and later, supposedly Sumerian dynasties. It is true that Sargon and his successors belonged to that part of Lower Mesopotamia where Eastern Semitic (Akkadian) was spoken and that Sargon promoted first of all his own countrymen, many of whom, perhaps even the majority, spoke Akkadian. However, some of the much earlier dynasties also spoke Semitic. The Eastern Semitic language was commonly spoken not only in Kish but also as far south as Ur, at least since the Early Dynastic Period, if not even earlier. It seems that Lagash alone remained almost entirely Sumerian speaking. But in Sargon's time, and during the time of his successors, Sumerian remained the official language, while Akkadian was used only as a secondary language.

Legend tells us that Rimush was killed by his dignitaries, who pelted him with heavy stone seals; evidently, it was not proper to carry weapons in the presence of a king. Yet, his brother, Manishtushu, continued the same policies. He also had to cruelly suppress uprisings in his own country. Taking advantage of the difficult situation of the cities that had been devastated by the slaughter inflicted by his brother, Rimush, and by himself, Manishtushu expanded the state economy sector by forcing the citizens to sell him their lands at nominal prices. However, he did not consider it feasible to simply confiscate the land but proceeded with all the formalities required in private land purchases. The deals were consummated in the presence of witnesses—his own and those of the unwilling sellers. In cases of very large tracts of land, he sought approval from the local popular assemblies. This proves that the ancient kings did not own all the land in their country as property, regardless of the despotic character of their power, and had to follow the universally established rules when acquiring real estate. They were able to exercise their power only in setting extremely low, almost token, purchase prices.

Manishtushu ordered his land transactions to be recorded in writing on a huge stone obelisk, which has been preserved to our day. Since these sales involved large numbers of people, the text inscribed on Manishtushu's obelisk allows us to determine for Lower Mesopotamia in the twenty-third century B.C. the structure of society outside the state economy sector.

It appears that the community members at that time lived in extended-family household communes ("houses") comprised of one to three generations that were headed by a patriarch. This domestic structure is similar to the one that existed during the Early Dynastic Period. Each household commune owned its own land, from which individual family cells received their shares. Such a share, in its entirety or in part, could be sold only with the approval of the whole extended-family commune. The seller received a "price," and his relatives received all sorts of additional payments ("gifts"); these payments became their personal property. Such land as belonged to the entire family group could be sold, all or in part, only with the permission of all the related extended families whose patriarchs descended from a common paternal ancestor. In such cases, the payment was received by the patriarch of the selling community, and the additional payments and gifts were given to the other interested parties; that is, the relatives belonging to the kindred "houses." Finally, when lands that belonged to several "houses" were sold simultaneously, especially in cases where their men belonged to more than one lineage, the approval of the territorial community's popular assembly or of the assembly of the entire nome was required. The feast for the popular assembly was given by the purchaser; viz., the king.

The military campaigns, already begun by Sargon, into neighboring countries (Syria, Asia Minor, and Elam) were continued by his sons. Apparently, the kings regarded occasional looting of nearby countries more profitable than duties and earnings that could be exacted from trade. Manishtushu organized military expeditions far to the East, by sea as well as by land, and got as far as the Elamite city of Anshan, located deep within Iran, close to the present-day city of Shiraz.

In Elam at that time there flourished a civilization very similar to the Sumerian-Akkadian one of the Early Dynastic Period. The Elamite language was related to the Dravidian languages of today's southern India. The Elamite hieroglyphic writing developed for this language in the first quarter of the third millennium B.C. was to a certain degree influenced by the Sumerian writing system. It was apparently used for accounts (as was the case also in Sumer) in the economies of the temples. This writing has not yet been deciphered. Generally speaking, Elam followed the same developmental path as Lower Mesopotamia. However, the region of the Elamite civilization comprised not only the alluvial plain of the Karun and Kerkheh rivers but also the mountainous regions all the way to the borders of today's Afghanistan and Pakistan. One of the routes to the land of the ancient Indus civilization led through Elam.

Despite a series of military campaigns, the kings of Akkade were apparently unable to completely subdue Elam, and Manishtushu's nephew, King Naram-Su'en, finally signed a written agreement with the Elamites whereby Elam pledged to coordinate its foreign and military policy with the Akkadian kingdom, while preserving its own internal independence. This was the first known international treaty in world history. It is written in Elamite using Akkadian cuneiform script, which, since that time, began to spread throughout Elam.

Naram-Su'en (ca. 2236–2200 B.C.) was the mightiest of Sargon's descendants. Yet, his reign also began with a rebellion. The citizens of ancient Kish elected one of their own as king, and numerous cities of different parts of the vast country joined the insurrection. Young Naram-Su'en's quick and resolute action crushed the rebellion.

We know relatively little about other military events during the reign of Naram-Su'en. He apparently fought in Syria, Upper Mesopotamia, and in the Iranian foothills. In Syria, he destroyed the powerful nome of Ebla, inhabited by Western Semites, and gained hegemony in that region.

The changes in the organization of the state, which Sargon had already initiated, were completed under his grandson. Naran-Su'en finally discarded all the old traditional titles and called himself "King of the Four Quarters of the World." In fact, no former period had known such a vast state as his had become. Although he preserved the role of the *ensís* in the administration, as well as the state economies of the nomes, he appointed as *ensís* either his sons or his functionaries. As a result, the rank of *ensí* in Lagash was borne by a common scribe.

Serious consequences resulted from Naram-Su'en's quarrel with the priests of Nippur. Among other factors, the problem of the titles may have brought this about. Having discarded all previous titles, Naram-Su'en rejected *eo ipso* the priestly ratification of these titles. And, as if that were not enough, he was the first ruler who let himself be proclaimed a god and demanded worship. An *ensí* was now obliged to bear on his official seal the following address to his ruler: "God Naram-Su'en, King of the Four Quarters of the World, God of Akkade, I so-and-so, *ensí* of the city so-and-so, am your slave."

Social support for the Akkadian dynasty shrunk to a minimum toward the end of Naram-Su'en's rule. The community members were ruined by wars, by punitive expeditions against the cities of the king's own country, and by compulsory land purchases. The old nobility was, for the most part, physically liquidated. A substantial part of the middle stratum of royal servants was dispossessed of their land allotments and transferred to helot rations. And the priesthood was discontented, probably for ideological reasons. It was in these circumstances that the invasion of the Quti (Gutium) tribes from the Iranian highlands began. (These tribes may have been related linguistically to peoples of present-day Daghestan east of the Caspian Sea.)

Gudea

From this time on, the Akkadian dynasty gradually declined. Initially, the struggle against the mountain people proceeded with varying success. But, eventually, Naram-Su'en's son was forced to yield his title "King of the Four Quarters of the World" to the king of Elam (whose kingdom at that time was unified), probably in exchange for his help against the Quti. Soon after, however, all power in Mesopotamia passed into the hands of Qutian chieftains, who although they also called themselves kings, actually seemed to have been elected in tribal assemblies of warriors for a limited term (from two to seven years). The Quti ravaged almost the entire country with the exception of Lagash, which was somewhat removed from the main thrust of the invasion, and, perhaps, also Uruk and Ur, which were protected by a stretch of marshland.

The Quti did not create their own central government in Lower Mesopotamia. Once they stopped their armed looting, they continued to plunder the country by exacting tributes, which were collected for them by local Akkadian and Sumerian rulers.

Gudea, who lived in the second half of the twenty-second century in

Lagash, is thought to have been the son of a priestess who represented a goddess in the "sacred marriage" rite with a priest. Although Gudea officially had no human parents, such a birth probably was considered to be rather distinguished. Gudea's wife by his first marriage was the daughter of the *ensi* of Lagash, whose title he later inherited. The divinity of his birth along with his acquired title granted him entry into the priesthood of the nome.

Gudea's policy combined the traditional program of the *ensis* of a nome with the principles developed during the Akkadian dynasty. He rejected the right of the state ruler to own temple lands, following in this respect Uruinimgina's policies, instead of those adopted by Sargon and Naram-Su'en. However, he did not return to the system of multiple temple economies belonging to many gods but merged them into one statewide temple economy of the nome god Ningirsu. He kept the workers of this economy, as helots, on rations, as was the custom under the Sargonids. Gudea spared no resources for the erection of a new, magnificent temple to Ningirsu. Thus, he imposed new taxes and obligatory labor conscriptions on the entire population in the support of this project; even women were enrolled in the working teams. Based on certain indirect information, we can conclude that the council of elders of Lagash was active during Gudea's time and that it had the theoretical right to choose and depose a ruler. Gudea payed a high ransom to the Quti, but Lower Mesopotamia, not just the Lagash nome, was almost entirely at his disposal. He was now able to wage war against Elam and to trade with other Near Eastern countries and even with Melakha (India). But it seems that he imported only materials required for the construction and rich ornamentation of the Ningirsu temple. Many statues and inscriptions have come down to us from Gudea's reign. His son and grandson, however were unable to maintain his political status, and the might of Lagash diminished.

The Third Dynasty of Ur

Soon after Gudea, Utuhengal (according to legend, he was the son of a fish curer) fomented a general uprising against the Quti, whose extortionate rule had, for a long time, been hated by the Mesopotamians. The Quti were successfully and permanently expelled, but the brilliant beginnings of Utuhengal's rule suddenly came to an end. According to tradition, while inspecting the construction site of a new irrigation canal, a piece of ground caved in under Utuhengal's feet, and he drowned. The kingdom passed on to Ur-Nammu, who made the city of Ur his capital. Lagash fell into disfavor, and the Indian trade again returned to Ur.

The new state was officially called the "Kingdom of Sumer and Ak-kad." Although all inscriptions and administrative texts were written in Sumerian, spoken Sumerian at that time was dying out and being displaced by Akkadian. The dynasty founded by Ur-Nammu is re-ferred to by historians as the Third Dynasty of Ur (or Ur III).[2]

Ur-Nammu (ca. 2111–2094 B.C.) and, especially, his son, Shulgi (ca. 2093–2064 B.C.) created the classic and typical form of the ancient Oriental despotic and bureaucratic state. Hundreds of thousands of accounting documents from the economies of the kings of the Ur III dynasty can be found in museums all over the world. They probably represent at least one half of all the preserved cuneiform tablets.

During the initial stage of the Ur III dynasty, much attention was given to the reconstruction of the irrigation network, which had fallen into considerable disrepair under the sway of the Quti and their henchmen. But this was not the essence of the Ur III kings' political activities.

Their most important accomplishment was the unification of the state economy. All temple and state economies within the borders of the Kingdom of Sumer and Akkad, which soon included not only Lower Mesopotamia but also a significant portion of Upper Meso-potamia, as well as some of the lands beyond the Tigris and in Elam, were welded into a single economy. All its male workers (helots) were called *gurush*, "lads," and the female workers were called *ngeme*, "slave girl."[3] Altogether, they probably numbered between five hundred thousand and one million. The workers—farmers, porters, shepherds, and fishermen—were organized into teams. (The craftsmen were organized into workshops, sometimes of a considerable size.) They worked from sunrise to sundown without any days off. (Only the fe-male slaves were given time off during their ritually "impure" days, when they were probably locked up.) Each received a standard ration: 1.5 liters (about 2.5 pints) of barley daily for every man and half this amount for every woman. They also received a small amount of vege-table oil and a little wool. Any team, or part of one, could be arbi-trarily transferred to other work and even to another city. Weavers could be sent to tow barges, coppersmiths to unload ships, and so on. Boys were also put to work. This, in fact, was a form of slavery, al-though this word was not used to describe male workers. No records indicate that little children received any rations; it seems that women

2. Nothing is positively known about the ephemeral Second Dynasty of Ur, which is included in the King List, except that it belonged to the ED III Period.

3. Note, however, that in ancient Near Eastern languages a "slave" was not neces-sarily a person who was another person's private property but was anyone subject to the authority of another person, vaguely called his or her "lord."

had to support their children on their own rations. This increased the already high mortality rate. Evidently, the *gurush* and the *ngeme* had no families, so the labor force had to be replenished mainly through persons captured during military campaigns and collected at Ur, from where they were distributed among the local state economies. The captives, especially women and children, were frequently kept in camps for considerable periods, and many would perish there.

Skilled craftsmen, administrative employees, and soldiers were also primarily maintained on rations. These rations, however, were more generous than those issued to the ordinary *gurush*. The administration of the state economies was very reluctant to grant land allotments for service.

Such labor organization required enormous efforts of supervision and accounting. Accountability was extremely strict. Everything was put into writing. Each document, even a simple issue of two pigeons to a kitchen, had to be documented, with seals affixed by the person responsible for the operation and by the controller. Moreover, the accounting of the labor force was separate from the accounting of the work norms fulfilled by the laborers. A field could be divided into strips, lengthwise and widthwise, and the work in each direction could be controlled by a different person. This ensured a mutual, overlapping control. Documents accounting for single operations were summed up in annual reports, according to each team, each economy, etc.

The products of the harvest and the workshop were used to support the court and the army, to offer sacrifices in the temples, to feed the personnel, and to carry out the international exchange conducted by state trade agents, the *tamkars*. Trade, however, did not flourish, because the *tamkars* had to return an excessive portion of the profit to the administration.

Livestock raising, as well as state agriculture, was centralized. Herds were kept mainly for sacrifices to the gods and, in part, for leather and cheese production. The temple's continual supply of sacrifices was guaranteed by each district taking turns in providing the temple with cattle during a specific period of time. Thousands of heads of cattle, from all corners of the country, were herded into the center of the state for the Enlil temple in Nippur. This was clearly a form of taxation.

The entire country was divided into districts, which did not necessarily coincide with the earlier territories of the nomes. Each was headed by an *ensí*. The *ensí*s were now mere functionaries who were arbitrarily transferred from district to district by the royal administration. The traditional authorities survived only in a few border regions.

The position of the *ensí* was, nevertheless, quite profitable. They were allowed to own many slaves, even though these slaves had to help the state economy during harvest or in urgent irrigation tasks.

The community members—those not yet swallowed up by the state economy—were probably also subjected to the bureaucratic authority of the *ensís*. All we know is that such community members did, in fact, exist and that the state economy hired some of them as reapers during the harvest. Clearly, they must have been poor. Unfortunately, the important data sources about community life that we have from the Early Dynastic and Akkadian periods in the form of land sale contracts are not available for Ur III. The reason for this apparently lies in the fact that purchase of land was prohibited, as generally was any private profit.[4] And, although there was a community court—a remnant of the council of elders—no popular assemblies within the nomes were active.

What social stratum provided the support for this despotic state? As we mentioned earlier, the fact is that managing a unified royal economy that embraced the entire country required an enormous number of administrative personnel—scribes, team overseers, workshop chiefs, and managers—in addition to large numbers of skilled craftsmen. The community members, ruined during the Akkadian and Qutian periods, must have been eager to fill these positions, thereby ensuring for themselves a stable and secure subsistence, independent of luck, harvest, or credit. Available information about court cases that were tried during the Third Dynasty of Ur indicates that the number of private patriarchal slaves sharply increased in the economies of even the lower level personnel. This tells us that the participation of administrative personnel in the acquisition of the surplus product, which was generated by helots (the *gurush* and the *ngeme*) resulted in a good income for them and increased their personal well-being. Minor supervisors, functionaries, and skilled craftsmen who thus became part of the ruling slave-owning class, together with the army, the priesthood, and the administration, constituted the political support of the dynasty.

It must be pointed out that patriarchal slaves, who belonged to the slave owner's family, even if not enjoying full rights, enjoyed better living conditions than the helots. They still had some rights left. For example, they were allowed to sue even their owners in court. Quite a few documents of court cases record attempts on the part of the slaves to argue against their slave status. In all the known cases, however,

4. Some land purchases in Ur III times have been documented recently. Editor's note (PLK).

they were not successful. Patriarchal slaves were exploited less mercilessly than the helots, although they also were flogged.

The rule of the Third Dynasty of Ur lasted about one hundred years, and it seemed that no government could be more solid and durable. Even the cults of the gods were subject to regulation. The diverse and mutually contradictory systems of nome deities were reduced to a single general system headed by the king-god Enlil of Nippur—the patron of the state. The second position was occupied by the god of the Moon, Nanna of Ur, also called Zuen (Su'en in Akkadian). A doctrine was created—or, in any case, systematized—that was constantly instilled in the consciousness of the people: humans were created by the gods to nourish the gods with sacrifices and to free them from work. Starting with Shulgi, all the kings of Ur III were deified, so they ranked with the other gods in regard to the people's duties. It was during this time that the King List, mentioned earlier, was created, as was the doctrine of the divine origin of royalty, which supposedly descended from heaven in the beginning of time, henceforth remaining on earth in an unchanging succession that passed from city to city and from dynasty to dynasty until it reached the Third Dynasty of Ur.

The Fall of Ur and the Rise of Issin

The end was unexpected to all. The pastoral tribes of Western Semites—the so-called Amorites—were harassed by droughts in the sheep-trampled Syrian steppe and began to cross the Euphrates, threatening the settled population of Mesopotamia. Therefore, the kings of Ur built a wall to protect Lower Mesopotamia from the north, along the edge of the "Gypsum Desert," which stretched from the Euphrates to the Tigris. But the Amorite pastoralists did not attempt to cross the scorching desert to the south and to penetrate the wall constructed by the royal laborers. Instead, the Amorites (around 2025 b.c.) traversed Upper Mesopotamia from west to east, crossed the Tigris and then the Diyala River, and began to invade the fields of Lower Mesopotamia in an east-to-west direction.

The king of Ur, Ibbi-Su'en (2027–2003 b.c.), was at that time apparently in Elam, the cities of which occasionally submitted to the authority of the Ur kings, then again fell away, and later entered into agreements with them based on diplomatic marriages; often, they waged war against the kingdom of Ur. Ibbi-Su'en, carried away by his own military successes, seemingly underestimated the impending threat. The Amorites continued to drive their livestock into the Sumerian grainfields, surrounding the cities and blocking the roads leading to the center of the kingdom. Without help from Ur, the local *ensís* began to fall away from the central authority. The *gurush* teams scattered, looting (together with the Amorites) state property in order to feed themselves.

Upon returning to Ur, Ibbi-Su'en was faced with an incipient famine. Most of the people in the vastly expanded state sector economy had been deprived of any land of their own and lived on rations supplied by the harvests of the state fields. But these supplies had ceased to arrive from a good one half of the districts.[5] The king acted quickly by dispatching his official, Ishbi-Erra, to the still-intact western regions of the country in order to purchase grain from the local communities. Ishbi-Erra accomplished this task and collected the purchased grain in the small town of Issin, situated on a branch of the Euphrates not far from ancient Nippur. From there he sent Ibbi-Su'en a request for boats to ship the grain. But the king had none. Ishbi-Erra, sensing his position of strength, seceded from Ur and proclaimed himself king. At first, he was cautious and took only the title of "King of His Own Country," but later he proclaimed himself "King of Sumer and Akkad." The surviving *ensís* who still reported to Ur now recognized Ishbi-Erra as their king. Ibbi-Su'en held on for several years in the cruelly starving Ur, but in 2003 B.C. the Elamite king decided to take advantage of Sumer's troubles; the Amorites let his troops pass through the occupied lands, and the Elamites captured Ur. The Elamites kept a garrison in the empty and devastated city for many years before finally abandoning it. Ishbi-Erra was now the sole king in Lower Mesopotamia. In addition, several minor kingdoms emerged in Upper Mesopotamia along the Tigris, on the lower part of the Diyala, and along the road to Elam.

The new kingdom of the First Dynasty of Issin attempted to mimic the Third Dynasty of Ur in all its aspects. The state language remained Sumerian, although fewer and fewer people still spoke this language. The kings were deified in Nippur. And the workshops where the *gurush* labored remained the same. But there were many things that had to change and that indeed changed. For example, it was no longer possible to maintain the enormous royal field economies based on helot labor. The remaining fields were distributed among individuals who conducted the work as if on their own estates, ignoring the fact that the land in question was the property of the state. Occasionally, this "royal" land was even sold. The private econo-

5. The following is based mainly on a collection of letters purported to have been written by Ibbi-Su'en and Ishbi-Erra that became part of the school curriculum of future scribes during the Issin dynasty. The authenticity of the letters is not beyond doubt, but the overall picture that they draw seems realistic.

mies on community lands recovered, whereas the life of the state economies did not become normalized for a long time. Economic self-government returned to the temples. Since the centralized distribution of products became impossible, exchange and trade began to develop. The Amorites who had captured the fields did not maintain the irrigation systems, and as a result of this neglect, the arable land dried up. It soon became unsuitable even to graze sheep. In order to subsist, the Amorites started to hire themselves out as soldiers into the armies of the kings of Issin and others and to enter the service of the city rulers.

Toward the middle of the twentieth century B.C. it became clear that further historic changes were in the making. The attempts to resurrect the order of the Third Dynasty of Ur came to naught and were abandoned.

4

The Old Babylonian Period of Mesopotamian History

N. V. KOZYREVA

Political History

The time from the fall of the Third Dynasty of Ur to the conquest of Mesopotamia by the Kassites (2000–1600 B.C.) is conventionally called the Old Babylonian Period. It was during this time that Babylon rose above all the Mesopotamian cities and became the capital of a state that finally unified all of Lower Mesopotamia and part of Upper Mesopotamia. Although this particular kingdom survived in its full extent for only one generation, it persisted in the people's memories for many centuries to come. As long as the Akkadian language and the cuneiform culture flourished, Babylon remained the traditional center of the country.

The urban and rural settlements together with their entire cultivated territories occupied a comparatively narrow area of the Mesopotamian alluvial plain and were surrounded by desert or by grazing lands occupied by Western Semitic pastoralists. The latter were subdivided into a multitude of kindred, but independent, often mutually inimical tribes. Seasonally each year the pastoralists would intrude into the settled zones or on their borders. Depending upon where they grazed their sheep during the other season of the year, they appeared either in the summer, when the grass and sources of water in the steppe had dried up, or during the winter, when the pastures in the mountains yielded little food for the sheep and when it was difficult to protect them from the cold winds. As a matter of principle, each tribe had its own autonomous territory, but its frontiers were vague. The settled population regarded the pastoralists as barbarians, while the pastoralists, in turn, despised the peaceful settled life; however, both ways of life were necessary for each other and were connected by various economic, social, and political factors. The exchange of pastoral for agricultural products played an important role in the economy; it is also probable that some foreign merchandise reached Mesopotamia through the pastoral tribes.

The pastoralists also importantly influenced social developments in Mesopotamia. One constant factor was the gradual sedentarization of certain members of the pastoral tribes. The richer ones preferred settled life when the size of their herds began to exceed the possibilities of the pasturage zone; then, they became landowners, military commanders, etc., replenishing the urban elite. The poorer ones settled when the herd was down to less than the minimum required for sustaining their families, and they then entered the state or temple service, receiving land allotments or rations in kind for their work. Thus, they replenished the number of the poorest and most dependent persons. All this helped sustain the stratification of Mesopotamia's population.

Still more important was the influence of the pastoral tribes on the political life of Mesopotamia. During all of Mesopotamian history, the annual peaceful migrations of the pastoralists could be transformed into aggressive campaigns if the power of the centralized state was weak. Such a process was occurring during the time we are describing.[1]

With the downfall of the Third Dynasty of Ur, the huge centralized state, which had unified nearly all of the "Land of the Two Rivers," collapsed, and its administrative institutions fell into a state of decay. The city of Ur was now no longer the country's center; several other cities laid claim to this role. The weakening and fragmentation of state power was accompanied by the strengthening in power of the tribes and tribal chiefs. Pastoralists occupied extended zones that included certain cities that became political centers of tribes and tribal confederations. Thus, toward the middle of this period, the city of Terqa became the center of the Hanean tribe; the city of Larsa, that of the Yamutbala tribe; and Babylon, that of the Amnanu tribe.

Considerable territories, including ancient cities, belonged to the zones of influence of the chiefs ruling the strongest and richest tribes; such chiefs attempted to gain still more power. They expelled the local dynasties and formed their own, turning the autonomous tribal territories into independent states and themselves into kings, instead of tribal chiefs. Further political development could proceed in different directions: either the tribe retained its importance, and the king, besides ruling the state, continued also to be regarded as the chief of the tribe (e.g., as in Mari on the Middle Euphrates) or the strengthening of royal power led to the weakening of the tribe. In the latter case, everything returned to the initial situation: a centralized state arose that was based both on the settled population and on the tribes, which

---

1. The Amorites had no horses or camels, and their transhumant movements were limited; they cannot be called nomads. They exercised little influence on the cultural life of the urban population. The percentage of Amorites in the cities did not exceed 1–3 percent of the population, and they had no influence on the Akkadian language. (By that time Sumerian was only the language of the schools.)

were self-governing parts of the state (e.g., as in Larsa and later in Babylon).

During the years 1900–1850 B.C., a number of kingdoms headed by Amorite rulers arose in Mesopotamia. Their political ideal remained that of the Third Dynasty of Ur, and the kings attempted to present themselves as legitimate heirs to its power, using the titles of the Ur kings. Actually, the power of most rulers of this kind was ephemeral, and they retained their independence only so long as one of their neighbors with a base of stronger and richer tribes did not conquer them. Innumerable agreements were made; two allied rulers would through common efforts topple a third one, only to start fighting between themselves. In these struggles, the rulers who fought less usually preserved more power; the rulers retained more control in cities that were situated on the outskirts of the territories involved in the wars or that were located right in the middle of especially strong tribal formations. In the course of these interminable wars, some Amorite dynasties decayed, their kings "descending" to be solely tribal chiefs, who then depended on their former allies. Others flourished, uniting most of Mesopotamia under their power and turning from tribal chiefs into kings of independent states.

One of the strongest states was created in Upper Mesopotamia by the Amorite chief Shamshi-Adad I. This state comprised a territory that was quite extensive for the times: from the edge of the Iranian plateau to central Syria, and for a time it also included Mari on the Euphrates. One of the most important centers of Shamshi-Adad's kingdom was the trading city of Asshur on the Middle Tigris. Shamshi-Adad (ca. 1813–1781 B.C.) organized an effective, well-functioning military and administrative system, effectively eliminating the rights of the self-governing communities. However, after his death, the kingdom fell to pieces.

The number of competing powers diminished with time. At the beginning of the eighteenth century B.C., there remained only three that counted: Mari in the northwest, Larsa in the south, and Babylon in the center. Toward the end of his reign, the Babylonian king Hammurapi (1792–1750 B.C.) completed the task of unifying the country. His state included finally all Lower Mesopotamia and the greater part of Upper Mesopotamia; its capital was the city of Babylon.

Decades of incessant wars were disastrous to the country's economic life. The mainstay of Mesopotamian civilization, the irrigation system, which required vigilant attention and constant repair work, was in an advanced state of decay. Land that used to provide bountiful harvests was now ruined by salinization and was useless for sowing. All this had a very negative impact both on the state and on the private economies, but the latter, being the more primitive, were the first to revive. As for the intricate, unwieldy administration of the state economy, which fell apart with the collapse of the Third Dynasty of Ur, the new rulers were neither able nor inclined to restore it. It was easier to apportion out the conquered state lands, workshops, trading institutions, etc., to private persons who organized their economic enterprises on a virtually private basis, although they themselves may not have been proprietors of the land. Considerable control of trade and industrial establishments passed into the hands of private persons, and even the distribution of priestly prebends, paid in kind or in silver, ceased to be the function of the state power and became an object of trade, private agreements, and testamentary bequests. Some of the taxes were, no doubt, also farmed out to private persons.

All this had various important results. On the one hand, numbers of people were wandering around Mesopotamia in search of security and willing, in the face of hunger, to hire themselves out for work or to go into slavery. On the other hand, rich and enterprising men gained opportunities for independent business activities that they never formerly had. Yielding to the state a certain portion of the industrial produce, of the agricultural products, or of the profits derived from trade, these individuals could keep the rest for their own enrichment or for increasing their own prosperity. Even international trade, in spite of the nearly constant unrest in the country, developed to a greater extent during this period, because a private trader could more easily pay bribes to a local petty king or even bypass him. Formerly, during the Ur III Period, all trade in Mesopotamia was strictly controlled and regulated, leaving little room for private enrichment.

The maritime trade route through the Persian Gulf (for pearls, copper, etc.) was restored. This extremely lucrative trade was in the hands of private seafarers and workshop owners. However, the ships no longer sailed directly to India but only went as far as Dilmun Island (present-day Bahrain); here there seems to have existed a center for a transit trade in commodities from India, Iran, and Arabia. The seafarers brought rich (and, no doubt, obligatory) presents to the temples or to the king, but the bulk of the profits went to private entrepreneurs.

The possibilities for developing commodity production were still minimal, and there was little silver in circulation; the income from agriculture, the main source of food for the majority of the population, was seasonal. Under such conditions, the growth of the private economic sector meant that small households simultaneously became dependent on credit. Usury proliferated; loans on credit became one of the most profitable ways to invest capital, interest on the capital being one-fifth or even one-third. Usurious forms of credit led to the ruination of small households. Sale and purchase first of the date plantations and later of fields began to occur everywhere. (However, the kings of Larsa, like the kings of Ur before them, prohibited the sale of fields.) A sale of land was tantamount to the loss of civil rights in the community by the seller, so such a deal was only to be undertaken as a last resort. In case of need, one could sell a family member into temporary slavery or one could pledge a family member to the creditor as a guarantee for the payment of one's debt. This is the period when hired agricultural workers first appear in Mesopotamia in considerable numbers (although the state economy hired workers as early as the Akkade dynasty).

A strong centralized state power was not in favor of excessive growth of private individuals' independence. Moreover, any loss of land and means of sustenance by an important part of the population deprived the state of income in taxes and weakened its military power. Therefore, as soon as the tendency toward unification and creation of a stable state was nearing its goal, the state began to devise limitations to private activities. The kings issued special decrees aiming at putting a brake on land sales and enslavement of the poorer strata of the population. Such decrees, called "Decrees of Fairness" (or "Righteousness") or simply "royal decrees," were issued regularly, once every five to seven years, and announced the annulment of agreements involving slavery for debt, the liberation of temporary slaves, the return of immovables to the original owner, and the like. However, the creditors sought ways, often successfully, to evade the fulfillment of such decrees, since the debtors seldom had the means to sue in court.

Such a policy of limiting the private sector's activities is attested in Larsa. This city became the center of a strong kingdom embracing all of southern Mesopotamia in the late nineteenth century after the Elamite-Amorite chief Kudurmabuk seized it. He did not give himself a royal title but ceded the throne of Larsa first to one and then to another of his sons. His second son, Rim-Sin, attained great power and achieved victories over all his more important rivals. After that, he introduced certain reforms, limiting the development of private enterprise and commodity-money relations. Private trade and usurious activities in Larsa fell off sharply.

The tendency to strengthen royal control over a country's economy and to limit private economic activities was still more apparent in the reforms of Hammurapi, king of Babylon. Hammurapi, after destroying his last rivals, Mari and Larsa, unified in the 1760s to 1750s all of Lower and a considerable part of Upper Mesopotamia, creating a kingdom not inferior to Ur III in its size and power. Hammurapi's policies clearly show a conscious tendency toward the restoration in

Mesopotamia of a royal power universal in its authority and despotic in its character.

The state's administrative system was improved and strictly centralized. In the final analysis, the reins of management of all aspects of economic life were gathered in the hands of the king. He was personally involved in all affairs and problems. Hammurapi laid great weight upon the king's personal involvement in the management of affairs, and he corresponded extensively with his local officials; it was not unusual for private persons to appeal directly to the king with their complaints. An important reform was carried out involving the courts of law; here also the role of the king was strengthened. Royal judges were introduced into all major cities, where formerly only temple and community courts had acted.[2] Royal judges were chosen from among royal officials responsible directly to the king; they did not, however, completely supplant the community courts.

The temples with their vast economies, occupying a considerable part of Mesopotamian territory and having become virtually independent after the fall of the Third Dynasty of Ur, were now again completely subjected to the royal authority, both administratively and economically. Private international trade was prohibited, and the traders were reminded that they were royal officials. In most districts of the kingdom, sale of land was prohibited, except for city plots. All these measures, as well as the above-mentioned "Decrees of Fairness," were designed to stop the ruination of the people and the loss of their land.

Old Babylonian Society

There was a considerable difference between southern Mesopotamian society of the early second millennium B.C. and that of a millennium earlier. Now Mesopotamia was no longer divided into separate nomes; a tendency toward unification was clearly present. The main social aim was, as before, economic self-reproduction and self-sustenance, which also presupposed sustenance of the state unity. In order to achieve this goal all social forces were brought into action—social, religious, and economic.

It seems to us that the Old Babylonian economy can no longer be usefully subdivided into a state sector and a private/communal sector; now we ought to distinguish a state sector in the direct sense of the word and a state-and-community sector: both actually were under state control. Two distinct types of economy seem to have existed

2. Conflicts and litigations within the state economies were settled by royal officials administratively rather than judicially.

within both sectors: a large type and a small type. State and temple economies, as well as the private economies of the king, the dignitaries, and the major officials, belonged to the first group; the economies of the community members, the rank-and-file servants of the state economies, and the men who tilled state land for a share in the crop had small economies of the second group. Production in the small economies was of the in-kind type. Their reserve and exchange funds were composed of the small surplus of products that had accumulated during climatically favorable years after all taxes and requisitions had been paid. More surplus, which could serve as commodities for sale, accumulated in the big economies, but primarily it was the state itself that had such surplus at its disposal.

The character of production in the Old Babylonian Period was not essentially different from that under the Third Dynasty of Ur, but the economic milieu had changed due to the aforementioned reasons. The increase in the size of the state led to abundant growth in administrative personnel and the state economic sector. Commodity-money relations, which might have served as a regulating factor for the entire economy, involved mostly international trade; the big economies of the state and the temples were autarchic. The small economies were, if possible, still more so. Thus, society had to develop other means or methods for regulating the economy and, specifically, the exchange of commodities. The means had to be able to operate within the framework of the main social goal: to maintain a stable, unchanged society under changed economic conditions.

Some of these methods were inherited from the Sumerians; others were developed during the Old Babylonian Period itself. These included the following: a fixed interest on credit; a system of state credit for private persons (through the *tamkars*, who were first and foremost tax collectors, but who were also responsible for trade and other state incomes); a periodic restoration of certain sold immovables to their original owners and a liberation of people who had become slaves for debt; compulsory prices fixed by the state.

It is well known that Mesopotamia, being poor in natural resources, always had to import certain vital materials; metals, particularly, were needed for agricultural tools and for weapons. From time immemorial, international exchange was a necessity for Mesopotamia. Such exchange was a very important element of the country's economic structure; it was basic to the reproduction of society and its activities. Fulfilling its function of maintaining social stability, the state also controlled this element of the economic structure. International exchange formed one of the most important activities of state officialdom. The state used any surplus that was at its disposal for international trade. Different imported commodities were brought into the state treasury; they were expended for the needs of the state and also were distributed to administration and state economy personnel. The *tamkars* and other officials seem to have gradually invested some private means of their own and tried to conduct their own businesses while they fulfilled their official duties.

The international exchange of commodities (both state and private) was nonequivalent; the prices were determined spontaneously and bore little relation to production expenditures. Caravans of donkeys loaded with the same commodities were always moving along the same routes, returning with other needed commodities. Private international trade could develop only under the shelter of the state trade, applying its methods and making use of its possibilities.[3]

An internal exchange of commodities on a very limited scale also developed alongside private international trade. It seems that in years of natural calamities and poor harvests the commodity-money exchange tendencies could become stronger, but with the normalization of a critical situation, everything returned to its point of departure. All the private trade in southern Mesopotamia amounted to rather rare cases of sale and purchase of the objects of primary necessity for the small economies or, contrariwise, of objects of luxury. This trade was not based on special commodity production, and the profits did not as a rule return to the production process.

Although the country was no longer divided into separate nomes, Mesopotamia could still be deemed worthy of its name "Country of Many Cities." These cities were dispersed along the banks of the Tigris and Euphrates and at the confluences of the large canals. Cities such as Nippur, Kish, Sippar, Ur, and Uruk already had a history of several hundreds of years behind them. There were also newer cities, like Issin and Larsa, as well as cities, like Babylon, whose history lay in the future. The buildings of these cities covered some two to four square kilometers (about a square mile or a mile and a half) and were inhabited by several tens of thousands of people. The center of a city usually consisted of a temple, including a ziggurat (stepped mud-brick tower) and temples dedicated to the city's patron god or goddess and to other of the more important deities. The temple area usually was surrounded by a wall. Inside it, the palace of the king or of the local ruler and the main utility buildings of the state economy were also situated. The rest of the city was occupied by private houses and other buildings. Dispersed among them stood small temples, or chap-

3. International commodity exchange outside of Lower Mesopotamia developed along somewhat different lines.

els, belonging to lesser deities. The houses were built close to one another and formed narrow, tortuous streets, 1.5–3 meters wide. A harbor with moorings for merchant boats and barges was located on the bank of the river or canal where the city had developed. Near the harbor there may have been a square which also functioned as a marketplace. The life of the townspeople was concentrated around the numerous temples and the palace, where many of them worked as clerks, soldiers, priests, craftsmen, and merchants. The living standard of the urban dwellers did not differ very much.

An urban residence usually consisted of a house and a lot of open land, the size of the individual houses ranging from 35 to 70 square meters. Many houses had two stories (utility rooms on the ground floor, living rooms on the upper level). Neighbors were mutually responsible for the upkeep of the common walls that bounded their properties. Some city dwellers also owned date plantations, which were either located next to the city or in nearby villages. These plantations were usually not larger than 1 hectare (2.5 acres). The townspeople, whose main occupation was in the administrative service or in some craft, often did not engage in garden work themselves and rented out their parcels. A month or two before the date harvest, the owners inspected their palm trees in order to estimate the expected yield. A written agreement was drawn up on the basis of this estimate, according to which the gardener was obliged to supply the owner with a certain quantity of dates.

Bread (actually flat cake) was the staple food of the city dwellers, as well as of the villagers. According to a southern Mesopotamian letter writer of that time, the fields were "the soul of the country." The provision of the cities with grain and, in the final account, the well-being of all their inhabitants depended on the crop yields of the fields. City life largely depended on the agrarian work cycle. Those urban dwellers who were servants of the state economy received land allotments for their services. Except for a few persons who held tens of hectares of land, most individuals received allotments amounting to some 2–4 hectares (5–10 acres). In addition to the land allotted for service, some townspeople also had land in the village communities by virtue of their membership in them. In addition to these two types of fields—state allotments and community land—some city dwellers owned large estates (*amirtum*), about the origin of which we have no accurate information. It is probable that these lands were awarded by the king personally to high officials or persons close to himself. The fields, like the orchards, were rarely worked by the townspeople. They usually rented them out to farmers who lived in rural settlements where the land allotments were located together with community land. The land parcels were either rented out for a fixed price or for a crop share, which usually amounted to one third.

Most townspeople kept no cattle (only a few sheep) and owned few slaves. The majority of the slaves were foreigners who were either captured by the local army or brought in from other cities by merchants, where they most likely had also been prisoners of war. A male slave could be bought for 150–175 grams of silver (1 gram = 0.035 U.S. ounce), and a female for somewhat less. In most instances, slaves worked on an equal footing with other family members (including production tasks), and their legal status was similar to that of minors under the patriarchal authority of the head of the house.

Thus, the property supporting a city dweller and his family comprised a simple house with the most essential furnishings and household implements, a small farming parcel that he owned by virtue of membership in some village community or that was allotted by the temple or state for his service, and sometimes a small date palm grove.

Another source of income for the townspeople were payments in kind: the temple and the palace supplied some of their employees with products in place of land. The payments were in grain, wool, vegetable oil, and sometimes small amounts of silver. In addition, special gifts were occasionally issued during temple feasts.

All Old Babylonian cities and most of the villages had temples. A temple in ancient Mesopotamia, as well as in other ancient societies, was not only a place of worship but also one of the most important components of the state's socioeconomic structure. The poor who lived within the temple's sphere of influence could depend on the temple to help them escape ruin or even starvation, and the rich found the temple a good place in which to invest or to save their surplus.

From the most ancient times, one of the important social functions of the temple was to be a sort of charity institution for people that were rejected by the highly regularized ancient society as physically or socially defective; for example, unmarried and parentless women, abandoned or orphaned children, physically handicapped people, and the elderly. In economically critical periods, such as at times of war or bad harvests, the poor would consecrate to the temple the elderly and sick members of their families or leave to it such children as they were unable to sustain. The main reason for such consecrations was a wish to get rid of the surplus mouths to feed (i.e., of family members unable to work at full strength), although the form the consecration took was a gift to the deity from his or her worshiper. When the economy was stable or on the rise, the number of people consecrated by the richer families would increase. Many of the rich would give their daughters to a temple. Here, religious and economic motivations were combined. Entering the temple cloister, a girl would take her dowry with her; she made use of it, even increased it by investing in different kinds of businesses, but after her death it returned to her family. Sometimes it was managed by her brothers during her life. The role of the temple as a social center also manifested itself in its duty to ransom community members captured by the enemy during royal campaigns if the family itself did not possess the necessary means for paying the ransom.

The role of the temple as a place where different kinds of controversies and litigations could be settled was also very important. Here, witnesses and the parties concerned produced their evidence on oath; here, before the divine symbols, the winning party was confirmed in its rights.

In addition to large and small cities, there were also many small rural settlements in Mesopotamia during this period. These villages were located on the banks of rivers and canals that connected the cities. The houses of the villagers could spread over an area of a few hectares. They were constructed of mud brick or, often, wattled reeds coated with clay. The villages were inhabited by fifty to several hundred people whose main occupation was agriculture. These people were members of territorial communities consisting of one or several villages with their corresponding land. Barley was the principal crop, and the yield was at that time on the average about 12.5 centners per hectare (1 U.S.S.R. centner = 220.46 pounds). Wheat was planted only rarely because it could not survive the increasing salinity of the soil. Other crops were dates, onions, and leguminous vegetables.

From the point of view of agricultural production, two main types of economies can be distinguished: state economies in the proper sense and the state-cum-community controlled economies. The former were not only controlled by the state but also organized by the state by administrative means; the workers on such estates were mainly dependent persons. However, they were not grouped into teams and, unlike the *gurush* of Ur III times, did not receive rations in kind; instead, they received group allotments in land. They were called *nashi biltim*, or "bringers of income," and were not regarded as slaves. About one third of the total cultivated land in Old Babylonian Mesopotamia can be estimated to have been fields of the state economies.

The second type, the state-cum-community controlled economies, were territorially organized by the state and managed on the spot along territorial and extended-family lines. The majority of workers were free, although the labor of slaves and other dependents could also be employed.

A process of pauperization and loss of land by a part of the free population was probably under way during the Old Babylonian Period. Several factors contributed to this. Among them were population growth, the splitting up of inherited parcels of land, and salinization. At the same time, however, new arable land was being created. The royal administration was undertaking large-scale projects to clear the old canals and dig new ones. The labor force consisted of community members and dependent persons. On the banks of the new canals, new state economies and territorial communities arose.

Life in the communities was governed by a council of elders, chosen by the inhabitants from the ranks of the most respected and wealthy families. The council was presided over by a village headman, usually appointed by the king. Some communities paid their taxes to the state in kind; others turned over a certain portion of their irrigated land to the state economy. The king, in turn, could allot some of this land to his officials and functionaries as remuneration for service. He could also settle these lands with workers from among the poor who sought his protection and who subsequently ceded to the king a significant portion of their harvest.

The main goal of most small economies was self-provision. Their marketable output was very small. But now and again they had to acquire necessary tools and implements that they could not themselves produce. Silver was used not only as a standard to establish prices but also not uncommonly as the means of payment, partly supplanting in this role the grain that had been used in earlier times. Everything was evaluated in silver: personal property as well as real estate, the income from priestly services (prebends), payments to a hired hand, and expenses connected with certain obligatory labor tasks. Yet, most townspeople, not to speak of people in small villages, owned no silver. Silver in bullion was basically available only to people engaged in commerce. Some decorative silver was owned by the more prosperous families. The silver jewelry included bracelets and anklets, earrings, and finger rings, often having a standard weight so that they could easily be used to settle money accounts in case of need. But the bulk of silver bullion was accumulated in the state treasury (i.e., in the palace and the temples). Part of this stock was distributed among the high palace and temple officials as payments for service and gifts.

Under conditions of low market output of the economies, the sale of agricultural products for silver was not everywhere or always feasible. This is especially true of the land beyond the bounds of large cities and far from the central offices and trading companies. In the absence of minted coins, silver bullion required weighing and calculations; that is, a certain degree of expertise, unavailable to the greater part of the population. This circumstance complicated the circulation of silver, especially in rural areas. Such problems did not arise in large cities, where there were money-changer shops and merchants in considerable numbers. Silver could circulate here more freely, and it seems that it could easily be exchanged for products, because the need for such exchange continued to rise as the economy developed.

The natural consequence of the low output of marketable goods was the increased need for credit. Since silver was not readily available, one could not lend it and hope for a payment of the debt with interest unless the debtor had trade capital or belonged to the elite of the state personnel; that is, unless he occupied a place in the small group of persons connected with trade or in whose hands the income from taxation and trade accumulated. The overwhelming majority of families did not belong to this group. They could not count on loans unless they could offer the creditor a sufficiently secure guarantee. Such a guarantee was the debtor's person or his estate. In these instances, the debtor could pledge or sell into slavery members of his own family or even himself; or (if he did not belong to the state personnel) he could mortgage (or sell)[4] his real estate. Sales of land and persons that were the result of a previous credit transaction were of a temporary character and, after a certain period of time or after certain previous conditions had been met, had to be canceled.

Besides private credit, ancient Mesopotamian society had also developed other important economic levers for promoting commodity circulation under conditions of the low level of development of commodity-money relations. One of these was the system of state credit. This system was represented by the tamkars, tavern keepers (often women), and bakers. Their activities supplied the rural and part of the urban population with their chief, sometimes only, source for commodity exchange.

The difference in the living and property standards among the various strata of Old Babylonian society was comparatively moderate, and the different levels that existed were relatively stable. The living standard allowed one to sustain oneself and one's family within the expected norm for that particular level of society.

Above the mass of people, there was a small group of wealthy families whose members occupied prominent positions in the state or temple economies (and also in the communities) or who were mem-

4. Leaseholders were not necessarily men who had lost their land. Not uncommonly, land was taken on lease by well-to-do persons in addition to their main allotment of property. Such persons had the means to pay for the additional expenditures incurred by leased land. Leased land was either worked by the family of the leaseholder and his slaves or, perhaps, could be subleased.

bers of the king's family or his close associates. These families owned many city buildings, dozens of hectares of date plantations and orchards, large estates providing income measured in the tens of thousands of liters of grain,[5] and, by the standards of that time, large herds of sheep. All work on these estates was conducted with the aid of leaseholders (in grain fields and orchards), hired hands (in herding livestock), and slaves, whose labor was used in all branches of the larger economies.

The lower social level was made up of the poor from among villagers and townspeople, consisting of people ruined by natural disasters or social misfortunes and those newly arrived from elsewhere. The latter owned nothing and survived only by rations issued from the palace or temple whose protection they sought. The numbers of the poor and the rich were small in times of peace relative to the bulk of the population, but their existence greatly affected the social life and the social development of the country.

The modest property status and income of the majority of the population determined their likewise-modest consumption. Norms defining the consumption requirement necessary to sustain a person were in use during the Old Babylonian Period in the private as well as in the state economies and are known to us. It was held that an adult working male required for his sustenance 1.5 liters of barley per day (or 550 liters annually). Yearly, an adult male used 2.5–3 liters of vegetable oil, chiefly for anointment, and he would wear out one set of clothing, requiring 1.5 kilograms of wool. A woman's maintenance ration amounted to one half of a male's barley ration and the same amount of oil and wool. Most people did not consume meat except when they participated in sacrificial meals during temple festivals.

The Mesopotamian society of this period was divided into three estates: free citizens with full rights (*awilum*), who owned real estate by virtue of belonging to some community (either urban or rural) or who had an official status in the palace or temple; persons with limited legal and political rights (*mushkenum*), who usually had no real estate as property but were allotted land by the state on the basis of conditional ownership for services but mostly for manual work; and, finally, slaves (*wardum*), who were owned as property by their masters. The top palace and temple aristocracy belonged to the *awilum*. The right to own land did not depend upon estate, and the *mushkenum* could also purchase land parcels, mainly houses, date plantations, and, very rarely and not in all parts of the country, fields.

5. In ancient times, grain and other similar products were measured in units of volume instead of weight (1 liter = 0.264 U.S. gallon).

The Laws

The main achievement in the reign of Hammurapi, king of Babylon, was the compilation of a code of laws.[6] Legislative activities are known in the Early Dynastic III Period from the so-called Oval Plaque of Enmetena and from the inscriptions of Uruinimgina (see Lecture 2). However, these texts only recount legislative acts and do not reproduce their exact wording.

The Laws of Shulgi compose the first legislative text known to us. (Formerly, these were known as the Laws of Ur-Nammu, but a short while ago it was established that they were promulgated by Ur-Nammu's son and heir.) This text, badly damaged, consists of a Prologue, followed by the legal regulations. We do not know whether or not an Epilogue also existed. The Prologue declares that the aim of the laws is the protection of the widow and the orphan, of the weak against the powerful, and of the poor against the rich. Such a declaration also exists in the text of Uruinimgina. It would be an error to dismiss it as social demagogy. The king in Mesopotamia long retained the features of a tribal chief whose duties included the protection of the poor and the wretched. Consequently, this feature was rooted in the social psychology of the population, and thus did the king himself visualize his duty. Of course, political necessity was also operative; no society can exist without a minimum of social equity.

Less than three dozen of Shulgi's legal regulations remain, partly damaged. Among other regulations, the laws prescribe punishment for adultery (§4), rules of divorce (§§6–8), punishment for false denunciation (§§10–11) and for perjury (§§26–27), and rules concerning marriage (§§12–13) and bodily damage (§§15–19). Especially interesting are the laws referring to slaves; for example, the obligation to return fugitive slaves (§14) and the regulations concerning the slave girl "who deems herself equal to her mistress" (§§22–23). It should be noted that such a slave girl could be punished only by due process of law and not by her master and mistress at will. In other words, during that period, the slaves were still regarded as persons, not as objects. From the legal documents of this epoch, one can see that slaves could even dispute their slave status against their master in court. (However, they usually lost the suit.) §§27–29 are devoted to the protection of the landowner against illegal actions of other persons, as well as against unconscientious leaseholders. The main punishment in the Laws of Shulgi is compensation paid by the culprit to the victim.[7]

The next legislative text known to us was issued by Lipit-Ishtar,

6. This section was written by V. A. Jakobson.

7. Note that the numeration of paragraphs in these and other Mesopotamian laws has been introduced by modern scholars and does not exist in the originals.

king of Issin (see Lecture 3). The text, considerably damaged, is in Sumerian (although the former existence of an Akkadian version is not impossible). It consists of a Prologue, forty-three legal paragraphs, and an Epilogue. In the short Prologue Lipit-Ishtar states that he has established a "liberation" of the "sons and daughters" of Nippur, Ur, and Issin and also of (all?) the "sons and daughters" of Sumer and Akkad. This liberation refers to obligatory labor and perhaps also to debts. The subsequent text suggests that the liberation was only partial and consisted of a reduction in the duration of obligatory work.

The laws themselves refer to property relations (§§1–3, heavily damaged); the payment for hire of a cart and ox and driver (§4); punishment for burglary (§6: who breaks open a door shall die; §7: who breaks through a mud-brick wall shall die and be buried under the break); and rules for hiring ships (§§8–9) and leasing plantations (§§11–13); and punishment for trespassing on another's plantation (§14: 10 shekels; i.e., 85 grams of silver to be paid) and for felling a tree (§15: 0.5 mina; i.e., 250 grams of silver to be paid). According to §16, a neighbor can be held responsible for thieves' breaking into another's house through his plot; if, although warned of the danger, he did not take precautions to stop the burglary, he must make restitution for the price of the stolen goods.

A number of laws refer to slaves and dependent persons. Thus, harboring a fugitive slave is punished by the delivery of another slave by the culprit to the owner (§17) or by the payment to him of 15 shekels of silver (§18). If a slave girl has borne children by her owner and he has manumitted both herself and her children, they still are not co-heirs of the estate (§20). However, if he married the slave girl after the death of his former wife, the children are co-heirs with the children of the first wife. §19, which is very poorly preserved, seems to have referred to certain conditions pertaining to emancipation.

Scholars seriously differ among themselves as to the meaning of the term *migtum* in §§20–21. In I. M. Diakonoff's opinion, this is a category of dependent persons working in a private economy. If a *migtum* has come by his own free will, he is free to leave by his own will; but if he is a present of the king, "he cannot be taken away." In §23, it is established that a person who has taken over another person's untilled plot of land and has tilled it for three years, paying the "income" (*biltum*, Sumerian *gu-un*) due from this land, can keep the plot. It is most probable that service land is meant, but it is not certain that the law does not refer to community land.

§§25–38 are devoted to family law; §§38–43 fix the compensation for damage to another person's draft ox. It is interesting to note that in §22 it is established that a false accusation involves a punishment for the accuser equal to that which would have been meted out to the defendant were the accusation true. This is the first time we meet with the so-called lex talionis; that is, retribution on the principle of an "eye for an eye," etc., a principle widely used in the Laws of Hammurapi.

And last, the direct predecessor of Hammurapi's laws are the Laws of the Kingdom of Eshnunna in the valley of the Diyala River (about 1800 B.C.). They have been preserved in two damaged copies written in Akkadian; the readings that differ in the two copies are unimportant. The text consists of a (nearly completely destroyed) Prologue and sixty paragraphs of law. It is not clear whether or not an Epilogue existed. The Laws of the Kingdom of Eshnunna open with a sort of "tariff," or, better, list or index of equivalency relations between the main commodities and silver (§1) and barley (§2). The prices listed correspond to the actual average prices of the period; the index probably was used for accounting purposes in the state economies.

§§3–4 fix the price for hire of a cart and a boat; §§3–11 fix the amount of payments for the hire of workers and also the punishments to be inflicted for diverse infringements of the law in connection with the hire of objects and men. Theft of movable property belonging to the *mushkenum,* from his house or fields, is punished by the payment of a compensation of 10 shekels of silver; but a similar theft made at night is punished by death (§§12–13). According to §15, male and female slaves are not entitled to make any sales, and according to §16, a minor "son of a man" or of a slave cannot borrow (cf. the comments on §7 in the Laws of Hammurapi below).

§§17–18a and 25–35 are devoted to family law. On the whole, they coincide with the corresponding paragraphs in the Laws of Hammurapi (see below). §§33–35, which deal with an attempt of a private or palace female slave to give away her child to a free person as a foster-child (presumably to set it free), are especially noteworthy. The law is that such a child should be returned to slavery and that the illegal foster-parent should pay two slaves, which is the same penalty as that for the theft of a slave (§49).

The laws concerning debts (§§19–24) are also practically the same as in Hammurapi's code, but not so detailed. We may note §20, which prohibits the requirement of a payment in silver for a loan in grain, and §24, which aims at protecting the *mushkenum* from a dishonest creditor. The legislator also attempts to prevent the economic ruin of community members. Thus, it is established that a brother has the first option in buying his brother's property if the latter has to sell it (§38). An analogous priority is given to the former proprietor of a house, if the new proprietor is selling it (§39); the law mentions specifically that the house has been sold because of an "enfeeblement," or destitutions, of the proprietor.

For bodily damage of various kinds, a compensation in money is provided (§§42–48 and 54–57). The Laws of the Kingdom of Eshnunna mention only one case of manslaughter (a wall collapsing because of the negligence of the proprietor), in §58. The verdict in this case is to be pronounced by the king, according to the general rule concerning "cases of life" (§48). Finally, we should note that according to §59, a man who divorces a wife who has borne children to him loses all his property in favor of the wife (if she is not to blame for the divorce).

The previously mentioned texts can be regarded as consecutive stages within a single tradition of Mesopotamian law. This does not imply that there did not exist local differences (though these were not essential). One can observe how methods for systematizing legal norms gradually evolved. The ancient Mesopotamian law books certainly were not codes of law in the *modern* sense. What we encounter here is the pretheoretical stage of legal development. At this stage, some of the main legal principles and concepts have not yet been formulated; for example, the most important principle of *nullum crimen sine lege* (there is no crime except that which is stated in law). Therefore, the Mesopotamian "lawyers" did not strive for completeness when compiling their "law books." (Or, more exactly, they did not see the necessity for completeness.) At the same time, they were convinced that justice is eternal and unchangeable, that justice is the order of things established from the beginning of time and cannot depend on the actual issues of the day. For this reason, they thought it possible to include in the laws even tariffs on prices and payments for hire, despite the fact that we know from the documents that such prices and such payments fluctuated considerably under the impact of the actual economic situation.

The most ancient laws in the history of humanity attest to the first and—most importantly—most difficult steps of jurisprudence. Therein lies their human value for all times. The development of Sumero-Akkadian cuneiform law culminated in the Laws of Hammurapi (hereafter referred to as LH).

The LH compose the largest and most important corpus of cuneiform law. No theoretical treatises on Mesopotamian law have come down to us. (They probably did not exist; we have no theoretical treatises for any of the sciences.) But the LH are the result of a tremendous work of collecting, unifying, and systematizing legal norms. This work was based on premises essentially different from those current in modern law, but its own principles were followed consistently enough. The norms are systematized according to the subject matter regulated, and the passage from one norm to another is by association. Thus, the same object is discussed in contiguous laws from different legal aspects. Cases that seemed obvious and indisputable are not mentioned in LH at all; for example, murder, theft, and sorcery. Such cases were decided in court according to custom. At the same time, the Babylonian lawyers had difficulty in formulating general principles and definitions of law, although they did have a certain understanding of the fact that such principles do exist. However, they expressed them casuistically. Thus, the principle that in one legal case there cannot be two decisions (verdicts) seems to be expressed in §5, in which the judge is punished for "changing the decision" after it has once been made and a document attesting it has been delivered. Or, again, the general principle that a minor or unfree person has no legal capacity seems to be expressed in §7, in which a person is punished for acquiring any kind of property "from the hands of a minor son of a man (*awilum*) or from a slave of a man . . . without witness and agreement" (since such an acquisition could not be made (i.e., was not legal) before witnesses who knew the status of the vendor).

The LH begin with a Prologue wherein Babylon is stated to be the "eternal habitat of royal power"; this is a change from the earlier principle, according to which "royal power" could move from one city to another. Hammurapi's merits are mentioned not in regard to the entire state but only in regard to every particular nome city of Mesopotamia; specifically, in regard to their tutelary deities. (The aim of the promulgation of the LH is stated in the Epilogue as follows: "So that the strong should not oppress the weak, so that orphan and widow should get justice.") Then follow the laws proper.[8] The laws can be divided into the following sections: (1) main principles of justice (§§1–5); (2) protection of property—that of the king, the temple, the "men" (community members), and the royal servants (§§6–25); (3) laws concerning service holdings (§§26–41); (4) operations with immovables and offences connected with such (§§42–88); (5) trading and commercial operations (§§89–126); (6) family law (§§127–95); (7) bodily harm (§§196–214); and (8) operations with movables and hire of persons (§§215–82). There follows an Epilogue with curses on everyone who should deviate from the laws. Both the Prologue and the Epilogue are written in a solemn and archaic language, reminiscent of poetic texts. The laws themselves are couched in a precise and clear business-like style.

8. The division of the text into 282 separate paragraphs is the work of the Assyriologists who published it; there is no formal subdivision in the original.

Babylonian law, like any ancient law, was not divided into civil, criminal, procedural, public law, etc. The text of the LH is "synthetic," proclaiming both positive laws and the punishment for their infringement.

As mentioned above, the society depicted in the LH consists of free community members (*awilum*), royal servants (*mushkenum*), and slaves (*wardum*). Practically, the conditions of royal servants could differ greatly: those belonging to the upper strata could obtain very considerable allotments from the king and were treated as community members; those belonging to the lower strata received tiny service allotments or only rations in kind, differing but slightly from the slaves. In other words, there were numerous steps between slavery and freedom within the category of royal servants. Life, honor, and personal inviolability of a *mushkenum* have a lower price than was the case for the *awilum* (§§196ff.). At the same time, the property of the *mushkenum* was better protected; after all, it was actually a part of the royal property.[9] Some vestiges of legal capability still linger with the slave: thus, the slave of the palace or of a *mushkenum* was allowed to marry a free woman, and the children of their marriage were free (§§175–76). A slave owner could declare his children from a slave woman legally his own (with all the rights ensuing from such a legal act); but even if he did not make this declaration, both the children and the mother were emancipated at his death (§§170–71). A slave who was bought abroad was to be freed without ransom if it appeared that he was a Babylonian. For assault and battery of a free man or for questioning his slave status, a slave was not subject to a reprisal out of court but was punished according to a verdict in court. (His ear was cut off, §205, §282.) Moreover, slavery for debt was limited by a three-year term. (Either the debtor himself or his family member or his slave could become slaves for debt.) A free person could be sold into slavery, but only for a term of three years (§117). In connection with a debt, there was also another type of temporary loss of liberty: pledging (§§114–16). A pledged person, apparently, could be forcibly apprehended by the creditor, who then held him in a kind of private jail until the debt was paid.

Creditors were usually the trading agents (the *tamkars*). They were state officials, but at the same time they could conduct different business using their own private means. Each important city had an organization of trading agents (*karum*, literally "quay"). It had the power

9. This is also the reason why the property of the *mushkenum* was specifically protected in the Laws of the Kingdom of Eshunna, whereas the protection of the property of a citizen was relegated to customary law.

of administrative surveillance over the *tamkars*, and it settled their mutual accounts and their accounts with the state. The *tamkars* traded internationally both in person and through their aids, the *shamalls*. The latter were wandering traders, not owning means of their own. Another field of activity of the *tamkars* was usury, as mentioned above.[10] Loans in kind were granted for an interest of one third of the sum, and loans in silver, for an interest of one fifth. The loan was usually for a short term, typically until the harvest. Business documents appear to document the existence of other types of loans, including those with compound interest. To a certain extent, the LH attempt to protect the debtors from the creditors' abuses: in some cases, payment of the debt could be deferred (§§48); one could pay in kind in lieu of silver (§49); the harvest of a field or of an orchard could not be seized to pay a debt (§66); giving false measure or weight in lending or in receiving payment for a debt was punished (§94?).

Agriculture was the basis of all life in Mesopotamia; no wonder that the LH pay great attention to it. The main type of agricultural economy was the small one; large landowners either used for work certain royal servants set at their disposal or rented out the land in small plots for a share of the harvest (one third or one half of the crop, §46) or for a fixed payment in advance (§45). The tenant was obliged to work carefully, ensuring a reasonable income (§§42–44). The term could be prolonged if the tenant suffered losses owing to natural disaster (§47). The farmer had to maintain the irrigation system in good order, and if his neighbor's land was damaged through his carelessness, he would be responsible (§§53–56). Cattle and sheep were usually entrusted to special herdsmen (royal or hired men), and they were responsible for damage caused by the animals as well as for any damage to the herd owing to the herdsman's actions (§§263–67). Work for hire seems to have been widely practiced; one could hire freemen as well as slaves.

The LH list wage rates for many types of labor, beginning with the most skilled (wages for physicians, veterinary surgeons, house builders, ship builders), to the wages for craftsmen (brickmakers, smiths, carpenters, shoemakers, weavers), down to unskilled labor (§§215–24, §§253–74). Workers were usually hired for a short period—for the sowing or, much more frequently, for the harvest or for a specified piece of work on a pay-by-day basis. In the LH the prices for hire given seem to be for a day's worth of work. The hired man was responsible (both materially and "criminally") for any eventual

10. They were also responsible for the collection of taxes, although this is not mentioned in the LH.

losses that the owner might incur through the hired worker's fault. The payment to a hired worker made it possible for him to sustain his family during the period of his work for hire.

The LH devote considerable attention to the family as the primary nucleus of Babylonian society (§§127ff.). A marriage was legal only if certain legal formalities were observed (§128); a marriage settlement must have been agreed upon before witnesses; the agreement was usually oral, but under certain circumstances (see below), it could also be written. The family was monogamous, and the wife's infidelity was punishable by death (§129). The LH establish detailed rules for the examination of such accusations (§§130–36). However, the husband could cohabit with his female slaves and could declare the children borne by them to him as legally his own (§170). Under certain conditions (illness of the wife, §148; marriage with a priestess to whom childbirth was prohibited, §145), the husband could take a second wife. A written agreement was drawn up when one married a priestess or some other rich woman; such an agreement could refer to the status of the children and the possibility of taking a second wife. The aim of marriage was the procreation of heirs to the family property and keepers of the funerary cult of the ancestors; if this cult was not maintained, the ancestral dead would experience famine in the underworld. The LH recount detailed provisions for the property relations between husband and wife: of the dowry and the bride-price (§§159–64?) and of the wife's property (§150).

Despite what is sometimes stated, Babylonian marriage did not consist of the purchase of a bride: the amount of the dowry exceeded the amount of the bride-price (§§163–64). The act of marriage formally resembled the act of purchase, but this similarity existed only because in ancient law purchase constituted the only conceivable form of passing power over a person or object from one patriarchal authority to another. (Even in Roman law the emancipation of the son from under the father's patriarchal authority took the form of a fictitious act of sale and purchase.)

The LH also devote much attention to problems of inheritance (§§165ff.). Disinheritance was permitted only after a son repeated a serious offence (§§167–68). If the marriage was childless, the adoption of other people's children (according to an agreement with the blood parents) or of foundlings offered a solution (§§185ff.).[11] The

---

11. The child could, however, be reclaimed in court by his real parents, unless he had been adopted by a eunuch (there were many at the royal court and in the temples) or by a *zikrum*. The *zikrum* was a woman, probably performing a male role in certain cults, who could not have children of her own.

property situation of the priestesses is discussed in some detail. It was customary in Babylonia to consecrate little girls to the temples for service to the gods; these girls subsequently became priestesses, sometimes of high rank. They were entitled to a certain share in the parental property (§§176ff.), and after their deaths the brothers usually inherited this share.

As noted above, the Babylonians did not distinguish between civil and criminal law, but the LH give much attention to punishments for offences and crimes: from breach of duties connected with royal service to infringements of property rights and crimes against persons. In the LH the number of crimes punishable by death is very considerable and applied to very diverse offences, ranging from felons' acquiring other persons' property to adultery. For some especially grave crimes, the LH prescribe particular means for carrying out the death penalty; for example, burning for incest with one's mother (§158) or impaling for the complicity of the wife in the murder of her husband (§156). In some other cases, a punishment according to the principle of talion was prescribed. This could be a "mirroring" punishment—that is, retaliation by inflicting the same injury that the criminal had inflicted—or symbolical—for example, cutting off the hand that has "sinned." In other cases a compensation in money was fixed.

The principle of talion was known in earlier Mesopotamian legislation, but only in the LH is it applied so widely and consistently. The widespread idea that the talion represents a survival of the vendetta is false. The vendetta is based on the principle, inherited from primitive society, of collective guilt and collective responsibility. As the concept of individual personality develops, so does the concept of individual guilt and individual responsibility. Moreover, it is in the developing civic society's interest that feuds should not continue indefinitely, which is, of course, the case in a vendetta. Therefore, the principle of money compensation is introduced, and only later the principle of talion, which for the legal consciousness of that epoch was perceived as the most just solution. In other words, the development of responsibility is toward individualization, and that of punishment is toward its public execution.

The proceedings of law in Babylonia were oral and competitive. This means that an action could be brought against a party only through a complaint from the other interested party, and in the course of the trial, each of the parties had to prove its statements. No written minutes were kept, but certain important moments of the trial could be fixed in writing. The main proofs were the evidence of the witnesses (see, e.g., §§9–11) and documents. In a few cases, if no other means of establishing the truth were available, recourse was made to a deity. This supernatural help could take two forms: ordeal by water and oaths in the names of the gods. The ordeal by water consisted of dipping the defendant into a river: if he sank and drowned, it was considered that the god of the river had punished him; if he swam, he was acquitted.[12] In the opinion of the times, perjury in an oath to the gods would inevitably bring about the gods' punishment of the guilty. Therefore, such an oath was considered sufficient for acquittal, whereas a refusal to swear an oath was regarded as proof that the accusation had been justified. A false accusation and false evidence were punished according to the principle of talion; that is, the accuser bore the punishment that would have been meted out to the defendant had the accusation been justified.

The LH were considered to be model legislation for as long as the "cuneiform culture" of Mesopotamia endured. They were copied and studied until the Hellenistic and, even, Parthian period of Babylon's history. About forty copies (or fragments) of the LH are known to us, which is more than can be said of most other ancient texts.

Finally, it should be noted that the opinions of the experts on Mesopotamian law differ widely. Some of them believe that what we have before us are not laws in the proper sense of the word but royal self-praise that aims at publicizing the king's wisdom and justice; others feel that they are no more than theoretical exercises of Mesopotamian scholars with no practical value. According to this latter, rather widespread, opinion, actual laws were not promulgated in Mesopotamia at all, but imaginary laws, which had no other practical value than that of extolling the justice of the kings, were written down, even incised on stone, and then copied and studied by scholars for hundreds of years. We find this point of view quite unacceptable. The texts of law were, no doubt, supposed to be learned by rote in the schools: that was the way all sciences were studied in Babylonia.

Opinions also differ among those scholars who actually do regard them as actual laws. (Some believe that they were applied to the entire population; others that they were valid only for the royal servants.) In the Soviet Union, the opinion is dominant that these texts were actual laws (albeit primitive ones) and that they were binding for the entire population. However, they did not duplicate customary law, and where the legislator thought the latter sufficient to guarantee justice and did not require amendment or change, it continued to be applied. At the same time, the royal laws paid special attention to the interests of the royal sector, including royal servants, and especially to cases of possible conflicts between the interests of the state and of private persons.

12. In the European Middle Ages, the reverse was true: the one who swam was considered guilty.

The End of the Old Babylonian Period

Hammurapi's reforms and legislative activities, far-reaching in their scope and aims, made a great impression on his contemporaries, and he was long remembered by future generations of Mesopotamians. All his measures, frequently innovative in form and execution, were not, however, really aimed at changing the society but, rather, at preserving the traditional social institutions, such as the in-kind economy, community land ownership, and so on. Consequently, what actually happened was that Hammurapi systematically counteracted all that was new, all that was regarded in his time as destructive of the state and undermining of its social and economic foundations. By imposing severe restrictions on private activities that led to the enrichment of some and the ruin of others, Hammurapi's reforms, in essence, were aimed against increasing the production and circulation of commodities and money. Although such increase did indeed lead to the growth of usury, as well as to the abuse of political power, and undermined community land ownership, it was the only possible avenue of economic development under the then-prevailing conditions. Therefore, all attempts to curb this development had no chance of lasting success.

Hammurapi was, no doubt, one of the most prominent statesmen in the history of Mesopotamia, and his personal qualities played a significant role in the rise of Babylon and the longtime preservation of its authority over a large part of Mesopotamia. However, the same forces that undermined the Third Dynasty of Ur and that caused its demise continued to operate even after the establishment of the Babylonian kingdom. After Hammurapi's death, the state that he had established continued for over two hundred years, although attacks perpetrated by external, as well as internal, enemies gradually weakened its stability. The role of the Amorites of the earlier period was now taken over by Kassite pastoral tribes who infiltrated Mesopotamia from the east—from the central Zagros Mountains. The onslaughts of the Kassites, the difficulty of defending the extensive borders, the economic hardships caused by the government's inability to control usury, and the loss of land by the common people weakened Babylon and spurred the separatist trends of the tributary regions.

The first city to fall away from Babylon was Terqa, situated at the mouth of the Khabur River, the region formerly roamed by the pastoral Hanean tribes of the Amorites. Here a large contingent of Kassites now settled. Then all the southern cities revolted, supported by the Idamarats and Yamutbala tribes. This rebellion was cruelly suppressed in 1739 B.C. by Hammurapi's son, Samsuiluna. Many cities of the south were completely destroyed and remained uninhabited for a long time. Among these were Larsa and the ancient centers of Sumerian civilization, Uruk and Ur, guardians of the millennium-long cuneiform cultural tradition. Babylon was never to reintegrate the south completely. The kingdom of the Sealand that formed on the shores of the Persian Gulf existed for over two hundred years.

Powerful rivals of the Babylonian kingdom, which was still the largest in Mesopotamia, appeared toward the middle of the seventeenth century B.C., reducing the territorial size of the state even more. In the south, Lagash and Ur, together with their adjoining territories, became part of the kingdom of the Sea-Country. The northern Babylonian frontier was moved to the south of Mari and Asshur. Beyond the Tigris, Babylon still controlled the territories of the Idamarats and Yamutbala tribes. The Hanean kingdom, centered in Terqa, remained strong in Upper Mesopotamia, but in this area the Kassite dynasty replaced the Akkadian-Amorite dynasty. A new king with the Kassite name of Kashtiliash assumed power there and ruled until the end of the Babylonian dynasty. From there, the Kassites infiltrated southern Mesopotamia in small groups. Many of them hired themselves out for seasonal work in cities and villages or entered the military service. After the invasion of the Hittites, led by Mursilis I, who, in 1595 B.C., apparently deposed Samsuditana, the last king of the Babylonian dynasty, the Kassites seized royal power in Babylon. Their reign lasted for over four hundred years.

5

Sumerian Culture

V. K. AFANASIEVA

The Religious Perception of the World and the Arts in Early Lower Mesopotamia

In the early Chalcolithic (Copper-Stone Age), humanity's emotional and intellectual perception of the world had greatly advanced since the time of their Stone Age forebears. However, people's fundamental method of generalizing continued to be an emotionally conditioned process of expressing the essence of a phenomenon by metaphor; that is, in order to express an abstract characteristic, one identified and matched two or more phenomena having some typical feature or characteristic trait in common. For example, the sun was a bird, because both soared in the sky. Likewise, earth was a mother. From these emotional associations, myths were born. Myths were not only metaphorical interpretations of phenomena, they were also actual emotional experiences. When verification by common everyday technical experiments was impossible or insufficient (for instance, if it was beyond the abilities of commonly accepted production methods), sympathetic magic was practiced. Such magic is practiced by peoples who cannot distinguish, either in judgment or practical actions, between logical and nonlogical connections.

Meanwhile, people also began to realize that certain things and events concerning life and work followed a natural order, that there were certain regularities determining the "behavior" of nature, animals, and objects. The only way in which one could explain this order was by assuming that such behavior was induced by intelligent actions, because it was only in human actions that the connection between cause and effect could immediately be observed. In nature, such actions were ascribed to powerful beings who were the metaphoric expression of world order. People imagined these mighty living principles not as an ideal "something," not as spirits, but as physically active and, hence, substantial beings. Therefore, it was perceived as possible to influence their will; they could, for example, be placated. It must be pointed out that actions based on logic and those based on magic were considered to be equally reasonable and useful to human life, including productive activities. The difference was that logical actions had practical, empirical, and obvious explanations, and magical actions (rituals, worship) had a mythical explanation. In the mind of ancient people, any magic action was a repetition of some action performed by a god or an ancestor at the beginning of time and still enacted under the same conditions. Thus, this was an epoch when historical changes were imperceptible, when development was extremely slow and the stability of the world depended on the rule of acting as the gods or ancestors did in the beginning of time. The criterion of verifying by practice, as we know it, was not applicable to such actions and concepts.

Magical activities were attempts to influence the personified laws of nature through the emotional, rhythmical, and "divine" word, sacrificial offerings, ritualistic body movements, and so on. Such activities, like any other socially essential actions, seemed to be necessary for the life of the community.

During the Neolithic Age (the latest period of the Stone Age), it appears that the existence of certain abstract connections and laws governing the real environment began to be perceived. This new consciousness may have been reflected in the introduction of geometric abstraction into art, depicting the world of humans, animals, plants, and motion. Abstract ornamentation replaced the disorderly conglomeration of magical drawings of animals and people (though the earlier images sometimes were accurate and faithful in their details). The geometrical image, however, retained its magical purpose and, at the same time, was not divorced from human daily activities.

Artistic creativity was present in the manufacture of necessary household objects, whether pottery, colored beads, or statuettes of gods, goddesses, and ancestors, but it was especially evident in works intended for magical and cultic feasts or for funerary use (so that the deceased could use the objects in the afterlife). The making of objects for cultic and household use entailed a creative process through which an artist was guided, consciously or unconsciously, by a certain instinct or flair, which developed as he or she worked.

The pottery of the Neolithic and Early Chalcolithic ages reveals a most important stage of artistic generalization, where the principal feature is rhythm. The sense of rhythm is probably inherent in human nature, but it was a long time before people began to embody it in images. Rhythm is hardly felt in Palaeolithic images. It begins to appear during the Neolithic Age as an attempt to order and organize space. Painted pottery shows how people learned to generalize their impressions of nature by grouping and stylizing objects and phenomena and transforming them into harmonious, geometric, plant, animal, or abstract ornaments that were rigorously controlled by rhythm. Starting with the simplest dotted- and incised-line ornaments that decorated the earliest pottery and culminating in the complex, symmetrical designs that, as if in motion, appear on vessels of the fifth millennium B.C., we can see that all these compositions are organically rhythmical. It is as if the rhythm of colors, lines, and shapes echoed the rhythm of motion—the rhythm of a hand slowly turning the clay vessel to form it (since the potter's wheel had not yet been introduced)—and perhaps even the rhythm of an accompanying song or tune. Ceramic art also provided the opportunity to fix or imprint an idea or a story by using conventional representative symbols; even the most abstract ornament conveyed some information derived from tradition.

In studying Neolithic and Early Chalcolithic sculpture, we confront even more complex forms of generalization (even beyond the artistic level). Figurines with an emphasis on female and especially maternal features, found in granaries and hearths, phalli and figures of bull calves, frequently found in association with human-like figures—they all represented a syncretic image of the fertility of the earth. The most complex expression of this concept appears in the male and female statuettes from Lower Mesopotamia at the beginning of the fourth millennium B.C. They have animal-like snouts, and their shoulders and eyes frequently have added-on pouches or inserts for actual vegetation (date seeds or grain). These figurines cannot yet be called fertility deities; they represent a stage preceding the creation of the image of the community's tutelar deity. We find such images at a later period, paralleling the evolution of architectonic structures, which started with outdoor altars and progressed to temples.

The culture of the Protoliterate Period can safely be called Sumerian, or, at least, proto-Sumerian. This culture is found throughout Lower and Upper Mesopotamia. The following are among the greatest achievements of this period: temple building, glyptic art (engraving of seals), new forms of plastic arts, new principles in figurative art, and the invention of writing.

All the arts of that time, as well as people's consciousness of the world, were colored by worship. However, we must point out that when dealing with the community cults of ancient Mesopotamia in general, it is difficult to draw any conclusion about a system of Sumerian religion. It is true that the same cosmic deities were worshiped everywhere. These were An, "Heaven" (Akkadian Anu); Enki, "Lord of the Earth," the deity of the World Ocean, upon which floats the Earth (Akkadian Ea); and Enlil, "Lord-Breath-of-the-Air," the deity of the forces between the Earth and the Heavens (Akkadian Ellil). Enlil was also the god of the Sumerian tribal union centered in Nippur. There were also deities of the sun and the moon and different mother-goddesses. But more important were the local tutelary deities of each community, usually with a spouse, son, and retinue. There were innumerable minor gods and evil deities associated with grain, cattle, the home, and the granary, as well as with illnesses and disasters. They usually differed from community to community, and different, contradictory myths were told about them.

Temples were not erected to every deity—only to the most important ones and, mainly, to the tutelary god of the community. The outside walls and platforms of a temple were decorated with alternating recesses and salients. (This technique was repeated each time the temple was completely rebuilt on the same site.) The temple itself was composed of three parts: the central part was a long court with an image of the god at the far end, and two rooms were attached symmetrically at the sides of this court. The altar was at one end of the court and the table for sacrificial offerings at the other. During this period, the temples of Upper Mesopotamia all had a similar layout.

Thus, a certain new type of sacred architecture developed in the north, as well as in the south, of Mesopotamia. It embodied certain building principles that soon became traditional for all future Mesopotamian religious architecture. The main principles were as follows: (1) The sanctuary was always rebuilt on the same site (all subsequent reconstructions incorporated the previous ones, so that the temple always remained in the same place). (2) The central temple was placed on an elevated man-made platform and was made accessible by staircases on two sides. (It is probably the custom of always erecting a temple on the same site that resulted in three, five, and, finally, even seven receding platforms, one on top of the other, with the temple on the very top—the so-called ziggurat.) The raising of the temple high up emphasized its antiquity and the indigenous character of the community, as well as the connection of the sanctuary with the heavenly abode of the god. (3) The temple complex consisted of a tripartite temple with a central hall and a roofless internal courtyard surrounded by auxiliary chambers (in northern Lower Mesopotamia such courtyards could also be covered). (4) The external walls of the temple and of the platform or platforms were segmented into alternating projections and recesses.

From ancient Uruk, we know of a very special structure, the so-called Red Building, which featured a sort of stage with columns decorated in mosaics. This may have been a place for meetings of the popular assembly (in the courtyard) and of the council (on the stage).

The beginning of urban culture, even if still primitive, introduces a new stage in the development of figurative arts in Lower Mesopotamia. The culture of this new period became richer and more diverse. For example, new cylinder seals began to appear in place of the earlier stamp seals.

The plastic arts of early Sumer are closely related to glyptic art. The seal-amulets in the shape of animals or animal heads that were so widespread during the Protoliterate Period may be regarded as an art form combining glyptics, relief, and three-dimensional sculpture. All these objects were functionally seals. The lower side of the figurine was flattened and incised with images. The incised images are usually related to the main figure: on the reverse of a lion's head we may find carved small lions, and on the reverse of a ram's head we may find horned animals or a figure of a man (apparently a shepherd).

Another trait of early Sumerian art is its narrative character. Each frieze of a cylinder seal represents a story, and each image can be read in sequence. The story can be about nature, the animal world, or about the artist—about humanity. It is only in the Protoliterate Period that the motif of the human being first appears in art.

Although people were depicted in art during the Palaeolithic Age, the resulting images were very stylized. In Neolithic and Chalcolithic art people appear as integral parts of nature: people had not yet consciously detached themselves from it. Early art typically presents syncretic representations: human-animal-plant images (e.g., figurines of frogs that have niches in the shoulders for holding grains and fruit pits or figurines of a woman feeding a young animal); or human-phallic representations (man represented by a phallus alone, as a symbol of reproduction).

In Sumerian art of the Protoliterate Period we can see how people began to distinguish themselves from nature. Thus the art of Lower Mesopotamia during this time constitutes a new qualitative stage in the relation between the human being and the environment. It is typical that objects of art in the Protoliterate Period give the impression of an awakening human energy, of people's consciousness of their newly discovered potential and of the power of their attempts at self-expression in a world that they were able to control with increasing success.

From the Early Dynastic Period we have many archaeological finds that provide more reliable information about certain common trends in the arts of that period. A definite type of temple style had emerged. This was the temple placed on a high platform. It was sometimes surrounded by a wall. (The entire temple area usually was walled in.) The ancillary rooms were clearly separated from the central hall or courtyard of worship, and their number decreased. The columns and semicolumns disappeared, and, along with them, so did the mosaic facings. A fundamental artistic design in temple architecture continued to be the breakup of the external walls in projections and recesses. It is quite possible that the concept of a multistory ziggurat of the main deity of a city was developed during this period, gradually replacing the temple on the high platform. There were also temples that were dedicated to lesser deities. These were smaller, without platforms, and were usually also built within the temple precinct.

A novel architectural structure was discovered in Kish. It is a secular building, the first example of a Sumerian structure combining a palace and a fortress.

Sumerian sculpture, in most cases, is represented by small figurines (25–40 cm.) made from local alabaster and other softer stone (limestone, sandstone, etc.). They were usually placed in niches inside the temples. The bodily proportions of these figurines differ according to region. In the northern cities of Lower Mesopotamia they are exaggeratedly tall, whereas in the south they are disproportionately short. They all have highly distorted bodily proportions and emphasize one or two features—most frequently, the eyes, the nose, and the ears. Such figurines were placed in temples probably so that they might pray—as proxies—for those who placed them there. These figurines did not have to be actual portraits of their owners, as was the case in Egypt, where the development of portrait sculpture was affected by the requirement of magic. (Otherwise, the "double" might not know its body.) In Lower Mesopotamia a short identifying inscription on the statuette was considered to be more than sufficient. The deliberate emphasis of facial traits probably served a magical purpose: large ears (the Sumerians considered ears to be the receptacles of wisdom); wide-open eyes with a pleading gaze combined with the amazement of a magical enlightenment; and hands folded in a gesture of prayer. These features often give life and expression to the otherwise-clumsy figurines. Apparently, it was more important to convey the inner state rather than the bodily form; the latter was elaborated only to the degree to which it accomplished the intrinsic aim of sculpture: to create an image endowed with supernatural qualities—all-seeing and all-hearing.

In the official art of the Early Dynastic Period, that peculiar—at times, free—interpretation characteristic of the best artistic creations of the Protoliterate Period is no longer found. Sculptured figures of the Early Dynastic Period, even if they represent fertility deities, completely lack sensuousness; they aspire to be superhuman or even inhuman.

The continuously warring nomes had different pantheons and rituals. There was no uniform mythology for the whole country (except that the main function of all deities of the third millennium B.C. was to promote fertility). Therefore, despite the common general type of the sculptures, the representations widely differ in their details. Cylinder seals begin to predominate in glyptic art, depicting heroes and also animals rearing up on their hind legs.

Our knowledge of the goldsmiths' art of the Early Dynastic Period is mainly based on the excavations of the royal tombs at Ur. Objects from these excavations can rightfully be included among the greatest creations in the art of jewelry making.

Art of the Akkadian Period probably can be best characterized by referring to its central motif; namely, that of a deified king, who first appears in history and, later, also in ideology and the arts. In history and in legends he appears as a man of nonroyal ancestry who acquired power, gathered an army, and became the first ruler in the history of the Lower Mesopotamian nomes to rule all of Sumer and Akkad. Artistically, we find a sculptured portrait: a manly head with straight, clearly outlined lips and a small, aquiline nose on a lean face. It is an idealized portrait, possibly even generalized, but clearly expressing the king's physical type. This portrayal clearly reflects the image of the historical and legendary victorious hero, like Sargon of Akkade. (Such is the copper bust from Nineveh, supposedly a likeness of Sargon.)[1] The stele of Naram-Su'en celebrating his victory over the mountain tribes shows the deified king conducting victorious campaigns at the head of his army and ascending a steep slope, ahead of his warriors. He is larger than the other figures, and the symbols of the Sun and the Moon, attesting to his own divinity, radiate above his head. A favorite theme of Akkadian glyptic art is a mighty hero with long curly locks and a beard who fights a lion. The hero's muscles are taut; with one hand he restrains the lion, who is standing on his hind legs with his claws helplessly grasping the air, and with his other he holds a dagger that pierces the predator between the shoulder blades. To a certain extent, the changes occurring in the art of the Akkadian Period may be related to the artistic traditions of the northern centers of Lower Mesopotamia. Scholars occasionally speak of the "realism" of Akkadian art. This is not realism as we understand it today; the attention of the artist was not focused upon the real, even if typical, traits of a given subject, but rather on those that express its essential idea. Nevertheless, the lifelike character of the represented subjects is fascinating.

The interest in the individual that began to emerge in the arts was brought on by events of the kingdom of Akkade which undermined the established traditions of the Sumerian priesthood. The influence of Akkadian art lasted for centuries. It is still evident in the artwork of the last period of Sumerian history, the Third Dynasty of Ur and the Issin dynasty. However, the overall impression left by the objects of

1. The identification is doubtful: artistically and archaeologically, Sargon the Ancient's time belonged to the Early Dynastic III Period. Naram-Su'en is a more likely candidate for the original. Editor's note (IMD).

this later time is that of monotony and stereotype. This also reflects the reality of that time: the seals were made by *gurush*-craftsmen in the huge collective workshops of the Third Dynasty of Ur. With great skill and faith they reproduced, over and over again, the same conventional and prescribed motif—a scene of man worshiping his god.

Sumerian Literature

Today we know more than 150 Sumerian literary works. (Many are preserved in fragmentary form.) Among them we find mythical tales in verse, epic poems, psalms, nuptial love songs related to the sacred marriage rite of deified kings and priestesses, funereal laments, complaints about calamities, hymns honoring kings (beginning with the Third Dynasty of Ur), and literary imitations of royal inscriptions. There are numerous didactic texts: precepts, moral instructions, debates in dialogue form, collections of fables, anecdotes, proverbs, and popular sayings.

Hymns constitute the best represented genre of Sumerian literature. The earliest hymns appear toward the middle of the Early Dynastic Period. Hymns are, without a doubt, among the earliest collective means of addressing the deity. They had to be written down with the utmost punctiliousness. Not a single word could be changed arbitrarily, because not one image in the hymn was fortuitous—each had some specific mythological content.

Hymns were intended to be read aloud by a single priest or by a choir.[2] The emotions that the hymn expressed and induced were collective. Such compositions fully reflected the power inherent in rhythmic language, perceived magically and emotionally. Hymns usually praise a deity and enumerate the deeds, names, and epithets of the deity. Most hymns that have come down to us stem from the school tradition of Nippur[3] and are, in most cases, dedicated to Enlil (the patron god of the city) and to other deities in his entourage. There are also hymns to kings and temples. Hymns could, however, be dedicated only to deified kings, so not all Sumerian kings qualified.

Along with the hymns, laments also belong to texts of public worship. They are very typical of Sumerian literature (especially laments

---

2. The texts were not read directly from clay tablets. They were memorized from the "word" of the scribe. Priests of the third and second millennia B.C. were, as a rule, illiterate.

3. These compositions were recorded and, more often than not, composed in Nippur itself. They provided reading material for students and graduate scribes. The library of Nippur belonged to a school or schools, the so-called *e-dubba* (house of tablets). Although this was a secular institution (it prepared scribes for the civil service), it was natural that in such an important center of worship as Nippur, priests were also very influential in the school teaching.

about national disasters). However, the oldest work of this type that we know of is not related to divine worship—it is a lament about the destruction of Lagash by Lugalzagesi, king of Umma. The lament tells of the calamities inflicted upon Lagash and condemns the culprit. The other laments that have come down to us—those over the fall of Sumer and Akkad, the destructions of Ur, Nippur, Eridu, and Uruk—are all connected with ritual. Such literary works were usually composed when the destroyed cities were being rebuilt or on the occasion of the pulling down of a temple before a new one was to be built in its place.

Among the texts of worship, we find the remarkable series of poems (or religious songs) beginning with "The Descent of Inanna into the Netherworld" and ending with "The Death of Dumuzi," which narrate the myth about the dying and resurrected deities and which are related to corresponding rituals. The goddess of carnal love and animal fertility, Innin (Akkadian Inanna), fell in love with the shepherd god (or shepherd hero), Dumuzi, and took him for her husband. Later, she descended into the Netherworld, apparently, to challenge the power of its queen. Inanna was killed but was returned to life by means of a trick played by the gods. She was allowed to return to earth (where, in the meantime, all living creatures had ceased to reproduce) under one condition: she had to pay a live ransom to the Netherworld. Inanna was revered in different Sumerian cities, and in each one she had a husband or lover. All these deities fell on their knees worshiping her and begging for mercy. Only Dumuzi proudly refused. Dumuzi was surrendered to the evil messengers from the Netherworld. In vain did Utu, the solar god, fulfilling the prayer of Dumuzi's sister, Geshtinanna ("The Vine of Heavens"), turn him into an animal and hide him three times. Dumuzi was finally killed and carried off to the Netherworld. However, Geshtinanna, sacrificing herself, achieves Dumuzi's release back to the living for half a year, while she herself descends into the world of the dead. While the god-shepherd rules the world, the plant-goddess dies. The structure of the myth is much more complex than the simplified versions of the death and resurrection of the fertility deities that are featured in our popular books.

The Nippur tradition also includes nine verse legends about the feats of heroes who, according to the King List, belonged to the semi-legendary First Dynasty of Uruk: Enmerkar, Lugalbanda, and Gilgamesh. It seems that the Nippur tradition began to be created during the Third Dynasty of Ur, whose kings were closely connected with Uruk. The founder of this dynasty traced his family line to Gilgamesh. The Uruk legends were probably included in the Nippur tradition because Nippur was a cultural center, and whatever nome happening to be the seat of a kingdom always desired to be connected with it. During Ur III and the First Dynasty of Issin, a uniform Nippur literary tradition was perpetuated in the *e-dubba*s (schools) of the other cities.

All the heroic legends known to us from those times were at the stage of forming series or cycles, a process typical of epics (e.g., the grouping of heroes by their birthplace is one stage in such a serialization). However, these stories are too heterogeneous to be easily grouped together as epics. The compositions stem from different periods; some are more finished and perfect (like the remarkable poem about Lugalbanda and the monstrous eagle) and some less so. It is very difficult to determine, even approximately, when these stories were composed; some of the motifs could be later additions. The legends may have undergone transformations over the centuries. In any case, it is clear that they constitute an early literary genre that eventually developed into the epic. The hero of such compositions is not yet the typical epic hero, monumental in his proportions and often tragic but, rather, the lucky lad of a magical fairy tale, related to gods but not a god himself; or he is a powerful king with certain divine features.

Historians of literature often contrast the heroic epics (or their precursors) with the so-called mythical epics (in the former, the heroes are men; in the latter, gods). Such a classification is not applicable to Sumerian literature, in which the image of the fighting deity is less typical than that of the mortal hero. In addition to the above-mentioned compositions, two more epic or pre-epic tales with divine heroes are known. One tells about the fight of the goddess Innin (Inanna) with the personification of the Netherworld—"Mount Ebekh," as it is called in the text. The other describes the war fought by the god Ninurta against the evil demon Asak, also an inhabitant of the Netherworld. At the same time, Ninurta appears as an ancestor-hero. He builds a dike from a huge pile of rocks in order to protect Sumer from the waters of the Primeval Ocean that spill over the fields, and so diverts them into the Tigris.

More common to Sumerian literature are the so-called etiological (explanatory) myths, which deal with the creative actions of the gods. Among other things, they describe the creation of the world as the Sumerians visualized it. Sumer probably did not produce comprehensive cosmogonic legends (or, at least, they have not been written down). It is difficult to explain why this is so. It is unlikely that the idea of the struggle of the titanic natural forces (the gods and the giants, the senior and the junior gods, etc.) had no place in the Sumerian apprehension of the world, especially since the motif of the death and the resurrection of nature (when a deity departs for and then returns from the Underworld) was actually well developed in Sumerian mythology, as shown by the stories of Innin-Inanna and Dumuzi and of other gods, such as Enlil.

The arrangement of life on earth—the establishment of order and prosperity—was probably the most favored subject in Sumerian poetry. Such compositions include stories about the creation of gods, whose duty it was to supervise the earthly order, assign divine duties, establish the divine hierarchy, populate the earth with living beings, and even to create the various farming tools. The principal deities acting as creators are usually Enki and Enlil.

Many etiological myths are structured in the form of dialogues between representatives of various branches of the economy and even between various objects in daily life, each trying to prove its superiority over the other. The Sumerian *e-dubba* played a large role in launching this literary genre, which is typical of many later Oriental literatures. We know little about this school in its early days; we only know that it did exist. (Many didactic aids from the Protoliterate Period are available.) The *e-dubba* became a clearly defined institution at least as early as the third millennium B.C. Its basic aim was purely practical: the school prepared scribes, surveyors, and other such professionals. As the school developed, its teaching became more universal, so that toward the end of the third and beginning of the second millennium B.C., the *e-dubba* became the academic center of its time. All the existing branches of knowledge were taught: mathematics, grammar, singing, music, and law. The studies included learning by rote lists of medical, botanical, geographical, pharmacological, legal terms (also laws), etc., as well as lists (catalogues) of literary compositions.

Most of the compositions mentioned above have come down to us in the form of texts written down by teachers or pupils at school. But there are also some literary texts specifically called "*e-dubba* texts." These are literary essays describing life at school and its rules and didactic works (precepts, moral admonitions, and instructions). Directed primarily at students, they frequently took the form of verse dialogues, but some were texts of folk wisdom, aphorisms, proverbs, anecdotes, fables, and sayings. (The only known example of a Sumerian fairy tale in prose is an *e-dubba* text.)

We can infer the richness and variety of Sumerian literature even from this short summary. This tremendously diverse material, stemming from different times (most of it was written down at the very end of the third or, perhaps, in the beginning of the second millennium B.C.), preserved much of the style of oral literary art. The basic device of most of the mythical epic and pre-epic stories is a continuous reiteration of the same dialogues, which are couched in the same words but are delivered between different interlocutors in succession.

This was not merely the typical three-fold repetition of the epics and fairy tales (in Sumerian literature, this repetition is sometimes nine-fold) but, most importantly, an aid to memory. This device obviously was inherited from the oral transmission of myths and poems, a feature of rhythmical and magical speech, reminiscent of the invocations of the shamans. The compositions, mostly constructed from monologues and repetitive dialogues, where the action is slow, appear to us as loose, crude, and thus imperfect (though surely the ancients did not regard them as such). If a story written on a clay tablet was intended as a kind of synopsis to guide a storyteller's memory, why was it necessary to repeat the same sentence nine times over? This is even stranger because the written tablet was heavy and unwieldy. This fact alone should suggest the need for brevity and conservation of space (which actually is taken into account in Akkadian literature toward the middle of the second millennium b.c.). All this suggests that Sumerian literature, to a considerable degree, was nothing more than a record of oral literature. The writers did not intend to deviate from the spoken word, which they set in clay, preserving all the stylistic characteristics and peculiarities of the spoken poetic word.

Nevertheless, it is important to note that Sumerian "literati"—the scribes—had no intention of reproducing in writing all the oral lore and all its genres. The selection was conditioned by the needs of the school and, in part, of the cult. Parallel to the written protoliterature, oral compositions continued to exist, but they have remained unrecorded. The spoken art might perhaps have been even richer than the written.

It would be erroneous to conclude that the incipient Sumerian literature lacked artistic and emotional value. The metaphoric way of thinking itself fostered imaginative speech and so did the use of parallelisms, a typical feature of ancient Oriental poetry. Sumerian poems are actually rhythmical speech. They have no rigid meter; we fail to find any indication of qualitative versus quantitative counts of foot, pauses, or stressed syllables. The main poetic devices used to emphasize rhythm were reiteration, rhythmical enumeration of divine epithets, sequential anaphoras of the first words of a line for several lines, and so on. All these are actually attributes of oral poetry, whose emotional effect was here preserved in written literature.

The written Sumerian literature also reflected the evolution from primitive ideology to that of the new class society.

When examining ancient Sumerian texts, especially mythological compositions, we are struck by the lack of "high-style" poetic images. Sumerian gods are not simply earthly creatures on a grand scale. Their world is not the world of human feelings and deeds. But it is easy to see how primitive people, with their sense of powerlessness in the face of greater, indomitable natural forces, seeing themselves helpless, at the mercy of these forces, could well have imagined the gods as beings who created living things from the soil under their fingernails, as beings who could and would, on a whim, send a flood to destroy all humanity. And the Sumerian Netherworld? From the available descriptions, it appears to be a particularly chaotic and hopeless place. There is no judge of the dead, no scales with which to weigh people's deeds. There are little or no illusions about "justice after death." An ideology that was to counter this natural feeling of horror and hopelessness was, however, itself at first rather helpless.

The written compositions mimicked the subjects and forms of primitive oral poetry. As the ideology of the class society developed and gradually came to dominate in Lower Mesopotamia, the content of the literature also changed. It began to develop new forms and genres, and the gap between the written and "oral" literatures grew wider and became quite obvious. Already at the later stage of development of Sumerian society, the didactic literature and the serialization of mythological subjects show a growing independence, exhibiting different directions of development for the written word. This new stage in the literature was, however, elaborated no longer by the Sumerians but by their cultural heirs—the Babylonians (Akkadians).

6

The Predynastic Period and the Early and the Old Kingdoms in Egypt

I. V. Vinogradov[†]

The Emergence of the State in Egypt

We do not know for certain whether Sumer or Egypt was the first cradle of civilization. However, we have reason to believe that the civilization that arose in Northeast Africa on the shores of the great Nile may have been the more ancient.

The boundaries of ancient Egypt are very distinctly outlined by nature: in the south (in the vicinity of today's Aswan, some 1,200 kilometers from the Mediterranean) lay the almost impassable First Cataract of the Nile; in the west the Libyan plateau's sandy ledges trace a line relatively close to the Nile; to the east the Nile Valley borders on lifeless and rocky mountain spurs. Below the First Cataract, the Nile flows directly north along a narrow and long valley (Upper Egypt). Its width varies from 1 to 20 kilometers. Some 200 kilometers from the mouth of the Nile, the river divides into several branches, and the valley widens, forming the famous Nile Delta (Lower Egypt). The source of the Nile, located thousands of kilometers from Egypt, was unknown to the Egyptians. But it is here we find the reasons for the specific hydrological regime of the river, the peculiarities of which exerted an enormous influence on many aspects of Egyptian life for millennia. Two thousand kilometers south of the First Cataract, not far from the present city of Khartoum (the capital of Sudan), two rivers merge to form the Nile: the White Nile and the Blue Nile. The swift Blue Nile flows from Lake Tana, high in the mountains of Ethiopia. The quiet and wide White Nile passes through a chain of large lakes and boggy plains in Central Africa. In the spring, when snow melts rapidly in the mountains of Ethiopia and when tropical Africa has its rainy season, the swollen waters of the Blue and White Nile carry downstream tiny suspended particles of mineral substances from the mountains and organic residues from the lush tropical vegetation. Toward the middle of July, the high water reaches the southern borders of Egypt. At times, the flood carries ten times more water than normal, and having overcome the bottleneck of the narrow straits at the First Cataract, it gradually inundates all of Egypt. The flood peaks in August and September, when the water level rises 14 meters above normal in the south and 8–10 meters in the north. In the middle of November, the waters recede rapidly, and the river returns to its normal banks. During this four-month-long deluge, the Nile deposits suspended mineral and organic particles over the entire flooded region.

Over the span of thousands of years, the Nile's uninterrupted annual cycle produced the alluvial soil of Egypt. The once narrow and rocky valley of Upper Egypt and the plain of Lower Egypt, which at one time was a bay of the Mediterranean, are now covered with a deep layer of fluvial deposits—the soft and porous Nile silt. This fertile, easily tillable soil is the country's primary resource and the reason for its secure and plentiful harvests. The soil, ready for plowing, actually glitters as if it were coated with a black varnish. The ancient inhabitants called the entire country Kemet, "the Black." The name is quite appropriate, because it was the blackness of its alluvial soil that made the Nile Valley the only region able to sustain human life in the severe heat and aridity of North Africa. Although surrounded by hostile, arid, and rocky red deserts, this fertile land—created and watered by the Nile—provided the ideal conditions for people to settle and sustain themselves by irrigation agriculture.

The wetlands of the Nile at first must have appeared inhospitable to the first settlers. The region was covered with thick, impenetrable groves of Nile reed (papyrus) and acacia that grew along the banks of the river; the vast swamps of the Delta lowland were swarming with insects, predators, and poisonous snakes; and large numbers of crocodiles and hippopotamuses thrived in the river. The Nile itself was indomitable during the flood season, when its waters would sweep everything in their path. It is therefore not surprising that the first people settled in the valley proper only during the Neolithic Age, when they already had sufficiently effective stone tools at their disposal and had acquired various skills. It can be surmised that they came here only in order to escape harsher environmental conditions.

Ten to twelve thousand years ago the climate of North Africa was less arid than it is today. The ice that had covered part of Europe and Asia during the end of the Ice Age was finally melting. Winds carried moisture toward North Africa, producing abundant rainfall. Much of today's deserts were savannahs, covered with tall grasses that sustained abundant animal life. Tribes of hunters, who were at the Mesolithic and Early Neolithic stage of development, inhabited the area of today's Sahara. These were the people who made the rock drawings of elephants, ostriches, antelopes, and buffalos, as well as lively hunting scenes. None of these animals are desert dwellers; numerous wadis (dry riverbeds that formerly fed the Nile from the east and west) provide evidence of a milder climate in the past.

Toward the fifth millennium B.C. the moist northern winds weakened, and North Africa became increasingly more arid; the water table dropped, and the savannahs gradually transformed themselves into desert. By that time some of the hunting tribes had learned to domesticate animals and had become herdsmen. The onsetting drought forced these tribes to migrate toward the tributaries of the Nile, which, meanwhile, were drying up. Archaeologists have discovered numerous campsites of Stone Age tribes along the wadis.

The desert continued to expand. As the last of the Nile tributaries dried up, people were forced to move closer and closer to the edge of the Nile. The Neolithic Age saw the settlement of pastoralist tribes at the edge of the Nile Valley and the first attempts at agriculture.

Archaeological excavations of Late Neolithic settlements of the sixth to fourth millennia B.C. show that their inhabitants led a completely sedentary life. That they engaged in farming is attested by the hand grinding stones, wooden scythes with flint teeth, and barley and emmer grains found by archaeologists. (Emmer was an early variety of wheat.) Discoveries of the bones of cattle, sheep, and pigs testify to the existence of stock breeding. Hunting, fishing, and gathering wild plants were also important activities. The inhabitants of these settlements, which were usually located along the edge of the valley, still shied away from the Nile and did not attempt to tame the river.

With the advent of the Chalcolithic Age and the invention of copper tools, people began to move resolutely into the Nile Valley. The sedimentation from thousands of annual floods raised the banks of the Nile above the level of the actual valley floor, forming a backslope away from the river and allowing water to flow naturally into the valley during flood seasons. In order to tame the river and to control the water flow into the valley, people strengthened the riverbanks, erected dikes along the river, and built transverse earthen dams from the banks to the foothills, so that the water would be retained in the fields, allowing the silt to settle and the earth to be soaked with sufficient moisture. Drainage canals were also dug in order to route the water back into the Nile before the sowing season.

These were the beginnings of the development of a basin irrigation system during the first half of the fourth millennium B.C.; they laid the foundation for the country's irrigation system for thousands of years to come, until the first half of our century. The ancient irrigation system was dependent upon the hydrological pattern of the Nile and ensured one yearly harvest, which, under the prevailing conditions, ripened during the winter (sowing beginning in November, after the flood); it was reaped in early spring. Plentiful and stable harvests were ensured because the yearly silt deposits guaranteed an annual regeneration of the Egyptian soil. In the heat of the sun the deposits produced the nitrogenous and phosphorous compounds necessary for the following harvest. Consequently, Egyptian farmers did not have to maintain the fertility of their fields by artificial means; the soil did not require any additional mineral or organic nutrients. The harnessing of the river and its adaptation to human needs was a long process that probably lasted throughout the fourth millennium.

Each community and tribe that dared to descend into the Nile Valley and to settle on one of the few existing elevations—inaccessible to the floodwaters—immediately embarked on a heroic struggle with nature. The gained experience and habits, the organized effort, and the relentless work of an entire tribe were eventually crowned with the success of mastering a small portion of the valley. This resulted in the creation of local irrigation systems—the base for the economy of the community that had built it.

It is likely that in the course of creating the irrigation system, important changes in the social life of the clan or tribal community also occurred. This metamorphosis came with the change in living conditions, work habits, and production organization in the distinctive environment of the Nile Valley. Since we have virtually no information about the events of that time, we are forced to reconstruct them quite hypothetically. It is most probable that the social structure consisted of communities of neighbors.[1] The traditional functions of tribal chiefs and priests were also in the process of changing. The organization and management of the complex irrigation economy was now their responsibility, and they, together with their closest associates, took hold of the economic advantages giving them power. Inevitably, this led to the development of a social stratification based on property status. The group prevailing in the economy needed to ensure the preservation of a social structure favorable to itself. Ways to maintain political supremacy over the majority of community members must have evolved, undoubtedly influencing the character of the entire community itself. The conditions necessary for the development of irrigation systems were responsible for the creation of a specific type of aggregation in the framework of each irrigation and economic unit. Such an aggregation would combine the characteristics of a rural community with those of an incipient state. Traditionally, such social organizations are given the Greek name "nomes."

1. No traces of autonomous village communities during the historical period of pharaonic Egypt have been discovered.

Each independent nome had its own territory, which was confined to the local irrigation system and represented a single economic unit. It had an administrative center—a walled city where the monarch resided with his retinue. The city also housed a temple of the local deity.

There were about forty such nomes by the time the united Egyptian state was first formed. In the narrow valley of Upper Egypt each nome, located on the right or left bank of the Nile, bordered directly only on northern and southern neighbors. The nomes of Lower Egypt were often separated from each other by marshes. Available sources do not provide us with sufficient information to trace the history of the nomes before they became part of a united Egypt and served as its local administrative and economic units. However, we do know that the nomes maintained their distinctiveness and tendency toward isolation for many centuries. Symbolic images in relief on flat shale tablets that were preserved from that time depict scenes of internecine strife between the nomes. We see bloody battles on land and water, processions of prisoners tied with ropes, and captured herds of long-horned cattle and sheep and goats. This long and persistent struggle resulted in the subjugation of weaker nomes by their stronger neighbors. These wars produced large unions of nomes in Upper and Lower Egypt that were headed by the ruler of the strongest, victorious nome. Of course, such conquests do not preclude the possibility of the peaceful alliance of some individual nomes with their stronger neighbors.

Finally, some time during the second half of the fourth millennium, the nomes of the south and the north formed the kingdoms of Upper and Lower Egypt. One of the southernmost Upper (southern) Egyptian nomes, centered in the city of Hieraconpolis,[2] united the Upper Egyptian nomes. The task of uniting the north was undertaken by one of the nomes in the western Delta, centered in the city of Buto. The kings of Upper Egypt wore a high white headdress, and the kings of Lower Egypt, a red crown. With the creation of a unified Egypt, the symbol of royal power for the duration of ancient Egyptian history became a red and white crown.

2. Because ancient Egyptian writing (in contrast to the Mesopotamian cuneiform script) does not express vowels, scholars must reconstruct the ancient pronunciation of Egyptian words and proper names by indirect methods—mainly from the pronunciation of Egyptian names in languages of other nations in later periods (second to first millennia B.C.). These reconstructions are very unreliable; most Egyptologists continue to use a conventional pronunciation, fully aware of its imprecision. In this book we use such conventional spellings of most Egyptian proper names. Some names are given in their ancient Greek equivalents, and some cities are called by the names that the Greeks and Romans gave them during later antiquity: Memphis (in the conventional Egyptological reading it is Men-nefer), Thebes (Waset according to the conventional Egyptological pronunciation), Buto, Hieraconpolis, Heliopolis, etc.

The history of both kingdoms is almost unknown; we are acquainted with only a few dozen royal names, mostly from Upper Egypt. We know very little indeed about the fierce struggle between the two kingdoms for hegemony, a struggle that lasted many centuries and ended with the victory of the cohesive and economically strong Upper Egypt. It is thought that this victory took place at the end of the fourth millennium, although our chronology for early Egypt remains very unreliable.

The efforts of the individual nomes, and even those of larger unions of nomes, were not sufficient for the proper maintenance of the economic structure of a country that comprised separate, unconnected or marginally connected irrigation systems. The merger of several nomes and, eventually, of all of Egypt into one state (which was accomplished as a result of lengthy and bloody wars) made possible the improvement of the irrigation system, the organization of its regular and effective maintenance, the widening of canals, the strengthening of the dikes, the development of the Delta marshlands by common efforts, and, generally, a rational use of the waters of the Nile. All this was an absolutely necessary foundation for the future development of Egypt, and it was made possible only by the country's unification under a single central administration.

Nature itself seemed to have made Upper and Lower Egypt economically complementary. Whereas the narrow valley of Upper Egypt was almost entirely used for fields, making land for grazing very scarce, the wide expanse of the Delta and its land reclaimed from swamps could also be used for herds. Later documents attest to the Egyptian practice of sending cattle, at a certain time of the year, from Upper Egypt to the pastures of Lower Egypt, which became the livestock-breeding center of Egypt. Moreover, most of Egypt's orchards and vineyards were also concentrated in the north.

The long, so-called Predynastic Period of Egyptian history began when the first farming cultures appeared close to the Nile and lasted until the unification of the state. The groundwork for the Egyptian state was laid during the Predynastic Period and was economically based on the organization of irrigation agriculture throughout the valley. Toward the end of the Predynastic Period in Egypt, writing was invented, primarily, perhaps, to serve the economic needs of the emerging state. This development marks the beginning of the history of dynastic Egypt toward the end of the fourth millennium.

The people who developed the Nile Valley and created, so early in history, such a unique and great civilization spoke Egyptian, a language that is now extinct. The first written records in this language come from the end of the Predynastic Period; the last hieroglyphic inscription is dated to the fourth century A.D.[3] The Egyptian language belonged to a branch of the Afrasian (Afro-Asiatic or Hamito-Semitic) language family. However, many indirect data indicate that the tribes that settled in the Nile Valley were ethnically heterogeneous and spoke different dialects. Naturally, this ethnic heterogeneity gradually disappeared over the millennia.

The physical appearance of Egyptians of the Predynastic Period is well documented. Multicolored reliefs and wall paintings and statues show them to have been of average height and slender build with broad shoulders and straight black hair (but often these are wigs). Traditionally, in dynastic times, Egyptian men are painted in brick red and women in yellow. We also find numerous depictions of other tribes and peoples who were in frequent contact with the people of the Nile Valley. In the west their neighbors were the light-skinned, blue-eyed Libyans. In the east there were tall people with yellowish-tan skin, prominent noses, and thick facial hair, including short beards, typical of Western Asia. Their southern neighbors, who inhabited Ethiopia on the Nile,[4] or Nubia, were of a dark violet complexion. Representatives of the Negroid tribes of southern Sudan are depicted with black, curly hair.

The periodization of the history of dynastic Egypt, which covers approximately the thirtieth century to the end of the fourth century B.C., from the semilegendary King Menes to Alexander the Great, is closely connected with Manethonian tradition. Manetho was an Egyptian priest who lived in Egypt shortly after Alexander the Great's campaigns. He wrote a two-volume *History of Egypt* in Greek. Unfortunately, only quotations from his book remain, the earliest of which are found in works by historians from the first century A.D. But even these bits, although frequently distorted, are extremely valuable in that they are fragments of a work written by a man about his own country and its great history, based on original documents that were easily accessible to him and are lost to us.

Manetho divides the history of dynastic Egypt into three broad periods: the Old, the Middle, and the New Kingdoms. Each of these kingdoms is divided into dynasties, ten for each kingdom—thirty in all. Manetho's division of Egyptian history into three periods reflects certain actual qualitative stages in the development of the country, but his uniform distribution of dynasties among the kingdoms is con-

3. The later Egyptian language, called Coptic, coexisted with Arabic in Egypt during the Middle Ages and survived in some regions until the beginning of the modern age.

4. In ancient times the name Ethiopia (Kush) designated today's northern Sudan, not the contemporary state of Ethiopia.

ventional. Although many of Manetho's dynasties actually comprise members of one ruling family, some of them include several unrelated ruling houses. In one case, two royal brothers were placed in two different dynasties. Regardless of such problems, scholars continue to adhere to the convenient Manethonian dynastic scheme. A few corrections have since been introduced into the periodization of ancient Egyptian history: the first two Manethonian dynasties are treated separately as the Early Kingdom, and the last ones, starting with the Twenty-first Dynasty, are classified as the Late Kingdom.

The Early Kingdom

The Early Kingdom of Egypt includes the First and Second Manethonian dynasties, which cover more than two hundred years of history (ca. 3000–2800 B.C.). Manetho regards King Menes, founder of the First Dynasty, as the unifier of Egypt. He was probably the same king who is identified in the most ancient Egyptian chronicle as Hor Aha ("Horus the Champion").[5] However, he was not the first ruler in Upper Egypt who claimed to rule over all of Egypt. The so-called Na'rmer tablet, found during the excavations at Hieraconpolis, gives a symbolic account of this king's victory over the inhabitants of Lower Egypt. Na'rmer was one of the last predynastic rulers in Upper Egypt. The relief on this tablet depicts him triumphantly wearing the unified crown of Upper and Lower Egypt. It seems that some of Na'rmer's predecessors were also inclined to consider themselves conquerors of the north and pretended to the united crown. The reason that Manetho placed Menes at the top of his list of Egyptian kings is probably due to the fact that a stable annalistic tradition began in Egypt under the reign of this particular king. But under Menes, as well as under his predecessors and even his successors, the unity of the country was not finally achieved. For a long time, the subjugated Lower Egypt refused to accept its defeat, and during almost the entire period of the Early Kingdom bloody battles continued to be fought there.

The kings of the first two dynasties were apparently natives of the Upper Egyptian nome of Thinis, situated in the middle of Upper Egypt. In the vicinity of this nome, near the city of Abydos (which later became the center of worship of Osiris, the god of the Dead), archaeologists discovered royal tombs of the Early Kingdom: those of Djer, Semerkhet, Ka'a, and others. The written names of these kings

---

5. Horus is the name of one of the principal Egyptian solar deities and was represented as a falcon. The king was considered to be the incarnation of Horus and bore, in addition to his own name, a special "Horus" name.

included the image of the Falcon god, Horus. This god was the patron of most of the rulers of the Early Kingdom.

We can assess the development of the productive forces by the abundant finds of tools in the Early Dynastic tombs. The artifacts are mainly of copper: flat-work axes, knives, adzes, harpoons, fishing hooks, saws, blades for wooden hoes, battle axes with rounded cutting edges, daggers, cups, and vessels of different shapes and uses. In addition to the copper items, many stone (mainly flint) tools and objects of daily use were also found, as were wooden work tools, ivory objects, Egyptian faience,[6] ornaments, and different types of ceramics made before the invention of the potter's wheel. The basic construction materials were adobe bricks and wood; the use of stone was still very limited.

Thus, Egyptians of the Early Kingdom lived in the Chalcolithic or Copper-Stone Age. The irrigation system of the country was already functioning and was constantly being improved and expanded; therefore, all the natural conditions offered by the Nile Valley could be fully exploited. This led to an enormous growth of labor productivity, especially in agriculture, in spite of the society's low level of technical development. Surplus produce was generated, and the potential for its accumulation and utilization led to all the usual consequences.

The fact that the Egyptian population was able to find all the necessities in the valley itself, or not far from it, was also favorable for the country's early progress. The Nile Valley contained a large variety of stone, including the soft and easily workable limestone. The acacia groves, still extensive at that time, compensated to some degree for the continuous shortage of construction timber, which, since very ancient times, was delivered to Egypt by sea from the Lebanon. The papyrus groves provided a seemingly inexhaustible source of raw materials. Papyrus was widely used in Egypt to manufacture a sort of paper, as well as for wattle to make boats that were used to fish and hunt waterfowl in the quiet backwaters of the Nile Delta. Young papyrus shoots were even used for food. The Nile was famous for its abundance of fish—the basic nonvegetable food of the Egyptians.

Since predynastic times, Egyptians extracted copper from the mines in the Sinai Peninsula. Gold was mined east of the valley, in the desert, and later in the south, in Ethiopia on the Nile.

The principal cultivated grain in Egypt was barley, which partially replaced emmer.[7] Livestock raising reached a new level of advance-

6. Egyptian faience is a special, hardened, composite mass with a glazed surface, usually of a light blue collar.

7. Emmer and spelt are very similar species of wheat and among the oldest cultivated cereals. Emmer was later replaced by more productive species.

ment. Ancient sources indicate the existence of several kinds of horned cattle, sheep, goats, donkeys, and pigs. Vegetable gardening and viticulture were also being developed, especially in the Delta. The linen found in the tombs of that time testifies to the cultivation of flax and to a well-developed weaving industry. Apart from their agricultural and farming activities, Egyptians also fished, hunted, and raised waterfowl.

The formation and consolidation of a unified state is a lengthy and complex process. In Egypt it took practically the entire period of the Early Kingdom. The unification of Egypt obviously brought important changes to the structure of the country's administration. The management of the vast irrigation systems—their expansion, maintenance, and improvement—became the responsibility of royal officials.

The Early Kingdom was the epoch when the single-state machinery of Egypt was developed. Inscriptions from the First and Second dynasties abound with terms for numerous officials and official posts. Some of these had existed earlier, and others were newly established in response to the increasing complexity of economic and administrative tasks, in the capital as well as in the nomes, during the entire span of the Early Kingdom. These changes apparently attest to a search for the best ways to manage the production, accounting, and distribution of goods.

Our knowledge of the social structure prevailing in Egypt during the Early Kingdom is very sparse. We know that there was a large royal economy and that it had many branches; it included arable and grazing land, vineyards and orchards, a food administration, craft workshops, and shipyards. Impressions of seals from the royal economy have reached us not only from the royal tombs of the First and Second dynasties but also from the tombs of nobles and of a number of lower functionaries, who apparently received allowances in kind from the royal economy. It is reasonable to assume that there must have been other, nonroyal economies that existed side by side with the royal, but we have practically no information about them. However, judging by the lavish burials of the elite, which were not much different from the royal tombs, it seems that these prominent people, originating in the nomes and being closely connected with them, maintained considerable economic independence and probably still disposed of significant inherited estates in their respective nomes.

We have no information about the people who worked in the royal economy and in the economies of the elite, nor do we have any data about the exploitation methods to which the workers, drawn into these economies, were subjected. The later period of the Old Kingdom provides much more information regarding the state of the workers. An examination of the tombs from the First and Second dynasties leads to the conclusion that there already existed considerable inequality in wealth. Apart from the rich tombs of the elite, we also find more modest burials of persons who apparently held positions within the economies of the king and the noblemen. Very modest tombs of people from the lower levels of Egyptian society have been discovered as well. These burials are simply shallow pits on the edge of the desert.

Little is known about the historic events that took place in these remote centuries. The kings of the first two dynasties fought continuous wars against the Libyan herdsmen and captured many animals, as well as numerous prisoners. The Egyptian army also operated in the Sinai mountains, where it defended the Egyptian copper mines from the incursions of Western Asiatic tribes. The Egyptians also invaded the land beyond the First Cataract—Nubia. But most of the available information tells us about battles in Egypt itself, where the struggle with the recalcitrant and rebellious north lasted until the end of the Second Dynasty. The "White Walls"—the city of Memphis—whose founding is attributed to Menes, played an important and strategic role in this period of war. The city was situated on the west bank of the Nile in Upper Egypt, at the opening of the valley into Lower Egypt. From this fortress the southerners could rule over the Delta. The many years of war in the north eventually culminated in the south's final victory during the rule of King Kha'sekhemui of the Second Dynasty, who brutally suppressed the last uprisings in the Delta. He symbolically commemorated his victory on the pedestals of his two statues, where he inscribed the number of enemy dead in the last battle; according to the inscription, they numbered about fifty thousand.

Some sort of interdynastic struggle also took place during the Early Kingdom. It was marked by a change in the patron god of the royal throne: the god Horus (the divine patron of the Early Kingdom rulers) was replaced by the god Seth. Seth (or Sutekh), the god of the Desert, was Horus's eternal rival. Later on, a compromise was reached by which the names of Horus and Seth appeared together in the throne name (title) of one of the Second Dynasty kings. But Horus eventually triumphed over his enemy, and Seth's name was subsequently eliminated from the throne name of the kings.

The defeat of the north and the end of the dynastic squabbles resulted in the final unification of the country, beginning a new epoch in Egyptian history—the Old Kingdom. The "White Walls" of Menes—the city of Memphis—became the capital of the unified kingdom. According to a widely accepted opinion, the Greek word *Aigyptos* and today's "Egypt" were derived from one of the names of this city: conventionally vocalized *Het-ka-Ptaḥ,*[8] meaning "Estate of the Double of Ptaḥ," the principal god of the capital city.[9]

The Old Kingdom

The epoch of the Old Kingdom (from about the beginning of the twenty-eighth century B.C. to the middle of the twenty-third century B.C.) covers a five-hundred-year period of Egyptian history. It is the time of the Third, Fourth, Fifth, and Sixth Manethonian dynasties. The Egypt of the Old Kingdom evolved from the Early Kingdom but represented a qualitatively new stage in the development of the country. The focal event was the final consolidation of the country into one single political unit. There were no substantial changes with regard to production tools: the changes here were mainly quantitative. But even the sharp increase in the number of copper tools, among other things, caused great changes in construction; soft limestone began to be used on a grand scale as a building material. The limestone was cut up into blocks by copper saws that were made from special forge-hardened ingot copper. Large numbers of various copper tools and their small-scale replicas were found in Old Kingdom tombs. The abundance of copper tools did not, however, preclude the existence of stone tools, which were still in use, as were wooden implements such as hoes, scythes with flint teeth, and primitive plows.

The complete unification of Egypt and the more effective organization of production within the unified land contributed enormously to a general improvement in all branches of the Egyptian economy.

The texts of the Old Kingdom shed the first rays of light on some important aspects of social relationships in the Egyptian economy. Numerous documents confirm the existence of a royal estate, temple estates, and, especially, of economies belonging to private persons—nobles or dignitaries—who occupied high positions at the royal court and in the administration (in the capital as well as in the local nomes). Innumerable colored reliefs, accompanied by explanatory inscriptions, cover the inner walls of the impressive tombs of noblemen. They disclose a picture of life as it may have been on the large estates, "the own house" (*per djet*), of the dignitaries. The images found in the tombs are closely connected with the Egyptian cult and reflect the Egyptian concept of the Hereafter as an eternal continuation of earthly life;

8. Actually, at least in the later period, the name of the city was pronounced *He-ku-Ptah.*

9. In the belief of the Egyptians, the *Ka,* or more exactly *ku'* ("double"), was a magical substance of any image. It was thought to possess its own independent existence.

hence, they provide detailed illustrations of normal everyday activities, yielding a picture of the real economic situation surrounding the deceased.

The reliefs tell us about the dignitary himself and his immediate household. He is usually shown as the head of an extended family, including his wife and children, brothers and sisters, his elderly mother, other relatives, and other household members. Here we also see numerous servants, singers, dancers, barbers, fan-bearers, and bodyguards. It is interesting to note that the junior members of the family served the master of the estate together with the household servants and sometimes participated in the running of his economy.

The vast economic establishment of a dignitary consisted of a main estate and many other properties (single households and villages) situated in different parts of the country, in Upper as well as in Lower Egypt. A large staff of different kinds of employees—scribes, foremen, accounting clerks, keepers of documents, and managers—all reported to a "House Superintendent," or manager, who directed the entire economic life of "the own house" and controlled the labor of a multitude of people who worked in the different branches of the master's economy. These included farmers, herdsmen, fishermen, bird keepers, gardeners, orchard keepers, bakers, beer brewers, coppersmiths, jewelers, potters, stonecutters, weavers, sandalmakers, carpenters, joiners, shipbuilders, artists, and sculptors. The vivid reliefs depict all these specialists in the process of going about their daily chores in the field, in the pastures, in the workshops, and in the master's house.

During the Old Kingdom, workers in the fields were typically organized into gangs employed in sowing and harvesting the crops. As far as we can judge from the scenes of farm work and from the explanatory texts, the grain for sowing was supplied to the farmhands from the master's granaries, and the draft animals (usually two long-horned cows per worker) were assigned from his herd. The harvested grain belonged to the master and was hauled to his threshing floor on donkeys and later stored in the granaries.

Detachments of workers were also assigned to hauling heavy objects and loading ships (the main mode of transportation in Egypt) and were engaged in many other tasks; when necessary, they could be transferred from one type of work to another.

The industrial production of a dignitary's economy was concentrated in common workshops (the "Hall of Masters") where artisans specializing in diverse crafts were employed. Only the men worked here; the women worked in separate weaving workshops. (There was also a special food complex where various provisions were prepared.) In all crafts, there was a division of labor: often each artifact was treated by different craftsmen at various stages of production. All the means of production in the workshop belonged to the owner of the economy, and all the goods produced by the craftsmen went into his warehouse. Consequently, all those who worked in a dignitary's economy were dispossessed of property in tools and means of production.

According to the tomb reliefs, the workers in the noble's household economy received their food rations—grain, fish, bread, vegetables, beer, etc.—from the master's warehouses, orchards, cattle ranges, fisheries, granaries, and food-processing shops. The pictures show farmers being issued clothes—a short apron—and a special ointment, which the farm workers used to protect their exposed bodies from the hot sun when toiling in the fields, almost naked, under the cloudless Egyptian sky. We do not know whether the master's laborers had any other sources of subsistence with which to supplement their rations.

However, the same tomb pictures show us retail markets where the same laborers seem to be exchanging goods. We see a lively trade in cereals, bread, vegetables, and fish, exchanged for fishing hooks, sandals, mirrors, beads, and other articles. Price was measured in units of grain. The existence of such markets suggests that at least some workers disposed of a certain surplus of food products and that probably craft production consisted in part of a system of fixed tasks. The work norm, no doubt, was very high and unlikely to have been below the full productive capacity of a craftsman. Egyptian workers frequently were driven on with lashes or canes. But it is probable that any worker able to fulfill his assigned task (productive norm) could produce a surplus that, by right, was his to dispose of at will. He could barter his personal savings at the market in exchange for the items he needed. Workers who were involved in the dignitaries' economies were thus entitled to some personal movable property. As far as we can judge from the relatively scanty information we have, the royal and temple economies of the Old Kingdom were organized along the same lines.

Keeping in mind the undoubtedly important role played by the economies of the dignitaries in the overall economy of Egypt during the Old Kingdom, we must now attempt to explain their relationship to the royal (state) economy. Egyptian texts teach us that "the own house" of a nobleman was something "external" with respect to the "internal," or state, economy. A dignitary's "own house" included lands and properties inherited from his parents. It was usually the eldest son of the family head who inherited the estate upon his father's death. This was why the dignitary's younger brothers had to work in his household and were sustained at the expense of his economy. Moreover, a dignitary could own properties inherited from other persons, as well as obtained as a "reward"; that is, purchased property. We get the impression that the inherited and purchased properties and lands were the dignitary's personal property; he had the right to dispose of it as he wished. It was his "in truth." A portion of it was automatically set aside for the cult of the Hereafter, which required the maintenance of a large staff of funeral priests to serve his tomb.

In addition to this property "in truth," a dignitary also had property "for service," which he did not have the power to dispose of at his own discretion, because it was not his personal property; it could be taken away from him together with his position or post. For this reason, he kept both types of properties clearly separated. Nevertheless, available records indicate that a dignitary's well-being depended primarily on what he received by virtue of his rank, and it is difficult to imagine a dignitary's career during the Old Kingdom as being outside the state service. We must note that Egyptian state ranks were, as a rule, hereditary and passed from father to son, although each of these transfers had to be sanctioned by the king. In this manner, the personal and official aspects of a dignitary's "own house" became closely intertwined. It is not by accident that the Egyptian term for "own" (*djet*) had a broader meaning than ours: it could designate full property rights.[10] But it could also designate property possessed for use by virtue of service.

It is natural that the large staff of production organizers of the royal, temple, and dignitaries' economies—clerks, scribes, accountants, and controllers—had a different status than the people who physically labored in these economies. Many of the first but not the latter held government posts, so that they had land estates and dependent people who worked for them at their disposal. This category must also have included the low and middle levels of temple personnel and the numerous priests connected with the cult of the dead. (The top priestly functions were concentrated in the hands of the royal court and the local provincial administration.) This category could also include sculptors, architects, painters, physicians, and other talented craftsmen who had become wealthy in the royal, temple, and dignitaries' economies. Many burials (some quite rich) of people from this middle level in the society of the second half of the Old Kingdom have been discovered.

The word for slave (*bak*) was known not later than the Early Kingdom. Documents from this period show that slaves could be bought and sold (e.g., a document from the Sixth Dynasty mentions the purchase of slaves); hence, there existed a slave market. For the most part, the slaves were people of Egyptian origin, though some were

10. According to our definition, this consists of one's right to prevent any other person from possessing, using, and disposing of property at one's own will and in one's own interest.

foreigners. It must, however, be conceded that it is difficult to re-construct the mechanism by which persons of Egyptian extraction could have been enslaved under the conditions that prevailed in the Old Kingdom. The predominance of enormous and relatively closed self-sufficient economies, which produced all that was needed from production tools to consumer goods, could not but hinder the development of commodity-money exchange relationships. Given the nature of the economies, there was little reason for the appearance of enslavement for debt, which was typical of some later Near Eastern societies. It is likely that most of the household slaves were descendants of the inhabitants of the Nile Valley who had been captured and enslaved by the victors in the wars between the nomes and between both the early Egyptian states. But there also must have been some means of enslaving fellow countrymen. We know that there was a tendency among high-ranking persons of the second half of the Old Kingdom to broadcast their virtue by bragging that they did not enslave a single Egyptian in their lifetimes. This conscious demonstration of ethics leads us to believe that the possibility of enslaving inhabitants of the Nile Valley was indeed not excluded, although it was clearly considered reprehensible and was possibly banned by the royal authority. Indirect information about the enslavement of Egyptians comes mainly from the end of the Old Kingdom, when the decline of the central power was already being felt.

There is no doubt that the royal, temple, and dignitaries' economies were predominant in the economic structure of the Old Kingdom. Were these large economies the sole organized labor sector in the country or were there other, perhaps quite minor, autonomous private/commercial economies? It is difficult to answer this question on the basis of available Egyptian sources, because all of them refer only to the royal, temple, and dignitaries' economies. It is only on the basis of a few indirect data that we can assume the existence of such an economic sector. For instance, a nobleman who lived around the end of the Third Dynasty apparently bought land from a group of *nisutiu* (plural, "persons belonging to the king"), who therefore must have enjoyed some kind of individual or collective rights to their own land and were able to dispose of it at their discretion. It is possible that some inscriptions of noblemen from the end of the Old Kingdom point to the existence of small individual economies. According to the texts, the dignitaries helped some obviously poor agriculturalists with draft animals and seed during the plowing season. It is difficult to imagine such aid within the framework of the royal and dignitaries' economies, which, as we have mentioned, were based on entirely different principles. Finally, is it possible that, once ruined, such small individual owners became dependent on large estate owners and were

transformed into *bak*-slaves? Was it from among these that the numerous funeral priests were recruited, serving in the dignitaries' cult that
guaranteed the dignitaries' existence in the hereafter? Were there,
perhaps, among the traders in the markets depicted on the tomb wall
paintings, in addition to the workers of the large economies, small individual producers? All this is just speculation. The available material
is too scanty and contradictory to draw any solid conclusions.

The Egyptian state was headed by the king, often called pharaoh.
This term comes to us from the Greek but stems from an ancient
Egyptian (New Kingdom) allegorical royal epithet: *per-'o,* meaning
"big house" (i.e., palace). The king's actual proper name was considered sacred, and its utterance was taboo.

The Egyptian king possessed unlimited economic and political
power and the dignity of high priest. All important actions within the
country and abroad were carried out in the name of the pharaoh:
major irrigation and building projects, extraction of metal and stone
from the surrounding deserts, and wars and trading expeditions. The
king was revered as a god and was deemed to be similar in every respect to the gods; in fact, it is quite possible that to the Egyptians, he
was even more powerful. During the heyday of the Old Kingdom the
grandeur of the kings' final resting places—the pyramids—eclipsed
the temples erected to honor the gods. The royal titles were lengthy
and were constantly embellished with new epithets. The full title of an
Egyptian king contained five royal names, including his personal and
throne names. Until the end of Egyptian history, a pharaoh presented
himself as king of Upper and Lower Egypt in commemoration of the
formerly independent kingdoms of the north and south. The dual
system of some administrative state offices was a remnant from the
two predynastic kingdoms.

The most important aide of the king was the high official called
tchati, who managed, in the name of the king, the overall economic
life of the country and presided over the highest court of justice. At
certain times the *tchati* could also occupy some other top posts; for instance, he could be the head of the administration in the capital. However, during almost the entire span of Egyptian history, he was not
entrusted with the armed forces, which were placed under a separate
top functionary—the commander of the army.

The once-independent nomes became administrative-economic
units of the kingdom. In the floruit of the Old Kingdom (during the
Fourth Dynasty), the nomes became totally subordinate to the central
power. The king could transfer the "nomarchs" (nome rulers) from
one nome to another at his discretion. A ruthless central control was
imposed on all the activities of the local administration. During the
Third and Fourth dynasties, the supreme aristocracy in the capital

consisted of a tight circle of the king's blood-relations. The highest state functionaries—the *tchati*, the military commanders, the chiefs of the various offices and work projects, the supreme priests of the most important Egyptian temples—belonged to the royal house and represented the ruling dynasty. This centralized administration operated through a huge and complex bureaucratic apparatus.

The infantry constituted the only military branch in the standing army of Egypt, the formation of which went back to the Early Kingdom. Its soldiers were armed with bows and arrows and carried short swords. The troops were frequently transported to the battle sites on freight riverboats. Egypt's northern and southern borders were protected by defensive lines of forts that housed military garrisons. It is interesting to note that the police functions were performed in Egypt since the earliest times by people of north Nubian origin whose country had long since been conquered by Egypt. These were the Medja.

Egypt is frequently given the figurative name "The Land of the Pyramids." These grandiose funerary structures of the rulers of the Old Kingdom—silent witnesses of the unheard-of power of the Egyptian kings—are scattered around Cairo and south of it. They were erected for the eternal glorification of the names of the pharaohs who rested in the underground chambers of these peculiar mausoleums. The first pyramid, still of the step type, is sixty meters high and was built near the present town of Saqqara, south of Cairo, for Pharaoh Djeser (Third Dynasty), founder of the Old Kingdom. It was built by a gifted architect, physician, and *tchati*—the famous Imhetep. The Greeks later identified him with the patron god of medicine—Aesculapius.

In the Giza suburb of Cairo still stands the impressive Great Pyramid of the mightiest king of the Fourth Dynasty—Cheops (Khufu). It is the only remaining structure of the Seven Wonders of the Ancient World. This structure was built using 2,300,000 perfectly fitted giant stone blocks and reaches a height of 150 meters. Nearby stand the pyramids of Khufu's successors: his younger son, Chephrenes (Kha'f-Ra'), whose pyramid is only 3 meters lower than his father's, and the much smaller (66 meters) pyramid of another pharaoh of the same dynasty, Mycerinus (Menkau-Ra'). Each king of the Old Kingdom began building his tomb as soon as he ascended the royal throne. Each pyramid's construction could have lasted for several dozens of years. Herodotus, who traveled through Egypt in the fifth century B.C., left us a vivid, although not entirely accurate, account of the construction of Cheops's pyramid as it was imagined by distant descendants of the people who witnessed the building.

According to Herodotus, Cheops plunged the country into an abyss of disaster by forcing all Egyptians to work for him. Some of the workers hauled huge boulders toward the Nile from quarries in the eastern desert, while others loaded them on ships and ferried them to the left bank of the Nile. Another multitude of laborers dragged the stones to the foothills of the Libyan plateau—the construction site. One hundred thousand people supposedly labored, day-in and day-out, in three-month-long shifts. It took ten years just to build the tomb proper and the road over which the boulders were dragged. The pyramid itself took twenty years to erect.

Actually, the main building material used for the pyramid was local limestone, quarried right at the foot of the future monument. It was only the high-quality white limestone used for the finishing of the interior chambers and for the exterior facets that was hauled from across the river. A limited number of working teams were engaged in the actual construction of the pyramid. These were permanent, trained workers. Special work gangs labored in the neighboring quarries. There is no doubt, however, that great numbers of unskilled laborers were used for auxiliary tasks and that many workers were taken away from their daily productive duties.

Nestled near the Fourth Dynasty pyramids stands the Great Sphinx. Cut from a cliff to a height of twenty meters, its face, partially erased by the ravages of time, is said to resemble the face of King Chephrenes, in whose time the statue was probably carved. The City of the Dead—the burial site of the nobles from the golden age of the Old Kingdom who, even after death, wished to remain near their master at the foot of his monument—spreads out over a large area close to the pyramids.

The kings of the Fifth and Sixth dynasties also erected their pyramids. Those of the Fifth Dynasty stand near Abusir and in the Saqqara region; the pyramids of the Sixth Dynasty kings were also built in the Saqqara region.

The Old Kingdom did not leave us very many royal inscriptions. However, there are a number of biographical inscriptions of dignitaries and nomarchs that tell about military campaigns, trade expeditions, and the exploitation of useful minerals outside Egypt.

King Snefru, founder of the Fourth Dynasty, undertook a great military campaign into Ethiopia on the Nile, from where he took 7,000 Nubian prisoners and brought back 200,000 head of livestock. From his Libyan campaign he brought into Egypt 1,100 Libyan prisoners and more livestock. The kings of the Fifth Dynasty—Sahu-Ra' and Unis—fought the Asiatic tribe in the Sinai and also organized campaigns into Libya. On the walls of the memorial temple of Sahu-Ra' there are depictions of ships with Asiatic and Libyan prisoners being transported to Egypt. These reliefs give us our first glimpse into Egyptian travels to the distant and mysterious Punt,[11] a place possibly located in present-day Somalia. At that time the canal between the eastern branch of the Nile and the Red Sea had not yet been dug. Thus, the voyage had to start in the city of Coptos in Upper Egypt, from where the Egyptians followed the dry riverbed Wadi Hammamat, on foot, to the shore and then traveled by sea to Punt, from where they brought myrrh, frankincense, and gold.

The kings of the Sixth Dynasty also undertook military campaigns. Pepi I, the second king of the Sixth Dynasty, fought Asiatic tribes beyond the Sinai Peninsula, mobilizing his forces on land and on sea. The son of Pepi I, Meren-Ra', conducted expeditions into Ethiopia on the Nile.

Many of the inscriptions that were made by functionaries at their work stations in the mines and quarries tell about the organization of "peaceful" expeditions to obtain minerals, about the struggles with the pastoralist tribes in the steppes during the expeditions, and about victories over them. As in the past, the mountains of the Sinai were exploited for the mining of copper and for the extraction of turquoise.

Stone was available everywhere, but in many cases, rare varieties of rock had to be brought from afar. For instance, lapis lazuli arrived in Egypt by way of a multistage exchange from today's Afghanistan. Numerous expeditions were organized to bring Lebanese cedar from the shores of the eastern Mediterranean. Ebony, ivory, and lion and leopard skins were brought from Nubia. As of now, we have no information about the Nubian gold fields that were extensively exploited by Egyptians in later times. During the Old Kingdom, gold was mined in the desert east of the Nile Valley; it was also brought from Punt via the Red Sea.

Despite the Old Kingdom's uncontested might, the internal situation was not without its worries. For some reason, the period of the Third Dynasty is shrouded in darkness. We know only about its founder, Djeser. During the Fourth Dynasty, the unfinished pyramid and the ruined statue of the elder son of Cheops, Djedef-Ra', may indicate an internecine war between two brothers that ended in Chephrenes' victory. But the dramatic end of the powerful Fourth Dynasty and the ascent of the Fifth Dynasty and its founder, Userkaf, are once again hidden from us.

The rule of this dynasty led to important ideological changes that were connected with the introduction of the cult of Ra', the Sun god. He was worshiped throughout the Egyptian state. Ra' was the prin-

11. The reading of this name is conventional and dubious; it probably sounded more like "Pawane."

cipal god of the Heliopolis nome, where the Fifth Dynasty probably originated. The king no longer was identified only with the god Horus, the traditional patron of the Early Dynastic Egyptian kings, but was now represented as the son of Ra'. Each king of the new dynasty erected temples to the Sun, in honor of Ra'. Such temples featured enormous obelisks built within their walled yards. Important political changes also marked the Fifth Dynasty, the external signs being the promotion of persons from aristocratic families but unrelated to the king to the highest state offices (contrary to the situation during the preceding dynasty).

Finally, the entire second half of the Old Kingdom saw the hidden but tenacious struggle for political and economic autonomy of strengthening nome administrations against the excessive domination of the central authority. For this struggle, there is no direct, written evidence, and evidence may never have existed in written form. But we can gain valuable insights if we observe the tombs of the Upper Egyptian nomarchs of the Sixth Dynasty. Necropoles of the hereditary nomarchs of that time were discovered all over Upper Egypt. Their tombs became increasingly wealthier from generation to generation (especially those situated farther from central Memphis), whereas the royal tombs of this time—the pyramids—cannot be compared in grandeur with the impressive structures erected by the powerful pharaohs of the Fourth Dynasty.

The nomes gradually undermined the authority and power of the central government, and the royal administration had to compromise more and more with the governments of the nomes. A redistribution of material and human resources was evolving in favor of the nomes and at the expense of the center; the economic power of the kings of Memphis was crumbling; their political power waning.

Soon after the death of Pepi II, a Sixth Dynasty pharaoh who ruled Egypt for almost one hundred years, the power of Memphis over Egypt became merely nominal. Around the year 2200 B.C., the country broke up into many independent regions: nomes. Thus ended the Old Kingdom.

7

The Middle Kingdom of Egypt and the Hyksos Invasion

I. V. VINOGRADOV[†]

The First Intermediate Period

It is customary to define the Middle Kingdom as the epoch of a new unification of Egypt at the end of the third millennium, rebuilt from the ruins of the Old Kingdom by natives of a southern Upper Egyptian nome, that of Thebes. This was achieved by the last kings of the Eleventh Dynasty, and the kingdom was consolidated by the pharaohs of the Twelfth Dynasty. This dynasty's dominion lasted for two hundred years and saw the florescence, as well as the rapid decline, of the kingdom.

The end of the Old Kingdom and the beginning of the Middle Kingdom are separated by an almost two hundred and fifty year period called the Intermediate Period. This was a time of fragmentation of the state, of great social upheavals, and of violent internal struggles for the reunification of Egypt. It is in this period of transition that we probably ought to look for the explanation of the differences between the Middle Kingdom and the Old Kingdom.

The dissolution of the unified state, the development of the nomes toward economic and political isolation, and the resulting rivalry and armed conflicts among them had a deleterious effect on the entire economic structure of the country and on the irrigation system: the basis for Egypt's material well-being. Records of the ephemeral Seventh to Ninth dynasties are full of accounts of famine years, of arable land turned into swamps and overgrown with impenetrable thickets, and of fields abandoned by the farmers, leaving no one to cultivate them. Even the once-wealthy and flourishing parts of the country had become depopulated. The interminable struggles between the nomes aggravated Egypt's already difficult situation and wrought further destruction and calamity upon the land. Naturally, this situation had the potential to create serious social upheavals among the laboring groups, who, no doubt, must have borne the brunt of pain and deprivation. Many documents and literary sources from that epoch hint at the increasing frustration and ensuing disturbances among the lower classes of Egyptian society.

It seems that socially induced mass actions of the people are reflected in two literary compositions that can be dated to this period. It
was a time of growing recognition of the need for the country's political and economic reunification.

A large but badly damaged papyrus (preserved in Leiden, the
Netherlands) contains a passionate appeal by a man called Ipuwer
who may have been closely connected with the ruling circles of the
north. He calls for the restoration of the old Egyptian order and for
the reunification of the country into one single state. Ipuwer describes
in poetic form the calamities, perhaps exaggerated, that befell the divided land: the prevailing hostility and mutual hatred, the plundering
and murdering, the desolation and famine, people eating grass and
washing it down with water, people eating foods that in the old days
were fed to the pigs, and even cases of cannibalism. The poet-narrator
mourns the destroyed cities and the ruined nomes, the fallen palaces
and the desecrated tombs. He is saddened by the interruption of the
age-old trade with the eastern Mediterranean region (there is no
longer even any cedar lumber left to make sarcophagi for the well-
born!) and by the disruption of internal relations: the south, torn by
discord, does not, as before, supply the north with grain, handicrafts,
fruit, and aromatic oils. The inhabitants of the surrounding oases no
longer descend into the valley to bring their gifts. Ipuwer is distressed
at seeing Asiatic and Libyan barbarians taking advantage of Egypt's
weakness by invading and plundering the defenseless Delta. Most of
all, he is concerned about the widespread uprising of the people. Either these rebellions took place during Ipuwer's lifetime, or they were
still vivid in the memories of his contemporaries. In Ipuwer's own
words, the land has turned like a pot spinning on a potter's wheel: the
poor have grown wealthy and the rich have grown poor; he who had
no bread has become the owner of granaries; he who had no animals
to pull his plow has come to possess a herd; he who had not one boat
has come to own ships; he who had no hut now owns a house; he who
did not weave, even for his own needs, dons the finest linen, while
noble persons wear rags; he who could not even make his own coffin
now has his own mausoleum, while the bodies of the former owners
have been thrown out into the desert. Ipuwer proclaims that only with
the restoration of the old order would Egypt be rid of all these calamities; harmony would again prevail once the old state offices were re-
established. People would again build pyramids, dig canals, and tend
the orchards. With the position of the aristocracy regained, the rob-
beries and rebellions would disappear, and the roads would again be
safe for travelers. The rise of Egyptian power would reduce the foreigners to barbarians trembling before its might.

Another papyrus, kept in Leningrad's State Hermitage, echoes the

Leiden document. The Hermitage papyrus text takes the form of a prophecy that was supposed to have been read to Pharaoh Snefru, the founder of the powerful Fourth Dynasty, in his palace by the learned priest Neferti. This document tells of the same sad events so vividly described by Ipuwer. Again, we read of the general decline of the country, the destruction, murders, looting, hunger, misfortunes, internal discord, and incursions by foreigners. Neferti's prophecy had the same intention as Ipuwer's pronouncement—a call for the restoration of a single authority and the return of the old order to Egypt. There is, however, an important difference: whereas Ipuwer's appeal has the quality of an idealized vision and is not addressed to any specific person, Neferti's prophecy is more concrete. It predicts the arrival of a southern king, born in Upper Egypt, who will place upon his head the double crown of Egypt, who will unify Egypt, pacify the internal strife, restore the truth, and banish falsehood. He will defeat the Libyans and Asiatics and restore the border fortifications. Neferti calls this future unifier of Egypt "Ameni"—a shortened form of the name of the founder of the Twelfth Dynasty, Amenemhet I.

It is reasonable to assume that Neferti's prophecies were written down during the final stage of Egypt's reunification under one ruler and that they originated from circles directly connected with the founder of the new dynasty. Ipuwer's appeals, however, may have been written earlier.[1]

Egyptian texts make it possible to establish the fundamental milestones of the struggle for unity long before Amenemhet I ascended the throne. In the middle of the twenty-second century B.C., Achtoes (Kheti) declared himself pharaoh. He was the ruler of the Heracleopolis nome, situated some 120 kilometers south of Memphis (Ninth Dynasty). Achtoes I and, especially, the kings of the Tenth Dynasty managed to unite part of the Upper Egyptian valley.[2] Later, the Theban nome gained strength in the south. Egypt saw the simultaneous rule of the Tenth Dynasty in Heracleopolis and the Eleventh Dynasty in Thebes. Achtoes III, king of Heracleopolis, wrote or dictated advice to his son, persuading him to live in peace with the southern

1. We must point out that both documents are later copies made during the New Kingdom. The Leiden papyrus was written during the Nineteenth Dynasty and the Leningrad papyrus around the middle of the Eighteenth Dynasty. However, there is no doubt that the texts of both papyri stem from an earlier time. Formerly, opinions differed in dating the events mentioned in these documents. Today, most Egyptologists confidently attribute the events to the First Intermediate Period—the time preceding the Middle Kingdom.

2. Manetho's Seventh, Eighth, and Ninth dynasties belong to the troubled period that spanned the time between the Sixth and the Tenth Dynasties. These three intermediate dynasties left no written evidence.

kingdom. But a showdown was unavoidable; the Heracleopolis kings sought and obtained support from some of the nomarchs in their struggle with Thebes. And finally, around the year 2040 B.C., the king of Thebes, Mentchuhetep I, became pharaoh of all Egypt. Here begins the history of the Middle Kingdom.

The Middle Kingdom

During the Intermediate Period, when centralized management of the irrigation system collapsed, we find a considerable increase in local initiative in Egypt. This is the time when a more efficient plow appeared in the fields, making it easier to prepare the soil and to improve cultivation. There also appeared many new tools used in farming and crafts. Invented in nomes that were often separated by large distances, these new tools spread gradually throughout the entire country as a result of internal trade. Old tools were also being improved. Toward the end of this period, the Egyptians began to use bronze (a copper-tin alloy), although pure copper remained the main industrial metal for a long time to come. A new, more productive, and larger breed of horned cattle appeared and gradually completely replaced the earlier long-horned variety. This progress was stimulated by the need to free as many able hands in the nomes as possible in order to compensate for the problems created by the disruption of the centralized economic organization. All these new inventions and methods were assimilated and continued to develop during the reunited Egyptian state of the Middle Kingdom.

Internal Egyptian trade grew during the First Intermediate Period, though it would appear that the conditions were far from propitious.[3] This growth was connected with the decline of the self-sufficient large economies belonging to the Old Kingdom's aristocracy, rooted at the capital. It was simultaneous with the rise of the role of smaller economies. At some time, the owners of these economies may have become supporters of the nomarchs in their struggle against the kings at Memphis and then were promoted for their service into the ranks of the numerous independent regional rulers of the First Intermediate Period. The number of persons who received their material sustenance for their service in the administration, at the court, and in the army grew considerably. It is natural that the numerous small and medium-sized economies of the new functionaries in the service of

3. The fact is that the stronger and more extended an ancient kingdom was, the worse were the conditions for trade, because strong royal power laid its hand arbitrarily on the profits by way of taxation or by submitting the trader to administrative control. Editor's note (IMD).

the local and the central administration did not dispose of the productive resources of the earliest dignitaries' large economies and were unable to produce all the tools and products they needed. This shortcoming could be compensated for only by some degree of specialization, which was conducive to the rise of an intensive exchange between the different economies. Internal trade also was characteristic of the entire period of the Middle Kingdom.

The Middle Kingdom inherited from the First Intermediate Period the increased influence of the local administrations on the economic and political life of the country. The independence of the nomarchs was so great that even at the end of this epoch, some of them continued to date events according to the count of their own years of rule, to preside over the worship of the local gods, and to call themselves sons of the local deities, as formerly did the pharaohs. The nomarchs headed the local armed forces, whose strength was frequently quite significant, and surrounded themselves with large and splendid retinues of courtiers, bodyguards, and servants. The position of the local rulers did not weaken even during the rule of the pharaohs of the Twelfth Dynasty; their power may have actually increased. Their tombs became richer under the first pharaohs of that dynasty. During the Middle Kingdom, the nomarchs were no longer simple executors of the central administration's will at the regional level, as was the case under the mighty pharaohs of the Old Kingdom, but had gained a significant amount of independence within the new, united state. Their rule became hereditary, and the pharaoh's appointment of a new nomarch became a mere formality.

Naturally, the position of the new pharaohs, who were forced to share their power with the local nomarchs, was less stable than that of the Old Kingdom pharaohs. It was therefore not surprising that hidden conflicts between the local rulers and the central authority, internal disorders and disturbances, court conspiracies, and intrigues abounded during the entire course of the Twelfth Dynasty.

Many important positions at court and in the administrative machinery of the Middle Kingdom were held, not only by the hereditary aristocracy of the capital, who had family ties to the new dynasty, and by persons from the local nome administrations, but also by persons of simple extraction who held important posts and owed their well-being entirely to the pharaoh. "The king is food," said a top functionary, not one of the nobility, in the middle of the Twelfth Dynasty. Obviously, it was precisely this class of people who were most interested in strengthening the central power; they were the main support of the Middle Kingdom rulers. It is quite probable that one of the incentives to build the enormous irrigation system in the Fayum Oasis was to ensure the material well-being of a large number of these people. The Fayum irrigation project significantly expanded the area of the country's arable land. It is characteristic that this newly developed acreage lay fairly close to the Egyptian capital and the royal court.

The reunification of the country and the consolidation of the central authority brought with it a reactivation of extensive building projects, expeditions to mines and quarries, and exploitation of new mineral deposits. The Egyptians continued to obtain their copper and turquoise supply from the Sinai mountains, but by the time of the Middle Kingdom, other mines between the Nile and the Red Sea in Nubia had been discovered. Gold was no longer extracted only in the eastern desert of Upper Egypt but was extracted in northern Ethiopia on the Nile as well. The interrupted relations between Egypt and other countries were renewed. Egypt recommenced its trade with the countries of the eastern Mediterranean region. Lebanese cedar was shipped to Egypt mainly via the Phoenician city of Byblos, and Egyptian traders began to import tin. The Cretan pottery found in Egypt and the Egyptian implements discovered in Crete demonstrate the existence of commerce between both countries during the Middle Kingdom. Furthermore, Egyptian ships resumed their visits to distant Punt.

On the basis of comprehensive and complex investigations of Middle Kingdom texts, O. D. Berlev was able to identify the social stratum of the people who produced the material wealth of the country; the Egyptians described them with the general term *hemwew nisut,* "the royal *hemwew.*" [4] Berlev succeeded in determining the position of the royal *hemwew* in Egyptian society, their relationship with similar social categories, the methods used to exploit the royal *hemwew,* and their connection with state institutions.

The term *hemwew nisut* encompassed practically the entire working population of the country. The main duty of the royal *hemwew* was to work in a specific profession or trade. They were exploited by the royal and temple economies, as well as by private persons: people who held positions in the central, nome, and temple administrations. The connection of each royal *hemew* with one certain profession was typical of this social stratum. This is the reason why the royal *hemwew* were most frequently mentioned not as such but in their professional capacity: as agricultural hands, herdsmen, orchard keepers, gardeners, fishermen, bird catchers—all those who toiled the fields and in the grazing lands and who practiced other outdoor trades. They could also be servants, dancers, singers, musicians, barbers, and teachers—that is, people who served the master directly, as well as his relatives

---

4. The term *hemew* is usually translated "slave," yet such an interpretation is not accurate. In order to avoid incorrect associations, we use this term in its conventional Egyptological reading, *hemew* (plural, *hemwew*).

and close associates, in their houses or in the palace. The fields were worked exclusively by men, whereas domestic tasks could be performed by men or women. The royal *hemwew* also worked in the specialized food production establishments (the *shnau*) as well as in the workshops of the royal, temple, and dignitaries' economies.

The royal *hemwew* were assigned to their duties in their early youth and could not choose a profession. Special inspection reviews were conducted in the nomes, in the name of the royal administration, to assign professions to young people who had, according to Egyptian notions, come of age. All the children of the royal *hemwew* were inspected, regardless of their parents' occupation. First, the strongest and toughest young men were chosen for the army. Some royal *hemwew* children were also assigned into the lower priesthood. Naturally, any acquired trade skills were taken into account when a youngster was selected, and so the son of a craftsman would usually also become a craftsman. A great portion of young people became farm laborers or were distributed among other basic professions, depending on the needs of the Egyptian economy. For most young men, such compulsory assignments were for life, although reassignments could also be made during the inspections. Thus, an old, ailing farmhand could be given a lighter duty—that of a doorkeeper, for instance.

Documents of the Middle Kingdom enable us to elucidate the social status of the royal *hemwew*. People belonging to this social class constituted the country's general working population. Deprived of property in tools and means of production, they worked in economies that did not belong to them and together with the production tools and means, they were in the possession (*djet*) either of an individual functionary or of temple or state (royal) institutions. The exploitation and provision methods were the same regardless of profession and employer, whether royal, temple, or private. Therefore, the Egyptian workers did not perceive any particular difference in their own status, wherever they worked. However, in order to clearly understand the economic and social structure of Egyptian society, it is important to point out that the relationship of the master to the royal *hemwew* who worked in his private establishments was somewhat loose, because they did not actually belong to him but, rather, to his official position. They were assigned to him, together with the land and other property, for his service as a royal functionary. Under this arrangement the master could not dispose of the royal *hemwew* at his discretion. We know that the children of the royal *hemwew* were assigned professions, during the inspection, in economies of other officials or institutions, but not necessarily those where their parents worked. Consequently, the master had no right over the offspring of the royal *hemwew* who were in his employment.

Another social category of dependent people, quantitatively insignificant in comparison with the royal *hemwew*, were the *bakew*, whom we remember from the Old Kingdom. The *bakew* were actual slaves in every sense of the word: they were exploited exclusively by private economies and differed from the *hemwew* in that they were the property of their masters; they were excluded from the overall state economy and not subject to the country's labor force distribution system; they did not take part in the inspections for vocational assignments and were not assigned professions by the royal administration. Naturally, they lacked any strictly professional designation.

While the royal *hemwew* performed their assigned work in the different branches of the private economies, the *bakew* were their masters' personal household servants or were given different occasional tasks. A master had the right to dispose of a *bakew*'s fate at his discretion, and the *bakew*'s children were his full property; a slave market existed where *bakew* could be freely bought and sold. It is interesting that a nobleman, who had hundreds of royal *hemwew* in his employ, found it necessary to widely publicize his purchase of even a single *bak*. This clearly underlines the difference between a royal *hemew*, owned by the master only on condition of his state service, and a *bak*, who was owned by the master as a personal possession.

It seems that enslavement of Egyptians, especially of young people from among the broad working population—that is, their conversion to the condition of *bakew*—was quite common when the central authority was losing its strength at the end of the Old Kingdom and, especially, during the difficult times of the First Intermediate Period. Once the country had achieved its new political unity during the Twelfth Dynasty, the attempts at enslavement began to be suppressed by the state. But it is unlikely that it could have been completely eliminated.

There was no exploitation of foreign prisoners to speak of during the First Intermediate Period, and there was not much of it during early Middle Kingdom times. But from the middle of the Twelfth Dynasty, the influx of aliens into Egypt increased significantly. They appeared in the establishments of the aristocracy and wealthy functionaries and even in the employ of modest Egyptian officials. Among the dependent Egyptian population, we find foreigners (almost exclusively Asiatics; i.e., Western Semites) who were captured by the Egyptian armed forces near the northeastern Egyptian border. Their situation was somewhat peculiar. The foreigners were registered with the rest of the labor force by the central administration, just as the royal *hemwew* were, and like the rest of the laboring population, the Asiatics could be employed by the royal, temple, and private establishments. But in private economies they often had no specific profession and were used for any available odd jobs at the discretion of their master, as were the *bakew*. The few available documents are sufficient to conclude that the labor of foreigners was used mainly in the house for personal service and in the royal and noblemen's food production establishments (the *shnau*), as well as in artisans' shops, including special weaving shops (where only women worked, including those taken captive). As a rule, foreigners were not used for farm work, such as work in the fields, gardens, and orchards and animal herding. All such work in the royal, temple, and private economies was mainly assigned to the royal *hemwew*.

The so-called royal works were a major factor influencing Egyptian society. Their raison d'être and organization were also discovered by studying Middle Kingdom materials. The royal works were carried out through a labor conscription for the state or the king, a burden that also lay on the royal *hemwew*. It meant diverting the men from their everyday professional tasks, regardless of where they used to work. The diversion was temporary, perhaps for the duration of a few months. The conscripts were forced into special guarded camps where they were assigned their new tasks. The exploitation under the regime of the royal works was heavy; the labor was hard, so everybody tried to escape conscription, which, however, was unavoidable for the royal *hemwew*. Among the royal works, heavy construction and earth-moving jobs were the fundamental occupations. This included work on the irrigation system and the exhausting work in mines and quarries. A royal obligatory labor was serving as oarsmen in the large royal rowing fleet; another royal work was watering the state gardens and orchards, which were situated above the naturally irrigated arable land. These plots required a continuous, manual supply of water. (During the Middle Kingdom, Egyptians did not yet use mechanical water-lifting devices.) The administration and management of the royal works were in the hands of the *tchati,* who was in charge of coordinating the functions of the different state departments that were responsible for the punctual delivery of qualified and auxiliary workers, tools, and provisions. People enlisted in the royal works could, when required, also be assigned to private economies—during harvest time, for instance.

From the above, it becomes obvious that within the entire socioeconomic structure the royal *hemwew* played the leading role in the life of the Middle Kingdom. There is no doubt that this extensive social stratum of the working population, so clearly described in the Middle Kingdom documents, could not have first appeared during this relatively brief period; it must have existed earlier, and it continued to function during the subsequent stages of Egyptian history. The social status of the royal *hemwew* during the Middle Kingdom was very simi-

lar to that of the workers exploited in the royal, temple, and dignitaries' economies of the Old Kingdom. It is probably true that the
workers of the Old Kingdom were more closely tied to certain of the
large economies, and it is also probable that the all-inclusive centralized labor force distribution, prevalent during the Middle Kingdom, did not exist earlier. Sources from the New Kingdom suggest
that this social stratum of the working population continued to exist
throughout the entire history of that period under the new general
designation of *semdet,* meaning "professions"—that is, people classified by professions or specialization. Naturally, the conditions of most
of the Egyptian working population must have changed throughout
the centuries, and such changes must be investigated in detail for each
individual epoch. But the royal *hemwew,* as described in the sources of
the Middle Kingdom, with all their relationships and social interconnections, also enable us to throw some light on some still-obscure
problems concerning socioeconomic relationships during the preceding Old Kingdom and the later New Kingdom.

We can now answer the question of who established and expanded
the irrigation system during the early periods of Egyptian history, and
who built the magnificent mausoleums of the pharaohs—the pyramids—during the golden age of the Old Kingdom. All the great Egyptian achievements from the earliest times were accomplished through
the efforts of the Egyptian working population, people exploited by
basically the same methods used during the Middle Kingdom. However, during the Middle Kingdom, some substantial changes appeared
in the organization of labor. The Egyptian farm laborers of the Middle
Kingdom, much like their Old Kingdom predecessors (cf. the agricultural workers in the dignitaries' economies), did not own means of
production (land, draft animals) as property; they had no right to the
harvested product and received their sustenance from the granaries
and warehouses of their master's economy or from those of the institution that employed them. But, whereas the agriculturalists of the
Old Kingdom worked in gangs when plowing, sowing, and harvesting, each agricultural laborer in the Middle Kingdom now worked an
individual parcel of land assigned to him and for which he was personally responsible. The gang production system became obsolete not
only in agriculture but also in many other branches of the Egyptian
economy.

A deep chasm separated the Egyptian working population from the
ruling class of Egyptian society. It was, in fact, only the latter who controlled the means of production. Very few royal *hemwew* managed to
cross this social chasm. It was no coincidence that Egyptian schools,
which instructed only children of functionaries whose career in the
administrative service was ensured, made the students copy texts that

told of the heavy lot of people assigned to the different professions by the state. This had a didactic purpose, because according to royal decrees, functionaries who committed a misdemeanor could be sent to work as farmhands in temple economies; that is, they could be demoted to the level of the royal *hemwew*.

Now we must briefly review the political history of the Middle Kingdom. The last three kings of the Eleventh Dynasty, all of whom bore the same personal name, Mentchuhetep, ruled for some forty years over a united country—from Elephantine in the south to the Delta in the north—and renewed the disrupted external relations. Under Mentchuhetep I, Egyptians again began to work the Sinai copper mines, and Egyptian armies successfully fought Asiatics along the northeastern borders of Egypt. Mentchuhetep I also conducted an expedition into the Wawat region—part of northern Nubia that bordered on Egypt. Striving to consolidate his position in the country, this new king of a united Egypt began to erect temples to the local Egyptian gods all over the land. The increased power of the royal authority was marked by intensive construction projects using stone, the greatest example of which is the splendid funerary temple of Mentchuhetep I in Deir el-Bahri on the west bank of the Nile, close to Thebes. This structure forms an architectonic ensemble at the center of which stands a two-tiered rectangular building surrounded by a colonnade and crowned by a small pyramid.

The Middle Kingdom reached the peak of its power during the Twelfth Dynasty. Since the year 2000 B.C., only eight kings ruled over Egypt, their rule covering more than two hundred years. Amenemhet I's founding of the Twelfth Dynasty was marked by the transfer of the country's capital from the southern city of Thebes (the residence of the Twelfth Dynasty kings) to the north. The new Egyptian capital had the typical name It-Tawi ("Possessor of Both Lands"; i.e. of all Egypt). It was located on the west bank of the Nile, near the Fayum Oasis at the junction of Upper and Lower Egypt. The transfer to the new capital was dictated by the desire of the kings, who came from the south, to consolidate their power in the Delta region and thus to strengthen the unity of Egypt. This was the goal of Egyptian rulers since the beginning of the country's history.

Having achieved significant progress in firmly establishing their rule over the entire Egyptian territory, the kings of the Twelfth Dynasty led successful military actions to the west and east of the Delta. They fought Libyan and Western Asiatic tribes, who had repeatedly invaded and ravaged Lower Egypt. But most of the Egyptian kings' attention was focused on Nubia, a country that had already been coveted by the rulers of the Old Kingdom. They wanted Nubian gold, copper, ivory, and rare varieties of wood. The most bellicose ruler of the Twelfth Dynasty was Senwesret III, who conducted several large military expeditions south of the First Cataract and who brought northern Ethiopia on the Nile into a close dependence on Egypt, a connection that would last for a long time. In order to facilitate the passage of the Egyptian military ships through the cataracts, he ordered the cutting of a bypass channel through the cliffs. In the eighth year of his reign, Senwesret III reached the Second Cataract and built fortresses to the south of it on both banks of the Nile. His inscriptions instructed his successors to stand fast at this new border. Another inscription, dating to the time of Senwesret II, tells of a large Egyptian campaign, probably the only one, to the Asiatic country of Retenu, which was situated somewhere in the territory of today's Israel or southern Syria. Future generations of Egyptians combined the image of this mighty Twelfth Dynasty pharaoh with the even more warlike pharaohs of the New Kingdom, creating the image of Sesostris—the legendary conqueror of half the world.

The Middle Kingdom reached its zenith during the almost fifty-year-long rule of Amenemhet III, son of Senwesret III. His reign spanned the end of the nineteenth and beginning of the eighteenth centuries B.C. It was during his reign that the work on the vast Fayum Oasis irrigation project, begun before him, was completed. He also built an imposing stone building at the entrance to the Fayum that was later admired by the Greeks, who called this enormous structure, with its endless halls and passages, the "Labyrinth." It was probably Amenemhet III's funerary temple. It is possible that some of these numerous rooms were intended to display statues of the numerous local and pan-Egyptian deities, making this structure a symbol of the solid union of Egypt under the ruling dynasty.

Amenemhet III was the last great pharaoh of the Twelfth Dynasty. After his death, the Middle Kingdom began its rapid decline.

The rulers of the Middle Kingdom were never able to gain complete control over the separatist tendencies of the hereditary nome administrations, which also held important positions at the royal court. This tense internal strife continued throughout the Twelfth Dynasty, spilling into the country's capital. An assassination attempt on Amenemhet I may have been successful, and according to Manetho, Amenemhet II was murdered by a court eunuch. Sinuhe, a dignitary in the court of Amenemhet I, was the hero of an adventure story of that time. Apparently, while in the army of the royal successor and future pharaoh, Senwesret I, that was operating in Libya, he received news of the pharaoh's death and decided to flee Egypt in fear for his own life, since the risk of being assassinated during dynastic power conflicts was very great.

In order to lessen to some degree the threat of revolt, the kings of the Twelfth Dynasty, starting with Amenemhet I, introduced the practice of appointing coregents during their lifetime. Neither were matters peaceful at the local level. The powerful nomarchs had large military forces at their disposal and the ability to challenge the king himself. It was for a good reason that the capital It-Tawi was built as a fortress (quite strong by the standards of that time). Amenemhet III, the strongest ruler of the Twelfth Dynasty, was finally able to limit significantly the power of the nomarchs by means of harsh measures and with the help of his officers of nonaristocratic descent, the backbone of his army. But this was the ruling dynasty's last success. A few years after the death of Amenemhet III and after the brief rule of his sister, Nefrusebek, the Twelfth Dynasty ceased to exist. The first kings of the Thirteenth Dynasty, who were probably related to the preceding dynasty, held sway in the Nile Valley up to the Second Cataract and maintained relations with the eastern Mediterranean countries. But soon Egypt apparently divided into two parts (Thirteenth and Fourteenth dynasties). At this point, Egypt embarked on a new stage in its history that is customarily called the Second Intermediate Period.

The Second Intermediate Period and the Conquest of Egypt by the Hyksos

The Second Intermediate Period lasted for over two hundred years and was another dark epoch in Egyptian history. It was marked by internal instability, dynastic strife, and conquest by aliens. The king lists of that time are eloquent: they contain over two hundred names of pharaohs from this period. This abundance of rulers indicates that the royal throne became a toy in the hands of warring court cliques. There were even instances of nonroyal persons becoming pharaohs—especially military commanders who managed to advance their fortunes during the continuous revolts.

While the country suffered under the difficult conditions at the turn of the eighteenth and nineteenth centuries, the Hyksos[5] attacked and invaded Egypt from the east by way of the Sinai Peninsula. The Hyksos were a tribal union of inhabitants of southern Syria and northern Arabia who possibly represented several ethnic groups. The weakened Egypt was incapable of mustering any significant resistance to the invaders, who brought along battle chariots, never before seen by the Egyptians, and overran the eastern Delta, where they established their base in the city of Avaris, situated on one of the eastern

5. The name *Hyksos* comes to us from the Greek. In the conventional "school" pronunciation, the term is pronounced *heqa-hasut*, meaning "rulers of the desert highlands" or "rulers of foreign lands," because any foreign land, except Nubia, is located above the level of Egypt and, in comparison to the fertile Nile Valley, is desert.

branches of the Nile. From here the Hyksos conducted their raids southward, burning cities, destroying temples, and killing and imprisoning many Egyptians.[6]

The Hyksos remained in Egypt for over 110 years. But their kings, traditionally assigned to the Fifteenth and possibly even the Sixteenth Manethonian dynasties, were unable to fully subdue the country. It was only under two of the Hyksos kings—Khian and Apepi—that the rule of the Hyksos extended far to the south, which otherwise remained basically independent. It is also probable that the western Delta did not entirely fall under the power of the Hyksos.

The Theban nome initiated the Egyptian struggle for independence. Thebes was situated about 800 kilometers south of the Delta. The kings of the Seventeenth Theban Dynasty, weak in the beginning, gradually began to rally around themselves most of the Upper Egyptian nomes and, once they had gathered substantial military and economic strength, headed the struggle to evict the Hyksos invaders.

An Egyptian legend, partly preserved in a later New Kingdom version, tells about the beginning of the liberation struggle and connects it with the penultimate king of the Seventeenth Dynasty, Seqen-ne-Ra', who apparently lost his life in this struggle. This is confirmed by the discovery of his mummy, which still shows the marks of mortal wounds inflicted with battle-axes. His son Kames appears to have had more success. He outfitted a large fleet, gathering detachments of bowmen and *medja*s, and advanced the fighting into the region of the Hermopolis nome, halfway between Thebes and the Delta. Though he reached the walls of Avaris, he was not fated to take the city. Disturbances in the far south of the country, probably precipitated by the challenge of the Nubian rulers to Kames, prevented him from delivering the final blow against the enemy. The Theban king was forced to terminate the siege of Avaris and to shift his armies to the south.

The final victory over the Hyksos was achieved by Kames' brother, Ya'hmes (Amasis I), founder of the Eighteenth Dynasty, who ascended the Egyptian throne around 1600 B.C. This marks the beginning of the New Kingdom.

6. Current excavations at Tell el-Dab'a, the ancient Avaris, have revealed that the Hyksos also engaged in profitable long-distance trade, linking the Nile Valley with the lands of the Eastern Mediterranean. Editor's note (PLK).

8

The New Kingdom of Egypt

I. V. Vinogradov[†]

General Outline of the Period

The epoch of Egyptian history illustrated by the largest number of ancient Egyptian finds covers three Manethonian dynasties: the Eighteenth, Nineteenth, and Twentieth. They extend from the sixteenth to the eleventh centuries B.C.

All branches of the Egyptian economy made significant advances from the very beginning of this period. Since the Eighteenth Dynasty, bronze was being introduced all over the country, although copper, stone, and wooden implements were still used. The invention of the foot-activated bellows put an end to the strenuous and dangerous work of the metalworkers, who previously had to fan their fires by blowing air through long tubes. A more convenient and efficient loom was developed. An improved plow with vertical handles, still rare during the Middle Kingdom, completely displaced the archaic plow. The shadufs (a long beam with a bucket on one end and a counterweight on the other) was now used to raise water, greatly increasing the productivity of the gardeners and orchard keepers, who until then had to carry pottery vessels this way and that for the watering. The manufacture of colored glass, a new craft for Egypt, began to develop rapidly. Archaeologists have found all sorts of small vessels and other items made of opaque, colored glass dating from the New Kingdom. Their appearance testifies to successes in chemical technology. Achievements in applied chemistry are also evident in the development of embalming techniques—the mummies of most New Kingdom pharaohs have been very well preserved. During a much later, troubled period of Egyptian history, they were taken out of their rock tombs and hidden from thieves and desecrators in a secret chamber near the Theban necropolis, where they were found only in the last years of the nineteenth century A.D.

Both the quality and the quantity of domestic animals underwent changes during the New Kingdom. This was due to an unprecedented influx of thousands of cattle of different breeds, sheep, and other domestic animals from countries conquered by the Egyptian armies. The first depictions of camels carrying loads appear on Egyptian reliefs from this time. Horse-breeding began in Egypt during the time of the Hyksos and gave rise to a new military arm—battle chariots—which became an important factor in pharaonic military expeditions into Western Asia. In the Egyptian economy the horse found no use; but wheeled carts appeared in increasing numbers, pulled by yoke oxen. Such vehicles were for transportation of heavy loads, as, for instance, in expeditions to stone quarries. However, the dragging of sleds on the ground remained the principal method of load hauling.

The entire economy of the New Kingdom was closely tied to the policy of conquest conducted by the pharaohs of the Eighteenth and Nineteenth dynasties. Occupied territories and, with time, entire countries were literally laid waste. Suffice it to say that the traditional Sinai mines no longer provided the main source of copper for Egypt; it was now brought mainly from Syria and Palestine or sent from Cyprus as gifts to the pharaohs. Gold, so lavishly used by the Egyptian court and in the temples, was the main item of tribute imposed on subdued Ethiopia, and it was also brought from the conquered lands of Western Asia. Silver was acquired there, but it is possible that it also was obtained by exchange from Asia Minor; silver was mined in the country of the Hittites. Timber continued to be felled in the mountains of Lebanon and, to some extent, in Nubia. Even the independent rulers of Mesopotamia sent presents to the mighty Egyptian kings. Contact with distant Punt became more frequent: communications with this country were facilitated by the construction of a canal connecting the eastern branch of the Nile with the Red Sea. For Egypt, Punt meant myrrh, frankincense, gold, rare varieties of wood, exotic plants, and animals. Egypt also received grain, domestic animals, and sundry food supplies in large quantities, either acquired through plunder by the Egyptian armies or as regular tribute payments. Some plants unknown in former times began to be cultivated during the New Kingdom.

In addition to the imported materials, local raw materials continued to be exploited as of old. We may especially mention the unprecedented increase in the extraction of sandstone from neighboring deserts, which was used as building material in the immense construction projects of the New Kingdom pharaohs. From the onset of the New Kingdom, not only mineral raw materials but also grain and animals began to flow into Egypt.

Returning from their military expeditions, the Egyptians brought unprecedented multitudes of prisoners. Hunting for captives became one of the main activities of the Egyptian army during their almost annual raids abroad. Certainly, the chase for captives during the New Kingdom was necessitated by the increased requirements of the Egyptian economy for additional labor. We have many accounts of the kings presenting thousands of prisoners to Egyptian temples after every successful foreign expedition—especially to the Theban god Amon, who became the supreme deity of the country. We also know that captives were used in the temple economies, where they worked in artisans' and weavers' shops, as builders in construction projects, and also as shepherds. Many foreigners also worked in the temple fields, which was not the case during the Middle Kingdom.

The labor of captives was widely used in the private economies of officials, especially on the small farms of priests, minor temple and government functionaries, and warriors. As soon as the pharaohs started their conquests, they began to reward the soldiers distinguished in battle both with land grants and with prisoners. It is thus not surprising that they went into battle "like lions" and "with a joyful heart" in expectation of generous rewards. It is interesting to note that not all prisoners were used to supplement the domestic labor force. It was mainly Asian prisoners who were used as workers, just as was the case in the Middle Kingdom; captive Sherden sea pirates, possibly natives of faraway Sardinia, frequently became royal bodyguards; Libyans and Ethiopians were recruited into the Egyptian army— initially perhaps only as auxiliary troops.

Of course, it was the native Egyptian laborers who continued to produce the bulk of material goods. They were compulsorily distributed among the different trades and remained in the same dependent condition and worked for their masters in the same way as they did in Middle Kingdom times.

The Egyptian Military Empire during the Eighteenth Dynasty

The principal historical sources for the New Kingdom are annalistic texts of the Egyptian kings carved on the walls of the temples they built and biographies of individual warriors written on funeral stelae. The New Kingdom is also remembered in later literary texts, which poetically re-created the past with vivid accounts of innumerable war expeditions, so typical especially of the beginning of this epoch.

What were the preconditions for the aggressive policies of the New Kingdom that were initiated by the first pharaohs of the Eighteenth Dynasty and that had such an enormous influence on all aspects of Egyptian life? To understand the reasons, we must return to the times of the Egyptian struggle for liberation from the foreign conquerors, the Hyksos.

The fight against this strong adversary required the creation of a numerous and powerful fighting force of an unprecedented size. We have no information about the number of soldiers in this army, but we do know that during the New Kingdom, ten out of each hundred young men mustered at the coming of age were assigned to be soldiers, whereas during the Middle Kingdom the ratio was one in a hundred. There is no doubt that the Egyptian army greatly increased in size during the wars of liberation.

In order to confront the enemy, the country had to be reunified and the central authority had to be strengthened; a concentration of all material and human resources was needed. Much had been done in this regard by the time of Kames, the last pharaoh of the Seventeenth Dynasty. However, at a decisive moment of the Theban king's struggle against the Hyksos, influential groups of the Egyptian aristocracy refused to support his effort to evict the invaders and to reunify the country. During a council meeting called by Kames, important state dignitaries suddenly announced that they had no desire to fulfill his wish to "punish the Asiatics." They declared that their life in Egypt was far from bad, since they owned the best farmland and their cattle grazed without obstacle on the vast meadows of the Delta, and that the power of the Hyksos, in their opinion, was illusory: it was they, the dignitaries, who governed Egypt; the Hyksos did not—they only ruled over the "country of the Asiatics." The nobles also told the king that they would oppose the Hyksos only if the Hyksos were to infringe on their own interests.

The angered pharaoh engaged the Hyksos in battle, disregarding the will of his dignitaries and without their support. All this can be understood if we keep in mind that the nobles of the court of that time—the aristocrats of the emerging New Kingdom—were very closely associated with their nomes, many of which only very recently had submitted to the authority of the new Theban king. The descendants of the Middle Kingdom nomarchs, who enjoyed a great degree of freedom in their nomes before the advent of the harsh reign of Amenemhet III, were not very eager to again have an excessively strong central government. The power of the nome administrations, which had consolidated their positions in the preceding times of trouble, continued to be strong. Texts from the end of the Seventeenth and beginning of the Eighteenth dynasties inform us that the local nobility not only did not help the Theban kings in their endeavor to evict the Hyksos and reunify the country under Thebes but actively opposed their aims by provoking rebellions in the south and north of Egypt. Under these circumstances, the Egyptian kings had to rely increasingly on the support of the growing army. Most of its members were young recruits who came from the working stratum of Egyptian society. Their fighting ability improved with each new battle. The new Egyptian kings also strove to consolidate their power by attracting

loyal subjects of nonaristocratic origin into the different state administrative offices in order to counterbalance the opposition of the old
nobility.

In this manner, the policy of centralization pursued by the Theban
kings at the end of the Seventeenth and beginning of the Eighteenth
dynasties created a new social base, consisting of soldiers and administrators whose new positions ensured material security. A gradual
compulsory redistribution of the country's material and human resources was taking place to the advantage of the new people and at
the expense of the old aristocracy in the capital and in the nomes. But
it was no mere chance that the land estates the new Egyptian elite received were smaller than the possessions of their predecessors of the
Old Kingdom, and that the nomarchs of the New Kingdom no longer
enjoyed in their nomes the amount of political influence that their
forerunners did. However, this internal redistribution of people,
land, and other property during the New Kingdom was not sufficient
for the accomplishment of the intended goals. It could not be made
radical enough, because the country's resources were not unlimited.
Thus, Egypt began to require a continual influx of wealth—material
and human resources from abroad—on an ever-increasing scale. The
interests of the Egyptian kings, who had by then consolidated their
power, coincided with those of the new stratum of civil servants who
supported the dynasty. At the very beginning of the Eighteenth Dynasty, the wars against the foreign invader, having culminated in the
expulsion of the Hyksos, developed into wars of foreign conquest.
These wars were conducted in Western Asia and in the far south, in
Nubia, over the span of many decades. The purpose of the military
expeditions was plunder of the conquered lands.

The roots of the stubborn struggle between the new elite of royal
servants, who rose from the ranks of a vast social layer of people who
supported the royal power, and the old local and metropolitan aris-
tocracies, who, though considerably shaken and exhausted, were still
able to maintain significant economic and political positions, must be
sought in the early period of the New Kingdom. In one form or another, this conflict continued throughout the entire New Kingdom.

In connection with this conflict, we must now turn to the situation
of the priesthood. As late as the fourth to third centuries B.C., the
hellenized Egyptian priest Manetho blamed the Hyksos for desecrat-
ing the Egyptian temples during their invasion. It was natural then
that the Theban kings could count on the support of the priesthood
in their war against the Hyksos. However, the higher priesthood was
inextricably tied to the metropolitan and local provincial aristocracy
by family relationships. The highest priestly positions were traditionally held by persons from the families of the dignitaries and

nomarchs; the head of a local administration was usually also the chief priest of the local cult. Therefore, the alliance between the Theban kings and the numerous influential Egyptian priests was apparently solid enough only during the struggle for independence from the Hyksos. This alliance began to weaken as the tension between the hereditary nobility and the new royal servants continued to mount. The kings of the Eighteenth Dynasty apparently tried to bolster this alliance with gifts; upon returning from foreign expeditions, they presented a good portion of the booty and prisoners to the temples. The first gifts went to the priests of the principal Theban god, Amon, who was identified with the ancient god of Heliopolis, Ra', and became the supreme god of Egypt, Amon-Ra', during the New Kingdom. Yet, it was the priests of Amon-Ra' who toward the end of the Eighteenth Dynasty became the principal adversaries of the new royal servants in their open struggle against the old aristocracy for positions closer to the source of power.

Under the new Theban dynasty at the onset of the sixteenth century B.C., Egypt was on the rise. Ya'hmes I (Amasis I), the first king of the New Kingdom, successfully concluded the war against the Hyksos, which began under his predecessor, Kames. The Egyptian warships, navigating through the canals, approached the walls of Avaris, and after several battles on water and land, the capital of the Hyksos fell. While pursuing the retreating foe, the Egyptians invaded southern Palestine, where for three years they laid siege to the fortified city of Sharuhen, probably the last stronghold of the Hyksos close to Egyptian borders. Eventually, Sharuhen was taken, and the incursions of neighboring Western Asian tribes were repelled. Thereupon, Ya'hmes I took his army upriver, south into northern Ethiopia (Nubia), and defeated the insubordinate Kushite tribes. He also fought against some unnamed rebel in Egypt itself, as well as against a certain Tetian and his "band of malefactors." These struggles within Egypt proper reveal the internal resistance of some local rulers to the central authority. Ya'hmes' successor, Amenhetep I (Amenophis I), continued the struggle against the obstinate resistance of the inhabitants of northern Ethiopia.

As a result of the military expeditions of the first two kings of the New Kingdom, Egypt extended its boundaries back to the old frontiers of the Middle Kingdom during its heyday: from the Sinai Peninsula in the north to the Second Cataract of the Nile in the south.

The beginning of the extensive military expeditions far beyond Egyptian borders is associated with the name of Pharaoh Thutmosis I.[1]

---

1. This is the Greek variant of his name. In the conventional Egyptological reading it is Djehutimesu.

Like his predecessors, Thutmosis I again turned his attention to unruly Ethiopia in order to "punish the rebels in foreign lands and to
repel invasions from the desert region." Having successfully accomplished this task, the Egyptian troops advanced farther south, reaching for the first time the region of the Third Cataract of the Nile,
where they built a fortress on the island of Tombos, establishing a
strong garrison. After the southern expedition, the Egyptian army
moved north into Western Asia and destroyed the small principalities
in the oases of Palestine and Syria, acquiring much booty and taking
many prisoners to Egypt. The army of Thutmosis I reached Nahraina
(Mitanni) on the Euphrates, where the Egyptians for the first time saw
a large river flowing in a north–south direction instead of the south–
north direction of the Nile, to which they were accustomed. This
greatly amazed the Egyptians and was reflected in the Egyptian name
for the Euphrates: "Reversed Water."

The successfully initiated campaigns were interrupted unexpectedly
for more than twenty years. The next king, Thutmosis II, was sickly
and short-lived. His son, by a concubine, Thutmosis III, was coregent
with his father while still a minor. After the death of Thutmosis II,
the real power passed into the hands of his widow, Hatshepsut, who
became the ruler of the country in the name of her husband's minor
son, but soon ascended the Egyptian throne as the ruler in her own
right, probably with the active support of the Theban priesthood.
During the rule of Hatshepsut, the army remained virtually inactive
for twenty years. The peaceful rule of the female pharaoh was marked
by intensive building activities that clearly reflected a special favoritism
toward the priests of the god Amon. Numerous temples consecrated
to the country's principal god were built at Thebes, as well as in the
southern and northern parts of the country. In Deir el-Bahri stands
Hatshepsut's beautiful funerary complex built by Senmut, Hatshepsut's architect and court favorite. Among her foreign activities only
one expedition, to Punt, is well known. It is vividly depicted on colored flat reliefs in her tomb.

Around 1500 B.C., after Hatshepsut died, Thutmosis III (who had
not even been officially mentioned during her reign) finally became
the sole ruler, formally in the twenty-second year of his reign. He
fiercely attempted to obliterate all mention of his stepmother, destroying her statues, chiseling away her name from the walls of
temples, and immuring between walls thirty-meter-tall obelisks that
had been built on her orders. Nor did he spare the men of her retinue, not even the deceased, such as Senmut, whose tomb he ordered
destroyed. Political life in the country drastically changed. The partisans of the new king began to gain preeminence within the ruling
group of the society. Thutmosis III sought support, as did his prede-

cessors, mainly in the army and in the new royal servants' elite. Thus
ended the short period of peace, so unusual for the New Kingdom,
and began a new era of military conquest launched by Thutmosis III.

Fragments of a chronicle written by an Egyptian scribe who participated in the campaigns of Thutmosis III were preserved on the walls
of the Theban temple of Amon-Ra'. The original text, written on
leather scrolls, has long since perished, but whatever remained engraved in stone and certain other documents allow us to follow the
military actions of Thutmosis III, which lasted for almost twenty
years.

In the very year of Hatshepsut's death the Egyptian army departed
from the frontier fortress of Tcharu[2] under the command of Thutmosis III. Ten days later, the troops reached Gaza in southern Palestine, where the king celebrated the twenty-third anniversary of his
formal reign. On the next day he proceeded into the interior of Western Asia, where he had to confront a large coalition headed by a
minor king of the city of Kadesh on the Orontes River. This time the
pharaoh met a unified force instead of the usual uncoordinated
efforts of individual minor kings and princes, typical of earlier times.

Thutmosis decided to engage in battle at the walls of the city of
Megiddo. Among the three possible approaches to the city he chose,
against the advice of his war council, the shortest but most difficult
route, which led through a mountain pass along a narrow path at the
edge of a precipice. "And he went at the head of his troops, showing
the path to every man. And horse followed horse, and His Majesty
was at the head of his army," recounts the chronicle. When the Egyptians came out of the gorge into the Megiddo plain, they built a camp
in full view of the enemy and spent the night. The next morning the
pharaoh himself, in a golden chariot, led the troops into battle. The
enemy could not long withstand the onslaught of the serried Egyptian
army. After a short time, the troops led by the ruler of Kadesh abandoned their chariots, weapons, and tents on the battlefield and hid
precipitously behind the city walls. Many of the retreating soldiers
had to be lifted by their garments and pulled over the city wall. The
Egyptians, however, failed to take advantage of the enemy's disarray,
proceeding instead to loot the abandoned enemy camp and to assess
the booty. Meanwhile, the city gates were closed. It was nevertheless
absolutely imperative that the Egyptians take Megiddo. "All the lords
of the northern countries are locked in this city," the pharaoh said to
his soldiers. "Thus the capture of Megiddo will be like taking thousands of cities." A long siege ensued—the Egyptians had not yet acquired the art of storming fortresses. Only after seven months did the

2. Cuneiform sources call it Tsilu.

starved city surrender. The rulers prostrated themselves before the pharaoh and begged for their lives. The pardoned and humbled "city lords" were sent to their respective cities mounted on donkeys, while the Egyptians again proceeded to count their spoils. The chronicle scrupulously enumerates the military trophies captured in Megiddo and its environs: "340 prisoners, 2,041 horses, 191 foals, 6 stallions." It goes on, listing hundreds of chariots, including the gold-plated chariot of the king of Kadesh, copper and leather armor, wooden props for royal tents, cows, oxen, goats, thousands of sheep, and an enormous amount of grain "delivered to His Majesty from the fields of Megiddo."

And so, year after year, from the twenty-second to the forty-second year of his reign, Thutmosis III led his troops each summer into Western Asia when the harvest was ripe and conquered further cities and regions of Syria. In one of their last expeditions the Egyptians once more took possession of Kadesh, but this time they stormed it through a breach in the city wall. The city of Carchemish became the northernmost limit of Thutmosis III's Asian campaigns. It was an advantageous strategic site at the junction of Mesopotamia, Asia Minor, and Syria.

As a consequence of his wars against the small Syrian principalities, it was unavoidable that Thutmosis III would eventually confront the Mitanni kingdom, situated in northern Mesopotamia. This kingdom served as a natural rear bulwark for Western Asiatic cities in their war with Egypt. On one occasion, Egyptian boats built in Byblos, on the eastern shore of the Mediterranean, were transported to the Euphrates on carts pulled by oxen. The Egyptians sailed downriver, destroying Mitannian cities and villages. After several clashes with the Egyptians, the Mitannian troops were forced to retreat far beyond the river.

In the south, the Nubian possessions of Thutmosis III extended all the way to the Fourth Cataract of the Nile. No successor of Thutmosis could ever go beyond his newly established boundaries—south or north. Egypt became the greatest world power, spanning, together with its tributary states, 3,500 kilometers from the north to the south.

The degree of dependence on Egypt of the conquered countries and cities varied. Ethiopia had the closest ties to Egypt. Directly governed by an Egyptian administration, it was headed by a vicegerent who bore the title Royal Son of Kush, although he was not a royal prince. In Western Asia, however, the Egyptians had not been able to establish such a strong position due to the difficulties of crossing the desert and the continual counteraction by neighboring empires. Nonetheless, Egyptian garrisons resided in important Asiatic cities, and the heirs of the local rulers were kept as hostages in Egypt and raised at the Egyptian court in a manner favorable to the interests of the pharaoh. The vicegerent of Egypt in Asia bore the title Chief of the Northern Countries.

Enormous wealth flowed into Egypt in the form of yearly tribute from the conquered lands and in the form of war loot from the territories that had not yet been subdued. The Egyptian warriors received a large share of this wealth, obtaining military decorations, land, and prisoners as reward for their prowess. The priesthood likewise was not neglected, as the pharaoh needed their support; the biggest share of the war booty went into the treasury of the Theban temple of Amon-Ra'. Vast construction projects were conducted in the main Amon-Ra' temple, as well as in other temples.

Thutmosis III died in the fifty-fourth year of his reign. He was succeeded by his son Amenhetep II, who also spent his time in military campaigns, quelling rebellions in various parts of his realm. This king claimed to have brought more than 100,000 Asian captives into Egypt, possibly during one single punitive expedition to Western Asia. His son Thutmosis IV also led several expeditions to Asia and subdued an uprising in Ethiopia.

The punitive expeditions of Amenhetep II and Thutmosis IV broke the resistance of the minor kings of Western Asia. The might of Egypt was now also recognized by independent states: Kassite Babylonia, the Hittite kingdom, and the city of Asshur. Following an armed confrontation, peaceful relations were established with the kingdom of Mitanni and sealed with the marriage of Thutmosis IV to a Mitannian princess. It is thus not surprising that the thirty-year reign of Amenhetep III, the successor of Thutmosis IV, was exceptionally peaceful. Only once, in the fifth year of his rule, did the new king conduct an expedition into Ethiopia. The reign of Amenhetep III was marked by grandiose building activities. A new and majestic temple was built in Thebes in honor of Amon-Ra'. On the west bank of the Nile, near the capital, Amenhetep erected a suburban royal residence. It was a large, luxurious palace, to the north of which stood the funerary temple of the king, with two enormous statues of the pharaoh rising in front of its pylons—the famous Colossi of Memnon.[3] An avenue flanked by sphinxes, sculpted from pink Aswan granite, was unearthed near the ruins of this temple during the last century. (Two of them are standing today on the bank of the Neva in Leningrad.) It was the incalculable wealth brought to Egypt from tributary and dependent states that allowed Amenhetep III to engage in such gigantic and lavish building activities.

3. Years later, when only the colossi remained standing, the ancient Greeks regarded them as images of Memnon, son of Eos, the goddess of dawn, because the morning breeze produced melodic sounds as it rushed through the cracks of the aging statues. The cracks were patched on the order of a Roman emperor.

However, we find that all was not well during the peaceful time of Amenhetep III. The internal stability of the kingdom was gradually eroding because of the continual, though still unobtrusive, struggle between the two mighty factions of the ruling class. On the one hand, the interests of the hereditary metropolitan and nome aristocracy and, on the other hand, those of the new social stratum of the new royal servants' elite continued to diverge. An open struggle was about to erupt. Its result was the so-called religious reform of Akhenaton (Amenhetep IV).

The Religious Reform of Amenhetep IV and the End of the Eighteenth Dynasty

While still a teenager, Amenhetep IV became coregent with his father, who in the last days of his life fell gravely ill. During this time, as well as in the first years of Amenhetep IV's rule, his intelligent and energetic mother, Queen Tiyi, a commoner, exerted a strong influence on the affairs of the state. The marriage of Amenhetep III to the daughter of an obscure cattle manager of a provincial temple was apparently not favorably regarded by the Theban priesthood and the metropolitan aristocracy. Personal enmity played a part in the events about to unfold, but this enmity was itself merely a manifestation of an old conflict that had been brewing in the upper stratum of the Egyptian aristocracy for many years.

Amenhetep IV became king about 1400 or 1375 B.C. His seventeen-year reign witnessed the harshest collision between the two mighty parties of the ruling class.

The initiators of this decisive confrontation were people of the vast stratum of royal servants, particularly those who were personally connected to the royal family. The texts of the New Kingdom call them *nemhu*.[4] The ablest representatives of this new group made distinguished service careers, consolidating their positions in all areas of the Egyptian administrative and economic bureaucracy, in the army and in the royal court. Their main goal became the removal of the old hereditary nobility as far as possible from the sources of power and wealth. The pharaoh, heading this new, loyal and dynamic faction, hoped to strengthen his autocratic power still further.

The task confronting the new royal servants' elite was not an easy

---

4. The original meaning of the word *nemhu* was "poor, destitute, insignificant." But with the beginning of the middle of the Eighteenth Dynasty this term appears with increasing frequency in the inscriptions of people who held very important positions in the Egyptian hierarchy. Thus, *nemhu* came to describe the people of the new stratum of royal servants (at least during the New Kingdom), its original meaning hinting at the social origin of the new elite as contrasted with the old aristocracy.

one, because their opponents still maintained secure positions at the capital and in the local centers. The influence of the powerful Theban priesthood, closely tied to the old hereditary nobility, was enormous. The priesthood of Amon-Ra', the principal god since the beginning of the Eighteenth Dynasty, became the most persistent rival of the new royal servants' elite and of Amenhetep IV himself. It was therefore inevitable that the struggle acquired the outward form of religious conflict; its focal point became the rivalry between the pan-Egyptian god Aton,[5] newly proclaimed by the pharaoh, and the Theban god Amon-Ra', along with other traditional gods of Egypt.

The bitter and irreconcilable position assumed by the Theban priesthood can be better understood if we take into account that by that time a new system of relationships had developed between the temple economy and the royal administration. This system, typical of the entire New Kingdom epoch, involved rigid control by the central government over all branches of the economy of the temples and demanded significant transfers of grain harvested on temple lands for the benefit of the royal administration. This was to maintain the ever-growing state machinery and the army. It seems that similar payments were also exacted from other productive temple enterprises. In addition, temples had to supply grain to their own workers and to various nontemple functionaries for their sustenance.

We know about the generous gifts presented by the pharaohs of the Eighteenth Dynasty to many Egyptian temples after each successful military expedition. But at the same time it is evident that the temple economies became an important source of wealth for the pharaohs themselves, helping them to continue their aggressive foreign policy and to consolidate the positions of the royal servants' elite. The control over the temples and the exactions of the central government probably increased as time passed, provoking the discontent and resistance of the priesthood in general and of the most powerful Theban priesthood in particular. About the time when Amenhetep IV ascended the throne, the confrontation between the opposing parties was reaching a climax, and an overt struggle became inevitable.

However, in the beginning of the new pharaoh's reign, events evolved comparatively slowly. The reforms, which would soon cause tremendous repercussions in all aspects of Egyptian life, were gradual. The introduction of a new countrywide state cult of the god Aton, who was worshiped as the personification of the solar disk, with its rays, like outstretched arms, radiating from its center and offering the

5. Aton or Aten is the traditional scholarly pronunciation of the name of this god. Actually, the Egyptological transcription of the name should have been Iten, and its actual New Kingdom pronunciation was apparently Yati.

country all the good things in life, by no means implied renunciation of the ancient Egyptian polytheism, especially since the first temple dedicated to the new god was built by the pharaoh in Thebes, near the sanctuaries of Amon-Ra'.

But the new countrywide state cult of Aton, especially patronized by the pharaoh, who proclaimed himself the new god's only son, meant new enormous temple construction projects and, correspondingly, grants to these new temples of land, cattle, and hunting and fishing facilities all over Egypt. The economies of the new temples had to be provided with labor and staffed with both high and lower priests to serve the new god. Texts of that time show that the new temples were mainly staffed by members of the new royal servants' elite. All of this required a significant reallocation of material and human resources in favor of the new god and at the expense of the priests who served the old traditional Egyptian gods (especially Amon-Ra')— the main opponents of the reformer-king and his supporters.

Apparently in the sixth year of Amenhetep IV's rule the struggle between the two factions strongly intensified, soon reaching its apogee. The king and his court left the unfriendly and hated Thebes, and a new capital was erected 300 kilometers downstream from the old center of Amon-Ra' worship. The new capital was named Akhet-Aton ("The Horizon of Aton," meaning the place where the solar disk rises above the world; today it is the archaeological site of Tell-Amarna). Somewhat earlier, as a sign that even the name of the god Amon should be avoided in his own name, he changed his personal name to Akhen-Aton ("Serviceable to Aton"; hereafter, Akhenaton).[6] The members of his family and his dignitaries whose names included the name of Amon or of any of the other old Egyptian gods received new names. The names of gods opposing Aton began to be erased from all monuments.

The Egyptian court, headed by Akhenaton, remained in the new capital for over ten years. Built in an unbelievably short time, Akhet-Aton became a large city with magnificent royal palaces, an enormous temple honoring Aton, vast gardens, and private residences for high royal officials who proudly advertised their humble origins in the inscriptions of their rich tombs.

Led by the king, the dynamic partisans of these reforms seemed to be winning the battle against their opponents. But the cult of Aton had no roots in the traditions and notions either of the noblemen or of the Egyptian populace at large. The replacement of the contradictory archaic cults of the old gods with the logically reasoned, prac-

---

6. Akhenaton is the traditional but incorrectly pronounced name. The Egyptological transcription is Ikh-ne-Iten.

tically exclusive worship of the solar disk, Aton, did not promise a better life for anyone but the appointees of the pharaoh, who competed with the old priesthood. It promised neither real nor imaginary benefits, such as, for example, more just rewards in the afterlife. Meanwhile, the priesthood of Amon remained strong not solely because of its material wealth, accumulated through the centuries, or its embodiment of the old traditions of national beliefs, but also because, since the time of the Middle Kingdom, the common people considered Amon the specific defender of the humble man and the safest refuge in time of tribulation. Also, there was no irreconcilable class contradiction between the two ruling-class groups: the adherents of Amon and those of Aton. And so, the period of redistribution of power and wealth was necessarily followed by a mutual agreement between the opposing factions.

It is not surprising that the premature death of the pharaoh (he had been ill since an early age) radically changed the course of events. Semnekhka-Ra' and Tutankhamen, the young and short-lived husbands of Akhenaton's elder daughter and the successors of the reformer-king, lacked the authority, fanaticism, and will of their father-in-law to continue his reform. A brief but stormy struggle erupted over the succession of Amenhetep IV during the rule of Semnekhka-Ra', whose reign lasted only three years. During this time, the cult of Aton underwent profound changes. The exclusive worship of Aton, which was the rule during the last years of Amenhetep IV, was abolished, and the old hierarchy of the gods was eventually restored. The worship of Amon as the principal god of Egypt was fully restored probably at the very beginning of the rule of Tutankhamen, who abandoned Akhet-Aton and returned to Thebes with his court.

The new boy-king, who had not yet reached even ten years of age, did not of course accomplish such an important action, a turning point in the country's life, on his own. An influential group of the former partisans of the reformer-king must have been active behind the scenes, and being fully aware of the changed situation, they were inclined to make peace with their former adversaries. Indeed, the most influential personality at the court of the young pharaoh was an old dignitary of Amenhetep IV, Ay, commander of the chariot troops, who until lately had been a zealous worshiper of Aton. The proof of his loyalty to this god was engraved on the walls of his tomb, which he erected early in his life at Akhet-Aton.

Tutankhamen died at the age of nineteen, having ruled for almost ten years, and was buried on the west bank of the Nile in the traditional burial place of the Eighteenth Dynasty kings—The Valley of the Kings, near Thebes. His tomb, hewn into rock, was discovered in 1922–24 by the English archaeologist Howard Carter. Fortunately, it remained almost untouched by ancient looters and yielded a wealth of remarkable art objects and other funerary items. The name of the owner of this wealth, the unremarkable and youthful king Tutankhamen, instantly became known to the entire world.

The Eighteenth Dynasty virtually ceased to exist, because Tutankhamen had no heirs, and after an unsuccessful attempt to offer the throne to a Hittite prince, the throne passed to the old favorite, Ay. Ay may have been related to Nefertiti, the principal wife of Amenhetep IV. Four years later, after Ay's death in the middle of the fourteenth century, the throne was seized by the powerful commander of the Egyptian army, Haremhab. This man, who was not even related to the ruling dynasty, was proclaimed king by the Theban priests on the occasion of a festivity honoring Amon.

The reign of Haremhab lasted for over thirty years and was an important postreform period in Egyptian history. This time provides some insights into the final fate of Akhenaton's reforms. The new pharaoh conducted a fierce campaign against the memory of the reformer-king, which had already begun under his predecessors. The city of Akhet-Aton, long since abandoned by the court and its inhabitants, was ruthlessly destroyed on his command. Everything was reduced to dust: royal palaces, residences of court officials, and workshops of sculptors.[7] The name of the "Apostate from Akhet-Aton" disappeared from official documents, and the years of Amenhetep IV's rule were merged in the royal chronicles with the reign of Haremhab. The king, seeking the support of the Theban priesthood and of the circles allied with it, erected monumental sanctuaries in the Karnak temple to the god Amon and presented the temples with vast land estates, as well as people, cattle, and a variety of implements. It seemed that the foes of Akhenaton's reforms achieved a resounding victory and that the royal court fully reversed its social orientation.

However, texts from the time of Haremhab also mention another side of his policies. He did not lack in attention to the social stratum that had supported the reformer-king. A decree issued by Haremhab and engraved on stone slabs in many Egyptian cities imposed severe punishment (the cutting off of a guilty party's nose and banishment to the desert fortress of Tcharu) on any official found guilty of arbitrary actions against a *nemhu*. Measures to ensure justice throughout the country were enacted; infringements were to be punished by death. The protection of the people of the middle, serving stratum, especially the soldiers, became a permanent concern of the pharaoh, and their material well-being was guaranteed by the wealth of the palace

7. In one of the workshops, that of the sculptor Djehutimes, archaeologists found the incomparable unfinished head of Queen Nefertiti, as well as other masterpieces of the so-called Amarna Period.

and the pharaoh's granary. It is interesting that many top positions in the royal court were still held, as before, by persons from the lower and middle echelons—functionaries not connected with the old hereditary aristocracy concentrated in Thebes. Egyptian kings of the postreform period were not predisposed to spend all their time in Thebes. Even Tutankhamen's court stayed mostly in northern Memphis rather than in southern Thebes. Haremhab moved north immediately after his coronation, and this tradition was continued by the pharaohs of the following Nineteenth Dynasty.

All this suggests that the long conflict between the old aristocracy, supported by the Theban priesthood, and the new royal servants' elite, which arose in the beginning of the Eighteenth Dynasty and gradually became entrenched, passed through a period of open struggle under Amenhetep IV and ended in a sort of temporary compromise after his death, resulting in a certain territorial delineation. The influence of the Theban priesthood increased in the southern portion of the country, whereas in the north, where the royal court remained most of the time and where the bulk of the Egyptian army was stationed, the strength was on the side of the middle stratum of service people—the *nemhu*. During that time, Lower Egypt, which had formerly ranked second in economic and political matters, entered a period of tremendous growth. Its importance increased especially with the resumption of extensive military operations in Western Asia by the pharaohs of the Nineteenth Dynasty, who succeeded Haremhab after his death.

Egypt during the Nineteenth Dynasty

The internal struggle that dragged on in Egypt for many years affected relations with its Western Asian possessions. The once-submissive minor local princes began to secede from Egypt. Documents from the diplomatic archive of Akhet-Aton (Tell-Amarna) tell us that Egypt was unable to provide timely military assistance even to its own Asian allies (and very few of these remained) when they were being attacked by neighbors who no longer recognized the authority of the Egyptian king. The Hittite kingdom, which began its consolidation in Asia Minor during the middle of the fifteenth century B.C., began to claim pharaonic domains in Syria and Palestine and thus presented a very serious threat to Egyptian interests in Western Asia.

The separatist tendencies of the local rulers, their internal wars, the military pressure exerted from the north by the Hittites, the continual incursions of bands of Hapiru (see Lecture 14 for a discussion of the Hapiru), and the utter passivity of the Egyptian army resulted in an almost complete loss, toward the end of Amenhetep IV's reign, of the great gains that had been achieved in Western Asia under Thutmosis III. The weak successors of the reformer-king—the last pharaohs of the Eighteenth Dynasty—were not capable of consolidating the foreign political position of Egypt, although an expedition was organized to Western Asia during the reign of Tutankhamen, probably under the command of Haremhab. Once the energetic Haremhab became king, he was forced to direct his attention to the internal consolidation of the country. His efforts were quite successful, and the kings of the next dynasty were able to direct their attention to foreign affairs. Wide-scale military operations were resumed in order to recover the lost territories in Western Asia. A direct confrontation between the Egyptians and the Hittites was unavoidable.

Seti I, the second king of the new dynasty, organized large expeditions across the Egyptian borders. This pharaoh succeeded his father, Rameses I, the founder of the dynasty, who reigned for only two years.

Western Asia had not seen an Egyptian king commanding the Egyptian army since the time of the redoubtable Amenhetep II. Seti I personally led his great army in a vast campaign, restoring Egyptian power all the way up to the Megiddo fortress—memorable since the campaigns of Thutmosis III. Seti I also conducted punitive expeditions deep into Nubia and west of the Delta, where he defeated Libyan tribes; thereupon he again crossed the Sinai. This time, the Egyptian troops entered the Orontes Valley and advanced to the city of Kadesh (Qinza), which had long since become a Hittite stronghold. This was the first confrontation between Egyptian and Hittite armies. However, the first clashes between the vanguards of both contenders for hegemony in Western Asia were merely a test of strength in anticipation of a future, decisive engagement.

Toward the end of the fourteenth or the beginning of the thirteenth centuries, after the death of Seti I, his twenty-two-year-old son Rameses II became ruler of the strengthened Egyptian kingdom. Rameses II's dream was to restore and expand the Western Asiatic possessions of Egypt. To accomplish his aims, Rameses II had to defeat the Hittites—no easy task.

For the first time the Egyptian army confronted a strong, disciplined armed force instead of the familiar and uncoordinated troops of the minor rulers of Syria and Palestine, or a weak coalition of these, as was the case during the reign of Thutmosis III. The Hittite kingdom was at the peak of its power, and its army was united under one commander, King Muwatallis, who also relished the opportunity to crush his competitor in the region. Several sources tell about the fierceness of this difficult war. Especially interesting is a detailed and vivid account of the first battle fought by Rameses II against the Hittites under the walls of Kadesh.

In the spring of the fifth year of his reign (probably in 1312 B.C.) Rameses II gathered a large army and departed from the frontier fortress of Tcharu. After marching for twenty-nine days the vanguard, led personally by the king, encamped one-day's march from Kadesh. The Hittite army positioned itself under the walls of this city, together with the allied troops of the small principalities of Syria and Asia Minor. The Hittites sent scouts to the Egyptian camp and misled Rameses II by convincing him that the armies of his adversaries were so scared of the Egyptians that they were hastily retreating to the north, far from Kadesh. Without waiting for the rest of his army, Rameses II and his vanguard detachment advanced to Kadesh, commenced battle, and narrowly escaped total destruction. A stroke of luck saved the Egyptians: the unexpected appearance on the battlefield of an Egyptian contingent of recent recruits that had been sent earlier by the king along the seashore in order to join the main force later. This fortuitous circumstance saved the situation. The counterattacks of the Hittite battle chariots were futile—they just interfered with one another, their wheels colliding in the narrow mountain passage. For some unexplained reason, Muwatallis held his infantry in reserve. The Egyptians managed to hold their positions until the evening, when their main force was to arrive. Eventually, neither army was able to prevail; the battle was a draw.

It took Rameses II fifteen years of tough fighting to dislodge the Hittites from southern Syria and to capture Kadesh and other cities, which the Egyptians were now able to take by storm rather than by siege. The northern portion of the former possessions of Thutmosis III remained in the hands of the Hittites. In the twenty-first year of his reign (ca. 1296 or 1270 B.C.) Rameses II signed a peace treaty with King Hattusilis III, which was later confirmed by the marriage between the Egyptian king and the daughter of the Hittite king.

Following the war with the Hittites, Rameses II continued to rule Egypt for more than forty-five years. (He had no peers in longevity, save for Pepi II, way back in the Old Kingdom.) In the tradition of his predecessors, Rameses II chose Lower Egypt for his permanent residence. He built a luxurious royal residence in the eastern Delta—the city Per-Rameses ("House of Rameses"). His extensive building activity involved Thebes, Abydos, and Nubia. In Nubia he ordered the carving of an enormous cave temple from a sheer cliff. Giant statues of the pharaoh, also hewn from the rock, flanked both sides of the entrance to the sanctuary. This famous temple—Abu-Simbel—had to be cut into sections, raised, and reconstructed above the waters of the great Aswan Dam water reservoir, where it stands today, majestically rising on the shore of the artificial lake.

Rameses II survived many of his sons.[8] After his death, his thirteenth son, the middle-aged Mer-ne-Ptaḥ, became king. During his reign (last quarter of the thirteenth century) Egypt was invaded from the sea and from Palestine by the "Sea Peoples" (see Lecture 14 for a discussion of the Sea Peoples). This emergency coincided with a major incursion of Libyan tribes into the western Delta. This first wave of Sea Peoples, some of whom probably came from western Asia Minor and from the islands of the eastern Mediterranean, was repelled by Egyptian troops led by Mer-ne-Ptaḥ. After his death serious internal upheavals occurred in Egypt, leading to another dynastic change.

Egypt during the Twentieth Dynasty and the End of the New Kingdom

The last 150 years of the New Kingdom saw the rule of the Twentieth Dynasty, which came to power after some tumultuous events obscurely mentioned in the narrative portion of one of the most important administrative-economic ancient Egyptian sources—the huge forty-five-meter-long Harris papyrus.[9] This papyrus was written during the time of Rameses III (in the twelfth century B.C.). It seems that the struggle between the opposing elites that reached a climax during the reign of Amenhetep IV flared up again. The compromise that had been reached after the open struggle during the reign of the reformer-king lost its force. Under the new circumstances, this struggle continued below the surface and gradually undermined the strength and unity of the country. The power of the central administration was radically weakened after the death of Rameses II. In addition, the invasion by the Sea Peoples was repelled at great cost. It is possible that a power struggle was brewing in the capital. The papyrus tells us that Egypt and its people, left to the mercy of fate, found themselves under the rule of "the great" and of "rulers of the cities"; the consequence was internecine wars that devastated the country. Murders were common. The victims included people from all classes—"the great" as well as commoners.

A Syrian named Irsu managed to assume power in the country, at

8. At the end of his life Rameses II married his own daughter. It was customary in Egypt (as in Elam and in some other Oriental states) for kings to marry their sisters to prevent the creation of relatives by marriage among the aristocracy, who could pose a threat by pretending to the throne along the distaff line. In his latter years Rameses II apparently had no living sisters.

9. Important papyri are traditionally designated by the name of the first modern owner—as in this case—or by the name of the first publisher.

least for a time. It is difficult to know what forces supported him, who were his adherents, and how large was the scale of his activities. We cannot exclude the possibility that the difficult conditions created by the internal struggle and the inevitable economic ruin caused a broad-based uprising among the Egyptian lower classes, with the participation of foreigners. Someone named Sethnekht finally managed to suppress the rebellion and to restore the authority of the central government.

Rameses III, son of Sethnekht and founder of the Twentieth Dynasty (middle of the twelfth century B.C.), was fortunate to inherit a pacified country; otherwise, he may not have been able to face successfully two major invasions of the western Delta by the Libyan tribes and, for a second time, by the Sea Peoples. They were repelled in a series of bloody battles on land and sea. Rameses III also fought in Western Asia with the intention of consolidating the weakened Egyptian positions beyond the Sinai Peninsula. The Egyptian army now included many more foreigners than before—Sherdens, Libyans, Philistines, and others. The need to recruit aliens arose because the pharaoh, yielding to pressure from the priesthood, whose support was essential during these difficult times, exempted the temple workers from military service (which involved the drafting of every tenth male).

The generous gifts and privileges granted to the temples (which had become increasingly opposed to the central power), the maintenance of a large, though now less numerous, army, the exhausting wars, and the arbitrary actions of local administrations resulted in a drastic deterioration of the internal condition of the country and sapped the treasury. On one occasion, the royal treasury was so insolvent that it was unable to distribute rations on time to craftsmen and employees working in the royal necropolis, and they went on strike. Various court cliques continued their infighting; eventually, Rameses III himself became their victim.

After the death of Rameses III and during the rule of the last eight kings of the Twentieth Dynasty (all of whom were called Rameses), the internal stability of Egypt and the Egyptian position abroad finally collapsed. Under Rameses IV, Egypt lost all its foreign possessions, except for Ethiopia. The central administration could not firmly hold the reins of power. The political separation of Lower and Upper Egypt (in the latter the Theban priesthood began to acquire absolute power), which had appeared soon after the reforms of Amenhetep IV, now greatly intensified. Rameses IX attempted, without success, to limit somewhat the rights of the high priest of Amon. Finally, under Rameses XI, the high priest of Amon, Herihor, assumed all the highest state offices. He became the supreme official (*tchati*) and commander of the Egyptian army. After the death of the last pharaoh of the Twentieth Dynasty, royal power passed to Herihor in the south. Lower Egypt, however, did not recognize the supremacy of the Theban ruler. The Delta eventually created its own dynasty, which ruled from the city of Tanis (Per-Rameses). By the middle of the eleventh century B.C., a united Egyptian kingdom ceased to exist.

9

The Culture of Ancient Egypt

I. A. LAPIS

Religion

Throughout the development of the Egyptian state the significance and character of its different religious cults changed. The beliefs of ancient hunters and farmers intermingled with ideas created by struggles between the different emerging and declining power centers of the country. The Egyptian religion preserved primitive concepts for a long time, and many very ancient cults remained important throughout the history of ancient Egypt.

The numerous deities that were worshiped in the different regions of Egypt personified diverse natural forces and social phenomena. The sky was represented by a woman or a cow; the earth and air were represented by male gods. The ibis-headed god Thoth was the patron of writing and sorcery. The goddess Maat personified Truth. Natural phenomena were perceived as manifestations of different deities.

In ancient times the Egyptians worshiped certain gods in the image of animals and birds. Since very early on, the falcon of Horus was associated with the notion of a mighty god of the sky. The falcon appeared on tribal standards and was also shown bringing victory over northern Egypt to Nar'mer on his stone relief palette.

After the formation of the Egyptian state, Horus appeared as the constant patron of the pharaohs, who began to adopt the denomination "Horus." The development of the cult of Osiris as that of the deceased pharaoh involved Horus in the Osirian myths and, thus, contributed to the merging of the cult of Horus with the royal cult. In addition, falcons, being objects of worship in different parts of Egypt, were involved in the emerging local cults of solar deities.

Vestiges of the original worship of animal deities can be observed in the animal and bird heads of otherwise anthropomorphic deities and in the headdresses of some gods (the cow horns of Hathor, the gazelle horns of Satit, the ram horns of Amon, and so forth). Later, the animals and birds in question came to be regarded as the "souls" of the gods and were actually kept at the temples. In order for a particular animal to be recognized as the incarnation of the corresponding god, certain signs had to be manifested: for example, the animal had to have a certain specific color; its spots had to follow a definite pattern; the horns had to be of a particular shape.

The bull was one of the most revered animals in Egypt. Since early times, the bull personified the reproductive force and fertility. The worship of the bull was typical of many localities; often it merged with the worship of the main local deity. Thus, in Memphis the bull Apis became the soul of the local god Ptaḥ, whose cult was connected with the worship of Osiris. In Heliopolis the bull Mnevis was regarded as the personification of the Sun god Raʿ. The bull Bouchis became the "living image" of the local god Mentu of Hermontis.

The animal representing Amon was a ram, which for a long time had been worshiped as the personification of fertility, like the bull. Sacred rams were kept in temples dedicated to a number of different gods. A ram was regarded as the personification of the god Khnum in Esneh, in Elephantine, and in the twenty-first nome; in Heracleopolis, it personified the god Herishaf. Mendes was a very important ram-worshiping center; here, the sacred ram was called Banebjed, "the Soul of the Lord of Djed" (Mendes).

The dung beetle, called scarab by the ancient writers, was widely worshiped. In trying to understand natural phenomena, the Egyptians developed the image of the beetle pushing the disk of the sun. The scarab was also depicted in flight, carrying the sun. It became the embodiment of the rising sun—Khepri—and was associated with the hope for life and resurrection. Beetles were worshiped in temples devoted to the sun.

The cult of the goddess Hathor originated in the worship of the cow. Hathor was usually represented as a woman, in some cases with a cow's ear and horns and, in others, with a cow's head. Deified cows were kept by certain temples. Because the sky was conceived, according to some legends, in the form of a cow, Hathor came to be regarded as the heavenly cow. She was revered as the goddess giving birth to the sun and granting fertility. In her role as fertility goddess, Hathor was also a tree deity.

Many gods were associated with an animal form: for example, sacred cats, monkeys, snakes, ichneumons (mongooses), ibises, falcons. After death, the bodies of these sacred animals and birds were mummified, wrapped in shrouds, and placed in tombs bearing the representation of the dead animal on the funeral slab. Many animal cemeteries have been discovered throughout Egypt, the most famous being the crocodile tombs in the Fayum, and those of the Apis bulls in the Fayum and of the Bouchis bulls in Hermontis.

Solar cults developed in many centers in very early times. The solar deities were represented by different images. In one region the image

was of a winged disk soaring in the sky; in another, an enormous beetle rolling the solar disk across the sky. Sometimes the solar deity was
depicted as a falcon or as a human with a falcon's head. The names of
the deities were Ra', Atum, Khepri, and Horus, but the cults were devoted to the same great heavenly source of light. Many solar deities
gradually merged together. Sometimes such mergers were rationalized; for example, it was argued that Khepri was the morning sun, Ra'
the sun during the day, and Atum the setting sun.

The Sun god Ra' acquired special importance from almost the very
beginning. The periodic disappearance of the sun in the evening and
its emergence in the morning were explained by its being swallowed
each evening and being born each morning, delivered by Heaven in
the guise of a cow or in the guise of a woman, named Nut. Other concepts coexisted. For example, Ra' voyaged across the sky in a boat
during the day toward the western mountains, where Ra' changed
boats and navigated throughout the night. Having completed his
nocturnal voyage, Ra' would transfer to his day boat, emerge from
a passage in the eastern mountains, and reappear in the sky. But
in order to rise, the sun had to fight his enemy—the dragon Apep.
Once victorious, Ra' made his appearance. Since very early times,
the cult of Ra'—the life-giving and all-protecting god—was a cult
of the pan-Egyptian state god, especially because of his connection
with the worship of the dead king resurrecting as Horus. Heliopolis
and Edfu were the principal centers of sun worship. In one form
or another, the cult of the sun remained the official state cult until
the end of ancient Egyptian history. And when at any time in history
some god acquired a pan-Egyptian significance, he was immediately
associated with the principal Sun god Ra' (Amon-Ra', Sebek-Ra',
Mentu-Ra').

During the Middle Kingdom, when Egypt was reunified under the
Theban nome, the cult of Amon acquired paramount importance.
The origin of this cult is not quite clear. On the one hand, the cult of
Amon was undoubtedly connected to that of the cult god of the generating forces of nature—Min in Coptos; on the other, Amon is
found among the most ancient gods of the city of Shmunu, capital of
the fifteenth Upper Egyptian nome. The cult of Amon was transferred to Thebes in order to strengthen the new dynasty and the new
capital. The local Theban deities, Mut and Khensu, were declared
Amon's wife and son. Because Thebes remained the Egyptian capital
for many centuries, the cult of Amon acquired a pan-Egyptian character. To enhance the authority of this god, he was associated with
Ra'. And as Amon-Ra', he became closely tied to the pharaonic cult
and was even endowed with the traits of a creator god. In response to

the political situation prevailing in the country during the Middle Kingdom and the beginning of the New Kingdom, Amon was imagined as the protector and patron of the common people. But his main traits were those of a conqueror and awesome lord—"King of the Gods." Certain acts of the king were treated as orders issued by Amon; even judicial sentences in court could be pronounced in the name of Amon.

The cult of the ruling king and the official deification of royal power was a specific phenomenon and one of the most important characteristics of Egyptian religion. Since early times, a pharaoh was considered to be of divine origin, being the terrestrial incarnation of the royal god Horus. A "Horus name" was part of the titles of the pharaoh. Already in the Old Kingdom, pharaohs began to be regarded as sons of Ra', and their name became enclosed in a protective circle. When Thebes had acquired the most important political role and the local god Amon had acquired a pan-Egyptian character, the king began to be likened to this god and was even declared the son of Amon. The miraculous conception and birth of the pharaoh was represented on temple walls. The power of the pharaoh was thought to extend not only to his country and subjects but also to natural phenomena. The pharaoh played the central role in the state agricultural festivities: when the Nile was about to overflow its banks, he threw into the river a papyrus containing orders to begin the inundation. He also initiated the plowing of the fields and cut the first sheaf of a new harvest.

The worship of the deceased king was most closely connected to the pan-Egyptian cult of the dead god, Osiris, who represented the annually dying vegetation. The myth of Osiris, as re-created from various sources, tells the story about his rule over Egypt in some distant past, and how he taught people how to cultivate fields and orchards. His brother, the god Seth, who himself wanted to rule, murdered Osiris. The wife of Osiris, the goddess Isis, gave birth after his death to his son Horus, who began the struggle for his succession. After lengthy litigations, the gods finally recognized Horus as the legitimate heir, and Osiris became king of the underworld. Osiris personified the waters of the Nile and was associated with cultivated plants—barley, spelt, and grapes. The connection of the living king with Horus and of the dead king with Osiris is traced to the earliest period of Egyptian history.

The principal places of worship of Osiris were Bousiris and Abydos, where the cult of Osiris completely absorbed the cults of the local gods. Here, at the end of the flood period, splendid festivals were celebrated, re-creating the fate of Osiris: his death, Isis's search for his body, his mourning, and his funeral.

In death, the pharaoh was likened to Osiris—even identified with him—and thus was granted eternal life. These beliefs are expounded in the texts carved inside the pyramids; they are records of the royal funerary rituals. These beliefs were also reflected in the coronation ritual, when the living king acted as Horus, and the mummy of the deceased king represented Osiris. The worship of Osiris preserved the character of a specifically royal cult for a long time. It was only after the end of the Old Kingdom, and especially after the Middle Kingdom, that participation in the cult of Osiris was extended to the dead in general. Not only the king but any ordinary person could become Osiris and receive eternal life with the help of special incantations. Faith in an afterlife was also strongly intertwined with the solar cult, which, similarly, was originally associated exclusively with the king. Ra', like Osiris, personified the source of eternal life, and a deceased person, who by means of sorcery became a passenger in the boat of Ra', shared the god's fate.

The image of an afterlife consisted of a complex combination of some very ancient and some more recent beliefs that were often contradictory and, at times, even mutually exclusive. The Egyptians believed that a person had several souls. One of these souls was called the Ka, a person's double, who lived in the tomb. Another was the Ba, which was imagined as a bird with a human head. The Ba could rejoin the body and revive the deceased after the performance of special rituals. This required the preservation of the body and led to the practice of mummification and to the construction of durable tombs built of stone or hewn in the rocks. However, it was not sufficient to perform the funeral rites and to provide the deceased with the provisions and the implements necessary in the afterlife. Eternal life depended on continued sacrificial offerings, which were the responsibility of the heirs, especially the eldest son of the deceased, who also had to bear the maintenance expenses of the tomb and the funerary priests. For this reason, kings, as well as private persons, apportioned the income from certain lands to cover the maintenance costs of the afterlife cult.

A person's name had enormous importance in Egyptian beliefs; the destruction of a person's written name would cause irreparable harm to that person in the afterlife. Necessarily, Egyptians always attached great significance to the preservation of names. The myth about Ra' and the dragon involves precisely this belief. It tells how Isis cunningly discovered the true name of Ra' and thus attained power over him.

The idea of judgment in the hereafter took its final form around the time of the New Kingdom. This belief existed earlier but in very vague terms. The concept of a posthumous judgment embraced ethical and magical elements in a typically Egyptian fashion. A written repudiation of one's sins was regarded as actually doing away with them. When a dead person's heart set the scales in balance during the judgment by Osiris, it meant that the deceased was righteous and was saved from being devoured by the monster Amemet.

The state after death was regarded as the continuation of earthly life. This was interpreted so literally that Egyptians used special incantations to protect a deceased person from death in the hereafter. The living communicated with the dead not only by sacrificial offerings and prayers but also by written requests and complaints presented to the dead. The intervention of dead people in the affairs of the living was regarded as an everyday occurrence. It was firmly believed that a deceased person could help the living or, conversely, bring about calamities. The dead were asked to help in court cases, to heal the sick, and to grant heirs. This last was especially important for the maintenance of the afterlife cult. One wished to be able to visit the earth after death and to spend time among the living. Special texts were thought to help achieve this and to ensure a dead person's "exit by day" from his tomb.

In hymns, in records of rituals, and in similar texts we sometimes encounter notions about the creation of the world. They are very contradictory, probably because they originate in different times and places. Although one doctrine could temporarily predominate over another, there was no canonic version of the creation story. The myth of Heliopolis held that Atum created the world, whereas in Memphis this role was attributed to Ptah. One myth tells that a mound rose from the primeval ocean and that a lotus grew on it and gave life to the Sun god. Another claims that the sun appeared in an egg laid by "The Great Cackler" on the same mound. The most widespread, however, was the Heliopolitan myth because of this city's special status as a very ancient political and religious center. According to this version, Atum (identified with the sun as Atum-Ra') came into existence from the primeval chaos, fecundated himself with his semen, and engendered through his mouth the first pair of gods: Shu, the air, and Tefnut, the moisture. Thus, Atum-Ra' became the archancestor of the universe, because Shu and Tefnut engendered Geb, the earth, and Nut, the sky, who in turn gave birth to Osiris, Isis, Seth, and Nephtys. These gods formed the Heliopolitan "Great Nine," who occupied a prominent place in the pantheon.

A later legend from Memphis dating from the state (i.e., dynastic) period of Egyptian history says that the local god, Ptah, created the world through his heart (the Egyptians considered the heart to be the seat of thought, i.e., the mind) and his word. Ptah created all things in the universe by naming them.

Architecture

Very little information is available about the domestic architecture of ancient Egypt. Certain pictorial and literary representations allow us to imagine a type of residential rural home made of adobe brick and enclosed within a fenced area. The entrance to the house opened onto a courtyard and was protected by a porch with supporting columns. Two or three doors led from the porch to the living rooms. The roof, which was either flat or vaulted, was supported by capitals in the form of plants. A pavilion was sometimes erected on a flat roof, eventually developing into a second story; some three-story houses were built with stairs attached to the outside. The enclosed courtyard often had a small covered pond. The houses were ventilated via windows or special cupola-type openings in the roof. The more complex houses featured a central hall with one to three columns. the hall was entered by way of a porch and was surrounded by private rooms. The stucco on the walls of the houses, as well as the columns, capitals, and wooden doors, were painted in bright colors. Windows were framed with grills, usually rectangular but, later, also ornamental.

The ruins of a settlement near the pyramid of Senwesert II near the modern town of El-Lahun give us an idea about the architectural and social planning of Egyptian towns. The settlement was surrounded by a common wall, and a second wall divided the town into two unequal portions. The houses of the poor quarter were clumped together in the smaller of the two sectors. The larger sector contained a palace, large residences of the nobles, and medium-sized houses. The largest houses contained up to seventy rooms used for different purposes and occupied an area of 60 × 40 meters, which equals approximately fourteen middle-sized or twenty-five small houses. There was a rectangular grid of streets and alleys, bordered by the blank walls of houses and courtyards.

A large house was usually divided into four sections: the rooms of the owners; a section for women; servants' quarters; and a household area. Each section was clustered around its own yard, which frequently featured a colonnade. The living quarters faced north. From the main courtyard, located in the heart of the house, one passed through a pillar-supported veranda into a reception hall. The living quarters—the dining room, the masters' and mistresses' bedrooms complete with lavatories and dressing rooms, and the children's rooms—flanked the hall. The larger rooms had columns. As the excavations at Tell-Amarna (Akhet-Aton) have shown, this layout of a wealthy mansion was typical throughout the New Kingdom. The inside walls of such residences were decorated with geometric and floral designs; floors, ceilings, and columns, which were sometimes crowned with capitals in the form of plants, were also painted.

The excavation site at the short-lived city of Tell-Amarna, with its main avenues running parallel to the Nile, constitutes an important source of information on Egyptian urban architecture and planning. But large, centuries-old cities that gradually expanded to include royal palaces, temples, and residences of the elite and of the common people could not preserve such a simple and clear-cut layout.

The design of royal palaces can be reconstructed for the Eighteenth Dynasty. The Theban palace of Amenhetep III, located on the west bank of the Nile, covered an enormous area and consisted of many spacious one-story rooms built at different times. The private rooms of the king included a reception hall, a banquet hall with the royal throne, a bedroom, a bath, and a lavatory. Similar rooms were built for Queen Tiyi. The palace ensemble included the houses of courtiers, the workshops of craftsmen and their homes, and a large hall used to celebrate the Heb-Sed.[1] The entire palace was richly ornamented with wall paintings.

More details are available about the Amarna palaces. The first thing that strikes the eye is their enormous size. It suffices to mention that the eastern facade of the formal part of the main palace, facing the street, was almost 700 meters long. The longer axis of this huge edifice was parallel to the Nile. A gigantic courtyard was located beyond the main entrance on the northern side and was followed by other courts and halls with columns and statues and stelae depicting the royal family's worship of Aton. One of the yards was paved with stone slabs that displayed images of captured enemies. This yard was followed by a deep, columned hall. This complex was connected to the royal living quarters by a bridge that spanned the road. A "window of appearances" was built at the center of the bridge. The king would stand at this window to be viewed by his subjects on certain official occasions. In contrast to the palace of Amenhetep III, which was built of adobe, the Amarna palace was constructed partly of stone. There were several palaces at Amarna, and all of them were splendidly decorated. The walls were covered with ornamental and figurative paintings and finished with colored tiles. Their floors, ceilings, and staircases were likewise brightly painted. Columns with elaborate capitals were also painted and inlaid with colored faience.

Rameses II and Rameses III built their Theban palaces near their funerary temples. The temple and palace were planned as a whole,

---

1. The Heb-Sed was a feast dedicated to the twentieth, thirtieth, etc., anniversaries of the pharaoh's reign. It is assumed that the object of this feast was the magical renewal of the pharaoh's vital forces, which, according to Egyptian belief, were necessary for the fertility of the land and the general well-being of the country.

and the portico of the temple courtyard also served as the portico of the palace. Both palaces essentially re-created the traditional layout of a residential house.

Structures dedicated to the funerary cult, particularly to the cult of the dead kings, are better preserved because they were built of stone. Stone was used for private tombs already during the Old Kingdom.

The oldest funerary structure surviving today, built mainly of stone, was the pyramid-tomb of King Djeser of the Third Dynasty. This structure was built by a daring architect, Imhetep. Tradition describes him not only as a builder but also as a sage. His memory reached the times of the Persians and the Greeks, who identified him with their god of healing, Aesculapius. Chapels were dedicated to him in numerous temples throughout the country.

The Djeser pyramid is surrounded by a large group of cultic structures whose exact purpose is not always clear. The pyramid was begun as a mastaba.[2] But the plan was later changed, and new smaller storys were added to the tomb, resulting in a pyramid with six steps. The Egyptian architects were still just beginning to learn how to use stone for building purposes and had not yet discovered the structural forms suitable to this material.

Many building details in the Djeser complex mimic in stone their wooden-structure prototypes: stone ceilings were made in the form of wooden beams; pilasters re-created the proportions of wooden columns. In places, walls were faced with colored tiles that imitated the woven texture of reed mats that used to hang on the walls of homes. The majestic fluted trunks of columns were connected to the walls with partitions, and in halls where the columns were free-standing, each pair was joined by a partition. The step pyramids served as the starting point in the development of geometrically regular pyramids, which for many centuries constituted the principal form of royal funerary structure. Such are the Snefru pyramids and the most famous pyramids of all—those of the Fourth Dynasty (Cheops [Khufu], Chephrenes [Kha'f-Ra'], and Mycerinus [Menkau-Ra']). These immense edifices and associated complexes demonstrate that the Egyptian architects had mastered the art of construction in stone and acquired a full understanding of the structural and decorative potential of this material. Free-standing columns of rectangular and round cross sections supported the heavy overhead covers, and different varieties of stone were used to decorate the interior spaces of the pyramid-temples. Since the Fifth Dynasty, temples were lavishly decorated with reliefs and columns with capitals carved to resemble plants. The layout of rooms was determined by the requirements of the fu-

2. *Mastaba* ("bench" in Arabic) designates the mud-brick and stone tombs of noblemen of the Old Kingdom. They are flat and rectangular in shape and have sloping walls.

nerary cult. By the time of the Fourth Dynasty, the mastaba became
the standard design of private tombs surrounding the pyramids. The
adobe bricks once commonly used in the construction of private
tombs were replaced with sandstone slabs. The room of worship,
which used to be built of brick and attached externally to the main
structure, developed into a complex array of hallways and rooms.
Their layout and design were influenced by the royal funerary structures, and private persons gradually adopted some aspects of the
royal funeral cult. The same trend emerges in the tombs cut in the
Giza cliffs at the sites of large quarries and in the mountains of Upper
Egypt.

Cliff tombs soon began to be used for royal burials as well. Such is
the burial place of Mentuhetep III. In front of his tomb, which was
cut into a cliff, a large funerary temple was built. This temple is noted
for its generous use of columns. Two-tiered porticoes graced the
building, in the center of which there probably stood a pyramid. A
colonnade encircled the central court, beyond which was a hall with
eight rows of columns. Trees of many varieties, specially brought and
planted within the perimeter walls of the structure, constituted an important feature in the overall design. A plan of the layout of this garden drawn by the ancient architect has been preserved.

The earlier form of royal burial was revived during the Twelfth Dynasty. But at that time, the pyramids were built of adobe bricks and
were simply revetted with sandstone slabs. The main attention was
now directed to the internal decoration of the funerary temples. Rectangular tombs of the nobility continued to be built around the royal
pyramids, but the independent elite, especially the nomarchs of
Middle Egypt, preferred to construct their burial sites in their own
districts. The rock tombs of these nomarchs had several rooms, many
of which were divided by rows of columns. The height of the aisles
was made lower than the height of the nave, and the ceiling was often
cut like a vault. The entrance to the tomb had the form of a porch,
and the columns used here eventually served as the model for the
Greek Doric order. Of special interest are the tombs of the nomarchs
of the Tenth nome. While repeating the main outline of the ancient
layout, they introduced a new architectural element—the pylon, which
was later widely used by architects of the New Kingdom. It is a
double, tower-like structure with slightly sloping sides.

In the Eighteenth Dynasty, funerary temples began to be built separately from the tombs, which were cut in cliffs in remote and hidden
places. Memorial temples began to play the central role in royal mortuary complexes. These temples seem to have had a rectangular
layout along one axis and entrances shaped like pylons.

The temple of Hatshepsut is the most prominent among such structures. It was designed by Senmut, a highly placed official who held extremely important posts at the court of this pharaoh. Her temple consisted of two portico-terraces, decorated with statues and reliefs. Elegant stairs gave access to the terraces, and a covered colonnade rose in the center of the second terrace, forming a small courtyard. This temple was adorned with bright paintings and ornaments, a wide variety of wood, bronze, carnelian, and gold inlays, as well as many statues and columns, creating an impression of luxuriance. The surrounding landscape was decorated with trees and ponds.

The tradition of erecting separate mortuary temples continued during the Nineteenth Dynasty. The temple of Rameses II (the Ramesseum), built by the architect Penra, was surrounded by a brick wall, behind which storage rooms, domestic workrooms, and the living quarters of priests and servants were located. The entrance was designed as a double pylon with a relief depicting a battle with the Hittites. An entrance from the first court led into the palace and into a second colonnaded court of the temple, and from here, three doors gave access into a colonnaded hall with skylights. This hall extended into a smaller colonnaded hall and rooms for worship and household use, as well as sanctuaries. The layout of this temple appears complex because of the great number of halls and rooms, but it was essentially a stone-built version of a royal palace, with its typical rectangular design and sequence of a colonnaded reception hall, throne room, and private rooms, where the spirit of the deceased pharaoh "resided."

The temple of Rameses III in Medinet-Abu is much better preserved. The temple and the surrounding structures were planned in the shape of a rectangle enclosed by a thick, fortress-like wall with an elaborately fortified gate. A channel was dug from the Nile to a pier near the temple. The tombs of the Sais kings of the Late Dynastic Period were located in the temple.

Private tombs of that time were often distinguished by their large size and original layout. They usually included one or two aboveground courts surrounded by walls and an entrance in the form of a pylon. The funerary rooms were carved into the rock. Colonnaded rooms, chapels, and hallways were built at different levels inside the rock; some tombs had more than twenty rooms.

The earliest urban sanctuaries were built of timber and reeds and were surrounded by fences. Many of the temples of the Middle Kingdom have been rebuilt beyond recognition. Many were taken apart, and the materials used in other construction projects. Later temples were built of brick and stone. The most important architectural elements were their symmetrical layout, pylon gates, gardens with ponds, faceted columns, stelae with reliefs, and not infrequently terraces and occasional obelisks in front of the entrance.

Toward the time of the New Kingdom, Thebes became the leading center of artistic life in Egypt. Gradually, a city temple style developed. The temple was laid out in a long rectangle, usually with a double pylon entrance facing the Nile leading into a colonnaded courtyard and followed by a colonnaded hall with a raised nave and skylights. There were numerous rooms for worship and a library. Various service structures were built nearby, and the entire complex was enclosed within a wall. The main elements of a temple re-created the fundamental elements of a residential house. This is reasonable, since a temple was intended as the residence of the god, to whom it was dedicated and whose cult statue stood there. Numerous sculptures, brightly painted reliefs, gilded obelisks, and flags flying from poles gave the temple a festive and rich appearance. The roads leading to the temple were frequently flanked by rows of sphinxes. Such was the main Theban temple to the god Amon: Karnak. It was built and rebuilt throughout the centuries on the old original site of a small Middle Kingdom sanctuary. Many pharaohs expanded this temple by adding halls and pylons. The Karnak complex, which included temples dedicated to a number of different gods, was connected by sphinx-lined roads with the Luxor temple dedicated to the Theban triad of deities. The latter was also built according to the above-described scheme. It featured a central hall with elegant columns designed as papyrus bundles. Architects of different times participated in the construction of these temples. (They also worked in places other than Thebes.) These architects were Ineni, Hapuseneb, Amenhetep son of Hapu, the brothers Hori and Suti, Amenhetep (the architect of Luxor), and many others.

The so-called peripteral temple became common during the New Kingdom. It was a small rectangular building on a stone socle surrounded by columns.

Cave temples appeared during the Middle Kingdom and became very common throughout the country in the New Kingdom. Originally, they were relatively small and resembled rock tombs with columned porches. During the time of Rameses II, such temples acquired enormous dimensions. Their layout became complex and came to include hypostyles (roofs resting on rows of columns), chapels, columns, and statues hewn within the cliff. The entrance to the cave temple at Abu-Simbel above the Great Cataract is in the form of a pylon and is embellished by four twenty-meter-tall statues of Rameses II glorifying the might of the pharaoh. It has been moved to a new location due to the flooding of the valley after the construction of the Aswan Dam.

Sculpture

The appearance of sculpture in Egypt and its development are closely linked to religious needs. Cult requirements dictated the creation of various types of sculpture, a certain fixed iconography, a particular location, and often even the selection of a particular material. The fundamental rules of sculpture representing deities and the deceased attained their final form during the Early Dynastic Period. These rules required symmetrical and frontal representations, precise postures, and a tranquil appearance—traits which best suited their religious purpose. These features were also dictated by the placement of the statues against walls and in niches. The most common attitudes—a sitting one with hands resting on the knees or a standing one with the left foot slightly forward—were developed quite early. The "scribe posture," appearing somewhat later, was that of a person sitting with crossed legs and was initially used only to represent sons of the royal family. Sculptures of married couples or family groups also made an early appearance. A series of rules applied to all sculpture: an erect head position, certain identifying attributes, and a specific coloration. Male bodies were painted brick red, and female bodies yellow. The hair was black. Eyes were often inlaid with bronze and stones.

The bodies of the statues exaggeratedly emphasized power and physical development, endowing the figures with a solemn nobility. The faces, however, were meant, in some cases, to express the actual traits of the deceased. This was the reason why portrait sculpture appeared so early in Egypt. The most remarkable portraits, now world famous, were hidden in tombs where no one could see them. But the statues themselves, according to Egyptian beliefs, could observe earthly life through small openings made at the level of their eyes.

Egyptian sculptors probably learned to master portraiture with the help of one of the methods used when trying to save a body from decomposition. The body of a deceased person would be covered with plaster, thereby forming a mask over the face. Since the eyes of the corpse had to remain open in order to represent the face of a living person, the mask required additional work. It seems that the practice of casting masks was also used by sculptors in their portrait work. Two kinds of statues were discovered in the same tombs: one type portrayed the personal traits of the deceased, who was dressed in the current fashion of the period, but without a hairpiece; the other type portrayed the face in a considerably more general, idealized way, and the figure was dressed in a short loincloth and wore a wig. The same duality is observed in reliefs. We do not yet have a reliable explanation for this custom. All we can say with confidence is that these statues represented different aspects of the mortuary cult. Wooden statues were found in a number of tombs; these were used during an important stage of the funeral ceremony when the statues were raised and lowered several times. After the rite of "opening the mouth and eyes" of the wooden statue was performed, the statue was considered alive, capable of eating and speaking.

Figurines of workers were placed in the tombs together with the statues of the deceased, especially during the Middle Kingdom. It was believed that the laborers were necessary to ensure the existence of the dead person in the next life. This imposed other demands on the sculptors; they had to represent people performing all sorts of work. In full compliance with the overall requirements of Egyptian art, the most typical moment was chosen for each occupation. This moment became canonical. Other general rules, such as the frontal representation and the conventional colors, were followed here as well.

Statues played an important part in the temple complexes: they flanked the roads leading to the temples and stood by pylons, in courtyards, and in halls. The statues that were used mainly for architectural and decorative purposes differed from the ones created for purely religious purposes. Their subject was treated in a generalized fashion, without much detail; moreover, they were often quite large.

The task of the sculptors working on religious representations of gods, kings, and private persons was different. Royal statues made up a large group: a pharaoh would dedicate his representation to his funerary temple in order to remain forever under the protection of the temple's god. Prayers written on such statues usually contained requests for good health, well-being, and, at times, requests of a political nature. The ideological changes that took place after the fall of the Old Kingdom brought about changes in the arts as well. The pharaohs, seeking to glorify their power, began to place their statues not only in their funerary shrines but also in temples dedicated to different gods. Such images served the purpose of glorifying the living ruler and had to portray him as faithfully as possible.

As tokens of the pharaoh's special favor, statues of noblemen were also dedicated to temples, especially statues of the temple architects. In the beginning, a person could dedicate his statue to a temple only with the permission of the king. But religious ideas changed. Some royal rituals were extended to the nobility and eventually to the middle stratum of society, and private persons eventually won the privilege of placing their statues in temples.

Already toward the latter part of the Old Kingdom, some regions developed their own characteristic styles of sculpture. Several artistic centers (such as the workshops of Middle Egypt) appeared during the Middle Kingdom, each with its own distinguishing features and traditions. For example, slender figures with elongated proportions were typical of Siut. The sculptures created in Meir were quite different, with their short heads and emphasis on pectoral muscles. And the statues of Abydos were softly treated and lacked sharp lines.

The Eighteenth Dynasty was the floruit of Egyptian arts in general, and of sculpture in particular. A new artistic style appeared during the last years of this dynasty, under the influence of the new religious philosophy and the new state cult created by Amenhetep IV (Akhenaton). The royal sculptors broke away from the old canons and began to develop new artistic principles. In their attempt to reflect the most characteristic individual features of their model, they tended to exaggerate and overemphasize these features. A new canon, based on the iconography of the reformer-pharaoh himself, began to develop. The latter part of the Amarna period has produced much finer and finished portrait images, lacking the earlier exaggeration. The most famous works of this time are the sculptured portraits from the workshop of Djehutimes, sculptor of Akhenaton and his queen, Nefertiti.

The time of the Nineteenth Dynasty saw the return of old traditions, especially in Thebes. The political situation in the second half of the New Kingdom led to the preeminence of the northern art workshops. Statues with mighty torsos and wide, flat faces offered a contrast to the elegance and grace of the elongated proportions of Theban sculpture; it was a style that was greatly influenced by the patterns of the Old Kingdom, which could be studied in the cemeteries of that period.

Reliefs

Many pictorial representations, in wall painting and in low relief, are preserved in the tombs of the Old Kingdom. At that time, the arrangements of scenes and the basic composition of reliefs acquired their final forms. The subjects of these works of art were determined by religious needs. For example, a representation of the deceased in front of a table of sacrifices seemed to reinforce and magnify the real gifts placed in the tomb. With time, reliefs grew in importance. More space was allotted to them, and the subject matter became more diversified. Scenes of people bearing gifts and sacrificing animals are ubiquitous. Eventually, probably as an expansion of this theme, the subjects began to include scenes of farming, hunting near the Nile and in the desert, and people feasting. As the political importance of the nobility began to increase from the Fifth Dynasty on, some royal cult rituals were extended to private persons. This resulted in the more complex layout of the tombs, and the previous range of topics developed into compositions that included a multitude of figures. The main purpose of such compositions was the immortalization of all that was of value for eternal life. However, some details that do not seem to have any direct connection to this age-old idea began appearing in the reliefs. For example, a scene of sacrificial offerings shows, under the list of sacrificial victims, farmers being punished for failing to bring their allotment of produce for the funerary cult. During the Middle Kingdom, the subject matter was further expanded to include military scenes and arrivals of foreigners, as well as new religious topics called forth by the wide propagation of the Osiris cult.

In addition to ensuring the well-being of the pharaoh after death, the reliefs of the royal and the city temples served to glorify him and immortalize his deeds; consequently, they claimed to depict real events that took place during his reign. This is particularly typical of the New Kingdom (the annals of Thutmosis III, the scene of the battle of Kadesh under Rameses II, and the battle with the Sea Peoples under Rameses III). Military subjects were depicted during the Old Kingdom, but the New Kingdom military reliefs are much more spirited and richer in detail.

Reliefs and wall paintings, like sculpture, were closely connected with the architecture of the tombs and temples. The imitative decor was selected to emphasize the purpose of each particular room. Even the scenes of sacrificial offerings, which at first glance appear so stereotyped, varied depending on which gods were being honored with sacrificial gifts, on their cult names, and on the types of offerings.

Two types of reliefs existed in ancient Egypt: convex and carved within an outline below the surface of the wall. All figures and their backgrounds were usually brightly painted, converting the walls into colorful tapestries of images (especially since the latter part of the Old Kingdom). Artists also took advantage of the decorative value of the Egyptian script and filled the empty spaces in their compositions or between the different scenes with inscriptions. The owner of the tomb always occupied a dominant role in the represented scenes. A composition was to be read rather than viewed as a whole.

The rules that applied to wall paintings developed simultaneously with those for sculpture during the Old Kingdom. The representation of three-dimensional space in a two-dimensional medium is not just a technical problem—the solution depends on a certain attitude toward reality. Egyptian artists reproduced reality as they knew it. A body or an object was not represented from a specific point of observation and at some fortuitous instant but showed each part of the depicted object in its most typical form. The face, elbows, and legs of a person were shown in profile, whereas eyes and shoulders were represented from a frontal view. A similar principle was observed in large compositions, where separate scenes did not all pertain to the same point in time. Large scenes depict a number of separate episodes to communicate to the fullest degree the idea of a represented subject. For example, a hunting scene could include separate topics relating to the hunted animal's life in the desert; a war theme could include scenes of life in a military camp, marching soldiers, battles, and so on.

All depicted people were imagined to come alive and all objects to be real; hence, they required bodily integrity. For this reason, artists generally avoided any overlapping of figures, at least of the main subjects of a composition. Separate scenes were arranged in strips, one above the other. Since the time of the Middle Kingdom, artists made wider use of the artistic potential of wall painting, and later, in some instances, would forego the use of contours in order to achieve special effects.

The existence of definite rules was essential to the preservation of artistic tradition, without which ancient Egyptian art would be unthinkable. Tastes and notions of what constituted an ideal changed with time and influenced the proportions of figures, the density of the details, and so forth. Although the overall scheme remained the same, there was always enough leeway to express the knowledge, the keenness of observation, the creative searching, and the imagination of the artist.

The Writing System

A writing system existed in Egypt by the Early Dynastic Period, its creation probably dictated by economic requirements. The repertory of signs shows the stages in the development of this ancient writing. The signs used for Egyptian writing were pictorial and phonetic, expressing one or more consonants. A sign became phonetic when it no longer conveyed only the general meaning of a sample of notions, as in a rebus, but was also used to convey just the consonants corresponding to the word represented by the pictorial sign. Although there were specific signs for each separate phoneme (consonants only, because vowels were not indicated in the Egyptian writing system), the Egyptians never evolved an alphabetic writing system. As a rule, they used a mixed logographic-phonetic system; that is, a word-sign (pictorial sign) was followed by signs used phonetically to indicate the consonants contained in the word represented by the word-sign. At the end they attached a sign (called a determinative) that was not meant to be read but that expressed the general semantic sphere to which the word belonged. Thus, the word *wn*, "to open," was written with the drawing of a hare (*wn* in Egyptian), the sign for water (*n*), and a picture of an opening door. These were followed by a picture of a papyrus scroll used as a determinative to indicate abstract concepts.

Hieroglyphic writing (as the Greeks called it, combining the Greek words for "sacred" and "carving") was used mainly for monumental inscriptions carved in stone, although hieroglyphics are also found on other materials. For everyday needs, for example, for economic documents, the Egyptians used a cursive script, the so-called hieratic script ("priestly," as the Greeks called it). The hieratic script was also used for works of literature and for scientific texts. The appearance of the cursive signs changed greatly with time. During the Late Dynastic Period, the demotic script came into use, developing from a late, simplified form of the hieratic script. It was originally intended for use by the bureaucracy for administrative texts but eventually also was used for literary and religious papyri and was even carved on stone.

Literature

No works of literature, in the strict sense of the word, remain from the Old Kingdom, save for "autobiographical" inscriptions found in tombs from the end of the Old Kingdom. Their widespread use is associated with the diffusion of the Osiris cult and with the appearance of new ethical concepts. These inscriptions became more and more extensive and came to include descriptions of the author's meritorious services not only to the pharaoh but also to the people of his city.

"The Story of Sinuhe," which dates from the Middle Kingdom, was written in this autobiographical tradition. Because of its great literary merit, this story was very popular in its time and has reached us in many copies. The hero of this story, a nobleman, lived during the reigns of Amenemhet I and Senwesert I. The story is told in the first person by a very well educated man, thoroughly familiar with the way of life at court and in the army of his time. After the death of Amenemhet I, Sinuhe, fearing civil war, fled from the retinue of the king's daughter. He eventually came to Syria, where he acquired great wealth and gained a prominent position. Life among the Syrian pastoral tribes is vividly described. Later, Sinuhe returned to Egypt at the invitation of Senwesert I and received a friendly reception at the royal court. Some scholars believe that Sinuhe was a real historical person, because the structure of the story is similar to other "autobiographies" and because it includes copies of documents and is told in a realistic fashion.

Egyptian fiction showed great progress, especially from the Middle Kingdom on, and produced *inter alia* a number of tales about all kinds of subjects derived from many different sources. "The Tale of the Shipwrecked Man" tells the story of a man cast ashore on an unknown island during a fierce storm. There he meets a serpent who presents him with rich gifts and foretells his return home. Upon his return, the king makes him his bodyguard. This story reflected the frequent travels of Egyptians. Historical persons and events may also have in-spired some folktales. Such is the story from the time of the New Kingdom about the quarrel between the Theban pharaoh Seq-ne-Ra' and the Hyksos king Apepi, as well as that of the officer Djehutiy, who seized the Palestinian city of Jaffa by ruse. The cycle of tales about the sorcerers and the pharaoh Cheops, whose feats are described by the sons of the pharaoh, stems from the Old Kingdom and may be re-garded as belonging to the same literary genre. Many tales are con-nected with religious conceptions. "The Tale of Two Brothers" echoes the myth about the god of the dying and resurrecting vegetation. In "The Tale of the Truth and Falsehood" we sense the influence of the myth of Osiris.

The genre of didactic sermons was very widespread; such sermons were used as school texts. They were usually written in the name of some well-known nobleman or sage. Such admonitions not only teach the rules of personal behavior but also explain the advantages of the position of an official scribe. The advice is often directed at young men starting their careers as officials and is based on the everyday service and experience of older high officials.

Occasionally, these precepts were written in the name of a king. Such are the instructions given by the king of Heracleopolis to his son Merika-Ra' and the instruction of Amenemhet I. In the former, the father relates to his son his ideas about royal power. The latter tells of a palace conspiracy against the king and is permeated with disap-pointment and bitterness. The appearance of such literary works was the result of events that took place during the end of the Old King-dom and the beginning of the Middle Kingdom and also as a result of changes in the worldview of the Egyptian people. "The Song of the Harpist," which was performed during banquets, is imbued with a sense of futility toward the traditional worldview. The author urges his listeners to enjoy life and to stop thinking about death and the fu-nerary cult, because the ancient tombs are empty and stand in ruins, and no one has yet returned from the other world to tell about the owners of the tombs, whose fate remains unknown. This literary pro-duction shares many traits with "The Conversation of a Disillusioned Man with His Soul." A man, disappointed with his life, desires death, but his soul tries to dissuade him, in the spirit of "The Song of the Harpist." In the end, however, the author makes the "soul" agree with the man's desire to die.

Two compositions recount a successful, but short-lived rebellion: "The Admonitions of Ipuwer" and "The Prophecy of Neferti" (see Lecture 7). The authors of both works were representatives of the elite and were naturally opposed to the rebels.

The social contradictions during the agitated time of the Middle

Kingdom are also expressed in "The Tales of the Eloquent Peasant," the most interesting part of which are the accusatory speeches in defense of truth, delivered by the unjustly mistreated hero of the story.

Historical literature flourished during the New Kingdom and is represented by royal chronicles and by "autobiographies" of noblemen, often written in a vivid and descriptive style.

Dramatic arts were not unknown in ancient Egypt. They were represented by dramatized funeral and temple rites and religious dramas on mythological subjects. At times, such performances transcended merely cultic limits and showed distinct propagandistic and political tendencies.

Among the rich Egyptian poetic literature we find hymns to gods and kings, songs of praise, and also, since the time of the New Kingdom, love poems. The rhythm of the verse was based on the counting of stressed syllables, whereas the number of unstressed syllables apparently had little significance.

The favorite poetic devices used were parallelism (each verse or couple of verses consisting of two sentences with a parallel structure) and alliteration, which was characteristic of prose as well. Literary works of all types were often ascribed to individual narrators and presented in a framework that included a prologue and epilogue. The Egyptians loved an elegant play on words, but to appreciate this device we must keep in mind that words had a special value to the Egyptians. According to legend, Atum-Ra' created people from his tears, but this was not just a play on words ("tears" and "people" sounded alike in Egyptian) but a manifestation of the belief that a word and the named object are closely interdependent.

Science

The ancient Egyptians made a valuable contribution to astronomy by creating the solar calendar. It was so accurate that we still use it today, with minor modifications. The year was divided into three seasons of four months each. A month had thirty days and was divided into decades. A year had thirty-six decades, each dedicated to a special deity (constellations). Five days were added at the end of each year. This calendar was devised in response to agricultural needs, which required the calculation of the flood stages of the Nile. The Nile overflowed its banks when the bright star Sirius appeared just before dawn. This coincidence was noticed by Egyptian observers. However, the Egyptians never brought the calendar year into concordance with the astronomical year, because they did not introduce leap years. For this reason, every four years the morning rise of Sirius diverged from a new year by one day. After 120 years, this error amounted to one month. The Egyptians had several projects for eliminating this discrepancy but never implemented them.

Another important contribution to astronomy was the division of day and night into twelve segments each. Sundials and devices for measuring time by the flow of water were used as early as the New Kingdom. The Egyptians mapped the sky and grouped the stars into constellations. They also observed the planets.

Egyptian mathematics was developed to satisfy the needs of the administration and economic management. The Egyptians used a decimal, nonpositional notation system that had special symbols for the numbers 1, 10, 100, etc. They used only unit fractions (fractions with a numerator of 1). We know that already during the Middle Kingdom, the Egyptians had school texts with arithmetical problems and their solutions. Most problems stemmed from practical needs. Egyptian mathematicians were able to calculate the length of a circumference and the volume of a truncated pyramid; some scholars believe that they could also calculate the area of a sphere. The Egyptian method of calculating the area of a circle gives 3.16 as the value for the ratio pi, although the specific concept of this number did not exist in Egypt. Calculations involving fractions were carried out with the help of special tables. The Egyptians were also familiar with arithmetical progression. An unknown quantity was designated with the word "heap."

Considerable knowledge of anatomy started to accumulate as early as the Old Kingdom (in part, because of the practice of mummification) and contributed to the appearance of physicians of different specialties—specialists in eyes, teeth, surgery, and so forth. Practical guides for physicians from later times have been found, but they frequently mixed science with magic. The greatest achievement of Egyptian medicine was their excellent knowledge of anatomy; they may have discovered blood circulation and had some knowledge about the functions of the brain. (They related paralysis of the legs with head injury.) Manuals for veterinarians were also available. Mummification techniques and especially recipes demonstrate a considerable knowledge of chemistry.

The most significant achievements of the social sciences were made in the field of history. Chronicles listing the sequence of rulers and recording the most important events have been preserved. The Egyptians compiled dictionaries, as well as aids used by the scribes to learn the Akkadian language.

Special schools were established in Egypt—the so-called Houses of Life—where sacred books were written and where medical research was apparently carried out.

10

The First States in India and the Pre-Urban Cultures of Central Asia and Iran

G. F. Il'yin[†] and I. M. Diakonoff

The Indian Peninsula in Ancient Times

Civilization arose in the Indian Peninsula later than it did in Egypt and Sumer, but it predated that of China by nearly one thousand years.[1] The modern and the ancient meanings of the word *India* are different. Today, India (more accurately, the Republic of India; Bharat in Hindi) is one of the states of the Indian subcontinent. In antiquity, the word *India* was the name given to all territories east of the Indus River (*Sindhu* to the Indians, *Hindu* to the Persians, and *Indos* to the Greeks), which are now divided among the states of Pakistan, India, Nepal, and Bangladesh.

The approximate size of ancient India was equal to the combined area of the territory of Egypt, Mesopotamia, Asia Minor, Iran, Syria, Phoenicia, and Palestine. Such a vast territory offered a great variety of geographic zones. The country can be divided into three principal regions, whose geographical differences have left an imprint on the history of their inhabitants.

1. The Indus region (northwest): It includes the lowland of the Indus River and its tributaries and the adjoining mountainous regions. The climate here is hot and dry. In the northern part the annual precipitation reaches 1,000 millimeters, but it gradually decreases toward the southwest. The lower course of the Indus receives only about 250 millimeters, making farming based solely on rainfall impossible. In ancient times precipitation was apparently more abundant.

2. The Ganges region (northeast): It comprises the valley of the Ganges River and its tributaries, the adjoining Himalayan foothills, and the mountainous region of central India. The climate here is hot

---

1. In this book the term *Central Asia* is applied to the countries between the Caspian Sea and the Tien Shan; the term *Middle Asia* is applied to regions between the Tien Shan and Mongolia.

The first five sections were written by G. F. Il'yin.

and humid. The annual precipitation amounts to about 700 millimeters in the west and up to 2,000–3,000 millimeters, or even more,
in the east. Before and during the second millennium B.C., this region
was covered with dense jungle.

3. The Deccan region (south): The term is derived from Sanskrit
dakṣina ("southern"). It includes the peninsular portion of the country
and is characterized by a complex topography. The climate is hot and
the precipitation irregular, but it does not drop below 700 millimeters
per year, even in the dry interior.

Most of the Indian territory receives over 500 millimeters of precipitation annually, mainly during the summer, a total that is adequate for dry farming. A considerable portion of the country enjoys
at least 700 millimeters of rain, allowing the growth of cotton without
artificial irrigation and, in many parts of the Ganges and Deccan regions, even of water-loving crops such as rice, sugarcane, and jute.
The water problem is clearly far from being as critical in India as it is
in Egypt and in some other Near Eastern countries. Although ancient
Indians were familiar with irrigation techniques, irrigation cannot be
regarded as the cornerstone of ancient Indian agriculture.

The abundance of water was not always a blessing. For people using
stone or even copper axes, the dense tropical vegetation presented a
serious obstacle to the occupation and improvement of agricultural
lands. The early Indian farming centers therefore appeared in the
less wooded northwest. The Indus region offered another important
advantage: it was more accessible to external communications and, in
particular, closer to the most ancient agricultural regions of the Near
East. Its location facilitated the exchange of cultural achievements
with other countries and contributed to more rapid technological
progress.

The Indus Civilization

The oldest farming settlements in India date from the fourth millennium B.C.—the Late Neolithic—and their number increased notice-
ably during the transition to the Copper Age (end of the fourth,
beginning of the third millennium B.C.).[2] These settlements were
located at the western edge of the Indus Valley in a hilly region. Here,
the climate is more temperate. Small streams served as sources for
economic and household needs, without presenting any danger of
flooding. This region also offered protection against enemies. The

2. The excavations presently being conducted at the settlement of Mehrgarh at the
foot of the Bolan Pass in Pakistan have pushed the origins of South Asian agriculture
back at least to the sixth, if not seventh, millennium B.C. Editor's note (PLK).

first settlements were small. Permanent dwellings were built of mud brick; copper was rare; the variety of agricultural crops was limited (barley and millet, for the most part); and artificial irrigation was occasionally employed.

With the advent of the Age of Metal, the agriculturalists, who settled originally in the hilly regions to the west of the Indus, acquired the ability to improve larger areas of land and expanded onto the plains. Agriculture appeared in the valleys of large rivers—the Indus and its tributaries—on lands that were irrigated by floodwaters. The rivers also offered a convenient means of transportation for the exchange of material and cultural goods and helped to fuse the communities into larger social aggregates. Although no permanent settlement from the first half of the third millennium B.C. has been found in the northwestern lowlands, a complete transformation occurred in this region by the second half of the same millennium. The cultural-historical complex that scholars call the Indus civilization, emerged toward the middle of the third millennium. This civilization spread beyond the boundaries of the Indus Valley to the east, almost as far as Delhi, and to the south, extending to the lower reaches of the Tapti River. Archaeologically, the golden age of this civilization is associated with the Harappan culture, named after the first discovered site and one of the largest urban centers of this civilization. Hundreds of settlements of this culture are now known, although most of them have not yet been studied.[3]

Certain Indus cities became quite large; the population in Harappa and Mohenjo-daro may have reached several tens of thousands. The cities probably were built according to a general urban plan. The streets were straight and ran parallel to one another, intersecting at right angles. Surrounded by strong walls, some of the cities contained a citadel that towered above the walls from its raised elevation. The citadel of Mohenjo-daro included a structure originally identified as a granary,[4] as well as administrative and commercial establishments. One of the largest and most elaborate buildings (230 × 170 meters) was probably the palace of the ruler. Another served as a covered

3. The absolute dates of the "mature" Harappan civilization are debated by specialists. Current excavations at Naushargo, Pakistan, will help clarify this problem. For the present, it is safe to say that at least part of the mature Harappan was contemporaneous with the Akkadian Period (twenty-fourth to twenty-first centuries B.C.) in Mesopotamia. Editor's note (PLK).

4. The traditional identification of many of the public structures of Mohenjo-daro and Harappa, such as granaries, has recently been questioned. Ongoing work by German scholars at Mohenjo-daro, in particular, has revised our understanding of this site, showing how many of its major buildings—whatever their purpose—were built on elaborately prepared brick platforms. Major portions of the site effectively were pedestaled in advance above the level of the floodplain. Editor's note (PLK).

market. The complex included a pool or bath (a watertight, sunken structure) that may have been used for religious ablutions. The adjoining structures also were probably for cult-related activities.

The granary at Harappa was located on the bank of the Ravi River. It was a huge building, possibly designed to hold many hundreds of tons (metric) of grain at one time. It measured 61 × 46 meters and was built on a brick platform to protect the grain from floodwaters. Floors for grinding grain were found next to the structure, as were the living quarters of the workers who serviced the harbor, the granary, and the grinding of grain.

The principal construction material was mud brick or fired brick. All two- and three-story residences in the central part of the city were built of brick and often formed residential complexes. The buildings were quite simple architecturally but were quite comfortable: they contained rooms for bathing; narrow slits were cut in the upper portion of the walls for ventilation; and staircases connected the upper and lower levels. The roofs were flat and covered with compressed earth; very likely, during hot summer nights, the inhabitants slept on the roofs. There were patios or courtyards within the houses that had fireplaces for preparing food and that provided space for children to play.

The city sewage system in Mohenjo-daro seems to have been the most advanced in the ancient East. Many houses had settling pits for wastewater, from where it was directed out of the city through special brick-lined channels.

Archaeological data suggest that people living within the walls of the central portion of the city enjoyed quite a high standard of living, although differences in wealth can easily be discovered. The city's poor apparently lived outside the city walls, and due to the frequent inundations that plagued the cities of the Indus Valley, their modest mud huts have not survived to our time.

The economy of the Indus society was based on agriculture. We do know that they cultivated wheat, barley, peas, and melons. Rice was planted outside the Indus Valley (in Gujarat) during the Late Harappan Period. Cotton was grown as well; it was initially domesticated in the hilly region west of the Indus (e.g., at Mehrgarh) during Neolithic times, which represents the earliest use of cotton in the history of the world. We also know that water-lifting wheels were in use, although there are no available data about irrigation structures on a large scale. The fields, located along the riverbanks, were most likely irrigated by the natural flooding of the river.

The development of animal husbandry can be traced from faunal remains. Domesticated animals included cows, buffalo, sheep, goats, pigs, donkeys, and fowl. The horse appeared only during the second millennium B.C.; that is, toward the end of this civilization. Hunting and fishing apparently no longer played an important role in the economy.

We know a little more about urban crafts. At its peak (end of the third, beginning of the second millennium), the Harappan culture belonged to the Bronze Age. In addition to bronze, lead was used, as well as gold and silver for ornamental objects. The urban dwellers received most of their copper and copper artifacts from abroad, apparently from Rajasthan (the neighboring region to the east). The local nonferrous metallurgy was also highly developed. The melting and soldering of copper and its alloys was known and practiced; swords, knives, spearheads, arrowheads, axes, and other tools were manufactured. The craftsmen of the Indus civilization also engaged in artistic casting, as demonstrated by such finds as that of a bronze statuette of a dancing woman. Stone continued to be used for the production of grinding stones, weights, plowshares, and weapons such as maces. Spinning and weaving were equally important; India was probably the first country to master cotton weaving. Already during this early time, India exported cotton fabrics and continued to do so during the next four thousand years.

Pottery was another important industry. All sorts of vessels and housewares were skillfully molded on potter's wheels, fired, and decorated with black pigment. There is a great variety of elaborate designs. Since cities and settlements were built mainly of brick, the production of brick must certainly have been an important branch of the economy.

Jewelers, who were particularly skillful, made various personal ornaments: bracelets, necklaces, rings, and beads. They used precious and other metals, precious and semiprecious stones, faience, bone, and shell. Toy making, stone and bone carving, and the crafting of seal-amulets were among the artistic endeavors.

Trade must have played an important role in the economy of the Indus cities. The discovery of large numbers of weights testify to this fact, as does the high development of handicrafts, which resulted, no doubt, in large quantities of items for sale. Another indication of trade is that many raw materials that were not available locally were used by the crafts. For example, copper, lead, gold, and precious and semiprecious stones had to have been imported from beyond the Indus Valley itself. Though some materials could have been acquired as war spoils or as tribute, trade probably was the most secure and constant supplier. The cities of the Indus Valley acquired what they lacked in raw materials through trade with southern India, Baluchistan, and Afghanistan. A Harappan colony was discovered on the banks of the Amu Darya River at the site of Shortughai (ca. 2300–

2000 B.C.). Evidence of trade with Lower Mesopotamia is found in various archaeological and cuneiform sources. The transshipment point for the maritime trade between India and Mesopotamia was the Bahrain Islands, called Dilmun in Sumerian and Telmun in Akkadian sources. India exported cotton fabrics, ivory, semiprecious stones, gold, and certain kinds of wood. We have less information about Indian imports, although some curious discoveries have been made; for example, beads from Crete dating to about the sixteenth century B.C. were found in Harappa.

Culture and Religion of the Indus Civilization

The existence of literacy in the Indus civilization is an important indicator of the level of cultural development. No less than 2,500 inscriptions, preserved on pottery, on metal objects, and, especially, on seals, have been discovered. Some seals had holes drilled through them, suggesting that they may have been used as amulets or as tags attached to merchandise. Many of the seals were carved by gifted artists and occasionally depict complex mythological scenes, with short inscriptions or simply a few signs.

Proto-Indus writing has attracted the attention of scholars for many years but has not, as yet, been deciphered. However, it has been possible to establish that the writing consisted of up to 400 pictorial signs that were read from right to left. In addition to the ideograms, Proto-Indus writing also included phonetic signs. The main difficulty is that we do not know what language was written with this script. Some Indian scholars speculate that this language was an archaic form of Sanskrit, a well-known but much younger Indian literary language belonging to the Indo-European family. Most contemporary scholars, however, believe it more probable that this script represents one of the earliest Dravidian languages, which today are spoken mainly in the south of the Indian Peninsula and in parts of Sri Lanka. A few Dravidian-speaking population groups, the Brahui people, are today dispersed in the area where the borders of Pakistan, Afghanistan, and Iran meet. Elamite, probably related to Dravidian, was spoken in antiquity in southern Iran.

Sculpting and carving reached a high level of development; bronze and stone statuettes have been discovered. Pieces of jewelry and toys made with exquisite artistic taste provide evidence not only of the skill of the artists but also of the high aesthetic standard demanded by the population.

Relatively few data are available about religious beliefs. On the basis of the large number of female terra-cotta figurines, one could conclude that there probably existed a mother-goddess cult. This seems very likely, because such cults are still widespread throughout present-day India. A three-faced deity surrounded by animals, shown on some Indus seals, reminds us of the later god Shiva in his image of Pashupati, "The Lord of Cattle" and may indeed have been that deity, perhaps with another name. Mythological scenes suggest that certain plants and animals also considered sacred today (e.g., the pipal, the bull) were deified. All this points to a certain affinity between modern Hinduism and beliefs that existed in India four thousand years ago. Excavations of burial sites offer some information about funeral rites. There was no strict uniformity; the deceased were usually buried directly in the ground and, in some cases, together with household implements.

This is the extent of the available information. No funerary structures even closely resembling those found in ancient Egypt have been preserved. Nor is there any extant structure that we can confidently identify as a temple or chapel. This distinguishes the Indus civilization from its contemporaries—the great civilizations of Mesopotamia and the Nile Valley, where structures for worship were the central features of cities.

The Social Structure of the Indus Civilization

When comparing the developmental level and the character of the Indus Valley civilization with that of the slave-owning cultures that existed simultaneously in Egypt and in the Euphrates Valley, we find many similarities. For this reason, scholars usually assume that the social structure of these civilizations must have been similar. Weighty arguments can be cited in favor of such a viewpoint.

The highly developed production forces, the large cities, and the existence of writing demonstrate that the society had progressed far from the primitive community level. The differences in the wealth of residential houses and between the burial sites of the wealthy and the poor attest to significant differences in property status. The production of enormous quantities of brick, the construction of large buildings, the installation of sewage systems and their maintenance, and the work performed in the enormous granaries and on the quays required a large labor force, part of which was certain to have been forced labor. It is not possible, however, to establish the composition of this labor force or the actual conditions of their dependence solely on the basis of archaeological remains.

The well-organized life of the city, which must have been controlled by a strong administration, and the existence of fortified citadels dominating the cities suggest a fully developed state with an effective social stratum of managers. The wide distribution of a uniform material culture over such a vast territory leads us to believe that the Indus Valley settlements were in communication with one another, and it is quite possible that during some periods in their history they may have constituted a single political unit.

However probable all this may be, it remains speculative. We must wait for new discoveries, especially for the deciphering of the writing, in order to prove or disprove the above hypotheses.

Decline of the Indus Civilization

After the end of the Harappan culture, a certain regression becomes manifest. Achievements of the Indus civilization, such as the building of cities, progress in the arts, and writing, were almost, if not entirely, lost. The reasons for this decline are still unclear, and different explanations have been proposed. The first one is the hypothesis (which still has adherents) about the destruction of the cities (and therefore of the civilization as a whole, because the cities were its mainstay) by an invasion perpetrated by inimical Indo-Aryan tribes. The proponents of this hypothesis refer to the discovery in the upper archaeological stratum at Mohenjo-daro of a few dozen skeletons of people who had been slain. Supporting evidence has been sought in the frequent mention in the *Rig Veda*, the most ancient Indo-Aryan collection of religious hymns, of wars between Aryans and the Dasyu, identified with the local aborigines (not always with satisfactory proof). Subsequent archaeological findings have not confirmed this hypothesis.

Today, the appearance of Indo-Aryan tribes in India is usually dated to the second half of the second millennium B.C. A significant time gap therefore exists between the final decline of Mohenjo-daro and the arrival of the Indo-Aryans, because the top stratum of this city, where the skeletons were discovered, cannot be dated later than 1750 B.C.

Archaeological data also point to the fact that the Indus cities were not all destroyed at the same time. Thus, if the fall of Mohenjo-daro occurred, as mentioned, in the eighteenth century B.C., then Lothal fell during the sixteenth to fifteenth century B.C., and Kalibangan even a few centuries later. Still later Indus culture sites seem to have existed. This gap of five to six centuries is so wide that it makes it completely impossible that all these cities should have been victims of one and the same invasion. Moreover, had all the Indus cities been destroyed by one ethnic group, the Harappan culture strata would have been superimposed by a single archaeological cultural layer. Actually, we find several such cultures; they are dissimilar and usually related to the cultures of Baluchistan, which cannot be classified as Indo-Aryan. In several cases, these cultures seem to represent a "degraded

Harappan culture" rather than one significantly different foreign culture (e.g., at Rangpur and Lothal).

Recent years have seen a sharpening attention to the environmental conditions of northwest India during the third and second millennium B.C. in order to determine whether climatic changes could have brought about the demise of the ancient society, which may have lacked the technical resources to cope with the new situation. There is good reason to expect new discoveries in this field. The ancient Greek geographer Strabo (first century A.D.) quotes Aristobulus, a participant in Alexander the Great's expedition to India (fourth century B.C.), as follows:

> He says that, having been commissioned with a certain assignment, he saw a land with more than a thousand cities with their villages abandoned by the inhabitants, because the Indus, having left its previous riverbed, shifted to the left into a new, deeper one, where it flows swiftly, dropping like a cataract.

All scholars have noted that the Harappan culture (at Mohenjo-daro, e.g.) did not suddenly vanish. The disappearance was preceded by a lengthy period of stagnation and decline, which may have begun as early as the twentieth to nineteenth centuries B.C. At Mohenjo-daro this can be seen from the desolation and impoverishment of the city and the decline of its economy. The city must also have weakened militarily, giving rise to internecine wars and uprisings of previously dependent tribes, as well as to incursions by independent foreign groups. However, we can only speculate about the character of the possible political and economic changes.

Which of the factors outlined here constituted the main reason for the collapse of the Indus civilization cannot yet be deduced with certainty. However, the Harappan civilization was the only early civilization to have declined and disappeared.

Prerequisites for the Creation of Pre-Urban Society in Iran and Central Asia

The Iranian highland—that is, the lands occupied today mainly by the states of Iran[5] and Afghanistan, west of the Indian Peninsula—

5. In modern times (before 1935), this state was called Persia. The change of name introduced some degree of confusion into scientific terminology. The official language of the state of Iran (which does not occupy the entire area of the Iranian plateau) is Persian, not "Iranian." The term *Iranian languages* includes many Indo-European languages spoken outside Iran, as well as beyond the Iranian plateau (thus, e.g., the Ossetic, Tajik, and Pamir languages). In antiquity, the Scythians, Sacae, and other tribes from the Black Sea region to Central Asia spoke "Eastern Iranian" languages.

was part of the region where agriculture and animal domestication originated. The same may be said about the narrow southern strip of land in present-day Soviet Turkmenia. However, the conditions for the development of farming (based mainly on mountain stream and pluvial irrigation) were less favorable in this region than in the Lower Euphrates Valley. While Sumer and Akkad had long since achieved the status of civilization and had become involved in the passions that the contradictions of a class society generate, a primitive society survived on the Iranian plateau throughout the Chalcolithic Age. It was only in the southwestern corner of today's Iran, in the arid plain created by the sediments of the Karun and Kerkheh rivers, that city-states (or nome states) appeared in the first half of the third millennium B.C. They were probably of the same type as those of Sumer. The principal city was Susa. Here a specific hieroglyphic writing, similar in many aspects to the Sumerian script, developed. Although it has not yet been deciphered, it is clear that it was used in large temple economies, as was the writing of the Sumerian Protoliterate Period.

The Karun and Kerkheh valleys were called Elam or, in the local idiom, Haltamti (Hatamti). Originally, it was the name of just one nome in this region, and not even the most important one. (Sumerians called this area *Adamdu*.) Only later was the name applied to the entire territory (Sumerians called it *Nim*, meaning "upland, highland"), which was united with Elam proper by a common language.

Until the twenty-second century B.C., a locally developed hieroglyphic script was used for writing Proto-Elamite; it remains undeciphered. Texts in this script have now been found at several sites in southern Iran up to the borders of Baluchistan. After the twenty-third century, Elam began to use the Akkadian cuneiform script for writing in their own language, as well as in Sumerian and, especially, in Akkadian.

Recent investigations by an American scholar, David McAlpin, appear to show that the Elamite language was relatively closely related to Proto-Dravidian—an ancestor of the Dravidian languages. We can assume that in very ancient times the Dravidian and Elamite languages were spoken in adjoining territories. This means that the Elamite-Dravidian population must have occupied the entire region extending from India to the Karun and Kerkheh valleys. Except for the inhabitants of the Karun and Kerkheh valleys, the people in this region had not reached the level of civilization by the second millennium B.C. The archaeological objects found at the various sites show that the culture was not homogeneous, although isolated centers of Elamite civilization proper did exist. One of the most important Elamite centers in the western part of the Iranian plateau was the city of Anshan (45 kilometers west of today's Shiraz), which had close relations with

Mesopotamia. In the east written sources reveal the existence of the city of Aratta. This site has not been located with certainty.[6] Other Elamite centers were even further away from Susa. The creation of such centers may have been facilitated by affinity between the language of Susa and the language (or languages) spoken by the local populations. These cities do not seem to be the result of indigenous development. Rather, they appear to be trading or military outposts of Susa or Anshan. Discoveries of tablets with Elamite hieroglyphics indicate that Elamite temple economies had been established here. The ancient names of these city-fortresses, which were surrounded by a primitive livestock-raising population, are unknown, and we have to use the modern names of their archaeological sites: Tepe-Sialk, on the road from Teheran to Shiraz (closer to the former); and Tepe-Yahya, near the region inhabited today by the Dravidian Brahui people. Documents discovered at both sites date from the first half of the third millennium B.C.

The ethnic affiliation of the inhabitants of Iranian bases outside the Elamite-Dravidian region is unknown. The entire Chalcolithic Age (and, to some extent, even later periods) was characterized throughout the Iranian plateau by pottery with highly artistic, multicolored ornamentation. This pottery was not produced by a single culture; nevertheless, all the archaeological sites on the Iranian plateau were traditionally classified under the general term "Painted Ware" culture, despite the significant differences in archaeological detail. Similar pottery is also found from the Protoliterate Period in Asia Minor, in Transcaucasia, in parts of Middle Asia, and in China. We believe that the reason for the similarity in pottery is similarity in sociocultural development in the highland regions rather than ethnic kinship among the pottery makers.

Cuneiform sources suggest that Hurrian dialects and Qutian were spoken in the northwestern parts of the Iranian plateau. Very little is known about the Quti language, but it is not improbable that, together with Hurrian, it was closely related to the Eastern Caucasian language family. The classification of the Kassite language is also unclear.[7] The Quti and the Kassites have been mentioned in earlier lectures, and more will be said about them later.

Fortified cities began to appear on the western slopes of the Iranian plateau toward the end of the third millennium B.C. They seem to

6. Lately there have been suggestions, based on philological data, that Aratta may have been located in the northern continental part of the Indus civilization. Another suggestion identifies Aratta with the rich archaeological site of Shahr-i Sokhta in Drangiana. Ancient Drangiana lay in the present-day frontier zone between Iran and Afghanistan, around the Darache-yi Seistan and in the valleys northwest of it.

7. The Kassites may have originated in the Elamite-Dravidian region.

have been centers of small mountain states. Large, but not yet fortified, settlements of agriculturalists also existed during that time along
the northern foothills of the mountain range between today's Iran
and Turkmenia (the archaeological sites of Altyn-depe, Namazga,
Anau, and others).

Typical of the agricultural settlements of Iran and southern Middle
Asia during the fourth to third millennia B.C. were houses with many
rooms, probably serving as dwellings for extended-family household
communes. The Hurrians on the western edge of the Iranian plateau
lived in fortified towers.

Trade routes that passed through the Iranian plateau in the third
millennium carried to what is today northeastern Iran and southern
Turkmenia samples of Sumerian and Elamite crafts, which served as
models for locally made clay and gold statuettes and other small objects of religious character. Blue lapis lazuli from northern Afghanistan, Indian carnelian, and gold reached the various centers of Iran
and Western Asia via the same trade routes. But the most important
merchandise (and, at the same time, the most enigmatic) was, from
the end of the third millennium, tin.

Tin was probably the most important raw material for the advent of
the Bronze Age. For quite some time, people had known that copper
was too soft for many kinds of work (so that stone had to be used) and
that alloys (particularly arsenic alloys) were required to improve the
working properties of tools and weapons. But no metal other than tin
was able to greatly improve the strength of copper. Therefore, in
order to make bronze implements and weapons, tin had to be imported from far away, regardless of the danger and expense. Bronze
tools were much more durable than copper tools; working edges
could be made sharper and suffered less wear. Even razors could be
made of bronze, whereas, in the past, they could only be fashioned
from obsidian (volcanic glass). Bronze began to be used for the production of daggers and swords, helmets and coats of mail. This significantly increased the fighting ability of armies and increased the
exploitability of slave labor.

The end of the third and beginning of the second millennium saw
the coming of the Bronze Age in Western Asia. However, we still do
not know where the tin came from during this time. In the second
half of the second millennium, when the trade routes changed, we
know that tin began to arrive in Western Asia from the west; for example, from Spain.[8] Other deposits sufficient for industrial exploitation were known to have existed not closer than Malaysia and

8. A sunken Bronze Age ship laden with copper and tin has been discovered near
the port of Haifa, Israel.

southern China. Strabo, the Greek geographer of the first century
A.D., mentioned a source of tin in Drangiana, a country in the southwest of what is today Afghanistan, but modern geologists rejected this
possibility. It was only in the early 1970s that Soviet geologists discovered large tin mining sites in this area that had been exhausted at least
a thousand years ago. (Archaeologists have not yet visited this area, so
its absolute date has not been established.) One of the deposits, apparently quite ancient, was located north of Hamun Lake (Daryache-yi
Seistan). Since copper was also found there, it is possible that finished
bronze ingots were shipped from this source. Another very ancient
deposit was found in the Hilmand River basin. This secret of the
Bronze Age may thus prove to be uncovered.[9]

In the third millennium, an important new draft animal was domesticated in Central Asia—the two-humped camel. It was, among
other uses, harnessed to pull four-wheel vehicles. This was a time
when there arose in this area a comparatively well-developed farming
culture, although it was still based on smaller and shallower rivers
than, for example, the Amu Darya. The irrigation canals found here
(up to three kilometers long) resemble those dug in Mesopotamia before the Protoliterate Period.

Toward the middle of the third millennium, large settlements several dozens of hectares in area (1 hectare = 2.47 acres) appeared in
southwestern Central Asia, in the Murghab and Zeravshan river valleys. They had an irregular, urban-type plan, houses for extended
families, and large cultic structures that were enclosed in thick adobe
walls. City walls apparently were built at least as early as the second
millennium. Mention has already been made of a Harappan colony
on the southern banks of the Amu Darya. Around the bigger towns,
there were small villages consisting of one or a few extended-family
dwellings. Such farmsteads had already disappeared in Lower Mesopotamia at the beginning of the Protoliterate Period. A pre-urban (or
even early urban) culture is also observed in Drangiana (the sites of
Shahr-i Sokhta and Mundigak).

However, the process of formation of a class society, which was
clearly taking place over the entire Iranian plateau (in Iran as well
as Afghanistan) and in southern Turkmenia, was not accomplished
during the Bronze Age; a period of decline ensued. The causes are
not clear. In this region the second millennium B.C. was a time of
droughts and ethnic migrations. Indo-Iranian tribes appeared in Iran
around this time, if not earlier (more will be said about this in Lecture 18). Archaeological evidence of ethnic migrations, however, is
difficult to find, unless the migrations were accomplished by mass
slaughter and fires; there are no written records. It also remains unknown whether these migrations hindered the development of urban

civilizations or, conversely, whether some internal difficulties in the development of local societies contributed to the ethnic migrations. The early cultures of Iran and Central Asia are still obscured in mystery; archaeological data remain insufficient. Our only information about the western edge of the Iranian plateau comes from inscriptions of Mesopotamian kings, to whose history we are now about to return.

9. While the scale and significance of its production is still uncertain, the mining of tin in ancient times has now been documented for the central Taurus mountains of southern Anatolia. Editor's note (PLK).

11

Asshur, Mitanni, and Arrapkhe

N. B. JANKOWSKA

The General Character of the Region

Settlements along the middle reaches of the Tigris played an important historical role.[1] In this region the inclement conditions for which Lower Mesopotamia was famous did not exist; there were none of its deserts and none of its salty rivers and sea lagoons overgrown with giant reed forests. On the other hand, the region defined by the middle reaches of the Tigris did not yield the inordinately rich crops that were so characteristic of Lower Mesopotamia (once the floods of the Euphrates had been curbed).

For a long stretch the Tigris runs between steep rocky shores, a condition impeding human movement along the river. Nearly as inconvenient for travel are the valleys of the small rivers that flow into the Tigris from the northeast: the Bohtan Su, the eastern Khabur, the Greater (Upper) Zab, and the Lesser (Lower) Zab.

Two fertile agrarian districts lie along the Tigris. The northern forms the triangle of historical Assyria, bordered on the north by mountains cutting it off from the valleys of the Eastern Khabur and the Greater Zab (in that part where the latter flows from northwest to southeast) and on the east by the foothills of the Zagros Mountains and the valley of the Lesser Zab. This district is watered by rainfall and subterranean sources. Its western boundary is the Tigris, which for a long stretch is bordered on the west by a steep mountain ridge (continuing the Hamrin range to the southeast of the Tigris). Between this ridge and the western bank of the Tigris there is hardly even a footpath. It is upstream from this ridge that, in some places, possible routes open over the Tigris, connecting the hilly part of Upper Mesopotamia with the east.

South of the Lower Zab the second trans-Tigride agrarian district begins. It is watered by two additional tributaries of the Tigris: the Adhaim and the Diyala. The district is subdivided into two by the Hamrin ridge; north of the ridge lie heavily hilled territories, similar to those of historical Assyria, although stock raising and agriculture

---

1. The first section was written by I. M. Diakonoff; some of his materials were used in the third and fourth sections as well.

were somewhat less developed here. The center of these territories was originally Gasur, renamed Nuzi after the Hurrian conquest in the eighteenth or seventeenth century B.C.; the new center (modern Kirkuk) became Arrapkhe.

The Tigris cuts through the Hamrin ridge, forming an almost natural gate, at a place now known as Fatha. One of the most ancient regions of irrigation agriculture, where the waters of the Diyala River are led over the plain in a network of canals, is situated to the south of this ridge. In the third millennium B.C. this land was called Warium or Ki-Uri. (This name was also extended to cover the northern part of Lower Mesopotamia.) In the second millennium B.C. its central part was called Nawar and its southern part was called Tupliash (in Kassite).

The importance of the regions along the Tigris lay not so much in their agricultural potential, which already in the fourth millennium B.C. lagged behind the Lower Mesopotamian plains, watered by canals and the Euphrates, but in their fords over the Tigris and its tributaries. Here lay the trade routes into Iran and even farther east—to the tin mines of western and southern Afghanistan, to the lapis lazuli quarries of Badakhshan, to the gold of India, and to the regions of the proto-urban cultures of Central Asia and to the land of the early Indus civilization.

There were five fords for trade and military expeditions over the Tigris. The first was situated near present-day Mosul. (This city lies on the western bank of the river; in antiquity the ford was guarded by a city on the eastern bank—Nineveh.) From here the road coming out of Upper Mesopotamia continued to Arbela (now Erbil) and, over the Zagros passes, to Lake Urmia.

The second ford was located below Mosul, where the road leading west to east from the confluence of the western Khabur with the Euphrates and through Karana (now Tell Rimah) crossed the Tigris at Kalkhu (Calah, now Nimrud) and from there led to Arbela.

Before reaching the Tigris at Kalkhu, this road split, and one branch turned northeastward to the city of Asshur (now Qal'at Sherqat). This city lay on the Tigris in a very important place—where the northwestern continuation of the Hamrin ridge ends, and the road from Lower Mesopotamia could again turn toward the river. Being politically and naturally a part of Assyria, the city of Asshur was actually a bridgehead before the main, third ford, where the road led from the west over the river and eastward to the passes over the Zagros. This road went through the center of the Arrapkhe district (present-day Kirkuk) and into the valley of Sulaimaniyeh and over the Zagros passes to the south of the passes that were reached along the first and second routes.

A fourth, less convenient route served as an exit from the roads of western Arrapkhe. It led through the "Gate" of Fatha and, after crossing the Tigris, continued toward Mari on the Euphrates.[2]

Finally, the fifth ford could have been in several places where the fertile valley of Tupliash-Nawar opened toward the Tigris. From here the road could lead either to the southwest from the mountain ridges toward the city of Der (now Bedre) and farther on into Elam; or through present-day Khaneqin and over the southern Zagros passes to modern Kirmanshah and from there either to the south toward Elam or to the southeast toward Anshan; or, finally, the road could turn to the north toward Arrapkhe. South of the confluence of the Diyala with the Tigris, the latter probably entered, in antiquity, a region of swamps and lagoons, of little economic value.

Besides the main west–east roads, there also existed south–north roads, parallel to the mountains. One led from Kish, Babylon, and Sippar to the north along the Tigris, skirted the Hamrin ridge, and then returned to the Tigris at Asshur. A traveler could either cross the river here or continue to the north until Nineveh, joining the roads running across Upper Mesopotamia from west to east. This road was usually open to raids of pastoral nomads; moreover, in the south, the traveler had to pass over the Gypsum Desert and a series of other inhospitable arid stretches. Therefore, a preferred road was the one a long way to the east of the Tigris, which led across the Diyala Valley, through present-day Tuz-Humatli (ancient Kissuk?), across the kingdom of Arrapkhe, and fording the Lesser Zab at the site of Tell Mahuz (ancient Tursha).

The Tigris Valley forms the western boundary of the foothills of the Iranian plateau and was in antiquity the eastern boundary of the historical region of Upper Mesopotamia that now is divided between Turkey, Syria, and Iraq. On the east this region is bordered by the Middle Euphrates, from its "Great Bend," where it flows nearest to the Mediterranean, and southward until, after crossing the Gypsum Desert, it enters Lower Mesopotamia. According to the physical topography, Upper Mesopotamia can be subdivided into three east–west zones: (1) A northern mountainous and hilly zone, which in antiquity was covered by evergreen underbrush (maquis), is located south of the Upper Tigris. (2) A middle zone, which was crossed from north to south by the Balikh and the western Khabur, tributaries of the Euphrates, is relatively well watered until the Sinjar Mountain (Jebel Sinjar) ridge; along the southern slopes of this ridge, there is a belt

2. Perhaps it is near Fatha that the town of Sugage should be sought on the western bank of the Tigris; we also suggest that the town of Unabshe might be located inside the pass.

still suitable, to a certain extent, for sheep raising and primitive agriculture. (3) A southern desert zone stretches from the southern slopes
of the Jebel Sinjar to the borders of Babylonia.[3]

The ethnic structure of the most ancient population of these zones
is not well known. We have information on the sequence of archaeological cultures but much less on the sequence of languages spoken
here, although some hypotheses have been suggested.[4] It is certain,
however, that as late as the second half of the third millennium B.C. in
the region of the future Arrapkhe, there still existed in the city of
Gasur (later Nuzi, now Yorghan-tepe) a Proto-Tigridian, or "Banana-
language," population (the name is conventional). And about the
same time a Hurrian population is attested in the northern zone of
Upper Mesopotamia. (It has lately been proved that the Hurrians, together with the related Urartians, formed one of the branches of the
Eastern Caucasian family of languages. Other speakers of the languages of this family today inhabit the Soviet Autonomous Republics
of Daghestan and Checheno-Ingushetia.) There is good reason to
believe that the homeland of the speakers of Hurro-Urartian was
situated in central or eastern Transcaucasia, probably no later than
the fifth millennium B.C. After entering the territories of Upper
Mesopotamia, the Hurrians naturally mixed with the aboriginal
population.

Archaeological data also attest that during the fourth and early
third millennia, the Sumerians had their colonies or factories not only
in Mari but also far to the north along the valleys of the western
Khabur (Tell Brak) and the Euphrates, at least as far as the confluence
of the Upper Euphrates (Karasu) with the Arsanias (Muradsu).[5]

3. There are two main west–east routes across Upper Mesopotamia: one extends
from the city of Mari on the Euphrates (now Abu-Kemal, at the frontier between
present-day Syria and Iraq) to Asshur or to Fatha on the Tigris; and the other stretches
from the crossing of the Euphrates at the Great Bend near ancient Carchemish eastward through present-day Urfa (or more to the south through ancient Harran), up to
Mardin and Nusaibin (Mcbin, Nisibis) toward Nineveh and Asshur. There were also
two major south–north roads: the first went upstream along the Euphrates (not necessarily following the river itself) over to Mari, which was a gateway to western Syria, and
to Emar (another gateway to western Syria and to Ebla and Haleb) and Carchemish,
where the road turned to Asia Minor or led farther north onto the Armenian highland;
the second road, which has been discussed above, led along the Tigris.

4. Among others, there is a hypothesis ascribing the Tell Halaf culture (fifth millennium B.C.) to the bearers of Proto-Indo-European dialects. However, no traces of an
Indo-European linguistic substratum have been disclosed in the region; unimportant
traces of Indo-Iranian influence on the Hurrians (from the East) appear only in the
second millennium B.C.

5. The archaic Sumerian writing, which was invented about 3000 B.C., is still poorly
attested in Upper Mesopotamia, although recently fragments of archaic Sumerian
documents were discovered at Tell Brak. Editor's note (PLK).

Lately it has been shown that during the third millennium, a culture defined most characteristically by its distinctive ceramic goblets occupied the eastern zone of Upper Mesopotamia. And we have good reason to believe that this culture originated with a group of Semitic tribes occupying an intermediate position between the Western and the Eastern Semites and having their most important center in the city of Ebla. The sheep-herding population, both in western Syria and in Upper Mesopotamia, probably belonged to the group of the Western Semitic tribes conventionally called Amorites.

A considerable part of the population in Mari on the Euphrates was Eastern Semitic speaking, as was virtually all the population in Asshur on the Tigris, although it may have been preceded by Sumerian colonies.

To the east of the Tigris, in places that are mostly still unidentified, Hurrians are attested at least from the middle of the third millennium. We know the names of certain mountain tribes by name (the Turukki,[6] the Qutians, the Lullubeans, the Kassites, etc.). But it is hardly possible to connect these tribal denominations with individual ethnic entities. It has so often happened, not only in antiquity, that the same tribal denominations, when they are not self-denominations, are applied to completely different ethnic groups by neighboring groups who believe they all have something in common. Thus, for the denomination *Lullubeans* we know for certain that the term meant simply "neighbors, strangers" or "of an unintelligible language." It is quite probable that most of these tribes belonged to the Eastern Caucasian linguistic family, while others may have belonged to the Elamite-Dravidian one. But all this belongs in the sphere of guesswork.

Agriculture throughout the regions in question was mainly based on rainfall due to warm humid winds from the Mediterranean Sea. When artificial irrigation systems appeared, they did so only on a local scale. In the social field this meant that here there was little need for strong state centralization. The main economic role was played by family or clan communities (the communal-cum-private sector); royal economies, and big economies in general, if existent, were not structurally dissimilar.

Seen from the point of view of the entire economy of the Near East, these regions played a very important role, because it was through them that the leading agricultural societies—Lower Mesopotamia

6. The naive connection of the Turukki with the Turks should be ignored. Turkic ethnic domination appears only in the first millennium A.D. in Central Asia and does not reach the Near East before the florescence of the Middle Ages. The similarity of the words *Turukki* and *Turkic* is simply fortuitous. There has been some searching for Turkic toponyms in the ancient Near East for political reasons.

first of all—were supplied with necessary raw materials, most especially metals and timber.[7] It is therefore only natural that international exchange played the leading economic and, in the final
analysis, also the leading political role here. Thus, the early, short-
lived political federations were connected with the trade routes. The
first of these, dating from the late third millennium B.C., was the state
created by the Hurrian ruler Arizhen (or Adalzhen). It included
Urkesh, not far from modern Mardin, on the northern road through
Upper Mesopotamia; Hawal, on the Zagros north–south road, probably connected with the third route discussed above; and the Nawar
region in the Diyala Valley. Characteristically it bypassed the territory
of the Ur III police state, which would not permit any trade not cen-
trally controlled by itself.

We have more information on international trade from Asshur.

Early Asshur

The oldest political history of Asshur is quite obscure. The only thing
we know is that in the twenty-third century B.C. the town was dependent for a short time on the kingdom of Sumer and Akkad (Ur III),
which had its governor installed here; he left an inscription that has
been preserved. Much later a list of the kings of Asshur was compiled,
but it is quite untrustworthy in its initial part; it begins with "kings
who lived in tents," but this is simply a part of the genealogy of a line
of Amorite tribal chiefs, to which the ancestors of Shamshi-Adad I
were supposed to belong. However, Shamshi-Adad I ruled (in the
nineteenth century B.C.) not over Asshur alone, but over the whole of
Upper Mesopotamia, as will be related below.

The first historically attested indigenous ruler of Asshur[8] was Ilushuma, who lived in the twentieth century B.C. He had no royal title.
As the ruling high priest he was called *isshiakkum,* which is an Akkadian transcription of the Sumerian *ensi(ak);* and as the chairman in
the city council he was called *ukullum,* or *waklum.* A short inscription
of his that has been preserved long defied interpretation; a few years
ago I translated it as follows:

> Ilushuma the *isshiakkum* of [the city of] Asshur, for [the
> goddess] Ishtar, his lady, and for his own life, built a temple;
> the old wall which had leaned on one side(?) he restored; for
> the [citizens of] my city I distributed houses.

7. The city of Asshur probably had wool supplied from the east for its important
textile industry.
8. Its local deity was called Asshur after the town. The name means "the holy" or
"the hallowed" in the Assyrian dialect of Akkadian.

The inscription goes on to mention new sources of water discovered in the town; then follows:

> A liberation [*andurarum*] of the Akkadians and also of their sons I established, and I made clean their copper. From the borders of the *midru* [pl.], [namely] from Ur, Nippur, (H)awal, Kismar, Der unto the city [of Asshur] I established their liberation.

This has formerly been interpreted as the description of a supposed military raid of Ilushuma into Lower Mesopotamia. (It could not have been a durable conquest, because the documents from Mesopotamia of this period are numerous and contain no traces of an Assyrian invasion, however short-lived.) This assumption is erroneous. Moreover, the word *andurarum* does not mean "political liberation." It is a translation of Sumerian *ama-r-qi* "returning to mother," that is, "to the original situation." It does not mean liberation from some supreme authority but the canceling of debts, duties, and the like. Also, "cleaning" is a *terminus technicus* for "release from payments." Then, the "liberation" established by Ilushuma does not apply to the citizens of his own city-state, Asshur. It is more probable that the "liberation of the Akkadians and their sons" means a release from some duties, for example, custom duties. When the inscription says "Akkadian," it does not, of course, mean a linguistic entity. (Such use of the term would lack political sense, because in early antiquity, if a body of men was contrasted to another, it was by reason of their different political or religious loyalties but never because of a difference in language.) Neither can the "Akkadians" be the citizens of Akkade, the capital of Sargon the Ancient; this city had long ceased to exist. The "Akkadians" of this inscription presumably are the citizens of the cities listed immediately after, and the "sons of the Akkadians" must be understood as persons who politically belong to these same cities but who are not dwelling in them.

The word *midru* is a crux; it is nowhere else mentioned in the Akkadian texts. Nearly all scholars translate it as "swamp, lagoon," connecting it with Arabic *miṭr-, miṭir-t-*, "rain ditch," a derivative of *maṭar-*, "rain." We suggest its connection with the Aramaic *midr-*, "earth, soil, clay (as material), silt," and with the Arabic *madar-*, "silt, soil, clay, adobe (hut)." Especially interesting for the interpretation is the Arabic expression ⁽ahl al-madar wa- ⁽ahl al-wabar, "townsmen and nomads," literally "people of the adobe and people of the [tents of] skin/felt." Also, in Akkadian *wab(a)rum* means "stranger, noncitizen," *wabar-t-* "trading station (factory) outside the city walls."

We propose to interpret *midru* as "zone, belt of sedentary (town) population." Then the enumerated towns would be the main points outlining the border of a certain zone: Ur and Nippur in the south and southwest;[9] Der, a transit station of Babylonian-Elamite trade, in the southeast; Awal and Kismar[10] near the Zagros passes, in the east; and Asshur itself, in the north. It is well known that Asshur, too, was an Akkadian city. Note that the zone in question is not a political entity but should be understood as purely geographical; it stands in connection with trade routes, ignoring the existing frontiers of contemporary states. This duty-free zone corresponds to the territory where "Akkadian" merchants might have been active, being citizens of the towns of Lower Mesopotamia and of Asshur itself; beyond that belt the merchandise would probably be passed to traders from "outside" towns, those not included in the free-trade zone created by Ilushuma.

In other words, the "sons of the Akkadians" were citizens of Akkadian towns acting as trading agents or representatives of their respective trading societies on all the main trade routes, especially the south road to Lower Mesopotamia and the eastern route over the Zagros Mountains, and were admitted by Ilushuma to duty-free trade; what Asshur sent to these agents was probably wool, as attested later. That there was trade between Asshur and the towns of this zone (e.g., Gasur) is also attested by documentary evidence.

About the same time the merchants of Asshur started en masse for Asia Minor in order to take part in the trade there—at first, perhaps, selling textiles, but then for the most part making profit from the difference in the prices of metal (which were cheap in Asia Minor but expensive in the Lower Mesopotamian markets). Although most of the documents that have come down to us from the traders in Asia Minor of the twentieth to nineteenth centuries B.C. (see Lecture 13) refer to business matters in Asia Minor and only sometimes to those in Syria and Asshur, more distant connections can sometimes be traced (through Asshur to be sure). Among the persons mentioned in this connection are some from Gasur and Hawal.

The measures taken by Ilushuma were continued by Erishum I; it is probable that the first written deeds originating from the trading colony (*karum*) Kanish in Asia Minor can be dated to his reign. How-

9. About that time Nippur, the ancient center of the Sumerian religious federation, received certain privileges from the First Dynasty of Issin and was possibly the center for transit trade in the kingdom of Issin, as was Ur for the kingdom of Larsa.

10. Awal, or Hawalum (not to be confused with Awan in Elam, which lay far to the east in the direction of Anshan), was probably situated on the middle route over the Zagros. It is mentioned in the inscription of the Hurrian king Arizhen and in letters from Shusshara (now Tell Shemshar in the Sulaymaniyah Valley). Kismar may be identified with Hashmar, the "Falcon Pass," on the modern route from the Diyala Valley to Kirmanshah, not far from the Hurrian city of Karahar, or Harhar.

ever, in my opinion this was the moment when the trade of the Asshurites at Kanish came under the control of the rulers of Asshur; the
trade itself must have existed before that. The traders of Asshur took
their obligatory oath in the name of Erishum. Like his father,
Erishum left an inscription at Asshur. It was written "for my life and
the life of my city." It states that in connection with extensive building
activities in the temple of Asshur, "my city sat [in council] at my call; I
established [a] "liberation" [for] silver, gold, copper, lead(?), barley,
wool, and [everything else] unto the scrapings(?) of the pot and chaff."
Thus the liberation was now extended not only to specific groups of
merchants but to the entire turnover on the market.

City rulers of the line of Ilushuma continued to be heads of the government at Asshur until the late nineteenth century B.C., when great
changed occurred in Upper Mesopotamia due to the conquests of the
Amorite tribal chief Shamshi-Adad, son of Ilahkabkabuhu.

Shamshi-Adad I

By the beginning of the second millennium B.C. no traces were left of
Sumerian or substratum ethnic groups in Upper Mesopotamia and
the regions adjoining the valley of the Tigris from the east. The
northern zone of Upper Mesopotamia proper, as well as certain regions of Syria in the direction of the Mediterranean Sea, were, to a
certain degree, populated by Hurrians; the regions east of the Tigris
were predominantly Hurrian. The rest of Upper Mesopotamia, including the city of Asshur on the west bank of the Tigris, was inhabited by Semites; the sedentary Semitic population spoke Akkadian in
the following dialect forms: in Mari and the neighboring townships,
Middle Euphratian (close to Babylonian); and in Asshur, Assyrian.
Correspondingly, there existed two varieties of Akkadian cuneiform
writing, the Middle Euphratian and the Old Assyrian; the former,
with minor derivations, was used in all smaller towns of Upper Mesopotamia and also by Hurrians; the latter was used in Asshur, in the
trade colonies, and the eastern city-states of Asia Minor.

These were the languages and the writing systems of the urban
population, including royal and community offices and the traders.
But there existed a Western Semitic group of dialects conventionally
called Amorite; it was spoken by some of the sedentary population
but mostly by the seminomadic shepherd tribes in the inner regions of
Syria and Upper Mesopotamia.

Both the Hurrians of Upper Mesopotamia and Syria and the
Amorites of these regions probably did not at first control any city-
states. But it seems likely that they were often taken on by the city
rulers as hired warriors; this would lessen the military service burden

on the sedentary part of the Semitic population. But the result was that Amorite military chieftains with their consolidated detachments of warriors began to acquire power over the cities. (We have already seen in Lecture 4 what happened in Babylonia.)

One such chieftain was Ilahkabkabuhu, a leader whose origins are not known. But a much more important historical role was played by his son, Shamshi-Adad I (1813–1781 B.C.). Shamshi-Adad first acquired a territorial nucleus somewhere in the center of Upper Mesopotamia; then, in a number of successful campaigns, he was able to conquer a number of towns on the Middle Tigris and also Asshur. After that (or possibly already before that), he conquered a city of no less importance, namely, Mari, on the Euphrates, expelling the local dynasty. Apparently, Ekallatum, 40 kilometers southeast of Asshur, was one of his residences, although later tradition spoke of him as king of Asshur.[11] He kept his two sons as governors in the crucial economic and political centers of Asshur and Mari but kept a rigorous control over both. At the height of his power he also seized the important trading center of Qatna in southern Syria. His ambitions resulted in confrontation with three rival kingdoms: that of Yamkhad, in the Great Bend of the Euphrates; that of Babylonia; and that of Eshnunna, on the Diyala. With the last two, Shamshi-Adad managed to establish satisfactory diplomatic relations; only Yamkhad, giving refuge to the exiled representatives of the old Mari dynasty, remained inveterately inimical.

Probably no one among his contemporaries so consciously attempted to create such a centralized empire as Shamshi-Adad I. Until his time the city councils of elders and even popular assemblies played a considerable political role in the nomes of Upper Mesopotamia and in Asshur. Under Shamshi-Adad, the councils and assemblies were no longer summoned and lost all importance. Instead, an orderly system of military districts (*haltsu*) was consolidated, and the commanders of these were entrusted with efficient power. The army was reorganized and strengthened. All the economic, political, military, and temple systems were under constant control and supervision. What was desired of the administrative staff was personal loyalty to the king. Local offices were unified by Shamshi-Adad; in Asshur, the local variety of the official language and writing was supplanted by literary Babylonian, in its Middle Euphratian variant, and with the corresponding Babylonian form of cuneiform writing.

Of course, no independent trade organization, weakly controlled by the state, could be tolerated by Shamshi-Adad. When he seized a

11. Recently, Tell Leilan in northern Syria has been identified as Shamsi-Adad's capital of Shubat-Enlil. Editor's note (PLK).

trade center, this meant that the trading capital and the stock of merchandise became the king's. However, he was not able—or did not want—to organize a state-run international trade. The lively exchange of goods with Asia Minor and the East stopped. In Asia Minor the leading role was taken over by the local merchants, and in the East, probably, by Hurrian ones, although we also have information on Amorite trade groups.

The empire of Shamshi-Adad I, powerful as it seemed, did not survive its founder. Apparently, in Asshur his son Ishme-Dagan recognized after his father's death the supremacy of Hammurapi in Babylon. In Mari, the same Hammurapi expelled Ishme-Dagan's brother and set Zimri-Lim, a scion of the old dynasty, upon the throne—only to overthrow him a few years later and raze the city of Mari to the ground.

It is likely that the last attested period of the existence of the archives belonging to Asshurite traders at Kanish in Asia Minor dates from a period after Shamshi-Adad I. Their activities now continued on a much smaller scale, and soon the rise of the local Hittite kingdoms put an end to any possibility for the Asshurites to trade in Asia Minor.

Unlike Mari, Asshur did not suffer quite so much from the vicissitudes of the epoch; the citizens had amassed considerable riches during the preceding period; the city was intact and lay as before on the crossroads to all directions. As a result of the Kassite invasion into Lower and Middle Mesopotamia then under Samsuiluna in the middle of the eighteenth century, Asshur was cut off from Babylon and no longer exposed to Babylonian political encroachments. Therefore, although the city was governed by weak rulers and retained an archaic semirepublican political structure, the prerequisites for a future rise in prosperity were already in place.

The Kingdom of Mitanni

We do not know precisely when the movement of Hurrian tribes began toward the south and southwest from their supposed original homeland in the northeastern part of Transcausia.[12] (The word *Hurrians* itself seems to mean "those of the east" or "of the northeast.") The Hurrian tribes may have already been living in Lower Mesopotamia in the third millennium B.C. This would explain the great number of names referring to nonsteppe plants borrowed into Akkadian from Hurrian (such as "apple tree," "plum," "mint," and "wild rose"). The first reliable information on the Hurrians as such is

---

12. Some of H. M. Avetisyan's materials have been used in this section.

gleaned from inscriptions dating from the late third millennium B.C.: inscriptions on stone tablets (e.g., those of Tishadal, the *enda* of Urkesh; of Arizhen, the king of Urkesh, Hawal, and Nawar) and on seals (that of Arizhen, king of Karahar). Then, beginning with the early second millennium, we have various personal names, ranging from rulers to helot workers; they originate from the Taurus Mountains near their eastern passes (the country which later was named Kizzuwadna), from the northern zone of Upper Mesopotamia (the site of Chaghar-Bazar in the upper valley of the western Khabur), and from Alalakh near the mouth of the Orontes in Syria. But in the time of Shamshi-Adad I (nineteenth century) all the names of nomes and places and rulers in Upper Mesopotamia were still Semitic.

According to the linguistic data brought forward by Margaret Khachikyan, it seems possible that the migration of the Hurrians to Western Asia occurred in several waves. They first got as far as northern Palestine, most likely in the middle of the third millennium. Another wave was responsible for the creation of a Hurrian population at the geographical points just mentioned above. The movement continued in the next centuries; thus, in the twentieth to nineteenth centuries the center of the region north of the Hamrin ridge still bore its ancient name of Gasur, but in the sixteenth century this land was occupied by Hurrians, who gave it a new name, Arrapkhe, after its new capital (now Kirkuk),[13] and the city of Gasur was renamed Nuzi. The Hurrian population of Alalakh, Syria, increased greatly between the eighteenth and the fourteenth centuries (but it is not clear whether this was due to the influx of new Hurrian groups or to assimilation of the original Semitic population). Toward the middle of the second millennium the population of Ugarit, on the Syrian coast, was bilingual—Semitic and Hurrian.

It does not seem likely that the Hurrians annihilated or expelled the former population; clear evidence of the latter's continued existence can be found in all Hurrian regions, with the only possible exception of Arrapkhe, where the Akkadian population, if any, was small and in some instances obviously of late origin. No changes of appreciable importance can be shown to have taken place in the material culture. It is probable that the mountain-dwelling Hurrians, like the Amorite steppe-dwellers, were first hired as warriors by the local kinglets and later seized power in the nomes and merged or coexisted with the local population.

The political predominance of the Hurrians in Upper Mesopotamia is usually dated to the sixteenth century B.C.; however, a

13. Arrapkhe [Arrafkhe], from an older Hurrian *Ar(i)nakhewe*, means "(the city) of the Givers"; in Akkadian the city was called *Al-ilani*, "City of the Gods."

short time ago H. M. Avetisyan seems to have proved that the Hurrian kingdom of Hanigalbat already existed in the seventeenth century. To the end of that century is dated a big raid of the Hurrians of Hanigalbat into Asia Minor during the reign of the Hittite king Hattusilis I (who at that moment was engaged in a military expedition to the western part of the peninsula). Obviously, this Hurrian kingdom must have consolidated at an earlier date.[14]

The Hurrian raid was beaten off by the Hittite potentate, but not without difficulty. However, he secured for himself the territory between the Taurus Mountains and the Euphrates.

In the later texts Hanigalbat is always another name for Mitanni and is never attested in any other sense. Therefore, one may assume that Hanigalbat, originating not later than the middle of the seventeenth century, was the same kingdom that became well known in the middle second millennium under the names of Maiteni (the earlier form) and Mitanni. One may conjecture that Hanigalbat was the name of the country, and Mitanni was the name of a particular Hurrian tribe and its dynasty.

Mursilis I, son of Hattusilis I, made himself famous through his 1595 B.C. campaign against Haleb, Syria, and Babylon. He put an end to the state founded by Hammurapi and left it to be conquered by the Kassites. (Having settled before that in Hana on the Middle Euphrates, they must have been allies of Mursilis.) It seems that Mursilis led his army only along the river, not entering Hanigalbat; that is, into inner Upper Mesopotamia. There were only unimportant skirmishes between Hittite and Hurrian forces. The Hittite kingdom after Mursilis experienced a deep inner unrest, and this favored the upsurge of Mitanni.

We have already mentioned that the Hurrian tribes moved toward Upper Mesopotamia and Syria in waves; their approximate sequence can be established by the spread of their dialects and the peculiarities of the local pantheons. Not counting the wave that may have reached Syria and Palestine in the third millennium B.C., the earliest was that represented by the inscription of Tishadal of Urkesh; it still has much in common linguistically with the related language of the Urartians, who never left the Armenian highland. The last wave is represented by the language of Mitanni, preserved in an extensive letter from Dushratta, king of Mitanni, to the pharaoh of Egypt.

The most interesting feature of this wave is the fact that the Mitannian kings bore Indo-Iranian first names (and Hurrian second names) and worshiped, among a number of others, a few Indo-

14. The Akkadian text that discusses this war is in late Old Babylonian, not in Middle Babylonian, which was used for all later Akkadian texts from the Hittite Kingdom.

Iranian deities. Also, the widely spread use of Indo-Iranian forms of horse breeding no doubt goes back to the Mitannian tradition. The German scholar Annelies Kammenhuber has shown that all Indo-Iranian terms and proper names preserved by the Mitannian tradition reflect their Hurrian, not the original Indo-Iranian, pronunciation; the dynasty and its adherents preserved the Indo-Iranian tradition but could themselves speak only in Hurrian. Thus, the dynasty originated in a region where actual Hurrian–Indo-Iranian linguistic contacts were possible: the founders of the dynasty were probably of Indo-Iranian origin. The most probable region of such contacts seems to be the country near Lake Urmia in northwestern Iran, still called Matiane (Mantiane) or Matiene by the Greek historians and geographers of the first millennium B.C.

Attribution of "Mitannian-Aryan" to the Indo-Iranian linguistic group is open to doubt. The little material that has been preserved does not contain features specifically typical of Iranian languages; thus Mitannian-Aryan is usually described as Indian. Yet it has features that appeared in Indian languages only in the first millennium B.C. and that are absent from Sanskrit. Several conclusions may be drawn from this: (1) Mitannian-Aryan is a very ancient Indian language that has, however, developed certain features not appearing in other Indian languages until very much later; (2) Mitannian-Aryan is a dialect spoken by tribes who later spoke a dialect containing features specific to the Iranian group dialect, which, however, had not yet developed at that time; (3) Mitannian-Aryan is a dialect belonging to a linguistic group intermediate between Indian and Iranian—the Kafir. This branch, now preserved only in the high mountain valleys of northeastern Afghanistan and in Kashmir, is thought by experts to have been the first group to have separated from the Indo-Iranian linguistic entity, and the first to enter the Indo-Iranian region of habitation (this hypothesis may be attributed to the Norwegian scholar Georg Morgenstierne). Therefore, it is quite possible that their dialect had been widely spread all over Iran before they were superseded by later waves of Iranian tribes proper. The latter appeared here not later than the last centuries of the second millennium B.C. It is this last solution that explains all the specific features of Mitannian-Aryan.

Note the important fact that Indo-Iranian features in the culture, in the language, and in the proper names are attested only among the Hurrians of the Mitannian group; they are not attested in Alalakh, Kizzuwadna, Boghazköy (except in the diplomatic treaties with Mitanni), or Arrapkhe (except in the names of Mitannian envoys).

The first king of "Maiteni" known by name is Shuttarna I, son of Kirta. He is known by an impression of his seal on a document from the sixteenth century B.C. from Alalakh. He was succeeded by Parattarna (or Barattarna), known from the long inscription of Idri-mi, king of Alalakh. Idri-mi had to flee from his enemies to Emar on the Euphrates (which perhaps belonged to Mitanni) and was later re-installed in Alalakh by Parattarna. From this time, one may reckon the beginning of the Mitannian influence in Syria.

The most powerful king of Mitanni was Sausattar (or Sausadattar). He bore the title of "king of Maiteni (or of Hanigalbat), king of the Hurri-warriors." In his reign Arrapkhe east of the Tigris was either in the power of Mitanni or, at least, under Mitannian influence; it was the same king who concluded a treaty with the king of Kizzuwadna, south of the Taurus Mountains in Asia Minor. Self-governed Alalakh was dependent on him. It was also he who managed to seize and plunder Asshur. However, this city was not included in the kingdom of Mitanni, but the Mitannian envoy (*sukkallu*) had a place in the council of elders at Asshur, and, like the other elders, became in his turn a *limmu*-eponym of Asshur. A number of towns in eastern Asia Minor were dependents of Sausattar in the same way as Alalakh. The region of Kadmukhi on the Upper Tigris and possibly some districts along its northern tributaries were parts of the Mitannian realm.

During their campaigns to Palestine and Syria in the sixteenth and later centuries, the pharaohs of Egypt came into contact with local rulers bearing Indo-Iranian names, obviously kinsmen and protégés of the Mitannian ruling dynasty. The Egyptian inscriptions denote Mitanni by the term *Nahraina*, "The Two Rivers," which shows that they regarded it as stretching from the Euphrates to the Tigris (Meso-potamia, "The Land between the Rivers" of the Greeks). The clash between Egypt and Mitanni happened during the reigns of the pha-raohs Amenhetep II (fifteenth century) and Thutmosis IV (early in the fourteenth century); however, the latter pharaoh later entered into friendly relations with Artadama I, king of Mitanni, and, after long negotiations, received a Mitannian princess into his harem. (The transaction was probably treated in Mitanni as if the princess became the queen of Egypt, which was not the case.) The reason for the con-clusion of peace between Mitanni and Egypt has been thought to lay in their common enmity against the Hittite kingdom, which soon be-gan its advance south of the Taurus and into Syria, but internal condi-tions in both countries may also have played a role. The frontier between the spheres of interest of Mitanni and Egypt lay south of Tunip and Qatna in the Orontes Valley and north of Ugarit on the coast.

The next two kings of Mitanni, Shuttarna II and Dushratta, also sent their daughters to the next pharaoh, Amenhetep III. Dushratta acquired the throne through a bloody coup (in which the son of Shut-tarna was killed). He was especially interested in friendship with

Egypt because during his reign there appeared another pretender to the throne, Artadama II, who was allied to the Hittites. Dushratta sent an image of the revered Hurrian goddess Ishtar-Shawaushka of Nineveh (enjoying a cult in virtually all Hurrian communities), which was supposed to heal the sick Egyptian king. A very long diplomatic letter in Hurrian, the longest known text in that language, is concerned with the negotiations about the marriage of Dushratta's daughter to the pharaoh. The relations with Egypt deteriorated under the next pharaoh, Amenhetep IV (Akhenaton).

About the same time or somewhat later the new Hittite king, Suppiluliumas I (probably in agreement with Asshur, whose ruler, Asshuruballit I, now aspired to the title of king and to total independence from other powers), began a major offensive against Mitanni, capturing Carchemish on the Great Bend of the Euphrates and several other formerly Mitannian regions.

Dushratta was murdered by one of his sons, and during the following affray, the son of Artadama II (whom we always find inactive—he was probably a sick man), one Shuttarna (III) managed to take possession of Mitanni. Dushratta's surviving son, Shattiwasa (or Shattiwazza), fled with a detachment of charioteers to Arrapkhe (as we know from economic documents referring to provisioning there of Shattiwasa and his men); from there he tried to go to Kassite Babylonia, but the Kassites received him as an enemy. Losing his warriors, he fled back to Arrapkhe and from thence was sent off through the empty steppe to the Hittite frontier, which at that time had reached the Middle Euphrates. At last he appeared before Suppiluliumas with one single chariot and two men. Nevertheless, he got a royal reception; king Suppiluliumas gave his daughter in marriage (after having found out what kind of social position she would have in Mitanni). He also sent an army headed by his own son to Shattiwasa's aid. After the Mitannian forces were routed, the Hittite king, at Shattiwasa's request, made him heir apparent but left his sick uncle, Artadama, on the throne. The events brought about the end of Mitannian hegemony; in the west, domination belonged to the Hittites; in the east, Assyria rose, to the greatest detriment of Arrapkhe.

We know hardly anything about the inner political and social structure of Mitanni. The only thing certain is that it was not a monolithic empire but a loose federation of nomes united around Wasshukanne, the capital of Hanigalbat-Mitanni (the city's location is still uncertain). The nomes paid tribute to the king of Mitanni and aided him by sending military detachments. We also know that the "Men of Hurri" (military nobility?) played an important role in the king's entourage and were sometimes mentioned together with the king in state treaties and that in the army—perhaps also in the administration—a certain role was played by charioteers, the *marianna*. Although the chariot detachments and the chariot battle tactics were, no doubt, borrowed by the Mitannians from the Indo-Iranians, their charioteers, to judge by their names, were exclusively Hurrians. The term *marianna*, contrary to a very widely held opinion, is not a derivation of Old Indian *marya* "young man" but is purely Hurro-Urartian. This is proved not only by the Eastern Caucasian etymology of the word but also because the *marianna* as an institution existed not only among the Mitannians, who were influenced by Indo-Iranians, but also among all Hurro-Urartians, including Alalakh, Arrapkhe, and even Urartu, where no such influence can be observed. Note also that the *marianna* were not a "feudal aristocracy"; they were palace personnel, and even their chariots were delivered to them from palace storehouses. (The actual term was *mari*, but it is encountered with various Hurro-Urartian suffixes: *mari-anna, mari-a(h)he, mari-he*.)

The Hurrian Kingdom of Arrapkhe

The state Arrapkhe will be described in some detail because it serves as a good example of the peripheral nomes of the epoch, which usually did not leave any documentation at all.

When scholars first had the opportunity to read the archives of this kingdom from Al-ilani (modern Kirkuk) and later from Nuzi (third-millennium Gasur, modern Yorghan-tepe), they at once noted the specific legal features of deeds of immovable property transfers. Along with the usual Akkadian *alu* ("town, village, community") there were constant references to another type of community called *dimtu*, the sole Akkadian meaning of the word being "tower, pillar." Instead of the usual documents of sale and purchase, they encountered a great number of deeds transferring immovables by means of the adoption of adult independent persons (up to fifty deeds of nearly simultaneous adoption by different persons of one and the same man are attested). Such adoptions were being questioned in court by the next generation. The claims of the descendants of the adopters to the property were not recognized by the courts, but in the future a new form of transfer of property was introduced, which has no ready analogies; it was called *didennutu*, "apportioning" (from Hurrian *did*, "to divide") and has been identified as a form of mortgage with right for kinsmen of the debtor to get back the property after taking care of the debt.

These phenomena were at first explained in the following way: *dimtu* was supposed to mean not "tower" but "district"; this is a usage unattested in the whole corpus of Akkadian texts, but anything was thought to be possible when Hurrian aborigines were involved! As to the adoption, it was suggested that this was a way to circumvent a royal prohibition against selling fiefs. Since the party acquiring land through adoption (the most influential one) appeared to have been an official, it was suggested that this was a way to return the alienated fiefs to the crown.

Analysis of the key term *dimtu* makes it possible to avoid all these complications. Such tower complexes from all over the world have been studied in detail by M. I. Djandieri and are well known as extended family dwellings; it seems that the land pertaining to the extended family living in a dwelling tower could also be designated as *dimtu* of X.[15] Note that ownership based on adoption was always disputed by the kinsmen of the vendors ("adopters"), and the city-state authorities held aloof from these suits.

Arrapkhe had its palace archives like any other city-state of the epoch; but it also has left us two private archives, among the largest written in cuneiform. One of them extends to five generations; the other to three. The first, belonging to the clan of one Tehib-Tilla, was, from the beginning, the main object of study. The rise of the clan began when Tehib-Tilla's father acquired hundreds of hectares of garden land in the village of Nadmani (now Tell-Ali), near the town of Tursha (now Tel-Mahuz) and the ford over the Lesser Zab, on the main northern road of the country. Tursha lay in the rear of Asshur, whose role in international trade is well known. In a district like this a commercial orientation toward gardening could be of importance; the gardeners paid the state treasury in metals (i.e., in money) insofar as their production was not considered necessary food provision for the palace personnel. In the next generation, Tehib-Tilla was able to acquire, through "adoption," no less than a thousand hectares of land in seven different districts of the country (M. P. Maidman). He preferred parcels situated along the roads; roads are the backbone of commerce, the control of which gives power. According to the usage in Arrapkhe, an able-bodied worker had a claim to about one hectare of land; this was enough to sustain a nuclear family. This means that Tehib-Tilla could equip about a thousand warriors. A thousand warriors was the usual quota of a military district (*haltsu*). Apparently this is why Tehib-Tilla could be appointed district commander (*haltsuhlu*).

15. These archaic tower dwellings, often grouped inside one village (as in Unabshe, which lay near modern Fatha), must not be confused with "feudal castles" that have another structure and another social function. Archaic towers are usually subdivided into dwelling and defensive towers. The latter could not as a rule be alienated because they were part of the community's defenses, something like the state's fortresses, which is not true of the dwelling towers. The same system was well attested in the preconquest Caucasus, where the towers, alone and in groups, as well as stone rings for the elders, etc., are still to be seen.

The parcels were alienated by the owners mainly for a miserable compensation because this happened during a period of drought (at least three new canals bear the names of members of Tehib-Tilla's family). All Tehib-Tilla's deeds of acquisition of immovables took the form of adoption "as son" into the family of the former owner of the parcel. One could also be taken into the family "as brother" (as known from other archives), but this form was not used by Tehib-Tilla. The reason is that the two levels of kinship differed not only in their rights but also in their duties. Thus, a brother of Tehib-Tilla, acquiring a horse for the family at the price of a hundred shekels, divides the payments as follows: half of it he pays himself, and two sons of Tehib-Tilla pay twenty-five shekels each. This means that coevals are equal, but men belonging to an elder and a younger generation are not.[16] As to Tehib-Tilla himself, in practically all cases of acquisition of land through adoption, he was not liable to pay taxes and duties, if such were connected with the land in question. The liabilities were his responsibility only if he acquired the whole estate, not a single parcel. The privilege may have been connected with Tehib-Tilla's position as quasi son; that is, a person of diminished or no rights of participation in the family businesses.

The price of the land in cases of land transfer was called a "present." This is because according to cuneiform customary law, a present became private property; thus, for the transfer of the parcel, not the whole family, but only the holder of that particular parcel received a remuneration. The attempt has been made to graph the "prices of land" according to the size or supposed quality of the parcel, but the points fell in complete disorder. The market situation can be traced only in that the "present" for a house is, on the whole, higher than that for a garden and still higher than that for a field. Inside the communal-clan structures, and groups of coevals, what counted was not market value but a duty of mutual help. This is a social relation that is at once voluntary and obligatory. Mutual help does not mean delivery of equivalents but only readiness to help whenever needed and in whatever way is needed at the moment. If we try to understand a system that is not based on commercial account but on completely different values, we can also understand the transactions where no "present" at all is implicated. To get a remuneration equivalent to one crop and a half for one's parcel of land is a good price in a period of drought, so common in the Near East of the second millennium; to deprive the younger, inactive generation of a parcel of land

16. Tehib-Tilla had a third son, but he is not mentioned when the family's expenses are distributed. He must have belonged to yet another, still younger age-group.

still useless to them could be the only feasible way out for the elder, active generation in certain situations.

The community court, above which stood in each town of Arrapkhe only its popular assembly, was independent of the king and was made up of elders (former charioteers especially). This court was typically ruthless. Outside the palace sector, this was the real power of the communal-clan structures.

Having become a district military commander (*haltsuhlu*), Tehib-Tilla could register at once fifty deeds of transfer of immovables without applying to the elders. Contrary to what was usual for cuneiform legal documents, these deeds were attested by three seals only: that of Tehib-Tilla himself, that of the king's brother, and that of the head of a shepherd clan. Chronologically, Tehib-Tilla's land acquisitions were contemporary with the period of some of the mayors' most reckless, arbitrary actions. One mayor was tried (or at least interrogated) at the palace office; a series of records of confrontations with witnesses has been preserved. But the complaints of Tehib-Tilla's sons were lodged at the community court, not a court of palace judges. In a few points, the community members got their own from them. The wave of litigation coincided with the period when the younger generation, deprived of their land, became the mainstay of society. To this period should also be dated a royal decree on the annulment of debts (no doubt intended to lessen the social strain).

Tehib-Tilla's mighty clan was not unanimous; his youngest son, Agibtazhenni, was as unfortunate as his coevals. The two elder brothers oppressed him, and the son of the second brought Agibtazhenni's sons to ruin. This influential grandson of Tehib-Tilla, named Tarmi-Tilla, became a military district commander, like his grandfather. He separated himself from his kinsmen by a double wall, and he also separated his land. He used hired men to reap his harvest and paid them a miserable amount of barley, but assessed considerable fines if a worker was absent from work. Perhaps this kind of activity led to disobedience in his district; not a single person appeared when called up by him to clean a silted canal. The king punished Tarmi-Tilla by confiscation of an ox, but Tarmi-Tilla complained in community court against the irrigation inspector and the herald, claiming that they had failed to call in the men. The elders found the explanations of the two officials unconvincing and delivered them both to Tarmi-Tilla until that time when they should have restituted his loss of an ox. It is not impossible that the disobedience of the men was intended as obstruction.

One of Tehib-Tilla's great-grandsons, a descendant of his eldest son, was first a mayor, then a *shakin mati*—the most important official

in the country after the king and head of community self-government. He rose to that dignity at a moment when the international
situation of Arrapkhe had worsened sharply, when the Assyrians advanced and the route connecting Arrapkhe with her ally Mitanni was
cut. Mitanni had been the leading state for a long time. The possessions of Tehib-Tilla's clan by now extended beyond the ford over the
Lesser Zab at Tursha and even to Karana (now Tell-Rimah in Upper
Mesopotamia). All this was lost during the enemy advance.

One of the wings of the garrison fortress of Nuzi, which originally
was owned by the Tehib-Tilla clan, was now occupied by a new
haltsuhlu, Kel-Tesshub, who belonged to another clan. The border
fortress of Kissuk came under his authority, neighboring villages and
towers having sworn an oath of allegiance to him. They denied recognition to the son of their former commander, and the king ordered
the *shakin mati* to question all neighboring villages and to appoint the
person they selected, which was Kel-Tesshub. After the loss of Tursha,
the ford leading to Kassite territory became especially important; this
was where the Mitannian prince Shattiwasa tried to contact the Kassite king. The "new liberation" of the citizens of Arrapkhe from debts
is mentioned in a number of Kel-Tesshub's documents.

The second large private archive found in Nuzi belonged to the
clan of the princes. The subject of the documents is quite different;
they are mostly documents of accountancy. Prince Shilwi-Tesshub, the
most active of the clan, lent barley, but usually not to private persons,
as Tehib-Tilla did, but to big rural communities, without interest.
When he lent small sums, he usually took immovables as security,
which Tehib-Tilla never did. (He preferred to take debtor-slaves as
security for the debt.) The result was that at the beginning of his activities, the prince himself had to borrow barley for the sustenance of
his personnel. Nothing of the sort ever happened to Tehib-Tilla. The
prince confiscated the immovables of his insolvent debtors through
the palace office; Tehib-Tilla did it openly and publicly, through the
community court. Apparently, a reserve of moral credit was indispensable for the ruling clan. It is possible that the change in the form
of loan deeds is to be connected with the numerous cases of litigation
with Tehib-Tilla's heirs as a result of Tehib-Tilla's activities: Shilwi-
Tesshub was a younger contemporary of Tehib-Tilla.

Extended-family communes not only were the mainstay of the state
structure of Arrapkhe but were also the principal structure in the
field of production; the professional family communes of the weavers,
the potters, and the merchants had their own prestigious towers. The
prince was a patron of the potters; therefore, we know more about
this community than the others. A list of the potters enumerates

forty-six able-bodied men, which means that the entire population of the community was at least one hundred and fifty. That was also about the number of members in the community of Shelwikhe, which was incorporated into the princes' economy. There were about a dozen palace economies in the different cultic centers of the country; these ensured the sustenance of the escort during royal visits and also the sustenance of impoverished families. During a critical period caused by military activities, when all the personnel of the palace in Nuzi received "siege-time rations" (all men received the amount normally received by women), the king ordered the richer houses to give refuge to poor families and strictly prohibited misuse of their power over them.

Arrapkhe was drawn into the struggle between the two rival powers of Kassite Babylonia and Assyria; the latter began to lay claim to the status of a world power under Asshuruballit I. Asshuruballit meddled twice in Kassite internal affairs, but in the end the Kassite kings Kurigalzu the Younger and his successor, Nazi-Maruttash (fourteenth century), not only threw the Assyrians back but led campaigns deep into Assyrian territory. This means that military activities must have occurred more than once in the territory of Arapkhe.

The Culture of the Hurrians

It took nearly a hundred years to define the characteristic features of Hurrian culture, but finally we have a certain picture. Settled in the Zagros foothills, in Upper Mesopotamia, and in Syria, the Hurrians first and foremost functioned as intermediaries between the more ancient cultures; this has been clear from the beginning. But the conclusion that their culture was secondary in relation to Mesopotamia cannot be upheld. The originality and grace of the forms and decorations of Hurrian pottery found in considerable numbers at Yorghan-tepe (Nuzi) and at the mouth of the Orontes at Tell-Atchana (Alalakh) remind one of Crete, the elaborate style of the Hurrian carved cylinder seals, the invention of colored rolled glass for making small vessels and beads—all this distinguishes Hurrian artistic craft as belonging to the highest level of creativeness relative to other contemporary cultures. Later the Assyrians borrowed much from Hurrian art. To the later period of Hurrian art belongs a fine gold vessel from Hasanlu near Lake Urmia, depicting scenes from Hurrian mythology.

For crafts practiced by extended families, a high level of artistry is typical. (In craft shops of other types of organization, as, e.g., in the Late Sumerian ones, a callous uniformity and lower level of craftsmanship are more characteristic.) In contrast to the traditional Mesopotamian compositions, Hurrian artists preferred curved lines both in pottery decoration and in glyptic art; the figures are placed freely and unconstrainedly. The subject matter also often differs from that in Mesopotamia: there appear, for example, all sorts of "carnival masks" unknown to the glyptic art of Lower Mesopotamia.

The literature of the Hurrians is poorly preserved, and it is mostly in Hittite translations (see Lecture 13); some original Hurrian poetry is preserved in school texts unearthed in Amarna, Egypt, and in copies from Emar (now Meskeneh, on the Euphrates), Ugarit, and especially in Hattusas (now Boghazköy). The texts from Hattusas are mostly liturgical or incantational. A short time ago a long bilingual (Hurrian and Hittite) incantation was found. Also from Hattusas comes a fragment of an epic tale about the heroes Gilgamesh and Enkidu journeying to fight Huwawa, the keeper of the Cedar Grove. The episode seems to have been related in more complexity than in the Akkadian version, and its sense has not yet been fully interpreted. We have some proverbs and a unique lyric-religious text, with musical notation added, from Ugarit; charms against snakes and the like from Babylonia; and a fragment of what apparently was a didactic dialogue. These are only poor remnants of what must have been an impressively rich literature.

Central to the Hurrian mythology and cults seems to be a concept of the gods' wrath bringing about ritual impurity, which can be purified by sacrifice. There are traces of primitive communal feasts; individualization had started but had not developed very far.

The head of the pantheon was the Thunderer god, Tesshub (an analogue of Zeus). In the heart of northern Syria (in Haleb), his spouse was Hebat (it has been suggested that she is to be connected with the biblical Eve); their child was Sharruma. In Arrapkhe, Tesshub's spouse was also Hebat (although she appears only in the proper names of princesses);[17] their child was Tilla, the Calf. In Hurrian Kizzuwadna, a state adjoining the Hittite kingdom, the supreme triad was composed of Tesshub, his spouse Hebat, and his sister Shawushka. Shawushka was also very popular elsewhere. The two chief goddesses differ not only in their kinship relation to the supreme deity (the one his spouse, the other his sister) but also in their attributes (the Throne for Hebat, the Bed for Shawushka). Their respective priestesses were accommodated in different parts of the palace at Nuzi.

Opposite the temple of Ishtar of Nuzi is the palace entrance. To the right is the comparatively new display section of the palace; it belongs to the reigning queen (or, more accurately, the "lady king," Sumerian

17. No names commemorating a goddess were ever given in ancient Western Asia to boys, except for goddesses of the Ishtar type. The great majority of the proper names mentioned in the legal and economic documents are those of men.

mí-lugal).[18] Here was situated the harem, with children and wet nurses. One of the hills was decorated with masks of a bull, a cow, and a calf, symbolizing Tesshub, Hebat, and Tilla.

To the left is the utility section of the palace. It includes an archive of the army commissariat and the private archive of the *entu*-priestess, the "god's spouse." It is possible that the *entu* was connected with the cult of Ishtar-Shawushka, the deity of strife and love.

The Hurrian ancestor god was Kumarwe (corresponding to Kronos of the Greeks). This is a metonymic designation, meaning "the one of Kumme," so he is actually a nameless deity. Kumme was an important Hurrian cultic center situated in the Kurdistan Mountains at present-day Zaho near the Turkish-Iraqi border. He is the evil father of beneficent Tesshub and was dethroned by all the gods in concert, as related in the "Song of Ullikumme," preserved to us in a Hittite translation. The action of this dramatized version of the myth is set on the seacoast, and it was no doubt compiled in Kizzuwadna. Ullikumme is the "destroyer of Kumme." He is a child, analogous to the Greek Eros, son of Chaos. He was created in the form of a phallus and a sword. He grows swiftly and threatens to destroy the entire world. He is blind and deaf like passion itself, and even Ishtar-Shawushka, sent by the gods to seduce him, is powerless against him. He proves invincible against the warrior Tesshub and all his host, because his root is deep under water. Only Eia, the master of wisdom, manages to overcome him; he cuts off his root with the instrument that had been used to separate the sky from the rock. This cycle of myths, passed on through unknown intermediaries, reached the Greek poet Hesiod in the seventh century B.C.

The city of Urkesh is mentioned in the Kumarwe epic as being Kumarwe's city of origin. But in historical times Urkesh was the center of the cult of another god, probably connected with the underworld (identified with the Babylonian Nergal). He was symbolized by a sword. In Arrapkhe this god was worshiped under the name of Ugur in the town of Kuruhanni, where he had his *entu*-priestess. Nergal's spouse (and sister) was Shala. In a Hittite-Hurrian offering list, Nergal is identified with the grain offered to Tesshub. In the calendar of Arrapkhe the first two months of the winter half-year are the *shekhli* of Tesshub and the *shekhli* of Nergal, corresponding to the month of rain and the month of sowing. The last month of this half-year is that "of the sheaf" (*kurilli*, probably the last sheaf of the harvest hiding the "mother of the grain"?). The Hurrians of Arrapkhe began their year with the month of the fires in the braziers (*kinunu*).

18. There were *mí-lugal*s in different towns of Arrapkhe, and they, like the *entu*s, also had religious functions.

These fires were probably commemorative of the dead, exorcising their possible harmful influence before the hungry and dry summer season. The gods of the luminaries were more judging and punishing than beneficent deities: Shimike, the Sun, is a god of oracles; Kushukh, the Moon, the Light of the Underworld, is the guarantor of oaths. Ancestors were worshiped in the sanctuaries of the extended families; a month was set aside for the paternal gods (*attanashwe*); the offerings to them were probably made simultaneously by all families.

Mantic practices were as widely in use among the Hurrians as among other ancient Oriental peoples. But besides the usual extispicy of the Babylonians (fortune-telling using a lamb's liver), the Hurrians also practiced augury (fortune-telling by the flight of birds).

The malevolent character of the natural forces is apparent in the selection of the subject matter in Hurrian myths. In order not to die prematurely, one should never forget the offerings to the gods. The idea of sacrifice is central to the Hurrian cult.

The City-State of Asshur and the Emergence of the Kingdom of Assyria

The cities that later formed the nucleus of the Assyrian Empire (Nineveh, Asshur, Arbela, etc.) did not constitute a single political or even ethnic entity until the fifteenth century B.C.[19] Moreover, the very term *Assyria* was nonexistent in the fifteenth century B.C. Therefore, the appellation Old Assyrian used to refer to the empire of Shamshi-Adad I is erroneous; Shamshi-Adad I (1813–1783) never regarded himself as a king of Asshur, although later Assyrian king lists dating from the first millennium B.C. include him among the Old Assyrian kings.

At an early period Nineveh was a Hurrian city. As for Asshur, its name is probably Semitic, and the population of the city was mainly Akkadian. In the sixteenth to fifteenth centuries these cities were dependent (sometimes nominally) on Mitanni or Kassite Babylonia, but already in the late fifteenth century the rulers of Asshur regarded themselves as independent. Both the rulers and the city elite generally were very rich for these times. The source of their wealth was the mediation in trade between the south of Mesopotamia and the lands of the Zagros, the Armenian highland, Asia Minor, and Syria.

Asshur was the center of a comparatively small city-state. Although after the conquest of Upper Mesopotamia by Shamshi-Adad and of eastern Asia Minor by the Hittite kings, Asshur's trading posts in Asia

---

19. The sixth and seventh sections are by V. A. Jakobson.

Minor ceased to exist, Asshur preserved its great economic and political importance. Its ruler bore the title *isshiakkum* (an Akkadianized version of Sumerian *ensî*); his authority was practically hereditary. He was a priest, an administrator, and a military chief; in his position as *ukullum*, he was probably also the chief distributor of land and head of the city council. The *limmu* were elected for a one-year term from among the members of the city council; these were the eponyms of the year and possibly also the city treasurers. With time, the council consisted more and more of men from the ruler's entourage. We have no information on the existence of a popular assembly in Asshur. The more the power of the rulers grew, the less became the importance of the city magistrates.

The territory of the city-state of Asshur included smaller settlements—rural communities, each headed by a *hazannu*. The land was the property of the community and was apparently periodically redistributed between family communes, that is, extended families. The center of the extended-family estate was a fortified farmstead, or *dunnu*. A member of a rural community and a family commune was entitled to sell his plot, which thus was lost to the family commune and became the private property of the purchaser. However, such transactions were controlled by the rural community, which could prohibit the sale of that particular plot and instead allot another from the reserve fund to the purchaser. Moreover, the transactions had to be permitted by the ruler. This shows that the commodity-money relations were here more developed than in neighboring Babylonia; alienation of land was no longer reversible. This was probably the result of the Asshurites' having long been involved in international trade and having accumulated considerable financial resources.

Sometimes whole estates were sold—not only the field but also the farmstead house, garden, threshing floor, and well, with an area from three to thirty hectares. The land was mostly bought up by moneylenders and traders. Note that the money was not silver but lead (or tin?), paid out in hundreds of kilograms. The labor force seems to have been supplied mainly through debtor-slavery. There were also other means of acquiring dependent labor; for example, the "revival in grief" (*balluṭu ina lumne*). The "revived" was subjected to the patriarchal authority of the "benefactor" or to "adoption together with the field and home." Thus a few rich families concentrated more and more land for themselves, while the community fields dwindled. However, the community labor obligations were not taken over by the purchasers of land but rested, as before, on the very much impoverished extended families. The owners of the newly acquired lands seem to have lived in the city, and their labor obligations as community members (*alaiu*) were borne by the dependent inhabitants of the villages. Asshur was now called "the community among the communities," and the privileged status of its citizens was officially recognized by granting them immunity from taxes and labor obligations. (The date of this decree is unknown.) The *alaiu* in the villages continued to pay the taxes and to fulfill the labor and, especially, the military obligations.

Thus, Asshur became a small but very rich state. Its riches helped to make Asshur economically strong, but in order to become really strong politically, Asshur had to wait until its neighbors became weak, else they could stifle all its expansion attempts. The Asshur elite began preparing for further strengthening of the state by augmenting the authority of the ruler, who was also the military chief. In the late fifteenth century the wall of the "New Town" of Asshur, which had been destroyed by the Mitannians, was restored, and Mitanni could do nothing about it.

Although both the Mitannian and Kassite kings continued to regard the Asshurites as their tributaries, the ruler of Asshur established direct diplomatic relations with Egypt. As early as the fourteenth century the ruler of Asshur titled himself "king," though so far only in private documents; however, Asshur-uballit I (1365–1330) began to use the title "King of the Land of Asshur" (Assyria) also in his official correspondence and on seals (although not in his inscriptions) and called himself "brother" of the pharaoh, like the kings of Kassite Babylonia, Mitanni, and the Hittites. He took an active part in the events that led to the downfall of Mitanni as a major power, and time and again involved himself in the dynastic struggle in Kassite Babylonia.

Later on, in the relations between Assyria and Kassite Babylonia, periods of peace alternated with periods of war, and sometimes Assyria suffered serious defeats, especially in the late fourteenth century. Nevertheless, the Assyrian territory in the west (the valley of the Upper Tigris) and in the east (the Zagros Mountains) continually grew. The authority of the king as military chief was steadily on the rise, while the role of the city council waned; now the king virtually became an absolute monarch.

Adad-nērari I (1308–1275) added to his other titles that of the *limmu* (the eponym-treasurer) of the first year of his reign. He also was the first to use the title "King of Multitudes" and can thus be regarded as the real founder of the Assyrian (Middle Assyrian) Empire. He had at his disposal a strong army, whose mainstay consisted of the king's men, who received as their remuneration either rations or special plots of land. In case of need, a community militia could be added to the army. Adad-nērari's wars with Babylonia were successful, and the frontier of Assyria was moved a good distance to the south. A special poem was written extolling the king's accomplishments, although in the end his successes in the south proved to be unstable. Adad-nērari also campaigned twice against Mitanni, with success. The second campaign ended in the deposition of the Mitannian king Wasashatta; the Assyrian protégé Shattuara II was enthroned; the whole territory of Mitanni as far as Carchemish at the Great Bend of the Euphrates was now controlled by Assyria. Adad-nērari's successor, Shalmaneser I (1274–1245), however, also had to wage war with the Mitannians and their allies—the Hittites and the new group of Western Semitic shepherd tribes, the Aramaeans. Although the Assyrian army was surrounded by their enemies somewhere in a desert and was inadequately supplied with water, they managed to break through and gain a victory. All of Upper Mesopotamia was included in the Assyrian Empire, and Mitanni ceased to exist. In his inscription, Shalmaneser recounts how he captured 14,400 enemy warriors and blinded them (14,400 is 4 × 3,600, a round number for the Assyrians, whose number system used base 6). Here for the first time we meet with the savage reprisals that with terrible monotony are repeated in later Assyrian royal inscriptions. (The first to make such reprisals were, however, the Hittites.) Shalmaneser also waged war against the Uruatri mountain dwellers in the north (the first mention of the Urartians, a people related to the Hurrians).

In all cases the Assyrians destroyed the towns and villages, killed or mutilated the inhabitants, and looted and exacted a "heavy tribute" from the survivors. The captives (mostly qualified craftsmen) were seldom taken to Assyria. Some captives were blinded. It seems that the Assyrian elite could satisfy their need for a labor force with internal sources. The main aim of the Assyrian conquests was at that period to lay hold of the international trade routes and to enrich themselves, partly by exacting customs dues from the trade but probably much more often by looting the trading centers.

Under the next Assyrian king, Tukulti-Ninurta I (1224–1208), Assyria was already a great political power, encompassing all of Upper Mesopotamia. The new king was even bold enough to invade Hittite territory, from which he brought home no less than 8 × 3,600 (28,800) prisoners. He also waged war with the nomads of the steppes and the mountain dwellers of the north and east, for example, with the "43 kings [tribal chiefs] of Nairi" (the Armenian highland). Campaigns were now conducted yearly, not for extension of the empire's territory but for sheer plundering. But in the south Tukulti-Ninurta achieved a great feat, conquering the Babylonian kingdom of the Kassites (about 1223 B.C.) and ruling over it for seven years. The statue of

Babylon's tutelary deity, Marduk, was brought to Assyria, and continued to be a cult object there. A poem was composed to commemorate these deeds of the Assyrian king; his title now was as follows:

> Mighty king, king of Assyria, king of Kar-Duniash [Babylonia], king of Sumer and Akkad, king of Sippar and Babylon, king of Telmun and Melakha [Bahrain and India], king of the Upper and Lower Sea, king of the mountains and the broad steppes, king of the Subarians [the Hurrians] and the Qutians [the eastern mountain dwellers] and of the lands of Nairi, a king obedient to his gods and receiving the tribute of the four quarters of the world.

As we can see, the title does not at all reflect the real situation, but it does contain a whole political program. First of all, Tukulti-Ninurta leaves out the traditional title of "*isshiakku* of Asshur," but at the same time he assumes the ancient title of "king of Sumer and Akkad" and refers to the heavy tribute of the four quarters of the world like Naram-Su'en and Shulgi. He pretends to rule territories that were never part of his empire, including the main trading centers of Sippar and Babylon, as well as the trade routes to Bahrain and India. In order to liberate himself finally from all possible influence of the city council of Asshur, he transferred his capital to a specially built new residence town, called Kar-Tukulti-Ninurta, "the trading center of Tukulti-Ninurta," which probably shows his intention to establish a center for international and internal trade there. Here was erected a new palace on a grand scale, where the king entertained even gods as his guests (that is, of course, their statues). To appear before the person of the king was now the privilege of a few of the highest dignitaries (mainly eunuchs). Very strict rules were introduced to govern daily life in the royal apartments, including rules for magic rituals to avert evil from the king and the like.

However, the time for creating enduring empires had not yet arrived. The traditional elite of Asshur were strong enough to declare the king a madman and to depose and then kill him. The new royal residence was left to ruin.

Babylonian rulers were wise enough to make use of the inner turmoil in Assyria, and all the following Assyrian kings (except one) were no more than henchmen of the Babylonian kings. One of them had to return the statue of Marduk to Babylon.

However, Assyria did not lose her sway over all of Upper Mesopotamia, and when King Tiglath-pileser I ascended the throne, a new political situation, most favorable to Assyria, had developed in the Near East. The Hittite kingdom had fallen, Egypt was in decay, and

Babylonia was invaded by a group of southern Aramaean nomads, the Chaldeans. Thus, Assyria was actually the only great power left. It had only to hold out against the general chaos and then to begin new conquests. This was, however, a more difficult task than may have been thought. The tribes that had appeared in Western Asia as the result of the ethnic movements at the end of the second millennium B.C. were numerous and warlike. These were the Proto-Armenians (the Mushki of the Assyrian sources), the Phrygians, the western Georgian tribes, the Apeshlaians (probably the modern Abkhasians), the Aramaeans, the Chaldeans, and others. They even invaded Assyrian territory, so that one had to begin with defense. But Tiglath-pileser I seems to have been a good general. Very soon he turned to the offensive, moving farther and farther to the north. Some of the tribes submitted without battle and were "reckoned among the men of Assyria." In 1112 Tiglath-pileser started a campaign north from Mesopotamia, to the west of the Upper Euphrates. The exact route is unknown, but it must have followed the ancient trade route. The annals mention victories over dozens of "kings." It may be surmised that following the retreat of "60 kings of Nairi," the Assyrian army reached the Black Sea somewhere near modern Batumi. The vanquished were looted and had to pay tribute; in order to secure its regular delivery, hostages were taken. This was not the last campaign of the king to the north. One campaign is commemorated on a rock to the north of Lake Van.

Tiglath-pileser twice invaded Babylonia. In the second campaign the Assyrians managed to conquer and plunder a number of important cities, among them Dur-Kurigalzu and Babylon. However, in about 1089 B.C. the Babylonians managed to throw the Assyrians back to their own territory. But, as early as 1111 B.C., the main attention of the Assyrians was fixed on the Aramaeans, who had become a major threat. Slowly but inexorably they moved into Upper Mesopotamia. Tiglath-pileser campaigned against them many times, and he even managed to proceed west of the Euphrates. Gaining a victory over the nomads in the oasis of Tadmor (Palmyra), he crossed the Lebanon and passed down Phoenicia as far as Sidon. He even made a sailing tour along the coast hunting dolphins. His military glory was great, but the practical results of his campaigns were paltry. Even the land to the east of the Euphrates could not be kept, much less the territory to the west of the Euphrates.

Although there still were Assyrian garrisons in cities and fortresses of Upper Mesopotamia, the steppes were in the hands of the nomads, who cut the communications with Assyria proper. Later attempts of the Assyrian kings to ally themselves against the nomads with the

kings of Babylonia brought little success. Assyria was thrown back to
its original land, and its economic and political life decayed, a situation exacerbated by centuries of prolonged drought in Mesopotamia.
Between the late eleventh and the late tenth centuries B.C., nearly no
Assyrian documents or inscriptions have come down to us. A new period in the history of Assyria began only after it had overcome the
threat of the nomads.

The Middle Assyrian Laws

The Middle Assyrian Laws (abbreviated MAL) throw light on the cultural history and the everyday life of the epoch. They are probably
not actual laws of the Assyrian state but a kind of scholarly compilation, a codification of different legislative acts and norms of customary law of the Asshur community, meant to be used in education and
for practical needs. During the excavations in Asshur fourteen tablets
and tablet fragments of laws were discovered. They are usually denoted by the letters A to O. Some are in an excellent state of preservation; others in a very poor one. Some fragments (e.g., B and C) belong
to one original tablet. The copies date from the fourteenth to thirteenth centuries; the original texts probably date to before the creation of the Assyrian Empire.

The MAL combine very archaic features with important innovations. One innovation is the method of systematization of the legal
statutes. They are grouped by subject into very big blocks; a separate
tablet is devoted to each subject. The subdivisions in the Laws of
Hammurapi (LH) are smaller; in the MAL subjects are defined more
broadly. Thus, tablet A (fifty-nine paragraphs) is devoted to different
aspects of the legal status of free women ("the daughter of a freeman," "the wife of a freeman," "the widow of a freeman"), harlots,
and the slave women. These aspects include the different offences
committed by or against a woman, marriage, property relations of the
spouses, and rights toward children. In other words, the woman appears here both as the subject of rights and as their object, both as a
criminal and as a victim of a crime. Acts are treated that can be committed not only by a woman but also by a man (§10, murder in another person's house; §47, sorcery). Also included in this tablet is the
crime of pederasty (§§19–20). Such a grouping is, of course, more
practical than that of the LH, but it has its drawbacks. For instance,
theft is treated in two different tablets (A, §§1, 3–6; C+G, §8); the
same happens to false accusations and false denunciations (A and N)
and to the statutes relating to inheritance (A, §§25–26; O, §§1–3).
However, it is only from our modern point of view that this can be
regarded as a drawback.

An innovation in comparison with the Laws of Hammurapi is the very wide application of public punishment—flogging and "royal labor" (i.e., forced labor)—apart from money compensation to the victim. This punishment is unique for so early a period. It can be explained in two ways: either as a result of a very high development of legal thought or as the result of the retention of community solidarity. The latter would mean that many offences, especially in the sphere of agrarian relations or against the honor and dignity of free citizens, were regarded as touching the interests of the whole community.

The MAL also contain archaic features. Such are A, §10, and B+O, §2. According to these, a murderer is to be delivered up to the "lord of the house"; that is, to the head of the victim's family. "The lord of the house" was entitled, at his discretion, either to kill the culprit or to let him loose after having received a ransom. In more developed legal systems ransom for murder is not allowed.

So far as we can judge from the MAL, the mixture of archaic and innovative features is typical also of Middle Assyrian society itself. Asshur was a rich trading city. The considerable level of devleopment of commodity-money relations allowed the legislator to use money compensations widely (involving dozens of kilograms of a metal, which might have been lead or tin). But at the same time bondage for debt existed, and its conditions were very severe: after expiration of the term for payment, the hostage pledged as security for debt was to be regarded as received for "full price"; that is, as bought. He could be treated as a slave, corporal punishment could be inflicted on him, and he could even be sold "into another country" (A, §44; C+G, §3). Land could be bought and sold unreservedly (B+O, §6), although under control of the authorities. From business documents it can be seen that the community had a right to substitute another plot for the one selected by the parties for sale. This means that private property coexisted with the retention of certain rights of the community to the land.

The patriarchal character of family relations is obvious already from the above-mentioned types of punishment for murder. It is made still clearer in the statutes regarding family law. The extended family still existed, and the power of the paterfamilias was very considerable. He could pledge away his wife and children as security for debt, could inflict corporal punishment on his wife, and even mutilate her. He could treat his unmarried daughter "as he wished" for her having "sinned" (A, §56). Adultery was punished by death for both partners; having caught them in flagrante delicto, the wronged husband could kill both. If the case was brought to court, the correspondent received the same punishment that the husband chose for his adulterous wife (A, §15). A woman could become a legally competent person only if she was widowed and had neither sons (even minors!), father-in-law, nor any other male kinsman of her husband. Otherwise, she was left under the patriarchal authority of one of these.

The MAL establish a very simple procedure for turning a slave-concubine into a wife and for legalizing the children borne by her (A, §41), but in other respects the treatment of slaves was very severe. On pain of a very cruel punishment, slave women and harlots were forbidden to wear the veil, an obligatory part of the garment of a free woman.[20] But it should be noted that such severe punishments were inflicted on the slaves according to law, not according to the arbitrary wish of the owner. The MAL also mention some nonslave dependent persons; however, the exact sense of the terms in question is still debatable.

From the documents it can also be seen that the "voluntary" subjection of a person to the patronage of a rich and/or noble person (i.e., a change from freeman to client) was practiced.

In the Assyrian court procedure, a wide use was made of ordeal by water and of oaths. Declining to undergo the ordeal or to swear an oath was tantamount to admitting one's guilt or the groundlessness of one's claim.

The punishments meted out according to the MAL were very severe and were based on the talion principle, although not so consistently as in the LH. The principle finds its expression mainly in the wide application of mutilating punishments.

20. Note that in Lower Mesopotamia the women were not, as a rule, veiled. The custom may have been borrowed by the Assyrians from the nomads.

12

Mesopotamia in the Sixteenth to Eleventh Centuries B.C.

V. A. JAKOBSON

The Middle Babylonian Period in Lower Mesopotamia, the Kassite Kingdom, and Elam

As we saw earlier, the Old Babylonian Period of Mesopotamian history ended soon after 1600 B.C. with the Kassite conquest. The homeland of the Kassite tribes was in the mountainous regions of western Iran and along the upper course of the Diyala River and its tributaries near the northwestern borders of Elam. We do not know whether they were native inhabitants of this region or whether they came from elsewhere. Nor do we know about any possible kinship between the Kassites and other ancient peoples. One thing is clear: they were not Indo-Europeans. Toward the end of the First Babylonian dynasty the Kassites raided Mesopotamia through the Diyala Valley, and one of the Kassite tribal groups even advanced into northern Mesopotamia as early as the eighteenth century, settling in the Hanean kingdom (on the Middle Euphrates, near the mouth of the Khabur). It seems that some of the Kassite tribal chiefs entered the service of the local rulers, but eventually they seized power and became kings themselves. These chiefs were much later included in the lists of Kassite kings of Babylonia, although actually it was still far too early for them to have ruled Babylon. It was only following the destruction of Babylon by the Hittites in 1595 B.C. that this city came into the hands of the Kassites.

Very few documents are available from Mesopotamia from the sixteenth and fifteenth centuries. The first Kassite king in Babylon known to us is Agum (sixteenth century, the second of his name in the dynasty that originally ruled in Hana). He already ruled over a vast territory that included southern Mesopotamia (except for the Sealand) and the mountainous regions beyond the Tigris, although he did not adopt the title "King of Sumer and Akkad."

At about the same time the Hurrians created a new kingdom in Upper Mesopotamia, Mitanni, which was discussed in Lecture 11.

A curious document has reached us from the first quarter of the first millennium B.C., the so-called Synchronistic History. It enumerates the wars and peace treaties between Assyria and Babylonia. We find in this document that the successor of Agum II, Burnaburiash I, signed a peace treaty with the ruler of Asshur, on the Middle Tigris around 1450 B.C. This shows that Kassite Babylonia shared a border with this city-state. Two generations later Ulam-Buriash, brother of the Kassite king, conquered the Sealand and killed its last ruler. After the death of his brother, he apparently became king of Babylonia, thus once again reuniting all of Lower Mesopotamia into a single state. The Kassite kings now began to call themselves "King of Babylon, King of Sumer and Akkad, King of the Kassites, King of Kar-Duniash."[1] Some of the Kassite kings corresponded with Egypt in a rather favor-seeking tone. Their relations with Asshur were varied: sometimes the rulers of Asshur were their enemies, sometimes their tributaries or allies, and even occasionally their kinsmen.

The Kassite king Kurigalzu the Elder (beginning of the fourteenth century) built the city Dur-Kurigalzu ("Kurigalzu Fortress"), where he established his royal residence, separate from Babylon.[2] Babylon itself was exempted from the general royal taxes and became a privileged self-governing city. A similar privilege was apparently granted to Sippar already during the First Babylonian dynasty, to Nippur around 1250 B.C., and later to other important cities.

Since the middle of the fourteenth century, the Babylonian economy seems to have experienced an upswing, which is attested by the increase in the number of business and economic documents. But then the ruler of Asshur began meddling in the dynastic quarrels of Babylonia, twice managing to put his henchman on the Babylonian throne. Some later Babylonian military attempts against Assyria were unsuccessful, and the Kassite kings were forced to accept Assyrian control over the Babylonian-Mitannian trade. A lasting peace with Assyria was eventually established, and the Babylonian king Kurigalzu the Younger (1333–1312 B.C.) was able to conduct a successful war against Elam, taking Susa and other cities. This success, however, was short-lived, an independent and powerful state soon emerging again in Elam.

In general, Babylonia's political situation continued to deteriorate. A powerful Assyrian kingdom already existed in the north and con-

1. Kar-Duniash was the Kassite name for Lower Mesopotamia; it remained in use for several centuries. Another official name for Babylonia from that time on was Shinar, or Shinhara.

2. A cylinder seal with the name and title "Kurigalzu, king of Shinar" written in Egyptian hieroglyphics has been found in a somewhat later burial at the site of Metsamor, located as far north as the modern Soviet Republic of Armenia. A chalcedony weight in the form of a frog, with the name of Ulam-Buriash, was also found there.

tinued to expand its territory, threatening to cut Babylonia off from its trade routes. Elam, as mentioned above, posed a threat from the east. On the west, where the Kassites apparently managed to rid themselves of the stock-raising Amorite tribes, new nomadic tribes— the Aramaeans—began moving in from the steppes. This threat became especially serious.

To counter these developments attempts were made to forge an alliance, directed mainly against Assyria and the nomads, between the three "traditional" great powers: Egypt, the Hittite kingdom of Asia Minor, and Babylonia. The alliance did not succeed. Around 1225 the Elamite king conducted a devastating incursion into Babylonia, and the Assyrian king Tukulti-Ninurta followed almost immediately with his attack. The Assyrians routed the Kassite army, and King Kashtiliash was captured and taken to Asshur in chains. Then the city of Babylon fell; its temples and palaces were plundered, and the statue of its god, Marduk, was carried off to Assyria. Seven years afterward, the Babylonians recovered their independence, and the new Kassite king, Adad-shum-utsur (about 1187 B.C.), was able, in turn, to intervene in Assyrian affairs and to place his own protégé on their throne.

In the middle of the twelfth century, Babylonia suffered a series of new invasions, first from Assyria and then from Elam. The latter was particularly grave. Around 1158 B.C. the Elamite king Shutruk-Nahhunte invaded the Diyala Valley, crossed the Tigris, and led his army across Lower Mesopotamia, capturing a number of cities. The Kassite king was overthrown, and Babylonia was placed under an Elamite governor. Mesopotamian cities suffered terrible destruction and looting,[3] and on top of it all, tribute payments were imposed on them. The Babylonians tried to resist, but their attempts were brutally suppressed.

Later, a new Babylonian leader took advantage of internal strife in Elam and proclaimed himself king, but it was Issin he chose as his capital (the Second Dynasty of Issin). During this dynasty, whose most prominent representative was Nebuchadrezzar I (1126–1105 B.C.), Babylonia enjoyed a brief resurgence. The king even managed to subjugate Assyria and to destroy Elam, excluding the latter from the political game for a long time to come. All these successes were eventually brought to naught, first by the Assyrians and, later, by a massive invasion of southern Aramaean nomadic tribes (the Chaldeans). With these events the first stage of antiquity comes to an end in southern Mesopotamia.

---

3. The Elamites also carried away to Susa the big stela inscribed with Hammurapi's laws, and it was there that it was discovered by archaeologists.

The Society of the Middle Babylonian Period

The typical document of the Kassite and post-Kassite periods is a *kudurru*—a deed granting land from the royal fund to some individual, sometimes freeing the recipient from certain taxes and service duties. Such grants were, strictly speaking, not donations but cessions of property for temporary use. A *kudurru* could be transferred to future heirs, subject to royal sanction. However, with time this land came to be regarded as private property, especially since the kings became tired of resolving the endless litigations about inheritance rights and began to transfer the land for "times eternal." Thus, alongside community land, privately owned lands came into existence, lying outside the jurisdiction of the communal authorities. It was still not feasible to run small economies independently, and the new private owners tended again to form communal structures—"houses" or "brotherhoods." Extensive land tracts, as well as entire villages (more accurately, taxes and the service duties from them), were also given to temples.

These new phenomena were brought about by the disintegration of the state economies with their unwieldy and costly administrative machinery. Instead of keeping up such economies, the state imposed taxes and service duties on the entire population (or its majority). The difference between the community members and the beneficiaries of royal grants gradually disappeared; both in fact became private owners, equally subject to taxes and duties. This process was also accelerated by the fact that the old irrigated lands had to be abandoned because of increasing salinization.[4] New lands had to be brought under the plow. The kings considered such fields to be their own, since new irrigation canals were dug at the expense of the royal treasury and with the help of royal duty services. However, the cities, as noted earlier, were granted privileges and became autonomous entities. A new social division arose: on the one hand, there were citizens of urban communities exempt from general royal taxes and duties and large landowners enjoying the same freedom; on the other hand, a peasant population came into being, lacking civil rights, burdened with taxes and service duties, and living on royal land. This new social structure arose at this time; it fully developed in the first millennium B.C.

Because of all this, the royal economy virtually disappeared during the Middle Babylonian period. Numerous documents from temple economies of this period are available. (Unfortunately, they have not yet been studied thoroughly enough.) They show that even the temples

4. It has lately been suggested that the importance of salinization should not be overstressed.

probably no longer kept up their own field economies. The temple archives consist of income and expenditure records. The former registered the income from the dependents (*amelutu*) attached to the temple. The income due from them was called their task. Nevertheless, the temple workers had their own households, although it is apparent that the households were not their private property. From the socioeconomic point of view, these temple workers must be regarded as a variety of helot slaves. The accounts of expenditures registered the payments in kind to the priests and artisans of the temple.

Toward the end of this period, commodity-money relations began to revive. Note that the universal value standard was no longer silver but gold. The causes of this change are still unclear. In any case, gold was practically never used in actual payments. Payments were made in grain and other commodities and sometimes in silver and copper, but their value was determined in gold.

Moneylending again developed, this time without any restrictions. The unavoidable consequence was debt-bondage, even for free-born citizens, and now it resulted in permanent slavery, not, as earlier, in temporary slavery.

Thus, the economic circumstances of the poorest strata deteriorated sharply. It is, therefore, not surprising that it was not only the slaves or temple helots who fled from their places of residence to become exiles, *hapiru*, but even free community members. The groups of *hapiru*, recruited from different tribes and united by their common misfortune, wandered about the Zagros foothills and the steppes engaging in sheep breeding, occasional work for hire, and even robbery. The *hapiru* soon became known all over Western Asia. This rather violent social group was of considerable concern to the minor kings of Syria and Phoenicia, but it was no substantial threat to the Kassite kingdom.

Another important social group in Babylonia were the warriors. The core of the Kassite military force was composed of chariot detachments, a newly established arm. The Kassites considerably improved the design of the Western Asiatic battle chariot. Various craftsmen of high qualifications—carpenters, coppersmiths, tanners, and armorers—cooperated in the manufacture of the chariots. Other fighting gear, such as bows, were also improved; plate armor for infantrymen made its appearance together with armor for horses. But it would be erroneous to regard the Kassites chariot warriors as a kind of feudal aristocracy. Although they did indeed constitute an elite in the armed forces, they depended fully on the king's maintenance; it was the royal economy that supplied them with horses, chariots, and weapons.

13

The Hittite Kingdom

G. G. GIORGADZE

Discovery of the Hittites

Until the middle of the nineteenth century the existence of the Hittites was known only from biblical sources. The European translation of the Bible calls a pre-Hebrew nation of Palestine and Syria "Sons of Heth," or "Hittites." This initially made historians believe that Palestine or Syria was the homeland of the Hittites, but subsequent investigations showed this was an error. Classical authors, on the other hand, had no idea about the existence of the Hittites.

The fact that the Hittites were one of the greater ethnic groups in the ancient East became clear during the past century, following the successful decipherment of Egyptian hieroglyphics and Akkadian cuneiform.

Information about the Hittites was also found toward the end of the nineteenth century in the cuneiform texts of the Tell el-Amarna archive in Egypt, which contained the diplomatic correspondence, written in the Akkadian language, of the Egyptian pharaohs Amenhetep III and Amenhetep IV (Akhenaton) with various kings of Near Eastern states. As could be inferred from this correspondence, the Hittite kingdom appeared to have been a strong state whose center was somewhere in Asia Minor. Its political influence spread to the region of northern Syria, where Egyptian, Hittite, and Mitannian interests clashed. It became evident that the Hittite kingdom (Kheta in the conventional Egyptian reading; Hatti in Akkadian) was a major power in the ancient East that compared with Egypt and Assyria.

The hypothesis about a Hittite center in Asia Minor was fully confirmed only in the beginning of the present century when the German Orientalist H. Winkler directed the first archaeological excavations in the Turkish village of Boghazköy (ancient Hattusas, 150 kilometers east of Ankara) in 1906–12; at this site archaeologists discovered thousands of cuneiform tablets. Some were written in Akkadian, but most were written in what was then a still unknown ancient language that also used the already well known Akkadian cuneiform script. Scholars immediately embarked on its decipherment. Already in 1915 the Czech Orientalist B. Hrozný defined the character of this language and concluded that it belonged to the Indo-European family of languages. Scholars dubbed it the Hittite cuneiform language (in contrast to the Hittite hieroglyphic language—or, more accurately, Luwian—specimens of which had already been discovered in northern Syria and Asia Minor before the beginning of the century). The inhabitants of ancient Asia Minor called the Hittite cuneiform language Nesite (from the name for the city of Nesa). Texts written in other ancient languages of Asia Minor were also found in this archive.

The interpretation of Hittite cuneiform texts from Boghazköy developed into a new branch of science—Hittitology, a discipline that studies the history, languages, and culture of the inhabitants of Asia Minor from the earliest times to the middle of the first millennium B.C. Archaeological excavations, which still continue today at various sites in Asia Minor, revealed not only new cuneiform texts but also assemblages of material culture indicating that the roots of historical development in Asia Minor stretch back long before the second millennium B.C.; they are deeply entrenched in earlier millennia.

The Pre-Hittite Period in Central Asia Minor

The eastern part of today's Asiatic Turkey—the Anatolian plateau (called Asia Minor since ancient times)—is one of the cradles of civilization.[1] At Çatal-Hüyük, located in central Asia Minor, archaeologists discovered a Neolithic settlement of the urban type, containing houses and sanctuaries with small religious sculptures and decorated with murals. The most extensively excavated levels of the settlement date between the seventh and sixth millennia B.C. Its inhabitants were agriculturalists and animal breeders who maintained active relations with distant regions. The immediate ancestors of the Çatal-Hüyük culture apparently were among the earliest agriculturalists in the world; those appearing at about the same period or somewhat later in Thrace and Macedonia on the Balkan Peninsula may have had their roots in Asia Minor. Although the Çatal-Hüyük pre-urban culture did not survive, which was perhaps due to the severe droughts of the sixth to fifth millennia, cultural centers arose throughout the subsequent epochs and eventually resulted in individual cultural-economic zones in the western, eastern, northern, southern, and central regions of Anatolia. During the Chalcolithic and Early Bronze ages, the central and eastern parts of Asia Minor achieved significant progress in their economic and cultural development. This is seen from archaeological material, dated to the fourth and third millennia B.C., found at the

1. This section was written in collaboration with N. B. Jankowska.

sites of Alaca-Hüyük and Horoz-Tepe in central Anatolia. This region eventually saw the establishment of the great Hittite kingdom of the second millennium B.C.

Asia Minor served as a link, a kind of bridge, that connected the Near East with the Aegean world and the Balkan Peninsula. An especially important role in these relations was played by the city at the site of Hissarlik, commonly identified as Troy and located on the Asiatic shore of the Aegean Sea near the Hellespont, or the Strait of Dardanelles, which leads from the Aegean to the Black Sea. An exchange of influence between the cultures of the Balkans and Asia Minor was especially obvious at Troy.

Ancient Asia Minor benefited not only from its unique geographic location but also from its natural resources, which were a decisive factor in its economic and cultural development. From very early times, metals (copper, silver, lead, and gold) had a special attraction for neighboring countries of the Near East. Fortified settlements on the hills in eastern Anatolia were centers of economic, political, and cultural life for the tribes of Asia Minor already at the beginning of the third millennium. These older tribes were, however, not the later Hittites, or Nesites (Indo-Europeans), who appeared in Asia Minor somewhat later, probably around the end of the third millennium, according to written sources. Scholars call these ancient indigenous tribes Proto-Hittites (because they inhabited these parts of Anatolia before the appearance of the Hittite state)[2] or Hattians. The latter name is derived from the name of the center of their country: Hatti. (This name was later adopted by the Hittites-Nesites to designate the whole of their country.) Hittite cuneiform texts written in the second half of the second millennium call the language of these people Hattic. The city of Hattusas was the center of political, cultural, and economic life first of the Hatti and then of the Hittites.

The natural resources of Anatolia attracted merchants from ancient Near Eastern countries. According to a late Hittite legend, Akkadian merchants must have already appeared in Asia Minor in the twenty-fourth century B.C.—that is, during the reign of Sargon the Ancient, king of Akkade. Toward the beginning of the second millennium, merchants from different lands, most from Asshur on the Tigris and some from northern Syria, lived among the local population. This information comes from the so-called Cappadocian[3] cuneiform tablets that were discovered at the archaeological site of Kül-tepe

2. It now seems probable that the Hattians inhabited only the northwestern part of the peninsula before the Hittites, while some other tribes must have preceded the Hittites and Luwians in the center and the southeast. Editor's note (IMD).

3. Cappadocia is the later name of the eastern part of Anatolia.

(near today's Kayseri), where the ancient city of Kanesh (or Nesa) once stood, as well as at Boghazköy (Hattusas) and at Ališar-Hüyük (possibly the ancient city of Amkuwa).

According to the Cappadocian tablets, foreign merchants established two kinds of trading settlements in order to better organize their business activities in Asia Minor: *karum* (literally "harbor" or "quay"), a foreign merchants' colony enjoying an autonomous status with rights to self-government granted by the local city-state (*alum*); and *wabartum*, a trading factory. The center that organized all foreign trading communities was located in the *karum* of Kanesh.

There were also native traders among the merchants of the foreign trading colonies. Most traders, however, were from Asshur. The Assyrians were the ones who brought with them the first writing system and literary language used in Asia Minor—the Old Assyrian dialect of the Akkadian language. Though Asshur greatly influenced the commercial activities of these trading communities through its merchants, the *karum* of Kanesh was free to conclude its own agreements with the local rulers. The primary task of the trading colonies was to organize the export of silver-lead ore and gold.

The exported silver-lead ore was apparently refined in Asshur, and large quantities of lead consequently accumulated in this city—this metal was even used as a price standard. The lively trade in copper and bronze and also wool was carried on mainly within Asia Minor proper. Iron was also known here (apparently not just meteoritic iron), but the local people held the sites where it was extracted in utmost secrecy. Its exportation from Asia Minor was strictly prohibited until the second millennium B.C., although foreign merchants tried to smuggle it out. In exchange for silver and copper ore[4] the merchants imported to Asia Minor woolen and linen textiles and also great amounts of the metal *annakum*, which has been identified both as tin and lead. It abounded in Asshur on the Tigris, but its origin is still a subject of contention (see Lecture 10).

Goods were transported by donkey caravans. Their route passed through many city-states, where each minor king exacted a ransom or duty that consisted of a share of the transported merchandise. In spite of this, the merchants realized enormous profits, mostly from their trade in textiles and the operations of money exchange. *Annakum* served as money in Asshur; there its price in relation to silver was 15 : 1; in Asia Minor it was 7.5 : 1.

The technical properties of bronze are far superior to those of pure

4. Copper apparently was brought to Kanesh and the central plateau via Asshur, having been originally procured from mines located in eastern Anatolia. Editor's note (PLK).

copper and stone—only steel is better. Iron, once it became available, offered advantages over bronze only because of its lower cost and abundance in nature.

Since a commodity economy was not yet sufficiently developed and the transportation of precious metals was risky, intermediate accounts were settled through trade associations (or extended families) mainly on credit. Promissory notes were issued on clay tablets in cuneiform script.

It did not take long for the local inhabitants of Asia Minor to engage in these commercial activities and to accumulate financial resources in the process. This capital was used for issuing credit to local free farmers under debt-bondage conditions when bad harvests or other natural and social factors made it impossible to survive until the next harvest.

The Cappadocian tablets include quite a few proper names and occasional words of Indo-European (Hittite or Luwian) origin; thus, the Hittite and Luwian tribes must have appeared in Asia Minor earlier than the date of these tablets. Their appearance in Asia Minor and the routes they traveled to arrive there remain open to question. They may have migrated to Anatolia in very ancient times through the Balkans or via the eastern regions and the Caucasus; none of this has yet been definitely confirmed. One hypothesis even proposes that all Indo-European tribes may be indigenous to Asia Minor. It is beyond doubt, however, that toward the beginning of the second millennium B.C. the Indo-European Hittite and Luwian tribes had already separated completely. Several distinct ethnic groups are known. The Nesites apparently lived in territories to the south or southeast of central Asia Minor, from where they gradually spread north into the territory inhabited by the Hatti. The Palaians lived in the country of Pala in northern Asia Minor, where they also came into contact with the Hatti. And, finally, the Luwians inhabited the country called Luwia in the southern and southwestern portions of Asia Minor. The Luwians also spread to the southeast, where the Hurrian ethnic group appeared at about the same time or earlier.

The significant advances in agriculture and technology that had been taking place in the eastern part of Asia Minor since the beginning of the second millennium (especially during the nineteenth to eighteenth centuries) produced corresponding changes in the sphere of social relations. Differentiation of social and property groups and strata advanced very rapidly in the local society. It seems that political structures of the city-state type had already developed in the eastern part of Asia Minor as early as the third millennium. They were headed by *ruba'u* ("princes") or *rubatum* ("princesses"). The royal court included numerous "great persons" or "chiefs" who held a variety of state positions ("chief of the stairs,"[5] "chief smith," "chief cupbearer," "chief gardener," and many others). Writing and literacy were adopted from the merchants of Asshur.

The city-states struggled among themselves for political leadership. Purushkhanda was first in achieving hegemony. Its ruler came to be regarded as the "great king" among the city-state rulers of Asia Minor. Later, the situation changed in favor of the city-state of Kussara, situated somewhere south or southwest of central Anatolia. The first known rulers of Kussara were Pitkhanas and his son Anittas (ca. 1790–1750 B.C.). Kussara already began to expand its domain when Anittas was still "chief of the stairs." From a text written by Anittas, which reached us in a later version written in Hittite (Nesite), we learn that the "king of Kussara (i.e., the father of Anittas) with a great multitude of troops descended from the city and took the city Nesa[6] by storm during the night. He captured the king of Nesa, (but) caused no harm to the sons (citizens) of Nesa, and he made them his mothers and fathers." Anittas continued his father's conquests, capturing a number of neighboring regions of central Asia Minor. Twice he defeated Piusti, king of the Hatti country, and leveled Hattusas to the ground. Anittas also marched against Purushkhanda, whose king surrendered without battle and gave up the symbols of his power (his iron throne and his scepter). Anittas made the city of Nesa his royal residence, where he built fortresses and temples and proclaimed himself "great king." Indo-European and native Hattian gods were worshiped in his city.

The Kussara kingdom founded under Anittas was the most powerful political unit in central Asia Minor prior to the rise of the Hittite state. It seems that Anittas's conquest put an end to the foreign trading colonies and trading stations in all of Anatolia. It is also generally assumed that during Anittas's rule Indo-European Nesite tribes gradually spread throughout central Anatolia, which up to then was inhabited mainly by the Hattians.

During this contact between the Hittites and the Hattians, which lasted for several centuries, the newly arrived Indo-Europeans blended in with the indigenous population. The Hattian language was absorbed by the Hittite (Nesite) language, which, in turn, underwent considerable changes in phonetics, in vocabulary, and in morphology. This blending of Indo-European and aboriginal Hattian tribes gave rise to the Hittite ethnic group in central Asia Minor. To-

5. This probably meant the ascent to the citadel. It was a very important post, usually held by the ruler's son.

6. Nesa is apparently the same as Kanish.

ward the eighteenth century B.C. this group founded the mighty Hittite state that inherited the rich Hattian cultural tradition. Scholars conventionally divide the history of this state into three main periods: the Old, Middle, and New Kingdoms.

The Old Hittite Kingdom (ca. 1650–1500 B.C.)

Hittite tradition associated the earliest period of its history with Kussara, which was the capital of the early Hittite state. But certain cultural and social changes took place after Anittas that, among other things, led the Hittites to relinquish the Old Assyrian dialect of Akkadian as the official language and the Old Assyrian cuneiform script and to substitute their native language and a variant of the cuneiform script adopted from the Hurrian scribes of northern Syria.

In the Hittite historical tradition, Pitkhanas and Anittas, the first rulers of Kussara known to us, were not the founders of the state: the founder was one Labarna, a later king of Kussara. In the beginning of his reign, when the "country was small," Labarna subjugated the neighboring regions by armed force. He also fought in the northern and southern regions of Asia Minor, expanding the Hittite domain "from sea to sea" (from the Mediterranean to the Black Sea). The next Hittite ruler—Hattusilis I (also called Labarna II)—began his rule still in Kussara. He was called Hattusilis ("the one from Hattusas") because for strategic reasons he transferred the center of his kingdom from Kussara northward to Hattusas. From that time on, Hattusas, which seems to have been subjected to Kussara following its conquest and destruction by Anittas, now became the Hittite capital until the fall of the Hittite state. The name "Hatti" began to be used as a general designation for the country and the entire Hittite kingdom.

After conquering a number of regions in Asia Minor, Hattusilis marched against northern Syria. Following the subjugation of Alalakh (today, the archaeological site of Tell-Atchana), one of the strongest Hurrian-Semitic states in northern Syria, Hattusilis defeated two other cities in this region—Urshu (Warsuwa) and Hashu (Hassuwa)—and initiated a lengthy struggle against a third city, Haleb. But, because of illness, he was unable to finish this task, which was eventually accomplished by his successor, Mursilis I. After Haleb's defeat, Mursilis marched against Babylon, which at that time was ruled by Samsuditana of the Old Babylonian dynasty. He took the city and destroyed it in 1595 B.C., seizing much booty. During his expedition against Haleb and Babylon, Mursilis also defeated the Hurrians who lived on the left bank of the Euphrates in northern Mesopotamia. This vast country was at that time called Hurri.

The military operations of Hattusilis I and Mursilis I influenced the course of events for the entire Near East. Hittite victories over Alalakh, Haleb, and other cities formed the cornerstone of Hittite domination in northern Syria. After that, the Syrian question became one of the central factors in Hittite foreign policy. Mursilis's victory over Babylon ended the rule of the First Dynasty of Babylon. These important victories were of tremendous significance to the Hittites. Henceforward, their state was one of the great powers of the Near East—beyond comparison even with the "great kingdom" of Haleb or with Babylon.

During the reigns of Hattusilis I and Mursilis I the military clashes between the Hittites and Hurrians began. The Hurrians started to attack Hatti from the Armenian highland and from northern Syria, devastating the eastern provinces of Hatti. At the very beginning of Hattusilis I's reign, the Hurrians invaded the Hittite country from Hanigalbat (northern Mesopotamia). As a result, many eastern regions, formerly under Hittite rule, temporarily seceded. Only the city of Hattusas remained unharmed. Now and again, the Hurrians also attacked Hittite possessions in northern Syria, as was the case during the rule of the next Hittite king, Hantilis, when the Hurrians, after having devastated Hittite territories, took the queen prisoner and executed her along with her sons. Hantilis repelled the invasion, but the struggle against the Hurrians continued for a long time to come.

At the end of the Old Kingdom the last Hittite king of this period, Telepinus, was successful against Kizzuwadna, a strategically important region in the northeast corner of the Mediterranean. A peace treaty with the king of Kizzuwadna was concluded. From then on, Kizzuwadna oriented its policy toward Hatti and gradually liberated itself from the influence of Haleb and Hurri.

Throughout the Old Kingdom the Hittite kings struggled to consolidate their power, which was strongly limited by the popular assembly, the *pankus*. Initially, the assembly comprised all men capable of bearing arms; later, the circle of participants was considerably reduced to include only representatives from the upper aristocracy.[7] The assembly had the right to name the successor to the throne, to decide legal matters as a court of law, and so on. The king, who bore a high title of Hattian origin—*tabarnas*—could only nominate his successors. It was the *pankus* that had the ultimate power to confirm or reject his choice. Potential candidates to the throne were many, and the selection was not limited to the king's sons; the power could pass

7. Apparently, the *pankus* was originally the popular assembly of the city-state of Hatti (Hattusas); with time, as the scope of the Hittite conquests grew, most of the citizens of Hattusas acquired commanding posts in the army and in the administration, so that the *pankus* almost automatically became a council of dignitaries. Editor's note (IMD).

on (especially when the king had no son) to the king's grandson, to the son or husband of the ruler's sister, etc. Starting with Hantilis, usurpations of the throne became frequent.

The question of succession was finally resolved by Telepinus, who issued a "throne succession law," according to which the right to the throne was from then on held by the king's sons on a seniority basis. If the king had no son, only the husband of the king's daughter could ascend to the throne. All others were excluded from the succession, and the *pankus* was charged with enforcing this law. The law of succession greatly strengthened the royal authority and continued without change throughout the existence of the Hittite kingdom.

However, even in the time of Telepinus, during whose reign apparently other Hittite laws were issued in written form for the first time, the monarch's authority still was not absolute. The assembly continued to limit the royal power, although the king could be overruled by it only if he chose to break the succession rule or to execute arbitrarily his royal relatives. The *pankus* interfered in no other governmental affairs. During the New Kingdom, the assembly ceased to exist.

The New Hittite Kingdom (ca. 1400–1200 B.C.)

Because the history of the Middle Kingdom, which embraced a period from approximately 1500 to 1400 B.C., has not been sufficiently explored,[8] we will deal in what follows with the highlights of the New Kingdom period of Hittite history, a time when Hatti came to be regarded as a power equal to Egypt, Babylonia, and Assyria.

It was Tutkhalias III who began the aggressive policy at the end of the fifteenth century that continued successfully into the middle of the thirteenth century. Throughout almost the entire period of the New Kingdom the Hittites conducted military expeditions into the southwestern regions of Asia Minor, an area occupied by political units subsumed under the common denomination of Arzawa, as well as to the south, a territory inhabited by Luwians, who spoke a language related to that of the Hittites. Their country was called Luwia. Wilusa, which many scholars believe was the name of the region of Ilion, or Troy,[9] was in Arzawa country. In earlier times Arzawa main-

8. Some scholars actually deny the existence of the Hittite Middle Kingdom. Editor's note (IMD).

9. The Hittite texts mention, in the southwestern part of Asia Minor, a town called *Wilusa,* presumably the Greek (*W*ilios) or (*W*ilion), the "town of (W)ilius," and a town called *Taruisa,* presumably to be read "Troisa," which may be the Greek Troy. The Homeric epic identifies the two cities; this, however, may be a later reinterpretation of the historical tradition. Editor's note (IMD).

tained contacts with Egypt. This is attested by letters written by Pharaoh Amenhetep III in the Hittite (Nesite) language to the king of Arzawa requesting him to send his daughter to the pharaoh's harem.

As a result of the military operations by Suppiluliumas I, son of Tutkhalias III, and the former's son, Mursilis II, the lands of Arzawa were conquered, and peace treaties were signed with each of them. The rulers of the lands of Arzawa promised to send to Hatti on a regular basis auxiliary detachments and battle chariots, to pay annual tribute to the Hittite king, to extradite fugitives from Hatti, and so forth. In turn, the Hittites pledged their help to Arzawa against any eventual enemy. The peace treaties were confirmed by oaths of loyalty, but these were not to be relied upon, since we know that the rulers of Arzawa broke away from Hatti whenever they had the chance.

Hittite historical texts of the New Kingdom are also full of accounts about struggles against the Kaska tribes who lived north and northeast of Hatti in the mountains along the shores of the Black Sea. The accounts of the Kaska are especially numerous in the annals of Suppiluliumas I and the annals of Mursilis II. The Hittite texts tell us that "in the Kaska country the rule of one [person] was not customary"—that is, they had no king and were still at a primitive stage of development. After the reign of Mursilis II, however, some Kaska rulers (Pihuniyas in the Kaska region of Tibiya, for example) began to govern their country "in the royal fashion," instead of in the usual "Kaska fashion."

The struggle against the Kaska people became continual beginning with the reign of Tutkhalias III. It was provoked both by the frequent incursions of the Kaska tribes into Hittite territory and by the aggressive intentions of the Hittite rulers themselves. The Kaska not only devastated the border regions of Hatti but also invaded the country's interior, threatening the Hittite capital. No Hittite ruler was able to settle the Kaska question finally, though they did at times sign peace treaties. Hittite military expeditions against the Kaska tribes could only temporarily halt their devastating incursions.

The Hittites subdued the allied tribes of Azzi and Hayasa in the northeastern part of Asia Minor. Suppiluliumas signed a peace treaty with their people and their ruler, Hukkanas, according to which the latter was to marry the daughter of the Hittite king, but it forbade Hukkanas, among other things, to claim other women of the Hittite royal house. This shows that vestiges of very ancient marital relations survived in Hayasa (as, for instance, the right to cohabit with the wife's sisters and cousins).

During that period, the Hittites achieved significant results in their struggle for northern Syria. The kingdom of Mitanni took advantage of the temporary weakness of Hatti after the fall of the Old Kingdom, as well as of the weakening Asshur, a city that up until then had been dominant in northern Mesopotamia. Mitanni had also achieved great successes west of the Euphrates, particularly in northern Syria. Haleb, Alalakh, Carchemish, and other kingdoms came under Mitanni's political control. Led by King Saussattar (or Sausadattar), the Mitannians defeated and sacked the city of Asshur and laid claim to the lands east of the Tigris. The Mitannian rulers Shuttarna II and Dushratta maintained friendly relations with the pharaohs Amenhetep III and, to a lesser extent, with Amenhetep IV (Akhenaton). These relations were consolidated by marriages between the Egyptian rulers and the daughters of the Mitannian kings.[10] Mitanni, like the Hittite kingdom, comprised a number of semiindependent kingdoms and city-states that pledged tribute and military assistance to the supreme king of the Mitannian federation.

Suppiluliumas I put an end to Mitannian power. After crossing the Upper Euphrates, Hittite troops invaded the small Hurrian kingdoms of the river valley and approached the Mitannian capital of Wasshukanne from the north. The Hittites devastated the capital, but the Mitannian pretender retreated without accepting battle. Suppiluliumas installed his supporter Shattiwazza as heir apparent to the Mitannian throne and gave him his daughter in marriage. After a successful Hittite expedition into northern Syria, Mitanni lost all its possessions west of the Euphrates. Later, Mitanni was unable to resist Assyrian attacks, and toward the end of the thirteenth century Mitanni was included in the Assyrian Empire.

Suppiluliumas not only destroyed Mitanni but also managed to depose almost all its vassal rulers in the Syrian principalities, which extended all the way to the Lebanon Mountains. This period marks the beginning of a lengthy Hittite dominion in northern Syria. After conquering Haleb and Carchemish (an important crossing point of the Euphrates), Suppiluliumas installed his sons Piyassili and Telepinu as rulers of these cities. This was the beginning of the Hittite dynasties in Haleb and Carchemish, which endured for centuries. Suppiluliumas conquered Alalakh as well, which had also been dominated by the Hurrians. Hittite hegemony lasted here throughout the period of the Hittite kingdom. Other principalities of Syria also came under strong Hittite influence during the New Kingdom. This domination was supported by regular appearances of Hittite troops in Syria.

No tensions existed between Hatti and Egypt during Suppiluliu-

10. This did not mean that Mitannian princesses became queens of Egypt. The pharaohs merely included them among the ladies of their harems, where they served the actual queen, who was Egyptian by birth and frequently the pharaoh's own sister. Editor's note (IMD).

mas's time, a fact corroborated by a congratulatory letter sent by Suppiluliumas to Pharaoh Amenhetep IV on the occasion of his ascent to the Egyptian throne. Eventually, however, Hittite policies in Syria led to collision with Egypt.

Since the Nineteenth Dynasty, the aim of Egyptian policy had been the restoration of its past influence in Palestine, Phoenicia, and Syria, having been lost in the first half of the fourteenth century B.C. Hatti now became Egypt's main rival in Asia, and Pharaoh Rameses II began a prolonged war against the Hittites. In the fifth year of his rule (ca. 1312 B.C.)[11] Rameses II gathered an army of 20,000 and led it into Syria, where the Hittite king Muwatallis prepared an army of 30,000 warriors. Near the city of Kadesh (Qinza) the Hittite troops, which included militiamen from various tributary countries (including Dardanians, i.e., Trojans), ambushed the Egyptian detachments led by the pharaoh and thoroughly defeated them. Rameses managed to break out from the encirclement and repel the enemy but was unable to defeat the Hittites and to take Kadesh. Nor, for that matter, could the Hittites advance farther south. After many years of war, in the twenty-first year of Rameses' rule, presumably in 1296 B.C.,[12] when Hattusilis III reigned in Hatti, both countries signed a peace treaty providing for mutual nonaggression, aid against common foes, extradition of fugitives, etc. The treaty was confirmed by a marriage of Rameses II to Hattusilis's daughters. As a result, Egyptians and Hittites never again fought each other.

Hittite cuneiform texts from the New Kingdom contain information about Hittite contacts with the state of Ahhiyawa (apparently identical to the Akaiwasha mentioned in Egyptian hieroglyphic texts). Ahhiyawa is mentioned in connection with regions situated in western and southwestern Asia Minor. Some scholars identify the name of this country with the term *Achaeans,* which Homer uses to describe a union of ancient Greek tribes, although others vehemently oppose this equivalence as linguistically highly improbable. Ahhiyawa has not yet found a definite place on the map. Experts suggest that this country should be sought on Rhodes, Cyprus, Crete, or somewhere in Anatolia (southwest, west, or northwest). In recent times more and more scholars have tended to accept the original hypothesis that identified Ahhiyawa with Mycenaean Greece.

Friendly relations prevailed between Ahhiyawa and Hatti beginning with the reign of Suppiluliumas I. But the relations later deteriorated because of Ahhiyawa's determination to consolidate its power in southern and southwestern Asia Minor, especially in the city of

11. In 1286 B.C., according to other estimates.
12. Estimates of this date vary from 1296 to 1270 B.C.

Milawanda (possibly the later Miletus), and in Alasia (the island of Cyprus), where the interests of both states clashed. Toward the second half of the thirteenth century, "a man (from) Ahhiya(wa)" (i.e., a ruler of that country) began with increasing frequency to invade Hittite-dependent countries that were situated in western Anatolia.

It is during this time that the gradual decline of the Hittite Empire commenced. Kaska tribes continually attacked the northern regions of their weakened neighbor. According to some scholars, this was taking place under the pressure of Abkhasian and Georgian tribes that were migrating from the Caucasus toward the southwest. In eastern Asia Minor various political unions became active in the Upper Euphrates Valley (Pahhuwa, Zhuma, and others). An unfavorable situation for the Hittites also developed in the lands of Arzawa that strove for political independence. The increasing cultural-religious influence of the Luwian world in Hatti itself may have contributed to this situation.[13]

The Hittite state suffered an internal crisis toward the end of the thirteenth century. Continuous military expeditions strongly undermined the country's economy, various branches of which became ruined. A letter addressed by the Hittite king to the ruler of Ugarit reveals that Hatti suffered from food shortages. Aegean tribes invaded Asia Minor, further aggravating the situation. Egyptian sources call them the Sea Peoples.[14] "No country, beginning with Hatti, was able to resist their armies," declares an Egyptian inscription. Hittite sources do not give any information about this catastrophe that befell their country during the reign of the last Hittite king—Suppiluliumas II.

Around 1200 B.C., or somewhat later, the formerly powerful Hittite kingdom fell once and for all together with its capital, Hattusas.[15] Eastern Asia Minor sunk into decay for three to four centuries.

13. Actually, during this period Luwian may have completely replaced Hittite (Nesite) as the spoken language. Strong Hurrian influence was also felt in the Hittite capital at this time. Editor's note (IMD).

14. Egyptian sources name many of the Sea Peoples, but they are difficult to identify. Possible identifications are of the 'kywsh (probably to be read as Akaiwasha) with the Achaeans; the rk (to be read as Rukka, Lukka) with the Lycians in southwestern Asia Minor; the shkrsh (to be read as Shikulai) with the Siculi; the prst (to be read as Purusta or Pulasta?) with the Philistines and possibly the Pelasgoi; and the trsh (to be read as Tursha or Trasha?) with the Etruscans (Tirseni) or with the Thracians (Thrasici). Note that vowels were not spelled out in Egyptian. Editor's note (IMD).

15. Which of the migrating tribes actually destroyed Hattusas and the Hittite kingdom is not clear. In the opinion of I. M. Diakonoff, the Indo-European Mushki tribes were responsible. The Mushki belonged to a non-Hittite and non-Luwian group of Indo-European speakers. Later, according to this scholar, they merged with the Urartians and Hurrians and formed the Armenian nation, giving them their Indo-European language. Editor's note (IMD).

During the same critical period, the famous city of Troy perished in the war against the Achaeans. Troy had linked the civilizations of Asia Minor with those of the Balkan Peninsula. Legends about the fall of Troy eventually supplied the subject matter for the great Greek poems attributed to the legendary poet Homer: *The Iliad* and *The Odyssey*.

Socioeconomic Relations in the Hittite Kingdom

Farming and livestock breeding were the main occupations of the Hittite people. This is reflected in many paragraphs of the Hittite laws. The Hittites bred sheep, goats, pigs, and cattle. During the second millennium B.C. horse breeding began to spread through Asia Minor. The Hittites learned the most advanced methods for training battle horses from a text that had been translated into Hittite from a "textbook" written by the Hurrian horse breeder Kikkuli. Hittite laws established the prices of various domestic animals: for example, a horse or a mule cost 15–40 shekels of silver; a sheep cost 1 shekel. (A shekel was a weight unit of approximately 8.4 grams.) Poultry and apiculture also played a role in the Hittite kingdom.

Agriculture was important in the Hittite economy. The working population cultivated arable land and orchards and vineyards. Compared with domestic animals, land was cheap; 1 *iku* (0.865 acres) of uncultivated land cost 1 shekel of silver; cultivated land cost 2–3 shekels.[16]

Alongside agriculture and stock rearing, the crafts also reached a high level of development in Hittite society, especially bronze metallurgy and pottery making. Archaeologists have discovered excellent examples of bronze agricultural implements and other tools, bronze weapons, and highly artistic ceramic artifacts. The high level of Hittite agriculture and crafts contributed to the development of trade.

Several forms of land ownership and land tenure existed in the Hittite kingdom. There were royal (or palace), temple, and private (community) lands. Royal and temple lands were the private property of the supreme power of the state, because the king was not only the supreme ruler of the country but also the high priest and, consequently, the principal owner of palace and temple lands. However, not all the land in the country was the king's property. Some land was outside the state economic sector. Such land could be alienated (by purchase-sale transactions, gifts, etc.).

16. These prices are incredibly low. Some scholars think that land in the Hittite kingdom, as in early Mesopotamia, was not involved in normal commodity circulation, and the above evaluations refer to cases when land was transferred from a debtor to a creditor to cover a loan. Editor's note (IMD).

State lands could be assigned to the various royal (or palace) and temple economies, usually as undivided tracts including several villages. The royal economy encompassed different estates, called "houses": for example, "the king's house" (sometimes called "house of the Sun"), "the queen's house," "the house of the palace." Land was tilled by people of different statuses. A certain number of the workers were permanently assigned to each house. Temple economies included estates called "house of a god" (temples proper), "stone houses,"[17] "bone houses," "seal houses," "tablet houses." Each house had its own staff of workers, who also were often permanently assigned to the land of the temple economies (or to economies connected with specific cultic activities, such as funerary rites). Houses could also be transferred to different royal and temple officials, usually together with the workers assigned to the land and their corresponding villages. Land could also be granted as such, without laborers.

The large houses of the state sector were subdivided into smaller economies: individual (nuclear) houses, which were the basic production cells of Hittite society. The possession and use of state land obligated the grantee to fulfill two kinds of state duties: the *sahhan* and the *luzzi*. The *sahhan* was an in-kind tax that required the individual producers or large houses to supply the king and high state functionaries ("the lord of the country," the district chief, the city mayor, etc.) with finished products (dairy and other foodstuffs, wool, etc.), as well as domestic animals. The *luzzi* was a labor duty involving work in the fields and vineyards, plowing, repairing fortifications, construction, and other state and public work for the benefit of the country's ruler or high state officials. The *luzzi* also included the obligation of royal employees and large houses to furnish troops for the Hittite army.[18]

A person could be freed from the *sahhan* and the *luzzi* by a special royal decree. Temple and various cultic establishments were usually free from state obligations, because their laborers worked only for the benefit of the deity. There were, however, cases of double exploitation whereby workers were forced to toil both for the king or his officials and for the temple.

17. These were apparently royal mausoleums and funerary temples.

18. Some scholars believe that the population outside the state sector was also subject to military service and some other conscription duties. They assume the existence of a private/communal sector on the basis of indirect allusions found in Hittite laws and on the dual jurisdiction of the courts of law. Some citizens were subject to the jurisdiction of royal functionaries and others to that of community elders, or *miyahwantes* (according to the "Instruction to the District Chief"). It must be kept in mind that no private documents have been preserved from the Hittite kingdom; probably having been written on wood, they did not survive. Editor's note (IMD).

In agricultural activities in the state sector there developed and continued to exist two types of economic relationships: the slave type and the serf type (by the latter we mean corvée labor). The methods of exploitation were mainly of a slave-owning type coexisting with an exploitation of the corvée type. Thus we can call the workers of the state sector dependent laborers of the slave and serf type.[19] We also should keep in mind that a Hittite "serf" did not constitute a distinct social class separate from that of slaves. The Hittites themselves, although they distinguished serfs from common slaves, still referred to them both as "heads of [female] and [male] slaves" (Sumerian *sag-geme-ìr;* Akkadian *ashtapiru*). For this reason, they are today often regarded as subcategories of one and the same class of nonfree persons.[20]

Hittite law divided its society into free persons and nonfree persons. From the very beginning people were referred to as free only if they were freed by the king from the state duties of *sahhan* and *luzzi,* not just those due to the king (or palace) and high officials but also obligations to temples and cultic establishments. People free of all obligations gradually became "noble, honorable, and well-born" and constituted the top echelon of the ruling hierarchy (royal servants, military chiefs, administrators, temple servants, who held large land estates). For them physical labor became a shameful occupation or a form of punishment.

Nonfree persons were those who were not liberated from obligatory labor—even if it were only one single obligatory duty. They all were therefore considered socially dependent. When such a person was freed from duties to the king and high state officials or servants, he was transferred to work for the temple; he remained nonfree, or dependent. The nonfree inhabitants comprised large numbers of direct production workers (plowmen, shepherds, craftsmen, gardeners, and so forth) and formed the lowest social stratum, in the Hittite kingdom. They included slaves and serfs (i.e., helots), hired hands, etc.—people in various forms of dependence.

War furnished Hittite society with an additional labor force and material goods. The Hittites took many prisoners during their military expeditions. Mursilis II alone brought back 66,000 captives from the lands of Arzawa. In the annals of Mursilis II they are described with the Sumerian term *nam-ra* (read in Hittite as *arnuwala*), meaning "deported" (captured inhabitants of a conquered territory). Some of these deported people were converted into different kinds of slaves,

19. In the earlier lectures of our book, this type of worker was called a helot. Editor's note (IMD).

20. They can also be regarded as members of the "slave class in the broad sense of the term." Editor's note (IMD).

and others were settled on land as subjects of the Hittite king and obligated to corvée labor. (They were sometimes also taken into the army.) After a certain period of time they could no longer be distinguished from the rest of the Hittite working population.

There were different categories of direct producers of material goods. Some were fully dispossessed of all property rights, including property in the means of production, and their labor was exacted by coercion. They were slaves, not subjects, but only objects, of law that were used in domestic service, to work the land of the houses, to tend livestock, and so on. Others had means of production at their disposal, but only as a conditional possession and not as their private property. Economically (but not socially), they differed from the previous category. They usually had certain legal rights and their own "houses" (economies), families, land (as a rule, only on the basis of possession, not property right), a few domestic animals and could have their own working personnel (i.e., slaves). For small producers this created an opportunity for incentive and economic initiative. From the legal viewpoint, all categories of direct producers constituted one exploited class—a stratum of dependent, nonfree people.

The Hittite state was loosely structured. In this respect it resembled Mitanni and other, relatively short-lived state confederations of Asia Minor, Syria, and northern Mesopotamia. Apart from the cities and regions directly under the authority of the king, there were semidependent kingdoms (under the king's sons and kinsmen), as well as regions placed under the rule of high officials. The entire state was headed by the king, *hassus,* who also (contrary to lesser kings) bore the title *tabarnas,* and by the queen, who could hold the title *tawanannas* if she was the mother of the heir apparent or of the king himself. The king performed important military, religious-cultic, legal, diplomatic, and economic functions. The *tawanannas* occupied an equally elevated position in the Hittite social structure; she was the supreme priestess, with a wide array of cult-related and political functions and rights. Moreover, she had her own independent income.

The royal court included many functionaries and servants: "sons of the palace," "bearers of the golden spear," "men of the scepter," "overseers of a thousand," "wine scoopers," "masters of repast," "cooks," "cupbearers," "barbers," "bread bakers," "milkers," and so on. Moreover, the king was served by "tanners," "shoemakers," and "makers of battle chariots." They were regarded as "slaves [servants]" of the king, although they were not slaves in the social sense of the word. They all received parcels of land for their sustenance.

Temples had large economies that were structurally analogous to the royal economy. Various categories of people worked for the temples. There were cult servants ("high priests," "minor priests," "annointed ones," "musicians," "singers"), servants of the "kitchen" ("masters of repast," "cooks," "bread bakers," "wine makers"), and direct producers of material goods (plowmen, shepherds, cattle herders, gardeners). They were all subsumed as "slaves" in regard to the god, although they also were not actually slaves.

Justice and Law

The Hittites believed the law was of divine origin, although this is not stated in so many words in the legal texts. The collection of laws that have reached us consists of two main tablets. The first had already been written in the beginning of the Old Kingdom. (There is also a later variant dated to the thirteenth century B.C.) Having a class character, Hittite laws stressed the protection of property, especially the private property rights, of the free persons. The laws established a fixed scale of prices, a sign of a certain degree of development in the commodity-money system. (Prices are also fixed for slave-craftsmen, including potters, smiths, carpenters, tanners, tailors, weavers, and bird catchers. They range from 10 to 20 shekels of silver.)[21]

A whole series of paragraphs is dedicated to family and inheritance law. The Hittite family was patriarchal. It was indisputably headed by the father: his authority applied not only to family property but also to his wife and children, although his rights over the family members were not limitless. Different forms of marriage existed. One type of marriage involved a payment of bride-money by the groom's family. Another, the *errebu*-marriage, was characterized by the son-in-law becoming a member of the bride's family, which paid a ransom. Finally, there was marriage by abduction. Marriage between free and nonfree persons was permitted under certain conditions.

Hittite Culture

The Hittite nation originated from the merger of Hattian and Indo-European tribes. Both ethnic groups also contributed their respective cultural achievements, giving rise to the Hittite culture, which from its beginnings was characterized by a wealth of local Hattian traditions. Hurrian and Luwian cultural elements also played an important role in the development of the Hittite culture. The same can be said about the influences of northern Syrian and Sumerian-Akkadian cultures.

A rich Hittite literature has been preserved in the Boghazköy ar-

---

21. These prices were probably not used by the Hittites, just as similar price lists were not used in Mesopotamia, for actual business transactions. More likely they served as estimates used by the courts in cases of damage and theft. As already mentioned above, there were almost no slave-craftsmen in Old Babylonia. Editor's note (IMD).

chive, which contains official texts (royal decrees, instructions, annals), as well as mythological and legendary texts and a great number of ritual texts. One of the world's first autobiographies is found in this archive: "The Autobiography of Hattusilis III." A considerable number of Near Eastern literary works were translated into the Hittite language during the New Kingdom (such as "The Epic of Gilgamesh" and a number of Hurrian myths). The most important are the Hurrian myths about the heavenly kingdom, which deal with the transfer of power from one dynasty of gods to another, and the "Song of Ullikumme," an originally Hurrian poem about the god Kumarwe. These literary works represent a link connecting the ancient Near Eastern literatures with the ancient Greek mythological and poetic tradition, especially with the *Theogony* of Hesiod. The subject of the "Song of Ullikumme" is the succession of four generations of gods in heaven, analogous to Hesiod's story of the transfer of power from Uranus to Cronos and from Cronos to Zeus. It is very similar to Hesiod's myth about Typhon.

Hittite mythological literature, which also includes myths of Hattian origin, is very rich. One of the mythological tales connected with the Hattian New Year ritual is "The Myth of the Serpent Illuyankas." The ritual re-created the battle between a divine hero and his enemy, the dragon Illuyankas. It was performed before the celebration of the New Year. This battle is to be compared with the ritual battles that were staged in later times in many countries of the world at New Year celebrations. Another myth traced back to Hattian tradition, "The Myth of Telepinus," is about a temporarily disappearing and resurrecting deity. One of the attributes in the cult of this god was an evergreen tree.

Hittite objects of art are characterized by the variety and originality of their designs and shapes (silver and bronze animal figurines, gold goblets and pitchers, gold ornaments, and so-called military standards, which sometimes depict a deer). Original idols have been found at Kül-tepe, together with pottery items (cups, rhytons, vases, etc.). The period of the New Kingdom saw the appearance in Asia Minor of a monumental style in different fields of art (architecture, stone reliefs, and animal sculptures, such as lions and sphinxes). Stoneworking reached a high level of sophistication in Hatti; a beautiful example of this is the gallery of sculpture carved in high relief into the rock at Yazilikaya. Original examples of Hittite glyptics have also been preserved. They include royal seals with inscriptions in Luwian hieroglyphics and in the Hittite cuneiform script.

Hittite religion played an extremely important role in the ideological and economic life of the society. In the words of the Hittites, there were "a thousand gods of Hatti," among whom were gods of diverse origins: Hattian, Indo-European (Nesite, Luwian, Palaic, and also Aryan), Hurrian, Assyrian, Babylonian, Sumerian, and others.[22] The principal deity was the Thunder god, "King of Heaven, Lord of the Hatti Country." His wife was the goddess of the Sun from the city of Arinna, "Lady of the Hatti Country, of the Heavens and Earth, Lady of the Kings and Queens of Hatti."

The traditions of Hittite culture did not vanish after the fall of the Hittite state.

22. Reliable references to Aryan (i.e., Indo-European) gods can be found only in a long list of deities mentioned in a treaty between the Hittite kingdom and Mitanni. Mitanni, as mentioned before, was ruled by a dynasty of Indo-Iranian origin. Thus, these Aryan gods may not have been part of the Hittite pantheon at all. Editor's note (IMD).

14

Syria, Phoenicia, and Palestine in the Third and Second Millennia B.C.

I. M. Diakonoff

The Emergence of Civilization

In this lecture the terms *Syria, Phoenicia,* and *Palestine* will be used exclusively to refer to ancient geographical (not political or ethnic) regions. During this period Syria comprised only the western part of the present Republic of Syria (from the Euphrates to the Mediterranean Sea) and part of the adjoining region of Turkey south of the Taurus Mountains. Ancient Phoenicia approximately corresponded to the modern state of Lebanon. Ancient Palestine included not only the territory now assigned by the United Nations to the state of Israel and the territory of the Palestinian Arabs but also part of today's Jordan. (The latter part of ancient Palestine is also known as Transjordan.)

The natural features of these regions are very diverse. A desert separated ancient Palestine from Egypt. Palestine itself is a land of natural contrasts: west of the Jordan there are mountains interspersed with oases and fertile valleys. Along the shore of the Mediterranean stretches a fertile plain. In the north, high, frequently snow-capped peaks rise. Transjordan is separated from the rest of Palestine by the deep depression of the Jordan and by the bitter-salt Dead Sea with its sun-parched, almost lifeless shores. In the third and second millennia the Jordan Valley was covered with damp forest and papyrus thickets. The hilly and mountainous regions of Transjordan, covered with steppe vegetation, gradually merge with the Syro-Arabian semidesert.

The region of ancient Phoenicia was separated from the rest of Western Asia by the high range of the Lebanon Mountains, with its cedar and other forests, alpine meadows, and snow-capped peaks. The western slopes of the Lebanon Mountains, facing the sea, were covered with evergreen Mediterranean vegetation. The moist sea breezes that brought the rains made artificial irrigation unnecessary.

Syria lies east of the Lebanon. It is cut in a north-south direction by the Orontes River (today called Al-'Asi), which flows along the valley between the Lebanon and the Anti-Lebanon Mountains. Beyond the

Anti-Lebanon, toward the Syrian semidesert, lies the large Damascus oasis and, farther east, barren lava fields. A caravan route, usually threatened by tribes of pastoralists, passed from Damascus through the small Palmyra oasis toward the middle course of the Euphrates.

The Great Bend of the Euphrates formed the ancient northeastern border of Syria. Northern Syria extended from the Mediterranean Sea to the Taurus Mountains of Asia Minor and to the fords of the Euphrates. The Orontes River passed northward through a region of swamps and lakes (which now no longer exist), then turned west, and discharged into the Mediterranean. The mouth of the Orontes offered a passage for the Mediterranean winds into a hilly region, making it adequately fertile.

Thus, the Eastern Mediterranean Belt (a term we use for all three historical regions discussed in this lecture) was not a uniform geographical area. Here were deserts, fertile lowlands, uplands, evergreen vegetation, marshes, and snow-capped mountains. But since there were no larger flooding rivers upon which to base an important irrigation system, no powerful centralized state developed here. In ancient times this region was rich in valuable species of wood, but at that time few valuable minerals had been discovered. Copper indeed seems to have been transported through Syria and Palestine; but it came either from the Sinai Peninsula in the south, from the upper reaches of the Tigris River in the north, or from Cyprus in the west. It was only some time later that copper, iron, and natural asphalt were discovered in southern Palestine and began to be exploited.

However, very important caravan routes passed through this land to and from Egypt, Asia Minor, and Mesopotamia. Although the word *caravan* usually conjures up images of a string of camels, the ancient caravans used donkeys to carry their merchandise. The hardiest of these animals were bred for sale in the Damascus oasis.

Palestine, Syria, Asia Minor, the mountains of Upper Mesopotamia, and the regions beyond the Tigris were perhaps the first homelands of animal husbandry and, especially, of farming. Prosperous agricultural towns existed as early as the eighth millennium in Palestine (Jericho) and in some parts of Syria. Some of these towns or villages were already encircled by strong stone walls during the Early Neolithic Period (Jericho, for example).

There is some reason to believe that the region of Palestine and Syria was the center of a group of tribes who spoke Afrasian (Afro-Asiatic) languages; namely, the Semites. From here they spread throughout the Arabian Peninsula (South Arabians and Arabs), along the coast of the eastern Mediterranean (Western Semites), and to Mesopotamia (Akkadians). None of these tribes were originally entirely nomadic, although as they penetrated deeper into the interior of the steppes and semidesert regions (which during the fourth to third millennia B.C. covered all of Arabia), they began to engage more in sheep breeding and less in farming.

Tribes were continually migrating, armies were marching along the roads of Syria-Palestine, and the raw materials required for the technological advances of the Chalcolithic and, eventually, the Bronze Age were lacking. This was the reason why there was a lag in social development between this zone and southern Mesopotamia and Egypt. However, city-states of the Sumerian-Akkadian type developed during the second half of the third millennium B.C., but, so far as is known, only in northern Syria. The most important of these were the flourishing cities of Ebla, which was closely connected with Middle and Lower Mesopotamia, and Byblos on the Phoenician coast, which was the export center of valuable cedar timber to Egypt.

Investigations of the earliest geographical names in this region and, to some extent, direct information found in the Egyptian and Mesopotamian texts indicate that the eastern Mediterranean region was inhabited by Western Semites at least as early as the third millennium B.C. They can be subdivided into three tribal groups on the basis of linguistic features. The three groups[1] are conventionally called Canaanites, Amorites, and Aramaeans. In addition, Hurrian tribes from Transcaucasia and ultimately from the mountains surrounding Lake Van (now in Turkey) and Lake Urmia (now in Iran) reached Upper Mesopotamia and northern Syria in the third millennium (see Lecture 11). During the second half of the third millennium, the first Hurrian wave seems to have reached northern Palestine.

Mesopotamian armies began to appear in northern Syria during the Akkade dynasty (twenty-third century). Later, during the Ur III dynasty (twenty-first century), the kingdom of Akkad and Sumer temporarily extended its power to northern Syria and Byblos.

The pharaohs of the Middle Kingdom of Egypt began their incursions into Palestine somewhat later, and Byblos became and for some time continued to be an isolated center of Egyptian culture in the midst of a Semitic population. (The ancient Egyptians spoke an Afrasian language of a non-Semitic branch.) However, toward the end of the third millennium Byblos was burned down, together with its Egyptian temple. This may have been the time when, if we are to believe a legend, a group of tribes from northern Arabia that spoke the Western Semitic dialect of the Canaanite group became established on the Mediterranean coast. They later became known as Phoenicians.

---

1. The placement of the Semitic language of Ebla within these groups is not firmly established, but in our opinion, Eblaite was a separate, early Western Semitic language.

Amorite-type speech was preserved north of Byblos, particularly in Ugarit, a city that later successfully competed with Byblos.

At the end of the third and beginning of the second millennium B.C. a network of city-states characterized by a society of the early class type appeared all over the Eastern Mediterranean Belt. These were walled cities. In the center of each city was a temple and a residence for the local ruler. These were surrounded by a complex of adobe and brick houses. The houses usually had two stories, with an open or grilled gallery on the upper floor, which was occupied by the owners, and a lower level for storage and for lodging slaves. Most of these towns were located in valleys. The uplands were sparsely populated.

In the areas at the edge of the desert, such as the Damascus oasis and Transjordan, people lived in tents. During the spring, when the steppes were in bloom, they migrated with their herds away from the sown fields of the oasis. The life of these tribes is vividly described in the ancient Egyptian "Story of Sinuhe" and in later biblical stories about the tribal patriarchs.

The social unit of the Amorite pastoral nomads of the period was the clan community. It formed part of a tribe or sometimes of a tribal union. The head of an extended patriarchal family had full authority not only over his wives and children but also over the nuclear families of his sons, over aliens who may have joined the tribe or were adopted by it, and, of course, over slaves. The patriarch had complete power over life and death, as well as over the personal belongings, of the family members. The affairs of the tribal community were managed by a council of "old men" and a chief, who was chosen in a meeting of all adult able-bodied and armed men. From time to time some leader could assemble a group of warriors that would form the core of a tribal militia. Arguments between neighbors were occasionally settled in single combat between strong men from each side.

Sedentary populations, however, were in the majority. At that time Hazor, a major city in northern Palestine, covered an area of some 50 hectares (about 125 acres), which was large for a city in those days. The traders of Hazor traveled far, even as far as Mari on the Euphrates. In Phoenicia and coastal Syria, Byblos and Ugarit flourished. A number of small settlements had developed into towns by this time, although they seldom exceeded one-tenth the size of Hazor. The cause of the growth of Phoenician towns was the early development of trade, especially with Egypt. The Phoenician merchants exported Lebanese timber, and for this reason the Egyptians endeavored to keep royal officials at Byblos. Overland trade between Egypt, Mesopotamia, and Asia Minor via Syria was also very important, as shown by the finds of objects at Ebla and, later, by the commercial correspondence from Kanish, Asia Minor. The same is attested by tales of Egyptian royal officials passing continually through the pastoral regions. Transit trade was, of course, the more important, but Syria also sold its own wood, pack donkeys, and ivory. (Elephants still inhabited northern Syria.) Egyptian influence was especially marked in the coastal regions (e.g., as shown by the numerous Egyptian inscriptions found in Byblos), while some Akkadian influence was felt in the interior, determined by the orientation of the trade routes. Many people could speak Egyptian, and some could use Akkadian cuneiform.

At the beginnings of the second millennium a powerful kingdom appeared in northern Syria called Yamkhad. Its capital was Haleb (present-day Aleppo). Its population was Amorite and its culture Akkadian. Southern Syria and even the Phoenician coast had felt the political influence of the Upper Mesopotamian king Shamshi-Adad I.

The social structure in the city-states of Syria, about which we have little written information (except for the still insufficiently researched archives from the city of Alalakh of the eighteenth century), was apparently very similar to that of the Hurrian society of Arrapkhe (discussed in Lecture 11). We know there were Hurrians in Alalakh, and both cities had a similar economy at about the same stage of development. It is interesting to note that here the king of a city would sometimes grant or "sell" entire villages to his agent or to his retainers. The documents recording these transactions were formulated as if the transactions were donations or sales, although we can assume that they were just transfers of the right to collect taxes and exact service duties from the villages in question. It also seems probable that such transfers—some of them reversible, others not—may sometimes have been a form of foreclosure of property for unpaid debts. Moneylending and usury were common. Individual owners and entire village communities appear as creditors. Obviously, the society was undergoing an accelerated stratification along property lines at the expense of ordinary community members who were sinking into poverty. Many fled to become Hapiru,[2] hiding in the Syrian semidesertic steppe (see the third section of this lecture for a discussion of the Hapiru).

As discussed earlier (Lecture 7, third section), groups of pastoral tribes, the so-called Hyksos, from Palestine or the Sinai, gradually infiltrated the Nile Delta between the end of the eighteenth and the beginning of the sixteenth centuries B.C. Armed detachments of the newcomers gradually seized power in the northern nomes of Egypt, and their leaders began to adopt pharaonic titles. The Hyksos soon lost their ethnic identity and blended with the local Egyptian popula-

2. The earlier opinion that the term *Hapiru* is an early form of the name *Hebrew* has been completely disproved and is no longer held by most scholars.

tion. The degree to which they preserved their supremacy in their original homeland remains unclear. In any event, the cities and rural areas of Palestine during this period showed signs of an improving standard of living. Yet, the wealthy, spacious, and comfortable houses of the elite sharply contrasted with the wretched hovels of the poor: a process of crass property stratification was in full swing. Palestine was not a political unit during that period. The mighty city fortifications and the archaeological signs of their destruction at different times testify to frequent internecine wars. It is possible, however, that the towns of Palestine gave nominal recognition to the supremacy of the Hyksos king in Awaris. The second Hyksos center may have been Gaza, in southern Palestine.

Mitanni and Pharaonic Egypt

During the second half of the seventeenth century B.C., the Hyksos kingdom (or kingdoms) of Egypt began to decline. In the beginning of the sixteenth century, several important new political factors appeared simultaneously in the eastern Mediterranean region.

In the north, the Hurrian kingdom of Mitanni swallowed the small Akkadian, Hurrian, and Amorite kingdoms, including the once-powerful Yamkhad kingdom beyond the Euphrates, which held the key to Syria. Idri-Mi, one of the kings of Alalakh of that time, tells in his inscription about a revolt in his city that forced him to flee in a single chariot driven by a faithful driver and to seek refuge among the Hapiru of the mountains. He lived among them for several years before regaining power in his city, but this time under the condition of recognizing the supremacy of Parattarna, the king of Mitanni.

It seems doubtful whether the state power of the Mitanni kingdom was ever firmly established west of the Euphrates, but its influence was very much felt. Although the dialects spoken by the inhabitants of Syria and Palestine remained Western Semitic (Canaanite in the south and Amorite in the north) and, to some extent, also Hurrian, nevertheless the dynasts of the different cities of both countries often bore not only Hurrian but also Indo-Iranian proper names up to the end of the fifteenth century B.C. The most likely explanation is that these rulers were kinsmen of the Mitannian kings, because at that time, except for Mitanni, Indo-Iranian was not a common language anywhere else in Western Asia, and the language must have been confined to the Iranian plateau.

The rise of Mitanni coincided with two inventions that could have contributed to the wealth of Syria and Phoenicia. About the eighteenth or the seventeenth centuries, the Hurrians of Upper Mesopotamia devised a method of making small vessels from opaque,

colored glass. This technique later spread to Phoenicia, Lower Mesopotamia, and Egypt, but for some time the Hurrians and Phoenicians
enjoyed an international monopoly in the trade of glass objects. The
second invention appeared no later than the end of the sixteenth century when the Phoenicians discovered a method of dying wool deep
crimson to violet, the coloring agent being extracted from Mediterranean shellfish.[3] As a consequence, the importation of cheap, undyed
wool into Phoenicia from the pastoral regions of Syria (probably also
from the island of Crete and, later, from all of Western Asia) became
a very important economic factor for Phoenicia. In turn, the Phoenicians exported very expensive purple-dyed wool. (The dye itself was
very perishable and unfit for transportation.) As a result of this trade,
large reserves of grain and metal artifacts accumulated in the small
towns of Canaanite Phoenicia. This enabled Phoenicia to embark on a
lively trade with distant regions of the Mediterranean (and also to engage in piracy).

Mycenaean and Cypriote pottery appeared in Syria and Palestine
beginning about 1400 B.C., probably attesting to the importation of
olive oil and wine. It is also quite possible that somewhat later the
Phoenicians began to import tin from or via Spain. This made the
manufacture of bronze in Western Asia less costly.

The increasing importance of the merchant impeded the development of monarchic governmental systems of the Egyptian or
Mesopotamian type. Although almost every town had a king, the governments were of an oligarchical character, with a certain degree of
surviving primitive democracy.

The economic growth of the Canaanite and Hurrian cities of Syria
did not reach the level of development that could have been expected
under these conditions because the Egyptian conquest of the region
began soon after 1600 B.C. The hold of the Hyksos on Egypt had been
broken, and after having conducted isolated raids into Western Asia,
the pharaohs of the new Eighteenth Dynasty began a systematic invasion of Palestine, Phoenicia, and Syria. Pharaoh Ya'hmes I captured
the last stronghold of the Hyksos in southern Palestine. During the
last quarter of the sixteenth century, Pharaoh Thutmosis I led his
army all the way to the Euphrates. Beginning with the time of Thutmosis III, who succeeded to the throne after the peaceful reign of the
female pharaoh Hatshepsut, the Egyptians began a lengthy, bloody,
and systematic devastation of Canaanite cities.

The Egyptian campaigns did not result in territorial annexations
but in the wholesale plunder of villages and cities (especially palaces)

---

3. These were the *Murex trunculus, Murex brandaris*, and *Thais haemastoma (Purpura)*.

and the capture of people and domestic animals. The administrative measures of the pharaohs were very primitive. A few Egyptian fortresses were established to control the main roads and mountain passes. The presence of garrisons encouraged the local rulers to appease the conqueror with gifts and tribute as long as possible. Their children were taken hostage to the Egyptian court as pledges; the sons were educated in Egypt in a spirit of loyalty to the pharaoh, and the daughters were sent to his harem. But the pharaohs never attempted to introduce the Egyptian administrative system in Palestine and Syria. Minor Egyptian military units kept by the Egyptian government at the courts of the petty local kings performed supervisory functions. They did not collect taxes: there was no regular imposition of taxes and tribute.

Valuables and manpower were pumped out of Palestine, Phoenicia, and Syria by continuous military expeditions. The booty is enumerated on the walls of Egyptian temples of the period (although the numbers cited are not entirely plausible). It included dyed fabrics, timber, chariots, ivory, gold and silver objects, large amounts of grain, oils, tens and even hundreds of thousands of captives, and still more numerous sheep and cattle. The minor kings and their aristocracy undoubtedly tried to recoup their losses by exploiting and bond-enslaving their own subjects, who found themselves trapped in a hopeless situation of insolvency. The city dwellers and inhabitants of the surrounding villages who fled into the ranks of the Hapiru must have constituted a significant part of the population. Toward the end of the fifteenth century, Syrian and Palestinian states must have lost a great percentage of their population because of the Egyptian invasions.[4]

Although the pharaohs were able to push the forces of Mitanni across the Euphrates, they failed to crush them. The Mitannian kings continued to maintain contact with the unorganized but relentless resistance forces in Syria and Palestine. On one occasion, Egyptian soldiers intercepted agents of the Mitannian king who carried cuneiform tablets—letters to a local ruler—strung around their necks. As the booty of the pharaohs grew richer, the trade along the Palestinian and Syrian trade routes dwindled, and the area became poorer and was no longer able to supply Egypt with valuables. Eventually, Thutmosis IV was compelled to make peace with Mitanni and to delineate the spheres of influence of the two powers. According to this agreement between the pharaoh and the Mitannian king Artadama I, northern Syria and its outlet to the Mediterranean remained in the Mitannian

4. It is interesting that despite the influx of hundreds of thousands of captives, the population of the Nile Valley did not seem to increase. This may mean that the mortality rate of the exploited population was very high.

zone. The Egyptian pharaohs now tried to extract resources from their sphere of influence without resorting to devastating annual military expeditions.

The period between the end of the fifteenth and the beginning of the fourteenth centuries B.C. is usually classified in the history of Palestine, Phoenicia, and Syria as the Amarna Period, because of the accidental fact this it is very clearly illustrated by the diplomatic cuneiform documents found at the archaeological site of Tell-Amarna, the ancient capital of the pharaoh Amenhetep IV (Akhenaton), and at Boghazköy, the ancient capital of the Hittite kings. The participants in the diplomatic exchange used the cuneiform script but several different languages. The Kassite kings used Akkadian, the Mitannian kings used Akkadian and Hurrian, and the Hittite kings used Akkadian and Hittite. The minor kings of the Eastern Mediterranean Belt used a strange, artificial language, part Akkadian and part Canaanite.

In the Amarna Period, the pharaoh resided at three locations: in southern Palestine, southern Syria, and northern Phoenicia. All aspects of Egyptian rule remained unchanged. Note that a local Syrian-Palestinian ruler could be called by three different titles. To the pharaoh he was "the Man of (such-and-such) city"; in diplomatic documents he called himself "mayor"; and to his own subjects he was "king." Only the ruler of Hazor was allowed to title himself "king" even in his letters to the pharaoh. The power of a city ruler was always limited by the council of elders, and in a number of cases this council or even the "sons of the city" (i.e., the popular assembly) could actually run the city without a king and communicate directly with other rulers and the great powers. Among the city-states of Palestine the most important were Gazru (Gezer), Lachish, Jerusalem, Megiddo, and Hazor. In Phoenicia, Byblos was dominant. An important trading center on the Mediterranean coast of Syria was Ugarit, which fell into the Mitannian sphere of influence. In southern Syria the city of Qinza, often given the epithet "the Holy," *qudshu* in Canaanite, was especially important. (It is usually known under the more familiar, conventional Egyptological designation of Kadesh.) Qinza-Kadesh guarded access to the Orontes Valley from the south.

The Popular Movement of the Hapiru

An extremely peculiar polity arose in the mountains between Phoenicia and Syria at the very beginning of the fourteenth century B.C. Its main population consisted of Hapiru. Since these people had no common tribal or territorial origin, the new polity acquired an unconventional name—Amurru, which up to the end of the fifteenth century simply meant "west" in Akkadian or the places inhabited by pastoral tribes (who for this reason were called "Amorites" or "Westerners"; their actual tribal name was apparently "Sutians"). Even earlier, the Hapiru formed their own self-governing communities whenever they had the opportunity to do so. Some of them entered the military service of local kings (as far away from pharaonic Egypt as possible). All of them were opposed to royal rule in general and to the authority of the pharaohs in particular.

The ambitious Abdi-Ashirta made use of these Hapiru to found the kingdom of Amurru. According to a report received by Amenhetep III, Abdi-Ashirta exhorted his adherents with the following words:

> Let us gather together and attack Byblos. And if there be no one there who would liberate it from the hands of the enemy, we will drive out the mayors from their lands and then all lands will unite with the Hapiru. And let there from then on be fairness [or justice] for all lands. Let the young men and maidens be safe [from bondage-slavery] forever. And if the pharaoh turns against us, then all lands will be inimical to him. What could he then do to us?

In ancient Western Asia "fairness" ("justice") meant, first of all, freedom from indebtedness and the return of bonded and pledged hostages and, whenever possible, the return of seized or sold immovable property. This meant that the subjects of all the small kingdoms were exhorted to kill their "mayors" (minor kings) and to become free Hapiru. Debtor bondage was to be abolished, and the pharaoh's military power was to be confronted by the resolve of the combined rebels. It is not surprising that from the very beginning the pharaonic governments pursued the Hapiru and tried to capture and send them into hard slave labor (e.g., in the stone quarries).

In their letters to the pharaoh, Abdi-Ashirta and, after him, his son Aziru were careful to appear as loyal servants of the pharaoh, while in the meantime their agents continued to urge the local population to kill their mayors. This actually happened in several places in Phoenicia and Palestine. In some areas groups of armed former slaves were active.

Meanwhile, in the 1460s, the Hittite king Suppiluliumas I began attacking the kingdom of Mitanni, Egypt's ally. Amurru became a buffer between the Hittites and the Egyptians, but its king took a pro-Hittite stance. From the onset of the Hittite invasion, it was clear that Hittite rule was easier to live under than the Egyptian. The Hittite king defined his relationships with his vassal kings in written agreements and authenticated them by terrible oaths invoking the names of all the gods commonly worshiped by both signatories; as a rule, he kept to the terms of these treaties. The tribute imposed by the Hittites and the military contingents they required were less onerous than the loot and plunder taken by the troops and functionaries of the pharaohs. Indeed, enormous was the price the peoples of the eastern Mediterranean paid for the luxurious, beautiful decorations of the pharaonic palaces and tombs. The Hittites were not yet accustomed to such luxury, and their state was a conglomerate of allied, although unequal, minor kingdoms, similar to the state of Mitanni earlier. Aziru, the second king of Amurru, now a large state in Syria, paid about five pounds of gold annually (the price of a hundred or so slaves) to the Hittite king. This was by no means a bargain, but he would have paid considerably more to the pharaoh. It is therefore understandable that almost everyone in the Eastern Mediterranean Belt, except for the pharaoh's henchmen among the elite, preferred the Hittite rule.

Amenhetep IV, busy with his utopian religious reform, did not want to or could not send enough troops to preserve the Asian possessions of Egypt. Suppiluliumas I had not yet started moving into these regions; he still had to finish with Mitanni. The Asian empire of the pharaohs was crumbling under the blows of Aziru and the ruler of Damascus, who also surrounded himself with Hapiru troops. In Phoenicia, the king of Sidon sided with the Hapiru; it is possible that Sidon's importance, surpassing Byblos, dates from that time. Despite the inaction of the pharaoh, most of the minor kings, completely compromised by their cooperation with the invaders, still maintained their loyalty to Egypt, but the ground was shifting under their feet. Following in the footsteps of the Hapiru, Hittite armies began moving south. They reached northern Palestine in the middle of the fourteenth century. Not much is known about the Hapiru after that. They obviously merged with the rest of the Canaanite population. Some may have managed to improve their living conditions, and some may even have been able to return to their original homes. Of course, no radical change in the social structure could have occurred. The Amurru kingdom became just another minor Syrian state, surviving until the twelfth century B.C. and maintaining its access to the Mediterranean Sea.

The Hittites and Pharaonic Egypt

The pharaohs of the Nineteenth Dynasty—Seti I and Rameses II— had to reconquer Palestine, Phoenicia, and Syria. The situation of the Hittites in Syria was not at all secure, and the Hittite kings had to engage in a complex political game. After the destruction of Mitanni, the crossings over the Euphrates into northern Syria were threatened by the recently established Assyrian kingdom. The Syrians realized that although the Hittite rule was more bearable than the Egyptian, it was more onerous than Mitannian domination. The agreements with the Hittite state included a stipulation that stripped the subject states of their rights to independent foreign and, particularly, military policies. Other clauses also severely limited their independence. Consequently, a number of Syrian states seceded from the Hittite kingdom, which was compelled to subdue them by military force. The Amurru kingdom found it necessary to maneuver between the Hittite and the Egyptian imperial aspirations.

The principal foothold of the Hittite kingdom in Syria was the city of Carchemish, on the Euphrates, which was ruled by Hittite princes. The Hittites sought to convert the coastal city of Ugarit into another such strategic center. The government archives of Ugarit supply historians with valuable information about Syrian society in the fourteenth to thirteenth centuries B.C.

A general outline of the social order of Ugarit can be gleaned from a diplomatic agreement between the Hittite king Hattusilis III and the king of Ugarit. It is clear from the stipulations proposed to Ugarit that Hattusilis considered the society of this city to be composed of the following strata: (1) "the slaves (i.e., servants) of the king"; (2) "the sons (i.e., free citizens) of Ugarit"; (3) "the slaves of the king's slaves," meaning slaves of the king's servants (this category may have included the entire lower level of workers of the royal economy who were under the supervision and authority of the royal employees); and (4) purchased private slaves. The document also stipulates that men of any category who have run away to Hapiru communities controlled by the Hittite king will be returned by the king.

From the documents we learn that collective taxes (mostly in kind, but also in silver) were exacted from Ugaritic communities, and its people were recruited for obligatory work for the state (called "the going," *ilku*[5] in Akkadian and *unusshe* in Hurrian). Obligatory labor included service in the army, service as rowers, and work on state projects. All persons recruited for state obligatory labor were maintained by the royal treasury. Members of family communes to be drafted for obligatory labor were apparently selected by the families themselves. The village and town communities were governed by elders and by a special mediator between the individual community and the royal

5. In ancient Babylonia the *ilkum* did not mean service by the population at large but military service in exchange for royal land grants.

authority called the *sakinu*. The governmental system of Ugarit as a whole was organized along the same lines, but Ugarit had a king in addition to the *sakinu*. This, however, did not prevent the council of elders or the *sakinu* from occasionally engaging in foreign relations directly.

The "king's men" (the Ugaritians did not call themselves royal slaves, the term used by the Hittite king) included plowmen, herdsmen, vine growers, salt workers, various craftsmen, and even soldiers, among whom were battle chariot troops designated by the Hurrian name *marianna*. The royal treasury supplied the chariots, horses, and all other equipment. Judging by their names, these soldiers were Amorites and not Hurrians or "Indo-Aryan feudal knights," as they have been represented by earlier historians. Each professional group had its own "elder." None of the king's men performed temporary obligatory labor (*ilku*); theirs was, rather, a "service" (*pilku*), and they paid their tax to the state in silver. Moreover, they could be awarded conditional land grants (*ubadiyu*). A person not performing his duty was declared a "lazybones" (*nayyalu*), and his grant could be transferred as "alimentation" to other high royal court functionaries, who were also king's men. Certain high officials, especially those connected with international overseas trade, acquired substantial land parcels for large sums of money, including royal land, that is, land constituting "alimentation" for some royal service. (This land bought from royal employees, but the king was recompensed.) The legal status of such properties, however, apparently remained unclear to the Ugaritians themselves. These transactions sometimes had to be reconfirmed when a new king ascended the throne.

Community members, as well as the king's men, were subject to universal military conscription; but some persons could be exempted by virtue of special privileges.

Ugarit's influence eventually decreased when it fell under the hegemony of Carchemish, whose power was on the rise. Meanwhile, the Egyptian offensive that started around 1300 B.C. under Pharaoh Seti I was intensified under Rameses II. The situation of the Canaanite cities of Palestine became worse than that of the Amorite-Hurrian cities of Syria. The pharaonic troops resumed their looting, murdering, and taking of captives. Rameses fell into a trap set for him by the Hittites at the battle of Qinza but still managed to defeat the Hittites and their allies. He continued the annual campaigns into the region for almost fifteen years, ravaging not only Palestine but Syria as well. In the end the Hittite king Hattusilis III, whose country was now threatened by Assyria, signed a peace treaty with Rameses II (in 1296 or 1270 B.C.).

The Migration of "Those Who Had Crossed the River" and the "Sea Peoples"

Soon after the reign of Rameses II (end of the fourteenth and beginning of the thirteenth centuries B.C.), a large group of pastoral tribes began invading Palestine from the Transjordanian steppes. This event is confirmed by sufficiently detailed archaeological data and is also described in the historical legends of the Bible, written some 400 to 500 years later from orally transmitted accounts.

The attitude toward the historical value of biblical stories varies from an unreserved acceptance of their veracity to a complete rejection of their worth to the historian. In fact, although these stories are legends that were used in the acute ideological struggles of much later times, each can be used by historians to the extent to which it can be confirmed by independent written sources or by archaeological remains.

Already by the middle of the nineteenth century A.D. it was quite clear that the biblical narratives about patriarchs (ancestors of various Hebrew, Aramaic, and Arab tribes) reflect legends of the type current among all Semites. Such stories are based on the memorization of tribal genealogies. Among the pastoral tribes, this was a necessary part of the training inculcating the essential mental outlook and awareness of one's identity. Such genealogies have come to us not only from the authors of the Bible but also from the dynasties of Hammurapi and Shamshi-Adad I of Mesopotamia, who traced their origins to Amorite (Sutian) ancestry. Ancestor lists of this kind are memorized even today among Bedouin Arabs. The most important biblical geneaologies are presented in Genesis. (This is the first book of the most sacred part of the Old Testament, the Pentateuch or Torah, venerated by Jews as well as Christians.) An analysis shows that these genealogies apparently belong to Sutian tribes; their mythical forefather must therefore be one Sutu, or Shutu, that is, the character known from the Bible as Seth, son of the first man, Adam. The Sutians are the Amorites. There are a number of other biblical legends implying the Mesopotamian origin of the Hebrew and related ancestral tribes; a few biblical myths are undoubtedly of Mesopotamian origin (e.g., the legend of the Flood).

This and other information make it probable that the tribes that appeared in Transjordan in the second half of the thirteenth century B.C. and later invaded Palestine were ultimately related to the Amorite-Sutian tribes living during the third and early second millennia B.C. in Upper Mesopotamia. They were displaced from there during the sixteenth to fourteenth centuries by the Mitannian Hurrians and the Kassites. Indeed, Babylonian documents of that time attest to a disappearance of Amorite pastoral tribes from Mesopotamia. The Aramaean pastoral tribes that replaced them (coming from oases further south, in Arabia) began to appear in the Transjordan in small groups beginning in the fourteenth century. By the end of the twelfth century many more were arriving.

Some of the Sutian tribes migrated as far as central Arabia; others appeared in Transjordan and Palestine. The Sutian tribes living in Transjordan in the thirteenth to twelfth centuries were called 'ibri, "those who had crossed (the river)." (The river in question was of course not the Jordan, which they had not yet crossed, at least en masse, but the Euphrates.) Thus, "those who had crossed" essentially meant "those from Mesopotamia." At that time the term 'ibri was by no means equivalent to "Hebrew" as the term was understood in later times; "Hebrew" included all the descendants of the legendary patriarch Abraham and even of his ancestor 'Eber. (This name actually means "crossing [of a river].") According to biblical and koranic accounts, Abraham was regarded as the ancestor not only of the Israelite but also of the Aramaean and Arab tribes. Some of the former Upper Mesopotamian tribes (e.g., the Didani, known in Mesopotamia since the middle of the third millennium B.C.) migrated to the Arabian Peninsula and merged with the Aramaeans and Arabs; others settled in Transjordan and never left it (the Moabites and Ammonites), and others settled south of the Dead Sea (the Edomites, also called Idumeans). All these lost the designation "those who had crossed (the river)," and only one tribal group retained this name. The Hebrews were a group of tribes who traced their ancestry to the legendary patriarch Jacob (also called Israel), grandson of Abraham, and had wandered longer than other tribes before finally settling.

According to a much later legend (which, however, was a matter of firm belief among all Israelites) their ancestors, migrating from drought and famine, settled on a stretch of land belonging to Egypt, somewhere on the fringes of the Nile Delta, where they multiplied fabulously. (Twelve men are supposed to have produced 643,550 warriors in just four generations!) They were made bondsmen or "slaves" by the Egyptian authorities and became "king's men," performing forced labor for the Egyptians. (The Bible mentions the building of two cities that were indeed founded under Rameses II.) Then they were miraculously led from there by the "prophet" Moses, an Israelite raised by an Egyptian princess and the husband of a Midianite woman. (The Midianites were apparently a northern Arab tribe.) Moses supposedly renewed a covenant (treaty) with the god Yahweh, which, it was believed, had originally been concluded by Abraham.[6] According to this treaty, Yahweh promised to give Palestine to the Israelites in exchange for a vow not to worship any other god. Since the Israelites did not keep their promise, Moses announced that they were to wander in the Sinai and the Transjordanian deserts for forty years until all those who had sinned had died and that only the new generation would enter Palestine. Moses also gave the Israelites, in Yahweh's name, ethical and legal instructions to guide their future settled life in Palestine.

The story is legendary and was told some three or four hundred years after the alleged events. No historical accounts are known to have ever been preserved correctly after four hundred years of oral transmission. So far, no independent evidence is known that could confirm this story, and it would be futile to attempt to discover if any of the elements of the story are historically accurate. The same can be said of any legend. There may be some truth in the tale, but we lack the criteria for deciding what the truth might be.

The Bible does contain legends that can be checked against archaeological data. To be sure, in the biblical accounts the events from the end of the thirteenth to the tenth centuries B.C. are presented in a distorted form, with dislocations of the historical perspective. This is normal for legends. Many events had been forgotten, many similar facts are telescoped into one, and reality is intermixed with obviously fictional events. Nevertheless, the basic outline of the events of that time as described in the Book of Joshua and, to a lesser degree, in the Book of Judges represents reminiscences of real events rather than pure folklore.

It is obvious that before invading Transjordan and, later, Palestine proper, the tribes must have consolidated to form the Israelite tribal union that recognized the common god Yahweh. The tribes most likely formed their union in the oasis of Kadesh-Barnea, suitable for sheep raising, in the northern part of the Sinai Peninsula. This tradition probably reflects historical reality, but the original composition of the tribal union is very doubtful. The real circumstances of the invasion, as revealed by archaeological data, were different from those depicted in the Bible, which tells of a coordinated and simultaneous march of twelve tribes headed by Moses' successor, Joshua, son of Nun. It was probably the first wave of the invading tribes who crossed

6. A not-implausible theory postulates that the cult of Yahweh was an entirely new one introduced ad hoc by a historical Moses in order to consolidate the tribes through a cult common to them all and to them alone. The new god was naturally identified with other former divine father figures. The theory can neither be proved nor disproved, owing to the lack of independent evidence.

the Jordan near the city of Jericho. The walls of the city crumbled in the face of the attackers, not because of the biblical trumpets, but because they were undermined. About the same time the city of Bethel was destroyed, and the invaders advanced into the center of Palestine. This particular group of tribes (Ephraim, Manasseh, and Benjamin) later claimed descent from Jacob and his favorite wife, Rachel.

Another invasion may have followed shortly. Although the first group traversed Transjordan without obstacle, the second, again moving from the Sinai, encountered resistance and had to fight their way through. Only some of the tribes of this group eventually crossed the Jordan. Two of these tribes, Issachar and Zebulun, settled in the regions west of the Jordan, and east and north of the Manasseh tribe. The third tribe, Judah (Jehudah), turned south, proceeding to destroy the towns in their path and eventually occupying the entire southern Palestinian upland southwest of the Dead Sea. The fate of the other two tribes is not entirely clear; at some later time they apparently lost their identity. Moreover, it seems that an Edomite (?) group, the Kalebites (or Kenazites), which entered the upland from the south instead of crossing the Jordan, merged with the tribe of Judah. The same may be true of the tribe of Simeon, later possibly merged with Judah or the Edomites. This entire group of tribes claimed descent from Jacob and his eldest wife, Leah. Four tribes[7] were said to have descended from Jacob's concubines. All these latter tribes lived at the outer edges of the territory of the tribal union and may originally have been local Amorite tribes who joined the union after it had become established in Palestine.[8]

In Palestine the Israelites (apparently a part of the Amorite-Sutian tribes) encountered a Canaanite and, to a lesser extent, Amorite population.[9] The Canaanites and the Amorites spoke very similar dialects of Western Semitic and worshiped many common gods. A much later tradition asserts that the invading Israelites butchered all of the Canaanite inhabitants at Yahweh's command. It is indeed true that the destruction visited upon Canaanite towns and villages was enormous. The population, however, was not exterminated, nor were all the Canaanite cities destroyed.

Why were the Canaanite city-states so easily conquered in spite of

7. These tribes lived in Phoenicia (Asher), where apparently no one worshiped Yahweh, in northern Palestine (Naphtali), and in Transjordan (Gad). The fourth tribe (Dan) initially lived in southwestern and, later, in northern Palestine.

8. Some of them had no tradition of ever having lived in Egypt.

9. The Bible mentions Hittites, Horites (Hurrians?), and some other, otherwise unknown tribes among the pre-Palestinian population but lumps them all together as Canaanites.

their longstanding cultural and military traditions? The reason is that they had been severely weakened by 350 years of massacres and pillage, which had pitifully decimated their population. And yet, the more important Canaanite cities were not conquered by the tribes "from beyond the river." Some Canaanite cities bought their freedom by ransom payments or pledges of labor service. Some remained independent, such as Jerusalem, the city of the Jebusites, which was located on top of an inaccessible cliff. The Manasseh tribe failed to conquer any important center, and one-half of the tribe had to return to the east of the Jordan River.

It is fair to say that the conquerors settled in the originally sparsely populated uplands and developed them. The valleys, to a large extent, remained in the hands of the Canaanites, who counterattacked the newcomers with some success. They received support from Pharaoh Mer-ne-Ptah, who invaded Palestine during the last quarter of the thirteenth century. His inscription represents the first written mention of Israel in history: "Canaan is ravaged by all kinds of misfortunes. . . . Israel is annihilated and its seed is no more; Hurri [this is what the Egyptians then called Palestine] has become a widow because of Egypt." The Bible makes no mention of this event despite its obvious significance. Having lost their initial drive and finding themselves pressured by new, more vigorous nomadic tribes from across the Jordan River (who by now had domesticated the dromedary camel), the population of twelfth-century Palestine found itself in a very difficult situation. Archaeological data show that Egypt still exerted influence in Palestine during this century. This was precisely the time of the final consolidation of the Israelite tribal union, the memory of which persisted even when most of these tribes (even the most important ones) ceased to exist during the eighth century B.C. But the membership of the union was still different from that of the later classical "twelve tribes." This is demonstrated by a fragment of an ancient Israelite epic from the latter part of the twelfth century preserved in the Bible called "The Song of Deborah." It tells of only seven tribes, headed by Barak and Deborah, that took part in the war against Yabin, king of Hazor, and his military commander Sisera:

> In the days of Shamgar, the son of Anath,
> In the days of Jael the ways were forsaken,
> So a path walker was walking by roundabout ways,
> Forsaken was the lowland in Israel, forsaken—
> Until I arose, Deborah, arising a mother in Israel!

Hazor, the largest and most important city of the Canaanites, was razed to the ground, a fact confirmed by archaeological data. The conquerors built a few squalid huts on the site of the city's ruins. But this was to be the last episode in the war between the Israelites and the Canaanites. A new situation arose when it became necessary to confront a common enemy. The victors and the vanquished joined together to form one people. The literary language of the Bible is based on a mixture of dialects. The ancient Hebrews did not call this language '*ibrith*, or *ivrit* (as they did later), but *Kena'nith*, "Canaanite."[10]

The events that radically changed the situation were also strongly influenced by another tribal invasion: that of the "Sea Peoples." This was the Egyptian name for a group of tribes of different origin. Some came by sea, sailing and rowing in ships; others came overland with carts. Among them were, no doubt, the Achaean Greeks (after having destroyed Troy); the tribes who put an end to the Hittite kingdom (possibly Proto-Armenians); and other tribes known to us only by names recorded in the imprecise Egyptian script. They are said to have "camped in the midst of Amurru."[11] They allied themselves with the Libyans, and the allies attacked Egypt both by land (from the east and the west) and by sea (from the north). The movement started at the end of the thirteenth century B.C., when Pharaoh Mer-ne-Ptaḥ fought them. It reached its peak in the beginning of the twelfth century, when the Hittite kingdom was destroyed. The advance of the Sea Peoples into Egypt was halted by Pharaoh Rameses III some time after the middle of the twelfth century. Two of the tribes belonging to the Sea Peoples, subsequently known as the Philistines,[12] settled the fertile Palestinian coast within a strip of land sixty kilometers long and twenty kilometers wide and formed a union of five self-governing cities: Gaza, Ashkelon, Ekron, Gath, and Ashdod. They brought with them the Late Mycenaean material culture, iron technology, and iron weapons. Soon their hegemony spread over almost all of Palestine. At the same time nomadic tribes of Semites (Aramaeans or Arabs) raided the land from the Sinai and from across the Jordan. Some of these tribes apparently settled on the frontiers of Palestine.

Apart from some military leaders whose authority was temporary, the Israelite tribes had no political power of their own and were ruled

10. Since that time, the term *Hebrew* has come to mean a general ethnic identity. The narrower term *Israelite* denoted membership in the tribal union and, later, in the state of Israel.

11. The fall of Ugarit was brought about by a completely different cause. When the Ugaritians sent their fleet to confront the approaching Sea Peoples, a catastrophic earthquake destroyed the city. The city of Carchemish was unscathed and became the center of a Late Hittite (Luwian) culture.

12. It is possible that "Philistines" is another name for Pelasgians. There were two types of plural morph in the region around the Black Sea: -ta and -k'a; hence, *pelash-ta- and *pelash-k'a. (See Lecture 15.) The term *Palestine* is derived from *Philistine*.

by elders. They were advised by prophets (*nabi*), who at that time had not yet become religious and political preachers and were not far removed from shamans or medicine men. In especially difficult situations, individual tribes or the entire union voluntarily subjected themselves to an elected or self-proclaimed leader and redeemer (*shofet,* "judge") to whom magical powers were attributed. Their names are mentioned in the Book of Judges (Samson, Jephthah, etc.), but not all of the biblical judges can be regarded as historical. The beginnings of statehood appeared during the time of the last judges (eleventh century B.C.).

The Israelite tribal union was traditionally considered to be composed of twelve tribes. Actually, the number of tribes in the union seems to have varied.

The union was first and foremost a cultic association welded together by the common worship of Yahweh, the god of the union. The maintenance of the cult was assigned to an intertribal organization, the Levites. Traditionally, they were one of the tribes, namely, the twelfth. Certain towns in the areas of the other eleven tribes were assigned to the Levites. Yahweh, as well as other gods, could be worshiped in any place but preferably on hilltops and mountain peaks. The Israelites believed that Yahweh dwelled invisibly on earth in the "ark of the covenant," which was kept in a tent, as it had been during the past nomadic life of the tribes.

During the early period Yahweh was still easily identified with local Canaanite gods, particularly because speaking the name of Yahweh, as well as the names of the Canaanite gods was very usually tabooed (not to be "taken in vain"; that is, without need), and the worshiper used apellatives instead: "god" (*el*) and even "gods" (*elohim*), "master" (*ba'al*), and "my lord" (*adonai*). Yahweh was not considered the only deity of the universe—neither then nor for a long time later. But he was a jealous god who had concluded a treaty (covenant) with his tribal union according to which he was not to be regarded as equal to other gods but rather was to be the only god worshiped by the tribes of the union. The symbol of this covenant was circumcision, a rite that originally was one of the initiation rites for an adolescent entering the community of full-grown warriors. Many Semitic tribes gave up this ceremony over time (e.g., the Canaanites, but not the Arabs). The Israelites performed this rite immediately after birth because the infant was ready to enter into the covenant. In some places Yahweh was regarded as "married" to the Amorite-Canaanite goddess Anath, even centuries later. Also, each family revered figurines or idols, the *teraphim,* of either gods or ancestors. In principle, praying to other gods was not deemed impossible, and certainly the power of other gods was not denied for the territories of other tribes and peoples.

Culture and Alphabet

The most ancient Israelites possessed neither architectural nor imitative arts. Only fragments remain of their epics, and their written literature, which in many respects is of the greatest interest, was yet to be created.

The Canaanites left a considerable cultural legacy, although some savage customs were also common among them. Each Canaanite-Amorite community had its own patron deities, usually a god, his wife, and son. As mentioned before, they were frequently designated by appellative nouns and were distinguished by the names of their places of worship, such as *Ba'lat Gubli*, "The Lady of Byblos." Certain deities, especially cosmic ones—for example, those of the Sun, the Moon, the Thunder and Rain, Fertility, and the sea—were worshiped all over the country, not being confined to any single community. Such was also the case of the "cultural hero," the inventor of crafts, Kuthar-wa-Husas. Also foreign gods were often worshiped (Egyptian, Sumerian, Hurrian, etc.). As various *els* (gods) began to be identified with each other, the notion of a common supreme god, *El*, emerged. *El*, however, had a different wife in each community.

Many deities were identified with animals, plants, and objects or had these as their permanent attributes (e.g., a bull, a heifer, a lioness, a serpent, a tree). Stone pillars were often used as cult objects, and it is not unlikely that they had a phallic origin. Orgiastic cults of fertility deities were common with participation of sacred harlots. Archaic rites such as the initiation of maidens and young men (by fire and maybe also by circumcision) were practiced. Male cult associations were also known. On occasions that were especially trying or important to the community (a siege, the founding of a new fortress, etc.), first-born children were sacrificed.

In the arts, the Canaanites were somewhat behind the other Near Eastern civilizations. During the third and beginning of the second millennium B.C., Canaanite and Amorite architecture of the north imitated the Mesopotamian; in the south and in Phoenicia Egyptian designs served as models. The second millennium, however, saw the development of large-scale and original fortress and temple construction across the entire Eastern Mediterranean Belt. The largest temples measured 30 × 20 meters and were supported by two rows of round columns. Stone slabs, stelae, or Egyptian-style poles were placed within the sanctuary proper before the shrine of the god or at its entrance.

Sculpture (representation of gods, rarely of kings) in the pre-Israelite period was at a stage where artists tried to imbue the statues with terrible and superhuman power, achieving (in the eyes of an observer of today) an impression of inhumanity and ugliness. They were usually small bronze statues; stone figures were less frequent. The Israelite god could not be represented because of a prohibition attributed to Yahweh himself: "Thou shalt not make unto thee any graven image or any likeness." This led to the almost complete disappearance of representational art, although small domestic terra-cotta idols continued to be made. However, the figurines of the naked goddess of fertility and birth, whose gestures emphasized her nudity or pregnancy, were replaced by fully clothed representations.[13]

Very little remains of Canaanite and Amorite literature of the second millennium B.C. What has reached us are religious poetic texts written in Ugaritic (a Western Semitic language) that were preserved in the temple library of Ugarit. The most interesting of these are the epic cult songs, such as the song about the god Aliyan-Ba'l. The song relates his defeat in his fight with the god of fading and death. Other gods intervened, death was defeated, and food became plentiful: "The heavens exude oil, the rivers flow with honey." Ugarit also had heroic epics. An interesting inscription from Alalakh stands apart— the "autobiography" of King Idri-Mi—which may have been influenced by the Egyptian "autobiographic" genre (see Lecture 9).

By far the most important accomplishment of the Canaanite-Amorite civilization was the invention of the alphabet. The common form of expressing information over time and space in use throughout the Eastern Mediterranean Belt for a long time was either the Egyptian language and writing or a Canaanite-influenced dialect of Akkadian and the cuneiform script. During the second millennium B.C., a syllabic linear script, commonly called Proto-Byblian, appeared in Byblos. It consisted of about one hundred signs, each representing a syllable composed of a consonant plus one of the three ancient Semitic vowels: a, i, or u. (Some of these signs were also used for consonants without vowels.) This form of writing could reproduce texts of practically any complexity and was much easier to learn than the Akkadian cuneiform script or Egyptian hieroglyphs. It could be learned in a few weeks instead of years. However, the new writing was difficult to read because the words were not separated. In the Egyptian script determinative symbols were used to separate words. These symbols indicated the group of concepts to which they belonged; they also marked the limit of each word. The cuneiform script also designated word boundaries.

The signs used in Proto-Byblian writing had no prototypes in any other writing system and apparently were designed ad hoc when this

---

13. In daily life Israelite women, including prostitutes, covered their faces, in contrast to the Canaanite women.

writing system was invented. Still, Proto-Byblian writing did not seem easy enough to Phoenician merchants and seafarers, who seem to have been willing to accelerate the learning process even at the expense of intelligibility. The ancient merchants engaged in international trade were never eager to make their documents easily understandable to strangers. Simplified variants of their writing system appeared gradually throughout the region, from the Sinai to Syria. The number of symbols decreased, so that each sign (letter) came to indicate one consonant (with or without a vowel). This resulted in an alphabet of thirty to thirty-two consonants.

Similarly sounding consonants could sometimes be represented by the same letter (*sh* and *ś*, ' and *gh*, *ḥ* and *kh*). The letters developed different shapes; the letters on the clay tablets used in Ugarit, like those of Babylonia, were formed of wedge-shaped lines. Canaanite Phoenicia developed a system of twenty-two linear consonant letters (probably about the thirteenth century B.C.). Another variant was developed in southern Arabia. A writing system without vowel signs was not at all "better adopted for Semitic languages," as, for some reason, is frequently asserted; it was actually a kind of merchants' cryptography. However, once the Phoenicians began to use the letters "'," "h," "w," and "y" to indicate the long vowels ā, ō, ū, ē, and ī and began to indicate word boundaries, this writing system became much easier to master and to use. Consequently, in spite of the fact that Phoenician writing did not unequivocally express the precise pronunciation of a given text and that cuneiform and hieroglyphic writing continued successfully to compete with it for a number of centuries, the new writing system eventually prevailed to become, after improvements introduced by the Greeks and other peoples, the precursor of all alphabets of East and West.

15

The World of Crete and Mycenae

YU. V. ANDREYEV

Minoan (Cretan) Civilization

The island of Crete was Europe's earliest cradle of civilization. The location of this mountainous island, which hinders access to the Aegean Sea from the south, is a natural outpost of the European continent facing the African and Asian shores of the Mediterranean. Sea routes connecting the Balkan Peninsula and the Aegean Islands with Asia Minor, Syria, and North Africa have intersected here since very ancient times. The Minoan[1] culture of Crete, situated at one of the most important crossroads of the ancient Mediterranean, was influenced both by the oldest civilizations of the Near East and by the Neolithic cultures of Anatolia, the Danube plain, and Balkan Greece. The Minoan civilization emerged at the end of the third and beginning of the second millennium B.C., that is, toward the end of the so-called Early Bronze Age. Part of Europe was still covered by dense forests and marshes, but in scattered spots there appeared isolated centers of farming and livestock-raising cultures (in the south and southeast of Europe: Spain, Italy, the lower Danube region, the steppes of southern Russia, and Greece). Around this time, elaborate buildings, usually called "palaces" by modern archaeologists, appeared in Crete. The first of these palaces was discovered by Evans in Knossos (in the central part of Crete, not far from the northern shore of the island). Legend has it that it was the residence of the mythical ruler of Crete King Minos. The Greeks called the palace of Minos the "Labyrinth" (a word adopted by them from some pre-Greek language). Greek legends describe the Labyrinth as an enormous building with countless rooms and corridors. A person who entered it could not find his way out without outside assistance and inevitably perished. The bloodthirsty Minotaur, a monster with a human body and a bull's head, lived deep inside the palace. The tribes subject to Minos were required each year to oblige the terrible beast with human sacrifices, until one day he was slain by the famous Athenian hero Theseus.

1. The name *Minoan* was introduced by the first discoverer of the ancient Cretan culture, Arthur Evans, who derived it from the name of a mythological king of Crete, Minos.

In fact, archaeologists unearthed a huge building, or a complex of structures, that covers a total area of 16,000 square meters and comprises some 300 rooms of different kinds and functions.[2] Similar structures were later discovered in other parts of Crete. The overall external appearance of the palaces reminds us of some ingenious theatrical set under the open sky: there are quaint porticoes with columns seemingly turned upside down, wide stone steps to open terraces, numerous balconies and loggias, ornaments carved in stone on the roofs, schematically depicted horns of sacred bulls, and bright patches of frescoed walls. The interior layout is very chaotic. Living quarters, kitchens, storage areas, workrooms, connecting corridors and staircases, internal patios, and light shafts are distributed without any apparent plan or system. But despite the seemingly chaotic nature of the palace, it is still perceived as a single architectural ensemble. One of the factors contributing to this unity is the large rectangular court in the center of the palace that connects all the main rooms of this enormous complex. This yard, paved with huge gypsum slabs, was apparently not used for any household purposes but rather for religious activities. It is possible that the famous games with the bulls were conducted here: we see them depicted on murals that decorate the walls of the palace.

The Knossos palace had to be repeatedly reconstructed due to frequent earthquakes.[3] New rooms were attached to existing ones. Rooms and pantries were strung together, forming, as it were, long rows of suites. Separate structures, or groups of structures, gradually merged to form one residential complex around the central yard. The palace had everything necessary to provide its dwellers with a placid and comfortable life. The builders even supplied running water and sewers. The ventilation and lighting systems were also well designed. The entire building was traversed from top to bottom by special shafts that allowed sunlight and fresh air to reach the lower levels of the palace. Large windows and verandas were built for the same purpose. Let us remember, for comparison's sake, that the ancient Greeks of the fifth century B.C., at the apogee of their culture, lived in badly lighted, stuffy dwellings and did not know such elementary comforts as bathrooms and toilets furnished with drains.

An important portion of the ground floor of the Knossos palace was occupied by storage rooms, where wine, olive oil, and other prod-

2. We must point out that only the first floor and the basement remain. The original building had two or three floors above ground level.
3. The Knossos palace and others were first built around 2000 B.C., and most of them were abandoned by about the fifteenth century; only the Knossos palace itself continued to be inhabited until ca. 1200 B.C.

ucts were kept. Here, there were pits in the floors, covered with big stone slabs for the storage of grain.

During the excavation of the Knossos palace, archaeologists found a great variety of works of art produced with exquisite taste and mastery. Many of these objects were made at the palace itself in special workshops by resident goldsmiths, potters, decorators of vases, and other craftspeople who served the king and the nobility of his court. (Such shops were found in many parts of the palace.) Of particular interest are the wall paintings, which graced the interior rooms, hallways, and porticoes of the palace. Some frescoes represented scenes from nature with plants, birds, and sea animals. Others show the inhabitants of the palace: athletic, sun-tanned men with long hair in fancy curls, thin "wasplike" waists, and broad shoulders, as well as ladies wearing enormous bell-shaped skirts with numerous pleats, tightly laced-up bodices, and bared breasts. Male clothing was much simpler and usually consisted only of a loincloth, but they wore splendid, feather-decorated headdresses, and gold necklaces and bracelets. The people represented in the wall paintings seem to be participating in some complex and little-understood rites. Some are shown marching ceremoniously in procession, carrying in outstretched hands sundry sacred vessels for libations to the gods. Others turn gracefully, performing a dance around a sacred tree. Another group sits on the steps of a "stage" and attentively watches a performance or ceremony. Minoan artists excelled in depicting people and animals in motion. Magnificent frescoes illustrating the so-called bull games are good examples of their artistry. We see a swiftly charging bull, with an acrobat performing a series of intricate leaps right on the animal's horns and back. In front and behind the bull, the artist has depicted two girls wearing loincloths, apparently the assistants of the acrobat. The meaning of this scene is not entirely clear. We do not know who participated in this strange, undoubtedly dangerous and life-risking competition between man and enraged beast and what the ultimate goal of this game was. One thing we can be sure of: the Cretan bull games were not a simple entertainment for an idle crowd, like the modern Spanish bullfights. They were a religious ritual connected with one of the principal Minoan cults—the worship of the Bull deity.

The bull game scenes constitute perhaps the only disturbing feature found in Minoan art. Cruel and bloody war and hunting scenes, so typical of the Near Eastern and continental Greek art of that time, were alien to Minoan artists.[4] Judging by what we see in the frescoes

4. Recently discovered Minoan frescoes on Thera, however, depict naval battles. Today, some scholars believe the idyllic character of Minoan civilization has been over-emphasized since the time of Evans's original discoveries. Editor's note (PLK).

and other Minoan works of art, the life of the elite must have been placid and unperturbed. It proceeded in a joyful atmosphere of al-most continuous festivities and colorful performances. Crete was se-curely protected from the surrounding hostile world by the waters of the Mediterranean. At that time, there was no significant maritime or any other hostile state close to the island. The feeling of security is the only explanation for the fact that all Cretan palaces, including Knossos, remained unfortified throughout their history.

Of course, the life of Minoan society was represented by the palace artists in an idealized and embellished fashion. Real life on the island also had its dark side. The natural environment was not always kind to the inhabitants. Frequent earthquakes shook Crete, often with devas-tating force. If we further consider the strong gales (quite frequent in this area) with thunderstorms and heavy downpours, dry and hungry years, and the epidemic outbreaks of illnesses, the life of the Minoans no longer appears as quiet and carefree.

The inhabitants of Crete turned for protection against the natural forces to their numerous gods. The central figure of the Minoan pan-theon was a goddess: the "Great Mistress." In Cretan works of art, usually statuettes and seals, she is shown in her various incarnations. We can see her as the ferocious Mistress of the Beasts, as the sovereign lady of the mountains and forests and all that inhabits them, as a be-nevolent protectress of plants, primarily of grain and fruit trees, and as the sinister queen of the Underworld, holding coiling snakes in her hands. In these images we can recognize the ancient deity of fertility, the great mother of people and animals, revered throughout all the lands of the Mediterranean region, at least since the Neolithic era.[5] In the Minoan pantheon, next to this great goddess who was the embodi-ment of femininity and motherhood and who symbolized the continu-ous renewal of nature, we find a god who embodied all the destructive forces of nature, the terrible earthquakes and the might of the stormy sea. The Minoans perceived these terrifying phenomena in the form of the mighty and ferocious god-bull. On some Minoan seals the de-ified bull is depicted as a fantastic being—a man with a bull's head—immediately reminding us of the later Greek myth of the Minotaur. To appease this terrible god and thus to pacify the angry forces of nature, sacrifices, apparently even human, were offered to him. (This barbaric rite is echoed in the myth of the Minotaur.)

Religion played an enormous role in the life of Minoan society and

5. Actually, the Great Mistress of Crete resembles rather closely the great goddess of love and strife and death, like the Mesopotamian Ishtar and her underworld double, Ereshkigal or the Hurrian Shawushka or the Greek Artemis (or even Athene); moth-erhood does not seem to belong to her attributes. Editor's note (IMD).

left its imprint on absolutely all aspects of its spiritual and practical activities. Archaeologists unearthed at the Knossos palace all kinds of religious items, including figurines of the great goddess, sacred symbols in the form of bull's horns and the double axe (the *labrys*), altars and tables for sacrifices, diverse vessels for libations, and so on. Many palace rooms were used as shrines for religious rituals and ceremonies. Among them were crypts, or secret rooms, where sacrifices were offered to the gods of the Underworld. Some rooms had pools for ritual ablutions; others served as small domestic chapels. The architecture of the palace, the paintings on its walls, and other works of art were permeated with complex religious symbolism. This was, in fact, a palace-temple where all inhabitants, including the king, his family, and the court ladies and gentlemen who formed their retinue, performed different priestly duties by participating in rituals depicted in the frescoes of the palace.

Thus, Crete had a special type of royal power that is termed theocracy. This is a variant of a monarchy and combines the supreme lay and religious authority in the same person. The king's person was probably regarded as sacred and untouchable. It is possible that he could not even be viewed by ordinary mortals. This may explain the strange circumstance that nowhere in Minoan art are we able to find any representation that can with certainty be interpreted as that of the king's person. The entire life of the king and his household was strictly regulated and elevated to a ritual status. The Knossos kings did not simply live and reign: they performed a religious ritual. The "holy of holies' of the Knossos palace where the king-priest condescended to meet his subjects, offered sacrifices to the gods, and decided the affairs of state was the throne room of the king, located near the large central courtyard. Before entering it, a visitor had to pass through a lobby containing a large bowl of porphyry for ritual ablutions. Apparently, prior to making an appearance before the king, a visitor had to wash all evil from himself. The throne room itself was a relatively small rectangular room. A gypsum chair with a high curved back—the royal throne—stood directly across from the entrance. The walls were lined with alabaster-faced benches on which the royal councillors, the high priests, and the functionaries of Knossos sat. The walls of the throne room are decorated with colorful frescoes of griffins—imaginary creatures with the head of a bird and the body of a lion. The griffins appear lying in solemn postures on each side of the throne as if protecting the ruler of Crete from harm.

The splendid palaces of the Cretan kings, the incalculable wealth amassed in their basements and storerooms, and the comfort and abundance surrounding the life of the kings and their retinue were all being produced by the labor of thousands of nameless farmers and craftspeople. Unfortunately, we know little about the working inhabitants of Crete. These people apparently lived outside the palaces in small villages scattered across the fields and hills and in squalid mud houses closely nestled together along narrow crooked streets. Such homes form a striking contrast with the monumental architecture of the palaces, with their luxurious appointments. The low standard of living and the cultural backwardness of Minoan villages, compared with the refined culture of the palaces, is evident in the simple and coarse funerary gifts, the human and animal figurines roughly modeled of clay, and other items found by archaeologists in remote mountain shrines. We have every reason to believe that the relationship between masters and dependents typical of early class societies had already developed in Crete at that time. Thus, we can assume that the farming population was subjected to taxation in the form of in-kind tribute and service duty for the benefit of the palace. The population had to supply the palace with livestock, grain, oil, wine, and other products. All this was recorded by palace scribes on clay tablets, which toward the time of the destruction of the palace (during the fifteenth century B.C.) formed a large archive amounting to some 5,000 documents. These supplies were delivered to the palace storerooms, where enormous quantities of food and other valuable goods were stockpiled. The same farmers probably built and rebuilt the palace, constructed roads and irrigation canals, and erected bridges.[6] We must not assume that they performed all this work by compulsion, only because the king and the nobility so desired. The palace was the main shrine of the community, and elementary piety required each villager to honor with gifts the gods who inhabited it, donating his household surplus for the celebration of festivals and sacrifices, and to work for the glory of the gods. Of course, there was an entire army of middlemen between the people and their gods: a staff of professional priests serving the sanctuary and headed by the king. In essence, this was an established and clearly defined stratum of hereditary priestly nobility, who stood in opposition to the rest of society. The priests, who disposed of the goods stored in the royal warehouses at their pleasure, could use a lion's share of this wealth for their own needs.

The accumulation of surplus produce of the community in the hands of the palace elite was not motivated solely by religious reasons, but also by strictly economic considerations. The accumulated prod-

6. Besides free community members whose dependence on the palace consisted of paying taxes, there probably also existed a nonfree population (slaves) or a semifree one (servants and dependents). On analogy with other early class societies—those, for example, of the Near East or of Mycenaean Greece—the palace personnel may have been quite numerous, hundreds or even thousands of trained craftspeople, etc.

ucts could serve as a reserve for times of famine. They were used to maintain the craftspeople working for the community. Any remaining goods were exported to Egypt, Syria, and Cyprus, where they could be bartered for the goods that Crete lacked: gold, copper, ivory, and purple-dyed textiles. Overseas trading expeditions were quite costly and risky in those days. The state, with its material and human resources, was able to finance such enterprises. Naturally, the rare goods acquired through this exchange were stored in the warehouses of the palace and from there distributed to master craftsmen of the palace and villages. Thus, the palace was multifunctional in Minoan society: it was the administrative and religious center of the community and, at the same time, its main commercial, storage, and artistic center.

The golden age of Minoan civilization covers the sixteenth century and the first half of the fifteenth century. This period saw the completion of the Cretan palaces with a heretofore unseen splendor. It seems that during this epoch, Crete was unified under the kings of Knossos and became a single centralized state. This is evident from a network of convenient, wide roads built throughout the island, connecting Knossos, the country's capital, with the most remote corners of Crete. This is also indicated by the already-mentioned fact that the Knossos and other palaces were not fortified. Had the palaces represented the capitals of independent states, they would certainly have been fortified in defense against any unfriendly neighbors. It is quite possible that Crete was unified from the Knossos palace by the famous King Minos, so often mentioned in later Greek myths.[7] Greek historians considered Minos the first *thalassocrates,* "sovereign of the sea." They said that he created a large navy, eradicated piracy, and established his supremacy over the entire Aegean Sea and its islands. This legend probably has some grain of historical gruth. Archaeological findings show that Crete began an extensive maritime expansion in the sixteenth century throughout the Aegean basin. Minoan colonies and trading stations emerged on islands of the Cyclades archipelago, on the island of Rhodes, and even on the shores of Asia Minor in the Miletus region. At the same time, Crete started lively commercial and diplomatic relations with Egypt and with the states of the Syrio-Phoenician coast. This fact is attested by frequent discoveries of Minoan ceramics in these regions. Objects from Egypt and Syria have been found on Crete. Egyptian wall paintings from the first half of the fifteenth century show the ambassadors of the country of Keftiu (the Egyptian name for Crete) wearing typical Minoan dress—aprons

---

7. However, it is also possible that this name was borne by several kings of Crete and was a dynastic name.

and half-boots—and bringing gifts to the pharaoh. There is no doubt that Crete was a very strong sea power at the time these pictures were painted and that Egypt was seeking friendship with its kings.

The situation changed drastically in the middle of the fifteenth century. Crete suffered a catastrophe unprecedented in its centuries-long history. Almost all the palaces and villages were destroyed; many were forever abandoned by their inhabitants and forgotten for millennia. The Minoan culture never recovered from this blow and from the middle of the fifteenth century began its decline. Crete lost its place as the leading cultural center of the Aegean basin.

The causes of this catastrophe have not yet been firmly established. The Greek archaeologist S. Marinatos suggested that the palaces and villages were destroyed by an earthquake and the ejecta of a tremendous eruption of the volcano situated on the island of Thera (modern Santorin) in the southern part of the Aegean Sea.[8] Other scholars are inclined to believe that Achaean Greeks who invaded Crete from continental Greece were responsible for this disaster. They plundered and devastated the island, whose fabulous wealth had attracted them for a long time, and subjugated its inhabitants. In fact, the culture of Knossos—the only place that survived the catastrophe of the fifteenth century—underwent important changes following this tragic event. A new people appeared on Crete. And with them the optimistic and realistic Minoan art yielded to an unemotional and lifeless stylization. The traditional Minoan ornamentation of vases with plants, flowers, and octupuses was replaced by abstract designs. At the same time tombs with all sorts of weapons—bronze swords, daggers, helmets, arrowheads, and lanceheads—appear near Knossos. None of these objects were typical of earlier Minoan burials. They indicate that persons of an Achaean military elite, now established in the Knossos palace, were buried here. Finally, one more fact unequivocally points to the penetration of Crete by a new ethnic element. Numerous documents (of the so-called Linear B script group) found in the Knossos archives were written in Greek (Achaean).[9]

These documents date mainly from the end of the fifteenth century. The Knossos palace was apparently destroyed toward the end of the fifteenth, or the beginning of the fourteenth, century and was never fully restored. Moreover, many remarkable Minoan works of art were lost in a fire.

8. Following the catastrophe, part of the densely inhabited and flourishing island disappeared underwater. Some scholars identify it with the legendary Atlantis. Editor's note (IMD).

9. A few dozen tablets written in the Linear A script in an unknown language are to be dated earlier.

After that, the decline of Minoan civilization was irreversible. It continued to degenerate and to lose its distinctive character. Crete became an obscure province, and the main center of cultural progress and civilization moved north to continental Greece, where the so-called Mycenaean culture reached its peak during that time.

Achaean (Mycenaean) Civilization

The Mycenaean culture was created by Achaeans, a Greek group, who invaded the Balkan Peninsula at the end of the third or beginning of the second millennium. They apparently came from the north, probably from the Danube lowland region. While advancing farther south through the territory of Greece, the Achaeans partly destroyed and partly assimilated the native pre-Greek population of this region, who were called Pelasgians by later Greek historians.[10] Initially, the Mycenaean culture was strongly influenced by the more advanced Minoan civilization. The following aspects of Minoan culture were adopted from Crete: certain deities and religious rituals, palace wall paintings, runing-water and sewerage systems, male and female dress styles, certain types of weapons, and, finally, the linear syllabic script. This, however, does not mean that Mycenaean culture was just a minor, peripheral variant of the Minoan culture of Crete and that the Mycenaean settlements on the Peloponnesus and other places were simply Minoan colonies in a foreign "barbarian" country, as Evans believed. Many characteristics of Mycenaean culture lead to the conclusion that it developed on Greek soil and was directly connected to the very ancient Chalcolithic and Early Bronze cultures of this region.

The earliest attestations of Mycenaean culture are the so-called shaft graves of Mycenae, in the northeast of the Peloponnesus. The first six tombs of this type ("Circle A") were discovered within the walled perimeter of the citadel of Mycenae by the well-known German archaeologist H. Schliemann. Many objects made of gold, silver, ivory, and other precious materials were found in these tombs. In the *Iliad,* Homer calls Mycenae "rich in gold" and the Mycenaean king, Agamemnon, is the most influential and powerful of the Achaean leaders who took part in the famous Trojan War. However, Schliemann erred in thinking that he had found the tomb of Agamemnon, who was viciously slain by his wife, Clytemnestra, after his return

10. The Pelasgians may have been related to the Minoans. Certain words of a lost language—whether it was Pelasgian or Minoan—were borrowed by the Greeks and inherited by the modern European languages; e.g., such plant names as "hyacinth," "cypress," and "narcissus."

from the Trojan campaign. The shaft graves date from the sixteenth century B.C., and the Trojan War, in the opinion of modern archaeologists, took place in the thirteenth or early twelfth century B.C. The very valuable items found in the graves of Circle A show that the Mycenaean kings ruled a warlike and violent people, greedy for the wealth of others. They undertook long land and sea expeditions and returned home loaded with booty. It is unlikely that any of the gold and silver found in the royal burial sites was acquired through peaceful trade; it was most likely captured in wars. The military inclinations of Mycenaean rulers are demonstrated by the extraordinary number of weapons found in their tombs and by the bloody war and hunting scenes decorating some of the objects found in the tombs and the stelae placed over the graves. One of the latter shows a warrior riding in a chariot and pursuing a footsoldier carrying a bow. Some objects are very rudimentary in their design (e.g., the golden funeral masks), revealing the lack of skill of local Mycenaean craftsmen. Other objects were made by the best Minoan goldsmiths.

Thirty years ago, another royal necropolis was discovered in Mycenae, outside the walls of the citadel. It consisted of twenty-three graves of about the same type as the six shaft graves found earlier. These burials were not as wealthy, although quite a few valuable items were found here too, such as vessels made of quartz crystal and beads made of amber. The earliest graves of "Circle B" are dated to the second half of the seventeenth century B.C. This places the beginning of Mycenaean culture earlier than formerly assumed. Apparently, a primitive state existed in Mycenae already by the seventeenth century, and its ruling elite, probably the royal clan itself, was clearly separated from the population at large.

The golden age of Mycenaean civilization can be placed in the fifteenth to thirteenth centuries. During this period, it spread over the entire Peloponnesus, central Greece (Attica, Boeotia, and Phocis), a significant portion of northern Greece (Thessaly), as well as to many islands in the Aegean Sea. This whole territory had a homogeneous culture represented by the same types of houses, burials, pottery, etc. From available information we can infer that Mycenaean Greece was a flourishing country with a large population, spread throughout the entire area and inhabiting many small and large settlements.

The main centers of Mycenaean culture were palaces, as in Crete. The most important palaces were discovered in Mycenae, Tiryns, and Pylos (Peloponnesus), in Athens, Thebes, and Orchomenus (central Greece), and, finally, in Iolcus (Thessaly). Almost all Mycenaean palaces were fortified and constituted veritable citadels, somewhat resembling outwardly the castles of feudal lords in the Middle Ages.

The advanced engineering skills of the Achaean builders are exhibited by the mighty, cyclopean walls[11] of the Mycenaean citadels, which were built with massive boulders without the use of mortar. The famous Tiryns citadel in the Argolis region, not far from Mycenae, serves as a first-rate example of Mycenaean fortification. Unfinished limestone boulders, some weighing as much as 12 metric tons, form the external walls of the fortress, which are up to 4.5 meters thick and 7.5 meters high (that is, in places where they have been preserved). In some places, vaulted galleries with casemates were built inside the walls. The casemates were used to store weapons and food supplies. (The walls can be up to 17 meters thick here.) Access to the main roads was designed so that an enemy soldier approaching the entrance had to turn his right side, which was not protected by his shield, to the wall. But in the event that an enemy should manage to penetrate the citadel, he would face an internal protective wall, which guarded the main part of the fortress, the acropolis with the royal palace. In order to reach the palace, he would have to pass through a narrow passage between the external and internal walls that was divided into two sections by two wooden gates. Here, an enemy would be subjected to a crossfire of missiles shot from all sides. To guarantee the defenders of the citadel an abundant water supply, there was an underground passage on the northern side of the citadel (the so-called lower city) that led to a carefully hidden spring situated 20 meters from the wall.

The most interesting of the actual palace structures of the Mycenaean epoch is the well-preserved "Nestor's Palace"[12] in Pylos, in the western part of the Peloponnesus. The palace at Pylos is similar in its interior decor to the Cretan palaces, but differs from them in its precise and symmetrical layout. The main rooms of the palace are situated along one axis, forming a closed rectangular complex. In order to reach the interior of this complex, it was necessary to pass through the entrance portico (propylaeum), a small inside yard, another portico, and a lobby, from which the visitor entered a spacious rectangular hall, the *megaron,* which was the most important part of a Mycenaean palace. A large, circular fireplace stood in the center of the *megaron,* from which smoke rose through an opening in the ceiling. Four wooden columns surrounded the fireplace and supported the ceiling. The walls were decorated with paintings. The *megaron* was the heart of the pal-

11. When the Greeks saw these walls in later times, they attributed their construction to the one-eyed giant Cyclops.

12. The name "Nestor's Palace" is conventional. According to Homer, Nestor, the old and wise king of Pylos, was one of the principal participants in the Trojan expeditions.

ace; it was in this hall that the king of Pylos caroused with his noblemen and guests. This was also the hall for official receptions and audiences. Two long corridors were placed along the *megaron* from the outside, and from here doors opened to numerous storage rooms, where several thousand vessels for keeping and shipping oil and other products were found. It seems that the Pylos palace was an important exporter of olive oil, a very valuable commodity in neighboring countries. Nestor's Palace had bathrooms, running water, and a sewage system.

The archive of the palace was kept in a relatively small room near the main entrance. It contained over 1,000 clay tablets inscribed in a linear syllabic script, very similar to that used to write the documents found in Knossos (Linear B) and mentioned earlier. The tablets were well preserved because they had been exposed to heat when the palace was destroyed by fire.

Among the most interesting architectural relics of the Mycenaean epoch are the majestic royal tombs called *tholoi*. They were usually built near the palaces and citadels and most probably served as burial places for members of the ruling dynasty, just as had the earlier shaft graves. The largest of the Mycenaean *tholoi*, the so-called tomb of Atreus, is located in Mycenae. (Originally it was thought to have been a treasure house.) The tomb proper is hidden within an artificial mound. To enter it, it is necessary to pass through a long, stone-faced passage called a *dromos*, which leads into the mound. The entrance to the tomb is covered by two enormous stone slabs (one of them weighing 120 metric tons). The interior chamber is a monumental circular room with a high, beehive-like vault some 13.5 meters high). The walls and the vault of the tomb are finished with superbly hewn stone slabs that were originally adorned with gilded bronze rosettes. A somewhat smaller, lateral chamber is connected to the main chamber. It is rectangular and not as finely finished. This was apparently the actual royal burial place, which had already been looted in ancient times.

The construction of such monumental structures as the tomb of Atreus and the Tiryns citadel could not have been accomplished, in our opinion, without the use of compulsory labor. In order to perform such tasks, it was necessary to have access to a cheap labor force in large numbers and, at the same time, have a sufficiently developed state organization to manage such a work force. The rulers of Mycenae and Tiryns obviously had both at their disposal.

The mystery of the internal structure of the Achaean state began to be disentangled in 1952 when a young Englishman, M. Ventris, deciphered the tablets of the archive of Pylos, as well as some of the tablets from the Knossos archive. He found that all these documents were written in an archaic Achaean dialect of the Greek language spoken by the people of Mycenaean Greece in the second millennium B.C.[13] The syllabic Linear B script that was used in these inscriptions most probably originated on Crete[14] and was based on the older Linear A script,[15] which existed there earlier. The Achaeans, who conquered Crete around the middle of the fifteenth century B.C., inherited from the Minoans the syllabic script and adapted it to their own language.

The tablets read by M. Ventris are bookkeeping accounting records, kept from year to year in the Pylos and Knossos palaces. The laconic records contain invaluable historical information allowing us to evaluate the palace economy, as well as the political and social structures of the states in question. We find, for example, that slavery already existed in Greece during that time and that slave labor was widely used in many branches of the economy. A significant number of documents from the Pylos archive enumerate groups of workers employed by the palace. Lists indicate how many women there were in each group; what their occupations were (grain millers, weavers, seamstresses, and even bathhouse attendants); how many children, both boys and girls, were with them (apparently, these children of the female slaves were born in captivity); what rations they were receiving; and where they worked (i.e., in Pylos or in some town of the dependent territory). Such groups of workers could be quite large, comprising a hundred persons or more. The total number of women and children in all the worker groups known from just one set of inscriptions of the Pylos archive must have been around 1,300. In addition to worker groups made up of only women and children, the documents also mention those composed exclusively of men; however, these were relatively smaller, usually not more than ten workers each. There were obviously more female than male slaves, a fact indicating that slavery was still at a relatively early stage in its development.

Documents from the Pylos archive also tell us that in addition to conventional slaves, there were "male or female slaves of a god." These people usually rented[16] small parcels of land from the community (*damos*) or from private persons. We can conclude from this that

13. Earlier, the opinion of Evans was universally accepted. Evans believed that all the inscriptions in the linear script were made by a people of non-Greek origin.

14. The Knossos archive is roughly two centuries older than analogous archives of continental Greece (Pylos, Mycenae, etc.).

15. The tablets written in the Linear A script, found in the Knossos palace and in some other parts of Crete, remain undeciphered. Most scholars are inclined to think they reflect a Minoan language not related to Greek.

16. The statement that the land granted to these people was rented cannot be considered proved. Editor's note (IMD).

they did not own land and, consequently, that they were not considered full-fledged members of the community, although they were not slaves in the strict sense of the word. The term "slave of a god" itself seems to indicate that people in this social subcategory were in the service of temples dedicated to the principal gods of the kingdom of Pylos and were under the protection of the temple administration.

An important portion of both the Pylos and Knossos archives is dedicated to accounting for the work of craftsmen, among whom we find a wide variety of specialists: blacksmiths, stonemasons, tailors, carpenters, potters, armorers, goldsmiths, and even perfumers. For their work they received rations from the palace treasury (barley and other produce). Cases of absence from work were recorded in special documents. "Loafers" were apparently punished, but we do not know how. Some of the craftsmen were probably considered "palace people" and were in the service of the state, like the numerous officials mentioned in the same documents. Their situation apparently was not much better than that of the female slaves.

Another group of craftsmen was composed of free community members whose work for the palace was a temporary obligatory service. According to the documents, periodic obligatory labor of this kind in Pylos and Knossos was imposed on the inhabitants of small villages located on the periphery of the main palace and economically dependent on it. Craftsmen drafted into state service did not lose their personal freedom. They could own land and even slaves, like all the other community members.

Blacksmiths occupied a special position among the craftsmen working for the palace. Thus, in Pylos they were exempted from delivering flax—the duty of all inhabitants of the Pylos kingdom. All blacksmiths residing within the territory of the state were under the supervision of the palace administration. The metal they required for their work was issued by the palace together with a task assignment. Blacksmiths were assisted in their work by slaves, who were apparently also assigned by the palace.

According to documents from the archives of Knossos and Pylos, the palace economy of the Mycenaean epoch appears to have been a powerful, widely branched system involving practically the entire society. The private economies, although they apparently existed in the Mycenaean states, were subject to taxation and obligatory service owed to the state sector and played a minor, subordinate role. The state monopolized the most important branches of the production of the craftsmen and established very strict control over the distribution of raw materials, especially metals. Not a single kilogram of bronze, not one arrowhead, escaped the watchful eyes of the palace bureaucrats. All metal, whether held directly by the state or in private hands, was carefully weighed, counted, and recorded on clay tablets by the scribes of the palace archive. All available information indicates that the economy that developed in Achaean Greece was analogous to the Near Eastern type.

The palace economy, based on the principles of strict accountability and control, required a bureaucracy in order to function. Documents from the archives of Pylos and Knossos show it in action, although many details of its organization still remain unclear. In addition to the staff of scribes who worked directly in the palace offices and archive, the tablets mention numerous officials who were in charge of the different types of work and who monitored conscription for obligatory labor. Thus, from the documents of the Pylos archive we discover that the entire territory of the kingdom was divided into sixteen tax districts, each headed by a governor, *koreter*. Each was responsible for the punctual delivery of tax payments from the district in his charge to the palace treasury. The payments mainly consisted of metals—gold and bronze—as well as different kinds of farm products. Functionaries of a lower rank managed the individual villages in a district and reported to the *koreter*. Such a functionary was called a *gwasileus* or *basileus*. They supervised production activities, for example, the work of blacksmiths in the service of the state. Both a *koreter* and a *basileus* were under the vigilant control of the central authority. The palace constantly sent heralds, messengers, inspectors, and auditors all over the territory.

The head of the palace state bore the title *wanaka*, which corresponds to the later Greek *wanax*, that is, "lord," "sovereign," "king." Unfortunately, the documents tell us nothing about the political functions and rights of the *wanaka*, but he certainly occupied a special and privileged position among the ruling elite. The land allotment (*temenos*) belonging to the king was three times as large as that of the highest functionaries. The king had a large staff of servants at his disposal, which, according to the tablets, included royal potters, royal fullers, royal armorers, and others.

One of the most prominent high-ranking functionaries under the king of Pylos was the *lawagetas*, "leader of the (armed) people," or "military chief." As his title indicates, his responsibilities included command of the armed forces of Pylos.

Other officials are also mentioned in the texts. Priests of the principal temples of the country and high-ranking military officers, especially those commanding the battle chariot detachments, formed part of the top elite, which was closely connected with the palace and constituted the immediate entourage of the *wanaka* of Pylos. Judging from all available data, farmers and craftsmen lacked all political rights and took no part in governing the state.[17] Only the slaves working in the palace economy had a lower status.

The decipherment of the Linear B script did not resolve all the questions about the socioeconomic and political history of the Mycenaean period. For example, we do not know the relations that existed between the separate small states. Did they form, as some scholars believe, a single Achaean state federation under the aegis of the king of Mycenae—the most powerful among the Greek rulers of that time—or were they completely separate and independent states? The latter seems more probable. It is not accidental that almost all Mycenaean palaces were surrounded by strong defensive structures that protected their inhabitants from a hostile outside world and, most of all, from their closest neighbors. The huge walls of Mycenae and Tiryns stand as witnesses to the almost uninterrupted hostility between these two states, which shared the fertile Argos Plain. Greek legends recount the bloody wars between the Achaean rulers. We are told, for instance, how seven kings of Argos intervened in the struggle between the sons of king Oedipus of Thebes, how they marched against Thebes, one of the wealthiest cities of central Greece (Boeotia), and how they managed to take and destroy the city after a series of unsuccessful attempts. Archaeological excavations have shown that the Theban palace of Mycenaean times was, in fact, burned and destroyed in the fourteenth century B.C., long before other citadels and palaces fell into ruin.

On occasion, the Achaean states were apparently able to join forces for common military enterprises. The famous Trojan War is a good example. Homer tells the story of this war in the *Iliad*. If we take this poem at face value, it appears that almost all the principal regions of Achaean Greece took part in this expedition—from Thessaly in the north to Crete and Rhodes in the south. The Mycenaean king Agamemnon was chosen as commander of the combined forces. It is quite possible that Homer exaggerated the actual size of the Achaean coalition and embellished the expedition itself. Nevertheless, today almost no one questions the historical authenticity of this event. Archaeological excavations in Troy (northwestern Asia Minor, not far from the shore of the Dardanelles, ancient Hellespont) revealed that one of the settlements on this site (Troy VIIa) was taken and destroyed after a protracted siege in about the middle of the thirteenth century B.C. or

17. According to one opinion, the term *damos* ("people"), which appears in tablets of the Pylos archive, stands for an assembly of the people representing the entire free population of the kingdom of Pylos. It appears more probable to this author that *damos* was one of the territorial communities (districts) forming the state (compare with the later Athenian *demos*).

somewhat later. (This date is close to the traditional dating of the Trojan War preserved by Herodotus.)[18]

The war of the Achaeans against Troy was just one, though the most significant, of the manifestations of the military and colonizing expansion of Achaeans into Asia Minor and the Mediterranean region. Many Achaean settlements appeared during the fifteenth to fourteenth centuries on the western and southern shores of Asia Minor, on the islands of Rhodes and Cyprus, and even on the coasts of Phoenicia and Syria. (They are identified by large accumulations of typically Mycenaean ceramics.) In all these places the Mycenaean Greeks took over the trading initiative from the hands of their Minoan predecessors. Crete iself, as we have mentioned, was colonized earlier (in the fifteenth century) by the Achaeans and became the main bridgehead for their further expansion to the east and south.

Successfully combining commerce with piracy, the Achaeans soon became a very prominent political force in that part of the ancient world. A document from the capital of the Hittite kingdom puts Ahhiyawā (probably one of the Achaean states in western Asia Minor or on neighboring islands) on the same footing with the strongest states of that time: Egypt, Babylon, and Assyria. The rulers of Ahhiyawā maintained very close diplomatic contacts with the Hittite kings.

At the turn of the thirteenth to twelfth centuries B.C., detachments of Achaean plunderers from Crete or the Peloponnesus participated in the invasion of Egypt by the coalition of the "Sea Peoples." Among the tribes of the coalition, the Egyptian inscriptions that recount these events mention the *akaywasha* and the *danauna* or *danawanna,* which could correspond to the Greek names Akhaioi and Danawoi, the names that Homer gave the Achaeans.

The Egyptians repelled the onslaught of the Sea Peoples from their borders, but meanwhile Achaean Greece was already on the threshold of serious troubles. The last decades of the thirteenth century were very agitated and alarming times, and the inhabitants of the palaces and citadels lived in fear. Mycenae, Tiryns, Athens, and other cities began hurriedly to rebuild their old fortifications and to add new

18. H. Schliemann, who discovered Troy in 1870, was mistaken in assuming that Homer's Troy was the settlement second from the bottom of the seven occupations discovered at the same site. In fact, it has now been established that Troy II belongs to the second half of the third millennium B.C.; that is, it was occupied almost a thousand years before the Trojan War. Troy VIIa was ignored by Schliemann. Even worse, the relatively well preserved stone walls of Troy VIIa were demolished to construct barracks for the workers hired by Schliemann; he even failed to sketch them. Thus, Schliemann succeeded in completing Agamemnon's work by destroying Troy and not leaving a trace. The (alleged) "backwardness" of archaeological science of that time is a poor excuse in this case, because archaeology had by then accumulated more than one century of experience. Editor's note (IMD).

ones. A massive, cyclopean wall was erected on the Isthmus (a narrow strip of land connecting middle Greece with the Peloponnesus), obviously intended to protect the Mycenaean states in the southern part of the Balkan Peninsula against dangerous threats from the north. Among the frescoes of the Pylos palace there was one painted not long before the destruction of Pylos. The artist depicted a bloody battle between Achaean warriors in armor, wearing their typical horned helmets, and some barbarians wearing animal skins and displaying long, free-flowing hair. Most likely these were the people whom the inhabitants of Mycenaean fortresses feared and against whom new fortifications were being erected.

Archaeological discoveries show that in the immediate proximity of the main centers of Mycenaean civilization, in the north and northwest of the Balkan Peninsula (regions called Macedonia and Epirus in ancient times), a completely different kind of life existed—very far removed from the luxury and majesty of the Achaean palaces. Tribes at a lower developmental stage lived there and apparently were still organized in clans and lineages structured by kinship. We can evaluate their culture by their crudely modeled pottery and primitive clay idols found in most burials of this region dating from this period. We must, however, point out that, in spite of such backwardness, the tribes of Macedonia and Epirus were familiar with the use of metals, and in the purely technical sense, their weapons were no less effective than those of the Mycenaeans.

At the end of the thirteenth century B.C., the tribes of the entire northern Balkan region had been set in motion by some unknown causes. An enormous multitude of barbarian tribes, including peoples who spoke different dialects of the Greek language (among them Doric and closely related western Greek dialects), and, apparently, also people of non-Greek origin (of Thracian and Illyrian origins), left their homelands to head south to the rich and flourishing regions of middle Greece and the Peloponnesus, as well as to Asia Minor. The route of the invaders is marked by destruction. The invaders conquered and destroyed many Mycenaean villages and towns that stood in their path. The palace of Pylos was consumed by a fire, and its site was abandoned and forgotten. The citadels of Mycenae and Tiryns suffered serious damage but were apparently not taken. The effect on the economy of the Mycenaean states was one of irreparable losses. This is evident in the precipitous decline of crafts and commerce in the regions most damaged by the invasion, as well as by a drastic decline in population. The Mycenaean civilization suffered a terrible blow from which it was unable to recover.

The ensuing rapid disintegration of the major Mycenaean states is explained not so much by the onslaught of the northern barbarians as by the instability of their internal structure, which was based, as explained earlier, on the systematic exploitation and subjugation of the working inhabitants by a small palace elite. A single blow was sufficient to destroy the ruling group, making the entire complex structure crumble like a house of cards.

The further course of events is unclear, because the available archaeological material is sparse. Most of the barbarian tribes who took part in the invasion apparently did not remain in the conquered territory (the devastated country was unable to sustain such a large number of people) and retreated north to their original homelands. Only small tribal groups of Dorians[19] and related western Greek peoples settled in the coastal region of the Peloponnesus (Argolis, the regions near the Isthmus, Achaea, Elis, Laconia, and Messene). Isolated pockets of Mycenaean culture continued to exist up to the end of the twelfth century B.C. in the midst of the newly established settlements of the newcomers. It appears that at that time the last Achaean citadels that survived the catastrophe at the end of the thirteenth century experienced their final decline and were forever abandoned by their inhabitants. To the same period can be traced a mass emigration—apart from the movements of the Sea Peoples—from Balkan Greece toward the east, into Asia Minor and nearby islands. The participants in this colonizing movement were the surviving Mycenaeans of the Peloponnesus and middle and northern Greece, who were now called Ionians and Aeolians, and Dorian newcomers. This migration resulted in the establishment of many new towns on the western coast of Asia Minor and on the islands of Lesbos, Chios, Samos, Rhodes, and others. Among the most important of the new towns were Aeolian Smyrna, the Ionian towns of Colophon, Ephesus, and Miletus, and the Dorian town of Halicarnassus.

19. Some modern scholars think that the Dorians did not participate in the first invasion, which culminated in the fall of Pylos. According to this view, they arrived later (in the twelfth century or even as late as the eleventh century), when the resistance of the Mycenaean Greeks was completely broken.

16
Greece of the
Eleventh to Ninth Centuries B.C.
in the Homeric Epics

YU. V. ANDREYEV

The period of Greek history following the Mycenaean Period is usually called "Homeric" after the great poet whose poems, the *Iliad* and
the *Odyssey*, constitute a very important source of information about
that time. The origin of the Homeric poems (the so-called Homeric
question) remains an unsolved problem in historical science. Homer
and his writings were the subject of heated debates in ancient and
modern times. This controversy was not entirely useless. Scholars
were able to determine, at least approximately, the time and place of
the creation of these poems. On the basis of a number of indications,
we know that both these poems originated about the eighth century
B.C. (the *Iliad* probably was written somewhat earlier than the *Odyssey*)
in one of the Greek towns of Asia Minor, on the Ionian coast of the
Aegean Sea.

The Homeric epics did not arise in a vacuum; the great poet had
numerous predecessors, nameless popular bards, called *aoidoi*, who
over the centuries passed by word of mouth, from one generation to
another, songs and tales about the Trojan War and related events.
Homer, who himself may have been one of the *aoidoi*, collected and
recast these legends, which became the foundation for two epic
poems of monumental scope and outstanding artistic value.

The historical material is included in Homer's narrative in a very
intricate manner. There is no doubt that it contains elements going
back to the Mycenaean Period, possibly even to times preceding the
Trojan War itself. This may explain the mention of swords and other
weapons of bronze (although the poet must certainly have lived in the
Iron Age), of battle chariots no longer used by the end of the second
millennium, and of such very important former centers of civilization
as Mycenae, Tiryns, Pylos, Knossos, and others. Some of these cities
had been razed during the Dorian invasion and never rebuilt; others
had become tiny villages of no importance.

However, the Mycenaean epoch as a whole remained for Homer a very distant past about which he had only a very vague idea. When the poet relates the events of the "Heroic Age," he generally places them in a much later historical milieu, belonging to a time probably not very distant from his own. This is attested by many details in the poems: references to iron-processing methods that became known in Greece no earlier than the eleventh century B.C., allusions to Phoenician seafarers and merchants, who arrived in the waters of the Aegaean Sea by about the same time or even later, his accounts of the comparatively recent custom of cremating the dead. All this demands great caution on the part of historians when treating the data contained in Homer's epics. When reading Homer, we must always bear in mind that we do not have before us a historical document but a work of art, where motifs and images from different ages of history, far removed in time from one another, appear in close proximity, combining in whimsical and, at times, surprising patterns.

The evidence of the Homeric epics can be checked and considerably augmented and corrected by archaeology. Excavations have shown that the so-called Dorian conquest threw Greece several centuries back, almost to the conditions that prevailed at the beginning of the second millennium B.C., before the birth of the Mycenaean civilization. The material and spiritual culture of this time is marked by signs of decline. The Mycenaean palaces and citadels were abandoned and lay in ruins; no one settled within their walls. Even the acropolis of Athens, a city apparently unaffected by the Dorian invasion, was abandoned by its dwellers as early as the twelfth century and remained uninhabited for a long time. We get the impression that the Greeks of the Homeric period had forgotten how to build houses and fortresses of stone, the building material used by their Mycenaean predecessors. Almost all the structures of the Homeric period were built of wood or adobe, which is the reason why none of them have been preserved; only their stone foundations give us an idea about their structure and appearance. In most cases, they were merely small rectangular or oval huts with a rudimentary stone fireplace in the center, a mud floor, and a roof made of reeds or straw.

As a rule, the burials of the Homeric period were extremely poor compared with the Mycenaean graves. Their entire contents usually were a few clay pots and an iron sword or knife and some lanceheads and arrowheads in the mens' graves, or cheap adornments in those of the women. They contained almost no beautiful, valuable items; objects imported from the Orient, quite common in Mycenaean burials, are absent.

All of this points to a sharp decline of crafts and commerce and to a mass flight of skilled craftsmen out of a country ravaged by wars and invasions. It also tells us that the sea routes that connected Mycenaean Greece with the countries of the Near East and all the other Mediterranean regions were forsaken. In their artistic quality, as well as in purely technical aspects, objects made by Greek craftsmen of the Homeric period are no match for the artifacts of Mycenaean masters, not to speak of those of the Minoans. This is particularly striking when we compare the pottery of the eleventh to ninth centuries with earlier specimens. The vessels of this period are invariably painted in the so-called geometric style. The elaborate drawings typical of Minoan and Mycenaean vase paintings were replaced with unpretentious geometric decorations made up of concentric circles, triangles, lozenges, and squares. Later, in the eighth century, these most simple elements began to be construed into compositions involving many figures, representing war scenes, funerals, chariot races, and so on. In their schematism and primitivism these vase paintings resemble children's drawings. A very wide gap separates these handicrafts from the great art of the Cretan and Mycenaean palaces.

This, of course, does not mean that the Homeric period failed to contribute anything new to the cultural development of Greece. Human history does not know absolute regression, and elements of decline are capriciously intertwined with a number of important innovations in the material culture of the Homeric period. The most important development accomplished by Greek craftsmen was in the field of iron-smelting and processing technology. Iron was known in Mycenaean Greece only as a valuable metal for the making of such items as rings and bracelets. The earliest specimens of iron weapons (swords, daggers, arrowheads, and lanceheads) found in Balkan Greece and on the Aegean Islands date from the eleventh century. The earliest discoveries of slag date from about the same time and prove that iron was being smelted in Greece itself and not imported from other countries.[1]

The acquisition of this technology and its large-scale utilization created a real technological revolution. For the first time, iron became cheap and widely available. (Iron deposits are much more abundant in nature than those of copper and tin, the main components of bronze.) With the dangerous and costly expeditions to the sources of the ores no longer necessary, the accessibility of iron enormously in-

---

1. Until recently, it was commonly assumed that the Dorians introduced iron to Greece. (This was the usual explanation for their victories over the Achaeans, who only had bronze weapons.) So far, however, this hypothesis has not been confirmed archaeologically. Another explanation seems more plausible: the secret method for smelting and treating iron was adopted by the Greeks from some of their eastern neighbors, most likely from one of the peoples of Asia Minor, where it was already known in the second millennium B.C.

cremented the production capabilities of the smallest economic unit of the society—the individual family. With the help of an iron axe, scythe, and other tools, each family was now able to clear much larger tracts of land for cultivation than was possible earlier when bronze was the principal metal for tool making. Toward the end of Homeric times (second half of the ninth century), Greek smiths had mastered the art of hardening wrought iron and converting it into a kind of steel (less resilient than the modern steels): Greece had reached the Iron Age. However, the beneficial effects of technical progress did not immediately reflect on the social and cultural development of ancient Greece, and on the whole, the culture of the Homeric period was clearly at a much lower level than the culture of the preceding period. This is clearly demonstrated not only in the objects excavated by archaeologists but also in the accounts of daily life found in the poems of Homer.

Long ago it was observed that the *Iliad* and the *Odyssey* present us, on the whole, with a society that was much closer to barbarism and whose culture was much more backward and primitive than the one we imagine when reading the tablets written in the Linear B script or when observing Minoan and Mycenaean works of art. The Homeric heroes, every one of whom was a king and aristocrat, lived in primitive wooden houses in yards surrounded by palisades. The dwelling of Odysseus, the principal hero of the second Homeric poem, is typical. At the entrance to the "palace" of this king rests, in all its splendor, a large heap of manure, upon which Odysseus, returning home disguised as a beggar, finds his faithful dog Argus. Beggars and vagabonds unceremoniously enter the house and sit by the door, waiting for handouts from the chamber where the master is banqueting with his guests. Trampled-down mud provides the floor of the house. The walls and the ceiling are covered with soot, because houses were heated by open fireplaces without chimneys or flues. The house even lacks a kitchen; all the preparations for dinner take place in the yard or in the dining chamber itself. Here the animals to be consumed are slaughtered, butchered, and roasted on a spit. The floor is littered with bones, leftovers, and freshly flayed oxen and sheep skins.

Obviously, Homer had no idea about the actual appearance of palaces and citadels of the "Heroic Age." Never do his poems mention the complex fortifications or the monumental cyclopean walls of the Mycenaean fortresses or the wall paintings and painted floors that decorated their palaces. He apparently knew nothing about running water and sewerage. Even the palace of Alcinous, king of the Phaeacians, which so greatly impressed Odysseus by its wealth and luxury, has little in common with the authentic palaces of the Mycenaean era and is more likely a product of Homer's poetic imagination.

The whole way of life of the poems' heroes is far from being the magnificent and comfortable existence of Mycenaean court aristocrats. The Homeric heroes led a much simpler, coarser life. The wealth of a Homeric "king," or a *basileus,* does not compare with the fortunes of his predecessors, the Achaean *wanaka.* The latter required an entire staff of scribes to account for and control their property, whereas a typical Homeric *basileus* himself knew perfectly well what and how much was stored in his pantry, how much land he owned, and how many head of cattle and slaves he had. His main wealth was his stock of metal artifacts: bronze kettles and tripods, as well as iron ingots, which he carefully kept in some secluded nook of his house. Thrift, economic prudence, and the ability to make a profit were not the least among his characteristic traits. In this respect, the psychology of a Homeric aristocrat was not much different from that of any prosperous farmer of that time (see below about Hesiod). Nowhere does Homer mention the numerous servants, divided by grades and ranks, that would have surrounded a *wanaka* in Mycenae and Pylos. The centralized palace economy, with its multitude of workers, supervisors, scribes, and inspectors, was completely alien to Homer. To be sure, the economies of some *basileis* (e.g., Odysseus and Alcinous) had a relatively large number of working personnel, fifty female slaves, as Homer tells us. But even if this is not a poetic hyperbole, such economies would still be far smaller than those of the palaces of Knossos or Pylos, which, according to the tablets, employed hundreds and even thousands of workers. It is difficult to imagine a Mycenaean *wanaka* sharing a meal with his slaves, or his wife being surrounded by female slaves while sitting at a loom. But to Homer, these were typical, everyday scenes in the lives of his heroes.

Homer's kings do not shun the roughest physical work: Odysseus is no less proud of his skill with the plow and the scythe than he is of his military prowess. We meet the princess Nausicaa for the first time when she comes with her servant girls to the seashore to wash the clothes of her father, Alcinous. Such facts tell us that slavery as an institution had little importance in Homeric Greece and that even the economies of the richest and most prominent persons did not employ very many slaves. We must also keep in mind that most of the slaves were females. As a rule, men were not taken prisoner in the wars of that period, because their "taming" consumed too much time and required too much persistence. Women, on the contrary, were readily taken because they could serve as both a labor force and as concubines. (This was not considered reprehensible even when a master had a lawful wife.) In Odysseus' house, twelve female slaves mill grain with hand mills, work that was regarded as particularly laborious and was assigned to unruly and refractory slaves as punishment.

Male slaves, in the rare cases when they are mentioned in the poems, usually tend domestic animals. The "divine swineherd" Eumaeus epitomizes the classical type of Homeric slave. Eumaeus is the first person to encounter and shelter the wandering Odysseus, who after a long absence has returned home, and helps him to deal with the suitors.[2] As a small boy, Eumaeus was bought from Phoenician slave traders by Odysseus's father, Laërtes. For his exemplary behavior and obedience, Odysseus made him the chief swineherd. Eumaeus figures that his diligence will be rewarded even further. The master gives him a parcel of land, a house, a wife, "and all else that a liberal master allows a servant who has worked hard for him and whose labor the gods have prospered as they have mine in the situation I hold."[3] Eumaeus can be regarded as the example of a "good slave" in the Homeric sense.

The poet also knows that there are "bad slaves," who do not wish to obey their masters. In the *Odyssey* they are represented by the goatherd Melanthius, who sympathizes with the suitors and helps them against Odysseus, as well as by Penelope's twelve female slaves who entered into an illicit association with the enemies of their master. Having disposed of the suitors, Odysseus and Telemachus then deal with the treacherous slaves. The female slaves are hanged on a ship's rope. As for Melanthius, he is thrown alive to the dogs after his ears, nose, legs, and arms have been cut off. This episode vividly testifies to the fact that Homeric heroes already had a strongly developed property sense in regard to their slaves, although slavery as an institution was at an early stage.

The typical Homeric community, *demos*, led a rather isolated existence, and its contacts with similar communities, even with its closest neighbors, were relatively rare. Commerce and crafts played an insignificant role. Each family produced almost everything it needed to subsist: agricultural and animal products, clothing, the simplest implements, tools, and possibly even weapons.

Specialized craftsmen, living from their own labor, very rarely appear in the poems. Homer calls them *demiourgoi*, "those who work for the people." Most of them probably did not even have their own workshops or permanent abodes and had to wander through villages from house to house in search of their earnings and food. Their services were needed only in special cases when some object of weaponry

2. The suitors are aristocratic young men of Ithaca, the island where Odysseus was born, and of neighboring islands. Taking advantage of Odysseus's absence, they settle in his house and try to coerce Penelope, the wife of the hero, into marrying one of them.

3. *Odyssey* XIV, 55; here and in the following cited Homeric passages, the quotations are from the English rendering by Samuel Butler.

had to be made—bronze armor or an oxhide shield, for example—or when some precious ornament had to be fashioned. In such cases a qualified master metalworker, tanner, or jeweler was needed.

The Greeks of Homeric times very rarely and reluctantly engaged in trade. They preferred to acquire any foreign objects or products they needed by force, and to this end they organized looting expeditions to foreign lands.[4] The seas surrounding Greece teemed with pirates. Piracy and robbery on land were not considered reprehensible activities in those times, a fact already noted by the great Greek historian Thucydides in the fifth century B.C. On the contrary, such enterprises served as opportunities to exhibit special daring and bravado, worthy of a real hero and aristocrat. Achilles openly brags that in the course of his battles on land and sea he destroyed twenty-three towns in Trojan lands. Telemachus is proud of the riches "looted" for him by his father, Odysseus. But even the intrepid pirates and plunderers did not venture too far beyond the boundaries of their native Aegean Sea. An expedition to neighboring Egypt seemed to the Greeks of those days to be a fantastic enterprise, requiring exceptional valor. The wide world beyond the borders of their own small universe and even such relatively close territories as the Black Sea region, Italy, and Sicily appeared to them as faraway and frightful lands. In their minds, these lands were inhabited by terrible creatures, such as Sirens and giant Cyclopes, about which Odysseus tells fantastic stories to his amazed listeners.

The only true merchants that Homer mentions are the "cunning guests from the seas"—the Phoenicians. In Greece, as in other countries, the Phoenicians engaged mainly in mediatory trade and sold all sorts of foreign goods, such as exotic and unusual items of handicraft, gold trinkets, amber, ivory, little flasks with scents, glass beads, and so on. The poet treats them with obvious distaste and regards them as crafty swindlers always ready to trick a simple-minded Greek.

Like so many other achievements of the Mycenaean civilization, the linear syllabic script was also forgotten during the troubled times of tribal invasions and migrations. The entire Homeric period was non-literate. So far, archaeologists have been unable to find a single inscription in Greece that can be attributed to the period from the eleventh to the ninth centuries B.C.

After this long gap, the first Greek inscriptions known to scholars appear only in the second half of the eighth century. These inscriptions, however, are no longer written in the Linear B script but in

4. Marketability was apparently more important in the economies of hereditary noblemen than in the economies of common community members. An aristocrat could at times exchange the surplus of his economy for bronze and copper, materials he needed for producing weapons, or for rare textiles, jewelry, foreign slaves, and so on.

letters of an entirely new alphabetic system of Phoenician origin that must have appeared at just about that time. Thus, we find no references in Homer's poems to writing. The heroes of the poems are all illiterate; they neither read nor write. The "divine" bards, or *aoidoi,* Demodocus and Phemius, both of whom appear in the *Odyssey,* were illiterate as well. As already mentioned, a close connection between the Homeric poems and the popular oral arts can clearly be perceived. In Greece, as well as in other countries, folklore undoubtedly preceded the birth of written poetry.[5]

The mere fact of the disappearance of writing in the post-Mycenaean era is certainly significant. The spreading of the linear script throughout Crete and Mycenae was principally dictated by the need of a centralized monarchical state to keep strict accounts and to control its material and human resources. The scribes working in the Mycenaean palace archives diligently recorded the receipt of produce delivered by the dependent population and the performance of labor duties of slaves and nonslaves, as well as all sorts of deliveries from the treasury and expenditures. The destruction of the palaces and citadels during the thirteenth to twelfth centuries was accompanied, beyond any shadow of a doubt, by a complete disintegration of the large Achaean states whose centers they were. Individual communities were freed from their former fiscal dependence on the palace and shifted to a completely independent economic and political path of development. With the collapse of the entire bureaucratic managerial system, the need for writing, which serviced this system, also disappeared. The art of writing was forgotten for a long time to come.

Relying on Homer's testimony, we can say that a fairly primitive territorial community was born from the ruins of the Mycenaean bureaucratic monarchy. This community was the *demos* and inhabited a very small territory, the political and economic center of which was the polis. In the Greek language of the classical epoch *polis* expressed two closely connected concepts in the consciousness of every Greek: "city" and "state." Yet, it is interesting that in the Homeric vocabulary, where the word *polis* is very frequent, there is no word that could be translated as "village." This means that there was as yet no difference between a city and a village in Greece during that time. The Homeric *polis* was simultaneously a city and a village. It resembled a city in the tight clustering of its structures within a small area and its fortifications. Such a Homeric *polis* as Troy in the *Iliad* or the city of the Phaeacians in the *Odyssey* already had walls made of stone or brick, or just

5. We do not know whether Homer wrote down his own work. There is no doubt, however, that both poems were recorded in written form very soon after their creation, or even at the same time, but hardly before the second half of the eighth century B.C. The canonical text took shape in the sixth century B.C.

earthen ramparts with palisades. And yet, the *polis* of the Homeric epoch can scarcely be considered a real city, because the bulk of its population was composed of farmers and herdsmen, not merchants and craftsmen. The *polis* was surrounded by uninhabited fields and mountains where the poet's eye saw only isolated huts of herdsmen and enclosures for domestic animals.

As a rule, the territory of each individual community did not extend very far. In most cases, they were limited to either a small mountain valley or some small island in the Aegean or the Ionian Sea. The boundary that separated one community from the next was usually the sea or the closest mountain range.

Thus, the Homeric poems describe all of Greece as a land fragmented into many small, self-governing units. Throughout many future centuries this fragmentation remained the most important characteristic of the political history of the Greek states. In Homeric times, the inhabitants of the next *polis* were regarded as enemies. They could be robbed, killed, and enslaved with impunity. Violent strife and border conflicts between neighboring communities were commonplace and frequently escalated to bloody and protracted wars. Stealing livestock from a neighboring community, for instance, could precipitate such a war. In the *Iliad* Nestor, king of Pylos and the most venerable of the Achaean heroes, relates his recollections about the feats he had performed as a young man. When he was less than twenty years old, he and his small troop of men attacked the region of Elis, Pylos's neighbor, and drove away a huge herd of sheep, goats, and cattle, and when, after a few days, the Eleans counterattacked Pylos, Nestor slew their chief hero and dispersed their entire army.

Strong traditions of clan society continued to play an important role in the social life of Homeric *poleis*. Clan unions, the so-called *phylae* and *phratriae*, were the foundation for the entire political and military organization of a community. The community militia was organized by *phylae* and *phratriae* during military campaigns and in battle. People gathered to discuss important questions by *phylae* and *phratriae*. According to Homer, a person who did not belong to a *phratria* was not protected by the law and could easily become a victim of violence or of other arbitrary actions. The ties between the various clan organizations were rather unstable, and the only reason why they stayed close together and lived within the walls of the same *polis* was because of a need to protect themselves from external enemies. In other matters the *phylae* and *phratriae* were completely independent; the community almost never intervened in their internal affairs.

Lineages and other groups continually quarreled with one another, and the barbarous custom of blood feud was commonly practiced. A person defiled by murder had to flee to a foreign land in order to escape persecution by the relatives of his victim. Among the heroes of the Homeric poems we frequently see such exiles who had left their homelands because of blood feuds and found refuge in the households of other kings. Thus, Patroclus, Achilles' best friend, in his early youth accidentally killed one of his playmates while throwing dice. He was forced to leave his native Locris and to flee north to Thessaly. There, he was kindly received by Achilles' father. A murderer who was wealthy enough could pay ransom to the relatives of the victim. Such a fine consisted of cattle or metal in ingots. An interesting scene of a judgment dealing with a fine (or blood money) for murder is found in Book XVIII of the *Iliad* (the poet includes this scene among those decorating the shield of Achilles, made by the Smith god Hephaestus):

> [497] Meanwhile the people were gathered in assembly, for there was a quarrel, and two men were wrangling about the blood-money for a man who had been killed, the one saying before the people that he had paid damages in full, and the other that he had not been paid. Each was trying to make his own case good, and the people took sides, each man backing the side he had taken; but the heralds kept them back, and the elders sat on their seats of stone in a solemn circle, holding their staves which the heralds put into their hands. Then they rose and each in his turn gave judgment, and there were two talents laid down, to be given to him whose judgment should be deemed the fairest.

As we can see, the authority of the community represented in this episode by the "elders" appears in the capacity of a simple court of arbitration, which acts as a reconciler of the litigants. Its verdict is not binding. In such circumstances, without a strong central power able to impose its authority on the opposing lineages, such quarrels quite frequently ended in bloody civil wars, putting the community on the verge of collapse. Such a critical situation appears in the closing scene of the *Odyssey*. Angered by the loss of their sons and brothers, their kinsmen rush to the estate of his father beyond the town, firmly resolved to avenge the dead and to eradicate the entire royal family. Both armed parties confront each other, and the battle begins. Only the intervention of the goddess Athena, patroness of Odysseus, stops the bloodshed and forces the contending foes to make peace.

Characterizing Greek society, Engels writes:

> Thus, in the Greek constitution of the heroic age, we see the old gentilic order as still a living force. But we also see the beginnings of its disintegration: father right, with transmis-

sion of the property to the children by which accumulation of wealth within the family was favored, and the family itself became a power against the gens.[6]

The monogamous patriarchal family, *oikos*, was the primary economic element in Homeric society. The gentilic, or tribal, property in land and other objects of ownership had, by all indications, already become outdated during the Mycenaean Period, although its vestiges continued to be present in Greece for a long time thereafter. Thus, as late as the beginning of the sixth century B.C., a law was enforced in many Greek states according to which the property of a deceased person who had no direct heirs passed on to his nearest relatives. It was strictly prohibited to bequeath property to nonrelatives.

The fundamental form of wealth for the Greeks of the Homeric period was land; and it was considered the property of the entire community. From time to time the community land was redistributed. In theory, each community member had the right to receive an allotment. (Such an allotment was called *klēros* in Greek; i.e., a "lot," because they were distributed, at least originally, by casting lots.) In practice, however, this system of land tenure did not prevent the enrichment of certain community members or the ruin of others. Homer already knew that there were rich people who had many allotments in the community (*polyklēroi*) and others with no land at all (*aklēroi*). Obviously, there were poor peasants who had no resources with which to run an economy even on their own small allotment. In desperation they ceded their land to rich neighbors and became landless hired hands, or *thētes*. The impoverished *thētes* wandered in villages, begging for alms or hiring themselves out for work in wealthy households under most difficult conditions in order to survive. One of Penelope's suitors, Eurymachus, turns to Odysseus, who has returned home unrecognized, having disguised himself as a beggar, and says:

> Stranger, will you work as a servant, if I send you to the wolds and see that you are well paid? Can you build a stone fence, or plant a tree? I will have you fed all year round, and will find you in shoes and clothing. Will you go, then? Not you; for you have got into bad ways, and do not want to work; you had rather fill your belly by going round the country begging. (*Odyssey* XVIII, 356)

Severed from his community and deprived of the support of his kin, a *thēs* was at the absolute mercy of the "strong men." Any of the latter could kill a vagrant or enslave him with impunity. When he

---

6. F. Engels, *The Origin of the Family, Private Property and State*, ed. by E. B. Leacock (New York: International Publishers, 1972), p. 169.

hired himself out for work, he could be dismissed without receiving the negotiated payment, and even maimed, should he be too persistent in demanding what was his due. The situation of a *thēs* was not much different from that of a slave and possibly even worse, because he was deprived of the protection given a slave by his master. The *thētes* were at the bottom of the social scale. At the top, we see the dominating group of the gentilic elite, people who in Homer's usage are called "the best" (*aristoi,* hence "aristocracy") or the "good," "well-born" (*agathoi*), as opposed to the "bad" or "lowborn" (*kakoi*), that is, the rest of the community members. In the poet's mind, a natural aristocrat is far superior to any commoner in every aspect, intellectually as well as physically. In the *Iliad* the aristocratic Odysseus disdainfully addresses a "man of the people," striking him with his staff as he speaks (the scene is a meeting of the Achaean assembly of people):

"Sirrah, hold your peace, and listen to better men than yourself. You are a coward and no soldier; you are nobody either in fight or in council." (*Iliad* II, 198)

The aristocrats laid claim to their special and privileged social position on the basis of their supposed divine origin. For this reason Homer usually calls them "divine" or "godlike." Many aristocratic families traced their lineage directly to one of the Olympian gods, or to Zeus himself (the supreme Olympian), not only during the Homeric period, but also in a much later time (in classical Athens of the fifth to fourth centuries B.C., for example).

Of course, the real source of the aristocracy's power was not its kinship to the gods but its great wealth, which set apart their social group from the common members of the community. Nobility and wealth are two almost inseparable concepts for Homer. An aristocratic person must be wealthy, and conversely, a rich person must necessarily be a noble man. Aristocrats boast before the common folk and before one another about their vast fields, innumerable herds of cattle, and rich stores of iron, bronze, and precious metals. Thus, in the words of the swineherd Eumaeus, his master Odysseus owned twelve herds of oxen alone and about the same number of pigs, sheep, and goats.

An aristocratic *oikos* stood out among the families of the other community members not only because of its wealth but also because of its size. It included the adult sons of the head of the family, their wives and children, as well as slaves and the so-called servants. (As a rule, the servants were aliens, adopted by the household out of mercy, and had the status of junior family members.) In addition, each noble family had an entire staff of followers and clients among the poorer peasants who had become dependent on an aristocratic benefactor when they were offered material support in difficult times or who had simply sought the patronage of a "strong" person. In case of need, a wealthy nobleman could assemble an armed troop of his dependents for his current enterprise of piracy or use them in some internecine struggle within his community.

The economic might of the aristocracy ensured their dominance in all affairs of the community, in war as well as in peacetime. The decisive role of the aristocrats on the battlefield was theirs simply by virtue of the fact that only a wealthy and noble person was able to acquire all the necessary heavy military gear (bronze helmet with crest, armor, greaves, heavy bronze-clad ox-hide shield). Weapons were very costly. Only the wealthiest of the community members could afford a battle horse. The natural environment and the lack of rich grazing land in Greece were not favorable for horse breeding. We must also add that only a man with good athletic training could hope to become proficient in handling the weapons of that time. This included systematic running, throwing the javelin and discus, and horse riding. Such men could be found only among the nobility. A common peasant, busy from sunrise to sunset with heavy physical labor, had no spare time to engage in sports. Athletics therefore remained a prerogative of the aristocracy in Greece for a long time. In battle the aristocrats, clad in heavy armor and advancing on foot or horseback (in chariots, in Homer's poems), took the front positions in the ranks of the community militia; the "common people" were massed together in no particular order. The rank-and-file soldiers wore cheap felt armor and carried lightweight shields, bows, and darts. When the two opponents approached one another, the *promachoi* (literally, "those fighting in the front," as Homer calls the warrior-aristocrats) advanced ahead of the ranks and fought in single combat. The poorly armed masses rarely engaged in the actual fighting, and the outcome of a battle was usually decided by the *promachoi*.

In ancient times the position, or ranking, that a man occupied in the battle line usually determined his status in society. By being the decisive force on the battlefield, the Homeric aristocracy also claimed a leading role in the political life of the community. As we already mentioned, the aristocrats treated the common community members contemptuously as people who were "nobody either in fight or in council." In the presence of noblemen, "common men" had to stay respectfully silent and listen to what the "best people" had to say. It was considered that their intellectual capacity was insufficient to make reasonable judgments in matters of "state." As a rule, kings and heroes of "noble birth" addressed people's assemblies, as is frequently mentioned in the poems. The populace attending these debates could express their opinion by exclamations or with the clatter of their weapons (when the meeting took place in a military situation). They were not unlike a theater audience or fans in a stadium and usually did not participate in the discussion proper. Only in one instance does Homer make an exception and present a representative of the masses with the opportunity to speak out. The assembly of the Achaean army, which is besieging Troy, debates the vital question affecting everyone: whether to continue the war, which in its tenth year is without any prospect of victory or to board the ships and head back home to Greece with the entire army. Unexpectedly, a common warrior, Thersites, addresses the meeting. The poet, obviously sympathizing with the noblemen, does not spare foul words and debasing epithets in portraying this "troublemaker":

> He was the ugliest man of all those that came before Troy— bandy-legged, lame of one foot, with his two shoulders rounded and hunched over his chest. His head ran up to a point, but there was little hair on top of it. (*Iliad* II, 212)

Moreover, he is an upstart and a loudmouth who disturbs the order of the meeting with no regard for the age-old rules of behavior, according to which he and persons of his position must not address the people:

> a man of many words, and those unseemly; a monger of sedition, a railer against all who were in authority, who cared not what he said, so that he might set the Achaeans in a laugh. (*Iliad* II, 212)

Thersites boldly exposes the greed and self-interest of the supreme commander of the Achaean army, Agamemnon, and urges everyone to sail immediately toward home, letting the proud *basileus* fight the Trojans alone:

> On this he beat with his staff about the back and shoulders till he dropped and fell a-weeping. The golden sceptre raised a bloody weal on his back, so he sat down frightened and in pain, looking foolish as he wiped the tears from his eyes. The people were sorry for him, yet they laughed heartily. (*Iliad* II, 265)

This curious episode illustrates the real relationship between the people and the aristocracy in the Homeric community. As soon as a common man uttered a single word in defiance of the will of the ruling elite, he was immediately stifled, and those in authority did not shrink even from physical reprisals. The scene with Thersites and many other episodes found in Homer's poems eloquently demonstrate the thorough decay and degeneration of the primitive democracy. The people's assembly, convoked to serve as the natural voice of the majority, appears here as a docile tool in the hands of a small group of kings. Although Thersites certainly expresses the thoughts of the majority of the Achaean army, he becomes their laughingstock. We see how the Achaeans, who moments before ran in panic to their ships so that they might return home as quickly as possible, vociferously welcome Odysseus's proposal to remain in place and continue the war to victory.

The will of the people, even when openly and directly expressed, by no means had legal force for a strong and willful aristocrat who was backed by many servants and partisans ready to support him. Thus, in spite of the clearly manifest will of the entire Achaean army, Agamemnon refuses to return Chryseis to her father, the old priest of Apollo. She had fallen to Agamemnon's lot when the loot was divided. This brings innumerable misfortunes upon the entire army: the angered god Apollo inflicts a terrible plague on the Achaeans that kills people and livestock.

When encountering open resistance to their schemes, the "best people" could simply dismiss the assembly. This recourse is adopted by Penelope's suitors in the *Odyssey*. The people's assembly had not been convoked since Odysseus sailed with his troops to Troy. (Twenty years had passed since then.) Finally, Telemachus, son of the hero, at last summons the citizens in the square to complain about the outrageous deeds being committed by the suitors in his house. (To force Penelope into marrying one of them, they consume cattle and wine belonging to Odysseus during their feasts.) The people gather, but at their first attempt to restrain the suitors, the suitors order the people of Ithaca to disperse and go home, and they dutifully obey. The people's assembly counts here for even less than in the scene with Thersites.

In the most dramatic and tense passages of the *Iliad* and the *Odyssey*, the people remain passive and mute witnesses to the violent collisions between the principal protagonists of the poems. (Such is the scene of the "quarrel among kings" in the first book of the *Iliad*.) Only in a few episodes of the *Odyssey*, written later, do the people appear as an awesome, chastising force that furiously hurls its anger upon whomever transgresses their will. Thus, the people of Ithaca assemble to deal with Odysseus and to avenge his slaying of the suitors, the pick of Ithaca's youth. However, the people do not act in such critical situations on their own but in reaction to the instigations of some aristocrat who seeks to settle accounts with his enemies. In this case, the instigator is Eupeithes, father of the slain leader of the suitors, Antinous. Eupeithes was once saved by Odysseus from an enraged mob of

Ithaca's citizens who attempted to plunder his house and to kill him for a crime he had committed against the community. The people's assembly thus became an arena used by contending groups of the aristocracy to settle accounts. Each faction tried to sway the people to their side and to represent their group's desire as the will of the entire community.

In considering all these facts, we must admit that the political organization of Homeric society was very far from being a genuine democracy. The real power was vested at that time in the hands of the most powerful and influential representatives of the gentilic nobility, whom Homer calls *basileis*. In literary works of later Greek authors *basileus* usually means "king," as in "king of Persia" or "king of Macedonia." Homer's *basileis* indeed have the appearance of kings. A *basileus* was recognized by the symbols of royal majesty: a scepter and a purple garment. "Scepter bearers" was the common epithet the poet used to characterize the *basileis*. They are also called "born of Zeus" or "reared by Zeus," epithets designed to show the special favor accorded them by the supreme Olympian. The *basileis* are endowed with the exclusive right to preserve and interpret laws, which was granted to them, believes the poet, by Zeus himself. Nestor addresses Agamemnon: "By glory, radiant son of Atreus, you are king of many nations; the Olympian handed you the scepter and the laws so you may judge and counsel the people."

In war, a *basileus* stood at the head of the troops and had to be the first in battle, setting an example of valor for his warriors. During great popular festivities, the *basileis* performed sacrifices to the gods and prayed to them for the well-being and prosperity of the entire community. In exchange for all this, the people had to honor the "kings" with gifts: an honorary share of wine and meat during banquets, the best and largest lot of land during the reallotment of community land, and so on. These "gifts" were formally regarded as voluntary grants or honors that a *basileus* received from the people in reward for his military valor (or for his fairness as a judge). In practice, however, this ancient custom frequently provided the king with a convenient excuse for extortion on supposedly legal grounds. Agamemnon is presented in such a light as a "king devouring the people" in the initial books of the *Iliad*.

But despite all the might and wealth of the *basileis*, their power cannot be considered royal in the strict sense. Consequently, the common use of the word *king* for the Greek *basileus* in modern translations can be accepted only as a convention. In the views of Marx and Engels,[7]

7. See ibid., pp. 167–69, where Engels cites Marx's viewpoint.

which concur with those of the prominent American ethnographer L. H. Morgan, a *basileus* was a tribal or clan chief. This assumption helps to explain a circumstance that, at first glance, is very strange. It was observed a long time ago that each Homeric *polis* had several persons holding the title of *basileus*, who each, so it seems, enjoyed all the privileges accorded this position. Thus, the fairy-tale island of the Phaecaeans, where Odysseus arrives during his wanderings, is ruled by thirteen "glorious *basileis*." One of them, Alcinous, kindly welcomes the wandering hero into his home and helps him to return to his homeland. We may assume that each *basileus* headed one of the thirteen *phylae* and *phratriae* that constituted the Phaecaean *demos*. Athens, even during a much later time, had four so-called *phylobasileis*, corresponding to the number of the ancient *phylae* (tribes) that constituted the Athenian nation.

Within the boundaries of his *phyle* or *phratria* a *basileus* discharged mainly priestly functions, since he headed the tribal cults. (Each tribal union had its special patron god.) As a group, the *basileis* formed something resembling a ruling collegium or council and jointly decided all matters of government before submitting the outcome for ratification to the people's assembly. (This formality was very frequently ignored.) From time to time, all the *basileis* of the community congregated in the town square (*agora*) and tried lawsuits in the presence of all the people. Such a scene is depicted, as we mentioned earlier, on Achilles' shield.[8]

In wartime one of the *basileis* (sometimes two) was chosen during the people's assembly to fill the position of commander of the community's militia. In military campaigns and in battles the commanders wielded vast powers, including the right of life and death over the cowardly and disobedient. But once the campaign was at an end, he usually renounced these powers. There were cases, however, when a commander who distinguished himself with deeds of prowess and who also stood out among the other *basileis* on account of his wealth and the noble lineage of his family succeeded in prolonging his extraordinary powers. When his military function was coupled with his function of supreme priest and principal judge, he became an actual king; that is, head of the community. Alcinous holds such a position among the Phaecaean *basileis*, as does Odysseus among the *basileis* of Ithaca and Agamemnon among the chiefs of the Achaean army. The position of a supreme *basileus*, however, was not very secure. Only a few managed to hold onto their power for long, and they were even less likely to pass it on to their offspring. This was usually precluded

8. The judges are called "elders" (*gerontes* in this episode). However, this term is used in the poems as a synonym for *basileis*.

by the rivalry and hostile intrigues of the other *basileis*, who tried in every possible way to prevent their rival from acquiring inordinate power.

A typical case history illustrating the political relationships in Homeric times is represented by the situation that develops during the absence of Odysseus from his native island of Ithaca. The power on the island is seized by the suitors of Odysseus's wife, Penelope. The one to succeed in overcoming her obstinacy is to be the heir of the missing Odysseus. Odysseus has a son, Telemachus, who is already of age. One would think that he would be his father's lawful heir and would occupy the vacant "royal throne." Yet, Telemachus does not voice any pretensions to the throne. To be sure, he admits when conversing with the suitors that, on the whole, "it is no bad thing to be a chief, for it brings both riches and honour" (*Odyssey* I, 388). But a strange reservation follows: "there are many men in Ithaca both old and young, and some other may take the lead among them." (The original Greek reads "many *basileis*, young and old.") Since Odysseus is no more, one of them may be chosen: "Nevertheless I will be chief in my own house, and will rule those [slaves] whom Odysseus has won for me" (*Odyssey* I, 388). We get the impression that Telemachus values his property much more than the "royal" power and the honors flowing from it.

It is also typical that neither Telemachus nor Odysseus himself ever accuse the suitors of usurpation, of seizing power illegally, of treason to the "head of state," and other such crimes. Addressing the suitors with a brief accusatory statement, Odysseus blames them only for stealing his property, for the violence inflicted on his female slaves, and for their attempt to force his wife into an unlawful marriage, without saying a word about his insulted "royal dignity" or the attempt on his power.

Apparently, the usurpation of "royal power" was not considered a crime, because there were no norms or laws establishing succession to the throne. In practice, any of the tribal or clan leaders (*basileis*) could become king, as could even any rich and noble person who managed to gain a sufficient number of supporters in the people's assembly.[9] However, the mere act of proclaiming a new king did not firmly guarantee his power. After a short time, the people could "change their minds" and hand the throne over to another pretender. (In reality, the decision did not of course depend on the will of the people but on

9. The confirmation of a new king in his office usually took the form of an agreement between the pretender and the people, whereby he promised to follow the customary law and not to step out of the bounds of power established by custom. Such agreements were made even in later times, in Sparta and in some other Greek states.

the competing groups of the elite.) Consequently, monarchy did not yet exist as a fully developed and firmly rooted institution.[10]

The Homeric period occupies a special place in Greek history.[11] The class society and the state, which already existed in Greece during the golden age of the Mycenaean civilization, are here born again, but on a different scale and in different forms. In many aspects, it was a time of decline and cultural stagnation. But it was also a time when Greece was gathering strength and was on the threshold of an energetic revival. Behind the outward appearance of quietude and immobility, a stubborn struggle between the new and old raged in Homeric society. An intense dislocation of traditional values and customs of the gentilic order took place together with a no less intense process of class and state formation. Extremely important for the future development of Greek society was the radical renewal of the technological base that the Homeric age witnessed. This was primarily reflected by the widespread use of iron and its introduction in industry. All these important advances paved the way for the transition of the Greek *poleis* toward an entirely new path of historical development. On this new road, in the course of the next three or four centuries, they were able to reach heights of cultural and social progress heretofore unseen in human history, leaving all their neighbors to the east and west far behind.

10. Only a few Greek *poleis,* including Sparta, had royal dynasties with firmly established rules of succession, although even here the royal power was strongly limited by law. In most of the other city-states, the office of "king of the community" had been eliminated in very ancient times (in the ninth or eighth centuries B.C.) and was replaced by an annually elected *archon,* as well as by other officials.

11. This period was typologically similar to the period of the judges (twelfth to eleventh centuries B.C.) in Palestine and to the period of the Aryan conquests in India (at about the same time). Editor's note (IMD).

17

Phoenician and Greek Colonization

YU. B. TSIRKIN

Many states in the ancient world undertook the establishment of new settlements in foreign lands. Such a settlement is called a *colony* (Latin, *colonia*, from *colo*, "I cultivate, inhabit"); the Greeks usually called it *apoikia* (from *apoikeo*, "to live or move away from home"). The city or the country of origin of a colony's founders was called a *metropolis* (Greek, "mother city"). Phoenician and Greek colonization played a particularly important role in the history of the ancient Mediterranean region.

Phoenician Colonization

As early as the second millennium B.C. Cretan and Mycenaean merchants frequented Phoenician cities and even established their trading stations there. At about the same time, the Phoenicians, in turn, settled on some of the Aegean Islands (from where they were later evicted by the Cretans) and worked the mines on the islands of Thasos. They even penetrated the Greek mainland, for example, to Thebes in Boeotia. Archaeological discoveries in Thebes indicate that relations existed with the east in the fourteenth century B.C., thus confirming that there is a grain of truth in the myths attributing the foundation of Thebes to the Phoenician Cadmus.[1] It is quite possible that during that time the Phoenicians also traveled to Sicily, but the Cretan and, later, Achaean domination of the seas restrained their expansion.

The situation changed at the end of the second millennium. At that time, the countries of the eastern Mediterranean experienced violent shocks caused by the downfall of kingdoms that had formerly seemed invincible and by great migrations of peoples. The invasion of the "Sea Peoples" also reached the Syro-Phoenician coast; among other cities, Sidon was destroyed, and the Sidonians fled to Tyre, although probably their city was soon restored. Although the great kingdoms declined, the small states revived more quickly. Tyre, which probably also had earlier contacts with the west, now completely took over the functions of the ruined city of Ugarit.

1. In the Phoenician language *qadm* means "east." Editor's note (IMD).

The flight of the Sidonians and others to Tyre probably contributed to the importance and power of this town, but it also would have increased demographic stress. Because the productive forces were at that time at a comparatively low level, the only solution to the problem of overpopulation would have been to force the emigration of some of the inhabitants across the sea. The collapse of Mycenaean domination in the eastern Mediterranean opened up new possibilities for Tyre. Its ruling circles capitalized on the situation by founding strong centers in foreign countries. These bases were needed for renewing and broadening trade and for exiling the more unruly and discontented elements from the *metropolis*.

The first stage of Tyrian colonization occurred in the second half of the twelfth and first part of the eleventh centuries B.C. The direction was twofold. One route led toward the island of Rhodes and then, along the western coast of Asia Minor, toward the island of Thasos with its gold mines; another led from Rhodes along the southern edge of the Aegean archipelago toward Sicily, thence to the northern promontory of Africa, and then at last along the northern African coast toward southern Spain. The gold of Thasos and the silver of Spain were two main goals of the colonists, but on the way there the Phoenicians founded intermediary bases; for example, on the island of Melos in the Aegean; on Cytheros, south of the Peloponnesus; on the eastern and southern coasts of Sicily; and in northern Africa (in Utica). A Graeco-Roman legend tells of the Tyrians thrice attempting to settle in southern Spain—probably meeting the resistance of the local population. Only on their third attempt were the Phoenicians able to found a town on a small island near the coast, west of the Pillars of Hercules (the modern Straits of Gibraltar). The town was characteristically called Gadir "fortress wall", the Romans called it Gades, and now it is known as Cadiz. Probably during these attempts to settle in Spain, they founded Lixus in northwestern Africa, also to the west of the Pillars of Hercules.

At this stage Phoenician colonization mainly had a commercial character. The principal materials that the Phoenicians desired were precious wares; what they sold in exchange were oil, knickknacks, products of the sea, and textiles—all goods that leave little archaeological trace. The trading was probably conducted via silent exchange, each party exposing their wares until the other party agreed to take them. But in a few cases the Phoenicians themselves could exploit the mines, as on Thasos.

The Phoenicians founded trading posts, temporary trading stations, and anchorages. A very important role was played by temples, whose founding not uncommonly preceded the emergence of the cities (as in Gadir and in Lixus); no international law existed at that time, and a temple probably gave the merchants a feeling of security and divine protection. Some temples, as that on Thasos, could also function as organizers of production. But already at that early time actual towns with stable populations were emerging. Such towns were Gadir in Spain and Utica in Africa.

There was an interval of about two centuries between the first and the second stage of Phoenician colonization. By the second stage, the Iron Age economies had so developed that they needed a great amount of metals—not only precious ones but also those for immediate use in production. The economic base of the first empires in the Near East was the unification under a single authority of different but complementary economic regions. Colonization enabled the transfer to the imperial economy of those sources of raw material that were beyond the reach of the military expansion of the imperial rulers. From the end of the second millennium B.C., the main point of contact between the Orient and the far west was Tyre.

A sociopolitical struggle arose within Tyre in the ninth century B.C. The rural population rebelled, and the slaves killed their masters. Rulers changed rapidly in Tyre, due to rivalry within the nobility. This gave a new stimulus to colonization.

Its beginning probably should be dated to the reign of one of the usurpers, Ithoba'l (second quarter of the ninth century B.C.). This ruler was interested in founding new towns in order to resettle his potential enemies there, including the supporters of the former dynasty. A legend ascribes to him the foundation of Bothrys in Phoenicia itself and Ausa in Africa.

The possibilities of Phoenician expansion in the eastern Mediterranean were limited. New great centralized empires had gained strength, and in the Aegean the Greeks and the Thracians had managed to oust the Phoenicians from the islands they formerly had held. In Greece itself, during the process of formation of the *poleis*, the Phoenicians could find no niche for themselves. The Phoenicians settled in the towns, but they did not form any specific organizations of their own and soon became hellenized. Sometimes they founded special quarters within foreign cities to serve as trading stations, such as in Memphis. In the eastern Mediterranean at this time, the Phoenicians founded proper colonies only on the south coast of Cyprus. The main field of Phoenician colonization during this second stage of development was the western Mediterranean.

The island of Sardinia now fell under Phoenician influence. Sardinia was important for its strategic location, guarding the way to central Italy, Corsica, and Gaul and also, via the Balearic Islands, to

Spain. It was also rich in metals and had a fertile soil. During the ninth century a number of Phoenician towns appeared on the southern and western coasts of Sardinia: Nora, Sulci, Bithia, and Tharros. At a comparatively early date the Phoenicians also gained a foothold in the center of the island.

The minor islands of Melita and Gaulus (now Malta and Gozo), which were situated between Sicily and Africa, offered another new field for Phoenician colonization. These islands served as the main connecting links between the *metropolis* and the westernmost parts of the Phoenician world.

The strengthening of the contacts between the Phoenicians and southern Spain made it necessary to found new strong points on the Iberian Peninsula. During the eighth and seventh centuries, the Phoenicians founded a number of settlements, varying in size and importance, on the southern coast of the peninsula east of the Pillars of Hercules, that is, on the Mediterranean coast. Some of them were relatively large cities, like Malaca (now Málaga) and Sexi; others were small, and we do not know their ancient names. Archaeologists refer to the latter by the names of the modern nearby villages, such as Toscaneo and Chorreras.

With the beginning of the Greek colonization of Sicily in the eighth century B.C., the Phoenicians left the southern and eastern coasts and concentrated themselves in the western part of the island. The cities founded here—Motya, Soloeis, and Panormus—guaranteed connections with the earlier colonized regions of Sardinia and Africa.

Meanwhile, in the central part of North Africa where Utica had earlier been founded, a number of Phoenician towns, among them the famous city of Carthage, now appeared. In northwestern Africa, south of Lixus, the Phoenicians settled around a bay to which the Greeks gave the name of Emporicus, the "Trading Bay."

The second stage of Phoenician colonization lasted from the ninth through the seventh centuries B.C., reaching its peak in the second half of the ninth century. It was a period when the Tyrians began colonizing Sardinia and dramatically increased their presence in Africa, founding Carthage and, possibly, other towns. The sphere of their colonization had now shifted: it included the far west of Sicily, southern and western Sardinia, southern Spain, the islands Melita and Gaulus, and the central and far western part of North Africa. The main goal was the same as before; namely, the acquisition of metals, not just gold and silver but also metals needed for production. Another aim of the colonization at this stage was the acquisition of land: the Phoenicians gravitated more and more from Spain to the center of the Mediterranean basin: to fertile Sardinia and the promontory of Tunis in North Africa, famous for its fecund earth. Tyre apparently remained the only metropolis (the participation of the Sidonians has not been proved), but the number of emigrants grew.

The character of the colonization itself also changed. Crafts, agriculture, and, of course, fishing developed in the colonies. The number of cities increased. Small settlements also emerged. Some specialized in a particular branch of economy. The Phoenicians also began to explore the hinterland of some of their colonies.

The character of the relations between the colonists and the indigenous population changed. The latter had by that time developed sufficiently to enter into the entire range of economic, political, and cultural contacts with the foreigners. A process of feedback began that led to the creation of local variants of the Phoenician culture. Thus, the local inhabitants came to be an important component of the process of colonization.

The emergence of the colonies and to a great extent their trade were indebted to the help or even the initiative of the metropolitan government. It was not the ships of Tyrian merchants but those of King Hiram of Tyre that sailed to far-off Tarshish (Tartessus) in southern Spain. Thus, the emerging cities were regarded as parts of the Tyrian Empire, although, at present, it is difficult to establish the degree and forms of their dependence on the *metropolis*. However, it is known that a governor set up by the king of Tyre was resident in Kition on the island of Cyprus and that an attempt by Utica to stop paying tribute called forth a punitive expedition from Tyre. With the gradual decline of Tyre, its empire weakened, and its domination became more or less nominal.

Carthage was founded under very special circumstances. According to the legend, a group of Tyrian aristocrats headed by the king's sister Elissa secretly fled from Tyre to Africa after having been defeated in a political struggle. At a place not too far from Utica, on the hill of Byrsa in the vicinity of an old sanctuary, they founded a city they called *Qart-ḥadasht*, the "New City," Carchedon of the Greeks, Carthage of the Romans. Because Carthage was not founded by the Tyrian government, it was never dependent on Tyre, although the spiritual ties with the *metropolis* were strong as long as Carthage existed.

An Orientalizing Civilization: Tartessus

The Phoenician colonies linked the civilized countries of the eastern Mediterranean with the usually less developed peoples of the central and western Mediterranean and the areas facing the Atlantic Ocean. But when the local populations, caught up in this process, had reached a relatively high level of economic and social development, there emerged the phenomenon of an "orientalizing civilization." The local aristocracy, having reached a high standing relative to their compatriots, was no longer content to adhere to the traditional forms of culture. Not having, so far, developed their own alternative forms, these men (or, more precisely, the artisans serving them) borrowed Oriental forms. In some cases such borrowings were not just of art forms but also of economic institutions.

The contacts of Greece with the Orient were not through the Phoenicians alone. The orientalizing culture in Hellas shows traces of influence from Asia Minor. The Phoenicians did play an important part in the emerging culture of Etruria. (If we adopt the hypothesis of the Oriental origin of the Etruscans themselves, then they must have brought some Oriental traits from their eastern homeland with them. However, this hypothesis is far from being proved and is not generally accepted.) The orientalizing civilization in southern Spain, in the Tartessian kingdom of the eighth to sixth centuries B.C., certainly owes its origin specifically to the Phoenicians.

Contacts between the Phoenicians and the southern Iberian Peninsula date from the first stage of the Phoenician colonization. At that period, the local inhabitants were not yet ready for establishing active mutual relations.

At the end of the second millennium, the southwestern part of Spain was dominated by the so-called Southwestern Bronze Culture. These people may have been related to the present-day Basques. This society shows little evidence of social stratification, and its structure was probably gentilic. Their economy was not so much in contact with that of the foreigners coming from the east as with those of the tribes of northwestern Europe. In the beginning of the first millennium B.C., new tribes appeared here, possibly speaking an Indo-European language. They brought a new type of pottery and new metallurgical and metalworking techniques. The new culture overlaid the old substratum, and the Tartessian ethnos was probably the result of a merger between the newcomers and the aboriginal population.

The contacts between the Tartessians and Phoenicians were at first sporadic; with time, they intensified and contributed to the further social development of the Tartessians. In the second half of the eighth century B.C., the Tartessian kingdom emerged in southern Spain. It included a number of different tribes at various levels of socioeconomic development. As to the Tartessians proper, the social stratification among them was already considerable. The elite consisted of a military aristocracy; the rest of society were considered by a Roman author to have constituted the "plebs" The "plebs" included the miners and craftsmen and probably the agriculturalists. Slaves no doubt also existed in the Tartessian kingdom, but we have no specific information on slavery. The city seems to have been the residence of the aristocracy, who dominated the rural countryside, but it was also the center of the organization of the plebs. This reminds one of Homeric society. The geometric style of decoration on the Tartessian funerary stelae and the repertory of the designs also remind one of the geometric style in the art of Homeric Greece.

However, as opposed to the late Homeric society in Hellas, the city of Tartessus was part of a broad federation: the Tartessian kingdom. To judge from the very scanty date of the sources, the king seems to have enjoyed supreme authority over the land of the Tartessians themselves and of their dependent tribes.

One may state that in southern Spain an early state had formed, which, of course, can in no way be compared with the great empires of the Near East. The Tartessian kingdom dominated the tribes of southern Spain, where the Tartessians had founded their own strongholds. These probably enabled them to control their dependents.

The economic base of the Tartessian kingdom was the mining and processing of metals and the great agricultural wealth of the Baetis River valley (present-day Guadalquivir). This enabled the Tartessians to conduct an active trade with the Phoenicians. The emergence of the state favored the development of mining and metallurgy, for those products the Phoenicians opened a capacious market in the Near East. As to the Tartessians themselves, they took over the oriental methods of smelting and founding ore. The demands of the Phoenician merchants made the Tartessians also seek wares which were not produced domestically, and this stimulated external trade. The Tartessians borrowed from the Phoenicians the potter's wheel, building techniques, olive cultivation, and the production of olive oil.

The Tartessian oligarchy now felt a need for newer forms of art, and they found them through the Phoenicians, while the local craftsmen lent certain motifs to those of the colonists. The Tartessians evolved their own writing system, certainly under Phoenician influence, and also borrowed some Phoenician cults and rites.

Thus, in Tartessus there emerged a syncretic orientalizing civilization. The main recipients of the Oriental influence were the aristocrats and those artisans who catered to them. Other artisans and the agricultural population were hardly influenced by the Phoenicians, these groups of the "plebs" keeping more to their own native culture.

Although orientalized to a degree, the Tartessian kingdom also maintained features of their own civilization. Some cultural phenomena, although originally borrowed from the Phoenicians, experienced a further independent development, as seen, for example, with certain types of pottery. Also the archaic handmade pottery was retained by the Tartessians. Their battle chariots were of an original European, not Oriental, type. Tartessian burial rites differed from those of the Phoenicians, although the dead were often given Phoenician amulets and vessels for their sojourn in the hereafter.

About 600 B.C. Greek colonies began to appear on the Tartessian shore. Although no Greek influence can be traced in the Tartessian culture, there were political and economic connections with the Greeks, and Tartessus entered into the complicated interplay of forces in the western Mediterranean. The result was that the Tartessian kingdom fell asunder, probably in the early fifth century B.C. under the onslaught of the Carthaginians.

Greek Colonization

The Greeks began their colonial expansion later than the Phoenicians. The eighth to sixth centuries B.C. mark the golden age of Greek colonizing activity. This period coincides with the Archaic Period of Greek history, the time when the ancient Greek *polis* was developing. We must search for the reasons behind Greek colonization in the circumstances prevailing in Greece during that time.

Among the causes we must first of all mention the general law of the correspondence of population size with the overall level of production forces. According to K. Marx, in the Greek and Roman world, an insufficient development of the productive forces made the granting of civil rights dependent upon a certain quantitative correlation that could not be ignored. The only alternative was forced emigration. This was the main reason for all cases of colonization in antiquity, although in every case there were also specific reasons.

The same is true of the great Greek colonization. Typical of Greece at all times was the poor development of agricultural technology, primitive methods of soil cultivation, and low fertility or small size of many of the regions in Greece. This led to a situation where part of the population was unable to subsist in the homeland. In the Archaic Period certain specific social causes also played an important role.

As the pre-urban society decayed, much of the land was usurped by the aristocracy, which misused its position as heads of clan communes; agriculturalists were forced to leave the *polis* if they did not wish to lose not only their land but also their free status. As their economic conditions deteriorated, debt-bondage increased. Moreover, the development of chattel slavery made it still more difficult for the peasants to find work in the towns. Of course, some of them found a way to adjust to the new conditions; that was why the Hellenic crafts and trades could continue to grow. But a great number of people found no other way out except by emigrating to foreign countries. In cities where trade was developing, the merchants' desire to gain a foothold along the trade routes and to become established was an important reason for setting up colonies. Merchants felt secure and protected only in cities connected with the *metropolis* by religious and economic ties. Such cities became their base for trading with the local population on the road to the more important trading centers. Initially, the colonies bought merchandise mainly from their countrymen who remained in the *metropolis*. They received merchants arriving from the *metropolis* and offered their goods to the local inhabitants.

Another significant factor in the colonial movement was the political struggle raging in the *metropolis*. During the period when the *polis* was emerging, this struggle reached a ferocity never seen before and was frequently accompanied by a most barbarous terror. In Miletus, during the ascendancy of the democrats, for example, the children of their adversaries were trampled to death by bulls, and the subsequently victorious aristocrats burned the democrats together with their children. In such situations, by no means rare, the defeated faction had only two alternatives: death at home or emigration to some distant land.

In the course of the development of Greek society during the Archaic Period, there emerged groups of low social standing who frequently became founders of colonies. Thus, once the Parthenii in Sparta, who lacked civil rights, failed in their attempt to gain legal equality with the Spartans, they founded Tarentum in Italy.

Another important reason for emigrating could have been defeat in war. The defeated had to choose between becoming a dependent population or emigrating. The latter was the course chosen by the Messenians after their defeat by Sparta, when they sailed to the west. Some of the citizens of Phoenicia, who did not want to submit to the Persian king, did the same.

The complex interaction of all these factors created a picture specially characteristic of the Archaic Period, the epoch of the creation of the Greek *polis*. Perhaps the most important factors were the dissolution of gentilic (clan) ties, which involved a "release" of a mass of peasantry, and the development of commodity-money relations, which led to a need for new markets and new sources of slave labor. When the gentilic relations became a feature of the past and the *polis* received its final form, the political struggle acquired new forms. The time of the great colonization came to an end. Emigration might still be necessary, but for different reasons.

Different regions, districts, and cities of Hellas took part in the great colonization; some, like Achaea, were less developed and mainly agrarian, and others, like the trading industrial centers of Miletus and Phocaea, were more advanced. According to the character of the *metropolis,* the colonial expansion was dominated by an agrarian or a commercial and industrial interest. The relative importance of one or the other factor should be explained by the degree of socioeconomic development of each particular *metropolis* and by the geographical environment of the colony and its relation to the neighboring population. Actually, colonization was neither purely agrarian nor commercial and industrial in its goal but always had a mixed character, with one of the two aspects predominating.

Trade during that period began to reach even the most backward regions of Greece, but we also know that all ancient cities were based on land ownership and agriculture. A colony could not survive without some land surrounding the settlement, no matter how meager. The colonists had their lots on this land, and sometimes lots were assigned to each colonist before the colonists had left the *metropolis*.

Such was the case during the preparation of the Corinthian expedition to Sicily, which resulted in the foundation of Syracuse. Which aspect of colonization was dominant would be decisive for the problem of relations with the local population. If the colony was to be mainly agrarian, then the colonists did not need collaboration with the indigenous population, which was even a hindrance. If the colony was founded for trading purposes, it was imperative that the surrounding population should be ready to trade with the Greeks, which meant that they had to be at a sufficiently high level of social development, but not too high. Where the Greeks encountered highly developed centralized kingdoms, the possibilities for founding new towns were extremely limited.

The preparatory stages of a colonization enterprise also depended on whether their predominant aim was commercial and industrial or agrarian. In order to find out what the settlers could expect in the new land, in some cases it was sufficient merely to reconnoiter the area; however, in other cases it was necessary to establish preliminary economic relations. The farmer-colonists sought fertile soil, whereas the traders looked for locations suitable for commerce, such as the estuaries of rivers which would enable them to reach the hinterland of the local tribes. The craftsmen were interested in the supply of the needed raw material. The Hellenes had some general rules for selecting places to settle. First of all, the site of the new town had to be on the seashore, or at least not far from it, because the sea was the only connection with the *metropolis*. The chosen place should be easily defensible, should have a supply of drinking water, and, if possible, should be surrounded by land that could feed the inhabitants of the colony. The land did not necessarily have to be suitable for grain cultivation, but it ought to be good, at least, for viticulture and olive plantations; that is, for foodstuffs customary for the Greeks, and yielding products that could be exchanged for goods needed by the settlers.

The colonists brought with them fire from the sacred hearth of their native city and, apparently, also some of the priests. The expedition was headed by an *oikistes,* who also became head of the new town. After his death, he might become the object of a cult.

Regardless of whether an expedition was at the initiative of the entire community or whether it was arranged just by some of its members, the colony still usually became an independent *polis.* In this, the Greek colonies differed from the Tyrian ones. There were, nevertheless, some exceptions. Corinth attempted to create a sea empire; the towns founded by the Corinthians were a guarantee of Corinth's domination over the western and northwestern sea routes. For some time Corinth ruled over the island of Corcyra. But the attempt to create a colonial empire failed. Although for a long time Corinth sent a deputy to Potidaea on the northern coast of the Aegean, this city was actually independent and sometimes acted against the interests of the *metropolis.*

Independence of the colonies was the rule, but they always felt spiritual ties with the *metropolis.* At a time when the concept of kin-structured society was still fresh in the minds of people, the inhabitants of the *metropolis* and the corresponding colony felt related, as people closely tied together in the face of an alien world. Embodying this kinship was the sacred hearth of the new city, which kept the fire taken from the hearth of the old city. As a rule, a colony did not wage war against its *metropolis;* usually cities founded by the same *metropolis* supported each other. Thus, even as late as the second century B.C., the inhabitants of Lampsacus in northwestern Asia Minor sought help from the citizens of Massalia (modern Marseilles, France) in their negotiations with Rome, because both cities were founded 500 years before by the same *metropolis,* Phocaea. Although a colony and its *metropolis* did not form alliances or share a common citizenship, any newly arrived metropolitan inhabitant became a citizen of the colony, and any colonist returning to his native hearth was reinstated to his original citizenship without much difficulty. Initially, the new colony copied the community the colonists had left, with the same *phylae* and the same state structure. But with time, as a result of internal social and political conflicts, everything could change, so that the paths of political development in the colonies could diverge completely from that of the *metropolis.*

Many colonies were established not by one but by several *metropoleis.* Thus in Italy, Cumae was established by the inhabitants of Chalcis and Eretria (both on the island of Euboea) and perhaps also by the Cymaeans of Asia Minor. Rhegium, also in Italy, was established by Chalcis and Messene; Gela, by people from Rhodes and Crete. But even if all the migrants sailed from the same city, it did not mean that they had all been its citizens. The populations of Greek cities were still quite small; nevertheless, quite a few *poleis* of Hellas founded several, even many, colonies. According to legend, Miletus was the *metropolis* for seventy-five colonies. It is difficult to imagine that the mother-city could have had enough people for so many migrations and still preserve its own existence. Therefore, it seems probable that these cities were transit distribution centers where the expeditions were initiated. The rule in such cases was, apparently, to consider the migration center as the *metropolis*. If there were several of them, the immediate initiator became the *metropolis*. (This was the case of Epidamnus, which was founded by Corcyra and Corinth: its *metropolis* was Corcyra.)

To start their lives in a new land, the colonists had to possess a certain degree of confidence in the future success of their enterprise. Therefore, besides reconnoitering the actual environment of a new region, they also sought to enlist divine patronage. Apollo pronounced his prophecy on the future of such expeditions at his oracle in Delphi. The temple of Apollo in Delphi, which enjoyed wide international connections and received a vast flow of information from all corners of the known world, gradually became a sort of regulatory center for the migrants and directed the flow of colonial expeditions.

The great Greek colonization proceeded in three main directions: (1) the western—the coast and islands of the Ionian Sea to northwestern Greece, Italy, Sicily, southern Gaul, and Spain; (2) the northeastern—the northern coast of the Aegean Sea, the Hellespont, the Propontis, the Thracian Bosporus, and the shores of the Black Sea (Pontus Euxinus); (3) the southeastern and southern—the southern coast of Asia Minor and Africa.

The first two directions were the main ones and were pioneered by people from the two Euboean cities: Chalcis and Eretria. In the first half of the eighth century B.C. these cities had already reached a high level of development. Situated on the coast of a strait that was a major sea lane connecting northern and middle Greece, these cities held an important share of trade in Greece. In addition, they possessed copper deposits and fairly fertile land, which was concentrated in the hands of the aristocrats. The importance of these two cities is illustrated by the fact that when war broke out between them in the last third of the eighth century B.C., many important Greek cities joined in, on one side or the other. Before this war, both cities jointly engaged in colonizing enterprises. In this they were followed by Corinth and Megara. These cities were important centers of trade and industry, but their lands were not fertile, so their inhabitants sailed overseas not only to trade but also to find and cultivate good land. This was the reason why rural dwellers from the village Tenea took part in the Corinthian colonization. Other centers of Greece followed the lead of the

first cities. By the eighth and early seventh centuries backward agricultural regions and communities, such as Locris, Achaea,[2] and Sparta,
also joined in the founding of colonies.

Initially, the Hellenes turned west, starting with the Euboeans. A
settlement of Chalcidians and Eretrians appeared in 774 B.C. on
Pitecussa, a small island near the western coast of central Italy. This
year can be considered the starting point of the great colonization.
After some fifty years, the Euboeans also settled on the mainland,
establishing Capua, which was followed by other cities, including
Naples. The region where these cities were established (Campania)
was the most fertile in Italy, but the Euboean colonization in the west,
especially the Chalcidian, was probably mainly oriented toward trade.
The Chaldcidians maintained active trade with the Etruscans and the
western Phoenicians. In order to gain control over the sea route between Etruria and Greece, they established their colonies on both
sides of the strait separating Italy from Sicily (Strait of Messina): at
Rhegium and Zancle. The Eretrians founded a colony on the island of
Corcyra, on the route from Greece to Italy and Sicily. The Euboeans
were also actively involved in colonizing the eastern coast of Sicily.

Syracuse became the major Greek city in Sicily. It was apparently
founded in 733 B.C. by a Corinthian expedition led by Archias, a
member of the ruling Bacchiad clan, who was forced to leave his city
because of discord at home. On their way to Sicily, the Corinthians
displaced the Eretrians from Corcyra. When they arrived in Sicily,
they founded a settlement on the small island of Ortygia off the Si-
cilian coast. it was only somewhat later that the city of Syracuse expanded to Sicily proper. For a long time Ortygia remained the
fortress and the administrative center for the city. Syracuse, which
had an excellent harbor, actively developed its crafts and, later, also
acquired fertile lands; soon it became a major center of Sicily and of
all western Greeks. A powerful state emerged under the rule of Syracuse that competed with Carthage and sought hegemony over all
western Greeks.

Other Greeks participated in the colonization of Sicily simultaneously with the Corinthians and Chalcidians. Thus the Megarians
founded Megara Hyblaea, to the north of Syracuse, and colonists
from Rhodes and Crete established Gela on the southern coast of the
island. Eventually, the Greek cities of Sicily themselves began founding more colonies on the island. In their colonization, the Greeks had
to fight the natives, the Siculi and the Sicani, as well as the Phoenicians, who later came under the rule of Carthage.

---

2. These are not the Mycenaean Achaeans, but the inhabitants of Achaea in the
northern part of the Peloponnesus.

The less developed agrarian towns and regions of Greece preferred the fertile land of southern Italy. Achaea founded Croton and Sybaris, a city which later became famous for its luxury; the Spartans founded Tarentum; the Locrians established Locri Epizephyrii. Among the more developed cities, only Colophon, in Asia Minor, dispatched an expedition to these parts. Under the threat of a Lydian invasion, some of the Colophonians sailed to Italy and founded Siris, a city whose wealth provoked the envy of the poet Archilochus, who compared the difficult life on the island of Thasos with the free and untrammeled existence of the citizens of Siris. Soon, so many cities appeared in southern Italy that this part of the Apennine Peninsula (sometimes even including Sicily) began to be called Magna Graecia.

Greek colonies were established in southern and middle Italy, as well as in Sicily, until the beginning of the seventh century B.C. After that time, new Hellenic cities were founded in these lands by already-established colonies. In the sixth century B.C., there were only isolated attempts by representatives from the original *metropoleis* to establish colonies in this part of the Mediterranean; men from Cnidus settled the Lipari Islands, and men from Samos settled in Dicaearchia.

The Phocaeans preferred to proceed farther west. At the turn of the seventh to sixth century, the Phocaean colonization followed two directions. The first was along the coast of Italy and then along the southern coast of Gaul and northeastern Spain. They founded a number of bases on the route from the *metropolis* to the colony of Massilia in Gaul and to Emporion in northeastern Spain. The second route passed along the "island bridge"—that is, via Corsica and the Balaeric Islands, directly to southeastern Spain, where the Tartessians had fought the Phoenicians for centuries and thus saw the Greeks as allies. With the approval of the king of Tartessus, the Phocaeans established a number of colonies, including Menestheou Limen, located beyond the Straits of Gibraltar, on the Atlantic coast. This settlement became the westernmost limit of Greek colonization.

As early as the eighth century B.C. the Chalcidians and Eretrians began colonization in the northeastern direction by settling on a large peninsula in the northwestern part of the Aegean Sea. The peninsula was named Chalcidice because the colonies were founded by the Chalcidians. To the east of Chalcidice, the inhabitants of Paros created their colony on the large island of Thasos, not far from the coast of Thrace. They later also attempted to settle on the Thracian coast. It seems that Thrace attracted them on account of its gold deposits. Among the Parians who settled on Thasos was the famous poet Archilochus, whose poems eloquently describe the difficult life of a colonist.

At the end of the eighth and beginning of the seventh centuries, the Greeks crossed the Hellespont and proceeded north. Here the *poleis* of eastern Greece (Samos, Chios, Mytilene, Phocaea, Miletus, Colophon), as well as Megara, began to play the leading role. Soon, a chain of Hellenic colonies spread along the European and Asiatic shores of the Hellespont, the Propontis, and into the Thracian Bosporus. Among these was the Megarian colony of Byzantium, located on the Bosporus, the strait that leads into the Black Sea; this city had a glorious future before it in late antiquity and in the Middle Ages.

The Iranian-speaking Scythians, who lived along the coast of the Black Sea, called this sea Akhshaina "Dark," but the Greek rendering of this name, Pontus Axinus, sounded like "Inhospitable Sea," in Greek. The lack of island chains, which in the Aegean could facilitate navigation, and perhaps also the suffering of the heroes whose adventures were thought to have taken place in this region, reinforced the Greek idea of the inhospitability of the waters and coasts of the Black Sea. Since the Hellenes believed in the magic of names, they felt that such a name boded ill. But during the seventh to sixth centuries B.C. they became convinced of the wealth of these shores and changed the local name to their own new name: Pontus Euxinus, "Hospitable Sea." By this name the Black Sea is known in history.

On the shores of the Black Sea colonies were founded mainly by the cities of Megara and Miletus. The Phocaeans also tried at first to gain a foothold there, but their colonies were soon taken over by the Milesians. The Megarians were active mainly near the outlet from the Thracian Bosporus, east and northeast of which appeared the cities of Heraclea Pontica, Mesembria, and Callatis. Only much later did the Megarians from Heraclea Pontica (on the southern coast of the Black Sea) cross the Pontus Euxinus and found Chersonesus Tauricus in southwestern Crimea (on the outskirts of modern Sevastopol).

Almost all the other cities of the southern, western, northern, and eastern Black Sea regions were founded by Miletus. The major Milesian colony on the southern coast was considered to be Sinope, the city that headed the Pontus union of *poleis*[3] (Pôṭ or Pûṭ in the Bible). Advancing along the western coast of Pontus Euxinus, the Milesians founded Apollonia, Odessus, Tomi, and Istros, and emerged in the northern region of the Black Sea. The first place settled here by the Milesians was an island, later called Berezan (now Schmidt's Island), 12 kilometers from the mainland. The settlement on this island seems to have been established in 643 B.C. Its inhabitants engaged principally in commerce, although crafts and farming were also developed.

Once familiarized with the local conditions and with the natives, the Greeks also settled on the mainland. There, in the mouth of the

3. Sinope and the allied *poleis* exported iron from the Chalybes of Asia Minor. They were founded at the end of the seventh or beginning of the sixth century B.C. Editor's note (IMD).

southern Bug River, at the very beginning of the sixth century B.C.,
The Greeks founded Olbia, which became the major Greek center in
the northwestern region of the Black Sea. Other settlements sprung
up around this city and began establishing close ties with the local
Scythian population. To the west of Olbia, at the mouth of the
Dniester River, the Greeks founded Tyras. Another center of Greek
colonization was on the Cimmerian Bosporus (Kerch Strait). Beside
the Milesians there were other Greeks, from Teos and Mytilene, who
settled here, but their settlements were insignificant. It seems that the
Greeks reached this area during the last decades of the seventh century B.C. The city of Panticapaeum (modern Kerch), the most important Hellenic city for the eastern Crimea and the Taman Peninsula,
was founded on the Crimean side of the strait. Other cities also appeared here in the sixth century: Myrmecium, Nymphaeum, and
Theodosia and, on the Caucasian shore (the Asiatic shore, to the
Greeks), Phanagoria, Cepi, Hermonassa, and Gorgippia (modern
Anapa).[4] To the south of the Bosporus sphere of influence, on the
eastern shore of the Black Sea there emerged the Hellenic cities
Pityous (Pitsunda), Dioscurias (Sukhumi), and Phasis (Poti). In this
manner, the entire coast of the Black Sea was covered by a dense network of Greek colonies.

The southern direction had never been important during the main
colonizing period, no matter how much the Greeks were attracted by
trade with Oriental countries and Africa. This is quite natural: the
eastern coast of the Mediterranean was in the hands of the Phoenicians. The wars between Assyria and Egypt discouraged foreign
trade, not to speak of founding settlements, and to the west of Egypt,
the Hellenes encountered resistance from the Carthaginians. Only in
the region of Cyrenaica, between Egypt and the Carthaginian dominions, were the Greeks able to found a few cities of their own. The first
was Cyrene, founded by the Therans (who, in turn, descended from
the Spartans) in 631–630 B.C.; the other was Barca, built in the sixth
century by the Cyreneans and Cretans. All our knowledge about the
colonization of Cyrenaica indicates that the colonies were purely
agrarian in character, despite the fact that the colonization took place
relatively late.

Quite different was the activity of the Greeks in Egypt. They acted
here in the capacity of hired soldiers and merchants. When Egypt
gained its freedom from Assyrian rule, the Saïte pharaohs, seeking

4. Around 480 B.C., all these *poleis* united to form the mighty Bosporus kingdom
with its capital in Panticapaeum. The Bosporites also explored the region of the Sea of
Azov, which they called Lake Maeotis, and established a settlement at its northwestern
corner, calling it Tanais, at the mouth of the river of the same name (now the Don).
This settlement became the farthest northeastern colony of the Greeks.

allies in the Greeks, offered them an opportunity to settle in Egypt. The main Greek settlement became Naucratis, apparently founded toward the end of the seventh century. This city was a very unusual sort of colony. It had no less than twelve *metropoleis* (Chios, Teos, Phocaea, Clazomenae, Rhodes, Cnidus, Halicarnassus, Phaselis, Mytilene, Miletus, Aegina, and Samos), but at the same time it was under the strict control of Egyptian authorities. The degree of internal autonomy of this city varied depending on the policies of Egypt (and, later, on the policies of the Persian satraps in Egypt), but Naucratis was never an independent *polis*. Possessing no farming territory, it remained strictly a commercial and industrial settlement, a center of importation of all sorts of Greek goods into Egypt and of exportation of Egyptian merchandise and its imitations to all countries of the ancient world. Probably the short-lived Greek colonies (or stations) on the Syrian coast at the modern sites of Sukas and Al-Mina had a status similar to that of Naucratis. The hostility of the mountain dwellers prevented widespread Greek colonization of the southern coast of Asia Minor. The Greeks were able to establish here only a few bases on the trading route from Greece to the Orient.

We have already mentioned that some colonies eventually became *metropoleis*. Thus the Bosporites founded Tanais, the Sybarites founded Poseidonia, the Massalians founded Nicaea (now Nice), and so forth. On occasion, the new *metropoleis* were helped by their own *metropoleis*. Thus, Corcyra established a colony with the help of Corinth, and the inhabitants of Gela founded Agrigentum together with the Rhodians. In other instances, the colonies acted on their own. A secondary colonization (or subcolonization) was frequently of a different character than the primary. Thus the Phocaean colonization in the west had a commercial and industrial character, whereas the Massalian subcolonization was more agrarian. The Achaean colonization in Italy was clearly marked by its agrarian character, but Achaean Sybaris established its colonies as bases for trade with Etruria and other regions of Italy in order to bypass the Chalcidians, who were firmly rooted on the Strait of Messina.

In the course of two and a half centuries, the Greeks founded a network of settlements along a significant portion of the Mediterranean coast, in the entire Black Sea region, and in the greater part of the Sea of Azov region. Greek colonies spanned an enormous territory, from Menestheou Limen, beyond the Pillars of Hercules (Straits of Gibraltar), to Tanais, at the mouth of the river Don, and from Massalia and Adria to Naucratis. Using these cities as their bases, traders and travelers penetrated farther, into the very heartland of a foreign-speaking world ("barbarian world" to the Greeks). They traveled upriver on the Dnieper, the Rhone, the Danube, and the Nile, and even reached the perilous waters of the ocean. The most enterprising among the inhabitants of *metropoleis* traveled to distant lands in order to establish colonies. Such persons made a great contribution to the rapid development of the colonies. Many new cities quickly became highly developed economic centers, far surpassing their *metropoleis*. Achaea remained a poor, backward region for a long time to come, while the Achaean colony of Sybaris became one of the wealthiest cities in Italy. The prosperity of this city was so great that despite its relatively short existence (it was destroyed by the rival inhabitants of Croton, also of Achaean origin, in 510 B.C.), the luxurious life of the Sybarites became legendary. Many cities founded by the Greeks still exist today; for example, Istanbul (ancient Byzantium), Marseilles (Phocaean Massalia), Naples (this name still continues the original Greek designation *Neapolis*), Kerch (Panticapaeum), Sinope, Poti (Phasis), and Sukhumi (Dioscurias).

The relation between the Greek colonists and the native "Barbarian" inhabitants varied, but both groups consistently influenced one another. Hellenic influence accelerated the economic, social, and cultural development of the Barbarians; for example, the Celts in Gaul and the Scythians north of the Black Sea. On the other hand, the new environments influenced the Greeks. This is especially apparent in the culture of the colonists. Historians specializing in the study of cultures classify the art of the Greek cities of the northern Black Sea region and of Magna Graecia as separate and, in many respects, distinctive variants of Greek culture as a whole.

The colonization also had an important influence on the *metropoleis;* Greek trade acquired a truly international character. Whatever the original aim of the founding of the colony in some far-off land, whether for trade or farming, the settlements founded there could not have existed without some links with Greece. From there the Greeks received merchandise they considered indispensable for a normal life: grapes and wine, olive oil, handicrafts, and artworks. Some of these products were resold to the local population, involving it, too, in international commerce. They exported to the *metropoleis* such vital wares as grain, metals, timber, slaves, and fish. This naturally led to the development of commodity-money relations, to the growth of artisan and trader groups in the archaic *poleis,* and to the strengthening of their social role.

Slaves were among the important commodities shipped to Greece from the periphery. Their increasing number created the economic possibility for the abolishment of slavery (bondage) for debts. Foreign slaves became a factor in the Greek way of life. This led to a further separation between Greek and foreigner, to the solidarity of the free against the unfree.

As the process of colonization went on, the *metropolis* was being left by the poor, who had nothing more to lose at home. One of the most important results of the great colonization was the fact that the relative overpopulation of the homeland had been overcome. For a certain period, the number of people was brought into accord with the level of development of production forces, and the middle strata of the population grew in importance. These were exactly the social groups that stood up for their economic, social, and political aims with more and more resolution.

Thus, colonization brought about, on the one hand, an aggravation of the social and political conflicts in the *metropolis* and, on the other hand, the preconditions for the stabilization of the society, for its unification into a natural association directed against the slaves—a definition of the classical polity that goes back to Marx and Engels.

Finally, we must note that the familiarization of the Greeks with faraway lands widened their outlook, cultivated their curiosity and interest in all that was foreign and unconventional, and set them thinking about a wide range of new subjects. The Greeks learned that although the outside world was not inhabited by awful monsters, it was more varied than they had believed; this became the psychological foundation of Hellenic sciences and Hellenic rationalism.

In closing this lecture, we should point out that the different subregions of the Mediterranean, as a result of the Phoenician and Greek colonizations, began to undergo a single historical process.

18

India, Central Asia, and Iran in the First Half of the First Millennium B.C.

G. F. IL'YIN AND I. M. DIAKONOFF

The Aryan Question

Today, almost all of northern and part of southern India are inhabited by peoples speaking Indo-Aryan languages (Punjabi, Gujarati, Hindi, Marathi, Bengali, and others).[1] In Kashmir, in the western foothills of the Himalayas, there is also an Indo-European Dardic-speaking population. Dravidian languages (Telugu, Tamil, Kannada, Malayalam, and others) are spoken in most parts of southern India; Munda languages are spoken by a relic population in middle India; and Tibeto-Burman languages are spoken, alongside Indo-Aryan ones, by the inhabitants of the Himalayan foothills. Moreover, in southern India there lives, or lived, a small number of aboriginal tribes speaking Veddoid languages. (The term is not related to the word *Veda*, denoting the religious books of ancient India.) The ancestors of the speakers of all these different languages migrated to India at various times. The most ancient were the Veddoid tribes.

The island of Sri Lanka[2] is inhabited by Indo-Aryan-speaking Sinhalese and by Dravidian-speaking Tamils.

The southern Iranian plateau was originally inhabited by Elamites, who were, perhaps, linguistically related to the Dravidians. The northern and western parts of the Iranian plateau were probably occupied by tribes speaking languages related to the Eastern Caucasian family. At present, Iran, Afghanistan, and part of Central Asia are inhabited by ethnic groups speaking Iranian languages, which, like the Indo-Aryan ones, belong to the Indo-European linguistic family: Persians, Tadjiks, Pathans (i.e., Afghans speaking Pashto), and different mountain-dwelling tribes speaking East Iranian and Kafir languages.

1. The first section was written jointly by both authors. The next four sections were written by G. F. Il'yin, and the last two by I. M. Diakonoff.
2. Sri Lanka, "The Sacred Island Lanka," is the Sanskrit name of the island formerly known by its garbled Sinhalese name Ceylon. Since the island is also inhabited by the Tamils, who call the island Ilam, or Ilanka, the ancient sacred name was selected as its new, official denomination, by way of compromise.

A Turkic-speaking population first appeared here during the Middle Ages. The Indo-Aryan, Dardo-Kafir, and Iranian languages form a common Indo-Iranian subfamily of the Indo-European languages. The ancestral homeland of the Indo-European speakers is usually considered either to have been in the deciduous forests of the eastern portion of central and southern Europe or in the vast steppes north of the Black and Caspian seas.[3]

The beginning of the disintegration of Indo-European unity is dated, with a considerable degree of probability, to the fourth millennium B.C. From that time on, the Indo-European tribes spread south to Asia Minor (the Hittites and Luwians), southwest to the Balkans (the Greeks and Thracians), and east (the Indo-Iranians).[4] These Indo-European tribes lived under comparatively primitive conditions, on the periphery of the ancient world.

Historical linguistics allow us to illuminate the natural environment and the level of the material and, in part, the spiritual culture, as well as—to a lesser degree—the social structure of the Indo-European tribes; for a somewhat later period, this can also be done in regard to the original Indo-Iranian tribes. Without at this time dwelling on the question of the pan-European tribal and/or linguistic unity, let us say a few words about the tribes during the time of the Indo-Aryan unity, which, according to linguistic data, must be dated around the middle of the third millennium B.C. The existence of this unity is indicated by the great similarity between the languages of the ancient Iranians and Indo-Aryans, as well as by many similarities in culture and religion. Their separation had occurred by the middle of the second millennium, when some of the tribes settled in Iran and the rest continued their advance to India.

Among the Indo-Iranians (and only among them) the term *arya*, "noble, wellborn," was widely used. This term apparently was a self-designation by those tribal members who held a leading position in the then-existing tribal unions. For this reason scholars often use the

3. Recently, a new hypothesis has been proposed that postulates that the homeland of Indo-European speakers is to be sought in Asia Minor, the Armenian highland (eastern Anatolia), and Transcaucasia. However, many linguists and practically all archaeologists do not accept this hypothesis; especially implausible is the localization of the Indo-European homeland in eastern Anatolia. According to this new hypothesis, the speakers of the main part of the different Indo-European languages are thought to have moved first east and then west, through Central Asia and then eastern Europe. Their migration from Transcaucasia to Central Asia is thought to have taken place in boats, which is highly improbable for so early a period. As to Indo-Iranians, they are thought to have arrived from the north according to all hypotheses.

4. A later migration is considered to be that to Italy (the Italics) and to the western regions of Europe (Celts, Germanic peoples), as well as to the forests of the Baltic region (Lithuanians, Latvians) and Poland, Byelorussia, and farther east (Slavs).

term *Aryan* for tribes that were Indo-Iranian by language. Those who remained in Iran[5] are called Iranians, and those who migrated to India are called Indo-Aryans; their languages are called Iranian and Indo-Aryan, respectively. An intermediate position belongs to the Dardo-Kafir languages, and it is thought that the speakers of Dardo-Kafir (or, at least, Kafir) reached the Indo-Iranian region before both the Indo-Aryans and the Iranians. Consequently, the term *Aryan* is linguistic and, in part, social, but by no means racial: there never existed an "Aryan" race in Europe, nor anywhere else. During the migration of tribes, an assimilation of languages of the Indo-European family by local tribes of different ethnic and anthropological types took place. It is not even clear whether the first tribes speaking the ancestral Indo-European language were anthropologically homogeneous.

It is certain that all the three eastern groups of the Indo-European tribes—the Dardo-Kafirs, the Indo-Aryans, and the Iranians—had to enter or cross the Iranian plateau; that is, the territories of the modern states of Iran and Afghanistan. There is unfortunately no unanimity on the problem of their origin or by what route they reached the edges of the plateau. There are no written sources, and archaeologists and linguists are still interpreting the available data on the material culture in different ways.

We can say with confidence that the Indo-Iranians were pastoral patriarchal tribes who also knew agriculture and, incidentally, raised not only sheep but also cattle. They were familiar with plows and with wheeled carts, probably harnessed to oxen. They were certainly also familiar early on with the horse and later with the camel. They may have had lightweight, horse-drawn battle chariots. Horseback riding (without stirrups, of course) was known at least since the second millennium B.C.,[6] but military cavalry troops probably appeared only later.

An important question is whether the migration date of the pastoral-agricultural tribes into India and Iran can be determined by archaeological data. There are cases when such migrations have been recorded by written sources. It is in such cases that archaeology, more often than not, fails to discover any evidence of these migrations. The

5. The ancient name of the Iranian plateau was *Ariana*. The term *Iran* is a newer form of the same word, *Ariana*. As we mentioned before, in ancient history the term *Iran* is used in a broad sense to designate the entire territory of the Iranian plateau, and not just the territory of the modern state of Iran.

6. Archaeological and osteological data from sites in the Ukraine suggest that horseback riding may actually have originated much earlier (fourth millennium B.C.) on the steppes north of the Black Sea, though its transport and military applications were not immediately appreciated. Editor's note (PLK).

exceptions are the cases when migrations were accompanied by mass slaughter and fires. More often, however, new settlers quickly and painlessly adopted the culture of the natives, which was better adapted to the local conditions. In Iran, also, attempts to determine the date of arrival of the Aryan tribes from archaeological materials have failed to convince scholars.[7] Therefore, it is clear that the Indo-Iranians probably did not advance south in a single, sudden invasion but in gradual stages separated by generations.

In searching for possible routes they could have taken, we must reject the then-existing areas of subtropical forests that were unsuitable for driving cattle—namely, the Black Sea coast and the southern coast of the Caspian Sea—as well as the highest mountain passes, those of the Greater Caucasus, the Hindu Kush, and the Pamirs. Such passes, it is true, are accessible to a light horseback troop without a baggage train, but they would have been inaccessible to heavy, primitive carts carrying baggage and children and also would have been very difficult to drive cattle over. We must also discount the regions where year-round cattle grazing with supplemental farming is not possible, that is, in regions with less than 250–200 millimeters of annual precipitation.

Only two routes remain to be considered. Without excluding the possibility that isolated Indo-Iranian (Aryan) groups may have infiltrated along the western shore of the Caspian route through eastern Transcaucasia, and farther over the high mountains of Iranian Azerbaijan, we must still regard the valley of the Tedzhen–Hari Rud River (in modern Turkmenia and Afghanistan) as the main route of penetration to the south of Kafir, Indo-Aryan, and, later, Iranian-speaking tribes.

It seems very likely that in their homeland, a patriarchal structure of society (also involving slavery), as a late stage of the primitive society, was characteristic of the Indo-Iranian tribes and, to a certain degree, of some related Indo-European tribes. On the basis of linguistic data and the evidence of later religious texts, it is also possible with

7. Until recently, it was very common to identify the earliest speakers of "Aryan" languages with the makers of gray ware at the end of the third millennium (in southwestern Central Asia), and in the second half of the second millennium (in southern, or Iranian, Azerbaijan). However, these identifications are today disputed. The Andronovo archaeological culture, attested in Kazakhstan, Soviet Central Asia, and southern Siberia in the second half of the second millennium, contains many cultural features that connect it with the culture reflected in the *Rig Veda* of India and the *Avesta* of Iran and, thus, can with considerable probability be ascribed to the future Eastern Iranians; the same may be true of the very similar Srubnaya culture to the west of the Andronovo area. But if so, that should mean that the Dardo-Kafirs, the Indo-Aryans, and at least the Western Iranians must have left these territories before that period—unless the people of the Andronovo culture were the forebears of all Indo-Iranians.

some confidence to reconstruct for this period some of the more complex peculiarities of the social structure common to Indo-Aryans and to a portion of the Iranians dating back to a time when they must have lived in eastern Iran or farther north. The evidence points to a relatively well developed and quite firmly settled (though, on occasions, mobile enough) cattle-breeding and farming society with permanent troops of warriors and a priesthood. From here stem the numerous patriarchal and legal institutions, common to the Eastern Iranians and Indo-Aryans, above all the same division of society into priests, warriors, and farmers–cattlemen with different social and cultic functions, and a fairly complex system of everyday customs. Some scholars, apparently without sufficient reason, date this three-way division of society back to the time of the ancestral Indo-European unity. But this division into three estates or cultic groups is, in fact, not attested by our sources for all Iranians; for the "Western" Iranians (the Medes and Persians) this division is not attested until a later period of ancient history. Actually, these seem to be features that must have developed while the Indo-Aryans lived close to a group of Iranian-speaking tribes under the conditions of a sufficiently well-developed civilization, at an early stage of stratification by property and estate (or class). Along the entire migratory route of Indo-Iranian tribes from their homeland to Hindustan, a similar civilization is attested only among the ancient cultures of southern Central Asia and eastern Iran, such as Namazga-depe, Anau, Mundigak, and others mentioned in Lecture 10. If we accept that the Indo-Aryans advanced gradually to the southeast, then we can allow for their penetration toward Hindustan already about the time of the Proto-Indus culture. At the time when the first Indo-Aryan religious texts emerged (*Rig Veda,* end of the second millennium B.C.), the Indo-Aryans had, in any case, moved far east of the Indus Valley. Thus they were no longer on the Tedzhen route, and their closest relatives—the Iranian tribes—must have started their own advance along it. Of course, we cannot preclude the possibility that some lagging groups of Indo-Aryans, and especially of the Dardo-Kafirs, remained within the Iranian plateau, and the same might be true of indigenous relic tribes belonging to the most ancient population of that land.[8]

Not so long ago, the picture of the arrival of Indo-Aryans in India was drawn as that of a conquering invasion by a superior race, which in part extirpated and in part enslaved and assimilated the local popu-

8. It is interesting to note that no traces of a pre-Indo-Iranian substratum can be discovered in the ancient Indo-Aryan languages. This might be due to the Iranian population overlapping not an unrelated linguistic substratum but a related one; for example, Dardo-Kafir or Indo-Aryan.

lation, which was, supposedly, dwelling in complete barbarism. The discovery of the Indus Valley civilization in the 1920s proved that the culture of the pre-Aryan population in the northeast of the country was superior to that of the newcomers. As was mentioned in Lecture 10, it seems that the Aryans bore no direct responsibility for the downfall of the Indus Valley civilization.

There are no data that would confirm that any one-time mass invasion of conquering Aryans into India took place. Apparently no later than the second half of the second millennium B.C., Indo-Aryanspeaking tribes began to infiltrate India in a slow and gradual process. Of course, the relations between the newcomers and the local inhabitants were not always friendly, but neither were the relations between the different indigenous groups themselves. But in the end, as a result of ethnic displacements and mutual contacts, an assimilation of the new arrivals by the native Indian population began to take place, the local inhabitants at the same time adopting the language of the newcomers.

Sources of Indian History: End of the Second to First Half of the First Millennium B.C.

As we said earlier, it still remains difficult to assert a direct continuity between the Indus civilization and the subsequent history of Hindustan. This is perhaps due to the limited number of sources, and, such as they are, they have not yet been sufficiently investigated. The character of these sources is also quite different. Although the source of our knowledge about ancient India of the third to second millennium B.C. stems almost exclusively from archaeological data, the information from literary sources is of decisive significance for the history of the end of the second millennium to the first half of the first millennium B.C. Moreover, these latter sources originate essentially from another historical region, the Ganges Valley.

The sources in question are very ancient Indian religious literary text collections. They comprise religious hymns, sacrificial and magical formulae, descriptions of rituals, and interpretations of and comments on sacred texts. The Indians bracket them all as the *Veda* ("Knowledge"); in modern literature the plural, the *Vedas*, also is used. The period of the first half of the first millennium B.C., to which the *Veda* probably date, is frequently called Vedic. Although most of this literature is primarily concerned with religious matters, it also gives some information about culture and economy; references to events of political history are extremely rare and sparse. The value of the *Veda* is considerably depreciated by the uncertain dating of its individual texts and passages. Nevertheless, most scholars agree that the mythological portions of the *Veda*—the *Samhitas*—were compiled in the eleventh to ninth centuries B.C. (the oldest *Samhita* is the *Rig Veda*); the explanations of rituals (*Brahmanas*), in the eighth to seventh centuries B.C.; and the most ancient interpretations of a religious-philosophical character (the *Aranyakas* and the *Upanishads*), in the middle and the later part of the first millennium B.C. Such time ranges are, of course, too broad for a historian to arrive at conclusions that would satisfy everyone. Also to the first millennium B.C. belong the beginnings of ancient Indian epic poetry, a source whose evaluation by the historian involves very considerable methodological difficulties.

The Indo-Aryans in the Ganges Valley

The most important process in the history of India between the second and the middle of the first millennium B.C. was the settling of the Indo-Aryans in the Ganges Valley and its economic development. Before the Indo-Aryan settlement, the valley was covered with jungle. There had existed here sparse settlements of hunters and farmers belonging, according to the archaeologists, to the so-called culture of copper hoards; these people are supposed to have penetrated the Ganges Valley from the southeast. It is possible that Himalayan tribes also began descending into the Ganges Valley at the end of the second millennium B.C. But the main direction of the colonization was from the northwest to the southeast, from modern Punjab and Rajasthan, along the Yamuna and the Ganges rivers. This is indicated by the spread toward the east of the gray-painted ware culture, which archaeologists associate with the Aryas, the creators of the *Veda*. Toward the middle of the first millennium B.C., the Ganges Valley was essentially settled, although considerable areas, especially the more remote districts, remained as jungle and marshes.

The main technological achievement ensuring successful settlement was the mastery of iron technology. This metal was apparently not brought to India by the Aryans, but, rather, iron metallurgy developed here independently; an ironworking center has been discovered in eastern India (West Bengal) and is dated to the beginning of the first millennium B.C. In southern India (Mysore) iron appeared as early as the twelfth to eleventh centuries B.C., perhaps too early for any close contacts with the northwest of the country.

Farming became the main economic activity in the Ganges Valley toward the middle of the first millennium B.C. A plow pulled by oxen was the principal cultivation tool. Canals for artificial irrigation were known; water-lifting wheels with buckets were also in use. The cereal crops were barley, wheat, different leguminous plants, and millets. The cultivation of rice was on the increase. Cotton was grown and sugarcane utilized. The oleaginous cultures were flax and sesame.

Livestock rearing maintained its importance. Among the domestic animals then known were cattle, buffalo, sheep, goats, donkeys, and camels. Horses appeared only in the second half of the second millennium, possibly with the migration of the Indo-Aryans to India. They were raised mainly in the northwest of the country. Even later, horse breeding did not take hold in the Ganges Valley or in southern India, because the climatic conditions there are not conducive for the breeding of horses or for their economic use; they were used mainly for military purposes. For the inhabitants of the Ganges Valley, just as for the Iranians, cattle were central to animal husbandry; in prayers addressed to the gods, the most frequent request was to grant an abundance of cattle.

In the Vedic Period, large cities, like those of the golden age of the Indus civilization, are not attested. Actual cities appeared in the eastern part of the Ganges Valley comparatively late. So far, no city that can be dated before the eighth century B.C. has been discovered. Even the later urban centers cannot compare with Mohenjo-daro or Harappa. However, such as they were, these cities were not merely administrative centers but also industrial ones. Certainly, almost all that was needed for a farming economy was produced in the villages themselves, except for weapons and other costly high-quality goods required by the elite (means of transportation, ornaments, textiles, pottery, etc.); these were manufactured in the cities. The available sources mention metal founders, blacksmiths, jewelers, weavers of mats and baskets, butchers, barbers, and viticulturists. There were also artisans specializing in narrower fields: wheelwrights, bowstring makers, embroiderers, and so forth. This proves the existence of a marked division of labor and specialization in the crafts.

We also know about the existence of professional merchants and moneylenders. Cattle were regarded as standards of value, and so were common golden or silver neck ornaments, called *nishka*. At the end of the sixth, beginning of the fifth centuries B.C., the first precursors of coins made their appearance: small silver bars bearing a mark certifying their quality. Trade was conducted mostly along land and river routes. The mention of ships with a hundred oars that we find in the *Rig Veda* (unless this is poetic hyperbole) suggests the existence of seafaring. Commercial relations with countries of the Near East continued, according to indirect evidence.[9] Linguistic analysis of the ter-

---

9. Assyrian kings of the eighth to seventh centuries B.C. were able to obtain elephant skins and ivory in the lower reaches of the Tigris and the Euphrates rivers, obviously

minology used in Western Asia shows that India exported varieties of precious wood and spices.

Social and State Structure in Northern India in the First Half of the First Millennium B.C.

A legend about the "four ages" was widely known among the ancient Indians. According to the legend, during the first of these ages, the "Perfect" (*Krita Yuga*), people lived happily, knowing no sickness, heavy labor, private property, or social inequality; everyone was virtuous, and thus there was no need for punishment or government. In each of the subsequent ages—*Treta, Dvapara,* and *Kali*—the virtue of the people diminished every time by one-fourth, and the living conditions worsened accordingly. The fourth age, *Kali Yuga,* the age in which we ourselves now live, was considered especially bad; it was called "dark" and "sinful." The former norms of virtue and rules of life were constantly being transgressed, because people became filled with all kinds of vices. They began to oppress, cheat, and insult one another. Only a king could now restrain people from mutual destruction. And he could only do so by means of severe punishment: thus arises the state.

This tale distortedly represents a real historical process. In the *Krita Yuga* we can perceive an idealized depiction of the primitive community structure. During the *Treta* and *Dvapara* ages, private property and social inequalities came into being. The *Kali* age is a period of developed class society with exacerbated social contradictions. We notice here an obvious similarity with the ancient Greek myth about the golden, silver, copper, and iron ages, but without the symbolism of metals.

Vedic literature contains the earliest written data on the social development of the Gangetic tribes. The time was still remembered when the ancestors, united in communities (*gana*), owned their property jointly, worked together under their chieftains (*ganapati*), divided the fruits of their labor equally, and appeared before the gods as a unity. But all had changed. The average free Indian seems economically to have been an independent proprietor or head of a family. Evidence of this is, for example, the performance of sacrificial rituals, in most cases, by private individuals; such individuals were able to assume the often significant costs of these ceremonies. Already during the early Vedic Period, usury was such a great evil that people prayed to the gods for deliverance from debt. Cultivated land was possessed

---

shipped from India. Attempts to introduce cotton cultivation in Assyria also probably indicate contacts and relations with India.

and used privately by free community members. Some relatively late information speaks about land being donated, but only to kings. There is still no information about sale and purchase of land.

A social stratification was taking place; the *Vedas* reflect even its extreme form: the appearance of slaves and slave-owners. Already the *Rig Veda* mentions that a person could own as many as a hundred slaves; later writings indicate many hundreds and even thousands. Of course, we must make allowance for poetic exaggeration.

The original meaning of the ancient Indian term *dasa*, "slave," was "foe," "alien," "barbarian." We can assume that the first slaves were prisoners taken in battle, as well as persons belonging to the noncombatant population of defeated tribes. Although the preconditions necessary for the appearance of slavery were laid down by the developing inequality within the primitive community itself, the members of a community were for some period of time still united by traditional tribal ties. Therefore, at first, the preconditions led to enslavement of strangers. Only later did enslavement of tribespeople by their own group occur. The *Brahmanas* mention the sale of children into slavery by impoverished free persons (even by the wellborn). However, war seems to have remained the main source of slaves. We have no information about slave trade. All this, as well as the existence of human sacrifice, allow us to assume that the overall development of slavery was still low. Obviously, we are dealing here with patriarchal slavery.

The disintegration of the primitive community was the cause not only of slavery but also of general social inequality. In ancient India it found its reflection in the division of society into *varnas*, or estates, castelike in their exclusiveness. There were four *varnas*: the Brahmans, the members of priestly lineages; the Kshatriyas, the warriors; the Vaiśyas, the other remaining free community members; and the Shudras, people with restricted rights. The traditional occupation of the first *varna* was the performance of priestly duties; the second group engaged in military matters and government; and the third *varna* consisted of farmers, herdsmen, merchants and moneylenders. The last *varna*'s duty was to serve the members of the other three. Membership in a *varna* was determined by birth and was inherited. Marriage between members of different *varnas*, especially between a man from a lower and a woman from a higher *varna*, was, in principle, illegal. The ancient Indians explained the inequality between the *varnas* by an inherent difference between people according to the degree of their natural nobility. The Brahmans were considered to be the highest. They were followed by the Kshatriyas. Below them were the Vaisyas. The Shudras were at the very bottom and embodied the basest qualities of the soul. Accordingly, it was explained that the Brahmans originated from the mouth of the mythical first human being, who was sacrificed by the gods. The Kshatriyas came from his arms; the Vaisyas from his hips; and the Shudras from the soles of his feet. In later times, the creation of the *varnas* was attributed to the god Brahma, who created them from the same parts of his own body.

The most striking feature of the ancient system of *varnas* was the contrasting of the three higher ones with the fourth. The members of the latter were the descendants of aliens or of persons who had lost their land, together with the protection and support of their kinsmen and members of their community. This group also included people of subjugated and dependent tribes. The low status of the Shudras was emphasized by the fact that in their childhood, they did not undergo the consecration or passage rite (initiation) that was viewed as a second birth. The members of the first three *varnas* were called twice-born. This circumstance imposed a number of limitations on the Shudras in religious worship. They were banned from reading and listening to the readings of the *Vedas* and from participating in sacrifices and memorial services for the dead. They were also limited in their social rights: they could not hold responsible positions in the government machinery, had no right to own land, and occupied subservient positions in economic activities.

The division into estates was also known in other ancient societies, but in ancient India it was uniquely clear-cut and stable. This can be explained by a particularly keen need for the ruling class to exercise extraeconomic coercion of the working people due to the specific conditions of the country. The natural environment of India was rich in food resources, and the products were relatively easy to obtain (plenty of game and fish, wild cereals, nuts, fruits, berries, and so on), and the requirements for shelter and clothing, given the mild Indian climate, were minimal. In these circumstances, the only way to force one group of people to work for another was by extraeconomic means. In the case of some workers, this was accomplished by direct enslavement, but for others who, for one reason or another, were not enslaved, a whole system of social and ideological compulsion gradually developed—the estate and later the caste system. Moreover, in an environment of ethnic diversity, frequent collapses of states and tribal unions, and the creation of others in their place, the ruling strata of society needed a most rigid system of estates. This was the only way to ensure the organizational structure necessary to preserve the privileges of the higher *varnas* and to maintain a class and estate solidarity, regardless of changes in the correlation of forces between the tribes or in the boundaries between the states or political disasters.

The bodies of state power arose gradually, emerging imperceptibly together with the exacerbation of social contradictions, from tribal and community bodies. The popular consciousness nevertheless preserved (as we mentioned above) the memory of a time when such power did not exist.

Toward the middle of the first millennium B.C., the states of the Ganges Valley assumed their final form. The majority were monarchies; institutions typical of the primitive community structure, such as tribal assemblies, community meetings, and people's courts, lost all their earlier importance or vanished entirely.

The king (*raja*) was the supreme manager of state property and, above all, of land; he commanded the army, headed the government, and was regarded as the principal protector of the *dharma* (rules of virtuous life). The royal power was hereditary, although sometimes a formal confirmation of his candidacy was required by a popular assembly—a relic from the time when the *raja* was a tribal or clan chieftain. In accordance with his role, the king's person was exalted in many ways, and his coronation developed into a magnificent ritual of a sacral character. Vestiges of tribal democracy survived better in republics, called, like the ancient communities, *gana* or *sangha*.

The machinery of the state was still simple, but some permanent posts had developed: the court priest, the commander of the troops, the treasurer, and the tax collector. The *Rig Veda* even mentions spying service. The oldest known tax was the *bali*, which was originally probably a voluntary contribution by the community members to support the tribal chief and the tribal cult, but we know it was an obligatory tax equal to one-sixth of the harvest.

The states of that time were not large, and the political map was complex and constantly changing. The process of a few large states absorbing smaller ones began only toward the middle of the first millennium. Tribes frequently changed territory, seized others' land, and lost their own. Some perished or dispersed; others, through military victories, grew at the expense of the weaker tribes. States emerged and fell apart, and their names, as well as their territories and reigning dynasties, changed. Thus it is not yet possible to write a coherent political history of the Vedic Period.

These states and some of their kings are not known from any inscriptions of theirs, or from documents, but from dispersed accidental references in religious literature; they are sometimes named in very heterogeneous sources, as, for instance, in Jainist, Buddhist, and Brahmanist ones, but the facts mentioned are, on the whole, compatible with each other. This shows that there must have existed a sort of historical tradition in this part of India.

The most important kingdoms seem to have been Koshala (in the present-day state of Uttar Pradesh) and Magadha (in the present-day state of Bihar). The Indus region was characterized by an even higher political and social instability, because it was more exposed to external dangers. For southern India, available data are not yet sufficient to provide even a sketchy historical appraisal.

Vedic Religion and Culture

The religion of the Ganges Valley tribes still bore a great similarity to the religion of the ancient Iranians. The cult of fire and the cult of ancestors were distinctive features of both religions, as was the use, during major rituals, of a specially prepared potion: *soma*. (The Iranians called it *haoma*.) Many examples of similarities in terminology and identical deities and mythical heroes can be found in both religions.

Like other ancient peoples, the Indians believed that the life of nature and of society proceeds according to the precepts of the gods, or *devas*, beings similar to humans but possessing supernatural powers. The most important gods were Indra, the Thunderer god and Warrior god, the *raja* of the gods; Agni, the god of Fire, protector of the home, intercessor between humans and gods; and Surya, the god of the Sun, the enemy of darkness and cold. Female deities were already losing their importance in the religion of the *Vedas*. Apart from the *devas*, the Indians recognized another group of deities—the *asuras*; but these deities, such as, for example, Varuna, the god of Heaven, and Mithra, the god of Light and of Treaties, were perceived as further removed from humanity and played a lesser role.

Because it was believed that the world exists and that people thrive only thanks to the gods, and because the gods live by sacrificial offerings, sacrifices were the main duty of believers. To please the gods people slaughtered animals, burned grain, and poured melted butter, milk, and *soma* into the fire. The god of the Moon, *Soma*, was also considered the god of this potion, which endowed the gods with unlimited life and power. Some rituals were very complex and costly; performing them and reading the appropriate texts and formulae required persons with special training. The importance of the Brahman *varna* resided in the importance of its members in worship and in their mastery of the "sacred knowledge" (*veda*). The expenses incurred in a ritual were defrayed by the ritual's beneficiary. The king bore the expenses of the state cult. There were no temple economies or actual temples as permanent places of worship in the Vedic religion.

The ancient Indians had the notion, preserved in modern Hinduism, that the body is mortal but the soul eternal; after death, the soul transmigrates to another body—to which body depends on the person's behavior in his past life. Thus, the concept of "action" (*karma*) not only means behavior but also retribution, so that both are inevitably one and the same. The soul of a virtuous person is reborn among higher beings, and that of a sinner among lower beings. The social significance of the *karma* teaching lies in the fact that the oppression of a working person is thought to be retribution for "sinful" behavior in his or her former life, so that their condition is their own fault. In turn, the privileged situation of the noble and wealthy is simply their reward for their virtuousness in previous lives. What is sin and what is virtue were defined by the prevailing ideology, which was declared to have been given by the gods. The teaching of *karma* turned out to be so convenient for the ruling class as a tool with which to influence people that it became the moral and ethical foundation of all Indian religions and is maintained up to the present time.

The first seeds of the scientific study of the real world appeared in India during this period, but characteristically still within the disciplines dedicated to the study of the *Veda:* phonetics, grammar, etymology, and astronomy. Thinking remained primarily religious. Yet, advances in the field of mathematics were impressive: the Indians knew the theorem bearing the name of Pythagoras long before the Greeks (but, apparently, later than the Babylonians). We have evidence of the existence of professional physicians who were able to diagnose and treat more than a hundred ailments, being familiar with the healing effects of many natural substances.

The ancient Indians did not erect temples or complex funerary structures, although their rituals were both elaborate and costly. Their way of life was still simple, including that of the wellborn, and the towns did not differ much from villages. There were no palaces, and the accomplishments of the Indians in the arts can be considered modest.

What has reached us from the Vedic Period is religious literature. The genres of this literature are manifold: hymns to gods, praises by the priests to generous donors, sacrificial formulae, incantations, descriptions of rituals, and mystic religious treatises. Some texts are characterized by colorfulness and a wealth of artistic devices. In the period under consideration, the *Veda* had not yet been rendered in writing but was orally transmitted from teacher to student; so far, no written literature, nor any written record, from the Vedic Period has been discovered. The ancient writing of the Indus civilization died out with the culture of Mohenjo-daro and Harappa. The first known texts in Indo-Aryan syllabic writing, apparently unrelated to the ancient writing system of the Indus civilization, date from as late as the fourth to third centuries B.C. Nevertheless, it is probable that the earliest Indo-Aryan writing evolved earlier, probably no later than the first quarter of the first millennium B.C. Palm leaves and similar perishable material must have been used for this writing.

Iran and Central Asia in the First Half of the First Millennium B.C.

Until recently, it was believed that a long interval of time passed between the arrival of Indo-Aryans in Hindustan and the arrival of Iranians in Iran. However, circumstantial evidence leads us to believe that the Iranians came to Iran in the immediate wake of the departure of the Indo-Aryans, or even that for some time they may have inhabited the Iranian plateau simultaneously. A certain group of Indo-Aryans (possibly, Dardo-Kafirs) who worshiped Indra and other Indo-Iranian *devas* came into contact with the Western Asiatic Hurrians (in all probability, in modern Iranian Azerbaijan) and, as we have seen (see Lecture 11), contributed an Indo-Iranian dynasty to one of the most important Hurrian states, Mitanni.

The "Western" Iranians, ancestors of the Persians and the Medes, had by the twelfth century B.C. still not reached their future habitat. But it is possible that the eastern part of the Iranian plateau, along the Tedzhen–Hari Rud Valley, had already been settled by Iranian tribes toward the middle of the second millennium B.C. Thus, it may be assumed that the inhabitants of the pre-urban settlements of southern Turkmenia (Namazga V), eastern Iran, and Afghanistan were, in the middle of the second millennium, either Indo-Aryans or Iranians by language. Another southern Turkmenian culture, Yaz I (dating to later than the ninth century B.C.), was probably Iranian. Somewhere in the great expanse of the Iranian plateau, Western Iranian-speaking tribes adopted the light battle chariots which, in the future, were to play a considerable role in their culture. The Eastern Iranian-speaking tribes (the Sogdians, the Khoresmians, the Bactrians, the Sacae, the Scythians, and others) continued at that time and during the first millennium B.C. to inhabit the entire expanse of the steppes from the Black Sea to Central Asia and the northern border of the Iranian plateau. By the beginning of our era these tribes had hardly made any advance into the territory of the Iranian plateau (in the broad sense) and remained, with the exception of the Bactrians, in Central Asia, Kazakhstan, and eastern Europe.

In appraising the culture of the inhabitants of Central Asia and Iran with the purpose of discovering some reflection of their ethnic history, it is of great interest to observe the changes in funerary rituals. These rituals apparently developed (at least for some of the inhabitants of the discussed region) from cremation (also brought to Hindustan by the Indo-Aryans) to the later Iranian ritual of leaving corpses to be torn to pieces by birds and animals of prey, whereupon only the remaining scattered bones were buried. The belief underlying this ritual was the tabu against defiling the purity of the elements—fire, water, and the fertile soil; this was probably due to the existence of a cult of fertile soil, water, and fire.

The ritual of exposing corpses has been attested by written and archaeological sources only for a much later period. The practice of cremation was recorded for graves of the fourteenth to thirteenth centuries B.C. between the mouths of the Kafirnigan and Surkhan Darya rivers in present-day Tadzhikistan. In the period of the Namazga VI culture a fire continued to be laid in the grave, but the body was not cremated; it was laid on its side in an embryonic position. In southern Tadzhikistan at the end of the second millennium B.C. cremation was replaced by the ritual of burial. The internment of bent skeletons together with funerary gifts was also still practiced in central Iran and most of Central Asia at the end of the second, beginning of the first millennia B.C. and later. But in southern Tadzhikistan in the first third of the first millennium, burials were conducted as follows. At the bottom of a pit a stone box was placed into which the dismembered corpse was laid, without any accompanying inventory, and covered with reeds. Such a burial reflects an attempt to preserve the purity of fertile soil from the contaminating contact with the corpse. Thus the Iranian custom of protecting the natural elements from a dead body's decay, also undoubtedly related to the worship of fire, came into being apparently in the settled southern regions of Central Asia or in eastern Iran during the first third of the first millennium B.C. By the middle of the sixth century B.C., this custom spread to Media and Persia, but it was still new there and not practiced by everyone. The ritual that requires that the elements be kept pure is closely connected with the Avestan civilization.

The *Avesta* and Zoroastrianism

The sacred book of the Iranian religion of Zoroastrianism is called the *Avesta* and is written in a language with characteristics of both Eastern Iranian (like Khoresmian, Sogdian, and Bactrian) and Western Iranian (like Median, Persian, and Parthian). The precise time and place of its creation are unknown. All that can be said is the following. To begin with, all parts of the *Avesta* antedate the emergence of the great Persian empire in the second half of the sixth century B.C., because no part of it contains any traces of knowledge of the Median or Persian empires or any awareness of the elaborate Persian administrative terminology, although the latter deeply influenced all languages from Greece to India between the sixth and fourth centuries B.C. Second, the compilation of the *Avesta* took quite a long time. Third, the most important part of the *Avesta*, the *Gathas*, verse sermons by the teacher of the doctrine, Zarathushthra (Zoroaster), appeared as a result of a religious and philosophical reform that could have taken place only within a civilized stratified society, even if still quite archaic. We shall see further on that these considerations force us to date the *Avesta* between the ninth and the beginning of the seventh centuries B.C. (although other dates have been suggested, ranging from the Neolithic period to the sixth century B.C.).

The farming cultures of the southern frontier of Central Asia and the northeastern part of Iran were expanding after 1000 B.C. A gradual transition from bronze to iron was taking place. Wide use was made of the waters of the mountain streams in the foothills and of the rivers, such as the Tedzhen, the Murghab, and the Amu Darya. These cultures are known to have existed between the tenth and seventh or sixth centuries B.C. in ancient Hyrcania (at the southeastern corner of the Caspian Sea), in Parthia, south of modern Turkmenia (probably also in Areia, or Haraiva—the Tedzhen–Hari Rud Valley), in Margiana (the Merv, or Mary, oasis), in Sogdiana, in Bactria (where the Amu Darya flows from the east to the west), and in Drangiana (southwestern Afghanistan).

The scattered and obscure information we have from the Greek authors leads us to believe that important political units existed in these regions before the Median and Persian empires. This seems to be corroborated by data gleaned from the *Avesta*. Can these units, dated to about the eighth to seventh centuries, be defined as states? Against such a definition is the fact that no written texts have yet been found in these regions from so early a period; but states that did not use writing are known (in Africa, for example). Moreover, let us not forget that the Elamite hieroglyphic script was known to the inhabitants of the Iranian plateau ever since the beginning of the third millennium.

The entire history of the ancient Orient shows that ancient states did not grow out of tribal unions, immediately assuming the form of empires. Rather, states emerged from territorial communities that naturally came under the influence of a single center (in a mountain valley, along a master irrigation canal, etc.) and formed city-states, or nomes. We must assume that in eastern Iran and in Central Asia, just as in western Iran, large political units were preceded by small urban settlements and small pre-state and state nuclei.[10]

10. Recently, Soviet archaeologists have uncovered evidence for an impressive number of Bronze Age urban settlements in Margiana (the now desiccated lower course of the Murghab River) and in Bactria (northwestern Afghanistan and southern Uzbekistan). The material culture of the settlements in Margiana and Bactria is quite

Avestan data, however, indicate the existence of at least one large and stable political unit at a time when small city-states no longer existed, but still in the pre-Achaemenid Period; that is, before the middle of the sixth century. Actually, this political unit must not have immediately preceded the Achaemenid Period, because there are no ancient data indicating a direct conquest of this older polity by Media or Persia.

One of the most ancient sections of the *Avesta*, a hymn to the god Mithra, the patron of Treaties, testifies to the fact that when the hymn was composed (presumably, in the ninth to seventh centuries) there existed a state, or rather a military federation of tribes and communities, called Aryoshayana occupying the Tedzhen–Hari Rud and Murghab river valleys (lying partly inside modern Turkmenia and partly inside Afghanistan), as well as the middle course of the Amu Darya and some surrounding regions, perhaps even as far as Khoresm (the lower course of the Amu Darya).[11] This federation was also called Aryanam-Vaejo, a name later transferred to Khoresm and, still later, becoming a half-mythical name for the distant northern homeland of the Aryans. According to legend, this union or federation was created by a person named Kavata, who bore the title of Kavi ("singer" or "soothsayer") and apparently hailed from Drangiana in southwestern Afghanistan. His tribal origin is unclear (except for the fact that he was Iranian-speaking). Aryoshayana was later conquered by a chief of the Tura nomads (Turanians, one of the Scythian-Sacae tribes, also Iranian, perhaps Khoresmian?), called Frangrasyan.[12] Frangrasyan, however, was killed near a "deep lake of salty waters" (the Aral Sea?) by Kavata's descendant, the Kavi Khausrava, who then unified all of Aryoshayana.

We have some superficial idea of the social structure of Aryoshayana from the *Avesta*. There were patriarchal slaves, though in small numbers. Like the Indo-Aryan society, that of Aryoshayana was divided into three estates: warriors, priests, and farmers-cattlemen. The fundamental economic unit, as in Western Asia, was

---

similar and exhibits striking parallels with materials uncovered farther south in Pakistani Baluchistan and in southeastern Iran. It is possible that the roots of later Zoroastrianism are to be sought in these second-millennium settlements of Margiana, such as Togolok 21 and Gonur-depe. Editor's note (PLK).

11. Note that the names of the countries mentioned by the *Avesta*, and later by the Old Persian inscriptions, referred originally to tribes inhabiting territories smaller than the limits of these later countries, and sometimes even different territories. Therefore, it is possible that we exaggerate the extent of Aryoshayana; that Khoresm was part of it is especially doubtful.

12. In the later legends he is called Afrasyab. The usage, widespread even in the twentieth century, of applying the denomination "Turanian" to Turkic-speaking peoples, is based on an old error.

the extended-family patriarchal community, the "house" (*dmana*). A group of houses—the gens, or the rural community (*vis*)—was also headed by a kind of patriarch. The next level, the tribe, apparently had lost some of its importance by this time. Still higher stood the "country" (*dahyu*, or *danghyu*), which was somewhat larger than a nome in Mesopotamia but similar to it in structure. The country was headed by a military chief (*sastar*), who ruled with the council of elders or a people's assembly.

Zarathushthra, the preacher who created a new religious and philosophical system, lived in Aryoshayana at the court of a later (and, apparently, considerably less powerful) ruler, Kavi Vishtaspa. We do not know the dates of Zarathushthra's life, although many attempts have been made lately to calculate them. A comparatively reliable legend placed his lifetime at ten generations before Alexander the Great; that is, in the seventh century.

The only reliable information about the teachings of Zarathushthra comes from his poetic sermons, the *Gathas*. From them we learn that Zarathushthra condemned the wasteful sacrifices (especially by the Iranian nomads) of cattle so vital to the farmers. They were offered to the *daeva*s (the *deva*s of the Indians), whom he regarded as false gods. But almost nowhere did he mention these deities by name. He preached the worship of a supreme creator-god, Ahura Mazda (later called Ahuramazda, Ormazd; in Iranian *ahura* means the same as *asura* in Indo-Aryan: one of two clans of deities).[13] Ahura Mazda, surrounded by the good spirits that personify virtues and the good elements of nature (fire, air, water, and fertile soil), struggles against Anghro Mainyu (Ahro Manyu, Ahriman), who leads the spirits that personify evil. The duty of each believing farmer is to protect the cattle (which have their own patron spirit), to till the land, to adhere to virtue, and not to defile the good natural elements. Then, after death, he will enter paradise—*Garo-dmana*—along a narrow path leading across the "bridge of souls," as narrow as a thin hair or a knife's edge. A miraculous savior, the descendant of Zarathushthra, will come at the end of time and Anghro Mainyu will be defeated. However, this latter belief, like the instruction to the faithful to kill harmful animals and insects and to leave corpses out for the birds to devour in an effort to avoid defiling the elements, was certainly introduced only after Zarathushthra.

Like other preacher-reformers of antiquity, Zarathushthra focused his attention on religious-philosophical and moral preaching. As a re-

13. Zarathushthra was not the first to worship Ahura Mazda: a deity with this name (Akkadian Assara-Mazash) was apparently worshiped in Iran much earlier. It is generally assumed that this epithet ("the wise *ahura* or *asura*") was applied to the god whom the Indo-Aryans called Varuna.

sult, it became possible to merge the most commonly comprehensible elements of his teaching with the ancient, traditional cults of Indo-Iranian gods. For the same reason, later Zoroastrianism also preserved many traits of the most archaic rites.

At the end of his long life, Zarathushthra was killed by the Hyaona (perhaps the Bactrian nomadic tribes later known as the Chionites), who fought against the kingdom of Kavi Vishtaspa; this kingdom also perished.

In the legends of later times, Kavi Vishtaspa (and Zarathushthra's) kingdom was erroneously identified with the kingdom of Bactria, located along the middle and upper course of the Amu Darya River. (The capital, Bactra, or Balkh, was located in the northern part of modern Afghanistan.) This kingdom existed until the middle of the sixth century B.C., when it was conquered by the Medes and Persians. The name Aryoshayana, or Aryanam-Vaejo, was used in the form Ariana as the general designation of a number of countries inhabited by Aryans. The Bactrian kingdom was better remembered, and in the later legend, Vishtaspa and his court were placed in Balkh.

The disciples and followers of Zarathushthra were not exterminated. To be sure, memory of the precise contents of his teachings faded, and many quite different and mutually contradictory beliefs were attributed to Zarathushthra. The *Gathas* of Zarathushthra and other early Zoroastrian texts were preserved in oral form for some 500 years. The sacred *Avesta* later also came to include hymns to Mithra, the god of treaties, to Anahita, the goddess of rivers and fertility, to the deified sacred potion *haoma* (the *soma* of the Indians; it was actually banned by Zarathushthra himself), and so forth. Some of these hymns (the *Yashts*) were probably composed long before Zarathushthra, but their inclusion in the *Avesta* was possible because the preacher left the rejected evil *daeva*s unnamed in his poetic sermons. Later, the *Avesta* came to include the *Yasna*[14] and the *Visprat*, ritual and prayer texts, as well as the *Videvdat*, a book of ritual prohibitions with penances and fines for their transgression. This latter book obviously dates from a much later time than Zarathushthra's but is still hardly later than the sixth century B.C. The *Avesta* also included other books, but they have not been preserved; we only have quotations from them in later legal and other texts, and their titles are listed in the general index of the *Avesta* from the fourth to sixth centuries A.D.

It seems that after the death of their leader, some of his disciples

---

14. The *Gathas* of Zarathushthra are also included in the *Yasna*. Note that the *Gathas*, as well as one prosaic part of the *Yasnas*, the *Yasna* of the Seven Chapters, are composed in a dialect different from the rest of the *Avesta* ("the late *Avesta*," including the obviously archaic hymn to Mithra and others).

resettled in Western Iran, in Media, where they converted one of the local Median tribes—the Magi. "Magus" later became synonymous with "Zoroastrian priest." Here in Media, the teachings of Zarathushthra as interpreted by the Magi became, in the seventh century B.C., the world's first official state religion. The Medes and the Persians had settled in the western and southern parts of the Iranian plateau not later than the ninth century B.C. Even earlier, they had contacts with the more ancient autochthonous civilizations. The Persians occupied Anshan, formerly an important part of Elam.

A culture of fortress-cities existed throughout the western and central Iranian plateau at the turn of the second and first millennium B.C. These were precisely the urban cultures that confronted the Assyrian conquerors in the ninth to seventh centuries B.C.

19

The First States in China

T. V. STEPUGINA

General Remarks

The emergence of the first civilization in the Far East—the Chinese—
also belongs to the period of early antiquity, although to its latest
part.[1]

It is supposed that most of the ancient tribes in China, Tibet,
Burma, Thailand, and North Vietnam spoke languages belonging to
the Sino-Tibetan linguistic family.[2] Only a small number of these
languages, especially those spoken in the basin of the Huang Ho and
the Yangtze Chiang, as well as to the south of that area, were the base
of the later Chinese language. It is thought that as early as the fifth
millennium B.C. the distant ancestors of the Chinese were living in
the Huang Ho basin. However, the Chinese had no common self-
denomination until late antiquity, when they called themselves *Han
jen* (the name of the Chinese writing systems, *Han tzŭ,* "Han writing,"
also dates from that period). The term stems from the dynastic name
of an ancient Far Eastern empire, Han (from 202 B.C.), although as a
national denomination it is attested only later. The European term

1. Materials supplied by colleagues have been used in this lecture.
2. At present, the Sino-Tibetan family includes Chinese (Han language), with its numerous, partly mutually unintelligible dialects, and the languages of the Tibeto-Burman branch. The latter includes Tibetan, Burman, Karen (in Burma and Thailand),
and a number of languages spoken in Nepal, Assam (India), Burma, and southwestern
China. The Thai languages may constitute other branches of the same family: Thai (or
Siamese) in Thailand, Shan in Burma, etc. According to a hypothesis of S. A. Starostin
and S. L. Nikolaev, the Sino-Tibetan languages, as well as that of the Ket on the Yenisei
River, belong to a linguistic phylum different from the so-called Nostratic, which
includes the Indo-European, Finno-Ugrian, Altaic, Kartvelian, and possibly the Afro-
Asiatic linguistic families. However, the division of languages into phyla does not correspond (as might have been thought) to the division of humanity into the major distinct
ethnic stocks or "races." Thus, the Mongols, belonging to the Mongoloid ethnic "race,"
speak a Nostratic language; the Hausa in Nigeria, belonging to the Negroid "race,"
speak an Afro-Asiatic language; the Northern Caucasians, Europeoid by "race," do not
belong to the Nostratic linguistic phylum. Vietnamese is supposed to belong to another
linguistic family, the Austroasiatic. The homeland of the speakers of Sino-Tibetan
should be sought in East Asia. (Southeastern Asia was long inhabited by tribes similar to
the Veddas of India, the Negritos of the Philippines, and the Melanesians of the
Pacific.)

China has its origin in the dynastic name of the empire preceding the Han: Ch'in.

The states emerging inside present-day China before the Ch'in dynasty, which unified the country, were not the result of the historical development of the Chinese people (the Han) alone. In this territory, ever since the Stone Age, there dwelled a number of tribal entities, presumably speaking not only Sino-Tibetan but also Tunguso-Manchurian and Austroasiatic. They created their own original cultures. Environmental factors were conducive to the creation of stable ethnocultural complexes in certain regions (the size of whole countries in other parts of the world). It was a synthesis of these cultures that was to form the unique cultural and historical phenomenon we call Chinese civilization.

Before the term *Han jen* appeared, the Chinese applied to themselves different self-denominations, of which the best known and perhaps the dominant one was a general ethnic term, the Hua. But judging from the earliest inscriptions, which date from the late second millennium B.C., there were also other self-demoninations used by the inhabitants of the Huang Ho basin, the cradle of Chinese civilization; namely, Shang[3] and Chou. Hua, Shang, and Chou can be regarded as the oldest known names for the creators of the Bronze Age culture in northern China.

The territory occupied by the Hua and the other ancestors of the present-day Chinese included only a minor part of what is now the People's Republic of China. Therefore, when discussing the ancient history of China, it is preferable to speak of Yin China, limited to the central part of the Huang Ho basin, and of Chou China, which included most of the Huang Ho basin and the northern part of the Yangtze basin. Only Ch'in-Han China was something of a "universal" empire including all China proper; that is, most of the land now inhabited by the Chinese. The Hua, or Proto-Han nation, were not the only inhabitants of this area; different ethnic groups and different social structures coexisted all through the history of "ancient China." But from the socioeconomic and political point of view, the unity of the Ch'in and Han empires is indubitable; the leading role of the Han nation inside this huge despotic state can be safely assumed from the end of the third century B.C.

China in antiquity was an independent closed sociopolitical complex, with its specific way of development inside the framework of the laws and stages of development typical of ancient society. At the same time, the Chinese civilization is one of the main links in the chain of ancient civilizations. There are some terms and notions typical of me-

---

3. Not to be confused with the Shan in Burma.

dieval and modern times that are misapplied when used of ancient China or have an incorrect connotation. Thus, ancient China did not know national, linguistic, or racial antagonism; the main antagonism was between the free and the unfree population. The notion of "slavery" was synonymous with "barbarian," "lack of culture," as contrasted with the "cultural," wellborn "masters" (*chun-tzu*). Persons of non-Chinese culture were by the same token (and not because of their nation, language, or race) treated as barbarians. It is characteristic that a national common denomination, *Han jen,* appears as the symbol of the consciousness of the unity of the Chinese nation only at the end of the ancient epoch. There was a consciousness of the inclusion of neighboring countries, tribes, and peoples in the cultural world, first of the Chou federation and, later, of the Ch'in-Han Empire. It took the form of an adoption, whether voluntary or compulsory (perhaps, at first, only nominally), of the official ideology and culture of this empire (at the end of the ancient epoch this meant adoption of the orthodox East Han Confucianism). Naturally, this meant, first of all, an assimilation of the aristocracy and their inclusion into the ruling class of the empire. The lower strata of the recent "barbarians" were simultaneously included into the *Han jen,* the oppressed mass of the aboriginal population in the empire. This is attested by the fact that the powerful explosion of the "Yellow Headbands" rebellion involved all the regions of the Late Han Empire, both in the center and on the periphery.

Both the Shang and the Chou in the basin of the Huang Ho and many other ethnic groups inhabiting, since the Stone Age, the vast area from Tibet to the East China Sea, from the Gobi Desert and the Steppes of Mongolia to the shores of the Pacific, hardly differed in their physique and their ethnic type from the present-day Chinese and other peoples dwelling in the People's Republic of China. All main anthropological types existing now in China and the neighboring countries have been there since the Neolithic. An ethnic and cultural continuity can be observed during the ancient epoch throughout Southeastern Asia. The ethnic and cultural unity of the population of southern China (including the Yangtze basin to the watershed between it and the Huang Ho) is undoubted; the tribes of northeastern China, Manchuria, and Korea formed, at the dawn of history, another historical and ethnological unity, the separate cultural world of Hsia. The population in the Huang Ho basin gravitated toward the latter, although it appeared on the scene of history, perhaps, somewhat later.

We use the term *ancient China* to refer to the entire territory in which the described historical processes occurred: east of the Tibet plateau, south of Manchuria and Korea, and north of the mountain ranges dividing China from Indochina. From an ethnic point of view, this China of antiquity was subdivided into two zones: a northern one centered in the Huang Ho valley and a southern one, from the Yangtze valley to the South China Sea.

According to the adherents of the polycentric theory of the origin of humans, China was one of the areas of the emergence of *Homo sapiens sapiens* and was the home of the eastern branch of humanity. China is also one of the homelands of agriculture and livestock breeding. Here can be located two independent centers of food production: the cultures of common and foxtail millet in northern China and of rice growing and kitchen gardening in southern China. The latter area had connections with the most ancient agricultural "hearth" or "focus" in southeastern Asia, possibly going back, at least for root-crop horticulture, to the ninth to seventh millennia B.C., if not earlier.[4]

Both in northern and in southern China separate cultures existed, each with its own history; this was partly due to diversity in the landscape, which led to a certain amount of isolation. This isolation, it must be admitted, was relative, because contact and mutual influence both inside the two zones and between them occurred since the earliest times. Moreover, the differences in climate between the south and the north have increased since the middle of the first millennium B.C. According to archaeological data, at an early period animals of the tropical and subtropical zone were still to be encountered in the Huang Ho basin, such as the elephant, rhinoceros, wild buffalo, tiger, leopard, antelope, tapir, and bamboo rat. The land was covered with deciduous forests, bamboo thickets, marshes, and lakes; the climate was hot and humid. The average annual temperature was 2 degrees centigrade higher than it is today. Thus the environment of the Huang Ho basin was in those long ago times similar to that in the regions farther south. This made contacts between north and south easier and livelier in the Stone Age.

Tin was mined in southern China and southeastern Asia, and the center of smelting copper and bronze discovered in Thailand existed no later than about 3000 B.C.[5] However, because of the humid tropical environment, the discovery of bronze did not bring about the spectacular progress it did in Western Asia. But, possibly the existence of this center helps explain the suddenness with which bronze industry appeared among the inhabitants of the Great Chinese Plain, an indus-

4. For example, the finds from Spirit Cave in Thailand are relevant for an understanding of the origins of horticulture in Southeast Asia. In spite of such early evidence for incipient agriculture in Southeast Asia, the level of class society and state was reached here at a considerably later date. Editor's note (IMD).

5. Early Southeast Asian bronzes, particularly those from Ban Chiang, are now dated later—to the first half of the second millennium B.C. Editor's note (PLK).

try basic to the creation of Chinese civilization. The second millennium B.C. in China was an epoch of the spread of local proto-urban settlements in the valleys leading into the Huang Ho in its middle and lower reaches.

Most favorable for agriculture were the great alluvial valleys of northern China with their fertile soil of river silt (now the provinces of Honan, Hopeh, western Shantung, and northern Anhui into the valley of the Huai Ho) and the loess plateaus, which were created over the millennia by sedimentation of very small particles of sand blown by the winds from eroded rocks in Central Asia (now the provinces of Shenhsi—in the valleys of the Wei Ho, the Ching Ho, and the upper reaches of the Huang Ho—and Shanhsi—the valley of the Fen). The monsoons brought enough precipitation, and irrigation was not a necessary precondition for agriculture, as was the case a millennium later. However, the plains farther away from the rivers suffered from droughts. As to the lowlands watered by the Huang Ho, the bed of the river was apt to change dramatically, flooding huge territories. It is characteristic that in the late second millennium inscriptions from Anyang, the sign "floods of water" also had the more general meaning of "disaster." Floods were also caused by typhoons blowing from the ocean. The forests required constant clearing because of the extensive use of land for agriculture by the Neolithic tribes. Precipitation was irregular; torrents of rain alternated with droughts. The unreliability of the weather was a constant factor. This helps to explain why agriculture could yield a surplus and become a basis for class stratification only as late as the second half of the second and first half of the first millennia B.C. This applied even in northern China, an area under cultivation as early as the late fifth and early fourth millennia B.C. The soil was light here, and even shallow digging with sticks was sufficient to yield grain harvests.

Southern China, from the great valley of the Yangtze to the shores of the South China Sea, was covered by subtropical and tropical evergreen forests. It belongs to the equatorial zone, and the environmental conditions have not changed much from ancient to modern times.

Archaeological finds attest to human activity in southern China throughout the Stone Age. In the sixth to fourth millennia B.C. specific Neolithic cultures are in evidence. This region was the homeland of a number of cultivated plants and domestic animals.

However, although very ancient foci of primitive agriculture and metalworking existed there, a number of factors hampered human settlement and economic development in these areas. Therefore the epoch of civilization began in the south, on the whole, at a later date than in northern China. But the country is so far not sufficiently explored by archaeologists, and the date of the first civilization here is still questionable. Some data point to the existence of an Early Bronze culture here as early as the fourth to third millennia B.C.

This was a period when in northern China there appeared several Neolithic complexes, of which the best known is the Yangshao culture. Its main area was the basin of the Wei Ho and the middle reaches of the Huang Ho and down the valley of the Huan Kiang toward the Yangtze basin. Typical of the Yangshao culture are painted pottery, transhumant, nonirrigation, forest-cutting (swidden) agriculture (the main cultigen being millet); and domestication of a number of animals (pigs, goats, sheep, dogs, fowl, and cattle). It is one of the Developed Neolithic cultures.[6]

The end of the Stone Age in the basin of the Huang Ho coincides with the Late Neolithic and Early Bronze Lungshan culture.[7] It is characterized by its gray and, especially, its thin, hard, black-polished pottery. Therefore, the Lungshan culture is also called the black pottery culture. Ethnically connected with the classical Yangshao of the middle reaches of the Huang Ho, the Lungshan culture extended east and northeastward, toward the Liaotung and Shantung peninsulas, and south southeastward, into the valley of the Huai Ho. This culture is more uniform than that of Yangshao. Typical are big fortified settlements, a more stable stick and hoe agriculture, and a considerably more important role for livestock rearing than was the case in Yangshao. There is some evidence for the separation of handicrafts from agriculture and for the beginnings of metalworking. The Lungshan villages were surrounded by walls made of stamped earth (up to 6 meters high and 10–14 meters thick). In Shantung a city wall was discovered that extended for 450 meters from north to south and for 390 meters from east to west. The inhabitants of the Lungshan towns had a sophisticated technique of fortune-telling using the shoulder bones of sheep, cattle, and pigs. It may be evidence of the emergence of an organized cult and of the priesthood as a specific group inside the gentilic community.

This was the beginning of the dramatic change that brought about the creation of proto-urban centers in the Huang Ho basin—centers of bronze industry characterized by a rapid development of surplus produce. The base for this change was the introduction of settled hoe and plow agriculture (perhaps applying the so-called *su-keng*, "double plowing," the plow being drawn by two persons) and of selective animal rearing (including horse breeding), not to mention metalworking, woodworking, and other crafts.

6. The earliest stage of the Yangshao, Panp'o phase, dates from about 5000 B.C. Some scholars regard the people of the Yangshao culture as Proto-Chinese.

7. Early Lungshan dates from the mid-third millennium B.C.

The fact that the settlements had to be fortified by walls shows that war now played an important economic role in the life of the Great Chinese Plain. One may expect that, correspondingly, a military nobility headed by a military chief must have emerged.

The Shang (Yin) "State"

The ancient written sources have preserved for us the term Yin, which was the name of the great tribal bodies that emerged in the middle and lower reaches of the Huang Ho during the second millennium B.C. The everyday life of the Yin tribal union had grown complicated enough to require the introduction of primitive writing, originally used in the cult. The writing was of an archaic pictographic type, but it can be shown that the modern Chinese script developed from it.

The growth of the productive forces was connected, first of all, with the beginning of the Age of Metal, but also with the improvement in the organization of the process of production; social functions were being delimited, and a group of organizers of productive labor was created: military chiefs, priests (whose activities at that stage were closely linked with economic life), and a community council of elders. The apogee of the social development was the adoption of slavery.

In northern China, with its wooded plateaus and foothills, agriculture was feasible only in the valley floodplains, where conditions allowed the drainage of excessive precipitation. Archaeological finds attest that in the second half of the second millennium, the first settlements of the early urban type, centers of bronze industry, appear in northern China. They appear along the rivers everywhere from Kansu to Shantung, from Hopeh to Hunan and Chianghsi. These urban foci were complexes of gentilic and/or neighbors' communities, in the process of becoming fortified cities. The early urban settlements of the Yin Period are found in the provinces of Honan, Shantung, Shanhsi, Hupeh, and Shenhsi. They are most numerous in the central plain (in Honan and southern Hopeh to the Huai Ho Valley and Shantung). Their southern limit extended to the middle reaches of the Yangtze; here, in the region south of the Tungt'ing and P'oyang lakes (Hunan-Chianghsi), two early urban centers of the same type as those in Honan have been found. Especially interesting are the excavations near the town of Huangp'i in Hupeh of a second-millennium settlement with a strong fortification wall and a palace complex. Such centers (up to six square kilometers) were built according to a certain plan, with monumental buildings of a palace or temple type and artisans' quarters, including bronze-smelting shops. The difference in the funerary inventory points to the existence of inequality in riches. Mass killings and sacrifices of slaves (prisoners of war) are characteristic of this period's society.

The first centers of civilization were small districts including one or several territorial communities (towns). The unification of the communities was dictated both by economic needs (as, e.g., collective efforts to stem the floods) and by military ones. The beginning of a period of fierce wars between the communities attests to their increased riches. The property stratification led to the replacement of the gentilic organization by that of the extended family; communities of neighbors took the place of the gentilic ones. In such pre-urban societies conflicts between the more and the less prestigious clans actually led to a stratification of the society into the poor and the rich, and the first class antagonisms began to emerge. Thus the pre-urban territorial communities were the precursors of early class society.

Toward the end of the second millennium B.C., the community of Shang headed a political entity of considerable size; it was ethnically uniform. The chief of Shang enjoyed extraordinary military powers and bore the title *wang* (with time, this title came to denote "king," who was also the high priest). The earliest major center of the Shang seems to have been Chengchou in the province of Honan, where a considerable walled town was discovered.

We learn about the community and city of Shang from the earliest Chinese inscriptions, discovered during excavations near the village of Hsiaot'un, near the modern city of Anyang in the province of Honan, and from other excavated material. But the inscriptions are the most important source for this period. Unfortunately, they are written in a very archaic script that is still rather unreliably deciphered, and their contents are mainly religious and magic; thus they supply few data for the reconstruction of the social order. There are major differences among historians in their interpretation of the texts and their evaluations of the overall character of Shang society.[8]

These earliest written texts date from the fourteenth to twelfth centuries B.C.;[9] that is, to the period of the existence of a large protourban settlement near Anyang. In it were discovered both poor dugout huts similar to the Neolithic dwellings and also foundations of big houses with bronze bases for columns. Foundries and furnaces were

8. The actual pronunciation of the signs on the oracle bones and tortoise carapaces and on the Shang bronze objects is unknown. The readings quoted are all conventional, representing the modern pronunciation of later hieroglyphics with which the scholars think it possible to identify the Yin Period signs.

9. The uncorrected radiocarbon analysis of the stratum containing the inscribed bones at Hsiaot'un pointed to a date of 1115 ± 90 B.C. Ch'eng-Chou, which has yielded only a few inscribed objects, may belong to a period up to two centuries before that.

also found. In the vicinity of the city burials were discovered that differed in their funerary gifts. Most were simple, with no weapons or bronze utensils, but a few were huge subterranean tombs in the form of overturned truncated pyramids, with broad roads leading to the tombs and descending inside toward the burial chambers, which were full of precious vessels, weapons, and artifacts of jade and gold.[10] In the pits there were hundreds of skeletons of murdered persons, and near such burials there were whole fields of beheaded prisoners with their hands bound behind their backs; also there were pits filled with thousands of skulls. Chariots were found buried together with horses and charioteers. Besides several big burials of this type discovered near Anyang, two similar burials dating from the Shang Period were found at Yitu, on the Shantung Peninsula; here dozens of persons were killed and buried, and also horses with their chariots. The pole-axes found in the burials bore names; apparently they were insignia of royalty, probably used by the chief of the local nome. In the same place a lesser burial was discovered with only a few sacrificed slaves. There was also a minor burial found near a Shang Period town in the vicinity of Huangp'i (Hupeh Province). Here, near the main burial of a man, a double coffin carved of wood containing more than sixty objects, including bronze weapons and utensils and three human skeletons, was discovered.

It has already been shown in the preceding lectures that human sacrifices were not rare in the early stages of ancient society. Nevertheless, the huge number of such sacrifices in the Shang society seems, at first glance, to be exceptional. Actually, however, the difference between the early Near East and the early Far East is that the military chiefs of Western Asia killed the prisoners after the battle, whereas the Shang chiefs left them alive and turned the massacres, usual for early antiquity, into a religious ritual. The cause was the same in both cases; namely, the incapacity of the ruling class to make use of great masses of prisoners in production while the means of coercion were still undeveloped.

The most important center of Shang society seems to have been Anyang, and the most interesting discovery here was that of the oracle archive. Here were found more than 100,000 inscriptions on animal shoulder bones and tortoise carapaces; 41,000 of them have been published. These bones and carapaces were used for fortune-telling. An indentation was made in the bone, and then the bone was scorched in fire; the cracks that formed were interpreted as the deity's answer to the question posed to the oracle—whether a hunt or a war would be successful; what were the prospects for the harvest, rain, or

10. The uncorrected radiocarbon date of one such burial is 1085 ± 100 B.C.

building projects; or whether the human sacrifices to the deities and to the spirits of the *wang*'s forebears would be favorable. No less than 2,000 inscriptions relating to human sacrifices have been identified. Near the crack on the bone or carapace, one scratched in the signs containing the question and the prediction of the oracle, its date, and sometimes a notice about whether the prediction had been correct. Thus, from such dated practical notes, the first historical chronicles emerged.

The inscriptions are in pictographs, but because the pictographs of the earliest inscriptions are already highly schematized, we can surmise that earlier forms had preceded them. Indeed, one can find more primitive forms of the signs on Shang bronzes. In the Old Chinese language grammatical relationships were expressed, not by prefixes, but by the order of the root words, and thus the Old Chinese writing consists solely of logograms (or ideograms); purely phonetic (syllabic) signs had not developed.[11]

The creation and preservation of this complicated writing system is connected with the peculiar features of the Chinese language: the one-syllable words did not consist of separate morphophonemic elements; therefore, the Chinese writing system did not develop alphabetic (letter) signs. Even a purely syllabic writing system would not be able to distinguish the great number of homophonous syllabic Chinese words, which in the spoken language are distinguished by melodic tones. Each sign in Chinese writing had to be equivalent to one monosyllabic word.

The study of the Anyang oracle inscriptions is also hampered because we are unable to reliably reconstruct Old Chinese phonetics before the middle of the first millennium B.C. It is supposed that the oracle inscriptions did not include signs denoting the "phonetics" of the language, being purely mnemonic and ideographic; that is, rendering the concept of a word independently of its sound.

Although nome centers must have been rather isolated politically (being part of a military and cultic federation and not of a unified state), the writing system seems to have been one and the same for the whole area of the "oracle bone culture." The center of its diffusion was the cultic union of Yin (a relic of entities of an earlier type). But it is quite possible that it was not necessarily invented by the Shang, who were the most stable part of the Yin tribal federation. Study of the signs and drawings appearing on Yangshao and Lungshan pottery has made some scholars think of other possible centers of creation

11. It was possible, in a developed Chinese writing system, to add, say, to the sign for "heart," which was used to denote different emotional concepts, the logogram for the "rising sun," which can be read *pa(k)* "white," and thus create a composed sign "heart + white (*pa*)" to be read *p'a*, "to be afraid."

of the pictographic writing. Dozens of graphic signs different from those at Anyang have been discovered on pottery and molds from Wuch'eng near Lake P'oyang in Chianghsi Province.[12] This makes it plausible that writing may have been invented by some of the southern tribes dwelling on the middle reaches of the Yangtze. It has also been suggested that another embryonic writing system may have been developed in Yin times by some inhabitants of the Huang Ho basin (possibly the Chou).

As pointed out above, understanding the Anyang oracle texts is a difficult task. The ideograms are often polyvalent, and some of them have not been deciphered at all. The same sign could mean different things depending on the context. Not every sign can be identified with the later hieroglyphs, and the terms used in fortune-telling are often obscure and conventional. The "cardinal points" mentioned in the texts are hard to identify; the social and political terms cannot be translated reliably enough. Therefore, one should not wonder that scholars are very much divided on the interpretation of the Anyang inscriptions, and that the historical reconstructions of the period differ considerably.

Nevertheless, a certain amount of information can be gleaned from the Anyang oracle archive. Thus, we know that the main figure in the Shang "state" (its military chief, high priest, and organizer of production) was the ruler of the "city of Shang," who bore the title *wang*. It is in his name that questions are directed to the fortune-tellers, and it is also usually he who interprets the answers of the deity.

The questions of the oracle refer to several "towns" (*yi*) and community entities (*fang*). Among them the Shang settlements are prominent: the "city/cities of Shang" (*shang yi*), the "capital [or "great"] city of Shang" (*ta yi shang*), "Central Shang" (*chung shang*), and Shang proper, a term used both as the name of a locality and of a people or tribe. These terms may indicate that the late second millennium B.C. city where the oracle was found was not the residence of the Shang *wang* and was not the center of the political entity of which he was the military leader. The site of the oracles was obviously an intertribal and intercommunity center, but it was not called Shang, which is a term for some region beyond it. To judge from later literary sources, the site of the oracle may have been called Yin. If this is correct, then we have a plausible explanation of the paradoxical fact that the term *Yin*, which was widely used by the later sources as a denomination for a district and for an ethnic unity and which we use to denote the earliest period of Chinese history ("Yin China"), cannot be identified with

12. So-called potter's marks on the painted Late Neolithic Yangshao pottery have also been considered precursors to the later Chinese writing signs. Editor's note (PLK).

any of the signs known from the Anyang inscriptions. These, however, mention the conventional names of nearly all the rulers of the
Yin dynasty, which we know from the much later list in the work of
the great Chinese historian Ssu-ma Ch'ien.[13]

As to the term *Shang*, it is used both in the oracle inscriptions and in
the later narrative sources to denote a political entity and its political
center, and also as an ethnic and local denomination; it is also used in
a sense equivalent to that of the "Yin dynasty." If the oracle center in
Anyang was called Yin, this explains why the sign *yin* is absent from
the oracle inscriptions; when questioning the oracle, there was no occasion to question it about itself. It is also possible that the name of
the oracle was taboo. Another possibility is that "Yin" was the self-
denomination of a tribe or tribal federation in the Huang Ho basin.

Shang society existed when the Chalcolithic or Early Bronze period
ended and the Bronze Age proper began. The Shang settlements of
the fourteenth to eleventh centuries B.C. were stable and lasting, in
contrast to those of the earlier periods. Shang society included not
only the Shang tribe proper; dozens of ethnic denominations are encountered in the oracle inscriptions, including the Chou, the future
conquerors of the Shang. The second great division of labor (between
agriculturalists and specialized industrial craftspeople) had already
occurred, even though the agricultural tools were still technologically
Neolithic. Agriculture played the leading role, and many of the questions to the oracle concern the prospects for the harvest. Like the
people of the Lungshan culture, the Shang cultivated sorghum, kao-
liang, barley, different subspecies of wheat, an edible species of hemp,
and foxtail, Japanese, and common millet. The main crops, however,
were common and foxtail millet, wheat, and sorghum. It is not quite
clear if rice was known, but if it was cultivated, it must have been a
dry-sown variety because no artificial irrigation existed, and harvests
depended solely on rain, a fact that can be deduced from the oracle
texts. Except for small drainage ditches known already from the excavations at Chengchou, no traces of the use of artificial irrigation
have been found in the Anyang tests or by the archaeologists, either in
the Shang region proper or in the area of other city-communities or
tribes in the zone of the fertile valleys of the Huang Ho basin. The
main hydrotechnical measure was regulating the river flow by overflow drainage channels. During the excavations at Anyang a system
of narrow (40–70 centimeters) transverse ditches, not longer than
60 meters or deeper than 120 centimeters, was discovered.

13. According to the Chinese historiographic tradition, the Yin dynasty reigned in
the second millennium, ca. 1766–1122 B.C. These dates do not contradict the archaeological sources; however, reliable dates for events in the history of China begin only
with the year 841 B.C.

Along with cereals, diverse kitchen garden plants were also culti-vated. Mulberry trees were planted for silkworm breeding. Linen and silk fabrics were woven; this was women's labor. The division of labor between men and women was clear-cut.

Animal raising played a prominent role in the society. The breed-ing of cattle, sheep, and draft horses for war chariots was very impor-tant: sacrifices of three to four hundred cattle at one time were not unusual. On the oracle bones we encounter special signs for sacrifices of "one hundred cattle," "one hundred pigs," "ten pigs," "ten rams," "ten white pigs," etc. Conflicts over grazing grounds were often the cause of wars between the Shang and their neighbors.

Hunting was still important, however. This can be seen from the predominance of animal motifs and compositions on the Shang bronze objects of art. The vessels in the form of animals—tiger, ele-phant, rhinoceros, buffalo, and owl—are strikingly realistic. The flora and fauna of the Huang Ho region in that epoch were very rich and various. Willow, elm, wild plum and pear, chestnut, cedar pine, and cypress trees grew. The low-growing forests and the marshes of northern China were rich in fish and fowl. Near Anyang skeletons have been found of deer, tigers, bears, snow leopards, rhinoceroses, buffalo, panthers, antelopes, boars, tapirs, monkeys, foxes, wolves, badgers, and hares. The inscriptions mention big battue hunts, when slaughtered deer and bears were counted in tens. The number of deer killed in a single hunt could reach 300. During one of the regu-lar hunts 164 wolves, 40 deer, and 1 tiger were killed. The hunts were collective; the entire adult population took part in them.

Workshops of considerable size were discovered by archaeologists near Anyang, Loyang, Chengchou (Honan), and Ch'inchiang (Chiang-hsi); they belonged to metalworkers, bone carvers, stonecutters, pot-ters, workers in wood and other artisans.

Cities were planned and monumental buildings were erected. Founding towns was one of the important functions of the *wang*, which shows that he had considerable human and material resources at his disposal. The most important industry was metalworking. Bronze was used to make all the ritual vessels, weapons, and certain chariot parts and to some extent, it was also used for making tools. Archaeologists have discovered a city quarter of Shang metalworkers, with their dwellings and their burial ground, where, characteristically, objects of cast bronze were laid in the graves. Ritual bronze vessels have been found, some of them weighing up to 875 kilograms. They are evidence of a high level of development of the art of making bronze alloys; they are diverse in their forms and vary in fabrication technique (different kinds of molds and the technique of *cire perdue* were used). It seems that the Shang originally had a monopoly on the secrets of foundry art in Yin China. The ritual vessels were probably made for the house of the *wang* and for the temples. The inscriptions mention a special group of the king's craftsmen (*wang-kung*), as well as a number of other groups of artisans. Of these the *kung-ch'en* and *ti-ch'en* may have been temple artisans, and the wo-kung, to-kung, and the *kung* may have been craftsmen of the community.

The hieroglyphic sign *shang* is also used for "trade," which may have been its secondary meaning, the sign itself depicting some handicraft object typical of the Shang, probably a bronze object. Perhaps this development of the sign's semantic realm points to a specific function of the Shang as intermediaries in intertribal and intercommunity trade; such a function could have contributed to the domination of the Shang over the other early urban societies of the middle basin of the Huang Ho.

Trade, however, was not highly developed and probably took the form of barter. However, there did exist a commonly recognized means of payment: namely, cowrie shells, both natural and bronze imitations.

The main form of exchange, however, between neighboring tribes or towns was not so much trade as seizure by force, the most primitive form of international relations. War was the normal way of life in Yin society. The oracle texts constantly mention military campaigns whose main aim was not annexation of new territories (as in later times) but looting—seizure of animals, grains, and prisoners—the last for mass sacrifices to the gods, up to five hundred at a time.

Sacrifices to the spirits of the *wang*'s ancestors, to the spirit of the Earth, and to other supernatural forces[14] were the essence of the cult as practiced by the dwellers in the Shang cities and were regarded as one of the vital activities. A very typical text on the oracle bones reads as follows: "Query: should the men of the tribe Ch'ing be sacrificed at the Altar of the Earth [*t'u she*]?"

"The city of Shang" headed a military confederation that united a number of early urban societies, which were probably obliged to supply military aid. From time to time, tribute was received from such allies—another form of compulsory international exchange. If they refused to pay, a campaign against them was in order. But it also sometimes happened that the allies attacked the Shang. The fact that the Shang occupied the central place in the confederation found expression in its special denomination: *Chung Shang*, "Central Shang." The oracle inscriptions reflect the concept of a universe oriented to the four cardinal points with *Chung Shang* at the hub.

14. The cult of mountains and rivers was especially popular among the Shang: there are dozens of names of mountain and river deities in the oracle texts.

The city confederation of the Shang was surrounded by inimical tribes, with whom constant war was waged, mainly to seize prisoners. The Shang aggression induced retaliatory measures by the tribes, who always threatened the Shang towns. The most intense and frequent wars were waged against the Tibeto-Burman Ch'iang tribe in the west. The questions to the oracle are full of anxiety: "Will the enemy reach the Great Shang?" The struggle with the neighboring tribes intensified at the end of the twelfth century B.C., when tribal pressure was most serious in the southwest. As mentioned above, here were also situated other urban communities of the Shang type. This does not imply that they were part of some "Shang Empire." It is more probable that they were independent city-states, although they might from time to time have been dependent on Shang and have paid tribute. Here, in the Huai Ho basin dwelled the Jen-fang tribes, which seem to have been both numerous and warlike. The prolonged wars between the Shang and Jen-fang and other inimical tribes and cities weakened the Shang and, in the final analysis, were one of the causes of their destruction. The decisive blow came, however, from another frontier, the western. In the eleventh century B.C. the Shang were routed by the Chou, who had long threatened them.

Shang Society

Extended families grouped together more according to the territorial than the gentilic principle were the mainstay of the Shang economic life. The economy of the *wang* was separate from the communal economies but was still closely connected with the community; it seems that the entire population, taking turns, had to work in it. However, there was also a permanent group of temple and palace workers; its members may have been to a great extent of non-Shang origin. An interesting group were the *sang* (literally "the lost," "the fugitive ones"), who were at the disposal of the *wang* and of officials called *ya* (temple administrators). The *sang* were probably persons from neighboring communities seeking refuge in the temple or in the *wang*'s economy.[15] They may have been junior kinsmen of the more impoverished family communes.

In ancient times, the greater the dependence on unruly natural forces, the more important appeared attempts to influence them, and the greater the role of ritual in sacral life. The irregular rainfall in the Huang Ho basin (while the agriculture here was based on pluvial, not

15. Compare the men "fled to the community" (i.e., refugees from neighboring communities), who composed a major part of the temple personnel of Early Dynastic Sumer (according to the texts from Shuruppak). Editor's note (IMD).

artificial, irrigation) and the catastrophic inundations of the river[16] were probably factors enhancing the power and authority of the chief. The reserve stocks of the chief's and the temple's economy were the security, exchange, sowing, and sacrifice fund of the Shang community, which was able to utilize it in times of crop failure or other disasters. The rituals were regarded as important means of safeguarding the well-being of the community.

The whole adult population, thousands of persons, could take part in the ritual feasts when hundreds of domestic animals were sacrificed. The *wang*, being the high priest, was, together with his entourage, the main consumer of meat. Indirectly but materially this strengthened his prestige and authority. Here the sacrificial rite appears also as a collective form of consumption parallel to the collective forms of labor. It is astounding how nearly every object of material wealth known to the Shang (such as domestic animals, bronze weapons and utensils, chariots, cowrie shells, gold and jade, agricultural produce, objects of hunting, prisoners of war) were recklessly expended in sacrifices to deities and ancestors and on funerals of the chiefs and the highest dignitaries. This is amply attested by the excavations at Anyang, near Huangp'i (Hupeh), in Hsiuchou (Chiangsu), and in Yitu (Shangtung). One can assume that because of the increasing wealth of some of the clans and noble families, such largesse not only was considered to lend them glory but was actually a form of evening out the extremes of the progressive economic inequality. This "equitable redistribution of wealth" was also to the credit of the world-organizing function ascribed to the *wang*.

The *wang* headed the field labor in the palace and temple economy. The productive function of the priest-chief (the predecessor of the king) was expressed in the image of the mythical ancestor Shen-nung, who was depicted as fulfilling agricultural rites. The participation in these works by the community members was not regarded as forced labor but as activity for the commonweal; moreover, it was part of a magical ritual that aimed at securing fertility for all the fields of the land. Work in the fields of the *wang* began by order of the oracle and at a time ordered by the oracle. Along with the temporary laborers in the *wang*'s economy (the *chung* or *chung-jen*), permanent personnel also worked. These were the *ch'en*, whom many regarded as slaves or helots. All of them took part in the agricultural activities headed by the *wang* himself or his agents, for example, the *hsiao-ch'en* or the *ya*. The tools seem to have been supplied by the temple or palace; this can be deduced from the finds of stores of stone sickles and other agricul-

---

16. In antiquity, the Huang Ho flowed near Anyang.

tural tools in Anyang near the temple of the *wang*'s ancestors; the temple fields should probably be sought in their vicinity.

Scholars do not agree on the social interpretation of the terms used for persons employed in agricultural work under the *wang*. Some think the *ch'en* were slaves; others regard them as free. It seems probable to us that the term *chung* was not primarily a social one but denoted all male persons of a certain age-group; namely, the group able to perform productive work (as distinguished from those still unable and those no longer able). At the same time, it is apparent that the *chung* were not confined to the *wang*'s economy, whereas the *ch'en*, the *hsiao-ch'en*, and the *to-ch'en* were connected with the *wang* only. It seems that among the *ch'en* there were persons of different status. Some were slave-type laborers; others (the *hsiao-ch'en*) were officials who in certain circumstances headed the community members (the *chung*) as their chiefs or overseers (e.g., during the period of their obligatory field work for the house of the *wang*). The *to-ch'en* were probably the *wang*'s bodyguard or his personal troops. The difference between the *chung* and the *ch'en* was that the latter were outside the community sector and were connected with the *wang* and bound to him by allegiance. It is possible that the *ch'en* were non-Shang by origin. The *chung* were connected with the collective economy of their own communities, but they also worked for the *wang*'s economy.

The fields were tilled by hundreds and thousands of men simultaneously. We read in a question to the oracle: "Should three thousand men be called up for field work?" The land was usually tilled with wooden tools: the furrow stick, the planting pick, the double-toothed hoe, and, in the best case, by a wooden plow drawn by human force (*su-keng*).[17] This was a very labor-consuming task for a considerable number of people. There even existed a special term that can be rendered as the "unification of common forces." We know an oracle mentioning "the great decree of the *wang* to the *chung-jen*," ordering them to engage in field work "all together." No other term for community members except *chung* has been found in the oracle inscriptions. It is clear that community members were the most important element of Shang society. Thus, it cannot be doubted that the *wang* was connected with the community, which must have played a leading role in the economic life of Shang society, and it was, no doubt, the

---

17. Some scholars think that the term translated as "double plowing" had nothing to do with a plow but involved the work of two men, one of whom made a hole in the ground with the planting pick, and the other placed the seed into the hole and covered it with earth. This is thought to have symbolized a magical act of impregnation and was part of the tilling and sowing rite.

community members who took part, in the thousands, in the wars and the big hunts headed by the *wang*. In war, the booty included thousands of prisoners (one inscription mentions the capturing of 1,656 people); the catch from the hunt could be hundreds of big animals.

The Shang were armed with bows and arrows of different kinds, hatchet-daggers, poleaxes, spears, helmets, shields and armor. Warriors on chariots played an important role (perhaps they were the *wang*'s bodyguard). The chariot was drawn by two horses and had a beam and two or four wheels (with 18, 22, or 26 spokes in the wheel); the box of the chariot was square or rectangular, the breadth between the wheels being three meters. There were three warriors for each chariot; the charioteer had an archer on his left and a spear-bearer on his right.

Leadership in war and in hunting was the *wang*'s most important duty. Wars made the *wang* and the other military leaders more powerful, concentrating great riches in their hands. But in a territorial community with collective distribution it was not the individuals who grew rich but the extended families. There were rich and poor clans among the Shang; the highest ranks of dignity, beginning with that of the *wang*, were inherited within the same generation, and then were passed on according to the degree of genealogical proximity. Some clans were hereditary priests. We have already mentioned that slavery had emerged, including private slavery, as attested by the burial of slaves with their master.

An analysis of the inscriptions allows us to assume that the power of the *wang* was limited by a council. The epic legends in *Shu Ching*, the most ancient collection of historical traditions, preserves a reminiscence of the dependence of the wang's authority on the popular assembly and the council of elders of the Shang. The election of the military leaders and the heads of the elders' councils (the *hou* and the *po*) chosen by the non-Shang communities (*fang*) that were inside the sphere of influence of the Shang had to be sanctioned by the latter's *wang*. Land was the common property of whole territorial communities; when speaking of harvesting, the inscriptions mention only general ethnonyms or ethnicons (names given according to the place of origin). But inside these territorial communities the means of production were, no doubt, ceded to separate extended-family groups.

The power and authority of the *wang* were not perceived as something alien to the people and above the community. In spite of the fact that a military and priestly elite had developed, the *wang* was regarded as symbolizing the unity of the body politic, as representing their common interests before the gods of the communities; and as soliciting for the community through his dead, deified ancestors. In his status as chief priest he was responsible for nature's fertility, securing the welfare of the land. The sources do not point to territorial acquisitions as being the aim of the military campaigns.

The administrative personnel employed in the government-temple sector do not seem to have received land or slaves for their service, which would have allowed them to start their own economies. More likely, they were sustained by deliveries in kind. This may explain the frequent questions to the oracle like the following: "Will community X harvest in a sufficient amount?" It seems that communities dependent on the Shang had to pay tribute in agricultural produce.

There did not exist any general term for the social category of people of high standing, but some of the *wang*'s closest retainers and trusted persons can be said to have constituted an elite; such as the *ya*, the *li*, the *pu*, the *shih*, and the *yin*. The same can be said of the chiefs (*hou*) and elders (*po*) of the non-Shang communities, insofar as such communities belonged to the sphere of Shang hegemony. To celebrate a victory over an inimical community the *wang* could sacrifice its leader to his own ancestors. Thus, according to the order of the oracle, were sacrificed "three community elders [*po*] of the Ch'iang."

Not only were male prisoners of war killed as a rule, but special manhunts were organized to supply victims for the sacrifices. The sign *fa* meant both "military campaign" and "human sacrifice"; it depicted an ax chopping off a human head. Note the use of this sign in an inscription, not very well preserved, but where the following sentence can clearly be read: "To sacrifice [*fa*] to the Ancestor Yi [the captured] . . . chieftain [*po*] of the Jen-fang."

The captured women were enslaved and became part of the economy. They were by no means considered to be the weaker sex; they were the main labor force in hoe agriculture, in pottery production, in weaving (including silk weaving), and in beer brewing (the last two being especially important for religious offerings). The women were not behind the men in such activities as driving big game and even participated in war, where the methods hardly differed from those in hunting. This may explain why Shang women enjoyed a position of esteem. Judging from the fact that in one of the big burials at Anyang a woman was buried with a big spear, women may have been leaders in war and in hunting. The same is attested by the oracle texts: one of them mentions a female military leader at the head of an army of 13,000.

The mass burials and the mass sacrifices of prisoners show that slave labor found little place in the economy. However, we have attestations of prisoner Ch'iangs being employed in hunting and animal breeding. Sporadically, prisoners of war seem to have been used for hard short-term labor (probably such as the construction of big tombs, rescue work after big floods, and city building). There seem to be hints of prisoners being used for spring agricultural work. They may even have taken part in the collective agricultural rite before being sacrificed, also according to rite. There is, for example, an oracle text with the following contents: "The *wang* ordered many Ch'iangs to fulfill the fertility rite on the fields."

There are inscriptions connected with the archive of a specific oracle where the fortune-tellers were women and the *wang* is never mentioned. They attest to a collective rite fulfilled regularly that may have been analogous to the sacred marriage rite. Here it was a fertility rite connected with the magical calling forth of rain. The rite included mass human sacrifices to Ancestress Keng (The Seventh").

The wives of the *wang*s are not infrequently mentioned in the inscriptions. They seem to have been high priestesses. The inscriptions attest to the high priestess having an agricultural economy of her own and even (as mentioned above) her own armed forces. A high priestess could also be the mother or the sister of the *wang* or a wife of one of the brothers of the *wang*'s mother. Sacrifices were made to the female ancestors in the clan of the *wang*, probably in their status as female chiefs and high priestesses, independent of the offerings to their husbands. This can be seen from the inscriptions on the oracle bones. Some scholars find in the inscriptions a special title for the high priestess–chief.

In this connection the excavation of one of the richest big burials found near Anyang is of special interest. Name signs on the sacred vessels found in this burial mention the "Royal Ancestress, the Eighth," "The Lady Hao." In this burial there were discovered nearly 1,500 artifacts of bronze, jade, and ivory, including a number of figurines of men and women representing, to judge from their clothes and exterior, persons of different social condition and ethnic origin. Here were also put to death and buried sixteen people—men, women, and children. The priestly rank of the central figure in the burial can be deduced from the great number (more than 200!) of ritual vessels, among them a pair of huge square vats, weighing 117.5 kilograms each, with the name of the owner engraved; also the earliest bronze mirrors found in China and different cultic musical instruments were found. Many weapons of every kind found in the same burial may point to the military dignity of the deceased "ancestress." There were also 6,000 cowries, indicating her great wealth. Note also that the largest ritual kettles found at Anyang (and mentioned above), which weighed 875 kilograms; also had inscriptions declaring the owner as a highborn lady: "Ancestress the Fifth," possibly another high priestess–chief. Several scholars think that both the Eighth Ancestress and the Fifth Ancestress were wives of Yin *wang*s.

In this society elements of ancient clan ideology were still very much alive. The cult of the fertility goddess, of the Great and High Ancestress, was very important. Abundant human sacrifices were due to her, so that special military expeditions headed by the *wang* were organized to capture prisoners, mostly from the tribes of the Ch'iang.

The office of the *wang* was hereditary but passed, not from father to son, but from one brother to another, or from an uncle to a nephew. We do not think that the rule of genealogical seniority was completely established at this time. Note that inscriptions are very common that mention sacrifices to the "many fathers" and the "many mothers" of the *wang*. That the Shang society was archaic is evidenced by its kinship system. The kinship terms are connected with age and marriage classes, and there is no differentiation of kinship relations inside one age-group. Cross-cousin marriages were obligatory between two exogamous dual-kinship groups. Eventually the transfer of the *wang*'s office within a generation (i.e., from an elder brother to a younger one) was replaced, and under the two last Shang *wang*s this office passed from father to son, demonstrating that the patrilineal principle had gained the upper hand.

The religious ideas of the Shang were closely connected with an identification of the magical power of the clan with political authority. Deities in Shang religion were perceived as human beings who, having passed into another world, still had their niche in the clan genealogy and, just as persons of this world, required food and care from the living. The ancestor cult, especially the royal ancestor cult, was the focus of all public activities in the Shang state. Along with the deceased rulers, their spouses also had their cults.

Because the *wang* was also the high priest, he alone (the "unique [or first] man," as he termed himself) could address the divine protectors of the Shang and could personally perform the necessary rites. His closest ties were with the nearest ancestors, who are called by name in the oracle inscriptions; they received from him the most copious offerings. At the head of the pyramid formed by the royal clan stood the First Ancestor and Supreme Deity, Shang-ti. The sacrificial rites to Shang-ti were performed comparatively seldom and were not especially splendid. The reason may have been that the *wang* thought it possible to influence the supreme deity through the mediation of the lower ranks in the divine hierarchy.[18] Five helpers of Shang-ti are sometimes mentioned, perhaps corresponding to the four cardinal points of the world and to its center. Also diverse local deities are mentioned in the oracle texts (spirits of the rivers, mountains, etc.). Some of them were deities of conquered tribes.

18. This may be an archaic feature in the Shang religion. In many archaic community religions, it is typical that the supreme deity is a *deus otiosus*, taking little part in running the world order. Editor's note (IMD).

Each community district that was part of the cultic federation constituting Shang society had its own tutelary deity, a *fang-ti,* who had
the gift of granting fertility and was probably regarded as the protector and ancestor of the population group in question.

A number of shamanistic features can be discerned in Shang religion. Shamanism is typical of many peoples but especially of groups
in northern Asia and America. Male and female shamans played an
important role in the royal rites, because they were thought to be able
to converse directly with the deities. They also could exorcise evil spirits. A number of typical features of shamanism are attested in Shang
religion: drums, fore-eyed masks, and horns (symbols of power). The
spirits of the dead are depicted in China as being horned. A bird
could be an intermediary between the world of the dead and the
world of the living (e.g., the swallow). The dynastic myth of the Shang
traced their origin from a certain "dark bird."

The Shang religion was the result of a very orderly *Weltanschauung.*
If we regard the archaic mythology and ritual as an attempt to introduce order into real life and to control the reality not dependent on
human activity, we can perceive that the Shang culture achieved a
structural ordering of the world after the pattern of relations dominating inside the clan. The main element was not the individual. It
was an order where everything had its place and functioned in a
systematic interplay. Typically, Shang art is characterized by a considerable degree of token conventionality and by the dominance of
symmetry and other forms of geometric stylization of images. The
contradiction between the increasing symbolization of religious ritual
and the ecstatic character of the shamanistic rites brought about, in
time, a crisis in the Shang ideology.

A few words ought to be devoted to the external connections of
Shang society. One should always keep in mind that the first foci of
urban class civilization in China lay more than 3,500 kilometers away
from the area of the closest, and more ancient, Oriental civilization—
the Indus Valley. Moreover, they were shut off from it, as well as from
other areas of Asia, by the world's greatest deserts and by practically
insurmountable mountains and rough plateaus. It must be regarded
as certain that China, so far beyond the reach of the ancient civilizations of Western Asia, could, at that early time, experience little influence from other class societies but had to develop quite independently, according to the general laws of history. That the Shang
culture evolved, in the main, quite independently is proved by the
clear continuity in the development of the local cultures, beginning
with the Neolithic ones, and by the high technological achievements
of the Lungshan pottery culture, whose creators were capable of

bringing the temperature of pottery baking to the point of smelting copper.

This, however, does not mean that the society of ancient China developed in complete isolation,[19] without any links whatsoever with other peoples. Like any other society, the Chinese could not have existed without international trade.

The middle reaches of the Huang Ho are a crossroads of routes leading toward the north-northwest, the Mongolian steppes and to the oases of Middle Asia, and toward the south, to the Yangtze Valley. Already in the Shang Period this region had links with southern China and the lands of southeastern Asia. The giant tortoises were brought by the tribes of the Yangtze Valley. Cowrie shells, used as a sort of primitive money, could have been brought from Burma. Tin ingots[20] were brought from the south to make bronze. Certain influences reached Shang China from the oases of Middle Asia. Moreover, some types of Shang pottery seem to have parallels as far away as Mohenjo-daro and Jemdet-Nasr. The jades of Anyang may have been brought from Middle Asia. Some zoomorphic ornaments remind one of Mesopotamian ones: serpents with interlacing coils, rampant tigers facing each other, and sundry other animals. There are archaeological data pointing to the arrival of merchandise from Xinjiang (Hsin-Chiang, eastern Turkestan) and from Siberia, probably through the mediation of steppe tribes. Trade may explain, to a considerable degree, the primitive riches of the Shang culture.

The State Federation of Chou (Western Chou)

To the west of Shang, in the valley of the river Wei (a tributary of the Huang Ho) in the modern province of Shenhsi, there lived during the fourteenth century B.C. a warlike Proto-Chinese tribe called Chou. A rivalry began between the Shang and the Chou that took the form of open military conflicts. It is assumed that the Chou entered the Wei Valley from the west.

In the first half of the second millennium B.C. the Chou were ani-

19. The use of wheat, barley, sheep, and goats is evidence for some diffusionary process from Western Asia, and the earliest unequivocal Chinese bronzes—dating mainly to the third millennium B.C.were found in Gansu Province, or west of the area later incorporated by the Shang "state." Although earlier diffusionist attempts to see Chinese civilization as "secondary" or somehow "derivative" cannot be maintained, questions still remain concerning the possible diffusion of technologies from west to east (e.g., metals) or, for that matter, east to west (e.g., sericulture) during the Bronze Age. Editor's note (PLK).

20. Recent research has shown the existence of a "tin belt" stretching through southern China, Burma, Thailand, and Malaysia.

mal breeders with a primitive form of agriculture. There are certain data pointing to the acquaintance of the Chou with bronze making at least by the second half of the second millennium. As their ancestress, they originally revered the goddess Ch'iang Yuan of the Clan of the Ram. Later, Hou-Ch'i, the "Chief of the Millet" (or "Millet Lord/Lady"), was considered to be the ancestor of the Chou.

The ethnic consolidation of the Chou was very complicated. Although the Chou later became a part of the Chinese ethnic entity, some scholars ascribe to them a Tibeto-Burman linguistic origin.

It seems that beginning with the second millennium the Chou slowly infiltrated into the neighboring territories of other ethnic groups, in a generally easterly direction from their original habitat, which meant also into the territory of the Shang. The Yin oracle attests to contacts with the Chou in the second part of the second millennium. We encounter questions to the oracle regarding the Chou; for example, "Will not misfortune befall the Chou?" It seems that Chou, at times, was part of the Shang federation. In the *Tales of the Kingdoms* (*Kuo Yu*) and in the *Tso Chuan*, written down in the fourth to third centuries B.C., there are reminiscences of the Yin and the Chou sacrificing to the same deity, Kun, which may point to their belonging to some common cultic union.[21] However, all the data are fragmentary and obscure. The sign *chou* (a field divided into parcels) appears in the oracle texts very rarely compared with references to other tribes, towns, and communities that must have been in frequent contact with the Shang. Therefore, the conquest of Shang by the Chou in the late second millennium at first glance seems surprising. According to legend, however, the Chou had "three hundred districts" (*chuhou*) as their allies, thus heading a strong military coalition. The date of the conquest is conventionally set at 1122 B.C., but it cannot claim to be exact and may be about a century too late.

If we take into consideration the inevitable weakening of Shang power in their struggle with the eastern tribes, the war becoming interminable and most exhausting by the end of the eleventh century and being followed by total devastation of the territories surrounding Shang proper, then Shang's defeat becomes understandable. It is even possible that the incapacity of the Shang to withstand the incursions of the eastern tribes might have been one of the causes that made their former satellites change sides and join the Chou. The decisive battle of Muye, which was lost by the Shang, may have been pre-

21. During the historicizing of the mythological heritage under the Chou, the image of Kun was reinterpreted: in the *Shu Ching* Kun has become a negative character exiled from the inhabited world by a deified ancestor, Shun, who was introduced into the pantheon of the Chou.

ceded by a prolonged struggle between the Chou and the Shang for domination in the middle valley of the Huang Ho.

The unusual military activity of the Chou at the end of the second millennium may have been connected with the acceleration of the process of class formation in the Chou society, prompted by the achievements of the early class society in Yin. The Yin made use of the rich potentialities for agricultural development on the alluvial lands of the Lower Huang Ho, and these lands may in the first place have attracted the Chou.

Vivid reminiscences about how the military chiefs of the Chou grew more powerful and how they created a mighty union of tribes (or districts) have come down to us in the poetic collection of songs *Shih Ching* and in the collection of historical texts *Shu Ching*.

In the *Shih Ching* and the *Shu Ching* the Chou tradition ascribed the mystic appropriation of the holy "Will of Heaven" (*t'ien ming*) to Ch'ang, also called Wen wang, "The Beautiful King," who ordered them to destroy "the city of Shang." The divine chastisement was fulfilled by his son, Wu wang, "The Warlike King." A much later tradition connects Wu wang with the creation of a vast "Chou Empire," projecting into that remote epoch the historical reality belonging to the second to first centuries B.C., when the Eastern Han Empire needed "proof" that an empire had existed from time immemorial and that it had a divine origin.

The Yin confederation of nome-type city-communities, headed by the "Great City of Shang," was replaced by a kingdom uniting the territory of the vast river basin of the lower and upper courses of the Huang Ho. The Chou community-tribal cult of Hou Chi became the state cult and eventually came to be accepted by all the communities within the dominion of Chou.

An entirely new cult appeared. It was not connected with an ethnic group but stood above all and everybody and united them. This was the cult of the Supreme Deity, namely, Heaven; it was connected with the cult of the Son of Heaven, the Chou *wang*.

There is some truth in the orthodox historical tradition about Chou. It was actually during the Western Chou Period (its beginning is traditionally associated with the time when Wu wang conquered the city of Shang) that the foundations of a new political order in northern China were laid, determining for many future centuries some of the typical characteristics of the states of ancient China.

From the very beginning Western Chou was not a unified state. Its hierarchical structure was in some respects reminiscent of the Hittite state, where princes, governors, and allied kings paid tribute to the supreme king but otherwise ruled their regions autonomously. After the Yin union was crushed, the Chou resettled the "recalcitrant Yin" on one of the estates of the Chou rulers. Apparently, the Chou had four such "capital-palaces." Three were in the Wei River basin, the main Chou base; one was in the Lo River basin. It was in the latter, Ch'eng-Chou, that the Yin were resettled and used as workers in the royal economy. The rest of the Yin remained in their former places, but their lands were granted to the relatives and companions-in-arms of the conquerors. The lands captured by the Chou in their further conquests were either given to the Chou elite (primarily to the relatives of the Chou ruling class) or remained under the management of the original rulers and chiefs, who were not supervised by special "observers" of the Chou *wang*. Thus the Chou *wang*s ruled their dependent territories indirectly.

Under Ch'eng wang (son of Wu wang, who died almost immediately following his victory over the city of Shang) the country was torn apart by quarrels between the top members of the Chou aristocracy and between the brothers of Wu wang, who were pretenders to the throne. The rule of succession was not firmly established, in spite of the fact that the later king list shows an uninterrupted line of successively ruling Chou *wang*s, beginning with Wen wang. It was only through the elimination of all his paternal uncles that Ch'eng managed to hold on to his power. In the future, the house of Chou again had to resort to armed force in order to assert its right to the throne.

As mentioned above, the early state structure of the Western Chou Period included, in addition to cities and regions that were directly subject to the *wang* and his governors, semiautonomous dominions. These were the territories conquered by the Chou and assigned to relatives of the Chou house and to companions-in-arms of the *wang*, as well as regions handed over to high functionaries. All such subordinate rulers swore allegiance to the *wang*. Special high functionaries of the court were charged with the supervision of the semiautonomous rulers (*chuhou*) of these regions, making sure that they performed their duties for the house of Chou, which included sharing any war spoils with the *wang*.

The drawing up of a penal code (apparently orally transmitted) is traditionally attributed to Mu wang (tenth century B.C.). It can be concluded from legend that the *wang* himself acted as judge in the most important cases. Fines could be paid in lieu of other punishment, including the death penalty. The allied rulers, subjects of the Western Chou house, were counted by the dozens and even hundreds (a legendary source even mentions eighteen hundred). Seventy-one such dominions (*kuo*) were placed under the members of the royal Chou family.

The Chou *wang* granted land, not because he had the supreme right to all land in the country, but, rather, because he exercised state sovereignty. The *wang*'s deeds of transfer to the high functionaries were officially registered as "gifts." This did not mean, however, that the transferred land became their private property. These lands were not regarded as withdrawn from the royal land fund. It was only the right to draw income from this real estate that was being transferred. When a new ruler ascended the throne, these deeds had to be renewed. After the middle of the ninth century B.C., granted lands could be passed to the holders' heirs, though still by the *wang*'s decree.

Sometimes not only land, settlements, and cattle were transferred but also "people of the *wang*, workers of different categories, "from stable hands to farmers." The "people of the *wang*" also included some functionaries. The number of people transferred could exceed one thousand. Workers (*ch'en*) were frequently transferred by families, from five to two hundred families of *ch'en* at a time. Although they were all called "royal people," not all of them were actually slaves. Some were individuals of high rank, although, in the eyes of their contemporaries, they were all equally subject to the *wang* and thus were not *personae sui juris*.

Large and complex royal economies appeared. They included farming, cattle breeding, and crafts enterprises, which were managed by special functionaries—"land overseers" (*ssu t'u*), "overseers of craftsmen," and so on. Royal-cum-temple economies were also common. The *wang* presided over the cult of Hou Chi and performed the sacred rite of tracing the "first furrow," a magical act in which the *wang* personified the fertility and well-being of the country. Free people (i.e., community members) were also called upon to work in these economies, but most of the work force was composed of large contingents of people with slave status. Some were convicted criminals condemned to slave labor, but most were prisoners captured during military campaigns. They were supervised by *shih* ("miliary chiefs," "commanders"). In general, the armed forces were the coercive arm of the state, and one of their duties was overseeing slave labor. The military ranks were invested with special production powers connected with organizing and maintaining forced labor in the vast royal economies. They were in charge of supplying this work force through military expeditions.

As the practice of granting lands expanded, and as very large economic entities developed that were virtually slaveholding, the aims and objectives of war also changed. The acquisition of territory was the primary aim, but capturing prisoners of war for slavery was just as important. The *wang* himself disposed of the captives by distributing

them among the participants of the military expeditions. He also enacted punitive measures and guaranteed the return of fugitive slaves
to their masters.

The main sources on the Western Chou Period are epigraphs;
namely, inscriptions on bronze objects such as decorative or ritual vessels. Among the texts we find direct references to the conquest of the
Shang state: "The *wang* conquered the Shang [country] and fortified
himself in Ch'eng-Chou," and Ch'eng wang "punished the city of
Shang and granted land to Kang Hou [the brother of Wu wang] in
the Yin region of Wei." But such inscriptions are an exception; mostly
they give no information about the political history of the period, a
history that still cannot be ascertained by reliable sources. Some scholars even think that the only reliable historical fact about the Western
Chou Period comes from its final year; namely, the resettlement of
the Chou people to the east in 770 B.C.

The sources from this period include Chou literary works, which,
however, have come down to us only in much later copies or versions.
These are the collection of historical legends, *Shu Ching*, and the collection of songs called *Shih Ching*. The latter is the most interesting
source. The work is a compilation of lively folk songs vividly reflecting
the life of people during Chou times. It is clear, however, that a single
collection of folk songs cannot convey a complete image of the social
structure of any society. One difficulty, in particular, complicates the
work of the historian. What is the precise meaning of the different
terms found in *Shih Ching* and *Shu Ching* and in the inscriptions on
bronze. The fact that some of the terms coincide formally with those
used in more recent epochs does not help much, because we do not
know what they meant during the Chou Period.

We can conclude from the songs of *Shih Ching* that marshes and
low-growing forests still covered much of the northern Great Chinese
Plain. Game was plentiful. Despite the fact that tools remained as
rudimentary as before, arable land was expanded around the settlements of the middle and the lower course of the Huang Ho. This increase in cultivated acreage was accompanied by a gradual draining of
swamplands. Just at that time the climate of northern China became
colder. The importance of cattle breeding diminished. This can be
concluded from the fact that many written signs relating to cattle
breeding and animal sacrifices disappeared from the vocabulary between the end of the second millennium and the eighth to seventh
centuries B.C. An important factor in the development of productive
forces was the expansion and improvement of bronze casting.

Urban-type settlements now spread over the entire region between
the northern steppes and the Yangtze basin. As a rule, they were built

near rivers and were surrounded by earthen walls protecting the inhabitants against enemy invasions and floods. These settlements were actually small towns or fortresses. The walled-in perimeter was no larger than 700–900 meters. These walled towns were laid out in squares or rectangles, with their corners oriented toward the four cardinal points. Each of the four sides of the wall had a gate.

According to *Shih Ching,* it can be assumed that these were territorial communities (judging from later information, they had collective self-governing institutions). The lands of the community were divided into those cultivated for the state (*kung-ch'ien*) and for the "private" sector (*ssu-ch'ien*). Keeping in mind the enormous role played by the extended family throughout the millennia, these "private" lands are to be understood as nonstate rather than as owned by individuals. The free members of the territorial communities outside the state sector constituted the main part of the population. They were obligated to make deliveries in kind to the state and also to take part in obligatory state labor.

The free men belonging to the Chou proper—the *po hsiang,* the "hundred families"—constituted a privileged category and enjoyed the right to receive free food distributed by the state. Systematic intracommunal land reallotments survived for a long time because there were no permanent irrigation systems that could have hindered such reallotment. The territorial and extended-family communities continued to be the collective owners of land.

It seems that private farms not included in the community also began to come into existence. The main labor in such economies, as was also the case in the royal economies, was performed by different categories of workers, but all of them were slaves or slave-type personnel. However, these workers were not always fully dispossessed of personal rights; this is typical of the early stage of the slave owner type of production system.

Excavations of burial grounds from this period attest to the consolidation of the power of the slave owner and the development of private slavery. A wealthy master would be found buried with several of his slaves (usually two to four) who had been bound and slain. At the same time, because slave labor had become an important factor in production, the mass sacrifices of slaves/war prisoners and their burials, so common during the Yin Period, completely disappeared during the Western Chou Period.

The early state of the Western Chou was too loosely organized to last for a long time. Within this system the power of the *chuhou* gradually increased and, with it, a desire for independence. This situation was aggravated by tribal incursions from the northwest and southeast.

At the beginning of the ninth century B.C., the Eastern Yi advanced all the way to the city of Ch'eng-Chou. And substantial pressure was exerted by the nomadic Tung tribes in the northwest (in Shenhsi). Attempts on the part of the Chou *wang* to sign a treaty with them provoked a counterreaction from the *chuhou*. The Chou were not able to resist the onslaught of the nomadic tribes, which came from the depths of Middle Asia. They began to retreat from their homeland in the Wei River basin (in Shenhsi). The last king of Western Chou, P'ing wang (770–720 B.C.), moved his capital east into Honan. During this time, some formerly dependent territories attained equality with the new and smaller Eastern Chou kingdom and became independent states. Thus began the period of "Many Kingdoms," Lie Kuo.

The Ideology of Chou

The passing of the power to Chou was connected with important changes in the public consciousness and the ideological traditions of ancient China.[22] The Chou introduced the notion of a supreme deity, whom they called T'ien.[23] In the original form the hieroglyph *t'ien* depicted a big man whose head was specially emphasized; it was probably used to denote the chief's ancestors. According to Chou myth, Hou Chi, the mother of the first ancestor of the Chou, became pregnant by stepping into the footprint of a giant. Before the conquest of the Shang state, there appeared among the Chou a legend that their kings were, through the maternal line, kinsmen of the Shang kings. After conquering Shang, they identified their supreme deity, T'ien, with the Shang supreme deity, Shang-Ti. But such a contamination implied the abandonment of the concept of a gentilic or clan deity. The notion *ti* could not be separated from totemic heritage, and its use in China was limited to the "clan body" of the individual dynasties. But the term *t'ien* in the sense of "heaven" served the new idea of a supreme active principle in the universe, not grounded in the archaic religion.

The historical fate of the idea of T'ien was predetermined at the moment of the Chou conquest, when the Chou tried to justify their actions by asserting that "Heaven" itself had decreed the punishment of the Shang ruler for his sins. The new dynasty stated that it was the supreme deity that invested them with the "Heavenly Command" (*t'ien ming*) to rule and to take away power from the Shang. In the same way, it was thought that the first Shang ruler took away the

22. This section has been written by V. V. Malyavin.

23. Some scholars of early China believe the Chou received their concept of a supreme deity from the Shang. (Editor's note (PLK).

Heavenly Command from the last ruler of the dynasty of Hsia, supposed to have ruled before Shang.

The new interpretation of state power had important consequences of long duration. From now on, the real justification of power was seen in the individual merits of the founder of the dynasty and his successors. In the terms of Chou ideology, the right to found a dynasty was grounded on the possession of a certain cosmic charisma, *teh*, another notion unknown in the Shang Period. The original hieroglyph *teh* represented the idea of the chief's magical powers inside the framework of gentilic (clan) religion. With time, however, the term assumed a more moral connotation.

Thus, Heaven was believed by the Chou to be a deity who meted out punishment for bad deeds and reward for good deeds. But the answer to the question, who is to be in possession of the Heavenly Command depended solely on men themselves. The Chou never tired of saying that the favor of Heaven is not guaranteed to them forever and that it is not easy to deserve it. The accent on the moral and absolutely impartial will of Heaven was responsible for the importance of the category "people" (*min*) in Chou ideology. In the Chou texts, the "people" are declared to be the bearers of the Will of Heaven, and care for the "people" is placed even above care for the spirits. The nonclan and nontribal character of Heaven allowed the Chou to incorporate the tribal gods into their religious-political system as local deities, or demons, mostly responsible for the fertility of the soil (the *she*).

The innovations of the Chou Period marked the beginning of a new stage in the interpretation of Universe and Man. The conception of a Holy Power in an individual manifestation gave way gradually to the conception of an absolute universal reality as the source of universal motion and of the immutable Fate of all that exists. Primitive magic, based on emotional experience, ceded its place to an emotional perception of cosmic links; to the ideology of genealogical succession, moral arguments were added. The cosmic power eclipsed the ancient deities, but unlike Western monotheism, it did not take over any of their anthropomorphic features. Heaven became an absolute anonymous and impersonal Judge, whose judgment is abstracted from the affairs of humanity. The relation between Heaven and the archaic deities was, as a matter of principle, not determined. Thus, the supremacy of Heaven allowed for the existence both of elements of archaic religion (such as the cult of the ancestors and the cult of natural elements) and also of other cults: local, familial, individual. The complex hierarchy of cults held together by the concept of Heaven as the focus of the hierarchic order became traditional for the Chinese religious system.

The concept of the cosmos as a real acting power led to a reinterpretation of the essence of ritual (*li*). In Western Chou ritual still preserved its archaic sense; it was, first of all, a sacrificial ritual, a way to communicate with the ancestors, and its sphere was limited to the ruler's clan. But already in that period the notion of ritual was rationalized in two ways: on the one hand, it was dramatized, and, on the other, its intimacy was accentuated. The Chou, however, interpreted communion with the deity as a mutual distancing. Their understanding of ritual can be seen from the classical sentence from the treatise "Notes on Ritual" ("Li Chi"): "To honor the deities and to keep at a distance from them." This resulted in the transformation of ritual into an ethical norm, a precondition of moral self-evaluation, and was one of the indications of the growing secularization of the Chou culture. The unity of form and content in Chou ritual was due to the accentuation of the necessity for restraint and self-absorption. The Chou themselves felt that this sharply distinguished their culture from the ecstatic cults of the Shang.

The rationalization of the categories and values of archaic religion was due to two main factors. One of them was the paramount importance of divination in China, which hindered the creation of a prophetic religion and made it impossible for an individualized revelational god to appear.[24] The transformation of archaic divination into a system of ethico-cosmic ideas can be seen from the fate of the ancient Chou mantic book *I Ching* (often called *The Book of Changes*). In the final analysis "divination" by *I Ching* was felt as cognition of the universal connectedness of things and a participation in the universal movement. In practice, it meant knowing what not to do.

The second factor was that, first, the chiefs of the clans and, later, the secular rulers were the centers of all religious life. Governing the state was a religious ritual; administrative documents were divine scriptures. Already in the Shang state there existed written memorials of the deeds of Shang kings. These memorials were designated by the hieroglyph *t'ien*, which later is an image of tied-together planks on a small table, indicating that they were especially revered. Such notes on earlier royal acts, which functioned as historical precedents, were composed also at the Chou court and later also in the capitals of the independent princes. Such notes, indicating the growing secularization of writing, were entered in the canonic book *Shu Ching;* but the entire, abundant corpus of archaic myths was not included in the Chou memorials. The canonic tradition relates these myths only

---

24. Compare the somewhat analogous opposition between the Babylonian cults with their "Omina" (which, however, did not exclude the existence of individual deities) and the prophetic religion of Israel. Editor's note (IMD).

in part and, moreover, in a form distorted beyond recognition by pseudohistorical and didactic treatment. The Chou activities revived the mythical characters, who now appear as kings, dignitaries, scholars, magicians from ancient times, and so on. This was achieved thanks to the continuity between the gentilic (genealogical) body and the state in ancient China. Thus the Chou epoch was the time of the discovery of the "mirror of history," which was a mirror of double depth: the metaphysical depth of the universe present in the idea of Heaven and the corresponding depth of humanity's self-consciousness.

Beginning with the eighth century B.C. the Chou state and, consequently, also the Chou ideology went through a deepening crisis. In the ideological sense, it was a crisis of confidence in the idea of Heaven as the supreme ethical power. There are a few indications of this in the canonic *Shih Ching.*

The apologists for the Chou tradition tried to find an answer by opposing rule through etiquette and moral influence, the so-called Way of the *Wang* (*wang tao*), and rule by power, the so-called Way of the Hegemon (*pa tao*). The Chou court tried to save itself by promoting the *wang tao,* even if it involved a voluntary retirement from actual politics.

The opposition of *wang tao* and *pa tao* had important consequences for Chinese history. It predetermined the development in China of a certain duality in political power, where politics balanced between ritualization of state life and overattention to the purely practical side of administration. But the concept of power could not defer the decay of the Chou idea of ritual, which was the main feature of public life and of the culture of the Chou state.

20

China in the First Half
of the First Millennium B.C.

T. V. Stepugina

Political History

Ancient society in the western part of the Old World reached its developmental peak in the first half of the first half of the first millennium B.C. Meanwhile at the easternmost end of the Old World, society was still undergoing processes that were typical of Western Asia in the second millennium B.C. but which had become outdated there by the first millennium B.C.

Western Chou was a loosely knit, early state formation that, to some degree, is reminiscent of the first big states in the Near East. Like many of them, Western Chou was also destroyed by an invasion of new tribes. Western Chou disintegrated in the first quarter of the eighth century B.C. under the pressure of western nomads from Shenhsi. The Chou people abandoned their former capital, the city of Hao near modern Hsian in the Wei River basin, and consolidated their position to the east, in the district of the modern city of Loyang. Here, P'ing wang formed a small kingdom with its capital in the city of Luoyi. This transfer (in 770 B.C.) traditionally marks a new stage in Chinese history, that of Eastern Chou. It is divided into two subperiods: Lie Kuo ("Many Kingdoms" or "Series of Kingdoms") and Chan Kuo ("Warring Kingdoms" or "Battles of Kingdoms"). The Lie Kuo Period is dated to approximately the eighth to sixth centuries and is sometimes called Ch'un Ch'in ("Springs and Autumns," so named after a chronicle of this period). The Chan Kuo Period is dated to the second half of the fifth to the end of the third centuries and is sometimes called the Preimperial Period.

Many separate and independent kingdoms (150–200) existed in China at the beginning of the Lie Kuo Period. These tiny city-states, or community states (*kuo*), were dispersed throughout the basin of the middle and lower courses of the Huang-Ho River and the Great Chinese Plain. A fierce struggle for supremacy flared up between them, following a relatively peaceful but short-lived period of coexistence. These internecine wars led to the absorption of small kingdoms by larger ones, and toward the end of the eighth century B.C. (more precisely, around 722 B.C., the first year covered by the *Ch'un Ch'in* chronicle), about a dozen of the most important kingdoms emerged, including Eastern Chou. The historical tradition of Chou considered them to be the Central Kingdoms (*chung kuo*) of the inhabited world (*t'ien hsia*, the "Universe under Heaven," usually translated in the West as "Celestial Empire"). Chung Kuo still remains the official name of China.[1]

Among the Central Kingdoms, those of Lu, Wei,[2] Sung, and Cheng were inhabited by descendants of the Yin people. All of them were under the nominal religious supremacy of the *wang* of Chou. It was a dual form of government, whose power, though divided, nevertheless allowed for the recognition of one spiritual leader. It constituted the legacy and further development of the early state order of Western Chou. This dual system developed in each of the numerous small states of the Huang Ho River basin. They were all essentially independent but formally recognized the *wang* of Chou as their military and religious leader. Eastern Chou, which survived as a relatively small state in the district of the modern city of Loyang, continued to be regarded as the cultic center of the Celestial Empire. Its rulers were called Sons of Heaven (*t'ien tzu*). The supreme royal title *wang* was held only by the kings of the Chou dynasty. The kings of all the other realms of the Chou world were recognized as "subordinate rulers" (*chuhou*), and each of them held one of the hierarchical titles granted by the *wang* to de facto independent rulers: *kung, hou, po, tzu, nan*. History, however, shows that the character of this hierarchy was formal, and that such a ranking of the rulers of the Chou kingdoms was practically irrelevant as early as the first half of the seventh century B.C.

After the transfer of the Chou capital to Luoyi, internecine wars and dissension within the ruling house of the *wang* weakened Chou to such an extent that other, stronger states of the Huang Ho basin placed it, as the cultic center of the Celestial Empire, under their own protection. The military and the priestly powers, which had earlier seemed inseparable, came to be regarded as independent from one another, and the militarily stronger ruler now acquired a new and important function: the military protection of the *wang* of Chou, the supreme religious leader of the Celestial Empire, the Son of Heaven. The concept of the "universal" character of the royal state power of

1. The concept of *chung kuo* was later interpreted as "the Kingdom [in the singular] central in the Universe under Heaven" and began to be contrasted with the rest of the world, which was conceived as that of "barbarians."

2. This kingdom must be distinguished from another, designated by a different hieroglyphic sign but read the same way, which arose in Shanhsi after the disintegration of the Ch'in kingdom.

the *wang*s of Chou developed precisely during this period. The fact that the competing rulers recognized the formal supremacy of the *wang* of Chou may be explained by their wish to gain the prestigious function of protecting him, and thus to place themselves above the other rulers who were practically equal to them. Any of these rulers, had he wished, might have put an end to the fragile supremacy of Chou.

The idea of the divine origin of the Chou dynasty was supposed to lay the foundation for a stable cultic leadership of the *wang*s of Chou. A story was circulated about the Hsia and Yin dynasties, which preceded the Chou dynasty, as "rejected by Heaven." Although on the Yin oracle bones the term *wang* actually refers to the ruler of Shang, it is revealing that the traditional dynastic list of ancient kings (in the version of the historian Ssu-ma Ch'ien, second to first centuries B.C.) recognizes the title of *wang* only for the rulers of the Chou dynasty.

We know much more about the kingdoms of the Chou world in the Huang Ho basin than about other ancient Chinese states of that time because of the specificity of the sources describing this period. The most important of them is the chronicle of the Lu kingdom, *Ch'un Ch'in,* and the commentary on it, *Tso Chuan.* The kings of Lu (in Shantung) claimed descent from the semilegendary Chou-Kung, uncle of Ch'eng, the *wang* of Chou, and his regent. Tradition ascribed to Chou-Kung the "merit" of the final subjugation of the Shangs and the establishment of the system of land distribution to high officials as the principle of the state order of Chou. His descendants declared themselves the protectors of the cultic traditions of Chou.

As a rule, the *Ch'un Ch'in* usually made reference to those kingdoms that were not part of the Chou world only insofar as they entered into contact with the kingdoms included in that world. But even this sparse information testifies to a progressive consolidation (at least after the second half of the seventh century) of states situated outside the Central Kingdoms. An important characteristic in the political history of the Lie Kuo Period was the political and, apparently, also the ethnic contrast between the southern kingdoms of the middle and lower courses of the Yangtze River (which were numerous in the seventh century) and the northern states of the Huang Ho River basin.

The first southern and ethnically non-Han kingdom to gain importance was Ch'u (along the middle course of the Yangtze); it was followed by the maritime kingdoms of Wu (in the Yangtze Delta) and Yue (located south of the Wu kingdom in the coastal region of modern Chechiang). They continued very ancient Late Neolithic and Early Bronze Age traditions that took shape among the tribes and peoples of Southeast Asia—the distant ancestors of the Vietnamese, the Chuang, the Miao, the Tao, the Thai, and other peoples that today inhabit this vast region. Later, Yue became the general designation of the maritime tribes, regardless of language, living in the region stretching from Chechiang to Vietnam.

Ancient Chinese sources use the general term *chiao chih* or *man* for the inhabitants of the Yangtze basin. What particular ethnic groups interacted here during this period is still unknown, but there is no doubt that they were alien to the Chou world. The *chiao chih* may have included speakers of Proto-Thai, Sino-Tibetan, languages of the Austroasiatic linguistic phylum, or even Proto-Austronesian languages. However, the comparative and historical linguistic research of Southeast Asia and Oceania is still in its initial stages, and at present, we can deal only with more- or less-probable hypotheses.

Ch'u, the most ancient state in South China, dating to at least as early as the eighth century B.C., gradually aligned itself with other, apparently Proto-Thai-speaking, kingdoms. Wu and Yue were probably founded by related tribes; we know that the people of both tribes "painted their bodies and cut their hair" (Ssu-ma Ch'ien).

Archaeological materials and written sources testify to a distinct and original civilization in Southeast Asia and in modern South China. Cultural achievements, such as the cultivation of rice, artificial irrigation, shipbuilding, the art of making lacquered ware, and others were adopted from the south by the natives of northern China. Archaeological data show that the Huang Ho River basin regions had contacts with South China and Southeast Asia since very ancient times. The south was especially important to North China because it had been, from very early times, a source of tin, the metal necessary for making bronze.

Under the conditions of constant wars between the kingdoms and pressure from the surrounding tribes, individual states of the north and south formed mutual foreign policy alliances and leagues. The military power of a state was measured by the number of its battle chariots. Thus the term *wan ch'eng kuo,* "a state with 10,000 four-horse battle chariots," expressed the idea of "the strongest state." The more powerful kingdoms gradually annexed vast territories by subduing their weaker neighbors. The Chou kingdom constantly lost territory in this process.

Some kingdoms of the Huang Ho and Yangtze basins, such as Ch'i, Chin, and Ch'u, expanded so much that they no longer can be regarded as city-states or groups of cities; rather, they embraced whole countries. The rulers of the state that, by the standards of that time, was the most powerful claimed personal supremacy over all the Chung Kuo and over the entire Celestial Empire. They proclaimed themselves "leaders" (*pa*) and tried to secure the confirmation of their new title from the *wang*s of Chou. In earlier times, the idea of "Heavenly

Command' (t'ien ming)[3] was developed in order to justify the power of
the wang of Chou over the conquered Yin or Shang. Later, it granted
the wang of Chou, in his capacity as the Son of Heaven, ceremonial
kingship over the entire world. The first leaders formally legalized
their power by nominally recognizing the supremacy of the Chou
king, because it was believed that it was he who embodied the magical
power of possessing the Heavenly Command, despite his meager territory and army. Real power, however, remained fully in the hands of
the leaders, who succeeded one another.

The first leader to be proclaimed was the ruler of Ch'i (in Shantung) in 679 B.C. This was one of the ten leading kingdoms in the beginning of the Lie Kuo Period. Chin (in the Fen River basin, Shanhsi)
became a "leadership" in 635 B.C. Although this kingdom was not part
of the Central Kingdoms at that time, it did have close relations with
them. From the very beginning it assumed the protection of the throne
of the wangs of Chou and, like Ch'i, became head of a military alliance
of kingdoms, in opposition to the Ch'u coalition of southern states.
Eventually, however, even states considered alien to the Chou world
began to claim leadership status. The southern kingdom of Ch'u,
strongest among these states, became a leadership at the end of the
seventh and beginning of the sixth century.

Traditional historiography segregates the time of the supremacy of
the leaders into a special subperiod, Wu pa, "Five Leaders." Apart
from the three kingdoms mentioned above (Ch'i, Chin, and Ch'u),
which were the most powerful during the Lie Kuo Period, some historical accounts also include other kingdoms among the competing
leaders.

The kingdoms that played such an active role in the Lie Kuo Period
were border states from the point of view of the original kingdoms of
the Great Chinese Plain and were more or less alien to the cultural
tradition of Chou. Apart from the already-mentioned maritime kingdom of Ch'i in the east, the kingdom of Chin along the middle course
of the Huang Ho River, the Ch'u along the middle course of the
Yangtze River, there were also the kingdoms of Ch'in in the west (Wei
River basin, Shenhsi) and Wu and Yue, which joined the internecine
struggle in the sixth century. Although the contacts of these kingdoms
with the Proto-Hans of the Chou world were becoming stronger, they
continued to exhibit certain peculiarities in their local cultures. Their
remoteness from the religious capital of Chou contributed to their increasing strength and striving for independence.

While individual states fought among themselves, they also had to

3. The term t'ien ming is translated in different ways: "Heavenly Command," the
"Will of Heaven," "Orders from Heaven," etc.

repel aggression from the outside. The tribes inhabiting the surrounding territories are presented in ancient Chinese sources under the generalized name "Barbarians" of the four cardinal points of the world: the Jung in the west, the Yi in the east, the Man in the south, and the Ti in the north. It is difficult to define the social orders of these tribes. It seems that they included nomads (in the west and in the north), jungle tribes (in the south), and settled and seminomadic groups of different ethnic origin. When the *wang* of Chou was unable to counter the incursions of these tribes, the leaders took upon themselves the task of resistance to the Barbarians. The first leader, Huan-kung of Ch'i (684–643 B.C.), announced his political motto: "Reverence for the *wang*, resistance to the Barbarians." And, in fact, at the head of a coalition of kingdoms, Huan-kung was able to repel an invasion of northern Barbarians (the Ti tribes).

It seems that the power of the *pa* was not solely based, at least in the beginning, on his military might. There is evidence that the leaders went through a sacred fraternization ritual—"sworn unity"—with the allied and dependent city-states. Thus the rulers of the Ch'i and Chin kingdoms invariably acted as heads of a military-religious alliance of eastern kingdoms of the Great Chinese Plain (Wei, Sung, Lu, Chen, Ts'ai, and others). The alliance was aimed against the aggression of Ch'u. The Ch'u already belonged to the leader states of what may be called "the new formation." Its rulers not only assumed the title of *wang* but also claimed the sacred title Son of Heaven. Of course, there is scarcely any doubt that aggression was directed not only from the south to the north but also in the opposite direction.

The leader kingdoms that had at their disposal thousands of battle chariots constituted the decisive force affecting the fate of all the other states of Lie Kuo China, many of which became their tributaries and were, in fact, unwilling participants in the struggle between the competing "great powers." The small Honan kingdoms found themselves under the greatest threat because they were squeezed between the major kingdoms of Chin, Ch'i, and Ch'u. Having acquired leadership status, Ch'u turned into the most powerful state in ancient China and began a vigorous advance to the north. But local noble families wielded great power in Ch'u and opposed its political centralization. Consequently, toward the middle of the first millennium B.C., the Ch'u kingdom was temporarily weakened and yielded its supremacy to the southeastern kingdoms—first to Wu and later to Yue. The predominance of these two, however, was short-lived. A new and terrible danger threatening all kingdoms appeared on history's horizon: the western frontier kingdom of Ch'in.

The internecine struggles between the kingdoms were accompanied by confrontations between political forces within the individual states that grew increasingly fierce. Starting in the sixth century B.C., noble families everywhere began to struggle for power within their kingdoms. The opposing tendency was that of rulers seeking to dominate the noble families (including their own) and to undermine the power of the strongest aristocratic clans. These aristocratic clans had virtually everywhere secured for themselves and their heirs the most important governmental posts. To weaken the power of the hierarchical aristocracy, the rulers attempted to enlist the support of men personally devoted to them. These men came from families of commoners, sometimes even from those of former slaves. They were rewarded for their services (in lieu of land) with a "salary" in the form of grain from the royal granaries. (Grain served as the basic standard for measurement of prices.)

These internal political struggles brought about different results. In some kingdoms they led to the displacement of the nobility and the rise of new people who were absolutely dependent on the ruler and, in others, to the usurpation of the throne by a representative of the aristocracy (as, for instance, in the kingdom of Lu in 562 B.C., where the ruler lost practically all his power, although preserving his sacral function). Another outcome could be the seizure of power by the strongest aristocratic family (as, for example, in Ch'i at the beginning of the fifth century B.C.). Finally, the struggle could culminate in the political disintegration of a kingdom, as happened in Chin, which broke into three independent states: Han, Chao, and Wei. (We prefer to date this event to 453 B.C., although 404 B.C. has also been proposed.)

The Social Order

Our knowledge about the Lie Kuo Period comes almost exclusively from narrative sources. Very few epigraphic data have reached us, and archaeological data are also scarce. The main source is *Tso Chuan*, a detailed year-by-year chronicle of events in the different kingdoms between 721 and 467 B.C. It is supposed to have been a commentary on the *Springs and Autumns* (*Ch'un Ch'in*) chronicle of the kingdom of Lu. No ancient chronicles of the other kingdoms have been preserved to the present day. However, it is known that the philosopher Mo-tsu in the fifth to fourth centuries B.C. had available for study the *Ch'un Ch'in* of several kingdoms. Also, the great historian Ssu-ma Ch'ien in the second to first centuries B.C. used different original chronicles of the period, among them that of Ch'in. Some information on the period in question can be gleaned from books written down in the third to fourth centuries A.D. It should be kept in mind that no Chinese treatise preserved to our time was written down earlier than that date.

Once written, books were commented on for centuries. On the one hand, the later commentators have preserved for us data from books long since disappeared, but on the other hand, they interpreted ancient terms and notions according to the spirit of their own age and thus often distorted the real picture of historical events. It is well known that narrative sources are always worth less than documents, which nothing can replace. However, very few documentary sources of the period have survived, which is why many important problems of Chinese history of this epoch are poorly understood.

Technological progress during that period induced further development in the division of labor. Although agriculture still remained at the former level of development and required an enormous expenditure of labor, we notice a rise in the cultivation of cereals and more abundant harvests toward the end of this period.

Crafts became subdivided into a multitude of specialized branches. The organization of production began on a relatively large scale; thus in that period, it can be especially noticed in saltworks, mining, and bronze casting, and in activities mainly connected with the royal economy.

As a rule, the centers of crafts were located near the sources of raw materials. The period in question saw the flourishing of the Bronze Age in China. The technology of bronze alloying improved; the melting process was combined with forging operations; multiphase casting became common; and the construction of dismountable molds (piece molds) improved. The manufacture of bronze tools expanded significantly. New types of weapons appeared: shields, armor, and bronze swords. Such armament made a soldier considerably stronger than a laborer with only his work tools. This facilitated the exploitation of prisoners of war and convicts as slaves.

Many towns of the Lie Kuo Period were quite small. They were encircled by walls that formed a perimeter of some 400–600 meters. As a rule, the towns were military, political, and religious centers. *Ch'un Ch'in* mentions that the construction of such fortified towns was one of the important activities of a ruler. The capitals (the residences of the rulers) were larger and constituted standardized architectural complexes. Such a complex focused on the palace and consisted of three courts aligned along a north-south axis. All buildings were rectangular, and their multiple-gabled roofs were supported by wooden columns. A socle, the typical feature of all public buildings, unified the entire complex. The palace quarters were situated in the northern portion of the central court, and the entrance faced north. Here, on a special elevation, the ruler performed ritual acts. The eastern side of the central court accommodated the temple of ancestors, and the western side, the altar of the god of fertile soil. This altar was used for sacrifices, often human, and for the execution of condemned criminals. On the eve of battles, soldiers swore their oath before it. The sacred central court symbolized the center of the universe. A market was located to the north of it, and the living quarters of artisans and of all palace servants extended to the south.

Following the practice of the *wang*s of Western Chou, the rulers of the kingdoms (the *hou* and *kung*) widely distributed lands from the state reserve in reward for services. Therefore, the larger aristocratic families strove not only to obtain the most important governmental posts but also to secure them for their heirs. There were usually about five to six such families in each kingdom.

A post was formally secured by casting a granting inscription on a sacred royal vessel. A typical inscription reads as follows:

> Pursuant of the order of previous *wang*s, I appoint you, in accordance with the post of your late father and of your ancestors, to be in charge of [horse harnesses, prisons and punishment, left and right wings of the army, or whatever].

In the ritual of appointment to high posts, the king handed the appointee a lump of soil from the royal altar of the god of earth taken from the cardinal point that corresponded to the location of the "granted" land allotment.

The allotments awarded to major officeholders could be quite sizable, but, as in earlier times, they did not represent private property in the true sense; the grantee was only empowered to collect tribute in kind that was due from the villages and towns placed under him and to dispose of such tribute at his personal discretion. Similar but smaller allotments were received by all sorts of officials, scribes, managers, and other servants of the ruler. Since the economy was not characterized by any significant market exchange of commodities, and since centralized politico-administrative management was lacking, such allotments constituted a convenient and perhaps the only imaginable method of maintaining the governmental machinery. Although all allotments formally remained the property of the king, who at any time could take them back from the temporary owners, they were, as a rule, inherited.

The highest elite, holding hierarchical posts, were obliged to participate in wars and large royal hunts (a sort of preparation for military service) together with their chariots and soldiers. They also supplied the court with labor and were responsible for delivering various kinds of goods to the palace: cattle and fowl for sacrifices, tortoise shells, cowrie shells, copper, tin, and other raw materials and commodities.

Justice was administered by the nobles according to customary law, which, however, gradually became inadequate for adjusting the relationships between the aristocracy and the mass of community members. Ch'i was one of the first states to attempt the introduction of written law. It was followed by Chin and a number of other kingdoms. Yet, everywhere, the introduction of written law was opposed by the aristocratic families, who saw in it a diminution of their ancient privileges.

As the kings continued to distribute land and thus grew weaker, the power of the hereditary high officeholders and military commanders grew. These groups strove to turn the members of neighboring communities (on lands allotted them for service) into their personal dependents by resorting to all kinds of petty gifts or by "forgiving" them their "grain debts." However, it is possible that such "good deeds" performed by those in power were actually in conformance with the age-old right of the people of a city-state (the *kuo jen*) to "bread and liberation."

In connection with the decay of the territorial community's land-ownership, the communal land reallotments gradually ceased in most of the kingdoms, and the land was inherited by individual families. This caused a complete change in the system used by the state to extract the surplus product from the bulk of the direct producers. The original system was the *kungt'ien*. According to this system, the community tilled a certain share of their fields for the benefit of the king. Now, instead, a grain tax on the entire land was introduced. This reform was first attempted in 594 B.C. in the kingdom of Lu (in Shantung) during the rule of Hsüan-kung; taxes began to be exacted from each *mu* (a unit of area). A similar measure was put into practice in 548 B.C. in the kingdom of Ch'u, and in 543 B.C. in the kingdom of Cheng (in Honan), where "they traced boundaries in the fields; houses with wells were grouped into five homestead units." Even earlier, "taxation in accordance with the land" was introduced in the Ch'i kingdom. In 483 B.C. Lu reaffirmed the "tax collected from [each family] field." The tax amounted, as a rule, to one tenth either of the average annual or of the real annual production.

The class stratification of community members intensified as the character of the community changed. The prosperous upper stratum of the community won a position that enabled it to further increase its wealth. The first evidence of the use of hired labor in agriculture stems from precisely this time. In spite of isolated records of the sale of estates and orchards, such sales did not become common until the end of the Lie Kuo Period. Unfortunately, we lack private documents, and the details of the differentiation process of the community members according to property and social position are unknown. With the introduction of a uniform tax (and, in general, with the transition to a

common tax system), the distinction between the state and private/
communal economic sectors slowly vanished.

A new trend took hold: the estates that had originally been granted
under conditions of service were being turned into private property.
Inscriptions from as early as the end of the tenth century B.C. tell us
about isolated cases of appropriation of land estates with the right of
their free disposal. The following documentary inscription on a bronze
vessel gives evidence of purchases of large land tracts (in exchange for
payment in kind):

> Ko Po gave a team of four horses to P'eng Sheng and re-
> covered thirty fields in exchange for them; this being certified
> by breaking [of a symbolic tally].

The end of the Lie Kuo Period was characterized everywhere by an
increased burden of taxes and service duties. A system of big royal
estates continued to survive in a number of kingdoms. They were
worked by dependent "royal men," but also the community population were recruited, in one form or another. The enrichment of the
hereditary elite and a trend toward luxury in everyday life, as well as
in funerary ceremonies, occurred; this is evident from archaeological
discoveries. There is an inscription on a bronze vessel that belonged
to the Wei family. It tells of its owner's acquisition of 1,300 *mu* (86.6
hectares, or 214 acres) of land in exchange for garments and jade val-
ued at 100 bunches of cowrie shells. Another vessel, belonging to the
same person, contains an inscription that announces the exchange of
some fields for 400 *mu* (26.6 hectares, or 65.7 acres) of land that belonged to the "ruler of Li." An inscription on yet another cast vessel of
the same man tells about his purchase from someone of a wooded
property; the payment was a carriage.

The private/communal sector did not disappear, but its character
changed. The old community village institutions of self-government
continued to exist in some kingdoms of this period and even much
later. These were the elders (*fu lao*), who were elected by the common
people (*shu jen*) of the communities (*li*); there was a collegiate authority of the three principal elders (*san lao*)[4] and the headman of a
village (*licheng*). The same institutions of self-government were apparently preserved even longer in cities and in groups of towns (*yi*), a
situation that can be compared with that in the nomes of Egypt and
Sumer.

The functions of the representatives of community government
were various. They were responsible for labor service obligations, tax

4. The authority of the original communal tripartite council later passed to a single
elder who, traditionally, kept the name of *san lao*.

collection, and law and order in the community and, at the same time, they headed the local cult. They could call out the local militia, organize the defense of their city, hold court to judge the people of their community, and even impose capital punishment. And in a number of kingdoms, they could even communicate on their own with the outside world. On occasion, with the support of the local militia, they could substantially influence the outcome of internal struggles between pretenders to the local throne.

The category of "free people" (actually "state people," *kuo jen*) played an important role in the political history of the Lie Kuo Period. These "commoners" were subject to military service, paid taxes, and fulfilled a number of labor obligations. They often came to the support of the ruler in his struggle against the powerful aristocracy, and their active, collective intervention in internal and external political affairs leads us to assume the presence of vestiges of a very ancient institution—the people's assembly. Available information about the activities of *kuo jen* in the kingdoms of Wei, Lu, Cheng, Sung, Ch'eng, Ch'u, and Chen indicates that these states preserved certain features of democracy. In some cases, the ruler of a kingdom even entered into agreements with the *kuo jen* about mutual support; however, eventually their role in the political life of the kingdoms came everywhere to naught; in large kingdoms, a centralized state governmental system evolved.

With regard to the socioeconomic relationships of this period, we can state with confidence that patriarchal slavery was predominant in private economies. The practice of pawning children for debts existed at that time, and it continued for centuries. In order to retain such hostages (*chui-tzu*) in the economy, they could be married to the daughter of the master. Another piece of evidence of the patriarchal character of slavery was the existence of slaves "begotten in the household" by female slaves (*nu ch'an-tzu*). Slave labor was also used in farming. We know from an inscription on bronze from the eighth century B.C. about a case in which a horse and a cut of silk were exchanged for five slaves for use as field laborers.

Problems of the status of the multitude of artisans—how many of them were slaves and what their general condition was—require more research. There is no doubt, however, that private slavery was not significant during this period. On the other hand, state slavery played a more important role, and the state used different sources for it, such as prisoners of war and people convicted in court. The most cruel exploitation of slave labor took place in state handicraft shops and in mines. Slaves were commonly designated, not as such, but by their occupations ("stable-man," "woodcutter," "porter," "herdsman," etc.) or by general terms such as "servant," "boy" (*liao, chung*).

Other categories of forced laborers (called *li* and *tsu*) were used widely in production; these were people who had lost their personal freedom. This condition of semislavery was mainly connected with their voluntary self-pawning for debt.

It is significant that during this period the "classical" term for slave, *nu*, appeared. It eventually became the standard word designating a slave in the later periods of Chinese history.

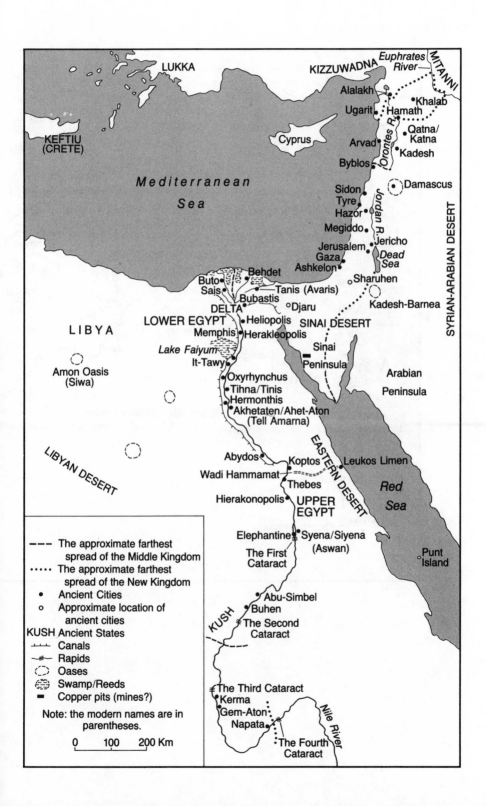

LUKKA

KIZZUWADNA

Euphrates River

MITANNI

Alalakh

•Khalab

Ugarit : Hamath

KEFTIU
(CRETE)

Cyprus

Arvad•

Byblos•

Mediterranean

Sea

Sidon•
Tyre•
Hazor•
Megiddo•

Jerusalem•
Gaza•
Ashkelon•

Behdet•
Buto•
Sais•
Bubastis•

Tanis (Avaris)

Qatna/
Katna
•Kadesh

Orontes R.

•Damascus

Jordan R.

Jericho
•
Dead Sea

Sharuhen

Kadesh-Barnea

SYRIAN-ARABIAN DESERT

LIBYA

Amon Oasis
(Siwa)

DELTA
LOWER EGYPT
Heliopolis•
Memphis•
Herakleopolis•
Lake Faiyum
It-Tawy•
Oxyrhynchus•
Tihna/Tinis•
Hermonthis•
•Akhetaten/Ahet-Aton
(Tell Amarna)

Djaru

SINAI DESERT

Sinai
Peninsula

Arabian
Peninsula

LIBYAN DESERT

Abydos•

Wadi Hammamat

Hierakonopolis•

Koptos•

Leukos Limen•

Thebes•

UPPER
EGYPT

EASTERN DESERT

Red Sea

Elephantine• •Syena/Siyena
(Aswan)
The First
Cataract

Punt
Island

- - - The approximate farthest
      spread of the Middle Kingdom
· · · · · The approximate farthest
          spread of the New Kingdom
•   Ancient Cities
○   Approximate location of
     ancient cities
KUSH Ancient States
‡‡‡ Canals
⇥ Rapids
⟨ ⟩ Oases
🪺 Swamp/Reeds
▬ Copper pits (mines?)

Note: the modern names are in
parentheses.

0   100   200 Km

•Abu-Simbel
•Buhen
The Second
Cataract

KUSH

The Third Cataract
•Kerma
•Gem-Aton
Napata•
The Fourth
Cataract

Nile River

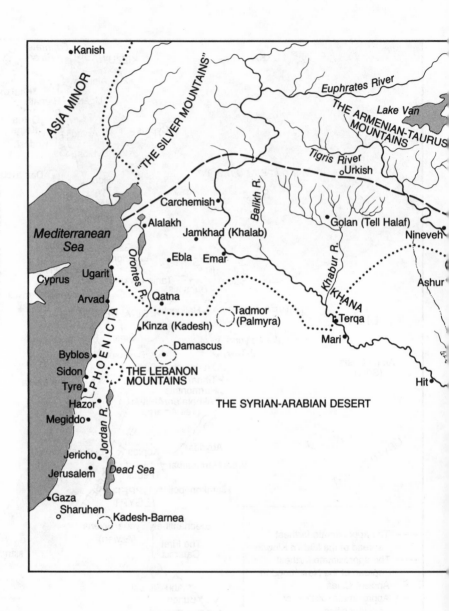

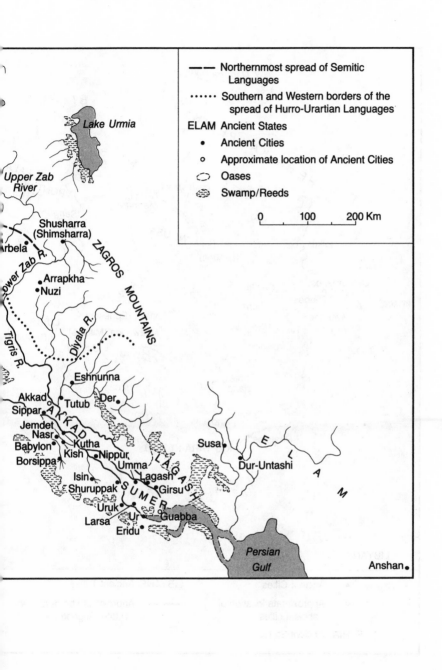

Legend:

- — — Northernmost spread of Semitic Languages
- • • • • • Southern and Western borders of the spread of Hurro-Urartian Languages
- ELAM Ancient States
- • Ancient Cities
- ○ Approximate location of Ancient Cities
- ⌒ Oases
- ⇔ Swamp/Reeds

0   100   200 Km

Lake Urmia

Upper Zab River

Shusharra (Shimsharra)

Arbela

ZAGROS MOUNTAINS

Lower Zab R.

Arrapkha

Nuzi

Diyala R.

Tigris R.

Eshnunna

Akkad

Tutub   Der

Sippar

A K K A D

Jemdet Nasr

Babylon   Kutha

Borsippa   Kish   Nippur

Isin   Umma   Susa

Shuruppak   Lagash

Girsu

S U M E R

L A G A S H

Uruk

Larsa   Ur   Guabba

Eridu

Dur-Untashi

E L A M

Persian Gulf

Anshan

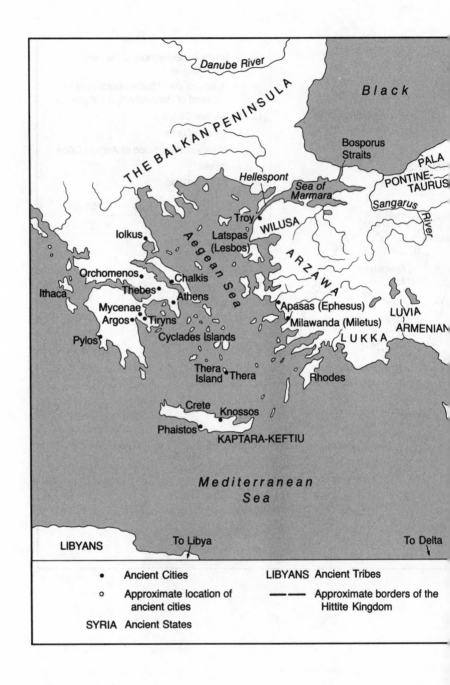

Danube River

Black

THE BALKAN PENINSULA

Bosporus Straits

PALA

PONTINE-
TAURUS

Hellespont

Sea of Marmara

Sangarus

WILUSA

Sangarus River

Troy

Iolkus

Latspas
(Lesbos)

ARZAWA

Aegean Sea

Orchomenos

Chalkis

LUVIA

Thebes

Apasas (Ephesus)

Ithaca

Athens

ARMENIAN

Mycenae

Milawanda (Miletus)

Argos

Tiryns

LUKKA

Pylos

Cyclades Islands

Thera
Island

Thera

Rhodes

Crete

Knossos

Phaistos

KAPTARA-KEFTIU

*Mediterranean
Sea*

LIBYANS

To Libya

To Delta

•	Ancient Cities	LIBYANS Ancient Tribes
○	Approximate location of ancient cities	—— Approximate borders of the Hittite Kingdom
SYRIA	Ancient States	

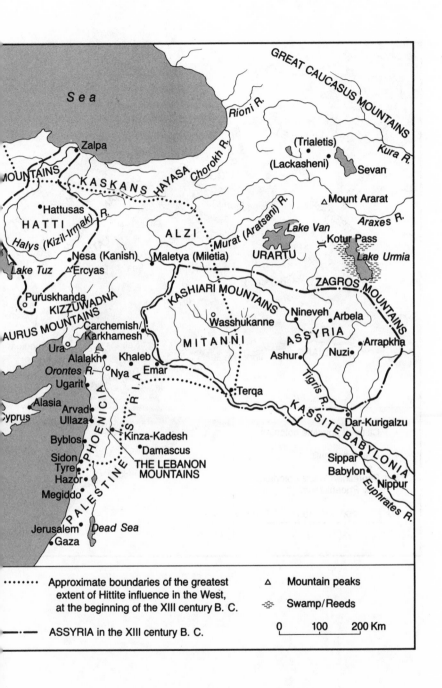

Sea

Zalpa

Hattusas

HATTI

MOUNTAINS

KASKANS

HAYASA

Chorokh R.

Rioni R.

GREAT CAUCASUS MOUNTAINS

Kura R.

(Trialetis)

(Lackasheni)

Sevan

△ Mount Ararat

Araxes R.

Halys (Kizil-Irmak) R.

ALZI

Murat (Aratsani) R.

Lake Van

Kotur Pass

Nesa (Kanish)

Maletya (Miletia)

URARTU

Lake Urmia

Lake Tuz

△Ercyas

Puruskhanda

KIZZUWADNA

KASHIARI MOUNTAINS

ZAGROS MOUNTAINS

AURUS MOUNTAINS

Carchemish/
Karkhamesh

Wasshukanne

Nineveh

Arbela

MITANNI

ASSYRIA

Ura

Alalakh

Khaleb

Ashur

Nuzi

Arrapkha

Orontes R.

Nya

Emar

Ugarit

Terqa

Tigris R.

Alasia

Arvad

Ullaza

KASSITE BABYLONIA

Dar-Kurigalzu

Cyprus

Byblos

PHOENICIA

SYRIA

Kinza-Kadesh

*Damascus

Sidon

Tyre

Hazor

THE LEBANON
MOUNTAINS

Sippar

Babylon

Nippur

Euphrates R.

Megiddo

PALESTINE

Jerusalem

Dead Sea

Gaza

.... Approximate boundaries of the greatest
extent of Hittite influence in the West,
at the beginning of the XIII century B. C.

—·— ASSYRIA in the XIII century B. C.

△ Mountain peaks

⚬ Swamp/Reeds

0   100   200 Km

Cities of principle colonies

Greek colonies

Shoreline/Coasts colonized
by Phoenicians

0   200   400   600 Km

Index

Aba (Amba), (god), 86
Abdi-Ashirta, King of Amurru, 295
Abkhasians, 257, 278
Abraham, 300
Abu-Salabikh, 75 n.8
Abu-Simbel, 189–90, 204
Abusir, 155
Abydos, 144, 189, 196
Achaea, 327, 355, 359, 360, 364
Achaean (Mycenaean) civilization, 317–27, 328, 335, 347; disintegration of, 326–27, 348; Mycenaean art in comparison to Homeric art, 330, 331; palace economy of, 322–23; palaces of, 318–20; socioeconomic and political history of, 320–24; and Trojan War, participation in, 324–25. *See also* Greece; Homeric Epics; Minoan (Cretan) civilization
Achaeans, 279, 304, 316
Achaemenid Period, 383
Achilles, 334
Achtoes (Kheti), Pharaoh of Egypt, 160
Achtoes III, King of Heracleopolis, 160, 161
Adad-nērari I, King of Assyria, 254–55
Adad-shum-utsur, King of Kassites, 263
Adhaim, 228
"Admonitions of Ipuwer, The," 211
Adria, 363
Aegean Islands, 309, 330, 347, 349
Aegean Sea, 46, 268, 309, 315, 316, 318, 328, 334, 348, 358, 360
Aeolians, 327
Aesculapius (god), 154, 201
Afghanistan, 79, 89, 156, 219, 222, 224 n.6, 226, 229, 241, 380, 383; and the Aryan question, 366, 368, 369; Bronze Age urban settlements in, 382–83 n.10; farming culture in, 382; and Indus Valley, trade with, 218
Afrasian dialects, 30–31, 71, 143, 287
Africa, 28, 29, 31, 49, 348, 349, 350, 362. *See also* Central Africa; North Africa
Agamemnon, King of Mycenae, 317–18, 324, 341, 343, 344

Age of Metal, 216, 393
Agibtazhenni, 247
Agni (god), 378
Agrigentum, 363
Agum II, Kassite King, 261
Ahhiyawā, 277–78, 325
Ahura Mazda (Ahuramazda, Ormazd), 384, 384 n.13
Aka, 75, 84
Akhenaton (Amenhetep IV), Pharaoh of Egypt, 58, 65, 66, 190, 207; religious reforms of, 182–87
Akhet-Aton, 184–85, 186, 187, 199–200
Akkad and Akkadians, 102, 113, 132, 136, 223, 232, 239, 252, 287, 288, 291; art, characteristics of, 130–31; fall of Ur and rise of Issin, 95–97; Gudea, rule of, 90–91; language of, 71, 85, 87, 99 n.1, 236, 272, 307; literature of, 135; religion in, 126–27; and Sargonids, Kingdom of, 85–90; Third Dynasty of Ur, 91–95, 97; writing in, 20, 92, 93, 113, 223, 244, 250, 266, 269, 290, 294, 307
Alaca-Hüyük, 268
Alalakh (now Tell-Atchana), 239, 241, 242, 244, 249, 272, 273, 276, 290, 291, 307
Alasia, 278
Alcinous, 331, 332, 344
Alexander the Great, 143, 222, 384
Al-ilani (now Kirkuk), 244
Aliyan-Ba'l (god), 307
Al-Mina, 363
Amarna, 200, 250
Amarna Period, 186 n.7, 294
Amemet, 198
Amenemhet I, Pharaoh of Egypt, 160, 168, 169, 170, 210, 211
Amenemhet II, Pharaoh of Egypt, 168
Amenemhet III, Pharaoh of Egypt, 170, 175, 266
Amenhetep (architect of Luxor), 204
Amenhetep (son of Hapu), 204
Amenhetep I (Amenophis I), Pharaoh of Egypt, 177

Amenhetep II, Pharaoh of Egypt, 181,
188, 242
Amenhetep III, Pharaoh of Egypt,
181–82, 200, 242, 275, 276, 295
Amenhetep IV. *See* Akhenaton
Amnanu tribe, 99
Amon (god), 174, 177, 178, 185, 186, 191,
193, 194, 195
Amon-Ra' (god), 177, 179, 181, 183, 184,
185
Amorites, 99 n.1, 100, 122, 232, 236–37,
288, 289, 290, 291; culture and alpha-
bet of Canaanite-Amorite civilization,
306–8; and fall of Ur and rise of Issin,
95–97; and Israelites, encounter with,
302; and the "Sea Peoples," 299–305
Amu Darya River, 33, 218, 226, 382, 383,
385
Amurru, 294–96, 297
An (god), 126
Anahita (goddess), 385
Anath (goddess), 305
Anatolia, 30 n.1, 267–68, 270, 271, 278,
309, 367 n.3. *See also* Asia Minor; Hit-
tite Kingdom
Anau, 225, 370
Ancestress Keng ("the Seventh"), 406
Ancient history: discussion of theoretical
problems in, 4–13; problems of an-
cient chronology, 21–25; problems of
sources for, 14–21
*Ancient Society: or, Researches in the Line of
Human Progress from Savagery through
Barbarism to Civilization* (Morgan), 6
Andronovo archaeological culture,
369 n.7
andurarum, 234
Anghro Mainyu (Ahro Manyu,
Ahriman), 384
Anittas, 271, 272
Anshan, 89, 223–24, 230, 386
Anti-Lebanon Mountains, 286–87
Antinous, 342
Anyang, 394, 395, 402, 406, 409; oracle
archive of, 395–98
aoidoi, 328, 335
Apennine Peninsula, 360
Apep, 195
Apepi, Pharaoh of Egypt, 171, 211
Apeshlaians, 257
Apis, 194
Apollo (god), 342, 358

Apollonia, 361
Arabia, 30, 101, 170, 300
Arabian Peninsula, 287, 300
Aramaeans, 255, 257, 263, 288, 300
Aratta, 224
Araxes River, 33
Arbela (now Erbil), 229, 252
Archaic Period, 354, 355
Archias, 359
Archilochus, 360
Argolis, 319, 327
Argos Plain, 324
Ariana, 368 n.5
Ariana, 385
Arinna, 285
Aristobulus, 222
Aristotle, 61
Arizhen (Adalzhen), 233, 235 n.10, 239
Arrapkhe (now Kirkuk), 229, 230, 231,
239, 239 n.13, 241, 242, 243, 250, 251;
Hurrian Kingdom of, 244–49, 290
Arsanias (Muradsu), 231
Artadama I, Mitanni King, 242, 293
Artadama II, Mitanni King, 243
Artemis (goddess), 312 n.5
Aryanam-Vaejo, 383, 384, 385
Aryans, 370, 371. *See also* Indo-Aryan
tribes
Aryoshayana, 383–84, 385
Arzawa, 274–75, 281
Asak (god), 133
Ashdod, 304
Ashkelon, 304
Asia Minor, 28, 29, 46, 83, 180, 187, 190,
263, 272, 287, 309, 315, 329, 352; and
Achaeans, military and colonizing ex-
pansion of, 324–25; and Asshur, trade
with, 235–36; culture of Hittite King-
dom in, 283–85; and Greek colo-
nization, 327, 357, 358, 360, 361 n.3,
363; discovery of Hittites in, 266–67;
Indo-European tribes, emigration into,
367, 367 n.3; justice and law in Hittite
Kingdom, 283; and Kingdom of
Mitanni, 240, 242; and Kingdom of
the Sargonids, 85, 86, 88; New Hittite
Kingdom in, 274–79; and New Kingdom of Egypt, trade with, 173; Old
Hittite Kingdom in, 272–74; and
Phoenician towns, trade with, 289–90;
pottery in Chalcolithic Age, 224; Pre-
Hittite Period in Central Asia Minor,

267–72; and Shamshi-Adad I's empire, 237–38, 252; socioeconomic relations in Hittite Kingdom, 279–83; Troy Villa, site of, 324–25. *See also* Central Asia; Middle Asia; Southeast Asia; Western Asia

"Asiatic mode of production," 5–6, 9–11

Asshur (now Qal'at Sherqat), 100, 123, 181, 230, 231 n.3, 242, 243, 262, 271, 276; and Asia Minor, trade with, 268–69; city-state of and emergence of Kingdom of Assyria, 252–58; early political history of, 233–36; and Egypt, diplomatic relations with, 254; and Shamshi-Adad I's empire, 233, 236–38

Asshur-uballit I, King of Asshur, 243, 249, 254

Assyria, 21, 48, 228, 243, 249, 266, 269, 274, 276, 297, 298, 362; and Babylonia, relations with, 254–56, 257, 262–63; city-state of Asshur and emergence of Kingdom of, 252–54; and India, trade with, 373–74 n.9; language of, 236, 285; Middle Assyrian Laws, 258–60; and problems of ancient chronology, 21

asuras, 378

Aswan Dam, 190, 204

Athene (goddess), 312 n.5, 337

Athens, 318, 325, 329

Atlantic Ocean, 351

Atlantis, 316 n.8

Aton (god), 183–85

Atreus, tomb of, 320

Atum (god), 195, 198

Atum-Ra (god), 198, 212

Augustus, Emperor, 18, 20

Ausa, 349

Austroasiatic linguistic family, 387 n.2, 388, 423

"Autobiography of Hattusilis III, The," 284

Avaris, 170–71, 177, 177 n.6

Avesta, 369 n.7; and Zoroastrianism, 381–86

Avetisyan, H. M., 240

Awal (Hawalum), 235, 235 n.10

awilum, 116, 117

Ay, Pharaoh of Egypt, 185–86

Azerbaijan, 369 n.7, 380

Aziru, King of Amurru, 296

Azov, Sea of, 362 n.4, 363

Azzi tribe, 275

Ba, 197

Babylon and Babylonians, 20, 136, 181, 230, 238, 240, 285, 379; end of Old Babylonian Period, 122–23; Hammurapi, Laws of, 112–21; Middle Babylonian Period in Lower Mesopotamia, the Kassite Kingdom, and Elam, 261–63; military operations of Hattusilis I and Mursilis I against, 272–73; Old Babylonian economy, 103–4, 108–10; Old Babylonian society, 103–11; political history of Old Babylonian Period, 98–103; and Shamshi-Adad I's empire, 237–38; social functions of the temple, 107–8; society of Middle Babylonian Period, 264–65

Babylonia, 231, 237, 249, 252, 254, 274, 308; problems of ancient chronology, 22; relations with Assyria, 254–56, 257, 262–63

Babylonian-Assyrian language, 71

Babu, archive of, 79

Bactria and Bactrians, 380, 381, 382, 385

Badakhshan, 79, 229

Baetis River valley (now Guadalquivir), 353

Bahrain Islands, 79, 101, 219, 256

bakew, 165, 166

Balearic Islands, 349, 360

Balikh, 230

Balkan Peninsula, 267, 268, 309, 317, 326

Balkans, 28, 30, 268, 270, 367

ballutu ina lumne, 253

Baluchistan, 218, 221–22, 223, 382–83 n.10

Ban Chiang, 390 n.5

Banebjed, 194

Bangladesh, 214

Barak, 303

Barbarism, distinguished from class society, 36, 37

Barca, 362

basileis (*basileus*), 323, 332, 343–46

Basques, 352

Batumi, 257

Bay of Bengal (Bangladesh), 31

Berezan (now Schmidt's Island), 361

Berlev, O. D., 163
Bethel, 302
Bible, 5, 16–17, 266, 299; and the migra-
tion of "those who had crossed the
river" and the "Sea Peoples," 300–5
Bithia, 350
Black Sea, 30, 222 n.5, 257, 268, 272,
275, 367, 368, 369, 380; Greek colo-
nization in region of, 358, 361, 362,
363, 364
Blue Nile, 137
Boghazköy (formerly Hattusas), 241,
266–67, 269, 271, 283, 294. See also
Hattusas
Bohtan Su, 228
Bolan Pass, 215 n.2
Book of Joshua, 301
Book of Judges, 301, 305
Bosporus and Bosporites, 362, 362 n.4,
363
Bothrys, 349
Bouchis, 194
Bousiris, 196
Brahmanas, 372, 375
Brahmans, 375, 376
Brahui, 219, 224
Bronze Age, 218, 225–26, 288, 388, 398,
427
Buddhism, 58, 59
Bug River, 362
Burma, 387, 409
Burnaburiash I, Kassite King, 262
Buto, 141
Byblos, 163, 180, 288, 289, 294, 295, 307
Byelorussia, 367 n.4
Byrsa, 351
Byzantium, 361

Cairo, 151
Callatis, 361
Campania, 359
Canaanites, 288, 291, 292, 296, 302–4;
culture and alphabet of Canaanite-
Amorite civilization, 306–8
Cappadocia, 268–69, 270
Capua, 359
Carbon dating, 25
Carchemish, 180, 231 n.3, 243, 255, 276,
297, 298
Carter, Howard, 185
Carthage and Carthaginians, 350, 351,

354, 359, 362
Caspian Sea, 90, 214, 367, 369, 382
Çatal-Hüyük, 29, 267, 287
Caucasus, 245 n.15, 270, 278
Cedar Grove, 250
Celestial Empire, 421, 423
Celts, 364, 367 n.4
Central Africa, 137. See also Africa;
North Africa
Central Asia, 13, 214 n.1; and the Aryan
question, 366–71; and the Avesta and
Zoroastrianism, 381–86; in the first
half of the first millennium B.C., 380–
81; prerequisites for creation of pre-
urban society in, 222–27. See also Asia
Minor; Middle Asia; Southeast Asia;
Western Asia
Cepi, 362
Chaghar-Bazar, 239
Chalcidice, 360
Chalcis and Chalcideans, 357, 358, 359,
360, 363
Chalcolithic Age, 33, 124, 139, 145, 223,
224, 267, 268, 288, 398; art during,
125, 126, 128
Chaldeans, 257, 263
Ch'ang (Wen wang), 411
Chan Kuo Period (Preimperial Period),
420
Chao Kingdom, 426
Chaos (god), 251
Checheno-Ingushetia, 231
Chechiang, 422, 423
Ch'eng-Chou, 394, 394 n.9, 398, 412,
414, 416
Cheng Kingdom, 421, 429, 431
Ch'eng wang, 412, 414
Chen Kingdom, 425, 431
Cheops (Khufu), Pharaoh of Egypt,
154–55, 201, 211
Chephrenes (Kha'f-Ra'), Pharaoh of
Egypt, 154, 155, 201
Chersonesus Tauricus, 361
Chesnaux, J., 9
Chianghsi Province, 393, 397
Ch'iangs, 405, 406, 407
Ch'iang Yuan (goddess), 410
Chief of the Northern Countries, 181
Ch'i Kingdom, 423, 425, 429
China, 5, 13, 28, 46, 214, 224, 226,
387–93; ancient geographical region

of, 389–90; ideology of Chou, 416–19; political history of Lie Kuo Period, 420–26; problems of ancient chronology, 23; Shang society, 401–9; Shang (Yin) "state," 393–401; social order of Lie Kuo Period, 426–32; sources of history for, 17–18; state federation of Chou, 409–16

Ch'inchiang (Chianghsi), 399

Ch'in-Han Empire, 388

Chin Kingdom, 423, 424, 425, 426, 429

Ch'in Shih Huang-ti, tomb of, 18

Chionites, 385

Chios, 327, 361, 363

Chorreras, 350

Chou, 388, 389, 397, 398, 401; ideology of, 416–19; and political history of Lie Kuo Period, 421–26; state federation of, 409–16

Chou-Kung, 422

Christianity, 59, 65

Chryseis, 342

Chuang, 422

Ch'u Kingdom, 422, 423, 424, 425, 429, 431

Ch'un Ch'in, 421, 422, 426

Chung Shang, 397, 400

Cimmerian Bosporus (Kerch Strait), 362

"Circle A" graves, 317–18

"Circle B" graves, 318

City of the Dead, 155

Clan of the Ram, 410

Class society: preconditions for formation of, 27–31; slave exploitation in, 40–43; in Sumer, 37–44

Claudius Ptolemaeus, 24

Clytemnestra, 317–18

Cnidus, 360, 363

Collingwood, R., 7

Colophon, 327, 360, 361

Colossi of Memnon, 181

"Conversation of a Disillusioned Man with His Soul, The," 211

Copper Age, 215

Copper-Stone Age, 145. *See also* Chalcolithic Age

Coptic language, 143 n.3

Coptos, 156, 195

Corcyra, 357, 358, 359, 363

Corinth and Corinthians, 356, 357, 358, 363

Corsica, 349, 360

Crete, 163, 219, 249, 277, 292, 308, 324, 325, 335, 346, 357, 359, 362. *See also* Minoan (Cretan) civilization

Crimea, 361, 362

Critique of Political Economy, The (Marx), 5–6

Croce, B., 7

Cronos (god), 284

Croton, 360, 364

Cumae, 357

Cymaeans, 357

Cyprus, 173, 277, 278, 315, 325, 349, 351

Cyrenaica, 362

Cyrene, 362

Daghestan, 90, 231

Damascus, 287, 289, 296

Danube region, 30, 309, 317

Danube River, 28, 363

Darache-yi Seistan, 224 n.6, 226

Dardanelles, 324

Dardo-Kafir(s), 367, 368, 369 n.7, 370, 380

dasa, 375

Dasyu, 221

Dead Sea, 286, 302

Dead Sea scrolls, 17

Deborah, 303

Decline of the West, The (Spengler), 7

Deir el-Bahri, 168, 178

Delhi, 216

Delphi, 358

demiourgoi, 333–34

Der (now Bedre), 230, 235

devas, 378, 380, 384

Diakonoff, I. M., 113

Dicaearchia, 360

didennutu, 244

Dilmun Islands, 79, 101, 219

Dilthey, W., 7

dimtu, 244–45

Dionysius Exiguus, 24–25

Dioscurias (Sukhumi), 362

Diyala River, 67, 95, 96, 114, 228, 229, 230, 237, 260

Diyala Valley, 71, 85, 230, 233, 235, 263

Djandieri, M. I., 245

Djedef-Ra', 156

Djehutimes, 186 n.7, 207

Djehutiy, 211

Djer, tomb of, 144
Djeser, Pharaoh of Egypt, 145, 156, 201
Dniester River, 362, 363
Don River, 362n.4, 363
Dorians, 327, 329, 330
Drangiana, 224n.6, 226, 382, 383
Dravidian languages, 89, 219, 366
Dumuzi (shepherd god), 132
dunnu, 253
Dur-Kurigalzu, 257, 262
Dushratta, Mitanni King, 240, 242–43, 276
Dvapara, 374

Ea (god), 126
Eanatum, 81–82, 83n.18
Eanna temple, 73
Early Bronze Age, 267–68, 309, 398, 422
Early Bronze Lungshan culture, 392
Early Neolithic Period, 287
East China Sea, 389
Eastern Caucasian languages, 231, 232, 244, 366
Eastern Chou, 420, 421. *See also* China
Eastern Han Empire, 411
Eastern Iranians, 370, 380, 381. *See also* Iran
Eastern Mediterranean Belt, 287, 289, 294, 296, 306. *See also* Palestine; Phoenicia; Syria
Eastern Semites, 72, 232, 287
Eastern Semitic language, 71, 81, 85, 87
Eastern Yi, 416
'Eber, 300
Ebla, 89, 231n.3, 232, 288, 289
Edomites, 300, 302
e-dubba, 131n.3, 134
Egypt, 13, 28, 45, 56, 67, 129, 214, 220, 250, 263, 266, 274, 277, 303; architecture of, 199–204; and Arzawa, contact with, 274–75; and Asshur, diplomatic relations with, 254; centralized administration under pharaohs of Old Kingdom, 153–57; and Crete, trade with, 315–16; Early Kingdom of, 144–48; early society, form of, 44–45; and emergence of civilization in Syria, Phoenicia, and Palestine, 287, 288, 289, 290; emergence of state in, 137–44; First Intermediate Period of,

158–61, 162, 165; first societal class differentiation in, 37, 38; and Greek colonization, 362, 363; and Hapiru, popular movement of, 294–96; Hittites and Pharaonic Egypt, 296–98; irrigation system in, 32, 33, 139–40, 145, 146, 161, 167; and Kingdom of Mitanni, clash with, 242–43; literature of, 210–12; Middle Kingdom of, 158, 161–70, 173, 196, 197, 203, 204, 206, 208, 210, 211, 213, 288; military empire during Eighteenth Dynasty, 174–82; Mitanni and Pharaonic Egypt, 291–94; New Kingdom of, 58, 167, 171, 172–92, 196, 197, 199, 204, 207, 208, 211, 212, 213; Nineteenth Dynasty of, 187–90; Old Kingdom of, 146, 147, 148–57, 168, 176, 197, 206, 207, 208, 210, 211; political history of Middle Kingdom, 168–70; Predynastic period of, 142–43; problems of ancient chronology, 22–23; pyramids of, 154–55, 167, 201–2; reliefs of, 207–9; religion of, 193–98; religious reforms of Akhenaton and the end of the Eighteenth Dynasty, 182–87; royal *hemwew*, position in Egyptian society, 163–68; royal, temple, and dignitaries' economies in Old Kingdom, 149–53; science of, 212–13; sculpture of, 205–7; Sea Peoples, invasion by, 190–91, 304, 325; Second Intermediate Period and Hyksos invasion of, 170–71, 173, 174–76, 177, 290–91; sources for history of, 15–16; Twentieth Dynasty and end of the New Kingdom, 190–92; war with Hittites, 188–90; writing system of, 209–10. *See also* Manethonian dynasties; Middle Egypt; Lower Egypt; Upper Egypt
Eia, 251
Ekallatum, 237
Ekron, 304
Elam and Elamites, 75, 81, 86, 90, 92, 95, 230, 235, 262, 263, 366, 386; First Dynasty of Issin, 96–97; and Gudea, rule of, 90–91; and Kingdom of the Sargonids, 88–89; language of, 219; Middle Babylonian Period in Lower Mesopotamia, Kassite Kingdom, and, 261–63; and prerequisites for the

creation of pre-urban society in Iran and Central Asia, 223–24; rivers of, 68, 68 n.2
Elamite-Dravidian languages, 232
Elbe, 30
Elephantine, 168, 194
Elis, 327, 336
Elissa, 351
El-Lahun, 199
Emar, 231 n.3, 242, 250
Emporicus, 350
Emporion, 360
Enentarzi, Ruler of Lagash, 82
Engels, Friedrich, 5–6, 9–10, 337–38, 343, 344, 365
Enki (god), 126, 134
Enkidu, 250
Enlil (god), 73, 86, 93, 95, 126, 131, 134
En-Menbaragesi, Ruler of First Dynasty of Kish, 74–75
Enmerkar, 132
Eos (goddess), 181 n.3
Ephesus, 327
Epidamnus, 358
Epirus, 326
Eredu, 132
Ereshkigal (goddess), 312 n.5
Eretrians, 359, 360
Erishum I, Ruler of Asshur, 235–36
Eros (god), 251
Eshnunna, 237
Esneh, 194
Ethiopia, 137, 143 n.4, 145, 155, 156, 163, 169, 173, 174, 177, 178, 180, 191
ethnogenesis, 19
Etruria, 352, 363
Euboea and Euboeans, 357, 359
Eumaeus, 333, 339
eunuchs, 42–43 n.6
Eupeithes, 342–43
Euphrates, 32, 44, 68, 79, 85, 95, 96, 100, 105, 178, 220, 228, 250, 257, 287; and city of Carchemish, 276, 297; and crossing of the "Sea Peoples," 300; and Kingdom of Mitanni, 240, 242; and Mitanni and Pharaonic Egypt, 291, 292, 293; and regions along the Tigris, 228, 229, 230. *See also* Lower Euphrates; Lower Euphrates Valley; Middle Euphrates; Upper Mesopotamia

Eurasian steppes, 30
Europe, 309, 367 n.4, 380
Eurymachus, 338
Evans, Arthur, 309 n.1, 321 n.13

"Falcon Pass," 235 n.10
Far East, 48, 386, 395. *See also* China
Fatha, 229, 230 n.2, 231 n.3, 245
Fayum Oasis, 162–63, 168, 169, 194
Fen River, 391, 424
Frangrasyan, 383
Freud, Sigmund, 61

Gadir (Gades, now Cadiz), 348, 349
Ganges River, 214
Ganges Valley, 371; and Indo-Aryans, settling of, 372–74; states of, 377–78; Vedic religion and culture, 378–80
Garo-dmana, 384
Gasur (Nuzi), 229, 231, 235, 239, 244
Gath, 304
Gathas, 382, 384, 385
Gaul, 349, 358, 360
Gaulus (now Gozo), 350
Gaza, 179, 291, 304
Gazru (Gezer), 294
Geb (god), 198
Gela, 357, 359, 363
Georgians, 257, 278
Geshtinanna, 132
Gilgamesh, 75, 84, 132, 250
Giorgadze, G. G., 11 n.10
Girsu (Ngirsu), 79
Giza cliff, tombs of, 202
Gobi Desert, 389
Godelier, M., 9
Gonur-depe, 382–83 n.10
Gorgippia (now Anapa), 362
Great and High Ancestress, 407
Great Bend of the Euphrates, 237, 243, 255, 287
Great Chinese Plain, 390, 391, 393, 414, 420, 424, 425
Greater Caucasus, 369
Greater (Upper) Zab, 228
"Great Mistress," 312
Great Sphinx, 155
Greece, 13, 28, 46, 58, 308, 318, 325, 367, 381; chronology of, 23–24; colonization by, 350, 354–65; in the Homeric Epics, 328–46. *See also*

Greece (*continued*)
Achaean (Mycenaean) civilization;
Homeric Epics; Minoan (Cretan)
civilization
Gregory XV, Pope, 62
Guaba, 81
Gual, 364
gwasileus, 323
Gypsum Desert, 230

Haifa, 225n.8
Haleb (now Aleppo), 231n.3, 240, 250,
272, 273, 276, 290
Halicarnassus, 327, 363
Haltamti (Hatamti), 223
Hammurapi, King of Babylon, 22, 66,
100, 102–3, 238, 240, 299; Laws of,
112, 115–22, 259
Hamrin mountains, 228, 229, 230, 239
Hamun Lake, 226
Hana, 240, 261
Hanean tribes, 99, 122
Hanigalbat, 240, 243, 273
Han jen, 387, 388
Han Kingdom, 426
Hantilis, Hittite King, 273, 274
Hao, 420
Hapiru, 187, 265, 290, 291, 293; popular
movement of, 294–96
Hapuseneb, 204
Harappa and Harappan culture, 216–19,
221, 222, 373, 379. *See also* India
Haremhab, Pharaoh of Egypt, 186–87,
188
Harris papyrus, 190
Hashu (Hassuwa), 272
hassus, 282
Hathor (god), 193, 194
Hatshepsut, Pharaoh of Egypt, 178, 203,
292
Hatti and Hattians, 268, 270, 271, 272,
273, 274, 275, 277, 278, 283, 284. *See
also* Hittite Kingdom
Hattusas (now Boghazköy), 250, 266–67,
268, 269, 271, 272, 273, 273n.7, 278.
See also Boghazköy
Hattusilis I, Hittite King, 240, 272–73
Hattusilis III, Hittite King, 189, 277, 297,
298
Hawal, 233, 235, 239
Hayasa, 275
hazannu, 253

Hazor, 289, 294, 303–4
Hebat (goddess), 250
Hebrew language, 71
Heb-Sed, 200, 200n.1
Hegel, G. F. W., 5, 10n.48
Heliopolis, 194, 195, 198
Hellas, 352, 353, 355, 358. *See also*
Greece
Hellespont, 268, 324, 358, 360, 361
hemwew, in Egyptian society, 163–68
Heraclea Pontica, 361
Heracleopolis, 160, 161, 194, 211
Herihor, 191
Herishaf (god), 194
Hermonassa, 362
Hermontis, 194
Herodotus, 154–55, 325
Hesiod, 251, 284
Hieraconopolis, 141, 144
Hilmand River, 226
Himalayas, 366
Hinduism, 59, 220, 378–79
Hindu Kush, 369
Hindustan, 370, 380
Hiram, King of Tyre, 351
Hissarlik (Troy), 268. *See also* Troy
Historians of antiquity, directions for fu-
ture research, 55–66
Historical materialism, 4–13; and Asiatic
mode of production, 9–10; and cycli-
cal theory of history, 6–7; and Ilyu-
shechkin's view of world history, 11–
12; and theory of universal history, 7–8
History of Antiquity (Meyer), 7
History of Egypt (Manetho), 143
Hittite Kingdom, 46, 123, 173, 181, 187,
203, 250, 252, 255, 256, 260, 302n.9,
304, 367, 411; and Ahhiyawā, diplomatic contacts with, 325; and the
Amarna Period, 294; Babylon, destruction of, 261; culture of, 283–85;
discovery of, 266–67; and Hapiru,
popular movement of, 294–96; justice
and law in, 283; New Kingdom, 274–
79, 284; offensive against Mitanni,
242–43; Old Kingdom, 272–74; and
Pharaonic Egypt, 296–98; Pre-Hittite
Period in central Asia Minor, 267–72;
problems of sources for, 14–15; socioeconomic relations in, 279–83; war
with Egypt during Nineteenth Dynasty, 188–90

Homer, 18, 277, 279, 317, 324, 325
Homeric Epics, 328–46; aristocracy in, 338–41; *basileis*, position of, 343–46; Engel's characterization of Homeric Period, 337–38; heroes in, 331–32; illiteracy in, 334–35; iron technology, development of, 330–31; slavery in, 332–33; sources of history for, 18–19
Homo sapiens sapiens, 27, 29, 64, 390
Honan, 391, 393, 394, 399, 416, 429
Hopeh, 391, 393
Hor Aha ("Horus the Champion"), 144
Hori, 204
Horoz-Tepe, 268
Horus (god), 144 n.5, 145, 147, 193, 195, 196, 197
Hou Chi, 410, 411, 413, 416
Houses of Life, 213
Hrozný, B., 266–67
Hsia Dynasty, 417, 422
Hsian, 420
Hsiaot'un, 394, 394 n.9
Hsiuchou (Chiangsu), 402
Hua, 388
Huai Ho, 391, 392, 393, 401
Huang Ho basin, 387, 388, 389, 390, 391, 392, 393, 397, 398, 400, 401, 409, 411, 414
Huang Ho River, 420, 421, 422, 423, 424
Huangp'i, 393, 395, 402
Huan Kiang, 392
Huan-Kung, 425
Hukkanas, 275
Hunan, 393
Hunan-Chianghsi, 393
Hupeh, 393, 402
Hurri, 272, 273
Hurrians, 224–25, 229, 231, 232, 236–37, 270, 283, 284, 285, 288, 302 n.9, 380; culture of, 249–52; and Hittites, military clashes with, 272–73; Kingdom of Arrapkhe, 244–49, 290; and the Kingdom of Mitanni, 238–44, 291; language of, 297; and Mitanni and Pharaonic Egypt, 291–94
Hurro-Urartian, 244
Huwana, 250
Hyaona, 385
Hydraulic Oriental civilizations, 8 n.4
Hyksos, 170–71, 173, 174–75, 176, 177, 177 n.6, 290; and Egypt, invasion of, 170–71, 173, 174–76, 177, 290–91;

and Mitanni and Pharaonic Egypt, 291–94. *See also* Egypt
Hyrcania, 382

Ibbi-Su'en, King of Ur, 95–96
Iberian Peninsula, 350, 352
'ibri, 300
Ice Age, 28, 138
I Ching (The Book of Changes), 418
Idamarat tribe, 122, 123
Idri-mi, King of Alalakh, 242, 291, 307
Idumeans, 300
Ilahkabkabuhu, 236–37
Iliad, The (Homer), 18, 279, 324, 328, 331, 335, 337, 339, 341, 343
Ilushuma, Ruler of Asshur, 233–36
Ilyushechkin, V. P., 11–12
Imhetep, 154, 201
Inanna (Innin) (goddess), 73, 77, 132, 133, 134
India, 13, 28, 46, 48, 58, 79, 81, 83, 86, 89, 91, 101, 229, 256, 346 n.11, 379; and the Aryan question, 366–71; culture and religion of Indus civilization, 219–20; decline of Indus civilization, 221–22; historical and geographical context of Indus civilization, 215–19; historiography of, 17; Indian Peninsula in ancient times, 214–15; Indo-Aryans in Ganges Valley, 372–74; problems of ancient chronology, 23, 25; social and state structure in Northern India, 374–78; social structure of Indus civilization, 220–21; sources of Indian history, 371–72; Vedic religion and culture, 378–80
Indian Peninsula, 222
Indo-Aryan languages, 366, 367, 368
Indo-Aryan tribes, 221, 369 n.7, 370, 371, 380; in the Ganges Valley, 372–74
Indochina, 28, 390
Indo-European languages, 30, 31, 270, 285, 366, 367
Indo-European tribes, 367, 368, 370
Indo-Iranian(s), 241, 244, 285 n.22, 291, 367, 368, 369
Indra (god), 378, 380
Indus River, 32, 79, 214, 216
Indus Valley, 31, 215, 216, 217, 218, 370, 371, 408
Ineni, 204
I-Nina-Gena, 68, 79, 81

Iolcus (Thessaly), 318
Ionians, 327
Ionian Sea, 358
Ipuwer, 159, 160
Iran, 13, 28, 58, 85, 89, 90, 101, 214, 219,
    225, 229, 241, 288, 378; and the Aryan
    question, 366–71; and the *Avesta* and
    Zoroastrianism, 381–86; in the first
    half of the first millennium B.C., 380–
    81; prerequisites for creation of pre-
    urban society in, 222–27
Iraq, 31 n.2, 67 n.1, 68, 230, 231 n.3
Iron Age, 328, 331, 349
Irsu, 190–91
Ishbi-Erra, King of Sumer and Akkad,
    96
Ishme-Dagan, 238
Ishtar, 31 n.5
Ishtar-Shawaushka (goddess), 243, 251
Isis (goddess), 196, 197, 198
Islam, 58, 59
Israel, 169, 286
Israelites, 300, 301, 302, 303–5
Issachar tribe, 302
isshiakkum, 233, 253, 256
Issin, 105, 112–13, 130, 133, 235 n.9; First
    Dynasty of, 96–97; Second Dynasty of,
    263
Istanbul (ancient Byzantium), 364
Isthmus, 326, 327
Istoriya drevnego Vostoka (Vasil'ev), 1,
    10–11 n.8
Istros, 361
Italy, 28, 46, 308, 357, 358, 359, 360,
    363, 367 n.4
Ithaca, 333 n.2, 342
Ithoba'l, 349
It-Tawi, 168, 170
Iturungal, 68, 81

Jacob (Israel), 300, 302
Jaffa, 211
Jakobson, V. A., 112 n.6
Jemdet-Nasr, 72, 73, 409
Jen-fang tribes, 401
Jericho, 29, 287, 302
Jerusalem, 294, 303
Jesus Christ, 24–25
Jordan River, 286, 300, 302, 304
Jordan Valley, 286
Joshua, 301–2
Judah (Jehudah), 302

Jung, C. G., 61
Jung tribe, 425

Ka, 148 n.9, 197
Ka'a, tomb of, 144
Kadesh (Qinza), 179–80, 188–89, 208,
    277, 294
Kadesh-Barnea, 301
Kadmukhi, 242
Kafir, 241, 366, 368, 369
Kafirnigan River, 381
Kalebites (Kenazites), 302
Kali, 374
Kalibangan, 221
Kali Yuga, 374
Kalkhu (now Nimrud), 229
Kames, Pharaoh of Egypt, 171, 175, 177
Kammenhuber, Annelies, 241
Kang Hou, 414
Kanish (Nesa), 235–36, 238, 269, 271,
    290
Kansu, 393
Karahar (Harhar), 235 n.10, 239
Karana (Tell Rimah), 229, 248
karma, 379
Karnak, temple of, 204
Kar-Tukulti-Ninurta, 256
Karun River, 32, 89, 223
Karun Valley, 31 n.2, 44, 46, 75
Kashmir, 241, 366
Kashtiliash, Kassite King, 123, 263
Kaska, 275, 278
Kassite Kingdom, 98, 122, 123, 181, 224,
    232, 238, 240, 243, 249, 254, 300; and
    the Amarna Period, 294; Middle
    Babylonian Period in Lower Meso-
    potamia, Elam, and, 261–63; society of
    Middle Babylonian Period, 264–65
Kavata, 383
Kavi Khausrava, 383
Kavi Vishtaspa, 384, 385
Kazakhstan, 369 n.7, 380
Kel-Tesshub, 248
Kemet ("The Black"), 138
Kerch (Panticapaeum), 364
Kerkheh River, 32, 89, 223
Kerkheh Valley, 31 n.2, 46, 75
Ket, 387 n.2
Khabur River, 122, 228, 229, 230, 239,
    260
Khachikyan, Margaret, 239
Khaneqin, 230

Kha'sekhemui, Pharaoh of Egypt, 147
Khensu (god), 195
Khepri (god), 194–95
Khian, Pharaoh of Egypt, 171
Khnum (god), 194
Khoresm, 383
Khoresmians, 380, 381
Kikkuli, 279
Kirmanshah, 230, 235 n.10
Kirta, 241
Kish, 79, 82, 83, 84, 87, 89, 105, 129,
  230; First Dynasty of, 74–75
Kismar (Hashmar), 235, 235 n.10
Kissuk, 248
Kition, 351
Kizzuwadna, 239, 241, 242, 250, 251, 273
Knossos, 309, 315, 316, 320, 321,
  321 n.14, 322, 328, 332
Korea, 389
koreter, 323
Koshala, 377
Krita Yuga, 374
Kronos (god), 251
Kshatriyas, 375, 376
Kudurmabuk, 102
kudurru, 264
Kül-tepe, 268–69, 284
Kumarwe (god), 251, 284
Kumme, 251
Kun (god), 410
Kura River, 33
Kurdistan Mountains, 251
Kurigalzu the Elder, King of Babylonia,
  262
Kurigalzu the Younger, King of
  Babylonia, 249, 262
Kuruhanni, 251
Kush and Kushites, 143 n.4, 177
Kushukh (god), 252
Kussara, 271, 272
Kuthar-wa-Husas (god), 306

Labarna, 272
"Labyrinth" (Knossos Palace), 169,
  309–11
Lachish, 294
"Lady Hou, The," 406
Laërtes, 333
Lagash, 79–83, 123, 132; and Gudea's
  rule, 90–91; and Sargonids, Kingdom
  of, 84, 85–86, 90
Lampsacus, 357

Larsa, 99, 100, 102, 105, 123, 235 n.9
Late Han Empire, 380
Late Neolithic Age, 214, 392, 422. *See
  also* Neolithic Age
Late Neolithic Yangshao pottery, 397 n.12
Latin, 20
lawagetas, 323
Laws of Hammurapi, 112, 115–22, 259
Laws of Shulgi, 112
Laws of the Kingdom of Eshnunna,
  114–15, 117 n.9
Leah, 302
Lebanon (modern state), 287
Lebanon Mountains, 173, 276, 286
Lebanon River, 257
Leiden papyrus, 159, 160
Lenin, Vladimir Ilyich, 6, 9
Leningrad papyrus, 159–60
Lesbos, 327
Lesser (Lower) Zab, 228, 230, 245, 248
Lévi-Strauss, C., 61
Levites, 305
Lévy-Bruhl, L., 61
Libya, 155, 174
Lie Kuo Period (Chu'un Ch'in), 420, 422,
  424, 425; political history of, 420–26;
  social order of, 426–32
limmu, 21, 253, 254
Linear B, 316, 321, 331, 334
Lipari Islands, 360
Lipit-Ishtar, King of Issin, 112–14
Lixus, 348, 349, 350
Locrians, 360
Locri Epizaphyrii, 360
Locris, 337, 359
Lo River, 412
Lothal, 221, 222
Lower Egypt, 44, 136, 138, 141, 142, 144,
  149, 168, 192; during Eighteenth Dy-
  nasty, 187, 189–90. *See also* Egypt;
  Middle Egypt; Upper Egypt
Lower Euphrates, 31. *See also* Euphrates;
  Middle Euphrates; Upper Euphrates
Lower Euphrates Valley, 32, 67, 73, 223;
  development of organized irrigation
  in, 67–69; first societal class differ-
  entiation in, 37–44. *See also* Euphrates
Lower Mesopotamia, 32, 44, 45, 46, 67–
  69, 72, 79, 98, 136, 229, 238, 263, 292;
  area defined, 67 n.1; and early Asshur,
  political history of, 234–35; Early Dynastic Period, 74–83, 112, 128, 129; fall

Lower Mesopotamia (*continued*)
of Ur and rise of Issin, 95–97; and
Gudea, rule of, 90–91; Hurrian art in
comparison to Mesopotamian art, 250;
and Indus civilization, trade with, 219;
Middle Babylonian Period in Kassite
Kingdom, Elam, and, 261–63; Old
Babylonian Period (*see* Babylon; Meso-
potamia); Protoliterate Period, 69–74,
126, 128, 129, 226; religious perception
of the world and the arts in, 124–31;
and Sargonids, Kingdom of, 84–90;
society of Middle Babylonian Period,
264–65; stratified societies in, 80–81;
Third Dynasty of Ur, 91–95, 96, 98,
99, 100, 101, 102, 103, 104, 122. *See also*
Akkad; Babylon; Mesopotamia; Sumer
Loyang, 399, 420, 421
Lugalanda, 82
Lugalbanda, 132–33
Lugalzagesi, 83, 84–86, 132
Lu Kingdom, 421, 422, 425, 426, 429,
431
Lullubeans, 232
Lungshan culture, 392, 396, 398, 408
Luoyi, 420, 421
Luwia and Luwian(s), 267, 268 n.2, 270,
274, 275
luzzi, 280, 281

Maat (goddess), 193
Macedonia, 267, 326
Maeotis, Lake, 362 n.4
Magadha, 378
Magi, 386
Magna Graecia, 360, 364
Malaca (now Málaga), 350
Malaysia, 225
Manasseh tribe, 302, 303
Manchuria, 389
Manetho, 143–44, 169, 176
Manethonian dynasties of Egypt: First,
144, 146, 147; Second, 144, 146, 147;
Third, 148, 153, 154, 156, 201; Fourth,
148, 153, 154–55, 156, 160, 201, 202;
Fifth, 148, 155, 156, 157, 201–2, 207;
Sixth, 148, 155, 156, 157, 160 n.2; Sev-
enth, 158; Ninth, 158; Tenth, 160 n.2,
162; Eleventh, 158; Twelfth, 158, 160,
165, 168–69, 170, 174, 202; Thirteenth,
170; Fourteenth, 170; Fifteenth, 171;
Sixteenth, 171; Seventeenth, 171, 175,

176; Eighteenth, 171, 172, 173, 174–82,
200, 202, 207; Nineteenth, 172, 173,
187–90, 203, 207; Twentieth, 173,
190–92
Manishtushu, 87–89
Man tribe, 425
Mardin (now Mobin), 231 n.3, 233
Marduk (god), 256, 263
Margiana, 382, 382–83 n.10
Mari (now Abu-Kemal), 99, 100, 102,
123, 230, 231, 236, 237, 289; and
Shamshi-Adad I's empire, 236, 237,
238
marianna, 244, 298
Marinatos, S., 316
Marseilles (Phocaean Massalia), 364
Marx, Karl, 5–6, 9–10, 343, 344, 354,
365
Marxist approach to history, 4–13
Massalia and Massalians (now Marseilles),
357, 360, 363
mastaba, 201, 201 n.2, 202
McAlpin, David, 223
Media and Medes, 380, 381, 385, 386
Medinet-Abu, 203
Mediterranean region, 273, 292, 293;
Greek colonization in, 360, 365; Phoe-
nician colonization in, 347, 348, 349,
350, 351, 365
Mediterranean Sea, 86, 137, 156, 180,
230, 236, 272, 286, 287, 296, 312
Megara and Megarians, 358, 359, 361
Megara Hyblaea, 359
megaron, 319–20
Megiddo, 179–80, 188, 294
Mehrgarh, 215 n.2, 217
Melakha, 79, 86, 91
Melanthius, 333
Melikishvili, G. A., 11
Melita (now Malta), 350
Melos, 348
Memnon, 181
Memphis, 147, 157, 160, 187, 198, 349
Mendes, 194
Menes, Pharaoh of Egypt, 143, 144, 147
Menestheou Limen, 360, 363
Men-ne-Ptah, Pharaoh of Egypt, 303,
304
Mentchuhetep I, Pharaoh of Egypt, 161,
168
Mentu, 194
Mentuhetep III, tomb of, 202

Meren-Ra', Pharaoh of Egypt, 156
Merika-Ra', 211
Mer-ne-Ptah, Pharaoh of Egypt, 190
Mesanepada, 77
Mesembria, 361
Meskeneh (formerly Emar), 250. *See also*
  Emar
Mesolithic Age, 29, 30, 138
Mesopotamia, 30, 56, 173, 180, 214, 220,
  226, 252, 257, 279, 282, 287, 409; area
  defined, 67 n.1; early despotisms in,
  84–97; end of Old Babylonian Period,
  122–23; Hurrian art in comparison to
  Mesopotamian art, 249–50; Middle
  Babylonian Period in Lower Meso-
  potamia, the Kassite Kingdom, and
  Elam, 261–63; Old Babylonian Period
  laws, 112–21; Old Babylonian society,
  103–11; political history of Old Babylo-
  nian Period, 98–103; problems of
  ancient chronology, 21, 25; problems
  of sources for, 14–15; sacred architec-
  ture, type of, 127; society of Middle
  Babylonian Period, 264–65; trade with
  Syria, Phoenicia, and Palestine, 287,
  289. *See also* Akkad; Babylon; Lower
  Mesopotamia; Sumer
Messene and Messenians, 327, 355, 357
Metsamor, 262 n.2
Meyer, Eduard, 7
Miao, 422
Middle Ages, 11–12, 25, 25 n.15, 57, 58,
  121, 361
Middle Asia, 214 n.1, 224, 225, 226, 227,
  229, 370, 409, 416. *See also* Asia Minor;
  Central Asia; Western Asia
Middle Assyrian empire, 46, 254–55. *See
  also* Asshur; Assyria
Middle East, 29, 31
Middle Egypt, 202, 206. *See also* Egypt;
  Lower Egypt; Upper Egypt
Middle Euphrates, 99, 230, 243, 260. *See
  also* Euphrates; Lower Euphrates;
  Upper Euphrates
Middle Euphratian language, 236, 237
Middle Mesopotamia, 288. *See also* Lower
  Mesopotamia; Mesopotamia; Upper
  Mesopotamia
Middle Palaeolithic Age, 27. *See also* Pa-
  laeolithic Age; Upper Palaeolithic Age
Middle Tigris, 100, 237, 262. *See also* Ti-
  gris; Upper Tigris

Midianites, 300
midru, 234–35
Milawanda, 278
Miletus, 278, 315, 327, 355, 358, 361, 363
Militarev, A. Yu., 30
Mill, J. Stuart, 5
Min (god), 195
Minoan (Cretan) civilization, 309–17,
  319, 330, 331; art of, 311–12; destruc-
  tion of, 316–17; Knossos palace, 309–
  11. *See also* Achaean (Mycenaean) civi-
  lization; Greece; Homeric Epics
Minos, King of Crete, 309, 315
Minotaur, 309, 312
Mitanni, 46, 180, 181, 252, 254, 261, 282,
  297, 299, 300; Adad-nērari's cam-
  paigns against, 255; and Hapiru,
  popular movement of, 294–96; Hittite
  destruction of, 275–76; Kingdom of,
  238–44; and Pharaonic Egypt, 291–94
Mitannian-Aryan language, 241
mitgum, 113
Mithra (god), 378, 383
miyahwantes, 280 n.18
Mnevis, 194
Mohenjo-daro, 216–17, 221, 222, 373,
  379
Morgan, L. H., 6, 344
Moses, 300–301
Mosul, 229
Mo-tsu, 426
Motya, 350
Munda languages, 366
Mundigak, 226, 370
Murghab River, 382, 382 n.10
Murghab Valley, 226, 383
Mursilis I, Hittite King, 123, 240,
  272–73
Mursilis II, Hittite King, 275, 281
mushkenum, 111, 114, 117
Mushki, 257
Mut (god), 195
Mu wang, 412
Muwatallis, Hittite King, 188–89, 277
Muye, battle of, 410–11
Mycenae, 292, 304, 317–27, 328, 335,
  347. *See also* Achaean (Mycenaean) civ-
  ilization; Greece; Homeric Epics
Mycerinus (Menkau-Ra'), Pharaoh of
  Egypt, 154, 201
Myrmecium, 362
Mysore, 372

"Myth of Telepinus, The," 284
"Myth of the Serpent Illuyankas, The,"
284
Mytilene, 361, 362, 363

Nadmani (now Tell-Ali), 245
Nahraina (Mitanni), 178, 242. *See also*
Mitanni
Namazga V, 380
Namazga VI, 381
Namazga-depe, 370
Nanna of Ur (goddess), 78, 86, 95
Naples, 359, 364
Naram-Su'en, 89–90, 91, 130, 256
Narody Azil i Afriki, 9
Na'rmer tablet, 144, 193
Naucratis, 363
Nausharo, 216 n.3
Nausicaa, 332
Nawar, 229, 233, 239
Nazi-Maruttash, Kassite King, 249
Near East, 13, 29, 30, 31, 46, 58, 215,
232, 246, 268, 308, 330, 353, 395, 420;
archaeological remains from, 15; eco-
nomic base of first empires in, 349;
Neolithic communication in, 69; prob-
lems of ancient chronology, 21–22, 25;
second way of development in late an-
tiquity, 48
Nebuchadnezzar II, King of Babylon, 20
Nebuchadrezzar I, King of Babylon, 263
Neferti, 160, 211
Nefertiti, Queen of Egypt, 186, 207
Nefrusebek, Pharaoh of Egypt, 170
nemhu, 182–87
Neo-Aramaic dialects, 71
Neolithic Age, 29, 69, 72, 217, 267, 309,
389, 391, 392, 398, 408; art during,
125–26, 128; settlement of pastoralist
tribes in Egypt, 138–39
Nepal, 214
Nephtys (god), 198
Nergal (god), 251
Nesa (Kanish) and Nessites, 268, 269,
270, 271. *See also* Kanish
Nestor, King of Pylos, 336, 343
"Nestor's Palace," 319–20
Nicaea (now Nice), 363
Nigeria, 71
Nikiforov, V. N., 13
Nikolaev, S. I., 387 n.2

Nile Cataracts, 137, 147, 169, 170, 177,
178, 180
Nile Delta, 159, 168, 170, 171, 188, 191,
290–91, 300
Nile River, 137, 138, 141, 142, 147, 155,
156, 163, 168, 169, 173, 185, 207, 363;
and Egyptian architecture, 200, 202,
204; flood stages of, 212; and Osirian
cult, 196
Nile Valley, 31–32, 44, 67, 137, 139, 140,
142, 145, 170, 220
Nineveh, 229, 230, 231 n.3, 243, 252
Ningal (goddess), 78
Ningirsu, 82, 91
Ninurta (god), 133
Nippur, 73, 77, 86, 90, 93, 95, 96, 105,
113, 126, 131, 262; and Asshur, trade
with, 235; literary tradition in, 132–33
Nora, 350
North Africa, 28, 29, 30, 58, 71, 138, 139,
308, 350. *See also* Africa; Central
Africa
North China, 423
North Vietnam, 387
Nostratic linguistic phylum, 387 n.2
Nubia, 143, 147, 155, 156, 163, 168, 173,
176, 177, 180, 188–90
Nusaibin (Nisibis), 231 n.3
Nut (god), 195, 198
Nuzi (formerly Gasur), 229, 231, 235,
239, 244, 249, 250
Nymphaeum, 362

Odessus, 361
Odysseus, 331, 332, 333, 342, 344, 345
Odyssey, The (Homer), 18, 279, 328, 331,
332, 335, 338, 342, 344, 345. *See also*
Homeric Epics
Oedipus, King of Thebes, 324
Olbia, 362
Old Assyrian language, 236, 252, 269,
272
Old Chinese language, 396
Old Indian language, 244
Old Stone Age, 29, 31. *See also* Stone Age
Olympiads, 23–24, 24 n.14
Orchomenus, 318
Oriental civilizations, 7–8, 8 n.4, 9,
21–22. *See also* China
*Origin of the Family, Private Property, and
the State* (Engels), 6, 10

Orontes River (Al-'Asi), 286, 287
Orontes Valley, 179, 188, 239, 242, 249, 294
Ortygia, 359
Osiris (god), 144, 193, 194; cult of, 196–98, 208, 210, 211
Ossetic language, 222 n.5
Oval Plaque of Enmetena, 112

Pakistan, 89, 214, 215 n.2, 219
Palaeolithic Age, 125, 128. *See also* Middle Palaeolithic Age; Upper Palaeolithic Age
Palaians, 270, 285
Palestine, 28, 29, 173, 177, 178, 179, 187, 188, 190, 214, 266, 277, 346 n.11; ancient geographical region of, 286, 287; culture and alphabet of Canaanite-Amorite civilization, 306–8; emergence of civilization in, 286–91; and Hapiru, popular movement of, 294–96; and Hittites and Pharaonic Egypt, 296–98; and the Kingdom of Mitanni, 238–44; and the migration of "those who had crossed the river" and the "sea peoples," 299–305; Mitanni and Pharaonic Egypt, 291–94; sources for history of, 16–17
Pamir language, 222 n.5
Pamirs, 369
pankus, 273, 274
Panormus, 350
Panticapaeum (now Kerch), 362
papyri, 15–16, 18
Parattarna (Barattarna), Mitanni King, 241–42, 291
Paros, 360
Parthenii, 355
Parthia and Parthians, 381, 382
Pashupati (god), 220
Pathans, 366
Patroclus, 337
Pelasgians, 304 n.12, 317, 317 n.10
Peloponnesus, 317, 318, 319, 325, 326
Penelope, 333, 342, 345
Penra, 203
Pensée (journal), 9
People's Republic of China, 388, 389
Pepi I, Pharaoh of Egypt, 156
Pepi II, Pharaoh of Egypt, 157, 189
Persia and Persians, 225 n.5, 380, 381, 385, 386. *See also* Iran
Persian Gulf, 83, 86, 101, 123
Phaecaeans, 344
Phanagoria, 362
Phasis (Poti), 362
Philistines, 191, 304, 304 n.12
Phocaea and Phocaeans, 355, 357, 360, 361, 363
Phoenicia and Phoenicians, 214, 257, 277, 334, 355, 359, 362; and Achaeans, military and colonizing expansion of, 325; ancient geographical region of, 286, 287; colonization by, 347–51; culture and alphabet of Canaanite-Amorite civilization, 306–8; emergence of civilization in, 286–91; and Hapiru, popular movement of, 294–96; and Hittites and Pharaonic Egypt, 296–98; and Mitanni and Pharaonic Egypt, 291–94; and Tartessus, contact with, 352–54
phratriae, 336, 344
Phrygians, 257
phylae (phyle), 336, 344
Pillars of Hercules (now Straits of Gibraltar), 348, 350, 363
P'ing wang, 416, 420
Pitecussa, 359
Pitkhanas, Kassite King, 271, 272
Pityous (Pitsunda), 362
Piusti, 271
Piyassili, 276
"Plebeians and Helots" (Struve), 7
Pleistocene Period, 28
Poland, 30, 367
Pompeii, 19
Pontus Axinus (Black Sea), 361
Pontus Euxinus (Black Sea), 358, 361
Poti (Phasis), 364
Potidaea, 357
P'oyang Lake, 393, 397
Precapitalist Economic Formations (Marx), 5
Precapitalist societies, 12
Preindustrial or urban societies, 12 n.12
"Problem of the Origin, Development, and Decline of Slave-Owning Society in the Ancient Orient" (Struve), 7
Production, 4, 9, 11; "Asiatic mode," 506
promachoi, 340
"Prophecy of Neferti, The," 211
Propontis, 358, 361

Proto-Armenians, 257, 304
Proto-Byblian writing, 307–8
Proto-Dravidian language, 223
Proto-Hans, 424
Proto-Indus, 370
Proto-Thai languages, 423
Ptah (god), 194, 198
Ptolemaeus, Claudius (Ptolemy), 24
Puabi (burial site of), 77–78
Punjab, 372
Punt, 156, 163, 173, 178
Purushkhanda, 271
Pylos (Peloponnesus), 318, 319, 320, 321,
  322, 323, 326, 328, 332, 336
Pythagoras, 379

Qart-hadasht, 351
Qatna, 237, 242
Qinza, 188, 277, 294, 298. *See also*
  Kadesh
Quesnay, F., 5
Quitians, 90–91, 224, 232

Ra' (god), 156–57, 177, 194, 195, 197
Rachel, 302
Rajasthan, 218, 372
Rameses I, Pharaoh of Egypt, 188
Rameses II, Pharaoh of Egypt, 200–201,
  204, 208, 277, 296, 298, 299, 300, 304;
  temple of, 203; war with Hittites,
  188–90
Rameses III, Pharaoh of Egypt, 190–91,
  200–201, 203, 208
Rameses IV, Pharaoh of Egypt, 191
Rameses IX, Pharaoh of Egypt, 191
Ravi River, 217
Red Building, 127
Red Sea, 156, 163, 173
Retenu, 169
Rhegium, 359
Rhodes and Rhodians, 277, 315, 324,
  325, 348, 357, 359, 363
Rhone River, 363
Rig Veda, 221, 369 n.7, 370, 372, 373,
  375, 377
Rim-Sin, 102
Rimush, 87–88
Robespierre, 60, 61
Roman empire, 47–48, 59
Rome, 13, 18–19, 23–24, 357
Rousseau, J. J., 5, 60–61

"Royal Ancestress, The Eighth," 406
Royal Son of Kish, 180

Sacae tribe, 222 n.5, 380
sahhan, 280, 281
Sahu-Ra', Pharaoh of Egypt, 155–56
Sais Kings, tombs of, 203
sakinu, 298
Samhitas, 372
Samos, 327, 360, 361, 363
Samsuditana, King of Babylon, 123, 272
Samsuiluna, 122–23, 238
sang, 401
Sanskrit, 219, 241
Saqqara, 154, 155
Sardinia, 174, 349, 350
Sargon the Ancient, 84–90, 130, 268
Sausattar (Sausadattar), Mitanni King,
  242, 276
Schliemann, H., 317, 325 n.18
Schmandt-Besserat, Denise, 69
Scythians, 222 n.5, 361, 362, 364, 380
Sea Peoples, 190–91, 208, 278, 325, 327,
  347; and the migration of "those who
  had crossed the river," 299–305
semdet, 167
Semenov, Yu. I., 12
Semerkhet, 144
Semites, 287–88, 299, 304, 305. *See also*
  Eastern Semites; Western Semites
Semnekhka-Ra', Pharaoh of Egypt, 185
Senmut, 178, 203
Senwesret I, Pharaoh of Egypt, 169, 210
Senwesret II, Pharaoh of Egypt, 169, 199
Senwesret III, Pharaoh of Egypt, 169
Sequen-ne-Ra', Pharaoh of Egypt, 171
Seq-ne-Ra', Pharaoh of Egypt, 211
Sesostris, 169
Seth (god), 147, 196, 198
Sethnekht, 191
Seti I, Pharaoh of Egypt, 188, 296, 298
Seven Wonders of the Ancient World,
  154
Sexi, 350
Shahr-i Sokhta, 224 n.6, 226
shakin mati, 247–48
Shala (goddess), 251
Shalmaneser I, King of Assyria, 255
Shamshi-Adad I, 100, 233, 236–38, 239,
  252, 290, 299
Shang, 388, 389, 410, 412, 416, 417, 418,

422; Shang (Yin) "state," 393–401; society of, 401–9
Shang-ti (god), 407, 416
Shanhsi, 391, 393, 424
Shantung, 391, 392, 393, 402, 422, 424, 429
Shantung Peninsula, 395
Sharruma (god), 250
Sharrum-ken, 84
Sharuhen, 177
Shatt-al-Arab River, 68
Shattiwasa (Shattiwazza), 243, 248, 276
Shattuara II, Mitanni King, 255
Shawushka (goddess), 250, 312 n.5
Shelwikhe, 249
Shenhsi, 391, 393, 409, 416, 420, 424
Shih Ching, 411, 414, 415, 419
Shilwi-Tesshub, Prince of Arrapkhe, 248
Shimike (god), 252
Shinar (Shinhara), 262 nn.1, 2
Shiraz, 89, 223
Shiva (god), 220
Shmunu, 195
Shnirelman, V. A., 30
Shortughai, 218–19
Shu Ching, 404, 411, 414
Shudras, 375, 376
Shu (god), 198
Shulgi, 92, 112, 256
Shun (god), 420 n.21
Shuruppak, 75, 76
Shusshara (now Tell Shemshar), 235 n.10
Shutruk-Nahhunte, King of Elam, 263
Shuttarna I, Mitanni King, 241
Shuttarna II, Mitanni King, 242, 246
Shuttarna III, Mitanni King, 243
Siberia, 369 n.7, 409
Sicani, 359
Sicily, 347, 348, 350, 358, 359, 360
Siculi, 359
Sidon, 257, 296, 347
Sieber, N. I., 7
Simeon tribe, 302
Sinai, 155, 156, 163, 173, 188, 301, 302, 304
Sinai Peninsula, 145, 156, 170, 177, 191, 301
Sinjar Mountains (Jebel Sinjar), 230–31
Sinope, 361, 364
Sino-Tibetan languages, 387, 387 n.2, 423

Sinuhe, 169, 210
Sippar, 105, 230, 256, 262
Siris, 360
Sirius, 212
Sisera, 303
Smith, Adam, 5
Smyrna, 327
Snefru, Pharaoh of Egypt, 155, 160, 201
Societies in early antiquity: characteristics of, 54–55; deities in, 50–51; first way of development, 31–43; further development of class societies, 46–49; mentality and worldview of people in, 49–54; mythology in, 51–54, 61; religion in, 53, 55–56; and rituals, importance of, 51–54; second way of development, 44–45; third way of development, 45–46
socium, 57, 57 n.9, 63, 64, 66
Socrates, 62
Sogdiana and Sogdians, 380, 381, 382
Soloeis, 350
Soma, 378
Somalia, 156
Song of Deborah, The," 303
"Song of the Harpist, The," 211
"Song of Ullikumme," 251, 284
Son of Heaven, 421, 424
Sources for ancient history, 14–21. *See also* Ancient history
South China, 423
South China Sea, 391
Southeast Asia, 390, 390 nn.4, 5, 422, 423. *See also* Asia Minor; Central Asia; Middle Asia; Western Asia
Southwestern Bronze Culture, 352
Spain, 225, 292, 309, 348, 350, 351, 352, 358, 360
Sparta and Spartans, 345 n.9, 346 n.10, 355, 359, 360
Spengler, Oswald, 7
Sri Lanka, 219, 366, 366 n.2
Srubnaya culture, 369 n.7
Ssu-ma Ch'ien, 398, 422, 423
Starostin, S. A., 387 n.2
Steppes of Mongolia, 389
Stone Age, 124, 125, 139, 388, 390, 391, 392. *See also* Old Stone Age
"Story of Sinuhe, The," 210, 289
Strabo, 222, 226
Strait of Dardanelles, 268

Strait of Messina, 359, 363
Straits of Gibraltar, 360
Struve, V. V., 7, 10
Stuchevskii, I. A., 10
Study of History, A (Toynbee), 8
Sudan, 137, 143
Sugage, 230 n.2
Sukas, 363
Sukhumi (Dioscurias), 364
Sulaimaniyeh Valley, 229, 235 n.10
Sulci, 350
Sumer, 32, 33, 36, 67–69, 104, 113, 137,
    214, 223, 285, 288; art and architec-
    ture, characteristics of, 128–31; disap-
    pearance of in Upper Mesopotamia,
    236; and early Asshur, 233; Early Dy-
    nastic Period, 74–83, 86, 87, 88, 128,
    129, 131; etiological myths of, 133–34;
    fall of Ur and rise of Issin, 95–97; first
    societal class differentiation in, 37–44;
    King List, 74, 92 n.2, 95; language of,
    71, 72, 81, 87, 113; literature of, 131–
    36; Marian and northern settlements
    of, 231; Protoliterate Period, 69–74,
    128, 129, 223; religion and sacred
    architecture, 126–27; religious percep-
    tion of the world and the arts in early
    Lower Mesopotamia, 124–31; Sar-
    gonids, Kingdom of, 84–90; Third
    Dynasty of Ur, 91–95, 96, 130, 131. See
    also Akkad
Sung Kingdom, 421, 425, 431
Suppiluliumas I, Hittite King, 243, 275,
    276, 277, 295, 296
Suppiluliumas II, Hittite King, 278
Suret-Canal, J., 9
Surkhan River, 381
Surya (god), 378
Susa, 223, 224, 262
Suti, 204
Sybaris, 360, 363, 364
Synchronistic History, 261–62
Syracuse, 356, 359
Syr Darya River, 33
Syria, 29, 30, 83, 169, 173, 230, 252, 266,
    282, 283, 309; and Achaeans, military
    and colonizing expansion of, 325;
    Amorites of, 232, 236–37; and Ana-
    tolia, trade with, 268; ancient geo-
    graphical region of, 286, 287; and
    Asshur, trade with, 235; and Crete,
    trade with, 315; culture and alphabet

of Canaanite-Amorite civilization,
    306–8; and Egyptian military empire
    during Eighteenth Dynasty, 178, 180;
    emergence of civilization in, 286–91;
    and Hapiru, popular movement of,
    294–96; Hittite domination of, 187,
    188, 189, 272–73, 275–76; and Hit-
    tites and Pharaonic Egypt, 296–98;
    Hurrians of, 236–37, 249–50; Hyksos
    of, 170; and the Kingdom of Mitanni,
    238–44; and Mitanni and Pharaonic
    Egypt, 291–94; and Sargonids, King-
    dom of, 88, 89; Sinuhe's residence in,
    210

tabarnas, 273, 282
Tadjiks, 366
Tadmor (Palmyra), 257
Tadzhikistan, 381
Tajik language, 222 n.5
"Tale of the Shipwrecked Man, The,"
    210–11
"Tale of the Truth and Falsehood, The,"
    211
"Tale of Two Brothers, The," 211
"Tales of the Eloquent Peasant, The,"
    212
Tales of the Kingdoms (Kuo Yu), 410
Taman Peninsula, 362
Tamil, 366
tamkars, 69, 81, 93, 104–5, 110, 117, 118
Tana, Lake, 137
Tanais, 362 n.4, 363
Tanis, 192
Tao, 422
Tapti River, 216
Tarentum, 360
Tarmi-Tilla, 247
Tartessus (Tarshish) and Tartessians,
    351–54, 360
Taurus Mountains, 239, 242, 286
tawanannas, 282
Tcharu (Tsilu), 179, 186, 189
tchati, 153, 154, 166, 191
Tedzhen-Hari Rud River, 369, 370
Tedzhen-Hari Rud Valley, 380, 382, 383
Tefnut (god), 198
Tehib-Tilla, clan of, 245–48
Tel el-Amarna, 266
Telemachus, 333, 334, 342, 345
Telepinu, 276
Telepinus, Hittite King, 273, 274

Tell-Ali (formerly Nadmani), 245
Tell-Amarna (formerly Akhet-Aton), 185, 199–200, 294. *See also* Akhet-Aton
Tell-Atchana (formerly Alalakh), 249, 272. *See also* Alalakh
Tell Brak, 231
Tell Halaf culture, 231 n.4
Tell Leilan, 237 n.11
Tell Mahuz (formerly Tursha), 230, 245
Tell Rimah (formerly Karana), 229, 248
Telmun Island, 79, 101, 219
Tenea, 358
Teos, 362
Tepe-Sialk, 224
Tepe-Yahya, 224
Terqa, 99, 122
Tesshub (god), 250, 251
Thai, 422
Thailand, 387, 390, 390 nn.4, 5
Tharros, 350
Thasos, 348, 349, 360
Thebes, 158, 168, 175, 178, 182, 184, 185, 318, 324, 347; city temple style of, 204; cult of Amon in, 195–96; during Eighteenth Manethonian Dynasty, 187, 189, 207; Eleventh Dynasty in, 160, 161
Theodosia, 362
Theogony (Hesiod), 284
Thera (now Santorini) and Therans, 311 n.4, 316, 362
Thermoluminescence, 25
Thersites, 341, 342
Theseus, 309
Thessaly, 318, 324, 337
Thinis, 144
Thoth (god), 193
Thrace and Thracians, 267, 360, 367
Thracian Bosporus, 358, 361
Thucydides, 18, 334
Thutmosis I, Pharaoh of Egypt, 177–78, 292
Thutmosis II, Pharaoh of Egypt, 178
Thutmosis III, Pharaoh of Egypt, 178–81, 188, 208, 292
Thutmosis IV, Pharaoh of Egypt, 181–82, 242, 293
Tibet, 387, 389
Tibeto-Burman Ch'iang tribe, 401
Tibeto-Burman languages, 366, 387 n.2
T'ien (god), 416
Tien Shan, 214 n.1
Tiglath-pileser I, King of Assyria, 256–57

Tigris, 32, 33, 67, 68, 71, 85, 92, 95, 105, 123, 133, 236, 242, 261, 263, 269, 276, 287; settlements along middle reaches, 228–33
Tilla (god), 250
Tiryns, 318, 319, 320, 324, 325, 326, 328
Tishadal, 239, 240
Ti tribe, 425
Tiyi, Queen of Egypt, 182, 200
Togolok 21, 382–83 n.10
Tombos, 178
Tomi, 361
Toscaneo, 350
Toynbee, Arnold, 8
Transcaucasia, 81 n.16, 224, 231, 288, 367 n.3, 369
Transjordan, 286, 289, 299, 300, 302
Treta, 374
Trojan War, 317, 318, 324–25, 325 n.18, 328
Troy, 268, 274, 279, 324–25, 325 n.18
Ts'ai Kingdom, 425
Tso Chuan, 410, 422, 426
Tukulti-Ninurta I, King of Assyria, 255–56, 263
Tungt'ing Lake, 393
Tunguso-Manchurian languages, 388
Tunis, 350
Tupliash, 229
Tupliash-Nawar, 230
Turkey, 81 n.16, 230, 267, 286, 288
Turkmenia, 28, 223, 225, 226, 380, 382, 383
Tursha (now Tell Mahuz), 245, 248
Turukki, 232
Tutankhamen, 185–86, 187, 188
Tutkhalias III, Hittite King, 274, 275
Tuz-Humatli, 230
Typhon, 284
Tyras, 362
Tyre, 347, 348, 349, 350, 351
Tyumenev, A. I., 7, 72

Ugarit, 239, 242, 250, 289, 294, 297, 298, 304 n.11, 307, 308, 347
Ugur (god), 251
Ukraine, 81 n.16, 368 n.6
ukullum (waklum), 233, 253
Ulam-Buriash, Kassite King, 262, 262 n.2
Umma, 81, 82, 83, 132
Unabshe, 230 n.2, 245 n.15
Unis, Pharaoh of Egypt, 155

Upper Egypt, 137, 138, 141, 142, 144, 147, 149, 153, 156, 157, 158, 160, 163, 168, 191, 202. *See also* Egypt; Lower Egypt; Middle Egypt
Upper Euphrates (Karasu), 231, 257, 276. *See also* Euphrates; Lower Euphrates
Upper Euphrates Valley, 278. *See also* Euphrates; Lower Euphrates Valley
Upper Mesopotamia, 72, 85, 89, 92, 95, 98, 100, 102, 123, 255, 287; Amorite-Sutian tribes in, 299–300; city state of Asshur and emergence of Assyrian Kingdom, 255, 256, 257; culture of Protoliterate Period, 126–31; Early Asshur, 232–36; Hurrian culture, 249–52; Hurrian Kingdom of Arrapkhe, 244–49; and the Kingdom of Mitanni, 238–44; and settlements along middle reaches of the Tigris, 229, 230, 231, 232, 233; and Shamshi-Adad I's empire, 233, 236–38, 252, 290; east-west routes across, 231 n.3, *See also* Mesopotamia; Lower Mesopotamia; Sumer; Akkad
Upper Palaeolithic Age, 29
Upper Tigris, 230, 242, 254
Ur, 74, 82, 87, 90, 105, 113, 123, 130, 132; and Asshur, trade with, 235; fall of and rise of Issin, 95–97; First Dynasty of, 77–79, 83; Second Dynasty of, 92 n.2; Third Dynasty of, 91–95, 96, 98, 99, 100, 101, 102, 103, 104, 122, 131
Uranus (god), 284
Urartians, 231, 255
Urartu, 244
Urfa, 231 n.3
Urkesh, 233, 239, 240, 251
Urmia, Lake, 229, 241, 249, 288
Ur-Nammu, 91–92, 112
Urshu (Warsuwa), 272
Uruinimgina, 82–83, 84, 85, 91, 112
Uruk, 73, 74, 90, 105, 123, 127; First Dynasty of, 75–76, 132–33; Second Dynasty of, 77, 83
Userkaf, Pharaoh of Egypt, 156
Utica, 349, 350, 351
Utu (god), 132
Utuhengal, 91
Uzbekistan, 382–83 n.10

Vaiman, A. A., 72
Vaisyas, 375, 376

Valley of the Kings, 185–86
Van, Lake, 257, 288
Varga, E. S., 10
varnas, 375, 376, 378
Varro, Marcus Terentius, 24
Varuna (god), 378
Vasil'ev, L. S., 10, 10–11 n.8
Vavilov, N. I., 28
Veda(s), 17, 371–72, 378, 379
Veddoid languages, 366
Ventris, M., 320–21
Venus, 22
Videvdat, 385
Vietnamese, 422
Visprat, 385
Voltaire, 5, 60
Vostok i vsemirnaya istoriya (Nikiforov), 13
Vsemirnaya istoria, 2

Wadi Hammamat, 156
wanaka (*wanax*), 323
Warium (Ki-Uri), 229
Wasashatta, Mitanni King, 255
Wasshukanne, 243, 276
Watson, J., 64–65
Way of the Hegemon (*pa tao*), 419
Way of the *Wang* (*wang tao*), 419
Wei Ho, 391, 392
Wei Kingdom, 421, 424, 425, 426, 431
Wei River, 412, 416, 420, 424
Wei Valley, 409
West Bengal, 372
Western Asia, 173, 176, 178, 179, 180–81, 187, 188, 191, 225, 291, 292, 295, 374, 390, 395; diffusion of technologies into China, 408, 409, 409 n.19; and the migration of the Hurrians, 238–39; tribes at the end of the second millennium B.C., 257. *See also* Asia Minor; Central Asia; Southeast Asia; Western Asia
Western Chou, 409–16, 418, 420
Western Chou Period, 411, 412, 414, 415, 416, 428
Western Iranians, 370, 380, 381. *See also* Iran
Western Semites, 98, 165, 232, 287, 288. *See also* Eastern Semites; Semites
Western Semitic language, 291
White Nile, 137
"White Walls" (Memphis), 147
Wilusa, 274, 274 n.9
Winkler, H., 266

Wuch'eng, 397
Wu Kingdom, 422, 423
Wu pa, 424
Wu wang, 411, 412, 414

Xinjiang, 409

Yabin, 303
Ya'hmes (Amasis I), 171, 177, 292
Yahweh, 301, 301n.6, 302, 305
Yamkhad, 237, 290, 291
Yamuna, 372
Yamutbala tribe, 99, 122, 123
Yangshao, 392, 392n.6, 396
Yangtze basin, 388, 389, 390, 391, 392,
    393, 415, 423
Yangtze Chiang, 387
Yangtze River, 422, 424
Yangtze Valley, 409
Yashts, 385
Yasna, 385
Yaz I, 380

Yazilikaya, 284
Yenisei River, 387n.2
Yin Kingdom, 388, 393–401, 411, 412,
    415, 421, 422
Yi tribe, 425
Yitu (Shangtung), 395, 402
Yorghan-tepe (formerly Nuzi), 231, 244.
    See also Gasur; Nuzi
Yue Kingdom, 423, 424, 425

Zagros Mountains, 122, 228, 230, 235,
    249, 252
Zaho, 251
Zancle, 359
Zarathushthra (Zoroaster), 382, 384–86
Zebulun tribe, 302
Zeravshan valley, 226
Zeus (god), 250, 284, 339, 343
Zimri-Lim, 238
Zoroaster, 65, 382. *See also* Zarathushthra
Zoroastrianism, 58, 59, 381–86
Zuen (god), 95

The internationally renowned Assyriologist and linguist I. M. Diakonoff has gathered the work of Soviet historians in this survey of the earliest history of the ancient Near East, Central Asia, India, and China. Diakonoff and his colleagues, nearly all working within the general Marxist historiographic tradition, offer a comprehensive, accessible synthesis of historical knowledge on the earliest period for which written evidence exists, from the beginnings of agriculture through the advent of the Iron Age and the Greek colonization in the Mediterranean and the Black Sea areas.

Features of Soviet historical scholarship of the ancient world are discussed by Philip L. Kohl in the Foreword, a theme I. M. Diakonoff expands upon in his Introduction to include debates on the periodization of antiquity and on the limitations of Marxist reconstructions of the ancient world. He also reviews the nature and quality of the sources available to historians for reconstructing early antiquity from area to area.

Several essays treat the history of early Mesopotamia, detailing, in particular, the emergence of the earliest Sumerian city-states